I Dare To Heal with Laughter

by Joel Vorensky

Nov 27th
To Mary Ann
Shalom
joy, much health
and many
blessings
Joel Vorensky

I Dare To Heal.
Subtitled: "With Laughter"

Library of Congress Number: 2013939508

ISBN: 978-0-9704510-8-8

This book was printed in the United States of America.

First Edition.

The information in this publication is not a substitute for professional medical or psychological advice or service. A physician or professional therapist should be consulted before attempting any of the suggestions or techniques discussed in this book. The author and publisher disclaim any liability arising directly or indirectly from the use of this book.

Published by:
Life's Breath Publications
6390 Rancho Mission Rd. Suite #207
San Diego, CA 92108

Additional copies of this book may be ordered directly from the publisher for $24.95 each, by calling: 1-619-584-8093.

Additional titles of the *I Dare to Heal* series can be ordered by order form in the rear of the book, or by PayPal on the website at www.idaretoheal.com
I Dare to Heal with Spiritual Power **$21.99**
I Dare to Heal with Compassionate Love **$14.95**

For email purchase please order by emailing the author at: jVorensky@sciti.com

Vorensky, Joel.
"I dare to heal" : with laughter / by Joel
Vorensky. — 1st ed.
p. Cm.
Includes bibliography.
ISBN: 978-0-9704510-8-8
Vorensky, Joel. 2. Self-Actualization
(Psychology) 3. Healer—United States—Biography.
4. Teachers—United States—Biography. 5. Counselors—United States—Biography. 6. Spiritual life.

Books by Joel Vorensky

I Dare To Heal With Compassionate Love
(Life's Breath Publications, 2001)

I Dare To Heal With Spiritual Power
(Xlibris, 2005)

This book is dedicated to my Mom, Helen Vorensky; daughter, Jonna; and granddaughter Lemonie; in addition to five friends who have made their transition and to the spiritual community of San Diego County.

Barbara Carey

May her sweet, kind, giving, soul and spirit rest in eternal peace.

Morris Kurtz

May his angelic good nature that embraced the world now embrace other angels and the loving spirit.

Thomas Sorrel

May his unlimited good humor enhance the eternal celestial realm in both spiritual time and space.

Beth Ivy

Her everlasting musical talent is now gracing the heavens for eternity.

Kirk B.

A Coda friend, and a loving, supportive friend to the community.

FOREWORD

THE ESSENTIAL ELEMENT OF ANIMATED LAUGHTER

I am in charge emotionally.

When human beings learn to effectively "let go absolutely" emotionally, the result is a multi-faceted human expansion: spiritually, mentally, in spirit, emotionally, physically, heart, soul, socially, creatively, and intuitively. There is an integration/interconnected result!

In achieving this success human beings' divine flexible intelligence expands as well. It facilitates a human being's ability to function better in the world. It enables humans to support each other's functioning and emergence from distress and dysfunctional issues.

My chief goal in writing the "I Dare to Heal" series is to encourage a humanistic, psychological, mind, body, and spirit approach to help others help themselves with the physical/emotional issues that affect their lives. "Animated Laughter with Feelings" is the third book in the "I Dare to Heal" series, and while the books can be read sequentially as each book builds upon the previous book I have designed the self-help programs as autonomous, self-contained methodologies that function both coherently and independently. My point of view is to always address the human side of the human being. Taking this point of view can facilitate clear thinking about humankind as a whole. It is quite challenging to find the human being behind a myriad of imprinted, embedded, ingrained, deeply rooted, hard-wired, genetically coded patterns that one has acquired in life. When someone willingly applies oneself consistently with a variety of self-help personal growth techniques to evolve, success is possible and probable.

The elegant solution to humanistic problems is to always address them in a humanistic holistic way! Humans have temperaments and personalities that are affected by the hurts and the traumas reflective of an individual's biological, environmental, developmental, experiential, and genetic components. Human beings and life itself becomes complicated when people experience emotional/physical hurt and trauma. Quite often it is unhealthy "Patterns" that inhabit and hide the essence of an individual.

An individual's ability to release and relinquish dissonant feelings and emotions reflective of dissonant patterns facilitates the integration and the evolution of self-realization. It also results in transforming, transcending, and moving behavior from rigidity to flexible cognitive thinking and emotional intelligence. It most certainly takes time, discipline, and effective/efficient practices to achieve self-realization. Ongoing personal growth practices enable individuals to achieve a deeper understanding of themselves and the human condition of others. Human beings' ability to alleviate physical pain enables them to lessen the burden of organic conditions (organic conditions can reflect issues with hip, knee, or diseases such as diabetes or cancer).

A humanistic approach based upon a profound understanding of the intensity of feelings reflective of a range of emotions and how this affects the expansion of flexible emotional intelligence results in an emergence from emotional and physical bondage. It is a mind-body-spirit approach, multi-dimensional in both depth and degree and results in an ever- unfolding self. However, it remains incumbent upon a human being to take and accept personal responsibility for one's own health and for one's own core beliefs that result in dysfunctional behaviors.

The use of emotional release techniques are a component of personal growth. When a human being has a healthy healing experience after consistently practicing emotional release, and "arrives" at experiencing the human side of the human being from the "inside out" it can be said that the quality of true "insight" has been achieved. It is a state of consciousness that can only be characterized as spiritual in nature.

In my writings I share and describe dynamic holistic methodologies that readers can choose from in order to address their own issues. It is my hope that by sharing my insights, my stories, and my individual and relationship examples, it will facilitate an understanding, a pathway for the reader's own direction toward wholeness on their life's journey. My desire is that readers will gain both awareness and insight into their own physical as well as emotional challenges. When one becomes aware of issues that create disharmony for oneself within oneself then it is possible to begin the quest of processing the feelings that create our compulsive and obsessive thoughts. "PEAR" is the key. "PEAR" is an acronym for "Process Everything And Recover." Recover and integrate the components of the self that are hidden from view by hurt and trauma. It is important to qualify "PEAR" by saying "Process (Almost) Everything and Recover." After all, let us not demand too much from ourselves but allow ourselves to process those core beliefs that are most dysfunctional in our lives and that keep us in severe emotional or physical bondage!

When we become aware of our issues we can also become alert to when and how our issues are triggered. What are the circumstances, situations, and present experiences that cause us to act out? Or what are the behaviors that do not serve our well-being?

Perhaps readers will learn to embrace their so-called undesirable experiences and their outcomes. We can learn to embrace, transform, and transcend our issues and our experiences so that the qualities of strong faith (even in oneself) courage, perseverance, persistence, patience, and resiliency have a possibility of prevailing.

It is true that many of our experiences may cause us "to feel" that we are more than challenged in our lives. In letting go of the intensities of feelings that reflect our range of emotions in relation to our experiences and outcomes (which may seem undesirable) we can gain spiritual and emotional strength to transform undesirable behaviors. In this way we learn to renew ourselves and keep on keeping on with added enthusiasm. We maintain the memories but discharge the painful emotions.

We learn to acquire necessary information for our well-being, infuse energy from within, take charge and act on our own and others' behalf. We learn to follow through with purpose and follow through with our given purpose in the most general sense and focus on the mission in our lives. As a result our fears, frustrations, disappointments, losses, all dissipate and we can experience a myriad of accomplishments. The secret is to consistently practice methods that resonate with ourselves that facilitate both transformation and transcendence, and going beyond from within! Simply said, we have learned to effectively feel our feelings.

Yet, another secret is to become aware and alert to our distractions that cause us to direct our attention elsewhere instead of staying focused upon our own issues. After all, it is our responsibility to stay conscious of what is working for us and what is working against us. It is possible in this way that we learn to never, ever give up but to take joy on our journey and in our lives.

The gain is in our self-esteem and self-worth. It is a desirable goal and it is in the nature of the human spirit! For example, I think of the experiences of the American soldiers taken as prisoners of war who express their personal and, more importantly, spiritual growth while being held captive during the Vietnam era at the so-called Hanoi Hilton, a North Vietnamese prison.

The essential element and goal of Animated Laughter (also to be known as ALWF i.e., Animated Laughter with Feelings) is for participants to address their issues, and core dysfunctional beliefs in a wacky, zany, outrageously ridiculous fun way, to heal, gain insight, release, relinquish, and let go from an authentic emotional base from within, and in the process have a great time while practicing ALWF and if need be even to seem juvenile and silly while in the process of distracting our defenses and to effectively access dissonant energies within ourselves. It is a case of whatever it takes to peel away the onion skins and reveal the hidden self, the authentic self. After all, Inner Child Work is to be expected in Animated Laughter with Feelings.

The process focuses on, and is spearheaded by, the circular connected healing breath. The "breath" anchors the participant so that he/she is in control, thus the "letting go," releasing, relinquishing, and discharging of dissonant feelings is productive, disciplined, efficient, and effective. The participant develops trust so that he/she dares to heal and transcend, transform, as well as go beyond any fear reflective of internalized self-consciousness/inhibitions and internalized self-judgments. The self-consciousness and judgments inhibit the person from "letting go." When we inhale the circular connected healing breath facilitates a movement through the bodily/emotional defenses and facilitates a connection with dissonant energies, and on the exhale results in the release of those feelings reflective of the range of emotions. The participant is free to have fun, and behave in a zany, silly, and ridiculous manner.

Attitude can be everything and your will to do, willing intention, willingness to act, and commitment to the process of learning to feel one's feelings is facilitated by simply having the mindset that "I will have fun," and "my process will be unbelievably hilarious without limit!" After all, Animated Laughter is the best of the best of medicine—it is no joke for as the saying goes 'Laughter is the best medicine'. Through our laughter we let go of what physiologically our body needs to release and relinquish.

In general, Animated Laughter with Feelings takes on several forms. With experience it can gradually develop into a more advanced Animated Laughter with Feelings session with primal sounds and elongated yawns.

In addition, one of the chief goals of Animated Laughter with feelings is to use the power of our breath to connect with our life force, our life energy, along with connecting to the intensity of our feelings and emotions. Traditional verbal therapy can only go so far in achieving a client's liberation of the self. It is in achieving this goal where Animated Laughter with Feelings finds its authenticity! After all, it is a healing process that we seek.

We have fun learning to naturally achieve this goal. There are times when our feelings/emotions are dissonant and toxic. They can keep us stuck and keep us from acting on our own behalf. They can be self-defeating and cause us to experience dysfunction, helplessness, hopelessness, and create a self-destructive attitude for ourselves and others. The recent economic downturn in the USA and the world has produced sudden reactive situations of mass disobedience by individuals who have accumulated repressed and suppressed feelings reflective of the range of emotions, sadness through grief, fear through terror, and acting out their anger through rage.

In addition, our physical pain can create emotional challenges for us. It can make our lives miserable. We can reduce our pain energy by applying a variety of methods that resonate with us and in fact hopefully bring about healing. It is then that we can use methods as our circular connected healing breath to connect with our life force along with our intensities of feelings/emotions, and begin the process of emotional release. As we do so, we become clearer in our connection with our life force, our primal energy, our spirit and our connection with our spiritual entity, whatever that may be.

We have then invoked a spiritual entity to foster miraculous healing of our issues. It states in codependency literature that "We admit our powerlessness and make a decision to turn our will over in trust to our higher power." The use of the circular connected healing breath with its emphasis on connecting with our feelings/emotions and learning the pattern of releasing them is a way for us to turn over our power in trust to a higher power and as it is well said "Let Go, let God in." It is part of the secret that we must do it again and again and again until we have achieved our goal. It is in processing "enough" of our dissonant feelings that we transform our self-defeating, dysfunctional behaviors. Again, let us not demand too much from ourselves but allow ourselves to process "enough" of those core beliefs which are most dysfunctional in our lives. Our patience, our persistence, and our perseverance add up to our tenacity in attaining our liberation, our complete humanistic liberation of the self. We have liberated ourselves from the accumulated stress, distress, and chronic distress that have plagued humankind and barred humans from their full and complete use of their divine flexible innate intelligence.

This is a dynamically fun way to connect again and again with our life energy, become more present and connect with enthusiasm, zaniness and zest. In achieving this goal our hurt and imprinted emotional and physical traumas can be addressed and we can begin the healing process. In fact, "Animated Laughter with Feelings" removes the edge from stress and distress, and facilitates connection with more profound feelings/emotions by using an animated primal laughter sound. It is a loving practice that facilitates access to deeper toxic feelings that in turn facilitates and enables our healing.

We sure do feel a lot better after a zany ten to twenty minutes Animated Laughter session. It is extremely hard to stay depressed or anxious after hilariously releasing our emotions with uncontrollable Animated Laughter regardless of the core dysfunctional belief! If and when healing is our goal, then daring to heal becomes significantly easier and enjoyable.

Many of us are plagued by anxiety and depression that can take charge of our beings. We can easily lose faith and move into emotional anxiety and depression when we continuously react and are not alert to and aware of the direction our emotions are taking us. Simply put, we may have reacted because of painful circumstances or situations whether they may be within or may not be within our control. We may have had a terrifying knee-jerk reaction in the blink of an eye from an imprinted, embedded, ingrained, deeply rooted, deeply seated, hard-wired, and genetically coded past trauma. These serious traumas can vary. For example a child may witness a parent's death, a parent having multiple personalities, abandonment, betrayal, separation, or a severe physical illness. It may result in a rigid, mechanical behavioral reaction that without our instantaneous alertness to take charge, the rigid behavioral reaction takes immediate charge of us. Often, we are not in touch and aware of how lethal our in the blink of an eye knee-jerk reaction has manifested itself into a rigid reactive behavior that just does not become us.

Animated Laughter with Feelings can, with the willingness and commitment of an individual, facilitate a person's taking charge of one's life when feeling anxious and depressed! It can also result in reaching "the understanding" of one's core dysfunctional beliefs! Willingness to partake in a new experience often occurs when an individual is desperate. A serious illness like cancer can be a catalyst for an individual to participate and succeed in ALWF. An individual becomes motivated to learn to reconnect with, and process, "feelings" and the result is that a participant then reconnects with one's life force within oneself! We can also develop the ability to move within a ten to twenty minute time span from a mood of helplessness, victimhood, and hopelessness to an attitude of zestiness, proactivity, positiveness, and feeling, sounding, and being emotionally in charge! As we shed layers of our onion skin we reconnect with our life force energy! Our senses become vibrant and we taste life again. The senses become alive. We live again and we even sound alive! We sound as though life is worth living! We produce an animated sound of life itself! Even our body language becomes animated! This in fact was a living reality we experienced in infancy and in our early formative years.

If and when because of circumstances and situations we become triggered, restimulated, or stuck in our "stuff" then we simply once again become proactive and embark upon a ten-minute "Animated Laughter with Feeling" session. We just initiate once again another laughter session. We keep on keeping on until we have broken the chain that holds us in bondage. It is a proven formula that works. I know because of my own experience with the process and as the leader/facilitator of many ALWF classes.

With Animated Laughter with Feelings we obtain an opportunity to expand our human qualities. The qualities are depicted in the pyramid which I describe in my book "I Dare to Heal with Spiritual Power" as the qualities of our mental, emotional, spirit, spiritual, physical, social, creative, intuitive, heart, and soul centers.

The psychological result can be profound as well. Some participants gain insight into their issues and subsequent to their release of toxic feelings and emotions become clearer as to how they view their hurt and traumatizing experiences. Participants reconnect with those parts of themselves that had become lost because of a traumatizing past or due to more recent events in their lives.

Finally, I use the term "Higher Power" in this manual. It is used consistently in Twelve Step programs. It has many meanings for participants. Divine Flexible Intelligence, "God." Great Spirit, Yahweh, The Awesome One, The Source, Emotional Intelligence, Spiritual Entity, Eternal Power. I am sure the reader can think of other terminology as well. When this book speaks of "Higher Power," the book refers to it in the above terms. Simply stated, subsequent to our effective emotional discharge, we have access to an expansion of our flexible intelligence. Some have defined our access to an expansion of our flexible intelligence as our connection to greater alertness, awareness, an awakening, a rising of consciousness or a "Higher Power."

While practicing Animated Laughter with Feelings we certainly reinvigorate the cells of our body because of the increase in oxygen levels and we release endorphins, opiates, dopamine and serotonin that strengthen the immune system.

At this time, please access the "Animated Laughter with Feelings!" video on YouTube.com. The video you shall see is but a ten-minute segment of a seventy-five minute plus class. I will refer to "Animated Laughter with Feelings" in the book as ALWF. At times, I refer in the book to Animated Laughter with Feelings as Spiritual Laughter.

Contents

Foreword .... **vii**

Chapter 1 .... **1**

The Practice 1

We strive for our own authenticity when we practice Animated Laughter with Feelings! 4

Effectively Addressing the Overwhelm and Our Emotional Shutdown. Our Emotional Disconnect! 6

The Process and Bio-Energetic Exercises 13

We are in Control of the Process! 17

Chapter 2 .... **19**

Educational Aspect 24

"The Great Result" 26

The Buried Feelings Reflective of Emotions! 27

The Trust Factor 28

HARRIET 29

Chapter 3 .... **31**

The Circular Connected Healing Breath 32

Moving Through the Body Armor and Igniting Our Funny Bone 33

Resting Normal Breath 33

Our Rigidities 34

The Power of Staying Focused 35

Slapstick, Mimicking, & Silliness 35

The Ballerina Knee Movement! 36

The Sound of the Clap 37

Wrist Movement 37

The Feather 38

The Tickle Effect 38

Use of Play 39

Music and Meditation 39

Our Scalene Muscles 40

Grounding and Anchoring Ourselves with Prayer and Activity 40

The Dreams 41

Carlos 42

Chapter 4 .... **43**

Sound as a Great Facilitator of Healing! 44

Why, Why, Why, Primal Sound?A Statement in Favor of Its Use! 46

Significance of Sustained Primal Sound in the form of Laughter 49

Beginning and End of Illusions! 49

Chapter 5 .... **51**

Defects of Character? ... 52
Distresses Influence Our Natures, Our Temperaments, and Our Sensitivities, which results in Our Vulnerabilities. ... 54
Transformation, Transcendence and Going Beyond ... 55
Category I ... 56
Category II ... 56
Category III ... 57
Addressing Post-Traumatic Distress Disorder of the Warrior ... 57
Phyllis ... 66
Mood Disorders, Depression, Persecution, Trust, Rejection, Birth Trauma, Anxiety ... 67
Jack ... 68
Frank ... 69
Developing Faith ... 69
Hysteria ... 70
Chapter 6 ... 73
Identifying Your Needs ... 74
MANIPULATION ... 75
Jennifer and Janet ... 81
Jeffrey P. ... 83
Doris ... 85
The need "to be" wanted, and the fears that reflect that need ... 89
Roger ... 89
Chapter 7 ... 91
Mary Ainsworth's Strange Situations! ... 91
Putting Aside the Judgments ... 93
Controlled "Uncontrollable"Hysterical Laughter ... 94
Additional Thoughts on Unfulfilled Needs ... 96
Phil's Inner Child Work ... 98
Chapter 8 ... 99
Jim's Chronic Need ... 99
Need/Addiction/Enabling ... 102
Peter and Petra ... 103
Will — Rage — Compliance ... 104
Chapter 9 ... 107
Spiritual Significance of Animated Laughter ... 109
The Spiritual Yawn ... 110
Acquiring Spiritual Abundance ... 111
Divine Compassionate Self-Love and Self-Acceptance ... 112
Tim ... 113
The Author's Experience ... 114
Becoming a Spiritual Crusader! ... 114
Manifesting Your Spirituality in a Humanistic Way by Feeling your Feelings. ... 115
Animated Laughter Produces Spiritual Synchronicity! ... 115
The End of Isolation ... 117

Turning our will over (surrendering) to our (Flexible Intelligence) Higher Power 118
Learning and Accepting Powerlessness over Others: A Spiritual Solution. 119
Felix 119
Finding the Will Power Within! 120
From Spiritual Empowerment to Self-Empowerment to Questioning to Acquiring Information to Discernment and to Clarity (Tom's Case) 121
Chapter 10 ..... **123**
The Dimensions, Degrees, and Depths of Feelings Reflective of the Range of Intensities of Emotions 124
Emotional Currents 125
Collision of Patterns 126
Terry 126
Paul 127
Fred 127
Chapter 11 ..... **129**
Responding, Reacting, Overreacting, Acting Out, And Being Out of Control 132
Chapter 12 ..... **133**
Ted, Mary, Fred, and Joan 135
Economic Downturn & Homelessness 136
Chapter 13 ..... **137**
Animated Laughter in Industry 138
The Abrasive Employee 139
Bill, Betty, Bradley, and Bessie 140
Chapter 14 ..... **143**
Autism 144
Learning to be Gentle with You 144
Donna and Diana 146
Carol and Barry 147
Chapter 15 ..... **149**
Chapter 16 ..... **153**
A Tale of a Toothache 154
Chapter 17 ..... **157**
Putting our unfulfilled needs into the Relationship 158
Evolving Together! 158
Paul and Pauline 159
Using ALWF for Conflict Resolution 160
Liberating the Self from Codependence Issues 160
Chapter 18 ..... **161**
David and Joan 161
Use of the Affirmation as a Contradiction in Order to Trigger our Toxic Feelings Within 162
Agitation 163
Agnes 164

Chapter 19 167
Video on YouTube 167
Theresa 168
Radiating Health in the World 169
Chapter 20 171
Chapter 21 175
Chapter 22 177
Chapter 23 181
Michael's Guatay Homestead 183
Miracle Retreats 183
Chapter 24 185
Getting It 186
Hard-wired 187
Rigidity and Control 188
Layered Multiple Traumas 188
Key Terms 190
About The Author 191
Humor References 195
Therapeutic Humor and Physiological Response 195
Therapeutic Humor and Medicine 196
Therapeutic Humor and Psychotherapy 197
Therapeutic Humor and Nursing 200
Humor in Crisis Situations 202
Therapeutic Humor at Work 202

Chapter 1

"I want some of that!"

While Tim was being treated with acupuncture at a downtown clinic, he suddenly broke out with "Animated Laughter"! His practitioner began to laugh as well. The patient behind the veiled screen next to Tim was overheard repeating the words "I want some of that!"

—Tim S.

Animated Laughter with Feelings!

Why Animated Laughter!

A Dynamic Healing Method to Address the Emotional Overwhelm, Shut Down, and Physical Disconnect Effectively?

The Two-Step Process and Bio-Energetic Exercises

We are in control of the process

The Practice

The practice of Animated Laughter with Feelings results in a healing of both physical and emotional wounds that are then replaced by complete joy and happiness. The use of ALWF can reduce organic pain in the body; for example, osteoarthritis. It also facilitates a crystal clear connection with the negative messages embodied within the self. It reflects unaware and unconscious dysfunctional beliefs that result in unhealthy behaviors. The result is a clear understanding of the messages that we have learned because of emotional/physical hurt and trauma. These messages can include: "I'm not good enough." "My world is coming to an end," "I do not deserve love," or "I'm unworthy."

It is time for a healing methodology that brings joy, happiness, completeness with self-forgiveness, grace, contentment, bliss and above all self-love. The practice results in the release of feelings reflective of emotions and experiencing more of one's authenticity. It frees oneself from the energy of emotional and physical bondage. This is a great challenge for many! When we learn to authentically go within, connect and release/relinquish feelings reflective of emotions the final result is an experience of self-love!

Striving for authenticity is essential in processing feelings reflective of emotions that are reflective of our issues. With authenticity, we can realize/empower ourselves and our connection with our higher power! Fear is the key emotion that gets in the way of realizing our authenticity. However, the more honestly we process our dissonant feelings, the more authentic our integration of mind, body, and spirit is!

The research has shown that as we age our frequency of laughter decreases. This decrease can affect our well-being and our health. Laughter is an important healthy quality that stimulates essential hormones, opioids, dopamine, endorphins, and serotonin. It strengthens our emotional well-being. Laughter strengthens our immune system because of the release of these hormones. Spiritual Laughter reinforces the empowerment of our spirit, our soul, and facilitates our connection to our higher power no matter in what way we conceive our higher power to be.

It is usual for human beings who are not experienced with emotional release manifestations to react uncomfortably while observing others releasing their feelings by "letting go." Our socialization process prevents us from "feeling our feelings," and from productively allowing and permitting ourselves to release and relinquish them. This book will promote, and encourage active participation in doing just that!

Animated Laughter with Feelings is different from other laughter methods because of several reasons. The focus is on experiencing healing in a fun way. It focuses on doing so repetitiously. It also focuses on developing adequate safety and trust to achieve sustained connection and release of intensities of feelings reflective of the range of emotions that consist of anger through rage, fear through terror, sadness through grief, and experiencing self-love through compassion. We experience a thorough release, emergence, and recovery from physical and emotional hurt and trauma by way of the circular connected healing breath! The recovery from emotional hurt and trauma is realized dramatically!

Ignoring our life situations and circumstances that call for emotional release is just unhealthy. There are many distractions that prevent us from taking the time to address our emotional issues. The result is an emotional disconnect and an isolation from the self. In psychology the term is Alexithymia. It is yet another inward obstacle, a step toward creating a wall that prevents oneself from living life, a step of retreating from reality, and a progression towards hopelessness, helplessness, depression, and frustration from never experiencing freedom from internalized bondage.

Humankind has resorted often to addictions as a substitute to learning to be present for each other and share with each other their inner pain. "Letting go" can reflect releasing pain by way of crying, tearing, anger sounds, hot/cold sweats, shaking, chattering, yawning, scratching (it's under my skin and I just got to get it out), animated verbal storytelling, anger release methods, and what this book is about: Animated Laughter with Feelings.

The reaction by many, at first, regarding the use of emotional manifestations to release, relinquish, discharge, and let go of stress and distress is "That seems unnatural" and "It appears odd." At first, it looks really unusual to most people. It is like anything that is new. It takes time to become accustomed to the pattern of emotional discharge. It is a natural physiological process. All human beings have the capacity to naturally heal hurt and trauma by manifesting their feelings through a variety of manifestations. It is an authentic process. Humankind becomes inhibited from naturally healing hurt and trauma by way of the socialization process and the so-called Freudian Defenses. The result is our body armor!

The use of the above manifestations to connect with and to release, relinquish, and let go of feelings is but the beginning of learning to become "comfortable" with feeling one's feelings reflective of stress and distress. We learn to trust ourselves so that we are comfortable connecting with, and discharging, our feelings. The key is to use the above methods as a bridge to practicing advanced methods of connection and release of embedded, hard-wired, ingrained, imprinted, deeply rooted, genetically coded, and compulsively unhealthy intensity of feelings. The feelings are reflective of the range of emotions that ultimately result in unhealthy behaviors.

We strive for our own authenticity when we practice Animated Laughter with Feelings!

What is "animated"? It simply means speaking with feelings and emotions! Some of our favorite songs are sung with feelings and emotions. Please think of some now! We also think of animated cartoons. The characters in the cartoons are pictured moving and taking actions as the story unfolds. I love to tune in and listen to the Spanish language romantic Latin love songs on a local popular radio station in San Diego while cruising around town or watching "Dora Exploradora," the Spanish cartoon series on Saturday mornings.

Animated is in contrast to monotone. There is intonation in the sound and the voice of the speaker. The sound of the voice is alive with passion! We can be motivated to act when we hear the sound of a person speaking with passion. Great salespeople, actors, musicians, opera singers and artists share a distinct passion that is transmitted by their voice in their message to the world. We are attracted to those who sound passionate. Our attention can be awakened and we can be affected and influenced by those who share their message in an animated voice. For example, we are motivated to buy an item from salespersons when they are animated and passionate about their goods and services. Have you ever visited a local county fair and listened to the salespersons offering their goods and services? Our life energy has been activated by listening to the salesperson's animated presentation and we become motivated to purchase the item. We may not need the item but regardless of the need we become motivated to act!

Alexithymia is a common condition that is prevalent in the humankind. The condition of Alexithymia (our disconnect with our thoughts and feelings), a condition common to both PTSD (post traumatic stress disorder) and chemical dependency, causes us to experience distress, confusion, disorientation, and dysfunction within ourselves and our relationships. We have issues that challenge us. Our issues can affect our well-being, our relationships, our employment, and affect others in a hurtful way. Nature motivates us to address our distresses. The emotional and physical traumas that lie within ourselves require that we connect to, access, go in, go into, those parts of ourselves affected by our physical and emotional hurts and traumas.

Animated Laughter with Feelings facilitates moving through our denial to access our feelings. "Denial" is a huge issue that prevents us from experiencing our feelings. Suppression and repression of our feelings is yet another way that we prevent ourselves from feeling our feelings. The socialization process is the most common way that human beings inhibit themselves from accessing their intensity of feelings and emotions.

Also, we accumulate daily stress just because of living. It is a reason for having a daily effective, efficient, and disciplined practice of emotional release. Some practices are tedious, boring, not a lot of fun, strenuous, and do not resonate with ourselves. It is very difficult to argue with a practice that transforms, encourages joy, zest, community, fun, and "letting go" in a harmless, effective, efficient, and disciplined way.

When we practice Animated Laughter with Feelings our resiliency to daily circumstances, experiences, and situations becomes stronger. We develop both emotional and cognitive flexibility. Our attitude becomes significantly more positive and we can better handle our upsets. Our ability to address our frustrations, disappointments, hurts and even traumas becomes far more emotionally manageable! We become more patient, persevering, persistent in and with our daily tasks, with ourselves, and with others. We genuinely develop a positive attitude of "looking forward" to the very next moment in our lives and then to the very next moment in our lives once again. Simply said, life works better on a daily basis.

Effectively Addressing the Overwhelm and Our Emotional Shutdown. Our Emotional Disconnect!

What do we use to go in, go into, and go within the feelings reflective of our emotions in ourselves? When we are not feeling well we can learn specific emotional healing methods. The methods enable and facilitate our access, connection, going in, going into, release, relinquishment, and letting go of our dissonant intensity of feelings. We can learn to expel the feelings reflective of our emotions in a dynamic, persistent, persevering, and patient way.

It is common for human beings to become overwhelmed by the stress present in our daily lives so much so that we disconnect from emotions. Animated Laughter with Feelings is an effective and efficient practice to facilitate a release of emotional stress that causes us to feel overwhelmed, emotionally disconnected, loss of energy, depressed and anxious.

The nature of a chronic distress is its underlying production of a constant tension that triggers those senses that were affected by the initial pattern of our physical and emotional hurt and trauma. The chronic distress is triggered when conditions, or circumstances, or situations are somewhat similar to the initial hurt and trauma.

The solution is simple. There is no option but to learn to feel our feelings. When we choose not to address effectively our feelings we stay in denial of our feelings, and likely in denial of parts of ourselves. It is those parts of ourselves that are hidden, misplaced, overshadowed, and possibly in darkness. Our potential for acquiring a codependent relationship becomes real because of our denial.

There are several key words to succeeding in the process of emotional release and Animated Laughter. Among them are effective and efficient. A key word is our learning to be "effective" in using methods that resonate with us. We can decide to address effectively our feelings and in doing so we learn our self-acceptance.

We are emotionally and spiritually uplifted when we consistently practice Animated Laughter with Feelings. It is an exercise that creates elasticity in one's facial muscles. It therefore follows that the process keeps the participant young looking, young at heart, young in soul, young in spirit, and young and agile in one's thinking as well! Methuselah lived until the age of nine-hundred. The daily practice of ALWF will enable us to experience an everyday rebirth and renewal. We renew and energize our cells within our bodies!

Efficiency is yet another word. We are efficient because as we focus on the word "again" it becomes a trigger to use the circular connected healing breath to help us reconnect with our feelings and our life force. When we constantly and continually focus our attention on connecting again and again our processing of our feelings becomes highly efficient.

Transcendent cognitive and spiritual solutions alone without the process of emotional release can provide some relief but invariably the pain returns. With past unfulfilled chronic frozen needs, past unfulfilled needs, and present unfulfilled needs, the pain energy may return again and again.

It just makes sense to learn to feel our feelings and let them go! However, it is a bit more complex than just to "let go." Persistence, patience, perseverance and daily effective, efficient processing of our toxic feelings transform our energy. The result is that we simply stay connected to ourselves. We stay connected to our life energy in an ongoing, moment-to-moment, instant-to-instant way. We strengthen our connection, we reinforce our connection, and we integrate the ten components that I describe in the pyramid in my book "I Dare to Heal with Spiritual Power."

It is the same connection that we were connected to when we were born. It is a time prior to our experiencing and acquiring accumulated stress, distress, beliefs and values that may not resonate with us. It is the accumulated stress and distress that can affect us in an unhealthy way as it influences our personality, temperament, and innate, inherent, genetic, biological nature. Our sensation in our world just does not seem to resonate with us in present time as it had resonated with us before experiencing accumulated stress and distress.

We can have a lot of fun with Animated Laughter with Feelings. It can begin at any time. At anytime we can decide to engage our feelings reflective of our emotions. We can learn the circular pattern of breath, the circular connected healing breath, a go-to method where we can find parts of ourselves long in shadow and in darkness because of a variety of unhealthy behavior patterns.

Asthma is a common ailment that can dramatically be addressed in an effective way with the combination of circular connected healing transformation breath together with Animated Laughter with Feelings. Asthma has an emotional component that can be diminished because of the release and relinquishment of toxic anxious intensity of feelings reflective of the range of emotions.

There are many triggers that can perpetuate the onset of an Asthma attack. For example, an allergic reaction to food ingredients; environmental components like rag wheat, dust, cat hair; or emotional facets like anger, abuse, sadness or fear; and sudden temperature changes. Since we address the feelings reflective of the range of emotions we can then effectively and efficiently address the emotional triggers of asthma as well.

Together, with our cognitive and emotional methods we can resolve issues and transcend and transform ourselves spiritually, and transform our dysfunctional behaviors so we experience healthy functional lives. When we discharge our feelings, our dissonant thoughts dissipate and we intuitively connect with our will, with a divine will, reflective of what is commonly known as spirituality. We can experience New Age thinking, an awakening, an enlightenment (releasing our physical and emotional baggage lightens us up!).

The process may result in greater awareness, alertness, and a higher state of consciousness. Minds stay clear, focused, and sharp. Our flexible intelligence operates at a high degree! Responding in an aware way to changing experiences, circumstances, and situations becomes commonplace.

We can call this a moment of profound immediate insight! This moment may bring a resolution to a problem, issue, or conflict, internal or external. The result is to emotionally reconnect with those parts of ourselves that were previously in darkness, in shadow, overshadowed or in other words those parts of ourselves that we have lost sight of!

We experience more self-realization. We experience a rebirth of those parts of ourselves that were previously in darkness, in shadow, obscured by painful feelings. We very simply find those parts to ourselves that were well, "misplaced." Our intuitive sense becomes stronger and more astute to situations and circumstances around us.

Practicing the process of Animated Laughter enhances and stimulates our appetite, sexual drive, and lightens our sense of humor. As with the practice of rebirthing (using the breath to focus on birth trauma), Animated Laughter with Feelings facilitates our hunger, happiness, and our sexual hormones.

The process of Animated Laughter can be achieved through circular connected healing breath, infectious laughter, and slapstick; a feather, visualizing a comical scene (visualizing a person tickling you), or faking it until you make it! Anyway it is produced is OK! It is all good and making it happen is OK too. There are no judgments to making it happen in ALWF.

The circular connected healing breath is used in many healing activities, yoga is the most common. Laughter is infectious. When I hear or see others laughing, I am also triggered into laughing. We can also visualize in our mind's eye a clown, a humorous time in our experiences, or a funny moment we experienced with a friend or member of our family. During ALWF sessions I tell groups of people to "just have fun with the process" and that will facilitate your laughter! The use of a feather pointed at the neck and, after participants remove their shoes, the balls of their feet, is also effective for these tender areas of the body are trigger points for the stimulation of laughter. Finally, we can even simulate laughter until the sound and the real feeling of it actually comes into reality.

We use Animated Laughter to open emotional doors that have been shut and feelings that have been buried for decades so that one can begin to look at them in an emotional upbeat mood! It is impossible to be emotionally stuck if and when one practices effectively Animated Laughter with Feelings. In addition, we can then begin to address and heal our hurts and traumas with a variety of methods that uniquely resonate with ourselves!

Animated Laughter becomes the cutting edge for healing our most traumatic of distresses but removes the edge from an all too common serious depressing and anxiety-filled point of view! It is a view that many so commonly experience in traditional therapy. We can learn to approach the hurt and trauma from a perspective that is creative and removes the painful pattern of looking at the feelings and emotions from an all or nothing devastating emotional state.

Nervous breakdowns are just not possible with ALWF but a stress/distress release and relinquishment of emotions when it is repeated enough times is certain!

Self-pity is a state that just cannot come about with profound Animated Laughter. The approach to relieving stress/distress becomes an uplifting exercise of an ever-expanding self-realization. Animated Laughter is a therapy that raises the insight gained from the aha moments of awareness to the ah ha...ha...ha...ha...ha... moments of controlled pandemonium. Insight becomes exhilarating and downright fun! It is impossible to feel depression, profound anxiety, or anger when someone has been effective in their access to their feelings and efficient in releasing and relinquishing them.

There are times that I watch the "Animated Laughter with Feelings!" video simply to transform my mood. It works and if you allow and permit yourself to let go it will work for you as well!

The buried feelings are reflective of our emotions. We effectively address toxic feelings reflective of our emotions everyday. Most individuals just do not realize the multiple dimensions, degrees, and depths of our buried feelings. We just do not realize how stress accumulates within the cells of our bodies on a moment-to-moment, day-to-day basis. We begin to recognize the accumulation of distress when we experience disease. Also, we begin to recognize the accumulation of distress when we have learned to trust the process.

Feelings are reflective of our emotions and upon connection to repressed energies by way of our circular connected healing breath, and the energies that are exhaled, they flow like culminating waves from the ocean onto the seashore. It is a rhythmic flow of movement of waves of energy rippling through us. They come from our pelvic area and end with the sound of their release through our mouth.

We need to become more sensitive to our blind spots and develop an alert, aware, and very conscious connection to how stress accumulates in our bodies, in the cells of our bodies, and how we are affected by the stress and how re-stimulated and triggered hidden emotions result in disease and dysfunctional behaviors that can facilitate addictive behaviors.

We cannot allow our dysfunctional behaviors to continue! We can ignite our will by igniting our funny bone. We can ignite our will by making a commitment to ourselves to stay connected to our life force and learn to process the hidden feelings and emotions we are unaware of. Emotionally stuck, repressed, suppressed hidden feelings and emotions in the cells of the body perpetuate dysfunctional behaviors.

We must learn methods that resonate with ourselves to address our distresses again, and again, and again. When we use methods that resonate with ourselves that are effective and efficient we just feel a lot better, and function a lot better in the world!

The indigenous people of Hawaii call mainland residents "Hollies." It is a word meaning shallow breathers. Mainland residents are in general shallow breathers. Participants in Animated Laughter with Feelings become, with consistent practice, deep breathers. Deep breathers facilitate access and connection with deeper feelings and their release!

The Process and Bio-Energetic Exercises

We gather round and stand in a circle. We practice several times the circular connected healing breath so those who are new to the connected breath have an opportunity to become comfortable with the process. The process begins by establishing a pattern of pulling oxygen into our bodies (nose and/or throat) and experiencing/learning to become conscious of our breath in our bodies. We practice inflating our stomachs by pulling in oxygen with the goal of connecting with feelings reflective of our emotions. The breath is the catalyst for us to become conscious of the connection, and the progressive integration, of our body, mind and spirit. It is the daily practice of ALWF that enables us to continually raise that level of consciousness and to release and relinquish more dissonant feelings and connect with spiritual energy.

The enthusiastic pulling in of oxygen is very important in our process. It is important to be patient with oneself when learning the pattern of the circular connected healing breath. As we pull oxygen into our bodies it is important to ingrain, embed, imprint, and consciously hard wire the words "Think Connection." The thought "Think Connection" facilitates the connection with dissonant feelings and energies within us. It is equally important to imprint, embed, ingrain, deeply-root, and softly yet consciously hard wire the words "Think Laughter" as we sigh with an attitude of surrender, slowly drop our chin and exhale. The use of the words "Think Laughter" has a goal of igniting the funny bone subsequent to the "connection" with feelings.

At first, participants stand in a circle and practice pulling oxygen into their bodies. With practice, participants become conscious of the mind, body, and spirit connection. Participant's goal is to learn how our breath facilitates connection with feelings reflective of emotions, and how participants can begin feeling secure and comfortable with connecting their breath to their feelings reflective of their emotions. We usually do two sets of five to ten counts of the breath exercises.

Pulling oxygen into our bodies has several purposes. Some of us breathe shallow while some of us breathe deeply. We develop an awareness of our breath as we pull oxygen into our bodies. We create a more profound connection of mind, body, and spirit by practicing connected breath. We learn the pattern of "connecting" with our life force and feelings that have accumulated, been suppressed, and repressed. Another reason is to become efficient and conscious as to the degree, and depth of our inhale and how it facilitates our connection with feelings reflective of emotions. We also learn the emotional dimensions reflective of our hurts and trauma that our breath moves us through. Our breath connects with different intensities of feelings reflective of the range of our emotions. With practice, we learn the nuances of feeling and emotional dimensions as it reflects the colors of the rainbow. Feeling different intensities of feelings reflective of emotions result in developing an understanding of how hurt and trauma have their dark and shadowy sides. Finally, with the release and relinquishment of our feelings we experience a dimension of clarity or "light" consciousness. We can learn to connect with feelings with one inhale or it may take several inhales and exhales before we begin to experience a connection with feelings reflective of emotions.

After we practice pulling oxygen in and inflating our stomach with air we begin the process of Animated Laughter with Feelings with the Bio-Energetic Exercises. Here again, the exercises are an attempt to bring oxygen into the body, and clear any emotional blockages in the so-called energy centers or chakras of the body, initiate the pattern of the circular connected healing breath, and prepare the individual to connect with feelings or energies that do not serve them. The pattern of breath is quicker, more rapid and staccato-like while practicing the Bio-Energetic Exercises. The seven chakras of the body include the pelvic, stomach, solar plexus, heart, throat, third eye, and top of the head. It is in the above chakras where feelings, emotions are blocked.

We also initiate the group process, make eye contact with each other, and prepare members to connect with their pure, clear, connected life energy.

Our second goal is to become comfortable, to trust ourselves with connecting to our feelings. It is scary to rediscover that we actually can connect with feelings/emotions in our body! We practice and learn to pull and hold in oxygen, to pull and hold, to pull and hold then slowly exhale dropping our chin, jaw, sighing, and igniting our two hundredth and seventh bone i.e., our funny bone with the thought "Think Laughter." The thought "Think Laughter" can be stated out loud, which is quite effective, or it may be said silently to oneself and it may be equally effective. One can then initiate a sharp clap, clap, clap with the goal of igniting our cognitive faculty and igniting the sound of our laugh!

Finally, we repeat the process with the word "again." Then an immediate, immediate, immediate pulling in of oxygen must take place. Immediate is emphasized because thoughts will distract the mind and patterns will take charge. It will prevent a participant from the release, discharge, and relinquishment of feelings reflective of emotions.

The laughter gradually comes as we are triggered by the words "Think Laughter," the sound of the clap, and the infectiousness of others beginning to "let go." The circular connected healing breath moves us through the body armor or defenses that prevent us from connecting, releasing, relinquishing our feelings! Our enthusiasm grows as we experience success with the process.

People have many thoughts and the thoughts prevent us from accessing our feelings and emotions present in our body. The Bio-Energetic Exercises are practiced to bring participants' attention to moving oxygen into their bodies and away from their compulsive thoughts. The practice helps us to discipline ourselves in the process of the use of the circular connected healing breath together with feelings/emotions and Animated Laughter. Many of our thoughts reflect our unaware emotional patterns. Our patterns are based upon our values, beliefs, culture, attitudes, emotional and physical hurts, environment, experiences, genetics, and our biology. Most people also have a need to move through the Freudian Defenses, our body armor. The body armor inhibits us from connecting, releasing, and letting go of our feelings and emotions. The breath, the circular connected healing breath facilitates access through the Freudian Defenses. The Freudian Defenses include rationalization, repression, denial, projection, reaction formation, regression identification, displacement, and sublimation. Please refer to a good psychology book for the specific definition of the Freudian Defenses.

Participants learn about the seven significant chakras of the body and the significance of allowing the throat chakra to stay open by not allowing objects to be placed under the head while lying on the floor. I advise participants to bring a mat or blanket. ALWF is best practiced lying on a mat or blanket. The throat needs to be left unrestricted. When participants place a pillow or an object under their head the throat chakra becomes in part shut off. It is also advisable to practice ALWF on an empty stomach since digesting food may restrict the release and relinquishment of intensities of feelings reflective of emotions.

We are in Control of the Process!

We learn to become comfortable accessing our feelings through the practice of circular breathing. Once again, it requires both a commitment and willingness to do the process. We learn to control the connection with the depth of our feelings by regulating how profoundly we pull oxygen into our body. We can consciously pull oxygen into our body in a shallow breathing manner or in a deeper way. We can decide to direct the oxygen to connect with pain in any part of our body. It is our decision in the final analysis. It is also in this way that we learn to control our connection with those energies that do not serve us. We are in control of the connection with the depth of our dissonant feelings and become comfortable, relax, trusting ourselves in initiating our release of them.

As we learn to trust ourselves, and our ability to control the release of our feelings, we then become more secure in addressing deeper feelings and emotions. It really becomes fun and we gradually, gradually, come to an understanding and a self-confidence that we are in charge of the connection between the thoughts in our minds and the feelings/emotions in our bodies. Our alexithymia thus begins to dissipate.

Tension needs to be triggered and the tension needs to experience a release. The use of the clapping sound along with the use of the circular connected healing breath, and the use of a feather, slapstick and a positive attitude about the process can trigger the feelings. Regardless, the physiology of the process will soon take charge and one will begin to naturally release feelings! Once the feelings are accessed effectively through Animated Laughter the movement of the tensions and the feelings or pain energy are facilitated by movement of the body, movement of the knees (like the ballerina) and movement or shaking of the wrists.

Chapter 2

"Learning to Process by Discharging, Releasing, Relinquishing, and Letting Go of Our Buried Feelings Make Us Human"

—Joel V.

The Greatest Challenge
Adjusting, Changing Our Belief System
Educational Aspect
A Great Result
Our Feelings
The Buried Feelings Reflective of Our Emotions
Denial
The Trust Factor
Harriet

When we feel our feelings effectively and efficiently our successful practice becomes a pathway to our empowering quest of oneness with our spiritual connection with a higher power.

Feelings, Feelings, Feelings, are we our feelings? What is the difference between our feelings and our emotions? Feelings and emotions are the same. There is no difference between the intensities of our feelings and the intensities of the range of emotions. There are five major emotions:

1. Anger
2. Fear
3. Sadness
4. Love
5. Joy

Each emotion has a variety of descriptive terms. For example; anger can reflect an irritation, frustration, fury, rage, being conflicted, and hot-headedness. There are ranges of emotions i.e., anger through rage, fear through terror, and sadness through grief, joy through ecstasy, and different intensities of feelings reflective of love. How shallow or deeply we have our feelings reflective of those emotions depends upon the emotional dimensions, degrees, and depths or range of our hurt, trauma, joy, and love. It also depends on how our personality, temperament, and make-up are influenced by our experiencing painful situations/circumstances. Human beings experience the dimensions, degrees, and depths of feelings and emotions in their unique individual ways. We also negotiate them in our unique individual ways as well.

Learning to address, access, connect with, go into, feel, move through, process, release, relinquish, and realize more of ourselves is an arduous task that can be addressed with an enlightened approach. It is a task to experience our pain reflective of our upsets. We can learn to surrender and therefore learn acceptance of those feelings reflective of our painful emotions. We can develop an attitude of the surrender of feelings reflective of an issue i.e., birth trauma, post-traumatic stress disorder, or trust reflective of separation, abandonment and betrayal, which are but a few examples. In so doing, ALWF can facilitate a connection with our higher power and can result in added spiritual strength. It is the added spiritual strength that can carry us through our painful experiences.

Denial is a barrier. The practicing of Animated Laughter with Feelings can make it easier for us to move from our denial to learning to effectively, efficiently, and with discipline, address and accept our tensions with enthusiastic zest!

When we permit and allow ourselves to accept painful feelings it is a way of surrendering and experiencing peace with ourselves. With consistent practice, it becomes a joy to dissipate our denial and look forward to addressing our tensions with encouragement. The result promises to bring us peace, serenity, and bliss. This is easier to do with hurt and less so with emotional and physical trauma. Healing trauma can be a lifelong process. However, our progress in achieving success can be measured by the experience of more awareness, better functioning, and greater consciousness in the daily activities of our lives. Simply said, we are more in control, happier and experience more joy. We become stronger.

It takes a will, a willing intention, a willingness of commitment, a wanting to, an enthusiasm, perseverance, persistence, patience, insight, finding our courage, and if need be support from another to "connect" with the intensities of feelings reflective of the range of emotions.

"It is scary. It is really scary," many say who are challenged by issues like codependency.

1. Control
2. Compliance
3. Denial
4. Avoidance
5. Self-Esteem Issues

It requires us to adjust and change our belief systems regarding feelings and emotions. We think of fear, anger, and sadness as negative bad feelings, and love, happiness and joy as the good feelings. We think that pain physical or emotional is also bad! If and when we begin to adjust our thinking and believing that feelings, emotions, and pain are energies that require attention then we can move away from the thought that they are bad and negative. Perhaps, we can begin to think that they are signals that require attention. Perhaps, we can begin to think that they are warnings that require us to take action. The warning signals require us to address the feelings, emotions, and pain by finding ways that resonate with us to effectively and efficiently address and release them! Gradually, our belief systems can adjust and change! When individuals begin to connect with their feelings one is quick to recognize the abundance of accumulated repressed and suppressed emotions. The first thought is "I certainly do not want to go there!" It is here where we must find the will and support to begin to do just that. Somehow we must find a way to go there again, and again. It is here where our rediscovering those suppressed parts to ourselves are hidden within our unconscious by our shadows and our dark sides. It is deadly to begin isolating from others when our feelings begin to pressure us for release and we chose to stay in psychological denial.

Our feelings have been labeled as good, bad, positive, negative, dark, shadow, and light. There are beliefs about feelings and many labels for feelings. The beliefs and labels regarding feelings prevent human being from accepting the reality regarding them. "Feelings" are dynamic energy that is more powerful then is generally thought to be. If we begin to think of certain feelings to be unnecessary and robbing us of our life energy than it is appropriate to not only transcend that energy, not only to transform that energy, and to transition from it. ALWF is an awesome modality to help us transition from energies that do not serve us by addressing, accessing, going into, surrendering, releasing and relinquishing them. We can then experience the impact of joy because we have taken the action to let go of the negative power of fear, anger, and sadness within and over us. We learn self-acceptance and self-affirmation.

Is it in the American Nature to connect with our feelings and process them? It would seem not. However, we are not helpless. Our taking medications and approaching the issues only with cognitive tools will not resolve our hurts and traumas. They just will not go away. They are like ghosts that will return again and again. We can try to "leave them behind us" and even perhaps succeed. However, that which is left behind just does not go away. We would so very much like to think so. Denial does in fact take many forms and our minds often are an incarceration of deception.

Psychology comprises the interaction of the cognitive, emotional, and social learning (motivational learning) elements. Human behavior is often influenced by patterns of thoughts and feelings reflective of a variety of emotions. We can also point to guilt and shame as significant emotions. Each emotion has dimensions that we can quantify through the variety of practices. These include: circular connected healing breath, primal sound, peer counseling and others. The circular connected healing breath methodologies, and peer counseling are strong emotional tools that are useful to have at hand in our emotional toolbox. The manifestations of emotional release, sobbing, yawning, Animated Laughter, stretching, shaking of the body, chattering, hot/cold sweats, storming, sobbing, tearing, active kidneys, scratching the head, and verbally connecting with feelings reflective of emotion and learning to surrender and release them are used for our deliverance/redemption. We feel better when we have learned to surrender and have learned to just let go! Is it just that simple. The answer without doubt is "no!"

Educational Aspect

Grade school children learn about electromagnetic, renewable, sun, wind, mechanical, and chemical energies. These energies have a quality of motion and many reflect chemical reactions. Grade school children, teens, and adults need to learn about the main and most significant energy that in fact has the word motion in it. In fact this energy is the only one that has the word motion within its word. This energy is "emotional energy." Unfortunately, the understanding of its power, its structure, its forces, its dimensions, and how to address this form of energy effectively, efficiently and with discipline by learning different methods are not an essential aspect of our elementary and secondary educational systems. It would be beneficial to our educational experience to learn effective and efficient methods that resonate with us to release and relinquish hurtful and traumatizing emotions. Learning different emotional methods to address our hurts and traumas are not learned in our educational institutions. There is just too much "CYA" (cover your ass) mentality. There is just too much denial by the general public, parents, students, and administrators. There must be a change in attitude! Unfortunately, people get hurt and become traumatized by their circumstances, situations, and experiences. One can no longer ignore, nor think of, nor put aside, put behind, repress or suppress the tragedies of life. The pattern of the violent incidents in Virginia Tech; Newtown, Connecticut; Tucson, Arizona; Aurora, Colorado; Columbine High School, Littleton, Colorado; Ladera Heights, California; other mass shootings and the corporate greed symptomatic of the Wall Street market crisis, are reflective of too much deregulation and greed and serve as examples, indeed serve as barometers to much that has gone wrong.

It is important for people to acquire a practice with which they can emotionally educate themselves based on a process of how-to in a focused, effective and efficient way to address, access, connect with, go into, surrender, and learn to let go of those feelings that do not serve them. The feelings must undergo an emotional processing by the individual. If the dissonant feelings are not let go of, then those emotional energies are self-defeating, self-destructive to us, and to others. The fun way to do this is through laughter with feelings, Animated Laughter!

We have dark emotions that are known as anger, fear, and sadness. The light emotions are joy and love. The dark emotions normally reflect hurt, trauma, past unfulfilled or present unfulfilled needs, daily stress, or physical pain that causes emotional distress. Our healing requires that we surrender and release enough of the feelings. In practice, it may be sufficient to release enough of negative emotions, depending upon the temperament of the individual. When we experience the dimensions of our range of emotions we come to understand that our feelings have intensities (mild to strong, even severe) akin to shades of color as these reflect the rainbow and the electromagnetic spectrum (categories of light, shadow, darkness, black holes, emptiness, voids), degrees (cold through hot), depths (shallow through profound or deep), and forms or pictures (dreams, nightmares). The intensities, shades of color, degrees, depths, forms, and pictures (mental images) of feelings reflect the range of emotions as previously described. Two additional ranges of emotions include infatuation through true love, and joy through ecstasy.

How can we conceptualize and quantify feelings reflective of emotions? How do we know and understand the anatomy of feelings reflective of emotions? Are they intangible? Can we experience feelings reflective of emotions in a tangible, concrete way? How can we visualize them? What are some examples?

We have experienced releasing and surrendering feelings, using a variety of methods, reflective of emotions collected over many decades. Individuals must have a consistent practice in order to come to grips with an understanding of their emotional body and how their emotions play a significant role in dysfunctional behavior.

There are many issues that I address in my practice of counseling. These include neglect, birth trauma, emotional and physical abuse, abandonment, betrayal, separation, trust issues, boredom, relationship conflicts, scarcity, alexithymia (disconnect in thought and feeling), PTSD, codependency, addiction, loneliness, persecution, and loss.

We have a lifetime relationship with a significant other and they suddenly pass. We are devastated. The loss is devastating. We experience severe feelings of intense sadness, depression and anxiety. The range of emotion is sadness through grief. In this case we experience profound grief. The issue is loss of a loved one. President Woodrow Wilson experienced profound depression upon the loss of his first wife, Helen.

On the other hand, when an acquaintance passes we experience mild feelings of sadness. The range of emotion is sadness through grief. Here, our feelings are significantly less intense.

I describe the healing processes in my books *I Dare to Heal with Compassionate Love*, and *I Dare to Heal with Spiritual Power*. The emotional release experiences have enabled me to experience the different range of dimensions of feelings reflective of the different range of dimensions of emotions.

"The Great Result"

How would the self be, how would you yourself be, where little or no feelings of intensities of fear, anger, and sadness exist? Can you ever imagine how a human being could ever experience an emotional state free of the above emotions? One can only speculate.

Can the Breath of Life exist without the shadow and dark emotions? The substance of the self is created because of the above emotions, and how we learn to effectively and efficiently address them.

We learn to take charge, process, and contradict our helplessness and hopelessness. Our faith, flexible intelligence, self-confidence, self-assuredness, compassion and forgiveness are challenged and manifested because of these emotions. Perhaps our peace, tranquility, and bliss would naturally manifest themselves as well?

The Buried Feelings Reflective of Emotions!

Denial

When asked, "How do you handle uncomfortable feelings of fear, anger, and sadness?"

The answer is, "I just allow them to pass by!"

Most of us just do not realize the multiple dimensions, degrees, and depths of our buried feelings! We just do not realize how stress accumulates within the cells of our bodies on a moment-to-moment, day-to-day basis. It is important to have alertness, awareness, and a very conscious connection to how stress accumulates in our bodies, how an individual is affected by stress and how feelings are re-stimulated (triggered) by situations, circumstances, and experiences that are ingrained from the past!

The different intensities of feelings of fear, anger, and sadness, as these reflect the range of emotions reflective of hurt and trauma, just do not pass by. It is "denial" of self that occurs. When we experience dissonant feelings it is at those times that we respond by reaching into our emotional toolbox and choose a method to address our feelings effectively and efficiently! Whether we like it or not, dissonant feelings are suppressed and repressed in and into our bodies.

It is important not to allow our accumulated feelings to be buried too long! Sooner or later our buried feelings create diseased organs.

Personal Growth, Self-Realization, and Consciousness Raising, are both transcendental and transformational life long processes. If we choose to embark on this path the journey may involve both sacrifice and pain, but transcendence and an experience of joy will also follow.

The Trust Factor

The "Animated Laughter with Feelings!" video on YouTube shows how people need time to feel safe and secure before they trust themselves to just let go, have fun, and laugh. Some groups and people just begin laughing from the very beginning once I initiate the music. The class is different every time. Many people have difficulty making sounds. We are not in a habit of making sounds. Perhaps we are uncomfortable in doing so? Sound is significant in Animated Laughter with Feelings. We relearn to make sounds that we have not experienced in a long time. Many participants are surprised at the sounds they make. When others in the class begin to make sounds of laughter, the group members feel safer to trust and just let go. I do my best to create a safe space for people to let go, feel their feelings, and release with laughter. I facilitate the Animated Laughter with Feelings in the class by leading the practice to an ignition of the funny bone at its primal source. I bring participants with me into the connection of the funny bone by way of the circular connected healing breath. I have not failed yet. In general, most people have succeeded in the class. There is no failure, only emotional blockage of dissonant energy.

The Animated Laughter class has always been successful. There are no rigid rules except to create a safe space for participants to permit and allow themselves to let go with laughter when they are ready to do so.

It is definitely not dangerous to connect with your funny bone and let go and have some fun. Unfortunately, most adults just do not laugh enough. It is most certainly time to change that habit. The old cliché is true: "Use it or lose it!" People may just need to learn, again, how to reconnect with their laughter. The good news is that laughter is a part of humankind. It is always present but latent. The history is that adults laugh less and less as they age. Adults will slow down the aging process by just laughing more and more!

Animated Laughter with Feelings works best when participants bring their enthusiasm, energy, and willingness to the class. The energy becomes contagious, as does the laughter.

HARRIET

Harriet had all the characteristics of codependency. She had a history of acting out in rage when others confronted her rigid pattern of control. She consistently behaved in a controlling manner. It reflected itself in her body language, verbal communication, and authoritarian attitude. Her ego (an acronym for Edging God Out) got in her way of recognizing and acknowledging to herself that she had an issue with control. Codependency Patterns are deceptive. They are unhealthy and hurt people.

It was common for her to boast about her sexual assertiveness with men! She had an expectation and an attitude that others would comply with her wishes. She was consistently manipulating others in word and in behavior. She seemed totally unaware of her controlling behavior. Perhaps, the pattern came from her demanding and authoritarian dad. However, when confronted by others about her controlling behavior she would shrink into rigid fear. Her fear and anxiety began to give her sleepless nights. Her unending fear and anxiety motivated her to seek self-help methods to alleviate the issue. She decided to address it by practicing ALWF. Harriet began to quickly access her underlying feelings and release, relinquish, and begin to let go of strong emotions. Gradually she began to change her demeanor and became more and more serene and personable with others.

Chapter 3

"Animated Laughter is infectious, wonderful, and freeing. It gave us permission to release all those tensions and anxieties in an acceptable and fun manner. What a hoot!"
—Sue Kelley, Parish Nurse

The Circular Connected Healing Breath
Moving Through the Body Armor
Igniting the Funny Bone
The Power of Staying Focused
Rigidities
Slapstick, Mimicking, & Silliness
The Sound of the Clap
The Ballerina Knee Movement
Wrist Movement
The Feather
The Tickle Effect
Use of Play
Music and Meditation
Our Scalene Muscles
Grounding and Anchoring Ourselves with Prayer and Activity
The Dreams
Carlos

The Circular Connected Healing Breath

The circular connected healing breath is used in many healing activities, yoga is the most common. The other modalities include: Tai Chi Chuan, Qi Gong, Vini Yoga, Primal Sound, Rebirthing, Transformational Breath, and even the Lamaze Birthing Practice.

Our inhibitions reflective of our defenses prevent us from accessing our feelings and emotions. The circular connected healing breath helps us move through the body armor. It helps us move through our defenses that prevent us from accessing our feelings. Our body armor begins to dissipate and fall away as we use the circular connected healing breath. We gradually, with persistence, become liberated from our inhibiting defenses that have prevented us from accessing our feelings. We develop an ability to access our feelings without inhibition reflective of our emotions. When our defenses dissipate enough as we gradually develop more inner safety, we become free to access and address our dissonant feelings at will. We have then created a transparency to our feelings. We have accomplished a powerfully empowered emotional state of being.

The circular connected healing breath can be performed in a variety of ways. One can take but one breath in (nose or mouth) and connect with both our life force and feelings within the pelvic area; or one can take two, three, or multiple short breaths into the pelvic area, inflating the abdomen in order to connect with feelings. Regardless of the nature of the inhale it is important to imprint, embed, ingrain, deeply root, and hard/soft wire the thought "Think Connect, Connect, Connect" with the feelings and energies within our bodies.

If one is experiencing pain in a part of one's body, for example the knee, then one can breathe into the area where the pain is located, connect with it, and connect at the same time with one's life force. Upon the exhale one can release, relinquish, discharge and let go of the feelings. When we release the oxygen gradually, slowly saying to ourselves, or saying out loud, the words "Think Laughter," the goal is to trigger the funny bone and the result is Animated Laughter. The words "Think Laughter" need to be said with conviction out loud or to oneself! We learn to develop as well as to ignite our funny bone as we gradually exhale. It seems to be a natural physiological inborn mind-body-spirit connection.

When we bring more oxygen into the body we can strengthen our immune system against disease.

When we are on the mat practicing ALWF it is important for us not to have anything under our heads that would close our neck chakra and reduce the flow of our breath. We do not want to restrict the throat chakra from obtaining enough circulating oxygen. It is preferable to lie on a mat that is approximately half an inch in thickness. This will allow our neck to reach over the edge of the mat and will allow our throat chakra to open.

Moving Through the Body Armor and Igniting Our Funny Bone

Our goal using the circular connected healing breath is to move through the body armor i.e., our Freudian Defenses, and access our intensity of feelings reflective of our range of emotions and ignite our funny bone. Upon the release and relinquishment of our feelings we experience a freedom from our individually held bondage. We also strengthen our two hundredth and seventh bone in our body, our funny bone. It is our goal to strengthen our funny bone to help us release and relinquish dissonant energies from within!

Resting Normal Breath

We use the normal breath to rest in between connected ALWF periods. We can pause after a ten-minute ALWF session and simply return to a normal breath pattern for five minutes just to give the body a chance to rest, accumulate feelings and energies that have been triggered, and to integrate the work that has been processed. After a five-minute pause we begin once again with the circular connected healing breath and continue the access, connection with, the going into, and the release and relinquishment of energies.

We can also fluctuate between a normal breath and the circular connected healing breath during our ten-minute session. When we take a short break between normal breaths and circular connected healing breaths it can help us to refocus our attention, anchor and ground us for our next "connected" breath.

Our Rigidities

Our emotional rigidities contain our defenses, our painful unfulfilled frozen chronic needs that are reflective of ingrained hurt and trauma. Our emotional rigidities also contain our feelings reflective of the intensities, and the range, of our dissonant emotions. Our body language and our rigid patterns of thinking and behaving reflect our beliefs as well as our emotional rigidities. Our ability to respond with flexible intelligence to each and every new situation becomes inhibited. Practicing Animated Laughter frees up, even if at first just for a short time, our flexible intelligence. We can better think through a situation, or a set of circumstances, with clarity. We can obtain significant insight.

We are often overwhelmed by circumstances and situations and sometimes become emotionally shutdown. We experience frustration often, and it is a significant reason for our disconnection from our feelings and emotions. We also experience disconnect from our feelings due to our daily stresses or the triggering of our past distresses. We can effectively and efficiently address our overwhelming emotional distresses with Animated Laughter with Feelings.

Our unlocking and releasing of our dissonant feelings and relinquishment of our stress and distress returns us to an emotional balance. Life returns to us. We experience a sense of joy, enthusiasm, and essentially just lighten up!

The Power of Staying Focused

It is important to stay focused on the circular process of pulling-in oxygen, connecting, dropping the chin, sighing consciously, stating "Think Laughter" and the word "again." The mind tends to wander, and is distracted by having other thoughts; or one can become distracted by others in the group who are laughing. The key is to just stay focused on pulling-in the oxygen, connecting with energies that do not serve us and learning the power of releasing and relinquishing them. Certainly, it takes time and practice to stay focused. If the mind does wonder it is important to always return to the foundation of the process again and again and again until "it," the process, becomes ingrained and second nature. It then becomes a go-to methodology that all participants in a group can experience as an integrative life-fulfilling and invigorating process.

The following components are used to amplify the access to, connection to, and especially the unlocking or releasing and then the relinquishment of feelings reflective of emotions.

Slapstick, Mimicking, & Silliness

Slapstick and mimicking are awesome practices that facilitate excellent expression of emotion. People express themselves spontaneously through slapstick and mimicking. It is a great opportunity to release suppressed and repressed feelings with actions.

We allow ourselves to be silly and silly with each other during the practice of ALWF. Silliness fosters connection to feelings reflective of emotions and it facilitates a lightening up, igniting the funny bone, and lightening up the process of ALWF. It contradicts "taking ourselves seriously," which is a pattern that many of us carry unconsciously around within us and are totally unaware of!

We can also use a feather to trigger our feelings through the provocative action of "tickling" another person. The feather can also be used as a tool in a prelude to accessing our feelings. The use of puppets and funny hats can also be used to trigger laughter. However, the main goal to be kept in mind is that our process is authentic and the connection with the processing of our feelings is our goal.

Comedy in the form of slapstick is very common. Some of the more famous slapstick comics include Laurel and Hardy, and Abbott and Castello. It is suggested that participants bring funny hats, big red noses, fake mustaches, and dress with humor in mind, and bring instruments of humor with them when they participate in class. Creativity and spontaneity is always encouraged.

The Ballerina Knee Movement!

Have you ever watched a ballerina on her toes, waving her hands with grace and discipline? Well, the ballerina is capable of sustaining her energy by rigorous training and by the rapid movement of her knees. The rapid movement of her knees enables her to move energy through her body and reinvigorate her body with connected primal energy. The Ballerina Knee Movement is effective in facilitating the movement of emotional energy out of our body as well. After we have connected with our feelings in our body, the movement of the knees, like the ballerina's movement, helps us to release and relinquish dissonant feelings. It also enables us to connect again and again with our life force that is our primal energy. Likewise, the movement of our wrists facilitates the movement of energies out of our bodies. The result is a circular flow facilitating an emergence and constant renewal of the self.

I have often watched how the ballerina rapidly moves her knees as she dances artfully on her toes. I have used the same movement of the knees when I have connected to and begun the discharge and release of energies from my body. The movement of my knees facilitates the movement of energy through and out of my body. It is then that I also begin the movement of my wrists to release and relinquish the energy that has been triggered.

The Sound of the Clap

The sound of the clap in the ALWF process has several significant meanings. It can function as a trigger by saying the words "Think Laughter" that provoke the laugh! Simply said, the action can be expressed as joy in the process. The sound of the clap repeated again and again can become a trigger that through and by hearing the sound we automatically find ourselves laughing. The sound of the clap facilitates the release of emotional tension. It can trigger the release of tension as we lower our chin and slowly exhale. It expresses "excitement" in and of the process.

The sound of the clap can also have a spiritual connotation. I believe that the sound brings forth a spiritual energy into the process. Devotional and spiritual singers bring forth spiritual energy by clapping as they sing out their words that produce melodies. It can trigger both a spiritual renewal and a rebirthing experience.

The sound of the clap brings us in touch with our life force along with the connection of our breath by way of the connection to our emotional core! Finally, clapping in unison with other members facilitates bonding and harmonic musical rhythms.

Wrist Movement

We use our wrists at times to facilitate the release and relinquishment of energy to help us process energy moving through our bodies. The wrist movement is useful because a lot of stressful and distressful tensions are released by way of the hands, wrists, and fingertips. They are our end points of the electrical currents that stream through our bodies. The fingertips begin to tingle and become alive as we process energy moving through our bodies.

The Feather

The feather is a means to an end. It is a versatile tool that can facilitate huge amount of laughter. The use of the feather is a simple tool to facilitate the connection with a participant's funny bone. Some participants just do not want to be touched by hand or a feather. Participants' wishes are respected in ALWF classes. The feather can be very effective at a distance. The leader can use the feather and just point it at the nape of the neck or at the ball of the foot with hilarious results. Once the funny bone is triggered it can facilitate the connection with feelings and facilitate their release. The feather is also an instrument that can facilitate participants' having fun and enjoying themselves in the group. Some of the participants have become quite silly in the use of the feather by utilizing it as an instrument of play.

The Tickle Effect

Often, participants begin to tickle each other to break through the defensive walls that inhibit individuals from letting go. Most people really like to be tickled so they can begin the emotional release process. Participants have a lot of fun in participating in Animated Laughter with Feelings when they begin to tickle each other.

Men have difficulty connecting with and releasing their feelings. However, when several women show them "tickle attention," men begin to open up and laughter is triggered. Men begin to dare to feel their feelings once they begin to feel safe enough to express their emotions. It is also a great way for those who are in relationships to learn not only to have fun with each other but also to reawaken a relationship that has become stagnant. It can lead to sexual foreplay at a later time during the day or even to breakthroughs to better verbal communication among the partners.

Use of Play

Play is shown to be essential in the development of a creative and a well-balanced life. Emphasis on play is given during the class. Participants who have not had fun in a long time enjoy a brief experience of zany interactions. Having "fun" becomes both a spontaneous and a refreshing experience. When was the last time you absolutely let go and had some playful, harmless interactive fun?

Music and Meditation

The use of music during ALWF class is essential. Music will facilitate the individual's and the group's experience. It will enhance the connection and the release and relinquishment of feelings. It will facilitate an ongoing, upbeat environment of a positive experience for all participants. I like using a variety of music, especially spiritual music, because ALWF can become a consciousness-raising experience for participants. In the "Animated Laughter with Feelings!" video on YouTube.com I use music sung in Sanskrit. The music facilitates healing of hurts and traumas.

The use of both a guided meditation and a silent meditation subsequent to an ALWF session is suggested. The meditation is enhanced with a deeper and more loving sensation because of one's release and relinquishment of feelings reflective of emotions. Meditation can result in more peace and bliss for participants.

Our Scalene Muscles

It is important to drink a lot of water when practicing ALWF. We place stress on our scalene muscles, the three muscles that connect the neck with the shoulder. Regardless, it is essential for a human being to drink enough water daily. It is significantly important for those who practice ALWF to drink enough water to keep the scalene muscles flexible and hydrated. One will avoid sore scalene muscles and it will facilitate the practice of ALWF.

Grounding and Anchoring Ourselves with Prayer and Activity

Following the two ten-minute ALWF sessions, a guided meditation, a silent meditation, blissful music, and participants sharing their experiences, comes the serenity prayer. Class always culminates with the serenity prayer.

One can select from a variety of guided meditations, either choosing one from a list on a search engine or one from a collection in a book. Meditations need to be spiritual in nature. They represent grounding in mind, body, and spirit. Some examples include: a healing garden, a walk in nature, hiking in the mountains, walking on the beach by the ocean, walking in the desert or a circular breath meditation.

It is important to have a silent meditation after the guided one. The silent meditation deepens the grounding experience in mind, body, and spirit. The silent meditation can last for ten to fifteen minutes.

Blissful music is played following the silent meditation so that a participant experiences a profound sense of peace and serenity in sound.

The facilitator then brings the participants consciousness back into the room by asking participants to slowly begin to move different parts of their bodies and then gradually, in their own time, when they are ready, to rejoin in a circle. Participants then begin a brief sharing round with each other. It is the participants' choice to share their experience or just to remain silent. The participants speak of feeling serene, happy, renewed, and invigorated.

The serenity prayer is as follows:

> *"God grant me the serenity to accept the things I cannot change, the courage to change the things I can and the wisdom to know the difference."*

The serenity prayer originates from Twelve Step programs like Codependents Anonymous. The prayer helps to ground people within themselves. The prayer helps seekers to find peace within and is an answer to one's powerlessness over others' dysfunctional behaviors.

Many times we are also powerless over the lack of flexible thinking and rigidities of systems that dehumanize people. Fear is one reason why people are powerless over rigid thinking originating from dehumanizing systems. The serenity prayer helps people to make sense out of powerlessness and rigid inflexible systems in society.

It is also important to find an activity like playing a musical instrument, cleaning the house, washing a car, or walking in nature to help emotionally ground and anchor a person during and after an ALWF session.

The Dreams

Anyone who practices ALWF finds that the richness and depth of their dreams increases dramatically! People can have very vivid colorful dreams and remember a variety of characters. Some people claim to have an out-of-body experience.

Carlos

"I practiced ALWF one evening before going to sleep and found myself having a wonderful dream of fantasy. I found myself in a room with very unusual people. They were wearing very colorful outfits and were socializing with each other. The people all looked very different from each other. The bodies and heads were very unique and outfits were very colorful. I entered a room where I found more unusual people who were seemingly interested in being together. I waited patiently until perhaps I could meet someone. Fortunately, I met someone who I resonated with. We left the room and embarked upon a beautiful romance together. I felt nurtured, secure, loved, content, and cared for. I have practiced Tantra in the past and the images described above remind me of the people and places while practicing that activity."

CHAPTER 4

"I've had enough of this stress! I need to clear my head with some ALWF!"
—*Peter K.*

Sound as a Great Facilitator of Healing

Animated Primal Sound-Our Life Force

Why, Why, Why, Primal Sound?

A Statement in Favor of Its Use!

Significance of Sustained Animated Laughter

Healing Empowerment of Sound!

Beginning and End of Illusions!

Infants connect with their primal energy through laughter, adults can too!

Animated Primal Sound, Our Life Force

Why, Why, Why Primal Sound? Sound used in the Healing Process. A Statement in Favor of its Use.

Significance of Sustained Primal Sound in the form of Laughter

Sound as a Great Facilitator of Healing!

Healing sounds are used in many venues. Humankind has found many ways to use sound to facilitate healing. Often, people just do not think about the significance of healing sounds. People enjoy humming, singing, playing musical instruments, chanting, and making primal sounds to facilitate emotional healing.

We all have a life force reflective of our primal sound that is inborn and innate. We need to learn once again to reconnect with it. It is our life force sound, our primal sound that liberates us from our post-traumatic stresses, and from our accumulated stress that harbors in the cells of our body. It liberates us from hurtful feelings regardless of their nature. It liberates us from traumatizing feelings regardless of their nature. It liberates us from our issues, from codependency (denial, compliance, control, avoidance, low self-worth/self-esteem issues, addictions), and from trust issues (separation, abandonment, and betrayal). The life force sound liberates us from being so-called emotionally stuck! We then use it again and again to do the job for our liberation! It is our essential tool that acts as a catalyst that facilitates access to our feelings! It is not an emotional tool per se but rather one that functions as a necessary and essential "sound" that becomes our go-to method to dislodge and process feelings reflective of emotions.

Prior to using this tool of the life force sound, it is important for us to have practiced the manifestations of emotional discharge. We can do this by learning peer counseling. In time, over time, gradually, we learn to trust our ability to process our dissonant feelings.

It is then time for us to use a tool that becomes a way for us to access deeper feelings reflective of our emotions. With the primal animated laugh we pull oxygen deeply into our lower stomach/pelvic area, hold it there, tighten our body muscles, and connect with emotional energies, and then allow and permit ourselves to slowly release a primal sound or a primal laugh. The laugh is life-sustaining and we experience a connection with our life energy. It also enables us to connect with divine energy as well. The sound also functions to contradict our denial! The sound enables us to begin the processing of our feelings.

The most important achievement of the animated primal laugh is connecting with the ingrained core frozen chronic intensities of feelings reflective of the emotions of our stresses, and our distresses. We begin the process of releasing and relinquishing our repressed, suppressed, accumulated charged energy that holds us in bondage and prevents us from functioning at our very best in the world. We have affirmed our connection with our dissonant emotions. The sound profoundly enables us to access our fears. We gradually learn to take charge of ourselves instead of the ingrained chronic distress taking charge of us and disabling our ability to effectively function on a daily basis.

Imprinted, physical and emotional traumas may be with us during our life span but they need not control our functioning at an optimal level on a daily basis. The research shows that human being have the capacity to take charge of themselves in relationship to their hurts and traumas. Only the necessary practices that are required. We can use those practices as tools that resonate with our unique selves, practices that are acquired and used effectively and efficiently, if need be, on a daily basis.

These are the unconscious patterns of fear, anger and sadness that have the tendency to take charge of the self. The so-called dark energies hold us in their emotional grasp to make our life unmanageable, dysfunctional, miserable, and perpetuate our suffering.

Our ingrained chronic distress perpetuates our knee-jerk reactions. It is extremely difficult to cognitively take charge of sudden, instantaneous knee-jerk reactions. The knee-jerk reactions are lightning quick, happening in the blink of an eye. We disable our knee-jerk reactions, our helplessness, our hopelessness, and empower ourselves when we become comfortable with accessing our feelings by using the animated primal sound by way of the Animated Laughter.

The oxygen that we bring into the cells of the body that harbor the distress nourishes the cells by cleansing them. The oxygen chemically alters the intensity of feelings reflective of the range of emotions that reflect the ingrained distress. We obtain an eternal renewal/rebirth and experience a sensation of youth as we process the feelings.

Why, Why, Why, Primal Sound? A Statement in Favor of Its Use!

Culturally and emotionally the wide world cannot cope with someone using the primal sound. Primal sound is lethal to ingrained deep-seated stored intensities of feelings that reflect a range of emotions. It is lethal in transforming dysfunctional behaviors and beginning the process of recovery. It is uncomfortable for many to hear the sound. The sound is unacceptable to people. People will alienate and invalidate those who use the sound. Most people react/overreact to the sound, and respond negatively to its use. Comments include: "it is not professional," "why do you have to do that," "go elsewhere," "you do not belong," and "it is not grown up to do that." Much of the foregoing is said in a condescending and invalidating tone of voice. It is the tone of voice that the individual uses that is the clue that the person who is stating the invalidation is the person whose feelings, in an unaware way, have been triggered. It is a statement of repression! Invalidation is a lack recognition of individuals' feelings and their emotions. It can be internally upsetting to other people, as well as to you, since invalidation reflects unaware hurts and traumas. The invalidation of individuals can come from beliefs, values, family of origin, or a rigid socialization process.

Fortunately, there are some people who understand the significance of connecting with feelings by way of the use of circular connected healing breath and the use of primal sound and its essential use in healing. Like circular connected healing breath, the use of healing sound is significant in the process of moving through the Freudian Defenses, the body armor, to access the different intensities of feelings and pave the way for their release and relinquishment.

The individual experiences waves of healing sound that move through the self again and again. Each movement and moment as it reflects a wave of emotion brings some relief from the painful feelings until one connects with oneself. The analogy is that of waves at the seashore or the ripples of a stone thrown into a lake. When there is enough release of feelings, an integration of the self occurs and a divine connection is created as well. Along with one's willingness, persistent practice is the essential element in our self-realization, personal growth, and spirituality. The primal groups around the world understand the significance of sound and its use. There are even those who although they never use the primal sound intuitively "get it" and encourage others to use primal sound for healing.

Another key element is our having a mindset, to permit, to permit, and to allow ourselves, to allow ourselves, to actualize the process. We must permit and allow ourselves to become comfortable with making sounds! If necessary, we must permit and allow ourselves to become comfortable with making any sound regardless of intensity and volume to succeed in our healing. When we learn/acquire those unique sounds to ourselves that facilitate our healing we have discovered significant secrets that are unique to our own freedom from emotional/physical bondage.

This includes loud sounds. The socialization process has created an environment where it is frowned upon to make loud sounds. It has become a pattern requiring a relearning process. We are not comfortable with making loud sounds in most cultures. We must change this mindset in order for us to succeed! We must create and change our mindset to succeed at ALWF. It certainly helps if and when we ingrain a mindset into our emotional body that it is OK to make whatever sound necessary reflective of the expression of our feelings! This mindset must become a part of our emotional body! It may take time to make a gradual change to a new mindset. Self-consciousness and inner judgment or judgment by others are emotional cognitive walls that participants must transcend/transform until the resistance dissipates.

People who have strong codependency issues are usually the ones who react and respond strongly against those of us who use the primal sound. The reason that they react in this way is because it reflects an insecurity, deeply-ingrained as it reflects a pattern of control. Codependency issues mirror the manipulations reflective of the patterns that reflect the categories of control, compliance, denial, avoidance, self-worth, and low self-esteem issues. These individuals usually have experienced profound persecution issues and who are in denial of them. They attempt to manipulate others by using patterns of control. Often, it is a reaction of glibness that is deceptive. It is usually those people who react and respond negatively to primal sound that are in denial. The sound disables their ability to control the person and it also triggers or stimulates their own deep seated and unfulfilled frozen chronic needs.

The primal sound is used in "Animated Laughter with Feelings" to address, connect with, access, go in, go into, the feelings reflective of emotions. It is used again, and again, and again to succeed in releasing, relinquishing the accumulated, suppressed, repressed deep seated intensity of feelings.

Primal sound facilitates the grounding/anchoring, and centering of the self. Its effect is to stabilize and ground the self after one has released and relinquished feelings reflective of emotions.

Significance of Sustained Primal Sound in the form of Laughter

The use of the word "again" gives emphasis to the significance of continual release by way of Animated Laughter. The word "again" is a significant trigger to facilitate sustained laughter. The result is a release of a great deal of suppressed and repressed tensions. We just cannot fathom the depth of our accumulated tensions until we connect again and again and discover to our surprise the degree of accumulated tensions that have harbored within ourselves. We learn quickly by processing our accumulated distress effectively, that sustained Animated Laughter is a fun-filled and efficient method of releasing and relinquishing our feelings.

Our unaware accumulated tension is huge. Participants speak about the anxiety that harbors around their heart area. Their chest feels heavy. They feel stressed and experience fatigue. As a participant releases and relinquishes their distress they experience liberation from it. They claim how relieved and how lighter they feel. Their burden of stress and distress has diminished and they just feel better. They have released, relinquished, discharged, and let go of significant baggage that they have been carrying around, perhaps for years!

Beginning and End of Illusions!

Often, we have perceptions of situations, circumstances, observations, and experiences that reflect our perceptions that are complicated by our feelings reflective of the range of emotions from fear through terror. The use of the primal sound facilitates the beginning and the end of our illusions that reflect our fearful perceptions.

It is impossible to maintain our feelings of fear when the primal profound sound is incorporated in our processing of feelings. Our illusions are the results of fearful perceptions. The primal sound begins the process that facilitates our processing our fears. Its use therefore becomes the beginning of the end of our fearful perceptions. The result is significant clarity in our thinking and feelings. We feel cleansed. It is the fear, the anger, and the sadness that we have cleansed. It is the exact same circumstances, situations, experiences, even our belief systems that before our processing seemed cloudy, dark, confused, and blurred and are now experienced with more clarity. Our flexible intelligence has returned.

CHAPTER 5

Liberate me from grief!
Liberate me from rage!
Liberate me from terror!
Allow Grace, Peace, Ongoing Serenity
and Bliss To reside within me!

"Inside my pain is the seed of my strength; it is there where I experience my authenticity"

"If and When I dare to feel my most profound of terrors; then I shall know 'Freedom from Bondage'"

"It feels like I'm going to die, but no, it's the trauma within me that I'm feeling is dying."

—Said by a participant of ALWF

Defects of Character?

Unnatural Nature of Hurt and Trauma and its affect on Our Natures, Our Temperaments, Our Sensitivities, which results in Our Vulnerabilities.

Transformation, Transcendence, Going Beyond!

Addressing PTSD and the American Soldier/Veteran

The Knee-Jerk Reactions

Migraine/Tension

Headaches, Domestic Violence Mood Disorders, Mania, Depression

Persecution, Trust, Rejection

Birth Trauma, Anxiety

Issues Developing Faith Reaction Formation or Hysteria

Emotional/Physical Abuse Developing Faith

Defects of Character?

Animated Laughter with Feelings has proven to be effective, and efficient in accessing feelings reflective of emotions with respect to many issues. We have addressed issues such as PTSD, bi-polarism, migraine headaches, persecution, Inner Child Work, codependency (self-esteem, denial, avoidance, control, and compliance), physical and emotional abuse, addictive behaviors, trust issues (separation, abandonment, betrayal), sexual abuse, panic disorders, a variety of beliefs/values reflective of phobias/fears, loss, and physical issues of recovery.

The term "Defect of Character" exists in the literature of Codependency Anonymous. There are many who are in denial of having ingrained character defects. Well, they do exist. Defects of character are ingrained in the psycho/emotional body of an individual. Defects of character are usually ignored by people. Humans often have an unaware defect of character reflective of a profound denial, self-righteousness and negative ego issues. However, when an individual becomes aware of a defect in character it is incumbent upon oneself to address it effectively. It is incumbent upon the individual to take responsibility for the self, and accept that in fact a defect in character exists. It is essential for people to learn methodologies to facilitate effective processing of feelings underlying the thoughts and resolve their defects of character. The defect may be a dysfunctional behavior that they are plagued by because it can and usually does recur. It may be triggered when the individual finds him/herself in similar situations or circumstances and the issue arises again and again and again. An example would be recurring feelings reflective of an emotion of fear, or anger or sadness or a repetitive knee-jerk reaction/overreaction to new circumstances and situations. The "persecution complex," the "I am a victim" issue is but one example.

The key for the individual is not to be in denial of the issue but to acknowledge it, surrender to the feelings that are triggered by it, learn to accept it as the individual learns to accept oneself. It becomes easier under these circumstances to release, relinquish, and let go of emotions and therefore turn the feelings reflective of the emotions over to one's higher power. The individual's issue then gradually dissipates. The issue is usually fear. It usually contains sadness and anger as well. The emphasis ought to be on doing the necessary ongoing processing of the feelings reflective of the issue. It is just not enough to become aware and alert to it.

There are many defects of character that are traumas. Physical and Emotional traumas can be addressed by an individual as long as the will, willing intention, willingness of commitment, the wanting, the desire, and the support from others are present. The key to addressing major upsets is learning effective, efficient, and disciplined tools that resonate while addressing them!

It is said in the literature of peer co-counseling that "When taking everything into account an individual has always tried to do their best and certainly does not deserve self-reproach." I believe this is true. The mind or pattern of self-reproach often deceives the individual to think otherwise. My opinion is that individuals, whether out of fear reflective of a hurt or trauma or lack of practical experience, make life choices based upon their histories.

The choices that individuals make often are dependent upon their evaluation of their mental and emotional present condition. There are many variables i.e., economic, cultural, emotional, physical, environmental, mental, genetic, biological, family, ideological and practical considerations.

Someone who is a leader of others has a responsibility to effectively address their defects of character. There is some degree of control that a leader must exert. Control can be a pattern reflective of the disease of codependency. Control has nuances. If and when the control reflects a leader's issue reflective of past unfulfilled frozen or chronic need reflective of neglect than control is irresponsible. A good leader will recognize it as such, own it, acknowledge it and process the underlying intensity of feelings reflective of the range of emotions with an ongoing commitment. A good leader will do what it takes to process codependent control issues relentlessly!

Distresses Influence Our Natures, Our Temperaments, and Our Sensitivities, which results in Our Vulnerabilities.

Fundamentally, distresses create a vulnerability of the self that negatively influences our temperaments, nature, and our senses.

In addition, there are certain stressors that the self has sensitivities too. Our sensitivities also reflect our temperaments and natures. For example, our temperaments can be introverted, extroverted, shy, bold, or spirited. Some of us may have vulnerabilities because of our upsetting experiences.

Upsetting experiences affect our temperaments as well. All of this affects our emotional body with imprints that become ingrained, embedded, hard-wired, and ongoing. The cognitive approach alone is insufficient to contradict the character defects that reflect severe disturbances and dysfunctional behaviors. It requires a mind, body (the emotional body) and a spiritual approach.

Our temperaments reflect our nature and the self. They are part of the self, and our genetic biological make-up. Our genetic and biological make-up can influence our developmental experience in our environment as well.

The major upsets we have experienced influence our temperaments inherent in and of the self. When we make choices and are exposed on a continual or intermittent basis to a sudden event (an automobile accident for example), to circumstances, situations, experiences, and environments that harmfully influence our temperaments/nature or physical being; the result may be dysfunctional behavior. The self may be affected in an unhealthy way.

It is common for one emotionally profound incident, situation or circumstance to result in Post-Traumatic Stress Disorder. The incident pushes us over the edge into the disease.

Disease is incongruent with our true nature. It is unnatural to us. The so-called diagnostic and statistical manual used for diagnostic purposes in the mental health community is filled with a list of those mental and emotional diseases. Post-Traumatic Stress Disorder is but one of those diseases.

Transformation, Transcendence and Going Beyond

THE THREE CATEGORIES

Many of us address our stress and distress in a variety of ways. The three main categories of addressing different intensities of stress and distress are as follows. Category I for example is for accumulated daily stress from employment. Category I methods help us to relieve daily stress. Category II methods help us to relieve mild to severe upsets but are essentially transcendent methods. Category III methods are essentially transformative methods and combining the categories facilitate helping a human being to go beyond the issues in their lives. In Transpersonal Psychology, it is said that we go beyond the surface or the mask. Going beyond does not mean putting aside or denying the dissonant energy. We can assert ourselves by acting with positive thought and taking positive actions to contradict the emotional pain within us as well. In this way, we can also go beyond the distress that has gotten in our way from functioning well in our lives. By our being, being proactive, we can effectively and efficiently process dynamically feelings/emotions, and move through, release, relinquish, discharge, and let go of our emotional energy lodged in our bodies.

Category I

Taking a vacation, Jacuzzi, casual walking, swimming, visiting a museum, walking your pet or acquiring a pet, reading a book, watching a film, walking on the beach beside the ocean, knitting, rowing, and social connections/relationships, flying a kite, experiencing nature, working in the garden, painting, playing a musical instrument, other hobbies or participating in a team sport.

The category II stress, distress reduction or resolution can come from family, employment, childhood or adult issues. Here we have both Eastern and Western Methods. They are as follows:

Category II

Family, Counseling, Dyad, Mirror Work, Relationship Counseling, Different Formats of Psychotherapy, Energetic Exercise, Power Walking, Nature Exploration, Acupuncture, Reiki, Massage, Shiatsu, Laughter Practices, Acupressure, Love, Tantra, Prayer, Yoga, Meditation, Reflexology, Rolfing, Spiritual Music, Hypnotism, Alexander Technique, Affirmations, Bio-Feedback, Bio-Energetic Exercises, Codependency Groups and other Twelve Step Groups.

The third group of distress release and possible resolution uses the power of the so-called circular connected healing breath, as do many Eastern Philosophies.

Category III

Primal Sound, Primordial Sound Circular Connected Healing Breath, Peer Counseling, Manifestations of Emotional Release (Animated Laughter with Feelings), Vini, and Kundalini Yoga. We learn to trust ourselves and connect, go into, and let go of the intensities of feelings reflective of the range of emotions!

My experience is that to address physical/emotional trauma (PTSD) effectively, methods from all three categories are necessary. The category III methods are essential to the effective and efficient movement of deep-seated, imprinted, ingrained, and suppressed denial of those feelings reflective of emotions reflective of PTSD!

Addressing Post-Traumatic Distress Disorder of the Warrior

The War for healing the Spirit and the Soul of the Soldier from the impact of PTSD is won by having continual practices. It is won by learning to connect, access with in an effective, efficient, disciplined way, repressed feelings/emotions on a continual, persistent/patient and ongoing way. It is then necessary to relinquish the intensities of those energies one session at a time! There is no doubt or reservation that victory is then assured!

There are many American soldiers, returning from Iraq and Afghanistan, and non-combat veterans, with PTSD. There are some veterans who daily are taking their own lives. The suppressed/repressed feelings reflective of emotions require a great deal of decompression. The depression, night sweats, nightmares, hyper-vigilance, and sudden outburst of knee-jerk anger or anxiety reoccur. The emotional and physical pain surfaces and traditional psychological methods and medications are used to address PTSD's impact. The traditional psychological methods are ineffective, inefficient, and for most diagnosed clients are marginal at best meaning not enough. The effects of PTSD may occur soon after the soldier returns from the theater of war or could occur at a later time.

Traditional Psychology has the following criteria for PTSD: "A" through "F" as stressor, intrusive recollection, avoidant numbing (disconnect emotionally) hyper-arousal, duration, and functional significance.

PTSD affects the mind, body, and spirit of an individual, possibly for an extended period of time or lifetime. It is time for a different point of view and approach in addressing the disorder. The power of learning and practicing Animated Laughter with Feelings consistently, effectively, and efficiently can dramatically alter the effects of this disorder. The major key is the ability/attention of the participant to learn the pattern and to practice the connection and then the release, mindset of surrender, relinquishment, discharge, and letting go of the underlying feelings reflective of the emotions. Participants so-called diagnosed by traditional psychology may or may not be ready for a different approach to addressing the disorder. There are many counselors and psychologists as well who are not prepared to implement approaches like ALWF.

Unfortunately, the methods that have been employed have fallen short of success. The best efforts of the traditional and pharmaceutical communities have experienced significant frustration. Two well-known senators chaired a Washington D.C. committee meeting whose topic was suicide prevention.

The top mental health military advocates explained what tools are being used to address the issue. One medical doctor explained that their go-to motivational speaker consulted with his nurse on Wednesday, his psychiatrist on Thursday, and his physician on Friday and on Saturday took his own life. The Physician explained that the staff was devastated.

There are other commanders who have called for "stand-downs." The "stand-downs" are an attempt by a commander to raise a sense of consciousness among their troops that soldiers need to become aware and alert to their fellow comrades who are having suicidal ideation. The "stand-downs" attempt to bring soldiers attention to the issues of suicide. Unfortunately, they are temporary band aids placed on a need for a comprehensive holistic approach to the issues of PTSD. Stigma is present and still flourishes in the military.

The thinking must change within the military and in society regarding the mental health approach to addressing distress. The stigma must end. A holistic approach must take shape and form and prevail. Even the present holistic approach used to address PTSD has fallen tragically short of success. Unfortunately, in a society that is highly competitive in nature, "stigma" of mental health issues has painful and devastating outcomes as it reflects advancement in the military, employment, relationships, and educational opportunities. An evolution and revolution in thinking and approach to distress must occur for humankind to conquer the hurts and traumas regardless of the society. The traditional DSM (The Diagnostic and Statistical Manual) diagnosis and approaches to treatment need to reflect a dynamic holistic approach that includes ALWF. Leadership is required to accomplish change. Peer pressure and its colluding with denial of mental health issues often reflect an insurmountable brick wall. Gender's biological nature also reinforces denial. Truly, it is extremely difficult for human beings to contradict their negative aspects of ego. Ego reflects the remnants of a childhood need to be "right" or more commonly known as self-righteousness. If and when one learns an attitude of surrender, and feels feelings, it is then that the negative aspects of ego and self-righteousness gradually fade away. The ability to think in a flexible way returns, resulting in an evolving and expanding human intelligence. We are at that point much happier in/with ourselves and in our relationships with others. Our connection with each other improves. Cooperation prevails with each other in a community and a society.

Mental health units attempt to stabilize individuals on medications with a prescribed short stay at an institution. They must begin to open the process to additional methods to help human beings learn to access their underlying intensities of feelings reflective of the range of emotions. They underlie the cognitive thoughts reflective of PTSD. Though it helps, silent meditation is insufficient as well! Circular connected breath and other effective and efficient methodologies must be added so that diagnosed individuals learn to let go absolutely, and begin the effective and efficient processing of emotional distress. The time has come! Of course, humankind must be willing to practice effective methodologies.

The mental health system does the best it can with its present system. However, the system cries out for significantly more flexibility and change. The bridges that are created are important but are not enough for resolution of the issue. Flexible bridges are necessary. Unfortunately, hierarchies have their inherent dysfunctional control, compliance and denial. Traditional academic oriented mental health educations stand in the way of effective and efficient solutions!

A possible holistic approach including Codependency Twelve Step Support Groups, Peer Re-evaluation Co-counseling practice, Bio-Energetic Exercises, Animated Laughter with Feelings Sessions, relationship methods such as Dyad, and Mirror work, Multi-Meditation Techniques, along with traditional psychotherapy, requires implementation at the Military's Program Centers for Psychological Health.

Most licensed practitioners are caring and concerned with their clients. However, some practitioners have patterns of power, position, and prestige. The patterns reflective of power, position, and prestige must end. It would be helpful for mental health professionals to learn circular connected healing breath methodologies to address human distress and to use them with their clients.

Clients and Consumers involved in the mental health system must do a better job by taking responsibility for their own mental health. The present mental health system has its rigid limitations that reflect the frustration felt by many caring and well-meaning practitioners.

Our emergence from distress is important to the health and well-being of ourselves and those who we have relationships with. Those who suffer from PTSD must be presented with alternative healing methods like Animated Laughter with Feelings.

The military mental health practitioners must facilitate practices for soldiers whereby they learn to effectively, efficiently and with discipline to address, access, connect, release, and let go of intensities of feelings reflective of the range of emotions. One branch of the military already encourages the use of support groups.

Mental health professionals must be "willing" to look at and address their own stress and distressful experiences dynamically, and learn to effectively feel and process them by using circular connected breath methodologies. Mental health professionals must also address their issues of control, compliance, denial, avoidance, and self-esteem issues. Mental health professionals employed to support the healing of American soldiers must be the example for the returning men and women from the theaters of war. The multifaceted approach to repressed/suppressed "fear" must be relentless!

Attitude is everything and the stigma attached to PTSD must

dramatically change. It should be commonplace to include effective and efficient emotional go-to training tools for American troops in order to facilitate the processing of feelings reflective of emotions before they are deployed to theaters of operations.

It is not possible to address issues effectively without a "willingness" to do so. Individuals need to become aware and alert of the fact that because of their military and life experiences, circumstances, and situations they might have issues that need effective attention. Denial is unacceptable. Individual attitudes must change and the attitude of the military towards expressing distress must change as well! The stigma must end! After all, it is the courageous soul who processes one's fear, anger, and sadness with productive practices that facilitates and strengthens the attributes of will power.

The issue of denial must be recognized and effectively and efficiently addressed by the attitude of military superiors! Individuals must acknowledge that their stressful and distressful experiences need to be processed both cognitively, and emotionally. Cognitive Behavioral tools are helpful but are not even the tip of the iceberg. It is therefore time for mental health professionals to get real! Behavioral Science must emerge from the dark ages. It is clear that cognitive behavioral statisticians favor their cognitive behavioral methods since measuring the effectiveness and efficiency of emotional tools are clearly time consuming and do not easily lend themselves to measurement.

The use of emotional tools like Animated Laughter with Feelings results in liberation from the painful emotions and therefore improves ones' health, happiness, and sense of well-being. It just follows that the resiliency and productivity of the American soldier expands as well! Healing takes place but healing does not necessarily mean that a traumatic imprint has dissipated.

The healing of the distresses consisting of imprints (that are hard-wired, ingrained, and embedded) reflective of emotional and physical trauma is dependent upon the nature of an individual's genetic, biological, developmental, environmental experiences. Some imprinted traumas can possibly be healed; some effects of traumas may not result in healing, but may result in lessening the dysfunctional effects, while other traumas may not lend themselves at all to any kind of healing. It all depends on the nature of the trauma. However, hope should never be lost because spiritual faith must prevail no matter the situation, circumstance, or experience.

The words that become ingrained, the cognitive pattern that one integrates into oneself are the words: pull-in, "Think Connect," "Think Laughter," and again! These words are significant because once repeated again, and again along with the circular connected healing breath they become the spearhead to connect with one's life energy and the release of toxic feelings reflective of the painful post-traumatic distress patterns and disorders. They become the "go-to" words that diffuse other words that come into the mind. It is this along with the circular connected healing breath, which facilitates the connection and release of toxic feelings reflective of the traumatic experiences of PTSD that results in healing.

We always strive to be effective, efficient, and learn discipline in our processing of feelings. The above words have proven to be cognitively effective for processing toxic feelings. Addressing of PTSD or for that matter any issue requires emotional effectiveness in the processing of toxic feelings!

Animated Laughter with Feelings is at the cutting edge of removing the feelings reflective of hurt and traumatic imprints present in the ingrained patterns and their range of emotions that have been manifested within the emotional body of an individual.

The power of the circular breath, the pulling in and the circulation of oxygen are not enough to resolve issues, even migraine headaches. The "connection" with the feelings reflective of the pain energy is truly the key to resolution along with the other components of emotional discharge. Without the "connection" there is no effective resolution of the issue. In order to achieve connection the participants must have the mindset of willingness and commitment to the process. Success reaps success and is gradual in its development.

The first step in ALWF is to become comfortable with the circular process of the breath and to experience how connection, release, and relinquishment of feelings through Animated Laughter can help one to help oneself.

Advanced ALWF involves use of primal sound to access deep-seated intensities of feelings reflective of emotions in addition to the use of the yawn as well as Animated Laughter to release and relinquish profound emotion! The release of endorphins, opioids, dopamine and serotonin occurs; healing takes place with daily, persistent, and patient practice. It does not take a scientist to realize that we initially feel better, and gradually chemical changes in the brain result. Yes, physiologically the emotional body gradually experiences nature's healing process!

Traditionally, a reaction formation is a Freudian Defense defined as expressing an impulse by its opposite. Hostility, for example, may be replaced by friendship. Frequently, however, the substitution is exaggerated, thereby calling into question the genuineness of the feeling (Engler, 1999, p. 51). Knee-Jerk Reactions are psychological challenges. They occur in the blink of an eye. They are very difficult to stay alert to and aware of because of how fast these reactions can take charge of an individual's behavior. Knee jerk reactions are learned false reactions, also fearful terror reactions reflective of profound insecurity. The individual experiences the knee-jerk reactions as defenses for sudden experiences of helplessness and hopelessness. Our thinking becomes locked up and we can react irrationally and negatively. The knee-jerk reactions normally reflect chronic distress.

Knee jerk reactions can be addressed if and when one stays alert to and aware of them occurring in the present moment. Then we can contradict the intensities of feelings reflective of the anger through rage, fear through terror, sadness through grief reactions by using an affirmation, for example, "I love and accept each and every cell of my body" and "take charge" because I am safe, secure, and in faith right now! The "taking charge" part is important because the possible power of the intensities of feelings reflective of the range of emotions may take charge of ourselves and cause us to react and respond in an unhealthy way. We act out. In the same way kids act out in classrooms and teachers find themselves having to "control" and discipline unruly behaviors. Positive contradictory affirmations need to be reinforced by saying them again and again and again until they are ingrained. Mirror Work is a great way to reinforce positive affirmations.

Animated Laughter is a go-to method that can dissipate fearful knee-jerk reactions. Physiologically the breath will take us to the accumulated repressed feelings of fear, anger, sadness, and on the persistent release of these feelings brings about human liberation from the emotions and its recurrent dysfunctional behaviors.

Attitude is essential! An enthusiastic go-into the feelings and release and relinquish and let go absolutely attitude is necessary. Persistence, patience, perseverance, tenacity, daily practice contradicting imprinted feelings reflective of emotional trauma is our daily goal!

Our thinking becomes flexible once again. We can then act rationally in the wide world. The secret is to do enough Animated Laughter, again and again and again. It is only enough if and when the pain within is effectively addressed and we begin to feel better. Often, the feelings are retriggered because of accumulated repressed, suppressed emotions and we must once again address them and experience a discharge, release, and relinquishment of emotions. It can take a long time but with each practice session we can feel substantive progress. Imprinted physical and emotional trauma melts gradually. The result is that we just become stronger in our daily functioning.

Our emotional reactions are a form of deceptive self-protection i.e., experiencing an emotional denial that disables an individual's ability to continue thinking rationally in the present moment, and stay in charge of a situation or a set of circumstances. Instantaneously, an individual's ability to think clearly is clouded by fear (sometimes intense), anger or sadness. At its very worst and individual's behavior is instantaneously taken charge of by intense feelings of rage, grief, and/or terror. If and when knee-jerk reactions are not effectively addressed individuals develop rigidities in their body, including physical symptoms and behaviors. This includes incongruent mannerisms disassociated from their natural personalities and temperaments. Simply said, they are not themselves. We can become emotionally paralyzed unable to maintain a clear channel to our emotional bodies. We become emotionally blocked! What we say and how we act can be construed as canned or rigid in tone and body language.

Phyllis

Migraine/Tension

There is no known cure for migraine headaches. However, when individuals with migraine headaches have practiced ALWF "enough," their migraine headaches have dissipated. Phyllis has had a history of migraine headaches for years. She attempted every possible natural remedy until she decided to practice ALWF. Phyllis became "willing" to practice ALWF. Phyllis was eager to laugh her migraine headaches far, far away. She made a commitment to herself to practice ALWF consistently. Gradually, the migraine headaches dissipated as her accumulated suppressed and repressed feelings rose to the surface. She realized that her migraine headaches were the result of childhood and adolescent emotional and physical abuse. It was terror in the most profound of cellular forms. "It was deep-seated energy requiring a unique methodology which enabled me to go into the feelings and release/relinquish them again and again and again that resulted in my resolution of the migraine headaches. It was also the fun I experienced in the process that facilitated my practicing it again and again and again." Phyllis was able to effectively address the emotions of her childhood abuse and release and relinquish the feelings through ALWF.

Mood Disorders, Depression, Persecution, Trust, Rejection, Birth Trauma, Anxiety

The Diagnostic and Statistical Manuel – IV lists mood disorders in a variety of categories. They include Major Depressive, Manic, Mixed, Hypomania Episodes, Dysthymic, Depressive Disorder Not Otherwise Specified, Bipolar I and II, and Cyclothymiacs Disorders. There are other mood and depressive/manic symptoms as well. They have a variety of symptoms including eating, weight, irregularities, erratic psychomotor activity, fatigue, self-worth, concentration, and suicidal ideation issues.

The result of ALWF is to have a profound stabilizing influence on the moods of individuals. The key is for a participant to practice consistently and daily.

Jack

I was just passionate about my wife Jane for twenty years. Jane was always healthy and outgoing but suddenly Jane became ill and

I became the caretaker. I worried so much about Jane's health and that she might leave me. I had been close with her for all our married life. I started to worry so much that I found myself fatigued, losing weight, experiencing sleep difficulties, my thoughts began to race, my concentration suffered, my judgments about business always seemed incorrect, and I was easily distractible. I found myself constantly talkative. My friends noticed the change in my mood and advised me to at least see a counselor. I started to visit a counselor who was caring and concerned. It was helpful for me but then I started practicing ALWF; I was able to connect to my underlying feelings of fear through terror, and sadness through grief. This was reflective of my thoughts of my wife's illness and her possible passing. The feelings of fear reflected my emotion of fear through terror and my emotion of feelings of sadness through grief. I feared the possibility of my being abandoned by my wife. I was depressed most of the time. I practiced ALWF daily during my wife's illness and found my mood changing for the better. I experienced a minor difference after each ALWF session. The minor differences gradually resulted in my healing of my depression. My wife did finally pass away. I experienced bereavement but continued to practice ALWF and in time my feelings reflective of my issues of bereavement dissipated. I also discovered that my abandonment issue had its origins in my youth. I credit ALWF and the counseling I received from Joel Vorensky that aided me and facilitated my recovery.

Frank

Frank is employed in sales and experienced a great deal of rejection. In addition, he experienced feelings of depression, anxiety, helplessness, hopelessness, consistent struggle, and frustration. His sales were low in volume. However, when Frank began his practice of ALWF he found a solution to his issue of rejection. He learned that it reflected his birth experience. The issues of hopelessness, helplessness, anxiety and depression all emanated from his infancy. He came to grips with a chronic terror reflective of his anxious feelings that his life would come to an end. In time, with persistent and consistent practice Frank learned to release and then relinquish his feelings of his painful birth. He experienced more emotional resiliency. His sales began to increase. He still experienced feelings of fear and sadness as it reflected his issue of rejection in relationship to his sales but he was able to take charge of himself and he succeeded in earning a living.

Developing Faith

Our faith in ourselves is stronger because of our ability to connect, release, access, surrender, and relinquish our feelings in our ALWF practice. Our doubts, reservations, hesitations, indecisiveness and procrastinations gradually dissipate and certainty, decisiveness, clarity of action and follow-up become commonplace. Our mood improves dramatically.

When we pull oxygen in, the effect is to pull in "oxygenated spiritual faith" and when we exhale the effect at times is to release dissonant energies in the form of fear. The practice of ALWF is more important now because of challenging economic times worldwide. Fear is quite prevalent and faith is a significant human and spiritual attribute necessary for our well-being. Fear weakens our immune system, making us susceptible to disease.

Gradually, we learn to ingrain a pattern of responding and reacting in the world with more self-faith and self-confidence. The achievement of this goal requires persistency, perseverance, practice, commitment, and resolve. The above qualities gradually develop as we succeed in our practice of ALWF along with other methods that resonate with us. The result is that we become more alert, aware, and focused. We are better able to respond and react to and therefore take charge of our everyday circumstances and situations in the moment. Our relationships, clear thinking, animated verbal tone, directness and emotional connection with ourselves is nurtured and therefore matures. We can better ask for what we need, desire, and want in this world.-As our hurts and traumas heal we deepen our development of more self-love, self-acceptance, self-forgiveness, self-compassion, and therefore develop a more positive attitude. In turn we gain more self-faith and self-confidence, and become more self-assured!

Hysteria

The following symptoms and rigidities of behavior can reflect painful conditions in different parts of the body such as: migraine headaches, arthritis, abdomen, back, joints, extremities, chest, or even rectum pain. There may be a history of sexual, emotional/physical abuse or even domestic violence, persecution issues, and depression. There may be pseudo-neurological symptoms as well like blindness, deafness, seizures, amnesia, and loss of voice, trouble swallowing, paralyzed muscles, lump in the throat or retention of urine (295, DSM-IV). The painful muscular-skeletal and neurological pain symptoms may reflect a diagnosis of hysteria. The above painful symptoms and the dysfunctional behaviors that result can be effectively addressed through ALWF. The key is to connect with the feelings reflective of the above issues. Animated Laughter with Feelings can facilitate the connection and release and relinquishment of the feelings reflective of these issues.

We can then strengthen ourselves mentally and emotionally through the practice of ALWF. As we connect, release, surrender, let go of absolutely, and relinquish the tensions that we accumulate our resiliency for circumstances that we do not have control over expands.

Chapter 6

"Unfulfilled Needs"

"I have freed myself from emotional bondage by turning over my emotional pain as it reflected my neediness. I have learned how to surrender and let go. I can now turn over a portion of my self-will and self-righteousness to my higher power. I am acting to do so, again and again and again (in a loving way) through release, relinquishment and letting go of my intensities of feelings. I am beginning to experience serenity within! The pain of my past unfulfilled needs created my issue. The result was my pattern of unaware neediness reflective of control and codependency. I was unaware of how I have hurt others and am now making my amends. I have developed compassion for myself. I realized, I was acting out my frightened insecure little girl. The intense feelings reflective of my birth trauma that my world is coming to an end, and the intense feelings that my world is ending in present time no longer has a paralyzing hold on me. I am hopeful and no longer have an attitude of my giving up."

—Petra S.

Identifying Your Needs

Manipulation

Detachment from Need

Jennifer and Janet

Doris

Jeffrey and Enhanced Laughter

Attempting to fill a need by having a Tantrum or Losing Control

Attempting to Control by Losing Control

Tell me, have you ever been frustrated because your needs have just not been met?

Learning to Set Healthy Boundaries With our unfulfilled Needs!

The Need to be Wanted and the Fear that

Reflects that Need!

Roger

Identifying Your Needs

We need to identify our needs. What are our needs in present time? Have we gotten them fulfilled? What emotional needs have been suppressed or repressed? In order to speak about needs; we must identify our present needs and whether or not we are fulfilling them. How can we uncover/discover our suppressed or repressed needs? For example, what needs are not being filled in our relationships, closeness, intimacy, trust, and honesty are but a few. We can better identify our past and future needs if and when we identify our present ones. ALWF is one method that can facilitate the awakening of our consciousness to our unfulfilled needs.

Manipulation

There are four types of unfulfilled needs. Our present, past, and chronic (sometimes frozen) unfulfilled needs can take charge of our behavior. Our unfulfilled needs can perpetuate a sense of or lack of self-acceptance. Our self-worth and esteem can suffer. This in turn can cause us to experience fear and a sense of anxiety. If we are not aware, if we are not conscious or mindful, of how our unfulfilled needs can trigger fear/anxiety, we can then experience ourselves struggling for emotional self-acceptance.

It is the unaware intensities of feelings reflective of the range of emotions as it reflects unfulfilled frozen needs which have been repressed, ingrained, embedded, and are imprinted to the point of them being hard-wired in our emotional bodies that cause us difficulty. They are hidden from our awareness. They prevent us from staying anchored and firmly connected to our truth, our self-acceptance. They become impulsive and compulsive. They can result in knee-jerk reaction and can also result in dysfunctional behaviors. Simply said, it is all suppressed/repressed underlying pain and fear.

The unfulfilled frozen chronic needs can reflect very "painful" feelings. Once again, we can adjust and change our belief systems and learn methods that resonate with us to think of "pain" as energy that requires attention and action. We must apply ourselves, our will and our will power, to achieve this result again and again and again! It is deceptive to the mind. With our effective methods we can address the pain energy. We can relinquish feelings/emotions that do not serve our well-being, our effective functioning, and can result in helping us stay emotionally clear.

Our unfulfilled frozen chronic needs reflect ingrained, imprinted, embedded, and hard-wired emotions like fear, anger, and sadness. It is often that different intensities of feelings reflective of the range of emotion from fear through terror can reflect unfulfilled frozen chronic needs that result in low or a struggle with self-worth and self-esteem. The net results are dysfunctional behaviors.

Unfulfilled frozen chronic needs can perpetrate and perpetuate ongoing intense anxiety! We are often in touch with the intense anxiety but not in touch with and connected to the feelings reflective of the anxiety. Nor are we in touch with the dimensions, degrees, and depths of the intense feelings reflective of the range of emotions.

Once we have begun to connect with the intense feelings reflective of the emotions and begun to "let go" emotionally we have begun the healing process. The work has begun. We have begun to process the intense feelings reflective of the deep imprinted, embedded, ingrained, genetically coded, deep-seated and hard-wired intense feelings reflective of the emotions.

The anxiety is overwhelming and it may lead us to "act out" and/or become addicted to whatever, for example gambling, tobacco, alcohol, sex, or substance abuse. As a result, it is understandable the reasons for masking our pain by way of our addictions. We begin to heal as we practice the circular connected healing breath and relinquish the pain reflective of the anxiety.

Dependent upon personality, vulnerabilities present, past, or chronic past needs may also facilitate addictions. However, the worst addictions are created with the past frozen chronic needs. ALWF has the capacity to facilitate the healing and resolution of all unfulfilled needs, regardless of the physical and emotional hurt or trauma, an individual experienced. The daily, consistent practice of ALWF can facilitate igniting our will and will power to take action to take charge.

We can experience grief and dysfunction. Our unfulfilled needs can result in both depression and anxiety and lack of self-acceptance. The DSM-IV diagnosis of manic depressive and bipolar is quite common as a result.

When we shed, release, relinquish our intense feelings, reflective of the emotions of fear then once again we begin to integrate ourselves and once again experience a sense of self-acceptance, enhanced self-esteem, and self-worth.

We can interrupt the pattern of low self-worth, self-acceptance, and self-esteem through and by practicing ALWF! Our fear creates pain! We can suppress our pain and it can become ingrained in our emotional body. We then can become unaware of how our ingrained fear and its relationship to our unfulfilled needs can take charge of our behaviors.

Our ingrained fear reflects our unfulfilled (chronic) needs that can result in an unaware attempt to manipulate others to fill them. We become desperately terrified of our being, and of being rejected by others. We commonly label this as "insecurity." The rejection amplifies our behavior to manipulate others to comply with and fill our chronic needs. They can cause us to irrationally manipulate others to get our unfulfilled needs (met) fulfilled!

It is our internalized fear of not getting our frozen needs met which can motivate us to become manipulative in our relationship with and to others. Our unaware frozen terror can perpetuate a behavior of manipulation and control over others. We can attempt to control others by laying our unaware guilt trips on others to fulfill our unfulfilled frozen chronic needs. For example, our attitude may be "How dare you not fulfill my needs!" This kind of behavior is all too common.

There are those who are unaware or aware of manipulating others with an attempt to control! They take advantage of others. They falsely empower themselves by attempting to control others and attempt to get others to comply with their unfulfilled chronic (sometimes frozen) needs. They can achieve control through intimidation of others as well.

Our unfulfilled present needs can be irritating and frustrating.

However, our unfulfilled past frozen chronic emotional needs can be very, very, painful! Our unfulfilled frozen chronic needs reflect rigidities in our behaviors. When our past needs go unfulfilled we can experience a great deal of emotional pain.

Present unfulfilled needs can be dramatically amplified by the pain of past unfulfilled needs and unfulfilled chronic frozen needs. When we are frustrated with daily activities it is wise to stay alert to how profoundly we react in present time. If we overact to our unfulfilled present needs than the odds are that our acting out reflects the amplification of our **past** unfulfilled needs and unfulfilled chronic frozen needs in present time. Our profound rigidities in our thinking and behavior reflect our reactions and especially knee-jerk reactions.

ALWF is a methodology that is profoundly effective as well as efficient in addressing our painful unfulfilled present, past, chronic and knee-jerk reactions to painful needs. We connect with the pain, release and relinquish again and again its energy. We can then better make healthy choices and maintain healthy fun behaviors. We accrue the cognitive, emotional, and spiritual slack to think through the results of our decisions and the outcomes of our behaviors for ourselves in our relationships. The practice of the method enables us to access our flexible intelligence and consider and be considerate of others' thoughts, feelings, situations, and circumstances. It becomes easier to take responsibility.

When we experience a frustration, Animated Laughter with Feelings is a simple method to address them. The key is not to wait but to feel the frustration before it begins to accumulate to any great extent. Daily frustrations can be numerous and we can create more well-being and patience for ourselves by releasing and relinquishing our frustrations shortly after we experience frustrating feelings. It does not matter whether those needs are practical or emotional. It is not unusual to discover that our present unfulfilled needs and frustrations are fueled by our past unfulfilled present, past, chronic, and unfulfilled frozen needs.

What are some other differences between unfulfilled past and unfulfilled past frozen needs? It has been my experience that unfulfilled past needs may be psychologically triggered intermittently, and unfulfilled past chronic frozen needs are far more ingrained, highly reactive (we act them out unaware), and far more controlling in our lives. Therefore, unfulfilled frozen needs are "chronic" and play us all the time. The CD is playing all the time with unfulfilled past chronic frozen needs and the CD plays sometimes with unfulfilled past needs. We are feeling them either all the time or when they are triggered based upon circumstances, situations, and our daily experiences.

A frozen need resembles a reinforced defense wall that separates the self emotionally. It is a separation and betrayal of the self. There is a great deal of emotional pain within the bricks and mortar of a frozen need. The power of the primal sound facilitates access to the feelings within the confines of the distress. An emotional frozen need requires a great deal of emotional work. The wall that may split the self requires daily work with perseverance, persistence, and patience before success is assured. It requires a great deal of time before the bricks and the mortar crumble. It requires knee-jerk awareness and alertness to the chronic need taking charge. Humankind can expect consistent victories as the frozen chronic wall dissipates and a whole human being emerges from the turmoil. It becomes a crusade for the self. When victory is achieved life becomes yet sweeter.

Our unfulfilled present, past and unfulfilled chronic frozen needs can influence our healthy behaviors. We can develop dysfunctional addictive behaviors because of our unfulfilled frozen chronic needs. It depends upon how significant those needs are as to how they relate to our genetic, developmental, experiential, environmental, and biological make-up. How is our temperament and personality affected by not getting our needs met? How hurtful or traumatic of a category of pain energy do we carry in our cellular makeup? Do we have awareness, alertness to the hurt or trauma and do we have the methods and or tools to contradict the pain energy effectively and efficiently so that we can dissipate its influence, take charge and be at peace in relationship to its affect upon and within us? How does the unfulfilled need affect our relationships with others, our significant other, friends, relatives, work relationships, and family? We need to stay alert and aware of the existence of our unfulfilled present/past chronic frozen needs and learn to effectively and efficiently address the pain energy that may be influencing our behavior.

Our denial is unacceptable and our acceptance begins the process of liberation from intolerable feelings of inadequacy.

We can begin to address our unfulfilled needs by expressing our "withholds" of them to others. Often, we harbor resentments reflective of unfulfilled needs. We can begin to resolve our resentments by finding within ourselves the courage to express so-called withholds or by making amends to those who we have hurt. ALWF facilitates our courage to express our withholds and make amends.

Women may be afraid of men's anger and men may be afraid of rejection. We hint at our needs, manipulate others to get our needs met, or outright take charge and control! Perhaps, many of the male/female conflicts result just from the non-expression of our needs to each other; our fears get in the way. It is a self-worth, self-esteem issue. Human being have not been educated to emotionally express their basic, natural needs in thoughtful and feeling ways! Ego (Edging God Out) and fear get in the way. The result is conflict, hurt, and trauma both physical and emotional.

In codependency groups, relationship issues are shared by participants. The core of relationship conflict comes from rigid belief systems, values, hurtful and traumatizing patterns usually resulting from putting our unfulfilled needs into the relationship.

Jennifer and Janet

Jennifer and Janet were twins. Janet hated Jennifer because of her controlling behavior. Jennifer traced her controlling behavior to her need for attention in her mom's womb! She claimed remembering the struggle she had to survive in her mom's womb and "needed" to control the "space" she occupied within the womb. Her sister Janet suffered her whole life because of a pattern of "compliance" with others control. Janet particularly hated the control that her sister Jennifer had over her. Janet also participated in ALWF and experienced the pain of her sisters Jennifer's control. She was also counseled by me to address her issue. Controlling people are very insecure and usually control out of their need, "neediness," authoritarian behavior, or outright internalized fear!

If and when we make a conscious decision to transcend, transform, and go beyond our destructive, destructive behavior that we perpetuate upon others, we then can become aware of our own underlying feelings reflective of our emotions, for example our suppressed terror. Our beliefs, values, and/or personality traits can also result in our manipulation and control. It is at that time that we can make the choice to begin to effectively and efficiently address all of it.

We can participate in ALWF to gradually release the intensities of feelings; our unfulfilled chronic needs can then begin to dissipate and our "need" to manipulate and control also diminishes. Our need to control and our need for others to comply with fulfilling our unfulfilled chronic needs dissipate. We empower ourselves authentically and reintegrate a part of ourselves lost when we were severely traumatized in and from the past.

When we meet human beings who have unfulfilled chronic

frozen needs who have the tendencies to exhibit controlling, manipulative behaviors we can learn to set boundaries by saying no! We can set our boundaries! It requires that we have enough self-confidence and trust in ourselves to set firm boundaries. We can accomplish this by staying alert and aware of our own feelings and emotions. If we are afraid to say no because of our own helplessness then we must address the intensity of our own feelings reflective of our own fear through terror and develop the emotional muscle to confidently say "no."

We can set boundaries without building walls between ourselves and those that harbor controlling, manipulative behaviors. When we set boundaries, we are not creating rigid behaviors but essentially saying no to unhealthy behaviors of others. We are saying no to others lack of integrity and perhaps failure to keep their agreements. We are essentially becoming flexible, and emotionally empowered. We are contradicting our own emotional rigidities, becoming flexible and contradicting others and perhaps our own compliance and codependency. Setting boundaries does not mean that you are rigid in your reaction to situations or circumstances. It means that you do not want to comply with unhealthy dysfunctional codependent patterns of behavior.

We can become emotionally strong "enough" to refrain from complying with others unfulfilled needs. We can address our own fears of rejection effectively and efficiently as well by practicing ALWF. In doing so, we develop the emotional muscle, trust, and self-confidence to stand-up for ourselves and refuse being manipulated and controlled. We just stop complying with others unfulfilled chronic needs. We take charge!

There is no room for denial in becoming aware of our frozen chronic needs. The denial prevents us from connecting with the cause of our need to control, the need to manipulate others, and the pull of our need to comply with our own unfulfilled need to be accepted by others. The denial also prevents us from owning our fear of rejection by others. We need to learn and learn again and develop more of our own self-acceptance. We can achieve this goal by addressing the underlying feelings and consistently releasing and relinquishing them.

Jeffrey's Restoration of a "Self" through Enhanced Laughter

I finally got it, that my terrors caused me to feel and think that my world was coming to an end! They were only, only my terrors and not reality!

Jeffrey P.

Jeffrey felt a deep-seated anxiety his whole life. Jeffrey was insecure around others. He was aware that as a child growing up terror was an everyday occurrence. Jeffrey had experienced daily and sudden maniacal outbursts by his dad. Jeffrey always felt on edge in his adult life. He never quite understood why he experienced ongoing constant anxiety. Gradually, over time he realized the reason for his ongoing anxiety. He was able to access, connect with, and go into the core of his intense feelings reflective of the range emotion from fear through terror by using ALWF, primal sound, and elongated yawns. As he released and relinquished his deep-seated core terror, he realized his ongoing anxiety came from the maniacal unexpected outbursts of his dad when he was a child growing up. He was constantly exposed on a daily basis to his dad's maniacal outbursts and developed a hard-wired, ingrained, knee-jerk reaction formation to others who just might behave in the same way. Jeffrey had no choice but to repress his terror. Jeffrey also understood that his unfulfilled past chronic frozen need for warm love and self-acceptance was a direct result of the emotional terror that he experienced. He experienced a shattered emotional body as it reflected his experience with his dad's ongoing sudden maniacal outbursts. He was able to experience a restoration of a lost part of himself through the practice of ALWF.

Jeffrey was nervous about being around other people for just the above reason! His nervousness was triggered when he sensed others were uneasy with what, how, and when he spoke or entered into discussions. Jeffrey was more or less always on his emotional watch and guard. His knee-jerk overreaction to others going over the emotional edge, and having a maniacal outburst was deep-seated and chronic! Jeffrey became emotionally triggered when others got upset and perhaps they, like his dad, would have a maniacal outburst? Perhaps, they would suddenly have a maniacal tantrum without warning? Jeffrey's self-confidence and self-esteem were affected by the constant underlying anxiety of unknown situations. Jeffrey just would never know. The unknown reaction of others when Jeffrey was in their presence would cause him to feel anxiety, more or less. Jeffrey would also experience nightmares because of the suppressed, repressed, and accumulated past intensity of feelings reflective of his terror. He just felt that others outbursts were prerequisites to his world coming to an end! He genuinely felt emotional devastation.

Jeffrey realized an awakening, and an emotional breakthrough from his anxiety by experiencing a deep-seated animated sustained relinquishment of dissonant feelings through maniacal laughter. He started to relinquish his pain again and again. Over time he was able to better relax with himself and others. He consistently worked out, worked through, and processed his intense feelings of terror through maniacal laughter until his healing process was sufficient for him to experience some serenity in his life. He experienced a restoration of a part of himself. He just could never tell anyone how really frightened his experience was when his dad had maniacal outbursts. Jeffrey relinquished his feelings by using "Maniacal

Laughter"! Jeffrey gradually liberated himself, found inner peace and tranquility because of ALWF.

Doris

Doris was unable to express her needs in her relationship with Jim. Doris would displace the expression of her needs by focusing on her family, and by focusing on material items. She just could not express her emotional needs to her partner Jim. Doris had a history of dysfunction in her marriages, and her indigenous family. Doris was just frightened of rejection. Her fear of expressing her needs started to affect her relationship with Jim. For example, she just could not bring herself to say, "I miss you Jim."

Doris started to practice ALWF and connected with the intensity of her fears that reflected the pain she experienced of just not getting her needs meet. She started to relinquish her accumulated pain reflective of her fear, anger, and sadness from her failed marriage, and from the pain of not getting her needs met in her indigenous family. Gradually, she began again to feel and express her needs to her partner Jim.

ALWF, dyad, mirror work, peer counseling, primal sound, Twelve Step Codependence Anonymous acting together can help to alleviate our inner conflicts and conflicts with each other. The above methods can be used to alleviate our fears that get in the way of our heartfelt expression of our needs. Often, we withhold expressing our needs to each other. Often, we withhold expressing what is needed to be said to each other because of our fears. When we relinquish our fears, it becomes easier to express ourselves to each other. We learn to take responsibility for our own issues, learn to express our so-called withholds to each other. ALWF facilitates relinquishing our fears and therefore expressing ourselves becomes easier. The goal is to improve our relationships and raise our self-esteem.

A goal is to learn to express emotionally our feelings and express our thoughts in a loving and compassionate way. This goal eludes most human beings but it is an essential element in our developing healthy relationship to ourselves and then with each other. We can learn to access, connect with, and release/relinquish our intensities of feelings reflective of our fears as it reflects our unfulfilled needs!

Often, our "will" can be fueled by our past chronic unfulfilled, past unfulfilled, and present unfulfilled needs. It is these unfulfilled needs that create our neediness/dependence, codependence. Our "will" can reflect our intensity of feelings that is indirectly fueled by our unfulfilled needs that create our neediness and impulsive/compulsive reactions. Our neediness emanating from unfulfilled needs can affect our will and our will power! The result can very well be the development of a so-called vulnerability by others to control us.

Our neediness can facilitate our compliance with control by others, and it can also facilitate and perpetuate our need to control others. The "neediness," the resulting insecurity can result in an authoritarian and power hungry personality trait or facet! The "neediness" can result in a rigidity reflective of the development of a compulsive need to control others, situations, and circumstances. Our neediness can result in illusions of others judging us or internalizing our judgments. It is also our unfulfilled needs that can cause us to feel "bad" about, and within, ourselves, our actions, and our behaviors.

Through Animated Laughter with Feelings we begin to become unstuck. We can learn to move the "needy" emotional energy that does not serve us "out" of our bodies. The Animated gut felt primal laughter is highly effective with all unfulfilled needs. If and when the profound pain reflective of the frozen need is chronic than the sound of animated primal laughter is truly the best of the best medicine for this issue! The key is to sustain the laughter with a persistent persevering attitude. The video on YouTube.com reflects sustained laughter among the participants. There is a continuing connection to our life force and a release and relinquishment of energies that do not serve the human being. In essence, we connect with our serenity by turning over our unfulfilled needs to our higher power! When a practitioner of ALWF has a good session their body experiences a serene relaxation. It is essentially the result of experiencing an emotional orgasm.

Unfulfilled needs are also reflective of trust issues. The trust issue is reflective of profound intensity of feelings reflective of the range of emotion from fear through terror. In any analysis it is the "I" who we do not trust!

Often it becomes a reflection of the issues of separation, abandonment, and betrayal. The "Neediness" that is present normally can reflect deeply ingrained, repressed, hard-wired, deeply rooted, embedded, and even genetically coded/suppressed accumulated intensities of feelings reflective of terror. The primal sound, the animated primal sound, and the sustained release and relinquishment of the intensities of feelings of terror by way of Animated Laughter is truly a renewing and exhilarating experience. It is also a lot of fun to use Animated Laughter with an extremely difficult chronic issue like unfulfilled frozen needs. It is the cutting edge of addressing an extremely "gripping" trauma in a highly effective and efficient way!

How can we tell the difference between the hurt and trauma of unfulfilled past intermittent needs and unfulfilled past chronic frozen needs? It is the practice of the circular connected healing breath, and it is the processing of the intensities of feelings reflective of the range of emotions as it reflects the ingrained painful chronic needs and the feelings of past needs. Remember, we control the process of our circular connected healing breath. We can inhale to a depth that connects with a degree of feelings and emotions. We are in charge. When we practice and process often enough we learn to experience the difference between frozen chronic and past unfulfilled needs. We get to come to grips with our rigidities, our flaws, our shortcomings, and gain a better understanding of our dysfunctional behaviors, our addictions. We can then better arm ourselves to contradict effectively our addictions. We learn to take charge in relationship of the unfulfilled needs and in doing so we gain the ability to set boundaries and learn to empower ourselves to take charge in relationship to its destructive dysfunctional behaviors that plague us.

Unfulfilled past chronic frozen needs and unfulfilled past needs may or may not require different approaches. Unfulfilled past chronic frozen needs may require access to the feelings reflective of the emotions by a primal sound while access to unfulfilled past needs may require just a connection by way of the connected breath and release by Animated Laughter, the yawn or other manifestation of emotional release.

Whatever the category of unfulfilled needs, their resolution may require the use of primal sound!

We can attempt to fill a frozen need or an unfulfilled need by acting out! Our acting out is a reflection of a human being crying out for help. Tantrums are attempts by human beings to share their unfulfilled needs or chronic needs. It is their attempt to share their desperation for loving attention. We just cannot get that loving attention by tantrums. When we embrace unfulfilled chronic needs and unfulfilled needs with warm love they begin to melt by way of our tears as well as Animated Laughter. When we attempt to control by losing control it is also our way of acting out. Our way of saying we are desperately frightened and need loving attention.

The need "to be" wanted, and the fears that reflect that need

John described his behavior as "acting out"! John could never really understand why he had feelings of neediness to be wanted. It was insecurity but he could not understand why he felt this way. After he was asked to leave school and attempted to reenter his program of studies the realization came to John after processing his intensities of feelings reflective of the range of emotions from fear through terror that he was afraid of rejection. He was afraid he would not be wanted. He was afraid that he was not good enough. He understood that it was a self-esteem issue for him. John realized that it was the intensities of his fears reflecting his need to be wanted that caused him to act out and not experience acceptance but to experience rejection. John had an issue with overeating as well. John processed his fears over time with ALWF and gradually came to an emotional state of security and self-acceptance. His neediness dissipated as he released and relinquished his fears reflective of his birth trauma.

Roger

Roger grew up insecure and terrified by his mom. The result was Roger would take things personally! He was fearful and lacked self-confidence. Roger practiced personal growth methods over a period of decades. He gradually realized that unfulfilled present, past, chronic, and chronic frozen needs resulted in his mom's reacting, overreacting, acting out, and controlling by losing control at him and others. Gradually, he learned to release, relinquish, discharge and let go of his fearful terrifying feelings and his self-confidence gradually increased. He learned to set healthy boundaries for himself as his self-confidence grew. He learned to powerfully interrupt other people if and when they irrationally reacted, overreacted, acted out, and attempted to control by losing control at him. In time with will, willing intention, and his willingness of commitment Roger became an emotionally secure human being. Roger processed his pain reflective of his own unfulfilled needs as well of his fears. He experienced those people who control by losing control had unfulfilled chronic frozen needs. He experienced them as very emotionally disturbed human beings and learned to stay away from them. It took Roger over four decades to develop and accomplish his self-confidence.

CHAPTER 7

Internalized Oppression
"Strange Situation"
Again Internalizing Your Own Thoughts
Internalizing Thoughts Derived from Your Relationships
Absorbing thoughts from others and internalizing them
"Judgments"
Controlled "Uncontrollable Hysterical Laughter"
Additional Thoughts on Unfulfilled Needs
Phil's Inner Child Work It just hurts really, really bad!

MARY AINSWORTH'S STRANGE SITUATIONS!

SEPARATION	CHRONIC FROZEN
	UNFULFILLED NEEDS
BETRAYAL	PAST NEEDS
	PRESENT NEEDS
ABANDONMENT	CHRONIC NEEDS

WHICH

LEND THEMSELVES TO PATTERNS OF BEHAVIORAL RIGIDITIES IN BOTH THOUGHTS AND FEELINGS!

Do you internalize dysfunctional, destructive, and negative thoughts? Have you a history of learned helplessness because of exposure to emotional or physical unstable situations or circumstances? Have you experienced your own internalized oppression (unconscious suppression/repression of feelings) with your own thoughts and feelings? If and when circumstances and situations occur, do they trigger dissonant feelings that bubble up from within?

There are times we absorb or buy into others' invalidation and judgments of ourselves. It could very well be based upon our "neediness." It is either a personality trait or trauma that facilitates our being hurt by others' judgments.

We can then internalize these destructive thoughts and harm ourselves. The reason we behave in this way is because we have been hurt or traumatized. The key is to become aware and alert to the internalization of our thoughts and commit ourselves to put a stop to it. It develops into a vulnerable ongoing pattern that we must address. It affects our ability to trust ourselves and others.

It is also true of the feelings that bubble up from within. Here, we must become emotionally strong enough to reach out and learn effective methods that enable us to address our dysfunctional thoughts and feelings. There are some who claim that they can automatically just go to their so-called truth. It is a claim that is debatable and is suspect of a behavioral rigidity of self-righteousness and denial.

We need support from the outside as well. It is tough going it alone. However, asking for support can be an issue with many of us. In such a case, we need to process those feelings that keep us stuck and prevent us from asking for support.

It is in the above situations and circumstances where we must learn to internalize self-compassion.

When we become aware and alert to our dysfunctional behavior then it is possible to learn a method or methods that resonate with ourselves so we can take charge. If and when our distresses take charge of ourselves then it is essential for our functioning that we learn to contradict them.

An example is when children can be invalidating to other children and those who are in peer groups can also be invalidating. There are incidences of put-downs, both verbal and unconscious, reflective of others' body language. Children can tune into other children's vulnerable natures and take advantage by putting each other down. Children can absorb the put-downs and they can become self-defeating. The result can be low self-esteem and low self-worth. The self-esteem issue can affect a person's grades in school or relationships.

Putting Aside the Judgments

Our own internalized judgments and others' (mothers) judgments of ourselves mean nothing. They mean nothing. It is we who are affected by others' judgments. We want to "fit in," or "peer pressures" are two reasons. Our fears of feeling our feelings, our beliefs, our values that we grew up with are a reason. We are affected by an authority figure or simply going for an interview for whatever the interview reason is, usually a job. Judgments can be devastating to our self-esteem and self-worth. They can prevent us from acting and doing what we need to do. Often, we victimize ourselves by imagined internalized judgments. Equally, we can be victimized by others who make judgments about us and we then internalize them.

We must work to *put aside our own judgments, as well as the judgments of others* and do what we need to do for ourselves. It means acting responsibly for and to ourselves. ALWF is an excellent method to facilitate our relinquishing of accumulated, repressed fearful judgmental feelings reflective of our internalized oppression that reflects the issue and consciousness of victimhood.

It is not unusual for observers to make judgments about those who use manifestations of emotionally "letting go." It is not unusual for others to gossip about those who feel their feelings and let go. Peer pressure creates a stigma. Can it be said by others that those who let go are emotionally unstable and cannot be trusted to do or get the job done? This is nonsense and again judgmental. It is not the reality. "Letting go" by way of the manifestations of emotional release is healthy and clearly the emotional body is nourished in doing so. I have heard often the comment that "she often has crying spells and feels better" or "he's emotional." In turn letting go facilitates clear thinking, great aware attention, alertness to others, and to one's surroundings in the wide world. The stigma of emotional disturbance and mental illness is a cornerstone requiring understanding and contradiction. When we learn to let go by way of the manifestations of emotional release, we come to gradually understand that it is a healthy and liberating practice. The stigma created by some of those in the academic community, some of those who practice traditional psychology (cognitive and/or behavioral), some of those who apply peer pressure, upon and to others is biased and unwarranted.

Controlled "Uncontrollable" Hysterical Laughter

"ALWF" may include letting go with "hysterical" laughter. Cultures do not readily react/respond positively, nor do people's beliefs and values, and are judgmental to "hysterical" laughter. One may hear the judgment that "hysterical" laughter is not professional. Well, for therapeutic purposes it is a very valid manifestation of emotional release of distress and I encourage participants to use it.

The use of the circular connected healing breath makes hysterical laughter a viable vehicle to facilitate dynamic processing of feelings reflective of emotions in ALWF! "Hysterical" laughter most certainly is a very dynamic form used in the processing of emotions.

Some people will react and respond judgmentally to "hysterical" laughter. Some participants may be frightened by "hysterical" laughter. Well, it is nothing to be frightened of! "Hysterical" laughter is certainly getting "It" out. If "It" is present in the nervous system then there certainly is a need to get "It" out. The participant may have been consistently exposed to an anxiety ridden hysterical family member, employer, or an authoritarian individual. Can you think of anyone in your experience that fits into this category?

The pattern is one of "fear." The participant may physiologically have a need to effectively and efficiently "connect" with the feelings reflective of the range of emotions from fear through terror and let it go. In ALWF the participant gradually develops the sense of security to address any feelings reflective of emotions. It is here where ALWF differs from other processes. The participant develops their own individual "emotional muscle" to go emotionally where they need to go and dare to heal even with hysterical laughter! It is in essence a controllable "uncontrollable laugh." It certainly is a lot healthier to feel ones' feelings and relinquish them in a group or when the individual feels secure "enough" to relinquish his/her emotions than to allow the feelings to stay within, accumulate, and create disease, suffering, and misery for oneself and others.

It has been my experience that those who make judgments are just uncomfortable with what they are observing. Simply put, it is their issue! If we are affected by others' judgments it is time for us to fight for ourselves and do what we need to do! "Hysterical" laughter is healthy, significant in the relinquishment/discharge process, and most certainly acceptable in ALWF! In the video participants require a sense of safety before they begin to "connect" and release, surrender, and relinquish their feelings. Once the safety is "felt" and "experienced" they begin to let go of their self-consciousness. As a result, their group process is enhanced! Initially, the participants may be hesitant to "get involved." However, when they experienced others letting go participants began to let go as well. Even to let go hysterically! I would say that "hysterical" laughter is an example of a freed-up participant who is Very involved in their healing and doing what he/she needs to do to heal!

There can be other reasons as well. For example, birth traumas, trust issues reflective of separation, abandonment, betrayal, or lack of nurturing, and "need issues."

Additional Thoughts on Unfulfilled Needs

Are you in practical need of money, a job, material items like clothes, auto, home, furnishings in the home, and other material needs? Are you in emotional need of nurturing? Have you been hurt or traumatized by not getting enough touch, nourishment, eye contact, play, verbal acknowledgement, approval, or encouragement in your formative years? A lot of our core dysfunctional behaviors come from not getting those basic needs met in our formative years. The past unfulfilled needs are triggered by our present circumstances, experiences, and situations and like knee-jerk reactions they bubble up like lightning bolts!

What is the basic difference between the pain of unfulfilled present and past needs and unfulfilled past chronic frozen needs? Unfulfilled past needs reflect emotional hurt and unfulfilled past chronic frozen needs reflects emotional or physical trauma. I am repeating it here only because it is an essential concept in understanding the difference. There may be some internal emotional connection with unfulfilled chronic needs, where there is disconnect with emotional unfulfilled frozen chronic needs.

Unfulfilled chronic frozen needs can be ingrained in the cells of the body. The pattern of dysfunctional behavior can be expressed in our body language and how we carry ourselves in the world. It is a pattern that we have accepted for ourselves. We have taken the pattern for granted pretending it is just the way we are in the world. However, it is not so. We are not the pattern reflective of a chronic frozen need. The pattern has taken charge of us. Our behavior is controlled by it and we are not in control; we are not in charge of ourselves.

I think the best example of the distress of unfilled past need and unfulfilled past chronic frozen need is "Mary Ainsworth Strange Situation" experiment. It is a classical experiment in attachment. It recognizes the infant's emotional tie to the caregiver as an evolved response that promotes survival. It is a great example of how our inadequacies manifest themselves in our present time reality. The experiment recognized four elements of attachment: secure, avoidant, resistant, and disorganized-disoriented attachment. The experiment describes four phases of attachment which are pre-attachment, attachment-in-the-making, clear-cut attachment, and the formation of a reciprocal relationship between infant and caregiver.

A significant disruption in creating a secure base for an infant can lead to separation anxiety and I believe unfulfilled chronic and chronic frozen need. Present/Past needs that go unfulfilled and past chronic frozen needs can cause emotional chaos within our cognitive faculties. Our hurtful traumatizing feelings affect us cognitively and cause us mental anguish and chaos. A person carries within oneself enormous pain because of profound neediness of attachment. It just hurts really, really bad.

Our unfulfilled present needs can be irritating and frustrating. However, our unfulfilled past chronic frozen emotional needs can be very, very, painful! Our unfulfilled chronic frozen needs reflect rigidities in our behaviors and also reflect addictive behaviors. When our past needs go unfulfilled we can experience a great deal of emotional pain.

ALWF is a methodology that is profoundly effective as well as efficient in addressing our painful unfulfilled present, past, chronic, frozen, reactive painful needs. We connect with the pain and release and relinquish again and again its energy. We can then make better health choices and maintain healthy fun behaviors. We accrue the cognitive, emotional, and spiritual flexibility to think through the results of our decisions and the outcomes of our behaviors for ourselves in our relationships. The practice of the method enables us to access our flexible intelligence and learn consideration of others' thoughts, feelings, situations, and circumstances. It becomes easier to take responsibility.

Phil's Inner Child Work

As a child Phil was overprotected by his parents, he came from a wealthy family and he claimed that he was always spoiled. Phil just never grew up and never matured into himself. He was very needy! He got on others' nerves and never understood why people refused to be his friends. Phil decided to participate in ALWF. As he began to relinquish his feelings he understood that he was never able to experience taking responsibility. He was still a needy, spoiled child. Phil never experienced healthy behavioral boundaries. He gradually learned to take responsibility for himself and own his feelings. He learned to relinquish his feelings reflective of fear, anger and sadness. He learned at an early age that to get what he needed and wanted he had to stay a needy spoiled kid. It did not work for him as an adult. It just turned people off. Phil just focused on Inner Child Work and gradually grew into himself. He learned to become an adult by taking responsibility, setting healthy boundaries for himself, and owning his feelings. He gradually began to develop a sense of self and own his life.

CHAPTER 8

"Animated Laughter: It felt good after the first ten minutes, but oh it felt *so* good after the *next* ten minutes."
—Betty S.

"Wow, I Experienced an Emotional Orgasm by practicing ALWF and that was just as good as....?"
—Freddy K.

"I experienced more of my authenticity by finding and experiencing more peace of mind by releasing my burdens."
—Robert B.

Jim's Chronic Need
Need/Addiction/Enabling
Peter and Petra
Will-Rage-Compliance

JIM'S CHRONIC NEED

The basic needs of women are different from the basics needs of men, according to a research study conducted at a community of men and women living together over a period of several years. The study resulted in a report showing that men have the basic needs of sex, a roof over their heads and food. Women have their basic needs as well. These included the biological need to reproduce, to nest, security in the nest, beads and bangles, (flowers, and jewelry), food, and a minimum twenty minutes of a man's attention or more each day. When the study says a woman needs attention from a man it does not mean that a woman needs to be in a contractual marriage with a man.

Jim and Jessica's relationship was undergoing profound stress. Their relationship had been filling their needs for eight years. Jessica had needed Jim's friendship because Jim was "there" for her meaning she was dependent upon him when she was emotionally needy for him! Jim filled her emotional neediness.

I counseled Jim on his relationship with Jessica. Jim was hurting because his eight-year relationship with Jessica was producing pain for him. Jessica was pulling away from him emotionally and physically. Jessica was anxious to begin a family. Jessica was celebrating her 35th birthday and she was feeling her biological time clock ticking. Jessica was angry. Now, she no longer needed or wanted to confide in him. She met another man by the name of Tim and she fell in love. However, Tim was involved with another woman. Tim was unavailable. Jessica wanted Tim and wanted a family with him.

Jim was unable to fulfill Jessica's need for children and family life. Jessica's unfulfilled need for relationship and family was unrelenting and painful for her.

Jim was in pain too. I counseled Jim and explained to him that he was not fulfilling Jessica's biological need for a family. Now, she wanted to alienate him because of her unfulfilled needs. Jim's presence reminded Jessica that the family she biologically needed would not manifest itself.

Jim was distraught and he needed to feel the sadness as it

reflected the loss of his wife. He needed to feel the emotional pain reflective of separation, abandonment, and betrayal in his present relationship with Jessica.

I told Jim that he was in a codependent relationship with Jessica. It was unhealthy. His self-esteem was being harmed, as was his wife's Jessica's self-esteem. Jim needed to realize that he was powerless over others actions, responses, and reactions to him. Jim began to realize that he was powerless over others behaviors when he processed his feelings reflective of separation, betrayal, and abandonment as it reflected the issue of loss. It is not enough to process intense feelings of fear, anger, and sadness cognitively; emotional processing is a necessity!

Jim needed to process his feelings emotionally as well. It was important and necessary for Jim to emotionally access and process his feelings reflective of fear, anger, and sadness. I advised Jim to begin learning the manifestations of emotional release and learn to let go. Therefore, he would be able to learn detachment from his present situation by releasing enough of his feelings reflective of his emotions. I suggested to Jim that he learn and use Animated Laughter with Feelings so that he could detach.

Jim learned that his pain reflected past unfulfilled needs (his need for nurturing) mostly triggered by past relationships with women i.e., former girlfriends, and his mom. Jim was receiving nurturing and attention from Jessica. Jim received that attention from his mom or step-mom. He realized that his strong reaction represented unfulfilled needs from the past, triggered by his present unfulfilled needs in relationship with his wife. It is very likely that his separation from Jessica was an opportunity for Jim to go deep emotionally and resolve the pain from his past relationships as well.

What an opportunity for Jim to emerge from codependence resulting from unfulfilled needs. Jim had an opportunity for emotional liberation and freedom. If and when he emotionally processed his past and present pain energy, Jim would succeed in liberating more of himself from his past as well as his present pain!

Need/Addiction/Enabling

Codependency can develop because of an enabling relationship. When we begin to enable someone it prevents them from learning to take responsibility for the self. It prevents them from maturing and could lead to dysfunctional behavior like acting out! An individual can begin to act out their immaturity in the world. It can even lead to addictive behaviors. The person who is enabled may return again and again to the person who enables them. They are challenged too as the cliché states "grow up" or "grow into themselves" as a whole person. For example, parents can enable their children, or a sponsor in a Twelve Step program can enable a person who is being sponsored.

Enabling can become a unfulfilled chronic need and an addiction. If and when one learns to feel ones feelings it is possible for the addiction to gradually begin to dissipate. Denial is the major defense as it reflects feeling feelings. Denial is in all ways deceptive. Human beings will rationalize their behaviors in a cognitive way. It is the reason why Animated Laughter is a magnificent practice to contradict the defensive umbrella issue of denial. Medications can also enable a person and also can become an addiction.

Primal Sound can help us heal the embedded, ingrained, imprinted, and hard-wired unfulfilled needs and addictions. Often, we are not aware of how deep-seated and ingrained our denial of our needs has become. Once we begin again to feel our feelings our denial and unfulfilled needs bubble up and become readily visible and apparent. It is painful and therefore it is important to have go-to methods to address the energy that is triggered.

Peter and Petra

We repress a lot of our natural needs in society. Petra had insatiable need for sex. Petra could never get enough sexual activity. Petra had an insatiable unfulfilled chronic frozen need that was in charge of her behavior. However, when Petra had sexual relations she just could not make an emotional connection with her partners. Her unfulfilled chronic frozen need was in charge of her!

Peter had an unfulfilled chronic frozen need for self-acceptance and self-worth, and attempted like Petra to get his need fulfilled from another human being. Peter's unfulfilled need of self-acceptance just could never get fulfilled from Petra because she needed many sexual partners to satisfy her unfulfilled chronic frozen need. Peter needed an emotional connection with a partner to experience both self-acceptance and better self-esteem. Unfortunately, neither partner could satisfy their unfulfilled chronic frozen needs for and with each other. Both of their needs never got fulfilled and both individuals were emotionally stuck in a diseased codependent relationship. Peter just could never have succeeded in connecting emotionally to Petra. Petra just was not there for him emotionally whether they engaged in sexual relations or not! Petra could never fulfill her frozen needs by finding enough partners to have sex with!

Both Peter and Petra committed themselves to practicing ALWF and gradually they were able to access their underlying feelings reflective of fear through terror, anger through rage, and sadness through grief as it reflected enormous underlying repressed emotional pain that they both experienced in their families of origin. In time, they both healed the severe traumas of their childhoods and were able to develop an awareness and understanding of their codependency issues. They fortunately ended up in a loving relationship with each other only because of their willingness and commitment to participate in ALWF and their commitment to each other.

Will — Rage — Compliance

Rage harms human beings' self-esteem in a negative way and is emotionally devastating. Have you ever been "raged" at? The will power of someone raging at you can inflict enormous emotional damage and emotional devastation. The rage can paralyze its victim into a state of traumatizing terror and/or a state of profound self internalized shame. The person who rages can then inflict his terrifying venom of intensity of terror to facilitate their control of and over their victim. The victim cannot help but to comply and please the perpetrator of the rage. This is especially true if the victim is a child. If the victim does not comply with the wishes of the person who rages, then the "threat" of terror can become a component of control.

The terror includes the laid in recordings of guilt, and manipulation. If and when the victim becomes strong enough to set boundaries to confront the person, a parent, or boss for example, who rages at them, the victim may experience a sense of guilt reflective of their own fear.

When the victim sheds their intensities of feelings reflective of their terror/shame by practicing ALWF, he/she can shed their self internalized guilt, empower themselves and set a firm healthy boundary and say a definitive no to the person who rages. The boundary interrupts the destructive pattern for the person who rages. It interrupts the person who rages from acting out their essential neediness to be loved just for themselves. The underlying neediness is also fear. The fear the perpetrator has is that of losing control. The setting of the boundary also raises the self-esteem of the person who was victimized by the person who rages!

A person may also be exposed to the silent person who rages. The individual, a boss, or a parent, may through their body language or mood express silent rage. The employees, spouses, and children of the silent rage are affected by it as well. ALWF is an excellent go-to method to negotiate and relinquish feelings reflective of rage and facilitate recovery from a rage issue.

Chapter 9

"My connection to my Higher Power Empowers Me!"
—Andrew S.

What is Spirituality?

Spiritual Significance of Animated Laughter

Spiritual Yawn

Acquiring Spiritual Abundance

Divine Spiritual Self-Love and Self-Acceptance

"Tim"

Animated Laughter Results in Spiritual Synchronicity: Tale of a Cockatiel

Becoming a Spiritual Crusader!

Manifesting Your Spirituality in a Humanistic Way by Feeling your Feelings

The End of Isolation

Turning our will over (surrendering) to our (Flexible Intelligence) Higher Power

Learning and Accepting Powerlessness over Others: A Spiritual Solution

Finding Will Power Within!

From Spiritual Empowerment to Self-Empowerment to Questioning to Acquiring Information to Discernment and to Clarity

What Is Spirituality?

When we are whole as human beings it becomes easier to connect with a spiritual power. If we harbor physical and emotional hurt and trauma then our dissonant feelings decrease our ability to connect fully with ourselves and connect as a whole person with the "One." As we embark effectively and efficiently to both transcend, transform, and go beyond ourselves by releasing and relinquishing painful and dissonant feelings reflective of emotions/patterns we gradually become whole in mind, body, and spirit as fully integrated human beings. We achieve our wholeness and become spiritually connected to a power greater than ourselves. I want to emphasize that it is a "power greater than ourselves."

There is recognition of the divine and recognition of our divine connection to the divine! We have attained supreme consciousness! It is known as a higher power in Twelve Step programs. We can describe it as a "knowing" that the "One" is there and that we are one with it. We can feel its presence. It is a supreme connection with energy greater than ourselves and we know it! The stronger our connection with the One the greater its presence and the greater experience of peace, bliss, and contentment. We walk with it, breath it, see with it, feel with it, and in an ongoing way function with it. We also delight in it! Our connection to our so-called higher power becomes more important if and when circumstances and situations are challenging and difficult. There is recognition of the divine and recognition of our divine connection to the divine! We have attained supreme consciousness!

The miracle of our connection with a higher power reflects the dissipation of our neediness. It is unexplainable! It just happens.

Emotional "need" or "neediness," present and past, intermittent and chronic, dissipates from our emotions and our souls.

Spiritual Significance of Animated Laughter

Animated Laughter with Feelings has great spiritual significance. Moslems pray several times a day for five to seven minutes each time. They claim praying several times a day keeps them connected spiritually. The practice of Animated Laughter several times a day for ten minutes each time also helps us to expand our spiritual connection to the "One"!

We experience a cleansing from a stress or distress that we may have experienced during the day for whatever reason. We reconnect emotionally with our life force and spirit. It is this reconnection that facilitates our connection in a clear and loving way with our higher power.

We usually are unaware of accumulated stress and how we suppress it. For example, if we drive to work in traffic we can experience stress. In fact, we can even experience stress driving period, with or without traffic.

Pentecostals have a process of spiritual laughter as well. They release their demons. There are participants that have a spiritual experience in practicing Animated Laughter with Feelings. The spiritual connection with the "One" is common for many who participate in the process. The so-called clearing of the storms, the clouds dissipate, and people claim that they are "brought home" by the process. Their sunlight has come through their distress. People claim to experience salvation, bliss, grace, forgiveness, deliverance, truth, beauty, peace, faith, and a connection with divinity.

Minds stay clear, focused, sharp, and alert. Our flexible intelligence operates at a high degree! Responding in an aware way to changing experiences, circumstances, and situations becomes commonplace.

The Spiritual Yawn

Yahweh, Yahwah, Yahawah, Yahovah, Yaheveh, Yahweh, Yahweh, Yahweh, Yahweh, Yahweh, Yahweh, Yahweh, Jahveh, Iabe, Yahweh, Iehouah, and Jehovah

Yawning has come to be synonymous with someone who is bored. However, yawning is a natural and common release of all kinds of tensions. Have you ever noticed a newborn infant naturally release tension by way of a yawn? The infant's yawn just seems to happen. There is no resistance to their yawn, no inhibition, it just occurs. This natural physiological emotional release occurs with adults when they practice ALWF as well. Some people begin to yawn prior to, during, and after laughing. It is fine when they begin yawning because it is a natural physiological reaction, release, and response.

The yawn is a reflection of feelings/emotions/tensions that we have been connected with, and results in a natural need to release and then surrender and relinquish. There are many who participate in Animated Laughter with Feelings who begin to yawn during the laughter intensive sessions. Some participants only yawn and do not laugh. Well, it is all good! The circular connected healing breath will facilitate connection with tensions so that participants naturally begin to release and relinquish those energies that do not serve them well. The result is that participants say they feel relaxed.

"YHVH" is the Old Testament Hebrew word. It is found 7,000 times in the Bible. The names above are also used by many as the names for God. It is certainly not unusual that the word yawn has similarities to the word above. I believe that yawning can be experienced as a spiritual process depending upon the nature of the emotional connection and release. The term that is commonly used is "Let Go, Let God In!"

We experience an ability to touch each other in a more gentle compassionate aware and loving way after an Animated Laughter session. We are able to touch each other spiritually. I think of the spiritual loving connection that is possible following an Animated Laughter session. All our senses awaken and our ability to communicate with each other by way of our touch becomes enlightened.

The world at large claims that the USA is not sensitive enough to global cultures. The mental health system in the USA finds it statistically and economically expedient to facilitate counseling rehabilitation mainly through cognitive applications at a variety of institutions. Unfortunately, separating mind from body reinforces alexithymia i.e., a disconnection of thought and feelings. It is clear to me that institutional cognitive approaches to mental health in most cases lead to dysfunctional behavior, inner conflict and unhappiness. It also leads to poor decision-making and choices by individuals affected by the system, our countries' leaders, and our so-called family of origin. It leads to reinforced denial of our pain, rigid thinking instead of flexible intelligence and sadness, anger, and fear and a variety of intense feelings.

If we dare, it is possible to manifest our liberation and spiritual freedom by taking a humanistic action. Do we dare to feel the intensities of our feelings? If we learn to gradually feel our feelings we can then heal ourselves. This will facilitate greater personal and cultural sensitivity to others throughout the world.

Acquiring Spiritual Abundance

It is natural for human beings to seek abundance in all areas of their lives. By achieving emotional liberation human beings can naturally manifest a spiritual connection with the divine. Human beings can then experience a sense of completion of self or self-realization within!

However, it is important to have a realistic point of view of self-realization. For example, we say in Codependence Anonymous that self-realization/self-acceptance is a progression and is not perfection. Nevertheless, a whole person can then manifest oneself in and into the world! There are other types of abundance that accrues to an individual who has attained an avatar (divine) state. These include clearer cognitive faculties, material abundance along with contentment, peace, inner compassion, self-kindness/acceptance, the essential quality of resiliency, self-assuredness and bliss.

Our emotional liberation facilitates our spiritual wholeness and connection with the divine. It becomes natural and effortless to then manifest other types of abundance in our lives.

Divine Compassionate Self-Love and Self-Acceptance

Participants in ALWF often process their feelings of rejection. An individual's experience of rejection can have occurred at birth. The birth trauma of rejection can be profoundly ingrained in the psychic cellular memory of an individual. Petra is a good example. Petra experienced a profound birth trauma and experienced chronic feelings of rejection most of the time. The sensation of rejection occurred in many facets of her life. Everything was a struggle. She always had doubts and reservations about her decisions. She always thought and felt she was doing it or saying it wrong. She always felt low self-esteem in relationship to others. Petra experienced a great deal of pain and grief from many of her daily activities and a lack of fulfillment in her life's dreams. Petra processed her feelings everyday by practicing ALWF and it helped her to take charge of her life. If and when a participant has adequately processed their intensities of feelings reflective of their emotions particularly fear through terror, a connection occurs of divine compassionate self-love and more importantly a connection of divine compassionate self-acceptance occurs. The self-acceptance becomes embedded, imprinted, and hard-wired! Authentic surrender of deep-seated feelings brought about Petra's experience of both divine compassionate love and divine self-acceptance.

The connection of compassionate self love and compassionate self-acceptance is significant in the development and achievement of peace, serenity, bliss, and inner contentment. After a lifetime of struggle Petra was able to effectively and efficiently learn how to contradict her sensation of rejection and for the most part to resolve it!

Tim

Tim suffered from a profound sensation of sheer terror in his adult life. He just could not understand why so many of his life's circumstances, situations and experiences had been such an ongoing struggle for him. His employment, relationships, marriage, practical daily functional activities were always a struggle. He felt an underlying sense of persecution and victimhood.

Tim participated in ALWF for many years and gradually understood that his experience of his war trauma reflected his arduous experience during the first gulf war in 1991. He was able to come to grips and release/relinquish/let go of his terror reflective of his military trauma and experience resolution of most of his pain. He was able to achieve an awareness of his trauma and how it manifested itself in his daily struggles. He learned to stay alert to his experience of anxiety and depression, which resulted in his feelings of powerlessness. The awareness of his helpless state enabled him to take charge of his daily circumstances and situations. Gradually, he was able to experience more peace, serenity, and bliss in his daily life as well.

The Author's Experience

I experienced sadness because of my inability to motivate a leader to act in a rational way. In Codependency Anonymous we learn that we are powerless over others behavior. Can the fear of rejection be a result of being powerless to control others or the expectation that others will respond rationally? We certainly have the right to ask and request others to meet our needs. However, we are powerless over others responding to fulfilling our needs. We cannot control others behavior in relationship to ourselves. The result was my experiencing an emotional sense of sadness.

I started practicing ALWF and after ten minutes the intensities of feelings reflective of the range of emotion sadness through grief began to lift. After twenty minutes I started to feel better and continued the practice. I started to connect with my spiritual power the last ten minutes and the words that I could use in relationship to him started to take form and shape in my mind. I wrote him precisely the words that came into my mind. I requested that he phone me and say precisely those words. I e-mailed my message to him never ever expecting to influence his behavior. To my surprise, the leader phoned me the same day and used the precise words I e-mailed to him. My issue was resolved!

Becoming a Spiritual Crusader!

We become spiritual crusaders through daily dynamic ritualistic practice. It is important to participate in a verbal activity that facilitates our spiritual connection. Peer co-counseling can be a great activity to manifest our spirituality. Peer co-counseling offers an opportunity to process feelings by dynamically manifesting them. I have had an ongoing successful Peer co-counseling relationship with a gentleman who lives in New York City since 1979. We have Peer Co-counseled by phone and in person when I have visited New York City. I have learned with experience to access the emotions and then to cognitively re-evaluate the hurt or trauma after discharging dissonant painful energies. My goal is to assertively release and relinquish dissonant energies from my body, feel better, and to become more connected spiritually. It becomes a crusade, reinforced by tenacity through a daily successful practice. My participation in spiritual group activities also enhances my spiritual and personal growth.

Manifesting Your Spirituality in a Humanistic Way by Feeling your Feelings.

When we feel our feelings effectively and efficiently our successful practice becomes a bridge to our empowering quest of oneness with the higher power. The power of transformation, transcendence, and going beyond our dissonant feelings occurs upon processing feelings reflective of emotions.

Animated Laughter Produces Spiritual Synchronicity!

A TALE OF A COCKATIEL

The practice of Tai Chi along with our practice of ALWF can produce spiritual synchronistic circumstances. The names of trees reflect street names in parts of the City of San Diego, California. Spruce, Redwood, Fir, Laurel, and Beech are some examples. Sixth and Upas is located on the north side of Balboa Park in San Diego. It is here every Saturday that our Tai Chi Group meets to practice Qi- Gong/Tai Chi. We meet on the south side of the old Marston House in a Eucalyptus Grove of Trees. The old brick house symbolizes a portion of San Diego history inhabited by a family who cared for the park and its preservation.

The group formed every Saturday morning for the past eighteen years under the tall Eucalyptus trees. The Eucalyptus grove was thus endowed with the spirituality and sacredness of the Qi-Gong/ Tai Chi practice.

The ongoing spiritual practice at the Eucalyptus grove had endowed the earth with a sacredness that could be felt by the faithful participants. It is the goal of the participants to share as a group in the Qi-Gong/Tai Chi practice in order to stay connected to themselves and to their spirit. The spiritual energy overwhelms those who step into its divine energy. Its sensation is dramatic!

The Eucalyptus grove is surrounded by the beauty of Balboa Park, the canyons and mesas are covered by chaparral and traditionally after winter rains the arid land blooms in large patches of yellow, white and blue with many small flowers of wild aden, sterna, sage brush, 'Spanish' violets, shooting stars, mimosas and white popcorn. The low-lying vegetation traditionally was home to coyotes, wildcats, rabbits, squirrels, quails and lizards.

The variety of the palm trees, sloping hill, the new building in completion at the corner named "Mi Abolition," and the building standing next to it could be easily named "Grand Arbor."

Barbara Carey, the creator of "Trees for Life" located in Balboa Park, is one of the individuals to whom this book is dedicated. Barbara, a member of the Tai Chi Chih/Qi Gong group, approached our class holding a cockatiel saying that the bird could not fly. She claimed that the bird had been frightened by a hawk and that she had found it walking around in the parking area. Barbara claimed that the hawk had zeroed in on the cockatiel's vulnerability and it was positioning itself for a morning breakfast. The cockatiel was definitely out of its environment and appeared helpless.

The bird had a grey and beige body with yellow and black at the top of its head. It appeared frightened and helpless. My classmate placed the cockatiel on the grass whereupon it strolled among the class participants for protection.

Suddenly, it approached me and I was totally surprised when it climbed atop my right foot! I just allowed the cockatiel to stay on my foot and stay at peace upon the laces of my Saucony tennis shoes. To my surprise, the cockatiel stayed on my tennis shoe throughout the thirty-minute class. At the end, the teacher requested that my classmates approach me and observe the cockatiel. The participants were very excited and could not help but to spontaneously shower me, and the cockatiel, with comments. I heard comments from the participants such as, "The cockatiel has now adopted you," "the cockatiel has adjusted to your energy," and "the cockatiel is your friend now."

I leaned over and without hesitation picked up the cockatiel and placed it on my right shoulder. The bird cooperated and clearly had no intention of flying. Tai Gong (the name I gave the cockatiel) began a grooming session. He started to nibble at my neck. How incredible. Clearly, the bird had a previous master and was well trained. My classmates were enthralled with the bird on my shoulder. I was totally in shock. They gave me money to care for my new-feathered friend. It seemed so happy to be connected to me. It seemed joyful.

Soon, the class disbanded and I walked up the slope of the hill towards my automobile. The bird stayed on my shoulder seemingly very happy and content. All this time the bird showed absolutely no indication that it could fly. However, to my surprise, upon opening the passenger's door of my automobile, the bird decided to take flight. I can only explain the story of the cockatiel as being a spiritual synchronistic experience.

The End of Isolation

The end of isolation from self occurs when we release, or unlock and relinquish our stressful and distressful feelings. Our reconnection with our spirit occurs but more importantly a deeper connection with a spiritual entity occurs. We simply can "feel" "it"! Harboring dissonant feelings prevents us from authenticating our spiritual connection within.

Turning our will over (surrendering) to our (Flexible Intelligence) Higher Power

We are surrendering our stress and distress as we let go with ALWF. It is in this way we are turning our will and our lives over to a higher power. We can think of our flexible intelligence as energy similar to our higher power. When we let go of the stress and distress that inhibits our access to our cognitive and emotional connection we then facilitate connection to spontaneous flexible intelligence. We think in a clearer way, which enables us to connect spiritually as well! The third step in Codependents Anonymous states:

"Made a decision to turn our will and our lives over to the care of God as we understood God." For those of you who do not have a connection with "God" then simply said it is developing trust in and for yourself when one encounters and responds in new instantaneous ways to circumstances and situations. Our effectively achieving this third step facilitates our increase in our flexible intelligence whereby we can then respond with many more alternatives to new situations and circumstances in our lives.

We achieve this realty as we consistently practice ALWF. We soon find ourselves manifesting and deepening our spiritual connection and our flexible intelligence. We deepen our connection and become one with a spiritual power. It is because of our developing the ability to release and relinquish stress and distress from within!

We come to realize the relinquishment of the emotions of fear, anger, sadness as these reflect the intensities of these feelings as it reflects rejections of employers, relationships, negative sides of will such as ego (an acronym for Edging God Out), attitudes, beliefs, values, judgments of self and others, unfulfilled needs (present, past and chronic), hurts, traumas physical and emotional, disappointments, internalized reproaches of self or of others, and defects of character.

We become alert and aware of them, so that we make our lives manageable! The result of clearing stress and distress from the self is to facilitate an energy flow that stimulates insight, empowerment, and actions that result in improved health, happiness, and abundance.

Learning and Accepting Powerlessness over Others: A Spiritual Solution

The use of ALWF and the range of emotional release manifestations facilitate a flexible bridge with our spiritual entity of our understanding. A great challenge for many of us is to realize how powerless we are over others' dysfunctional behaviors, situations, circumstances that are just not within our "control." ALWF and the practice of the manifestations of emotional release can bring us in touch with a spiritual power which then can facilitate our "accepting" of our powerlessness over others' dysfunctional behaviors, situations, and circumstances. It can expand our flexible intelligence that reflects our connection with our spirituality. Finally, it can terminate any and all compulsive obsessive mental activities and bring us to a state of mental and emotional serenity.

Felix

Felix received a phone call from his friend's daughter early one morning. Jane notified Felix that his long time friend, her mom, was hospitalized and was diagnosed with a terminal illness. Martha had been acting strange for many months but her illness had not been identified or diagnosed. Felix visited Martha in the hospital and felt horrified at seeing Martha's physical and emotional condition, which was terminal. The illness had been consuming her body. Felix leaned toward Martha and told her that he loved her and gave her a big hug. Martha spontaneously responded with great joy! The unexpected show of humanity and compassion facilitated a spark of life from her! The spark of life was expressed with great joy on her face! He then sat by her bedside and read from her favorite book. Martha made her transition soon after Felix's hospital visit.

Felix felt devastated at his loss. He cherished many fond memories that he shared with Martha! Felix sank into a deep depression because he was powerless over his loss! Felix began the ALWF process along with other manifestations of emotional release. Over time, with daily practice Felix was able to realize his powerlessness over Martha's illness and was able to effectively, efficiently, and authentically grieve the loss of Martha. Felix was able to connect with his spiritual power and experience peace and serenity. He was also able to connect spiritually with the spirit of Martha because of his ALWF practices.

Finding the Will Power Within!

We connect with and find our will power within by using methods that resonate with us to connect with our life's spark. The connection with our life spark results from practicing a variety of methods including ALWF. When our practices are consistent and we are successful in our lives then it is much easier to stay connected to our will. We are then more willing to venture out and take risks, some reasonable and maybe some unreasonable. We are therefore taking action and we are expressing our willingness to act in our lives and not act out! We also learn detachment from outcome because of our ability to surrender feelings by releasing, relinquishing, discharging, and letting go of emotions.

From Spiritual Empowerment to Self-Empowerment to Questioning to Acquiring Information to Discernment and to Clarity (Tom's Case)

Often, we cannot control or are overwhelmed by others' dysfunctional behaviors, unforeseen circumstances, and situations. Emotional overwhelm can result in enormous anxiety which can block our clarity, our decision-making, and actions. Animated Laughter with Feelings can help us experience spiritual empowerment, which can lead to our self-empowerment which can result in our better discerning of present or past situations. It is then that we can make better decisions and take actions. We can also effectively communicate with others our wants, desires, and needs.

Tom was hoping to have a total knee replacement and assumed that his health insurance would cover the surgery. He visited the physicians, and followed the necessary procedures. However, to his surprise his knee surgery was not a covered benefit in his insurance. Tom was overwhelmed with pain and it was beyond him as to how he could proceed. Tom addressed his pain effectively with ALWF. He was able to connect spiritually with his God and was able to empower himself. Tom was able to ask the correct questions, obtain accurate information, support, discern and gain clarity of his actions. He was able to act rationally and obtain the necessary health insurance that covered the cost of his knee surgery.

CHAPTER 10

"I attended the laughter workshop with Joel several years ago and found it to be well presented and a lot of fun. I would recommend it to anyone looking for a way to connect with their emotions in a joyful and pleasant way. Joel Vorensky is an experienced facilitator and it really showed in this class."

— *Jason L.*

"Pain go, go, go away and don't come another day."

Physical Benefits of Animated Laughter Releasing Somatic, Visceral, and Nerve Pain

The Dimensions, Degrees, and Depths of Feelings Reflective of the Range of Intensities of Emotions

Emotional Currents

Collision of Patterns

Terry, Paul, Fred

Physical Benefits of Animated Laughter Releasing Somatic, Visceral, and Nerve Pain

Animated Laughter with Feelings is a great way to strengthen the immune system because its practice facilitates the connection with and release of opioids, dopamine, endorphins, and serotonin into the blood stream. The immune system increases its resistance to disease. When opioids are released into the blood stream it relieves muscular-skeletal, visceral, and nerve pain. Physical and Emotional pain are most certainly connected.

Somatic muscular-skeletal pain is a category of pain that is often sharp and localized. It is usually felt when the area of the body is either touched or moved. Some examples of muscular-skeletal pain are arthritis, backache, headaches, toothaches, surgeries, and knee pain.

There is also organ pain which is reflective and referred pain to the lower, mid and upper back. Abdominal pain reflects pain to the mid-back. Organ pain feels like a vague deep ache, sometimes reflective of cramping or colicky in nature. Organ pain affects the following cavities — thorax, heart and lungs, abdomen, liver, kidneys, spleen and bowels, pelvis, bladder, womb and ovaries.

Nerve pain may be caused by such diseases as multiple sclerosis, stroke, brain hemorrhage, nerve pressure, and inflammation because of a torn or slipped disc, or viral infections such as shingles. The pain may originate from the peripheral nervous system (the nerves between the tissues and the spinal cord), or from the central nervous system (the nerves between the spinal cord and the brain).

The Dimensions, Degrees, and Depths of Feelings Reflective of the Range of Intensities of Emotions

The best way I have found to describe the dimensions, degrees, and depths, of feelings reflective of the range of emotions is by practicing, practicing, and practicing the circular connected healing breath. One comes to an intuitive understanding of an emotional sense of dimensions, degrees, and depths of feelings in the physical body as one connects with and relinquishes painful feelings.

I describe the dimensions of feelings by way of shades of color. The goal is to create a visual image of the different intensities of feelings reflective of the range of emotions, such as: anger through rage, fear through terror, sadness through grief, liking through joy, and affection through love. The more one becomes acquainted with an individual the deeper more intense the feelings become, and so follow the emotions.

Can one give a better visual image of dimensions of feelings to an interested party experiencing emotional/physical pain than by reflecting upon three categories of light, shadow, and darkness and the nuances of color that are the shades of the rainbow? I think not.

The degrees of physical and emotional hurt and trauma can be reflective of the intensities of feelings reflective of the range of emotions and it can best be described as it reflects the various degrees from freezing cold to boiling hot.

Finally, the depths of physical and emotional hurt and trauma can be reflective of the intensities of feelings reflective of the range of emotions that can best be described as a reflection from shallow to profound or even number from one through ten.

Emotional Currents

Emotional Currents reflect the underlying currents reflective of moods much like the ocean has currents and moods as well. A Human being can experience a tsunami of emotions. It is similar to an earthquake under the sea. Traumas can be triggered by situations and circumstances, and the effect is similar to a tsunami rising up from the pelvic area and creates a major emotional wave reflective of a major emotional reaction. There are also major emotional currents reflective of intensities of feelings that are triggered in the body.

Collision of Patterns

John experienced colliding patterns reflective of his ingrained, hard-wired, and imprinted traumas. His issues included a knee-jerk fearful reaction which caused him to demand too much of himself. This created a sense of helplessness and anxiety. The result was that John experienced a sense of low self-esteem. The above pattern reflected John's profound terror buried deep within himself. John was in turmoil and conflicted because his pattern was triggered under circumstances, and in situations, of stress. His pattern caused him to experience emotional and mental anguish! John was able to sort out his feelings of helpless terror by practicing ALWF. Gradually, he was able to productively sort out his feelings reflective of his emotions reflective of his issue by his effective practice of connecting and discharging of his feelings by way of the laughter process and peer counseling. Therefore he was able to experience more functionality in his daily life. As John connected with his helpless terror, he gradually was able to dramatically reduce his pain without the help of a counselor.

Terry

Terry had arthritis in her left knee that flared up during rainy weather. ALWF facilitated her healing process because of the dynamic release of the hormones into the blood stream. As well as the components of the process of bio-energetics, relaxation, emotional discharge by way of Animated Laughter with Feelings, group support, music, and meditation. She practiced Animated Laughter and breathed into her pain in her knee and relinquished it by way of her laughter. She relinquished it again and again until the pain dissipated. Terry also used a topical gel to suppress the pain. Her laughter therapy assisted her in letting go absolutely of her recurring pain and relieving it. The ALWF facilitated resiliency as it reflected addressing the physical pain she was experiencing. Therefore she was better able to think through her options to resolve her issue.

Paul

Paul experienced a great deal of frustration during a typical day on his sales job. It was difficult for him to make customer service calls to companies regarding client issues as customer service representatives would invariably transfer him to agent services and again to other sections. Paul learned that it was inevitable for him to experience frustration from day to day regardless of the patience and detail he exhibited by working with customer service and his clients. He was afraid of others acting out, or overreacting. This was an old terror Paul internalized from his family of origin. He internalized frustration and became aware of this unhealthy behavior. Since it was a sales job, Paul would daily experience rejection by clients. Paul used Animated Laughter to relinquish his frustration, and his embedded terror of demanding successful outcomes. Gradually, he developed a positive attitude regardless of the outcome of his service phone or sales calls.

Fred

Fred had a stressful job as an airline controller. He was often anxious after working eight hours on his job. He also found it difficult to sleep at night because of the accumulated anxiety during the day. Fred decided to practice Animated Laughter before going to bed at night. Fred learned the pattern of ALWF, and used melatonin before going to bed. The result was that Fred improved his ability to get a good night's sleep. If he was awakened during the night with anxiety Fred would practice immediately Animated Laughter with feelings for twenty minutes and would then fall back to sleep once again. He was successful in discharging his anxiety.

Animated Laughter with Feelings is a great way to get a dynamic workout as well. Exercise trainers claim that a sustained Animated Laughter session is similar to an intensive mind, body, and spirit workout of removing toxins. In fact, it is just as effective a workout as a good sweaty run because one can connect to and relinquish deep-seated repressed feelings in and from the cells of the body.

The immune system is stronger and can withstand the onslaught of disease. ALWF therefore triggers greater zest and life energy on a daily basis.

Chapter 11

The Integration of Self and Self-Acceptance, Self-Affirmation, Wholeness

Achieving Authenticity

Our Thoughts, Concerns, Feelings Reflective of Emotions

The Interruption of Obsessive/Compulsive Thought Patterns

Responding, Reacting, Overreacting, Acting Out, And Out of Control

Nature strives naturally to bring us to wholeness, to oneness. Nature strives to integrate the self by relinquishing stress and distress that can cause disease. Nature constantly attempts to remove our imperfections, our patterns of behavior that do not serve us. It strives to create within us an authenticity that we can express in the world. Our body armor, our defenses prevent us from accessing our feelings and facilitating their release and relinquishment. We cannot allow or permit our defenses to prevent us from achieving access to our feelings, our integration of self, our wholeness and our authenticity. It is through contradicting our distresses reflective of our patterns in a dynamic loving way that we can achieve effective enlightenment. When we receive enough loving support externally, reassurance from just one individual it facilitates our emergence from present or past issues. However, it is the individual who must take primary responsibility in addressing their issues. If and when our loving support from an individual who is "there" for us, flexibly using their intelligence to think about our emergence from distress, then our connection with our self-acceptance and affirming ourselves is amplified and manifested. Another human beings flexible intelligence when exercised with us in mind dynamically supports our integration of our mind, body, and spirit! We become conscious beings with magnificent awareness and alertness in our environments. It is a consciousness raising experience!

Denial reflective of fear, anger, and sadness are our emotions reflective of our patterns that usually stand in our way from succeeding at our integration of the self and therefore our self-realization and self-acceptance. We cannot nor should not minimize the reality of the difficulties that can arise because of patterns that can get in our way. Patterns are deceiving. The mind will prevent us from accessing our feelings reflective of the distress. It is a challenge to deceive the mind and repetitively permit and allow ourselves to connect with, and release/relinquish, the repressed and suppressed feelings reflective of the patterned emotions. It is the reason why learning and internalizing compassion for self is essential.

We are denied authenticity as long as we carry our patterns that are reflective of our emotions of fear, anger, and sadness. We cannot achieve our authenticity unless we develop effective and efficient use of tools that facilitate our transcendence/transformation. We learn to develop emotional tools to discharge feelings reflective of our traumatizing experiences in our lives from conception through the present. It is also true that we may have to address traumatizing experiences from our past lives as well.

We can attempt to focus on the present and leave behind or put aside the past. However, our dysfunctional patterns of behavior may take charge. Unfortunately, when past patterns of behavior take charge the word "fun" in dys"fun"ctional may not be possible. We may be forced to address the past if only because it requires our very existence and viability to live. After all in our final analysis, it is our choice. When we have effective tools that resonate with ourselves than our self-confidence expands as well as our self-esteem.

There is great opportunity to find more of our occluded selves by practicing ALWF. As we peel the so-called onionskin with each ALWF session, our life energy begins to reappear. We experience a rebirth of those parts of ourselves that were in so-called darkness and shadow. It is then that our life energy returns to us. It is when we progress towards perfection that we receive the encouragement to move forward again and again in our lives. After all it is the experiences in our journey that are of significance and not the journey's end point.

The daily practices of our effective methods bring about a daily affirmation and re-affirmation of the self. It is a healthy trend that we establish for ourselves when we practice personal growth methods that resonate with us.

Have you ever suffered from obsessive/compulsive thought patterns? Your thoughts would just not stop? The practice of ALWF can effectively interrupt obsessive/compulsive thoughts. The thoughts will begin to dissipate as one connects and releases/relinquishes feelings. As the participant connects with the feelings by way of inhaling the participant relinquishes them upon the exhaled Animated Laughter. The participant begins to take charge of himself/herself as he/she interrupts the obsessive/compulsive thoughts with one's sustained laughter session. If the pattern arises again then the practice can once more dissipate the intrusive thoughts until the participant finds peace and serenity in one's meditation.

Responding, Reacting, Overreacting, Acting Out, And Being Out of Control

John was a very emotional and sensitive person. As a child in his indigenous family he was frightened by people who suddenly reacted, overreacted, acted out, who also were out of control. As an adult John was in fear and insecure in the world. In fact, John reacted in sheer terror to people who were out of control. John became paralyzed with terror. He sought for years to find ways to alleviate his anxiety. John had no choice but to become a seeker of self. He needed to find himself and therefore learned a variety of self-help methods including peer counseling, primal sound, non-sexual nurturing touch, and Animated Laughter with Feelings. These methods facilitated his healing and personal growth but more importantly his healthy daily functioning. Gradually, John mastered his feelings through discharge and became more confident. He learned the difference between responding and reacting as it reflected self and others. He then became emotionally strong enough to set both internal and external boundaries in relationship to others. He became clear about overreacting, acting out, and those who were controlling with their out of control behavior. John was successful in processing his feelings of fear and gradually became a more secure individual.

Chapter 12

The Transformative Power of Animated Laughter
Transcendence, Transformation, Going Beyond!
Issues of Loss
Economic Downturn & Homelessness

Animated Laughter with Feelings has potent transformative powers as it reflects feelings and emotions. This is so in the case of the following participants as their present real-time experiences reflect the issues of loss. Marilyn lived some distance from her daughter Teresa and they had an ongoing relationship but had little interaction. They seldom visited each other or got together. They had contact mainly by telephone and computer e-mails. Marilyn experienced profound episodes of depressions. Marilyn had been divorced from her husband for decades but had strong emotional ties to her daughter. She was able to cope with her depression through service to others, silent transcendental meditation, verbalizing her thoughts to a counselor, and transforming her feelings of deep grief at the loss of physical and emotional connection with Teresa. Marilyn practiced Animated Laughter with Feelings on a daily basis. It was clear to Marilyn that both the personal presence of verbal communication and empathetic attention of another human being were as important as her daily practice of laughter. By practicing Animated Laughter with Feelings, the processing of her underlying feelings revealed neglect from her family of origin. It enabled her to effectively and efficiently release and relinquish her feelings reflective of the range of her emotions of sadness through grief and heal from the issue of neglect as it reflected loss.

Marilyn used ALWF especially during the holidays when the need to be with her daughter was the greatest. There was one holiday season when Marilyn was able to speak briefly with her daughter and experience profound joy because of the verbal and the emotional contact. The joy she experienced caused her deep depression. Marilyn could not understand the reason for her deep depression when she had experienced such overwhelming positive contact with Teresa. Marilyn practiced Animated Laughter daily and realized that the verbal communication she experienced though positive caused her to experience deep depression. She realized that her grief reflected unfulfilled emotional need. It was loss of emotional contact with her daughter that caused her depression—she experienced the depression because of the realization of her loss together with the neglect she experienced growing up in her family of origin. Her practice of Animated Laughter proved to be an important emotional tool to help her help herself get through her emotionally difficult periods of loss.

Issues of loss, and trust reflective of separation, neglect, abandonment, betrayal and a passing of a loved one are all common in the human experience. Peoples' tendency to repress/suppress the intensities of feelings of fear, anger, and sadness, as it reflects their issues, is all too common.

Animated Laughter with Feelings has shown itself to be a practice that is effective and efficient in connecting with and releasing/relinquishing the different intensities of feelings reflective of emotional loss.

Ted, Mary, Fred, and Joan

Ted, Mary, Fred, and Joan all grow up in a foster home and had experienced abandonment. They practiced Animated Laughter with Feelings and connected with different intensities of feelings reflective of their issues of need/neglect as it reflected the emotion of grief. They claimed their pain was ingrained in their cells, temperaments, and personalities. They all shared a lack of life energy. They had a lethargic attitude in respect to their daily activities. Gradually their attitudes changed as Animated Laughter with Feelings enabled them to use the circular connected healing breath to access their feelings within the cells of their bodies, and to begin the release and relinquishment of their pain.

Too often clients are emotionally stuck because their life experiences, their hurts, and traumas have been overwhelming. They have not been successful in other practices or have not fully become aware of the profound will it takes to address their feelings and emotions. It is important to emphasize that it requires a concerted effort to become unstuck emotionally. It requires a concerted effort to address emotional barriers that cause emotional bondage. Animated Laughter with Feelings has removed emotional walls/barriers and has facilitated connection with feelings. It has enabled them to begin the recovery of their life's libido.

Resolution of an issue requires the use of various tools. Often it is important for clients to verbally speak about their experiences as well. It is important for an individual to communicate their distress to another human being. Healing requires empathy and nurturing from another human being. Human beings must be listened to in an empathic and nurturing way. This can mean touching hands or nurturing eye contact at a significant point in time. Their story must be verbalized for the healing process to take place and for the healing process to reach an end point. It is clear that both the verbalization and the connection and release and relinquishment of feelings are essential in the healing process.

Economic Downturn & Homelessness

There is an economic downturn and an increase in homeless families presently in the United States, as well as globally. It is emotionally devastating to lose employment and to lose one's home. Young people and adults are experiencing painful feelings of fear, anger, and sadness reflective of the trust issues of betrayal, of the unknown, and of loss. ALWF leaders can spearhead group experiences for young people. Young people who have learned and practiced ALWF can in fact spearhead their own groups as leaders.

Young people feel betrayed by society when they have to compete with their fellow students whose parents still have a home and employment. The sense of "I am not as good as others" or "I am not good enough" prevails. Students' peers perceive easily their homeless comrades' emotional vulnerability reflective of their unstable circumstances and situations. In a competitive society homeless students' self-esteem suffers. The students' academic grades suffer and young people withdraw, isolate or act out their anxiety and depression by being uncooperative with others in the classroom. Students are not always compassionate and when social workers are laid off, a teacher must wear several hats and academics may suffer in the classroom. The daily practice of Animated Laughter with Feelings certainly can become an essential exercise in effectively and efficiently addressing, accessing, connecting, releasing, and relinquishing intensities of feelings reflective of the above emotions. ALWF can, with its practice, create resiliency for human beings if and when they have the maturity to practice the method. It is then effective for those who find themselves emotionally affected by an economic downturn and can effectively counteract the feelings reflective of the loss of self-worth that it produces.

Chapter 13

"I felt as though I had a vacation from my accumulated tensions after a group session of ALWF!"
— *Larry R.*

"I embrace reality as I process my feelings by practicing ALWF; the result of doing so is a reflection of perpetual serenity within!"
— *Joy S.*

"I just cannot live without this practice!"
— *William M.*

Animated Laughter in Industry
The Abrasive Employee
Animated Laughter before Bedtime and ALWF after we arise in the Morning!
Laughter Methods

Animated Laughter in Industry

The use of ALWF in industry and corporate settings can facilitate greater resiliency, a more relaxed work environment, productivity and enjoyment with employment. Management and labor unions can unite to make a decision to use ALWF in the work environment. When we develop the ability to release and relinquish our accumulated stress and tension from employment we can experience more relaxation and therefore have clearer use of flexible thinking in our jobs. We have access to more flexible intelligence, and are happier with ourselves in employment. We can bring our heightened awareness, alertness, and a happier perspective to resolving issues within ourselves. We can better understand how our issues influence our relationships with our fellow employees. It also directly affects issues that arise in our employment as well. An example would be the function of codependent relationships.

Our ability to cooperate with each other is heightened. We are more alert and aware of ourselves, and our attitudes improve. The result is a more cooperative and positive work environment. We might even look forward to our Monday mornings! When an employee radiates a positive vibration others in the work environment intuitively sense it, and tune into it! Absenteeism declines when employees are happier because their immune systems are strengthened. We therefore can become more productive.

The use of ALWF in industry and the corporate world helps to break the momentum of tedious and mechanical employment duties and responsibilities. The practice clears the emotions for participants so workers and management just feel better. The practice unites management and workers as one team, perpetuating a team effort towards a goal. It is best to have an ALWF "moment" during the workday. My suggestion is that before lunch fifteen or twenty minutes can be used to practice ALWF in a group experience. I suggest that workers and management participate together and have a group experience. The willingness of commitment must be present for this to happen!

Employment as a concierge enabled me to experience the service industry. A concierge helps guests with their needs. It could be arranging a plan flight, ordering a cake, a bottle of wine, and directions to a resort or local transit information. Animated Laughter with Feelings enabled me to resolve anxiety about learning the duties and responsibilities of the position.

Sales are a high-stress position and marketing products with prospects rejection has its emotional consequences. Animated Laughter with Feelings enabled me to facilitate the release and relinquishment of the anxiety and sadness of the issue of rejection. The result is my sales improved.

The Abrasive Employee

Ted complained about his fellow employee John all the time in counseling sessions. According to Ted, John was abrasive, and invalidating to everyone in the office. When office employees confronted John regarding his abrasiveness, John responded that he was brought up to be abrasive and condescending to everyone and his coworkers just needed to deal with it. Well, Ted had had it with John and so had all the members of the staff.

I told Ted that John was a frightened insecure little boy and it was his way of acting out his fear and abusive childhood. Ted agreed with my evaluation and even John was aware of the fact he was acting out his insecure childhood. However, John claimed he just had no control over his behavior and he had tried everything in order to resolve his insecurity but to no avail.

I suggested to his fellow employees that John could connect

with his feelings of fear reflective of his insecurities and release them by way of Animated Laughter. Ted and John agreed to try the methodology. It worked! John began to connect with his feelings reflective of fear through terror, anger through rage, and sadness through grief surrounding his frightened childhood and he began to release his feelings reflective of his emotions. However, John needed to verbally recount his memories in therapy again and again again. He needed to tell his story!

Bill, Betty, Bradley, and Bessie

Bill, Betty, Bradley, and Bessie are employed in industry as assemblers. Their work is tedious, and monotonous. They participated with eight others on their team three times a week in a group ALWF session. They shared a positive attitude and willingness as members in a group in ALWF sessions. They were able to learn the pattern of ALWF during the first session. The group bonded well together since they shared many hours working together and spending time with their families. They were able to release and relinquish many of their tensions at work and also family tensions brought with them from home. The enthusiasm for ALWF was positive so they shared their experience with their families and introduced them to the process as well.

ALWF is important to practice before going to bed and when one arises. We usually accumulate a lot of hidden stress in our body during the day. We can release and relinquish a great deal of that stress before going to bed in the evening by practicing ALWF. Stress or distress that is harbored in the body can, like bubbles, manifest themselves during sleep. Many of us process stress and distress by way of our dreams. It is important to begin our day with an AWLF session to release and relinquish stress that is still harbored in our body during the sleeping hours. If thoughts cause us to awaken in the middle of the night an AWLF session is ideal to release and relinquish any stress that triggers our compulsive or obsessive thoughts. The result is we can return to a deeper and more peaceful sleep. We can then awaken refreshed and ready to bring on the day.

The popularity of laughter methods introduces us to the possibilities of how laughter can lighten our load. Laughter exercises that facilitators teach help participants to learn to let go and help participants to develop a pattern of emotional release. ALWF can facilitate yet a deeper emotional discharge of our feelings reflective of our emotions and an understanding of how we can liberate ourselves from hurts and traumas. Different Laughter methodologies and Animated Laughter with Feelings complement each other and facilitate healing and enlightenment of ourselves.

CHAPTER 14

Animated Laughter with Feelings and Inner Child Work Autism

Aging Parents

Learning to be Gentle with You

Focusing on Twelve Step Goals

Donna and Diana

Carol and Barry

Animated Laughter with Feelings and Inner Child Work

We can use ALWF to focus on our Inner Child Work. Inner Child Work is the focus on hurts and traumas that we incurred as children. The hurts and traumas that we experienced that have emotionally disconnected and separated us as adults from our little ones within. If and when we as adults have consistently arising issues, then it is incumbent upon us to take responsibility and initiate Inner Child Work. When we become aware and alert to our prevailing present time issues Inner Child Work often results in productively addressing them. We can gradually reconnect with our inner child by practicing different personal growth methods. Of course, ALWF is one method where we can connect with our fear, anger, and sadness that has been repressed and discharged and let go absolutely of it. Participants in ALWF experience great joy when they reconnect with their inner child! We reconnect with a zest for life and experience each moment as new and reinvigorating.

Autism

ALWF may be an ideal therapy for certain categories of special education including neurologically challenged individuals. For example, autism challenged individuals have a repetitive pattern of behavior. ALWF is a repetitive practice and it may be helpful for those who are emotionally challenged and have the ability to learn the process. At the time of the writing of "I Dare to Heal with Laughter" an adult stroke victim participated in the process and he had extremely positive results. He felt better, looked better, and had a more positive attitude after his participation in the group ALWF experience.

ALWF is an excellent emotional tool when addressing the tensions younger people's experience with their aging parents. It helps in relinquishing participants' distress experienced in their relationships with elderly parents. There are many issues arising with elderly parents such as falls, Alzheimer's disease and living situations. ALWF facilitates ones' ability to improve personal relationships with elderly parents. More importantly, it facilitates learning detachment from patterns of distress reflective of enmeshment. The distresses could be in the form of parents' high anxiety, depression, loss of cognitive faculties, or physical illness.

Learning to be Gentle with You

The pattern of being harsh with oneself can be contradicted effectively with Animated Laughter with Feelings. We often have too high an expectation of ourselves. Often, we do not take into account or are thoroughly conscience of how our issues get in the way of our functioning in productive ways in our lives. Our high expectations can deceive us by demanding too much from ourselves. We lack compassion for our so-called human "failings." Often, we are unaware of the underlying repressed emotions that cause us to demand too much. If and when our expectations do not manifest themselves into reality we often have difficulty detaching from outcomes and therefore experience disappointment, depression and anxiety. After all it is not always easy to accept people as they are without our will and ego wanting them to change. Our will and ego often get in the way of accepting people and their perpetuating behaviors. We connect with our serenity, peace and bliss as we move our frustration and resentments out of our body. We learn to contradict our inner harsh feelings cognitively by thinking that we get to be gentle with ourselves regardless of situations, circumstances, outcomes, or experiences. We become more tolerant and patient with others' confusion and behaviors. Once again, we stay alert and aware of our thoughts and how situations and circumstances can perpetuate negative thoughts that translate into our self-invalidation and affect our self-worth. It is here that Animated Laughter with Feelings is a great go-to practice we can use to alter our mood and transform our attitude. We grow in our strength as we move fear and sadness as it reflects our self-esteem from our emotional body! We also address and become clear of any underlying pattern causing the harshness embedded in our emotional body.

Often I take leadership in Twelve Step Codependence Anonymous group. I like to stimulate participants' thinking by asking them goal-oriented questions. One basic question I enjoy asking is how will they accomplish their process of self-realization? The effect of this question and others is to facilitate individuals thinking. Perhaps the questions facilitate emergence from their issues using the Twelve Steps.

Donna and Diana

The five categories of codependency include: denial, low self-esteem, avoidance, control and compliance. Donna was controlling and Diana was compliant. Donna enjoyed being a bully. She bullied Diana at every opportunity. Diana complied with Donna by placing a higher value on Donnas' approval of her thoughts, feelings, and behaviors over her own. In addition, Diana put aside her personal interests and hobbies to do what Donna always wanted to do. Consequently, Diana had low self-esteem. Her self-esteem reflected itself by Diana being afraid and having difficulty making decisions, judged her own thoughts, employment, and actions harshly; she never thought nor felt that she was good enough. She was unable to ask Donna to meet her needs, and valued Donna's approval and thoughts, feelings, and behaviors over her own self-approval. Diana had a lot of difficulty standing up for herself and confronting Donna. Diana practiced Animated Laughter with Feelings consistently everyday for a month and was able to learn how to address her fears, and her resentments effectively and efficiently. Diana also needed verbal counseling as well. Gradually, Diana's fears began to dissipate and she was able to find more of herself. She was able to develop enough self-confidence to confront Donna effectively. Diana self-esteem grew because of her ability to confront Donna. Diana felt emotionally stronger and more in charge of her emotions. Confrontation was difficult for Diana but when she developed a willingness to connect release and relinquish her fears, she was able to connect with her will power. It was her will power that facilitated her ability to stand up for herself with Donna. However, Donna was unable to address her own insecurities and is still very much a bully. However, she no longer bullies Diana.

Carol and Barry

Carol and Barry were in an intimate relationship and participated in ALWF at home by way of accessing the video on the Internet. They had come to some classes as well and learned the pattern of pulling-in oxygen, “connecting” with feelings, ingrained the thought “Think Laughter” upon exhaling, and repeated the process again and again until it became second nature. They experienced more sexual attraction for each other, were happier in their relationship and found themselves to be hungrier with better appetites as well. Carol and Barry’s experiences were not unusual. There are others who are in intimate relationships who are experiencing better appetites, are improving their communication with each other and are experiencing more joy in their relationships.

Chapter 15

"I'm emotional! My stress accumulates during my daily employment. I practice Animated Laughter with Feelings after my tedious employment and "it" revives me!"
— *Bernice A.*

"It gave a person relaxation."
"Discharge, Discharge, Discharge!"
— *Jimmy M.*

Achieving/Accomplishing Cognitive, Emotional, Spiritual Flexibility

We achieve it through Effective Emotional Healing

The nature of emotional disturbance can occur because of constant exposure to distress on a routine basis. The hurtful pattern is laid into the nervous system. The disturbance becomes ingrained, imprinted, hard-wired, embedded, compulsive, repressed, and set within the cells of a person emotionally. It becomes emotional baggage that has both cognitive and spiritual negative effects on our functioning. The disturbance becomes anchored into the personality and temperament of the person. It is said to be a parasite but it is significantly more than a parasite. It can become a trauma that is an evil that requires daily effective, efficient, disciplined processing.

Loving the self is most certainly an answer as well. However, loving the self is most certainly not enough. The effective proactive processing facilitates the healing of the trauma.

There is hope if and when an individual finds emotional tools to heal themselves and if and when an individual finds effective loving support from the outside. The sensation of emotional disturbance is both a cognitive hell within the mind and an emotional hell that reflects on the physical well-being of the body. The sensation can dominate and resonate within and its overwhelming pain is felt when it is triggered by similar situations, circumstances, and experiences as it reflects the origins of the disturbance.

The disturbance should never under any circumstances be underestimated for its destructive power to the inner peace, serenity, and bliss that a healthy human being can experience on a routine basis. Nor should a disturbance ever be underestimated for the destructive power it can proactively create in the world.

In real estate the mantra is "location, location, location." In healing a hurt or in particular an emotional or physical disturbance the mantra is "emotional discharge, discharge, discharge." The goal is the quantity and quality of the "discharge, discharge, discharge." Persistence is necessary because healing takes time. The learning of the manifestations of emotional discharge, and becoming comfortable with the manifestations of emotional relinquishment of feelings is a priceless treasure. One can learn and develop go-to tools for a human beings' emergence from their dysfunctional energies. As always one's "willingness" is paramount in achieving success.

When a human being experiences both the quality and quantity of therapeutic emotional discharge he/she begins to realize the dimensions, degrees, and depths of a disturbance. More importantly, the individual begins to realize the emotional devastation that the trauma has provoked and created in their lives. The human being can perhaps realize how the trauma has permeated his/her very existence. The proliferation of Twelve Step programs has resulted because of the prevalence of individuals reaching out for help and support.

It is why practicing Animated Laughter with Feelings can very well effectively address an attitude of hopelessness and helplessness. Cognitive clarity comes with effective and efficient practice using the emotional discharge manifestations. It is also here where the human being experiences a profound spiritual connection. It is the law of attraction that then takes charge, and a human being becomes a magnetic presence in the world.

Learning surrender and humbly asking a higher power for help as well as reaching out for support from another human being is essential in realizing the self. Surrendering to a higher power and asking for support from another is essential in ones' personal growth.

Human beings are naturally attracted to those that radiate positive vibrations. With the daily practice of Animated Laughter with Feelings, one enters the zone of the law of attraction. People are happier to be within the zone of someone who is growing and experiencing happiness!

It has other benefits as well. Practicing Animated Laughter with Feelings increases the testosterone levels in the blood. Participants experience a detoxification of dissonant feelings reflective of emotions. The result is an increase in sexual drive. Human beings respond by communicating how they become happier, healthier, and far more sexually aroused after their experiences with the process.

Chapter 16

"It promotes euphoria, tranquility, peace of mind, releases tension, deals with your feelings, gives you a sense of well-being and gets rid of toxins in your body"!

— *Stan G.*

Recognizing Powerlessness over Others
A Tale of a Toothache

Often at codependency meetings the phrase "I am powerless over others' behavior" comes up! When human beings imprint, embed, hardwire, ingrain, and learn to accept as well as acknowledge powerlessness or the lack of control over others' behavior, it facilitates empowerment of themselves with the help of learning to set "healthy boundaries." We can then experience self-acceptance, compassion, affirmation, faith, bliss, peace, and serenity! It requires learning both humility and learning to set healthy boundaries in relationships. We set healthy boundaries to prevent others from hurting us. We set healthy boundaries to reinforce our own self-esteem and self-acceptance. We set healthy boundaries with the realization that we are powerless over others' attempts at manipulations. We set healthy boundaries as it reflects our alert, aware, intuitive, knowledge and best judgments. We set healthy boundaries because we are not ready to process the deeper hurtful feelings at present time. Most participants at meetings do not readily recognize how setting healthy boundaries directly empowers themselves over time! The realization gradually ingrains itself and manifests itself in the real world reality. Often we can harbor resentments when others succeed at manipulating us. We can intuitively perceive if and when we are manipulated. We are human and we have experiences where we comply with the wishes of others at the expense of ourselves.

For example, we can learn to strengthen ourselves by expanding our intuitive sense. This realization can be expedited through ALWF. After all we become aware and conscious as we release and relinquish those energies that keep us codependent in relationships and in doing so we learn to take charge as we experience more and more self-acceptance.

A Tale of a Toothache

Tooth number nineteen began hurting and I needed an evaluation. My last visit to a San Diego Dentist for an evaluation and extraction of tooth nineteen was very costly. My American dentist is very cautious and sent me for an evaluation. I live near the Mexican border and there is an abundance of dentists minutes away from the USA. It was time to visit a Tijuana Dentist. I have had previous positive experiences with both Lasik vision correction and a podiatrist in Mexico but had never experienced dentistry. Before visiting a Mexican Dentist homework is important and obtaining a referral is necessary. It is also important to bring someone as a support person along with you when crossing the border.

My friend Tom had a nightmare experience at a Tijuana Dentist who in fact was an American Dentist practicing in that city. Tom visited Kansas Dental in Tijuana with a friend and communicated to me his experience. He did not have any dental work performed at the location. I conducted an Internet research, phoned several times and spoke with several employees at Kansas Dental. It seemed like a reliable business.

My tooth was hurting so I decided to visit Tijuana on a Saturday morning. Tijuana has undergone street violence between the drug cartels and the police. Mexican military and police battle the members of the drug cartels weekly. Bodies would be found headless in open fields in the Tijuana neighborhoods. Street battles would suddenly and unrepentantly break out. Corruption is not uncommon on the Tijuana streets, and foreigners have been asked for money by uniformed officers. It is one of the wildest and most colorful cities in Mexico.

It was time for me to be courageous. It is but a twenty-minute drive from San Diego, Mission Valley to the Mexican border. I took a Mexi-coach across the border and arrived at the main bus terminal in Tijuana. There were very few people at the bus station. Perhaps it reflected the lack of security on Tijuana's streets? It was but a short two and a half blocks walk to Kansas Dental. I met Sam, the manager, and a dentist who were particularly pleasant. An X-ray was taken and nothing was found to be wrong with my tooth nineteen. I did not need a root canal. However, three crowns were necessary. I decided to do one crown. It was painful but successful. My fears got the better of me because of the experience.

The sign above the discotheque says "the most visited city in the world." However, my visit to Tijuana was a blend of boredom and underlying tension of sudden violence. Prior to the attack of the World Trade Center the main Avenida de Revolucíon was a crowded, noisy, and extremely active thoroughfare. The Avenida was quiet, few people walked the streets, police and military patrolled its neighborhoods and fear seemed to be present.

When I got home my head was aching from fear and a toothache. The dentist was excellent but my tooth pain and fear had gotten the better of me. It was time for emotional release. My

Animated Laughter with Feelings was the go-to emotional practice! After just one ten-minute session of Animated Laughter the pain began to dissipate. After two more sessions the pain had completely dissipated.

Sometime later, I had difficulty with my implant tooth thirteen. I went to an American dentist who referred me in an emergency to an American oral surgeon. The oral surgeon could not help me and my toothache increased during the day. The result was intense pain in the evening. I immediately went to the emergency room of a local hospital where I was treated. The following week, I confronted the American oral surgeon and requested that he pay the emergency room visit. He apologized but refused to pay my bill. Instead, he referred me to my oral surgeon in Tijuana.

Neither American dentist could find the problem with my tooth number thirteen implant. Once again, I ventured across the border and at this time Tijuana had calmed down considerably. The violence had moved further south. The streets no longer were crowded with police and soldiers. However, the streets still lacked the vitality of earlier years.

I returned to my oral surgeon in Tijuana who upon taking a high definition x-ray determined I had tooth decay in tooth fourteen. The oral surgeon immediately referred me to a Mexican dentist who resolved my issue. The American dentist and oral surgeon failed to discover the decay while the oral surgeon in Tijuana immediately determined the cause of my issue with implant thirteen; it was the decay of tooth fourteen! I still cannot fully understand why the American dentist and oral surgeon could not discover the issue.

Chapter 17

Animated Laughter in Relationships
Putting our unfulfilled needs into the Relationship
Evolving Together!
Paul and Pauline
Using ALWF for Conflict Resolution
Liberating the Self from Codependence Issues
Todd!

Animated Laughter in Relationships

Those who have a relationship can learn to access their issues by using ALWF, and agree to resolve them in a hysterical humorous way. It is much better to lie on a mat next to each other and connect and relinquish feelings reflective of emotions rather than come into conflict with each other over money, communication issues, beliefs, values, offspring, chores, responsibilities, and relatives. It is certainly useful to use mirror work (listening to your partner and repeating what is said), peer counseling, and dyad work (using structured affirmations and then stating specific needs) with relationship issues as well. Learning to use Animated Laughter to address relationship rigidities, irritations, and frustrations facilitates more rational communication. The result is more clarity, rationality, and a reduction in tension around issues that create conflict in relationships. It will also instill more rational thinking about issues.

After all, a relationship that has peace, harmony, compassion, and most of all cooperation for and with each other is preferable. It just may end in a blissful loving relationship experience.

Putting our unfulfilled needs into the Relationship

Evolving Together!

When we put our "unfulfilled needs" into our relationships they can become like creatures ready to take charge and negatively influence our communication with each other. The needs may be unfulfilled present needs, unfulfilled past needs, unfulfilled chronic needs and the monster of all creatures our unfulfilled chronic frozen needs present and past!

It is important to find methods so that we can process our feelings reflective of our unfulfilled needs and especially our painful ones. It is clearly a pattern when we sound needy, complain, demand, nag, react, overreact, and lose control to attempt to maintain control in the relationship. It is most certainly clear that a dysfunctional pattern has taken charge of us. Our relationships become confusing and disruptive when we put our needs, especially irrational ones into the relationship. The mind is deceiving because underlying the dysfunctional behavior is usually the range of emotion from fear through terror!

It is incumbent upon us to process our feelings reflective of our painful unfulfilled needs. We must take responsibility for ourselves and do our own work! Denial by way of procrastination is unacceptable. It is then that we can experience a more loving relationship with and to ourselves and then with and to each other! This is not an idealistic sentiment nor is it preaching, but a realistic reality if and when one takes charge and addresses the underlying feelings/emotions reflective of the issues at hand!

Paul and Pauline

Paul and Pauline were unhappy in their love relationship. The arguing just never stopped between them. They just did not listen to each other. They both felt frustrated in their relationship. However, Animated Laughter With Feelings enabled them to clear the unhappy feelings between them. The unhappy feelings reinforced their rigid thinking and behaviors toward each other. Upon relinquishing their strong feelings they were better able to "be" there for each other and begin to give each other loving attention. They gradually learned to listen to each other and respect each other's needs as human beings. They learned to modify their egocentric behaviors. They needed to release the tensions they experienced in their work environment, the tensions with their children, and the tensions with their parents.

They learned to have fun in their relationship and let go of the seriousness of paying bills, and caretaking of their elderly parents. Their sex life improved as well. Both Paul and Pauline experienced fears reflective of trust issues. The issues were abandonment, betrayal (severe jealousy), neglect, and separation. The release of tensions underlying their issues brought them to an awareness of how their irrational feelings affected their relationship.

Their awakened consciousness, because of their use of Animated Laughter With Feelings, resulted in more caring, more communication, and a more understanding relationship for each of them. Their individual egocentric attitudes dissipated when they both developed the willing intention and willingness of commitment to surrender their feelings and emotions. They continue to this very day to process their underlying feelings when their tensions get the better of them. It is unusual for two people in a relationship to maintain a commitment to process their underlying feelings reflective of their emotions. They are to be acknowledged for their ongoing commitment. They are doing what is necessary to maintain a loving relationship.

Using ALWF for Conflict Resolution

Liberating the Self from Codependence Issues

Todd!

Todd used ALWF to address his low self-esteem and low self-worth. Todd was born premature and believes his low self-esteem and low self-worth came from his premature birth. Todd experienced once again his premature birth and mother's drug addiction within the womb. He experienced developmental issues emotionally and physically because of his pre-natal situation and circumstances. Todd relived his experience in the womb because of his repeated practice of ALWF and released and relinquished his painful feelings reflective of his pre-natal experience. Todd explained that it was his release and relinquishment of the pain by way of ALWF that facilitated clear memories of his pre-natal birth trauma. He blamed his low self-esteem and low self-worth on his pre-natal birth experiences. Over time, with gradual daily practice, Todd was able to release and relinquish his pain; his self-esteem and self-worth unfolded, developed, and improved. His shyness began to dissipate and he became more assertive and self-assured out in the world. He also furthered his education and got a better job!

CHAPTER 18

Detachment & Detachment from Outcome
David and Joan
Cure for Anxiety through Laughter!
Use of the Affirmation as a Contradiction in order to Trigger our Toxic Feelings Within
Agitation
Agnes
Detachment & Detachment from Outcome

Detaching from outcome is an important goal in our lives. Individuals can have expectations regarding their dreams and their hopes. It is important to learn serenity when individuals' expectations, dreams, goals, and hopes are not manifested. It is easier said than done to have the above approach. However, Animated Laughter with Feelings practice can facilitate this way of being. We can release and relinquish our feelings of fear, anger, and sadness, and of anxiety when we experience disappointment from expectations, dreams, goals, and hopes that have not surfaced regardless of our best efforts.

David and Joan

David and Joan purchased their dream house in a middle class neighborhood and thought they would be happy and content the rest of their lives. Unfortunately, in 2008 and 2009 an economic crisis occurred in the United States and they experienced a foreclosure on their home. They were emotionally devastated and used ALWF to release and relinquish their fear, anger, and their grief at this disaster. Emotional, financial and family chaos entered their lives profoundly. It is common for people to experience the above emotions if and when they experience a major stressor of this kind. The consistent practice of ALWF helped David and Joan to establish a resiliency that facilitated a new strength in their character. The surrendering of their emotions facilitated the emotional, spiritual, and mental strength to move forward in their lives. It was not a one-time simple process for either of them to reinforce the strength of their character but an ongoing daily practice, morning and evening, for them to accomplish their resiliency.

They were able to begin again like the phoenix and rise from the ashes still holding a goal of purchasing a new home and perhaps a home that was even better than the one they were foreclosed upon! Above all, they learned to transform their loss into serenity and self-love by releasing their feelings of fear, anger and sadness, and grief. They were able to persevere and sustain their faith in themselves and emotionally support each other. The result was gaining the emotional and spiritual strength to move on.

Use of the Affirmation as a Contradiction in Order to Trigger our Toxic Feelings Within

We use affirmations in ALWF along with the circular connected healing breath to connect with and trigger our feelings. Powerful affirmations like "I take charge now," "I love and accept each and every cell in my body right now," again and again and again; or "I take charge," "I am safe, secure, and in faith now," again and again and again! The stronger the tone of voice and conviction when saying the affirmation the more emotional power is brought to bear on the repressed and suppressed feelings. There is greater potential for release and relinquishment of the dissonant feelings reflected of the emotions that manifest themselves in different forms of emotional discharge. I would like to repeat once again the myriad manifestations of emotional healing discharges: yawning, Animated Laughter, hot/cold sweats, shaking, anger sounds, tears, sobbing, connecting with feelings verbally and expressing the story, scratching (it is under my skin and I just need to get it out), and active kidneys.

Agitation

Agitation is common. It can occur for a variety of reasons. It is self-destructive when someone is exposed to too much noise in the environment. One may have experienced too much frustration with school, friends, family, employment, an illness, a computer, reading and understanding instructions, or experiencing traffic on the freeway. Too much agitation can leave a permanent imprint of emotional hurt or even trauma from the present, or can be caused by unfulfilled past needs! Emotional shutdown and disconnect can occur.

Agitation originates from fear. It is deceptive, hard to see, intuitively blocked, rarely felt, but the underlying feelings of agitation usually are ingrained, embedded, hard-wired, and deeply rooted in chronic compulsive fear! It causes constant irritation.

One's ability to think through an issue is hindered because of being in a state of agitation. If one is taking an exam and one is agitated, the test questions become far more difficult. Often, because of test anxiety one reads too much into the questions and creates even more anxiety.

Animated Laughter with Feelings is highly effective in contradicting a sense of agitation! A sense of agitation consists of different intensities of feelings. The connected circular healing breath facilitates access to the feelings of agitation and enables the release and relinquishment of them.

The ability to think returns as the feelings reflective of agitation are released and relinquished, flexible intelligence presents itself once again. The ability to creatively and dynamically think through an issue motivationally results in action. There is greater ability to discern situations, and circumstances. One can better make decisions because one feels better. One can communicate better with others. The communication is clearer, concrete, emotionally connected and is anchored to the self. One experiences more alertness, awareness, self-confidence, freed up attention in and for the environment. The recognition and connection one has to beauty in the environment becomes more apparent. Remarkably, beauty in the environment just seems to amplify itself. Flowers, birds, trees, bushes and even the sky profoundly become more endowed with color, shapes, forms, and meaning.

In addition, one experiences more compassion and empathy for another's situation and circumstances. There is more tolerance for others, for self, less self-stubbornness, less negative ego (the acronym for Edging God Out), and more flexible behavior. Agitation creates rigid inflexible thinking, feelings, and reactions instead of flexible intelligent responsiveness.

Agnes

Agnes grew up in Los Angeles, California. She was affected emotionally by her experience on the freeways in Los Angeles. Agnes experienced a great deal of agitation because of her constant stress on the roadways. The irritation just continued to grow within her from years of experiencing traffic congestion. The traffic in Los Angeles got to her again and again and again. She developed enormous anxiety corresponding to her traffic experiences. The experience included road rage. However, she had no choice but to use the freeways to continue her employment. She decided to use Animated Laughter with Feelings as a daily practice to address her agitation resulting from her anxiety. She practiced ALWF on a continual basis. She became comfortable with the method and learned to connect and discharge her feelings using a variety of manifestations, including: Animated Laughter with Feelings, yawns, anger sounds and even primal sound. It enabled her to address and access the feelings reflective of her distress. She learned to release and relinquish her agitation and let it go effectively and efficiently. In fact, she learned to connect with her irritation and discharge her feelings by way of yawning in the automobile while driving on the freeways. This enabled her to discharge tension and at the same time free up more attention for the freeway traffic. She learned to let go absolutely. Agnes learned to better handle the emotional frustration while in traffic in Los Angeles. Agnes continues to practice ALWF for other issues as well.

CHAPTER 19

"My initial resistance along with physical pain triggered my defenses causing me to experience denial. As I started to laugh, I could feel layers and layers of buried emotions. As I continued through the process of connecting to my core through Animated Laughter many emotions came out (pain, loss, frustration, joy, fears, loss, hopes, longing). By the end of the session, I felt emotional weights had been lifted because of my willingness to release and let go. The experience was exhilarating and I felt euphoric."

— *Scott M.*

Video on YouTube.com
And Veoh.com
Theresa
Radiating Health in the World

Video on YouTube

The video Animated Laughter with Feelings on YouTube.com shares with the viewer a brief ten-minute segment of an actual group exercise. It shows how an ALWF inexperienced, pristine group gradually allows and permits a connection with, and a letting go of feelings reflective of emotions. In addition, it shows how they experience the process with a fun filled, zany, and playful attitude.

For many, the healthy processing of intensities of feelings reflective of the range of emotions or practicing emotional release manifestations is "unusual!" The common judgments and reactions may include, "They are nuts" or "It is just not normal." "What are they about" as one views the video of participants practicing ALWF. However, the use of tearing, sobbing, yawning, shaking of the body, hot/cold sweats, active kidneys, scratching (it is under my skin and I need to get it out), release of anger through sounds/pounding of the fists, connecting verbally with feelings, expressing a story in an animated way, and yes, Animated Laughter, are healthy ways of relinquishing intensities of feelings reflective of stress, distress, hurt and trauma. For the observer it is a new experience to watch another individual connect with their emotions and begin to discharge their feelings. Often, the observer's unconscious fears are triggered when observing an individual process one's feelings.

Theresa

Theresa's reaction to first viewing ALWF was very common. "When I first observed the video, I thought to myself that the participants were really strange but then I found myself pulling-in oxygen, connecting with my feelings, dropping my chin, sighing, and guess what? Even I started to laugh and yawn with the group in the video." I began to realize that I needed to connect with and relinquish my stress from work as well! After I practiced AWLF a couple of times it just became second nature for me to do it on a daily basis. I just simply felt reinvigorated, recharged, and energized!"

One can view and participate in ALWF by going to YouTube.com or Veoh.com and writing in "Animated Laughter with

Feelings" and then click search. One can then participate and follow the instructions set forth by the facilitator who happens to be the author.

Radiating Health in the World

Those who practice ALWF find themselves radiating a healthy attitude and a young and healthy appearance. People respond to the positive healthy look of participants who radiate the law of attraction. The "Law of Attraction," like a magnet, draws people to those who practice ALWF with success!

Chapter 20

Achieving/Accomplishing Cognitive, Emotional, Spiritual Flexibility

We achieve it through Emotional Discharge!

Once Again experiencing our Unfulfilled Emotional Needs!

We are effective in our healing, in our learning genuine self-love

The practice of both primal sound and the manifestations of emotional release are essential in addressing chronic and frozen chronic ingrained, embedded, imprinted, and hard-wired distress. When we are successful in learning and consistently practice methods of emotional release and relinquishment of our underlying repressed feelings, we are assured of our gradual healing. The profoundest of distresses can be successfully addressed. The will, the willing intention, willingness of commitment, and connection to our will power, are achieved as we emotionally process our issues. Our flexible intelligence expands as our emotional release deepens and becomes both effective and efficient. Our emotional success facilitates expansion of our flexibility in a cognitive and in a spiritual way as well! We cannot help but experience the results of an integration of mind, body, and spirit.

It can take a great deal of practice moving through intensities of feelings reflective of anxiety and the range of emotions, anger through rage, fear through terror and sadness through grief. It is a gradual processing that occurs. Our processing of underlying feelings reflects different issues. It results in our reaching a realization that past unfulfilled chronic frozen needs, past unfulfilled chronic needs, past unfulfilled needs, and present unfulfilled needs are at the core of most imprinted, embedded, ingrained, and hard-wired traumas. It reflects unhealthy behaviors and compulsive/impulsive unhealthy reactions in present time in our lives. Our many addictions serve as examples. Simply said, we just needed to have had a healthy experience from conception through our formative years—from birth through age six. If we did not have this experience then our sense of safety in our life's development was compromised by emotional hurt and trauma.

It is quite a realization when we discover that unfulfilled needs lie at the core of most of our issues that result in a basic need for our own self-acceptance and approval. The result is that most of us have not received anywhere near the nurturing that we require for success in our present intimate relationships. It is the main reason why loving relationships experience pain and suffering.

We use ALWF to process the intensities of feelings reflective of the ingrained, embedded, imprinted, and hard-wired pain reflective of our unfulfilled needs as it reflects our issue of neglect. Our experience of neglect directly influences the dimensions, degrees, and depths of our depression and anxiety. Of course, our feelings of depression and anxiety decrease when we are disciplined, effective, and efficient in the processing of our pain.

We can address our pain energy through transformation by way of primal sound and the manifestations of emotional release; for example, having a good cry. We can also transcend our pain through prayerful affirmations, "God, grant me the serenity to accept." We can also learn to go beyond the pain and experience possible transformation and transcendence of its dissonant energies.

When we reach our core unfulfilled needs and begin to process our pain the connection with genuine, authentic love takes place. We have accomplished a great emotional feat! We have awakened from the darkness of our nightmare! We begin to experience our authenticity! Inner love begins to emanate primarily from within. It comes from the spark of our life creation. Our need or neediness dissipates and inner true love begins to flow from our spiritual core and begins radiating out. We experience authentic genuine inner peace. The result is that our need to fulfill love from the outside lessens and we experience more contentment. We have arrived at a more enlightened state of consciousness. This is not an idealistic thought but a result of daily practice as it reflects our journey to wholeness.

We can enhance/brighten our inner life spark and expand our inner love by dimensions, degrees, and depths simply by continuing our effective, efficient, and disciplined practices. This is truly a hopeful, promising, self-fulfilling, and uplifting experience! It works.

Chapter 21

Getting out of your Head and into your Body
Internalized Oppression
Internalizing your own thoughts
Internalizing thoughts derived from your relationships
Absorbing thoughts from others and Internalizing them

Thousands upon thousands of thoughts pass through our mind on a daily basis. Our erratic thoughts prevent us from addressing, accessing, and connecting with feelings reflective of our issues. Our thoughts just get in our way. In traditional psychotherapy the verbal is always the predominant method of processing an issue. Well, this method is just not enough. Many clients just go around and around with their thoughts in tangles without ever getting to the resolution of an issue. Traumas run deep and because of their nature it is incumbent upon an individual to learn methods that facilitate accessing hard-wired feelings reflective of emotions.

When a person is hurt or traumatized, the dimensions, degrees, and depths of their feelings reflective of their emotions is changed profoundly. This differs from person to person because of our different genetic, biological, experiential, developmental and environmental makeup. Hurt and trauma affect us differently because of human beings' temperaments which reflect their personalities. The temperament could be bold, shy, or good-natured; people normally have a combination of personality and temperamental traits. Our personalities and temperaments mainly come from our genetic makeup.

A goal of ALWF is to teach participants to "Get out of their heads" and allow and permit the use of their circular connected healing breath to help them get into their emotional body. The goal is to have participants **connect** with their feelings and begin the process of unraveling those issues that cause them constant aware and unaware stress. ALWF makes it much easier because participants have a fun and zany time achieving awareness.

Our thoughts and feelings are also influenced by our learned beliefs and values, accumulated as we grew up in our culture. All of these components can get in our way when we learn to process our feelings by way of ALWF. It is the reason why the pulling in of oxygen to access and connect with our feelings in our emotional body, and doing it repetitively, is so significant. We begin to experience ourselves! We begin to experience our emotional body. We begin to experience a reality that many of us have been disconnected from. We begin to realize that "Somewhere over the rainbow" is within and not outside ourselves.

CHAPTER 22

"I bring my will, willing intention, and willingness to my self-actualization by practicing ALWF, and process effectively and efficiently my imprinted, hard-wired, chronic, frozen, stuck feelings reflective of my emotions! It works and more importantly, I work."

— *Sam T.*

Advanced Animated Laughter with Feelings
AALWF
Integrating Animated Laughter with Primal Sound/ Elongated Yawns
Embracing the Power of Now with ALWF
Experiencing the Ageless Timeless Eternal Infinite Now!

After one has become experienced and mastered the Animated Laughter with Feelings process, one begins to realize that the circular connected healing breath is facilitating access to a natural and automatic movement to deeper feelings reflective of a range of emotions. It is a natural physiological and emotional progression. It is nature's way of facilitating deeper and more profound healing and personal growth. We cannot resist the natural physiological and emotional progression of personal growth, self-realization, and a movement to an enlightened state of spiritual consciousness in the ten components of the self: mental, emotional, spirit, spiritual, physical, social, intuitive, creative, heart, and soul centers.

Animated Laughter with Feelings and Advanced Animated Laughter with Feelings is proving to be an effective and efficient therapy to address both emotional and physical trauma. It is exciting to experience the dramatic changes that facilitate liberation in mind, body and spirit after effectively connecting with the feelings reflective of the range of emotions and releasing/relinquishing them through sustained laughter. This is also shared with elongated yawning as well as with other manifestations of emotional discharge.

It is even more effective and efficient to experience profound healing with Advanced Animated Laughter with Feelings, which facilitates both deeper connection with the intensities of feelings reflective of a deeper range of emotions, for example fear through terror, and learning disciplined, effective and efficient release and discharge. Naturally, experience is required practicing the process of the basic pattern first. Simply said, we build our self-confidence practicing the basic pattern of ALWF.

Advanced Animated Laughter with Feelings brings laughter, elongated yawns, and primal sound as the three key components to bear upon the effective and efficient addressing, accessing, connecting, release and relinquishment of deeper seated emotional and physical distress (pain) and its resolution.

The use of primal sound in the form of a so-called scream is useful in the practice of ALWF. The so-called scream in a primal sound is different from a scream that one would normally hear in a non-healing environment. The non-healing scream may not have the healing impact that a primal healing sound would have. There are many who have experienced an emotional release using the primal sound and never experience a sore throat. It is this kind of primal scream and sound that is the natural physiological healing sound of spirit. The sound, in fact, is the release mechanism that facilitates emotional discharge! It is the sound that “unlocks” the feelings and facilitates the discharge. It is “here” where we find the resolution of profound trauma like PTSD.

In achieving this goal one should not lose sight of imprinted traumas retriggered from similar situations, and circumstances that result in the re-stimulations of trauma. However, if and when individuals are "willing" to learn and practice on a daily basis an effective and efficient program of processing retriggered re-stimulations then healing is not only possible and probable, it is assured! It truly is a major human accomplishment to realistically emerge from distress!

A human being's flexible intelligence and clear thinking immediately returns until the next time the trauma is retriggered and re-stimulated by similar situations and circumstances. It is at that time when a human being's ability to use effective and efficient innate flexible intelligence reflective of their clear thinking is clouded and blocked.

Step three of Codependents Anonymous states: "Made a decision to turn our will and our lives over to the care of God as we understood God." This third step is significant as it relates to the serenity prayer: "God grant me the serenity to accept the things I cannot change, change the things I can and the wisdom to know the difference."

We can relinquish our conflicts and experience serenity by making a conscious decision to turn our unfulfilled present needs, unfulfilled past needs, unfulfilled chronic needs, unfulfilled chronic frozen needs, our unfulfilled wants, desires, dreams, our disappointments, our negative aspects of ego, our hurts/traumas, that can make our lives unmanageable, and then turn our lives over to the care of God as we understood God.

If and when we are effective in processing our unfulfilled needs as well as in turning over our disappointments, negative aspects of ego, our hurts/traumas—that could potentially make our lives unmanageable—to spirit, and manage our lives in a functional way, we can then ground ourselves in faith, peace, and bliss. This is a fluid process that comes and goes. When we are persistent and consistent we will evolve as the process moves us to a healthy state of consciousness. The culmination of quality and quantity of emotional discharge results in a realization and awareness that one's personal growth has no limits. It takes emotional work to experience our bliss and connection to our higher power. It is then that we can embrace the power of present time and the power of the now!

We can also embrace the empowerment of an ageless, infinite, timeless life!

CHAPTER 23

Animated Laughter Workshops
Sierra Club
Miracles Retreat
Christ Lutheran Church
First Spiritualist Church
San Diego Transformational Meet up Group
Michael's Guatay Homestead
Whole Being Weekends
Palomar Mountain
Sierra Club

It is October 31st, Halloween and the Sierra Club is having their holistic gathering in the Cuyamaca Mountains, San Diego County, California. Participants have canceled it twice in 2007 because of fires and in 2008 because of sharp increases in the price of gasoline, as well as cancellations. Animated Laughter with Feelings originated because of the Sierra Club's holistic gatherings.

The San Diego Sierra Club's Mt. Laguna Cabin Retreat is located along the Sunrise Highway. The beautiful Anza-Borrego Desert can be viewed from the location of the retreat. The Sierra Club is established nationwide and together with its affiliate Sierra Club Canada is committed to raising awareness and educating the general public about the protection and restoration of nature and its significance to the human environment.

The leader of another group recommended several participants to ALWF because of its healing, anti-aging and rejuvenating powers. Several participants decided to learn ALWF. A participant named Sidney claimed never "really" being able to experience "letting go!" Sidney commented after the experience that it left him exhilarated, renewed, and hopeful. Another participant, named Alexander, commented that he had a positive experience with the use of infectious laughter. He claimed, "The power of infectious laughter facilitated an empowered and a loving connection to himself." Judy claimed that, "she had bursts of overpowering joyful, sustained laughter!" Betty claimed, "that after forty years she finally "got it!"

I lead a rebirthing class at the Foster Lodge location in 2005. I successfully practiced and became expert in the myriad manifestations of emotional discharge. Since discovering the practice of peer counseling in 1972, Animated Laughter was one of the manifestations of emotional discharge that became prevalent as one of my practices. At Foster Lodge, I noticed one of the participants connecting with her negative, destructive, deep-seated, rooted, entrenched, feelings and relinquishing them by Animated Laughter during a rebirthing class. I realized it was a great way to guide people in their stress discharge, self-realization, personal growth and spiritual connection. There were other participants who began to laugh with animation as well. It dawned on me that ALWF was an easier way to achieve connection to deep-seated feelings reflective of emotions and to release and relinquish them. I began holding ALWF classes and workshops on a regular basis and continued having them at Miracles Retreats, Christ Lutheran Church, First Spiritualist Church, San Diego Transformational Meet up Groups, private homes and Whole Being Weekends with great success. They have proven especially popular with seniors.

Michael's Guatay Homestead

The leaves on the trees were beginning to change and the Laguna Mountains just east of San Diego were beginning to release their spiritual autumn power. The change in seasons, the shortening of days is symbolic of transition. It can be said that the earth indicates to human beings to make changes within themselves, their lives, their consciousnesses. Change is a natural evolution of human life span and life cycle. At this time, I find myself at the retreat home of Michael in this beautiful setting.

Michael holds his monthly meetings with different holistic themes. Today, it is ALWF. As I lead an ALWF class in Guatay, the mountains, valleys, and canyons echo with the laughter of twenty-five participants. The participants are in the house, on the patio, around the house on the asphalt. The twenty-five participants' laughter reverberates throughout the area in the canyons, from the mountains, and over the hills into the distant valleys. It was as though the mountains themselves were infected by the irresistible laughter.

Miracle Retreats

The Miracles Retreats have been held in San Diego County for many years. Mary Brenda McQueen and Syd Clopton originated the retreats. They are traditionally held at Angels Landing and Camp Marston near the old mining town of Julian, California. It is here that a group of about twelve participants experienced a pandemonium laughter session. The group laughed non-stop for forty minutes and just could not help surrendering to the ongoing gaiety. One participant claimed, "I am just amazed at the depth of laughter I experienced. I never thought I had it in me to laugh so hard and so long. The sounds came from an emotional depth within me that was totally new and refreshing!"

Chapter 24

Summary
Getting It
Hard-wired
Rigidity and Control
Layered Traumas

Is ALWF right for you? Does it resonate with you? Have you tried it once, twice? Have you given it a chance to work for you? Have you derived benefit in some way shape or form from it?

There are many personal growth methods that may or may not resonate with you. If the method or methods you use do not hurt or harm you or hurt or harm another person then it is all good!

Is ALWF work, labor of love, or just a zany fun activity? It all depends upon attitude. Yes, it can be all of the above! I experience it as an experience that is zany, fun, outrageous, and a special and unique group experience, as well as an opportunity to just let go and let the tensions out!

The practice of ALWF will facilitate a present time experience. Animated Laughter is a moment-to-moment processing of dissonant energies. The participant is immediately returned to a present time reality. It has the power to achieve this by the instantaneous experience of the laugh, a primal laugh, and its sound.

Sometimes the best humankind can hope for is to coexist with chronic distress and use its energy to grow in strength, wisdom and flexible intelligence. Compassionate self-love is especially significant for oneself. When we stay conscious of loving ourselves, no matter how we feel, then the intensities of our fear reflective of the range of emotions from fear through terror has a better opportunity to move through our body and dissipate. It is important for us to stay alert to the times when we are triggered and caught, gripped, and paralyzed by our fear. It is then that we must respond to it effectively and efficiently and address it with enthusiasm. Often, we may not "feel like" addressing it with zest. It is incumbent upon us to be a witness to our mood and realize that it is fear that is getting in our way. It is then we can make the decision to begin processing our feelings reflective of our emotions. Our awareness and alertness to our behaviors reflective of our moods is key to our processing our feelings or choosing to refrain from embarking upon proactively addressing our feelings. Our moods can effectively paralyze our taking action to help ourselves in our endeavors to process our emotions. We can better address efficiently and effectively our dysfunctional and unhealthy patterns of behavior by staying alert and aware of our moods. How we are impacted by situations and circumstances on a moment-to-moment daily basis.

Success using ALWF is based upon staying focused with the process, just like it is with anything else. When a participant has the willingness to just have fun and go with it, enjoy it, enjoy the group energy then success is assured!

Getting It

There is an opportunity by practicing ALWF of "getting it." We get the connection with our self and our life source. It is a connection that can take place immediately or it can take time. We are all at different states of awareness or consciousness in our lives so making and keeping our connection to our sense of connection with ourselves, and our connection to our spiritual oneness, is a major emotional and spiritual challenge. Our eyes are open to the present time realty of our significance of our being, being in the world. We then learn how truly fortunate we are to experience Life in and on an earthly dimension. When we have gotten this realization, our true appreciation for Life occurs! It is then that we become aware of the significance of the ten components of ourselves: the mental, emotional, spirit, the spiritual, physical, social, heart, soul, creative, and our intuition.

Self-Realization takes Time, Temperament and Tenacity. It is Patience, Perseverance, Persistence, and Perspiration. It is developing an attitude of Progress and not Perfection that results in a life well lived and its journey well traveled.

Hard-wired

The beauty of Animated Laughter with Feelings is that it removes the "covered razor edges of feelings reflective of the range of emotions" from our hard-wired dysfunctional imprinted and ingrained patterns. Our hard-wired unhealthy patterns could very well reflect our beliefs, values, and even our personality traits! We become safer, more comfortable, trusting, and "willing" to "engage" the patterned recordings of our stresses and distresses! In achieving this goal, we are encouraged to experience more of our dissonant feelings and experience more healing and therefore more emotional freedom of/for ourselves. We then learn that it is safe for us to delve deeper (breath deeper and connect) and experience yet more freedom through relinquishing dissonant energies. We experience more of who we are i.e., precious, and free. It is then that our consciousness rises to a point where we come to realize that we are whole human beings having a spiritual experience.

ALWF provides and facilitates peer pressures that encourage participants to engage together to have a spiritual experience reflective of a natural physiological release and relinquishment of dissonant energies. What is significant is that we learn to go beyond, transforming, transcending, transmuting (doing service work), transitioning and developing a transparency of our stresses and distresses. We go beyond to find a self that is viable, alive, vibrant, invigorated, functional, and whole. We then learn to experience more self-faith, compassion, love, and enthusiasm in the world. Healing wounds, hurts, traumas become practical, enjoyable, reinvigorating and most of all fun! Above all, we learn to become flexible in our actions.

Rigidity and Control

We can effectively, through the practice of ALWF, address the issue of rigidity as it reflects those who have control issues. Control is a major issue in codependency. Individuals using controlling behavior normally have underlying insecurities reflective of fear. Fear is an underlying cause of rigid behavior. Fear is an underlying cause of manipulative controlling behavior as well.

There are many forms of manipulations used by individuals who attempt to control others. These include using different healing methods as manipulative tools. Controlling behaviors form emotional recordings that reflect the following manipulative distresses. People having controlling behaviors can choose to use ALWF as a healing practice for themselves to access, connect with and facilitate the release, relinquishment, and the letting go of their repressed and suppressed accumulated intensities of feelings, reflective of the range of emotions, fear through terror, anger through rage, and sadness through grief.

Layered Multiple Traumas

Too often, our personalities experience layered multiple traumas reflective of experiences, genetics, biology, development, and environments. We are just not aware of how profoundly we are impacted by traumas from our indigenous families. Our vulnerabilities are not always apparent to ourselves until we begin to wake-up at night in hot or cold fearful sweats. Our anxieties begin to bubble up and begin to become apparent when we least expect them. Through ALWF we can begin to see our nature and how we have been impacted by stress and distress. We begin to awaken to our sensitivities and vulnerabilities and how we have been hurt and traumatized. We can then begin to give our issue a name. We can label it abandonment, betrayal, separation anxiety, or helplessness. We can understand that the way we have been impacted by layered multiple traumas reflect a distress issue. We begin to awaken to the damage that we have experienced. We begin to understand that the emotional damage we have experienced is sadly multi-layered. ALWF gives us hope! We can begin to effectively and efficiently address the feelings reflective of the patterns confidently! We can achieve this by way of accessing our multi-layered feelings through our connected circular healing breath. We can then gradually process our feelings layer by layer.

KEY TERMS

Advanced Animated Laughter with Feelings

Alexithymia

ALWF – Animated Laughter with Feelings

Chakra - The seven chakras of the body include the pelvic, stomach, solar plexus, heart, throat, third eye, and top of the head. It is in the above chakras where feelings, emotions are blocked.

Chemical Dependency

Discharge

Emotional Body

Emotional Release Manifestations

Emotional Toolbox

Enhanced Laughter

Flexible Intelligence

Freudian Defenses: The Freudian Defenses include rationalization, repression, denial, projection, reaction formation, regression identification, displacement, and sublimation.

Ingrained Core Frozen Intensity of Feelings

Inner Child Work

Knee-Jerk Reactions

Law of Attraction

Mirror Work

Peer Counseling

Pyramid – Ten Components

Rebirthing

Re-evaluation Co-counseling

Release

Spiritual Laughter

Spiritual Solutions

Tantra

Transcendent Cognitive

ABOUT THE AUTHOR

Joel Vorensky is the author of two recognized and reviewed classic inspirational books, *I Dare to Heal with Compassionate Love* (2001), and *I Dare to Heal with Spiritual Power* (2005). The books are inspirational treasures and have received five star reviews and awards. (idaretoheal.com). The books span the period of the '60s through 2005. *I Dare to Heal with Laughter* is his present book in progress. Mr. Vorensky has participated in myriad New Age activities since 1968, and writes about his experiences.

Mr. Vorensky embodies the understanding that wisdom comes through doing. His first "doing" was a childhood job shoveling snow. Since then he has worked as a typist, a taxicab driver in New York City and San Diego, California, a teacher of both adults and children in private and public schools in the United States and abroad; and as a retail salesman, registered securities representative, bank officer, insurance broker, publishing, senior public health advisor, immunization and communicable diseases, bookkeeper, beekeeper, baker, agricultural laborer, concierge at a five star hotel and casino, telemarketing, crowd control officer, ice cream cashier, hospital, liquor, mail room clerk, and restaurant busboy. He is presently marketing Medicare Health Plans, and other insurance.

Teaching holistic classes in Circular Connected Healing Breath, Peer Counseling (integrative emphasis), Primal Sound, Rebirthing, Tai Chi Chuan, and Animated Laughter, has been a consistent theme in his life; languages (English as a Second Language, Swedish, Spanish, and Hebrew) as well as Medical Terminology, Computer Software, and Marketing. He has taught at the American Language Institute at San Diego State University, National University in California, San Diego Community College Continuing Education, and adult detention centers. Mr. Vorensky has a forty-one year background as a peer co-counselor in English and Scandinavian languages.

Joel grew up in Queens, Brooklyn and New York City. He lived in Scandinavia for seven years and spent several years in the State of Israel living in the desert. For the past twenty-eight years he has made his home in San Diego, California. He has a daughter, now grown, and granddaughter.

Since 1968 he has been on a conscious path to heal the pain that began in the trauma of his birth, a path that has taken him on an odyssey through the various personal growth and healing modalities available in the Eastern and Western worlds.

Joel holds a degree in Business, Scandinavian Teaching Certification in Early Childhood Education, California teaching credentials in multiple subjects and community college credentials in English and Business. Joel has a recent formal academic background in counseling psychology classes and has obtained his Master's Degree in Psychology Human Behavior. He has a spiritual counseling practice in San Diego County and is an expert in the field of emotional intelligence (feelings reflective of emotions) with four decades of experience. The eclectic nature of his experience has afforded him social exposure leading to significant insights as to "what makes people tick." In his books he freely shares his wisdom with all who care to listen and apply it to the task of improving their own lives. His books are written to help others.

Joel has been interviewed many times on national radio and has been interviewed twice on Cable TV. Joel writes two blogs, one for spiritual counseling, and one for insurance that can be accessed by visiting his websites at healthplansinsandiego.com and joelvorenskyinsurance.com. For further information and to order other books, access his website at idaretoheal.com.

Humor References

Buxman, Karyn (ed.) Nursing Perspectives on Humor. Staten Island, NY: Power Publishers, 1995.

Cousins, Norman. 1979. Anatomy of an illness as perceived by the patient. New York: W. W. Norton.

Klein, Allen. (1989) Healing Power of Humor. Los Angeles CA: Tarcher

McGhee, Paul. (1996). Health, Healing and the Amuse System. Dubuque, IA: Kendall/Hunt.

Robinson, Vera. (1991). Humor and the Health Professions, 2nd ed. Thorofare, NJ: Charles B. Slack.

Wooten, Patty. (1996). Compassionate Laughter. Utah: Commune-A-Key.

Wooten, Patty. Humor: An antidote for Stress. Holistic Nursing Practice. 1996, 10 (2). pp. 49-56.

Therapeutic Humor and Physiological Response

Berk, L. & Tan, S. (1989). Eustress of mirthful laughter modifies natural killer cell activity. Clinical Research, 37, 115.

Berk, L.S., Tan, S.A., Fry, W.F., Napier, B.J., Lee, J.W. Hubbard, R.W. Lewis, J.E. & Eby, W.C. (1989) Neuroendrocrine and stress hormone changes during mirthful laughter. American Journal of the Medical Sciences. 298(6), 390-396.

Berk, L.S., Tan, S.A. Nehlsen-Cannarella et al, Humour associated laughter decreases cortisol and increases spontaneous lymphocyte balstogenesis. Clinical Resident 36

Cousins, Norman. Head First: the Biology of Hope. NY NY: Dutton, 1989.

Dillon, K.M., Minchoff, B., & Baker, K.H. (1985-86). Positive emotional states and enhancement of the immune system. International Journal of Psychiatry, 15(1), 13-18.

Fry, W.F. (1992) The physiologic effects of humor, mirth, and laughter. Journal of the American Medical Association, 267(13), 1857-1858.

Fry, William F. (1971). Laughter: Is It the Best Medicine? Stanford M.D. 10 16-20.

Fry, William F. (1971). Mirth and Oxygen Saturation of Peripheral Blood. Psychotherapy and Psychosomatics 19 76-84.

Fry, William F. (1977). The Respiratory Components of Mirthful Laughter. The Journal of Biological Psychology 19 39-50.

Fry, William F. (1994). The Biology of Humor. HUMOR: International Journal of Humor Research 7.2 111-126.

Fry, W., Savin, W.M., (1988) Mirthful Laughter and Blood Pressure, Humour: International journal of Humour Reasearch 1, p. 49-62

Kamei, T., Kumano, H., & Masumura, S. (1997). Changes of immunoregulatory cells associated with psychological stress and humor. Percept Mot Skills, 84 (3 Pt 2), 1296-1298.

Lefcourt, H., Davidson-Katz, K., & Kueneman, K. (1990). Humor and immune system functioning. International Journal of Humor Research, 3 (3), 305-321.

Sultanoff, S. (Summer, 1999). Examining the Research on Humor: Being Cautious About Our Conclusions the "President's Column" in Therapeutic Humor, Publication of the American Association for Therapeutic Humor, Vol. XIII, (3), P. 3.

Therapeutic Humor and Medicine

Black, Donald W. (1984) "Laughter." J Am Medical Association, 252:21, 2995-8.

Cousins, Norman. (1976) "Anatomy of an Illness." New England J of Medicine, v295, 1458-1463.

Cousins,Norman. (1989) "Head first: the biology of hope." New York: Dutton

Haig, R.A., The Anatomy of Humour: Biopsychosocial and Therapeutic Perspective, Springfield, IL: Thomas

Lambert, N.K., Lambert, R.B (1995) The effects of humour on Secretory Immunoglobin A levels in school aged children, Pediatric Nursing 21 p. 16-19

Levinson, W., Roter, D., Mullooly, J., Dull, V., & Frankel, R. (1997). Physician-patient communication; The relationship with malpractice claims among primary care physicians and surgeons. Journal of the American Medical Association, 277(7), 553-559.

Spitzer, P (2001) The Australian Family Physician journal Vol30, No.1, Jan 2001 the lead articles are on the subject of "Is Humour Medicinal?"

Van Blerkom, L (1995). Clown doctors: shaman healers of Western medicine. Med Anthropol Q, 9 (4), 462-75.

Weisenberg, M., Tepper, I., & Schwarzwald, J. (1995). Humor as a cognitive technique for increasing pain tolerance. Pain, 63 (2), 207-212.

Therapeutic Humor and Psychotherapy

Dunkelbau, Edward. "'That'll Be Five Cents, Please!': Perceptions of Psychotherapy in Jokes and Humor." Handbook of Humor and Psychotherapy. Eds. William Fry and Waleed Salameh. Sarasota, FL: Professional Resource Exchange, 1987, 307-314.

Eberhart, Elvin (Cy). "Humor as a Religious Experience" Advances in Humor and Psychotherapy. Eds. Fry, William F., and Waleed A. Salameh. Sarasota, FL: Professional Resource Press, 1993, 97-120

Engler, B. (1999). *Personality Theories. (5th Edition)* Boston: Houghton Mifflin Company.

Farrelly, Frank, and Michael Lynch. "Humor in Provocative Therapy." Handbook of Humor and Psychotherapy. Eds. William Fry and Waleed Salameh. Sarasota, FL: Professional Resource Exchange, 1987, 81-106.

Fay, Allen M.D. (1989, ©1978) Making Things Better by Making Them Worse. NY NY: Hawthorne Books.

Fry, William F., and Waleed A. Salameh, Eds. Advances in Humor and Psychotherapy. Sarasota, FL: Professional Resource Press, 1993.

Fry, William F., and Waleed A. Salameh. Handbook of Humor and Psychotherapy: Advances in the Clincial Use of Humor. Sarasota, FL: Professional Resource Exchange, 1987.

Gelkopf, Marc, and Mircea Sigal. "It is Not Enough to Have them

Laugh: Hostility, Anger, and Humor-Coping in Schizophrenic Patients." HUMOR: International Journal of Humor Research 8.3 (1995): 273-284.

Gelkopf, M. & Kreitler, S. (1996). Is humor only fun, an alternative cure or magic? The cognitive therapeutic potential of humor. Journal of Cognitive Psychotherapy: An International Quarterly, 10(4), 235-254.

Gillikan, L. S., and Peter Derks. "Humor Appreciation and Mood in Stroke Patients." Cognitive Rehabilitation. 9 (1991): 30-35.

Goodheart, Annette. Laughter Therapy. Santa Barbara, CA: Stress Less Press, 1994.

Grossman, Saul A. "The Use of Jokes in Psychotherapy." It's a Funny Thing, Humour. Eds. Antony Chapman and Hugh Foot. NY: Pergamon, 1977, 149-52. Haig, Robin Andrew. The Anatomy of Humor: Biopsychosocial and Therapeutic Perspectives. NY: Thomas, 1988.

Hageseth, Christian. A Laughing Place. Fort Collins CO: Berwick Pub Co, 1988.

Killinger, Barbara. "The Place of Humour in Adult Psychotherapy." It's a Funny Thing, Humour. Eds. Antony Chapman and Hugh Foot. NY: Pergamon, 1977, 153-56.

Kisner, Bette. "The Use of Humor in the Treatment of People." The Handbook of Humor: Clinical Applications to Psychotherapy. Malabar, FL: Krieger, 1994, 133-156.

Kubie, L. (1971). The destructive potential of humor in psychotherapy. American Journal of Psychiatry, 127, 861-866.

Lefcourt, H. and Martin, R. (1986). Humor and Life Stress. New York, NY: Springer-Verlag.

Marcus, N. N. (1990). Treating those who fail to take themselves seriously: pathological aspects of humor. Am J Psychother, 44 (3), 423-432.

Martin, R.A. & Dobbin, J. P. (1988). Sense of humor, hassles, and immunoglubulin a: evidence for a stress-moderating effect of humor. International Journal of Psychiatry in Medicine, 18(2), 93-105.

Martin, R.A., &. Lefcourt, H.M. (1983). Sense of humor as a moderator of the relation between stressors and moods. Journal of Personality and Social Psychology, 54, 520-525.

McGhee, Paul E.; & J.H Goldstein (eds). (1983) The Handbook of Humor Research (Volumes I & II). NY NY: Springer-Verlag.

Porterfield, A.L. (1987). Does sense of humor moderate the impact of life stress on psychological and physiological well-being? Journal of Research in Personality, 21, 306-317.

Prerost, F. J. "Evaluating the Systematic Use of Humor in Psychotherapy with Adolescents." Journal of Adolescents 7 (1984): 267-76.

Richman, J. (1996). Points of correspondence between humor and psychotherapy. Psychotherapy, 33(4), 560-566.

Rosenheim, E. & Golan, G. (1986). Patients' reactions to humorous interventions in psychotherapy. American Journal of Psychotherapy, 40(1), 110-124.

Salovey, P., Rothman, A., Detweiler, J. B., & Steward, W. T. (2000) Emotional states and physical health. American Psychologist, 55(1), 110-121.

Seligman, M. & Csikszentmihalyi, M. (2000). Positive psychology: An introduction. American Psychologist, 55(1), 5-14.

Seligman, M. (1998). Learned optimism: How to change your mind and your life (2nd ed.). New York: Pocket Books.

Shaughnessy, Michael F., and Terresa M. Wadsworth. "Humor in Counseling and Psychotherapy: A 20-Year Retrospective." Psychological Reports 70 (1992): 755-762.

Sultanoff, S. (May, 1994). Therapeutic uses of humor. The California Psychologist, Publication of the California Psychological Association, 25.

Titze, Michael. "The 'Conspirative Method': Applying Humoristic Inversion in Psychotherapy." Handbook of Humor

Valiant, G. E. (2000). Adaptive mental mechanisms: Their role in a positive psychology. American Psychologist, 55(1), 89-98.

Volcek, Mary Kay. "Humor and the Mental Health of the Elderly." The Handbook of Humor: Clinical Applications to Psychotherapy. Malabar, FL: Krieger, 1994, 111-122.

Therapeutic Humor and Nursing

Bellart, Judy. Humor: a therapeutic approach in oncology nursing. Cancer Nursing, 1989, 12:2.

Buckwalter, K. C., Gerdner, L. A., Hall, G. R., Stolley, J. M., Kudart, P., & Ridgeway, S. (1995). Shining through: the humor and individuality of persons with Alzheimer's disease. J Gerontol Nurs, 21 (3), 11-16.

Buffum, M. & Brod, M. (1998) "Humor and well-being in spouse caregivers of patients with Alzheimer;s disease" Applied Nursing Research, 1998 Feb, 11(1) pp. 12-18.

Dean, R. A. (1997). Humor and laughter in palliative care. J Palliat Care, 13 (1), 34-39.

Dossey, B.M., Keegan, L., Guzzetta, C.E., Kolkmeier, L.G. (1995), Play and Laughter, Moving towards harmony, in eds. Holistic Nursing: A Handbook for Practice, Kolkmeier L.G., Gaithersburg M.D., Aspen Publishers, , p. 315-330

Green, L. (1990) "Feeling Good: Humor in the facility." J of Long Term Care Administration, 1990:Fall, 5-8.

Herth, Kaye. "Contributions of humor as perceived by the terminally ill." Am J of Hospital Palliative Care, 1990, 7:1.

Hulse, J. R. (1994). Humor: a nursing intervention for the elderly. Geriatr Nurs, 15 (2), 88-90.

Hunt, A. H. (1993). Humor as a nursing intervention. Cancer Nursing, 16 (1), 34-39.

Kennedy, P., & Marsh, N. J. (1993). Effectiveness of the use of humor in the rehabilitation of people with SCI: a pilot study. J Am Paraplegia Soc, 16 (4), 215-218.

Klein, Allen. The Courage to Laugh. Los Angeles, Tarcher, 1998.

Kuhlman, Thomas. (1988) "Gallows Humor for a Scaffold Setting: Managing aggresive patients on a maximum security forensic unit." Hospital & Community Psychiatry, v39, 1085-1090.

Matz, A. Brown, S.T. "Humor and pain management." Journal of Holistic Nursing. 1998 March, 16 (1) 68-75.

McGhee, P. (1998). Rx: laughter. RN, 61 (7), 50-53.

Richman, J. (1995). The lifesaving function of humor with the depressed and suicidal elderly. Gerontologist, 35 (2), 271-273.

Ritz, Sandy. "Survivor Humor and Disaster Nursing" In Buxman, K. (ed), Nursing Perspectives on Humor. Staten Island,NY: Power Publications, 1995.

Robinson, V. (1991). Humor and the Health Professions, 2nd ed. Thorofare, NJ: Charles B. Slack.

Rosenberg, Lisa. (1991) "Clinical Articles: A qualitative investigation of the use of humor by emergency personnel as a strategy for coping with stress." J of Emergency Nursing, 17:4.

Showalter, S. E., & Skobel, S. (1996). Hospice: humor, heartache and healing. Am J Hosp Palliat Care, 13 (4), 8-9.

Simon, Jolene M. (1987) "The therapeutic value of humor in aging adults." J of Gerontological Nursing, 14:8, 9-13.

Simon, Jolene M. (1988) "Therapeutic Humor: Who's fooling who?" J of Psychosocial Nursing & Mental Health Service, 26:4, 8-12.

Simon, Jolene M. (1988) "Humor and the older adult: Implications for nursing." J of Advanced Nursing, v14, 441-446.

Simon, Jolene M. (1988) "Humor and Its Relationship to Perceived Health, Life Satisfaction, and Morale in Older Adults." Issues in & Mental Health Nursing, v11, 17-31.

Simon, Jolene M. (1989) "Humor techniques for oncology nurses." Oncology Nursing Forum, v16, 667-670.

White, C. & Howse, E. "Managing Humor; When Is It Funny - And When Is It Not?" Nursing Management, 1993, 24 (4), pp. 80-92.

Wooten, Patty. "Humor, Laughter and Play - Maintaining Balance in a Serious World" In Holistic Nursing Handbook. Dossey, B. and Keegan, L (eds.). Baltimore, Aspen Publishing, 1999.

Wooten, Patty. "Humor: An antidote for Stress." Holistic Nursing Practice. 1996, 10 (2). pp. 49-56.

Wooten, Patty. "You've Got to be Kidding! Humor Skills for Surviving Managed Care." Dermatology Nursing. 1997, 9 (6 pp. 423-428.

Wooten, Patty. (1992) "Humor as therapy for patient and caregiver" in Pulmonary Rehabilitation: Guidelines to Success. Philadelphia PA: J.B. Lippincott Co.

Humor in Crisis Situations

Klein, Allen. "How Can You Laugh at a Time Like This?" AATH. Oct. 2001 (online).

Harris David A The Jokes of Oppression: The Humour of Soviet Jews., Izrail Rabinovich. Northvale N.J.:J Aronson, c1988

Moran, C.C. and Massam, M. (1997) An evaluation of humour in emergency work. The Australasian Journal of Disaster and Trauma Studies, 3, 26-38.

Moran, C.C. (1990) Does the use of humour as a coping strategy affect the stresses associated with emergency work? International Journal of Mass Emergencies and Disasters, 8, 361-377.

Sultanoff, Steve. "Using Humor in Crisis Situations." AATH. Oct. 2001 (online).

Wooten, Patty, and Ed Dunkelblau. "Tragedy, Laughter, and Survival." Nursing Spectrum. Oct. 2001 (online).

Therapeutic Humor at Work

Barreca, Regina. (1991) They Used to Call Me Snow White . . . But I Drifted: Women's strategic use of humor. NY NY: Viking-Penguin Pub.

Blumenfeld, E., & Alpern, L. Humor at Work. Atlanta: Peachtree Publishers, 1994.

Kushner, Malcolm. (1990) The Light Touch. NY NY: Simon & Schuster.

Morreall, John. (1997) .Humor Works. Amherst, MA: HRD Press, Inc.

Paulson, Terry. (1989) Making Humor Work Los Altos CA: Crisp Publishing,.

Weinstein, Matt. (1997). Managing to Have Fun. New York: Simon and Schuster

Therapeutic Humour Skills and Development

Bates, Roger. (1995) How to be Funnier, Happier, Healthier and More Successful Too! Minneapolis: Trafton Publishing,

Lipman Steve (1991) Laughter in hell: the use of humour during the Holocaust.. Northvale, N.J:J Aronson Inc.

Humour and Well-being

Dossey, L (1996) N ow You are fit to Live: humour and health, Alternative Ther
99-100.

Kraus, P Lefcourt, Herbert M & Martin, Rod A. (1986) Humour and life st
adversity Lefcourt, Herbert M. New York; Berlin: Springer-Verlag,

Siegel, B Love, Medicine & Miracles Harper Perennnial

ANALYTIC FUNCTIONS

ANALYTIC FUNCTIONS

M. A. Evgrafov
Moscow Physical - Technical Institute

Translated by Scripta Technica, Inc.
Edited by Bernard R. Gelbaum

DOVER PUBLICATIONS, INC.
NEW YORK

Published in Canada by General Publishing Company, Ltd., 30 Lesmill Road, Don Mills, Toronto, Ontario.
Published in the United Kingdom by Constable and Company, Ltd., 10 Orange Street, London WC2H 7EG.

This Dover edition, first published in 1978, is an unabridged republication of the English translation originally published by W. B. Saunders, Philadelphia, in 1966. The work was first published in Russian by Izdatel'stvo Nauka, Moscow, in 1965, under the title *Analiticheskiye Funktsyi.*

International Standard Book Number: 0-486-63648-8
Library of Congress Catalog Card Number: 78-52149

Manufactured in the United States of America
Dover Publications, Inc.
180 Varick Street
New York, N.Y. 10014

Foreword

This book represents a healthy departure from traditional presentations of analytic function theory. Among the interesting features are the early introduction of Riemann surfaces, conformal mapping, and the applications of residue theory. The orientation of the author is "modern" in that he dwells at much greater length on those aspects of the theory that lead into the modern parts of research, rather than on some of the classical (albeit elegant) topics, whose relevance to further research is becoming less and less clear.

The book should serve the needs of all graduate students who wish to get a firm foundation in the theory of functions of a complex variable and who wish at the same time to be made aware of the most important lines of its modern development.

Bernard R. Gelbaum

Preface

The present text is designed for students and other readers acquainted with the fundamentals of mathematical analysis as presented in a year of advanced calculus.

The order of presentation of material in this textbook is significantly different from that of other texts in analytical function theory. We shall give a rigorous discussion of the theory of multiple-valued analytic functions presented on the basis of analytic continuation. This theory is presented toward the very end in many textbooks in use today, but it enters in the present book much nearer the beginning (Chap. III). A strong argument can be made for such arrangement of the material. First of all, from the point of view of logic, analytic continuation plays no less a role in the theory of complex variables than that of the theory of limits in analysis. Second, it is appropriate from the purely practical point of view, since the earlier utilization of analytic continuation allows great economy in space and time in the presentation to follow. The usual objection made against this arrangement is based on the opinion that analytic continuation is difficult to understand. However, the difficulty is greatly exaggerated. Moreover, whatever the difficulties, they must be overcome in any event upon the introduction of the elementary multiple-valued functions, and by more artificial (and therefore less intelligible) means.

In any case, my lecturing experience in the theory of analytic functions at the Moscow Physical-Technical Institute has convinced me that two or three difficult (but completely accessible) lectures were fully justified by the better understanding of the material that followed. The exercises could be gone over much more easily, since the problem of isolating analytic branches is laborious and difficult to understand.

It was also valuable in that the student developed from the beginning a correct and accurate point of view of the subject studied.

In the writing of the book I tried to make the separate chapters as independent as possible of one another. The object of this was to make the book available for a variety of courses with considerable variation in content. The volume of material presented in the text considerably exceeds the content of the courses usually given at the Institute. It is worthwhile to stress that all the chapters are written on a level completely accessible to third year students.

I will now point out the relations among the chapters.

Chapter I need only be employed for purposes of reference. Chapters II-IV are essential for all that follows. Chapters VI and

VII have no connection with V and VIII-X. Chapter VIII relies to a considerable extent on Chapter V, and itself serves as the base for the two that follow. Chapters IX and X have only slight connections with one another.

A subject and name index is included at the end of the book.

In conclusion I should like to thank all those who contributed to my work on this book. First of all, I thank my teachers: Corresponding Member of the Academy of Sciences of the U.S.S.R. A. O. Gel'fond and Academician M. V. Keldysh. My views took shape under the influence of my discussions with them, and this influence is more noticeable in this book than in other of my works. My students helped me very much: Candidates in the Physical-Mathematical Sciences I. S. Arshon and G. M. Mordasova, who carefully read all the variants of the manuscript as they made their appearance. V. V. Zarutskaya, the editor of this book, helped me very much in finishing the final version of the manuscript. I am very thankful to professors V. B. Lidskiy and B. V. Shabat, and to docents O. V. Lokutsievskiy and M. B. Fedoryuk for their helpful observations.

M. A. Evgrafov

Contents

I. INTRODUCTION 1

1. Complex Numbers 1
2. Sets, Functions and Curves 5
3. Limits and Series 9
4. Continuous Functions 12
5. Line Integrals 15
6. Integrals Depending on a Parameter 20

II. ANALYTIC FUNCTIONS AND THEIR PROPERTIES 24

1. Differentiable and Analytic Functions 24
2. Cauchy's Theorem 28
3. Cauchy's Integral Formula 32
4. Criteria for Analyticity 38
5. A Uniqueness Theorem 41
6. The Behavior of the Basic Elementary Functions 46

III. MULTIPLE-VALUED ANALYTIC FUNCTIONS 50

1. The Concept of a Complete Analytic Function 50
2. The Analytic Function $\ln z$ 55
3. Monodromy Theorem 62
4. Riemann Surfaces 68
5. Examples of the Construction of Riemann Surfaces 71

IV. SINGULAR POINTS AND EXPANSION IN SERIES 75

1. The Notation of a Singular Point of Regular Function 75
2. Removal of Singularities 80
3. Isolated Singular Points 83
4. Residues and Laurent Series 88
5. Expansion of Meromorphic Functions in Series of Partial Fractions 93
6. The Argument Principle and Rouché's Theorem 97
7. Implicit Functions and Inverse Functions 100

V. CONFORMAL MAPPINGS 107

1. General Information About Mappings 107
2. Linear Fractional Transformations 112

3. Conformal Mapping of the Elementary Functions 118
4. The Riemann-Schwarz Symmetry Principle 123
5. The Schwarz-Christoffel Integral 128
6. Approximation of Conformal Mappings Near the Boundary 135

VI. THE THEORY OF RESIDUES 144

1. Generalized Contour Integrals 144
2. Analytic Continuation of Contour Integrals 149
3. Evaluation of Definite Integrals 154
4. Asymptotic Formulas for Integrals 159
5. The Summation of Series 165
6. Basic Formulas Relating to Euler's Gamma Function 171

VII. THE LAPLACE TRANSFORM 177

1. The Inversion Formula for the Laplace Transform 177
2. The Convolution Theorem and Other Formulas 185
3. Examples of the Application of the Method 191
4. The Generalized Laplace Transform 198
5. The Use of Analytic Continuation 202
6. The Mellin Transform 208

VIII. HARMONIC AND SUBHARMONIC FUNCTIONS 213

1. Basic Properties of Harmonic Functions 213
2. Subharmonic Functions 219
3. The Dirichlet Problem and Poisson's Integral 226
4. Harmonic Measure 232
5. Uniqueness Theorems for Bounded Functions 241
6. The Phragmen-Lindelöf Theorems 246

IX. CONFORMAL MAPPINGS OF MULTIPLY CONNECTED DOMAINS 253

1. The Existence of Conformal Mappings 253
2. Corresponding Boundaries Under Conformal Mappings 260
3. The Automorphism of a Conformal Mapping 266
4. The Dirichlet Problem and Mapping Onto Canonical Domains 272
5. Mapping of the Plane with Deleted Points 279
6. Automorphic and Elliptic Functions 283

X. EXTREMAL PROBLEMS AND DISTRIBUTION OF VALUES 291

1. The Principle of the Hyperbolic Metric 291
2. The Symmetrization Principle 298
3. Bounds for Functions Univalent in the Mean 302
4. The Principle of Length and Area 310
5. Distribution of Values of Entire and Meromorphic Functions 315
6. Nevanlinna's Theorem of Defect 323

INDEX 333

CHAPTER I

Introduction

The study of the theory of analytic functions requires that the student have mastered a full course of mathematical analysis. It is therefore quite natural to assume that all the results needed for the presentation of the theory are already known from analysis. Unfortunately, all the questions treated in a course of analysis are presented in terms of real functions of real variables. For this reason, before we can present the theory of analytic functions, we must introduce at least the statements of the fundamental results concerning limits, continuity and integrals. Since the presentation of the proofs of a small number of theorems does not replace a full course in analysis, and since the reader who has studied analysis can readily prove the theorems stated himself, we have given only the statements of the theorems in the majority of cases. Exception to this rule is made only in a comparatively small number of cases where the theorem in question is not characteristic of analysis.

1. COMPLEX NUMBERS

By a ***complex number*** z we mean an ordered pair of real numbers (a, b).

We say that two complex numbers $z=(a, b)$ and $\zeta=(c, d)$ are equal, if $a=c$ and $b=d$.

The operations of addition and multiplication are defined for complex numbers by means of the following rules:

$$(a, b)+(c, d)=(a+c, b+d),$$

$$(a, b)(c, d)=(ac-bd, ad+bc).$$

By using the definition, verify that the operations on the complex numbers have the following properties:

1. Associativity, i.e.,

$$(z+\zeta)+w=z+(\zeta+w),$$
$$(z\zeta)\,w=z\,(\zeta w).$$

2. Commutativity, i.e.,

$$z+\zeta=\zeta+z,\quad z\zeta=\zeta z.$$

3. Distributivity, i.e.,

$$z\,(\zeta+w)=z\zeta+zw.$$

We shall define multiplication of the complex number $z=(a,\ b)$ by the real number c by means of the equation

$$c\,(a,\ b)=(ca,\ \ cb).$$

Then any complex number can be written in the form

$$(a,\ b)=ae_1+be_2,\quad e_1=(1,\ 0),\quad e_2=(0,\ 1).$$

The number e_1 behaves like an identity under multiplication, since $ze_1=z$ for all z. It is therefore reasonable to regard e_1 as the identity or 1. It is customary to use the notation $e_2=i$ for the number e_2 and to call it the imaginary unit. It is easily verified that $i^2=-1$. Thus, complex numbers can be written in the form

$$(a,\ b)=a+bi.$$

The complex number $a+0i$ is identified with the real number a, and the complex number $0+ib$ is called an *imaginary number.*

The notion of complex numbers may be considered as an extension of the concept of real numbers. The same basic axioms hold for complex numbers as for real numbers, with the exception of the order axioms and in particular the Archimedean property concerning order. The concepts of "greater than" and "less than" have no meaning for complex numbers.

The real numbers are represented by the points of a line, while complex numbers are represented in a natural way by the points of a plane. Specifically, the complex number $a+bi$ is represented by the point of the (coordinate) plane with abscissa a and ordinate b. Complex numbers can likewise be represented by vectors, particularly since they may be added like vectors. However, the analogy between complex numbers and vectors should not be carried much further. Neither the scalar nor the vector product have any relation to the multiplication of complex numbers.

We next introduce a series of traditional names and notations for the complex numbers.

The plane in which we represent the complex numbers is called the *complex plane.*

The axis of abscissas in the complex plane is called the *real axis*, and the axis of ordinates the *imaginary axis.*

Let $z=a+bi$. We shall employ the following names and notations:
$a=\operatorname{Re} z$—the ***real part of z***;
$b=\operatorname{Im} z$— the ***imaginary part of z*** ;
$a-bi=\bar{z}$—the ***complex conjugate of z***;
$\sqrt{a^2+b^2}=|z|$— the ***modulus of z*** (absolute value of z);
$\arg z$—the ***argument of z***; this is the number φ defined (modulo 2π) by the equations

$$\cos\varphi=\frac{a}{\sqrt{a^2+b^2}}, \quad \sin\varphi=\frac{b}{\sqrt{a^2+b^2}}.$$

All the quantities introduced have simple geometrical interpretations in the complex plane. Thus, the modulus of z is the distance from the origin of coordinates to the point z, the argument of z is the angle between the positive real axis and the vector issuing from the origin in the direction of z.

Let us note two important inequalities satisfied by the modulus.

Theorem 1.1. *For any complex numbers z_1 and z_2*

$$||z_1|-|z_2||\leqslant|z_1+z_2|\leqslant|z_1|+|z_2|.$$

Proof. Let us consider the triangle with vertices 0, z_1, z_1+z_2. The lengths of its sides are: $|z_1|$ (from 0 to z_1), $|z_2|$(from z_1 to z_1+z_2) and $|z_1+z_2|$ (from z_1+z_2 to 0), since the distance between two points z and ζ equals $|z-\zeta|$. We know that the length of a side of a triangle is not greater than the sum of the lengths of the other two sides and not less than the absolute value of their difference. Applying this statement to the side from z_1+z_2 to 0, we obtain the required inequality. [Ed.: A strictly analytic proof may be based on the Schwarz inequality for real numbers.]

It is now easy to describe various regions or lines in the complex plane with the aid of the notation introduced. For example:

The points z satisfying the inequality $|z-z_0|<R$ lie in a circle of radius R with center at the point z_0.

The points z satisfying the inequality $\operatorname{Im} z>0$ lie in the upper half-plane, i.e., above the real axis.

The points z satisfying the inequality $|\arg z-\theta|<\eta$ lie within an angle of 2η with vertex at the origin and with a bisector making an angle θ with the positive real axis. The points of the bisector are described by the equality $\arg z=\theta$.

Complex numbers are often represented in the so-called exponential or trigonometric form:

$$z=re^{i\varphi}$$

(here $e^{i\varphi}$ is to be understood according to Euler's formula as $\cos\varphi+i\sin\varphi$). It is not difficult to see that

$$\operatorname{Re} z=r\cos\varphi, \quad \operatorname{Im} z=r\sin\varphi,$$

$$|z|=r, \quad \arg z=\varphi+2\pi k, \quad \bar{z}=re^{-i\varphi}.$$

We can easily deduce the following result from the definition of the product of complex numbers:

The modulus of the product of complex numbers is the product of the moduli, and the argument of the product is the sum (modulo 2π) of the arguments of the moduli.

We shall usually be dealing with the so-called *extended complex plane*, the complex plane supplemented by the point at infinity, which corresponds to the conventional complex number ∞. The extended complex plane is also called the *complex sphere* or *Riemann sphere*. This name is justified in terms of the following geometric interpretation (stereographic projection).

Imagine a plane in the three-dimensional space and a sphere of radius 1/2 placed above this plane and tangent to it at the origin of coordinates. We denote the origin of coordinates by O and the opposite pole of the sphere by P. We now make each point z of the plane correspond to a point $A(z)$ on the sphere where the sphere with the line joining the points z and P intersect. Moreover, the set of points of the sphere with the exception of P are found to be in a one-one correspondence with the points of the plane. We readily observe that as $|z| \to \infty$, the point $A(z)$ approaches the point P. Therefore it is natural to say that the point P of the sphere corresponds to the point at infinity of the extended plane.

The formula expressing the coordinates of the point $A(z)$ of the Riemann sphere in terms of the coordinates of the point of the plane, sometimes finds application.

Theorem 12. *The point* $z = x + iy$ under stereographic projection *corresponds to the point* $A(z)$ *of the sphere* $\xi^2 + \eta^2 + (\zeta - \frac{1}{2})^2 = 1/4$ *with coordinates*

$$\xi = \frac{1}{2}\frac{x\,|z|}{1+|z|^2}, \quad \eta = \frac{1}{2}\frac{y\,|z|}{1+|z|^2}, \quad \zeta = \frac{|z|^2}{1+|z|^2}.$$

Proof. Since the projection of the point A lies on the line Oz, then, $\xi = \lambda x$, $\eta = \lambda y$, where λ is some real constant. We shall find ζ in terms of $|z|$. Let us consider the cross section of the sphere cut by the plane passing through the points O, P and z (Fig. 1). The

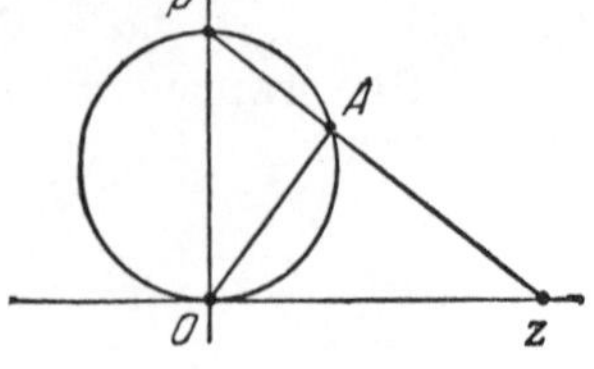

Fig. 1.

right triangles OPz and OAz are similar. The altitude of the triangle OAz is equal to ζ and its hypotenuse is $|z|$. The segment OA is a leg of the triangle OAz and the altitutde of the triangle OPz. From the similarity of the triangles OPz and OAz we have

$$\frac{\zeta}{OA}=\frac{OA}{OP}, \quad \frac{\zeta}{Oz}=\frac{OA}{Pz};$$

$$Oz=|z|, \quad OP=1, \quad Pz=\sqrt{1+|z|^2},$$

from which we find $\zeta=\frac{|z|^2}{1+|z|^2}$.

With the aid of the equation of the sphere it is easy to determine the value $\lambda=\frac{1}{2}\frac{|z|}{1+|z|^2}$, and after that ξ and η.

Corollary. We denote the distance between the points $A(z)$ *and* $A(w)$ by $k(w, z)$. We can easily obtain

$$k(w, z)=\frac{|w-z|}{\sqrt{1+|w|^2}\sqrt{1+|z|^2}}, \quad k(w, \infty)=\frac{1}{\sqrt{1+|w|^2}}$$

with the aid of the formula of Theorem 1.2.

The quantity $k(w, z)$ is called the ***chordal distance*** between the points w and z.

2. SETS, FUNCTIONS AND CURVES

We shall need to deal with a variety of sets in the extended complex plane, and to avoid ambiguity we shall define here the terms to be employed.

We shall usually write the formula $z \in E$ in place of the words "the point z belongs to the set E," and the formula $z \bar{\in} E$ in place of the words "the point z does not belong to the set E."

By the ***intersection of the sets*** E_1 and E_2 we mean the set E consisting of all points belonging to both E_1 and E_2.

By the ***distance between the sets*** E_1 and E_2 we mean the quantity

$$\varrho(E_1, E_2)=\inf_{z\in E_1,\ \zeta\in E_2}|z-\zeta|.$$

We shall call the circle $|z-z_0|<r$, where r is any positive number, a ***neighborhood of the point*** z_0.

We shall call the set $|z|>R$ for any R (the exterior of a circle)* a ***neighborhood of the point at infinity.***

We shall call the point z a ***limit point of the set*** E, if an infinite number of points of the set E are in any neighborhood of the point z.

The point z is called an ***interior point of the set*** E, if it has a neighborhood consisting entirely of points of E.

---

*We can also call the circle $k(z, z_0)<r$, for any $r>0$, a neighborhood of the point z_0. Then it is not necessary to single out the point at infinity.

The point z is called an *exterior point of the set* E if it has a neighborhood consisting only of points not belonging to E.

The point z is called a boundary point of the set E, if in every neighborhood of the point z are found points belonging and points not belonging to E.

The union of all the *boundary points of the set* E is called its *boundary*.

A set is said to be *closed*, if it contains its boundary.

It is possible to show that the boundary of a set is always a closed set.

The set obtained by taking the union of E and its boundary is called the *closure* of E and is denoted by $\bar{E}$.

A set is said to be *open*, if all its points are interior points.

We shall define the notion of connectedness for open and closed sets. The definitions are essentially different.

An *open set is called connected* if any two of its points can be joined by a polygonal line all of whose points belong to the set.

A *closed set is called connected*, if it is impossible to decompose it into two subsets which are a positive distance apart.*

A connected open set is called a *domain*.

The closure of a domain is called a *closed domain*.

A domain is said to be *n-connected* if its boundary consists of n-connected subsets.

In particular, a 1-connected (simply connected) domain has a boundary consisting of one connected set, i.e., roughly speaking, of one curve or one point. A multiply connected domain can be imagined as a simply connected domain in which holes have been made ($n-1$ holes in an n-connected domain).

Suppose we are given a set E in the complex plane and a rule by which a complex number $f(z)$ is made to correspond to each point z of the set E. Then we will say that $f(z)$ is a *function of the complex variable* z *defined on the set* E. The set E is called the *domain of definition of the function* $f(z)$.

If we use the notation $z=x+iy$, $f(z)=u+iv$, then we can study the function $f(z)$ of the complex variable z as a pair of functions $u(x, y)$ and $v(x, y)$ of two real variables x and y.

Functions of a complex variable can be studied geometrically as mappings of one complex plane (or, more exactly, a part of it) into another. The mapping given by the function of a complex variable $w=f(z)$ is equivalent to the real mapping

$$u=u(x, y), \quad v=v(x, y), \tag{2.1}$$

in which

$$u(x, y)=\operatorname{Re} f(x+iy), \quad v(x, y)=\operatorname{Im} f(x+iy).$$

The mapping (2.1) is called *nondegenerate* at the point (x_0, y_0) if the Jacobian $D(x_0, y_0)$ of the transformation is different from

---

*The definition is only appropriate for the extended plane.

zero. We recall that the *Jacobian of a transformation* is the quantity

$$D(x, y) = u'_x(x, y)v'_y(x, y) - u'_y(x, y)v'_x(x, y).$$

The linear transformation

$$u = b_{10} + b_{11}(x - x_0) + b_{12}(y - y_0),$$
$$v = b_{20} + b_{21}(x - x_0) + b_{22}(y - y_0),$$

where

$$b_{10} = u(x_0, y_0), \quad b_{11} = u'_x(x_0, y_0), \quad b_{12} = u'_y(x_0, y_0),$$
$$b_{20} = v(x_0, y_0), \quad b_{21} = v'_x(x_0, y_0), \quad b_{22} = v'_y(x_0, y_0),$$

is called the ***principal linear part of the transformation*** (2.1) at the point (x_0, y_0).

The transformation (2.1) is called *one-one in the domain D*, if the transformation takes distinct points of the domain D into distinct points of the plane.

In the study of topology it is shown that a one-one transformation defined by a pair of continuous functions $u(x, y)$ and $v(x, y)$ must take an n-connected domain into an n-connected domain.

We shall discuss in somewhat greater detail domains and the curves bounding them.

Let us begin with the general concept of a continuous curve.

Let $x(t)$ and $y(t)$ be continuous functions of the parameter t on the segment $[a, b]$, and $z(t) = x(t) + iy(t)$.

We shall call the equation $z = z(t)$, $a \leqslant t \leqslant b$, the ***parametric equation of a curve***. Moreover, we shall assume that two functions

$$z = z_1(t), \quad a_1 \leqslant t \leqslant b_1, \text{ and } z = z_2(s), \quad a_2 \leqslant s \leqslant b_2,$$

define the same curve only if there exists a monotonically increasing and continuous function $\varphi(t)$ on the segment $[a_1, b_1]$ such that

$$z_1(t) \equiv z_2(\varphi(t)), \quad \varphi(a_1) = a_2, \quad \varphi(b_1) = b_2.$$

The definition given says that we assume in general that a curve has a parametric representation. It is evident that this representation involves first, a set of points (of the plane) presented in the form $z = z(t)$, $a \leqslant t \leqslant b$ (it is easy to convince oneself that this set does not vary under the transition from one parametric equation to another); second, the order in which the points of this set are traversed (the order of the points is likewise maintained under the transition from one equation to another). Clearly, we have described a very special situation.

We call a curve defined as above a *continuous curve*.

Let us suppose that at least one of the parametric equations of a curve is such that the functions $x(t)$ and $y(t)$ are continuously differentiable on the segment $[a, b]$ with the exception of at most a finite number of points, at which the left- and right-hand limits of the derivatives exist. Then we call the curve *piecewise smooth.* (The exceptional points will be called *corners.*)

Since the points of the curve are ordered, we may speak of the beginning (initial point) and the end (terminal point) of the curve. These are the points $Z(a)$ and $Z(b)$ respectively.

The curve is called *closed*, if its initial and terminal points coincide.

An arbitrary curve may intersect itself any number of times. We can imagine it as a tangled thread lying on the table. It is clear that an arbitrary curve need not be the boundary of some domain. The following much narrower class of curves has significance.

Curves that do not intersect themselves, i.e., such that the function $z(t)$ takes on different values for different values of t, $a<t<b$, are called *simple curves* (it is not considered an intersection if the initial and terminal points coincide).

The following result is well known:

Jordan's theorem. A simple, closed curve divides the plane into two domains and is their common boundary.

It follows from Jordan's theorem that the following expression has meaning for simple curves: "motion to the left (or to the right) along the curve."

We shall define still some classes of curves that occur as the boundaries of domains.

Suppose that a given piecewise-smooth curve can be divided into a finite number of pieces, each of which is a simple curve. Suppose, furthermore, that there exists a division of the curve into simple parts such that two distinct parts either have only end points in common or completely coincide, but have opposite directions. We call such a curve a *piecewise-smooth curve with folds* (*folds* are the parts that coincide and have opposite direction).

Let C be a closed piecewise-smooth curve with folds, and let the set of points lying on C coincide with the boundary of a domain D. If the domain D remains on the left when we traverse any simple part of the curve C, then we shall say that C is the *boundary curve of the domain D.*

Folds of the curve inside the domain are called "cross cuts."

Example 1. We shall study the domain described by the inequality

$$|z|<1, \quad 0<\arg z<2\pi.$$

This domain is obtained by removing the radius $(0, 1)$ from the circle $|z|<1$. It is easy to make a model of this domain by cutting a circle out of paper and then cutting it along a radius. The boundary curve of this domain is a piecewise-smooth curve with a fold (the slit in the paper). The equation of the curve is easy to find, say, by expressing the points as a function of time as we move along the curve with constant velocity. One of the possible equations is $z=z(t)$, $0\leqslant t<3\pi$, where

$$z(t) = e^{it} \quad (0 \leqslant t < 2\pi); \quad z(t) = \cos^2 t \quad (2\pi \leqslant t < 3\pi).$$

Another class of curves, for which it is possible to define a concept of length, has great importance in questions connected with integration.

Suppose we are given an arbitrary continuous curve. We choose an arbitrary number of points on it (the first is the initial point of the curve, the last is its terminal point). We obtain a polygonal line by joining these points by lines in the order of their succession along the curve. If the set of lengths of the polygonal lines thus obtained is bounded, then we say that the curve is *rectifiable.*

The least upper bound of the lengths of these polygonal lines is called the *length of the curve.*

3. LIMITS AND SERIES

Since it is customary in analysis to study only the limits of real functions, we shall briefly present the basic facts about limits of functions of a complex variable.

Let the function $f(z)$ be defined on the set E, ζ be a limit point of the set E, and suppose that there exists a number A satisfying the condition: For every $\varepsilon > 0$ we can find a $\delta > 0$ such that for all z, $0 < |z - \zeta| < \delta$, the inequality $|f(z) - A| < \varepsilon$ is satisfied.

Then we say that the *function f(z) has a limit* A as $z \to \zeta$ in the set E. This fact will be denoted in one of the two following ways:

$$\lim_{z \to \zeta,\ z \in E} f(z) = A, \qquad f(z) \to A \qquad (z \to \zeta,\ z \in E).$$

If some neighborhood of the point ζ is contained in the set E, then we can omit the requirement $z \in E$ in these formulas.

The formulation is easily modified in the cases that $\zeta = \infty$ or $A = \infty$ (or both at once). For $\zeta = \infty$ we must write $|z| > R$, $z \in E$, in place of $0 < |z - \zeta| < \delta$, $z \in E$, and for $A = \infty$ we must write $|f(z)| > R$ in place of $|f(z) - A| < \varepsilon$.

The *limit of a sequence* is the special case of a limit of a function which occurs when E coincides with the set of positive integers.

We shall state some properties of limits, the proofs of which will be left to the reader. (Here the discussion is only about *finite* limits.)

If the limit of each of a finite number of terms exists, then the sum of the limits is equal to the limit of the sum of these terms.

If the limit of each of a finite number of factors exists, then the product of the limits is equal to the limit of the product of these factors.

If the limits of the numerator and the denominator exist and if the denominator and the limit of the denominator are different from zero, then the limit of the quotient exists and is equal to the quotient of the limits.

In order that the limit of a complex variable exist, it is necessary and sufficient that the limits of the real and the imaginary parts exist.

In order that the limit of f(z) exist as z approaches ζ *in the set E, it is necessary and sufficient that the following condition be satisfied: for any* $\varepsilon > 0$ *we can find a* $\delta > 0$ *such that for any* $z' \in E$, $z' \in E$, $|z-\zeta| < \delta$, $|z'-\zeta| < \delta$, *the inequality*

$$|f(z)-f(z')| < \varepsilon$$

holds (Cauchy's criterion).

In what follows we shall need to use the symbols $\sim$, o, O. The meaning of these symbols is as follows:

The formula

$$f(z) \sim \varphi(z) \qquad (z \to \zeta,\ z \in E)$$

denotes that

$$\lim \frac{f(z)}{\varphi(z)} = 1.$$

The formula

$$f(z) = o(\varphi(z)) \qquad (z \to \zeta,\ z \in E)$$

denotes that

$$\lim \frac{f(z)}{\varphi(z)} = 0.$$

The formula

$$f(z) = O(\varphi(z)) \qquad (z \in E)$$

denotes that

$$|f(z)| < C|\varphi(z)| \qquad (z \in E).$$

(Roughly speaking, $f(z) = O(\varphi(z))$ $(z \in E)$ means that the expression $\frac{f(z)}{\varphi(z)}$ is bounded on the set E.)

The concept of uniform convergence to a limit has great importance.

Suppose we are given a function $f(z, w)$ depending on the parameter w and suppose that

$$f(z, w) \to \varphi(w) \qquad (z \to \zeta,\ z \in G)$$

for any fixed value of $w \in E$. We shall say that the *convergence to the limit is uniform with respect to* $w \in E$, if for any $\varepsilon > 0$ we can find a $\delta > 0$, depending only on ε, but not on w, such that for $z \in G$, $0 < |z-\zeta| < \delta$, and for all $w \in E$ the inequality

$$|f(z, w) - \varphi(w)| < \varepsilon.$$

is satisfied.

The concept of uniformity can also be applied to the symbols o and $\sim$. It means that the convergence to the limit occurring in the definition of the symbol is uniform with respect to the parameter in question. For the symbol O, uniformity means that the constant C occurring in its definition can be chosen independent of the parameter in question. (Roughly speaking, that the expression $\frac{f(z, w)}{\varphi(z, w)}$ is uniformly bounded with respect to the parameter in question.)

We shall say that the *series* $\sum_1^\infty u_n$ *converges*, if the sequence $U_n = \sum_1^n u_k$ has a limit as $n \to \infty$. This limit is called the *sum of the series*.

The series $\sum_1^\infty u_n$ is called *absolutely convergent*, if the series of absolute values of the terms $\sum_1^\infty |u_n|$ converges. An absolutely convergent series converges.

We shall now introduce the basic facts about numerical series.

1. *A necessary and sufficient condition for the convergence of the series* $\sum u_n$ *is: for any* $\varepsilon > 0$ *we can find a positive integer* N *such that for any* $n > N$ *and* $n' > N$, *the following inequality holds:*

$$\left| \sum_n^{n'} u_k \right| < \varepsilon.$$

2. *A necessary condition for the convergence of the series* $\sum u_n$ *is that* $u_n \to 0$.

3. *If the series* $\sum u_n$ *is absolutely convergent and* $|v_n| < |u_n|$, *then the series* $\sum v_n$ *also converges absolutely.*

We often study series of functions $\sum u_n(z)$ also. The concept of uniform convergence has great importance for series of functions.

We shall say that a series $\sum u_n(z)$, convergent for all $z \in G$, *converges uniformly with respect to* $z \in G$, if for any $\varepsilon > 0$ we can find a positive integer N, depending only on ε, but not on z, such that for $n > N$, $n' > N$, and for any $z \in G$, the following inequality is satisfied: $\left| \sum_n^{n'} u_n(z) \right| < \varepsilon$.

The following criterion (bearing the name: *Weierstrass' criterion*) for uniform convergence of a series of functions is often applied:

If $|u_n(z)| < u_n$ *for all* $z \in G$ *and the series* $\sum u_n$ *converges, then the series* $\sum u_n(z)$ *converges uniformly with respect to* $z \in G$.

In conclusion, we shall present the necessary information about *power series*, i.e., about series of the form

$$\sum_0^\infty c_n (z-a)^n, \tag{3.1}$$

where z, a and c_n are complex numbers.

The following statement is called *Abel's first theorem.*

Theorem 3.1. *If the series (3.1) converges for* $z=z_1$, *then it converges absolutely and uniformly with respect to* z *in any circle* $|z-a| \leqslant R$, *where* $R < |z_1-a|$.

Proof. Since the series (3.1) converges for $z=z_1$, then, according to property 2, $c_n(z_1-a)^n \to 0$. But a sequence converging to zero is bounded in modulus. This means that

$$|c_n(z_1-a)^n| \leqslant M \qquad (n \geqslant 0).$$

Moreover, for any z from the circle $|z-a| \leqslant R$, $R < |z_1-a|$, we have the inequality

$$\left|\frac{z-a}{z_1-a}\right| \leqslant \frac{R}{|z_1-a|} = \theta, \qquad 0 \leqslant \theta < 1.$$

Therefore

$$|c_n(z-a)^n| = |c_n(z_1-a)^n| \cdot \left|\frac{z-a}{z_1-a}\right|^n \leqslant M\theta^n.$$

But the series $\sum M\theta^n$ converges absolutely for $0 \leqslant \theta < 1$. Applying Weierstrass' criterion, we obtain the statement of the theorem.

Abel's first theorem leads to the following important conclusion:

There exists a number R possessing the property: for $|z-a| < R$ the series (3.1) converges, and for $|z-a| > R$ the series diverges. (The number R may be either zero or infinity.) This number R is called the *radius of convergence of the series* (3.1) and the circle $|z-a| < R$ is called the *circle of convergence of the series* 3.1.)

We have the following formula giving the radius of convergence in terms of the coefficients of the series (3.1):

$$\frac{1}{R} = \overline{\lim_{n\to\infty}} \sqrt[n]{|c_n|},$$

which bears the name of the *Cauchy-Hadamard formula.*

4. CONTINUOUS FUNCTIONS

The function $f(z)$ defined on the set E is said to be *continuous at the point* $\zeta \in \overline{E}$, if for any $\varepsilon > 0$ we can find a $\delta > 0$, such that for $z \in E$, $|z-\zeta| < \delta$, we have $|f(z) - f(\zeta)| < \varepsilon$.

If the function $f(z)$ defined on the set E is continuous at each of the points of E, then it is said to be *continuous on this set.*

We shall list a series of properties of continuous functions:

The continuity of a function f(z) of a complex variable is equivalent to the continuity of the real functions $u(x, y)$ *and* $v(x, y)$:

$$u(x, y) = \operatorname{Re} f(x+iy), \qquad v(x, y) = \operatorname{Im} f(x+iy),$$

of two real variables x and y.

The sum and product of two continuous functions is continuous.

The quotient of two continuous functions is continuous at all points at which the denominator does not vanish.

If the values of the function f(z), continuous on the set E, lie in the set E_1, *on which the function F(z) is continuous, then the function* $\varphi(z) = F(f(z))$ *is continuous on the set E.*

Theorem 4.1. *If the function* $f(z, w)$ *is continuous on the set E as a function of z for all* $w \in G$, *and*

$$f(z, w) \to \varphi(z) \qquad (w \to w_0, \ w \in G)$$

uniformly with respect to $z \in E$, *then the function* $\varphi(z)$ *is continuous on the set E.*

Corollary. The sum of a uniformly convergent series of continuous functions is a continuous function.

The proof of all these assertions is left to the reader.

Let us note one more result, not usually presented in a course of analysis.

The sequence of functions $f_n(z)$ defined on the set E is said to be *equicontinuous*, if for any $\varepsilon > 0$ we can find a $\delta > 0$, depending on ε, but not on n, such that for $z \in E$, $z' \in E$, $|z - z'| < \delta$, and for all n we have the inequality

$$|f_n(z) - f_n(z')| < \varepsilon.$$

Arzela's theorem. It is possible to select from a uniformly bounded and equicontinuous sequence of functions* $f_n(z)$ *on the set E a uniformly convergent subsequence* $f_{n_k}(z)$ *for* $z \in E$.

It is easy to define continuity for functions of two or more complex variables. For example:

A function $f(z, \zeta)$ defined for $z \in G$, $\zeta \in \Gamma$, is said to be *continuous at the point* $z_0 \in G$, $\zeta_0 \in \Gamma$, *if for any* $\varepsilon > 0$ we can find a $\delta > 0$ such that for $z \in G$, $\zeta \in \Gamma$, $|z - z_0| + |\zeta - \zeta_0| < \delta$, we have $|f(z, \zeta) - f(z_0, \zeta_0)| < \varepsilon$.

It is clear that all the enumerated properties of continuous functions are valid for functions of two or more complex variables.

---

*Cf. I. G. Petrovskiy, Lectures in the Theory of Ordinary Differential Equations, John Wiley & Co., 1955.

The concept of uniform continuity enters in the usual way. The function $f(z)$ is called *uniformly continuous on the set E*, if for any $\varepsilon > 0$ we can find a $\delta > 0$ such that for $|z-z'| < \delta$, $z \in E$, $z' \in E$, we have the inequality $|f(z)-f(z')| < \varepsilon$.

A function continuous on a closed set is uniformly continuous on that set.

If a function is uniformly continuous on the set E, then it is possible to extend its definitions to the boundary of E in such a way that the new function is continuous on $\bar{E}$.

For convenience in studying functions continuous on domains with cross cuts we shall need a concept close to that of uniform continuity, but restricting the function less.

The distance in the domain D between the points $z \in D$ and $\zeta \in D$ is defined as the greatest lower bound of the lengths of the polygonal lines connecting the points z and ζ and contained in the domain D. We will denote it by $\varrho_D(z, \zeta)$.

Let the function $f(z)$ be continuous in the domain D. We shall say that the function $f(z)$ is *continuous in the domain D up to its boundary*, if for any $\varepsilon > 0$ we can find a $\delta > 0$ such that for $\varrho_D(z, z') < \delta$, $z \in D$, $z' \in D$, we have the inequality $|f(z)-f(z')| < \varepsilon$.

Since $\varrho_D(z, \zeta) \geqslant |z-\zeta|$, it is clear that continuity of a function up to the boundary of a domain is a much weaker requirement than uniform continuity on the function in the domain. On the other hand:

If the domain D is bounded by a simple curve, then continuity of the function f(z) in D up to its boundary implies uniform continuity for f(z) in D.

The statement for any simple curve is a rather refined result, roughly corresponding to Jordan's theorem (see 2); but it is rather evident for piecewise-smooth curves. The reader should attempt to prove it himself in this case.

Continuity of a function up to the boundary of a domain is not as strong a requirement as uniform continuity even for domains with cross cuts. The reason for this is that in domains with cross cuts we can have points for which $|z-\zeta|$ is arbitrarily small, but $\varrho_D(z, \zeta)$ is greater than some positive constant. Such points are situated on different sides of a cut. Therefore, we may conclude that there is a distinction between uniform continuity and continuity up to the boundary for a domain, since for uniform continuity for a function in the domain we must have unique limits as points approach a point of the boundary, independent of the side of the cross cut on which the approach takes place, but a function continuous up to the boundary may have different limits as approach is made to different sides of the cross cut.

We shall give the details on how to extend the definition of a function continuous up to the boundary of the domain to the boundary curve.

Let the domain be bounded by a closed, piecewise-smooth curve with folds (or by a finite number of such curves not intersecting one another), and let the function $f(z)$ be continuous in the domain D up to its boundary.

We choose some part D' of the domain D in such a way that the domain D' will be bounded by a ***simple*** piecewise-smooth curve. A part of the boundary curve of the domain D may be contained in the boundary of D'. As before, the function $f(z)$ is continuous up to the boundary in the domain D', since it is evident that $\varrho_{D'}(z, \zeta) \geqslant \varrho_D(z, \zeta)$. According to the above assertion, this implies uniform continuity of $f(z)$ in D'. Consequently, as noted above, $f(z)$ has a limit as z approaches any point of the boundary of D'; thus we can obtain a continuous function on $\overline{D}'$ by extending $f(z)$ to the boundary of D' and using the values of these limits. In particular, we can extend $f(z)$ by this means to that part of the boundary curve of the domain D contained in the boundary of D'. Moreover, the function obtained will be continuous on this part of the boundary curve.

Since each point of the boundary curve together with that part of the curve lying in some neighborhood of it is contained in the boundary of some part of the domain D, it is possible to extend $f(z)$ to the entire boundary curve, and the function obtained will be continuous. Of course, the function may take on distinct values at points on different sides of a cross cut, since these points constitute distinct points of the boundary curve.

We shall assume below that functions continuous up to the boundary of a domain are also defined on the boundary curve.

5. LINE INTEGRALS

We shall define the integral of a function of a complex variable on a rectifiable curve (see the end of 2).

$$z = z(t), \qquad a \leqslant t \leqslant b.$$

We choose an arbitrary number of points of the curve $z_k = z(t_k)$ in such a way that the point z_k follows the point z_{k-1} for each k, the first point coincides with the initial point of the curve and the last to its terminal point. We call the sum

$$\sum_1^n f(\xi_k)(z_k - z_{k-1}),$$

where $\xi_k = z(t'_k)$ is any point of the curve Γ lying between z_k and z_{k-1}, the ***integral sum.***

The limit of the integral sum as $\max_k |z_k - z_{k-1}| \to 0$, if this limit exists and is independent of the choice of the points z_k and ξ_k, is called the ***integral of the function f(z) along the curve*** Γ and denoted

$$\int_\Gamma f(z)\,dz.$$

(It is possible to give another definition in which sums analogous to the upper and lower Darboux sums are employed.)

The integral of the function $f(z)$ along the curve Γ can easily be expressed in terms of integrals of real functions. In fact, if $f(z)=u+iv$, $z=x+iy$, then

$$\int_\Gamma f(z)\,dz=\int_\Gamma u\,dx-v\,dy+i\int_\Gamma v\,dx+u\,dy.$$

We shall restrict our attention to one of the simplest results concerning the question of existence of the integral:

If $f(z)$ is continuous on the curve Γ, then the integral of $f(z)$ along Γ exists.

We note that if the integral is taken along the curve in the opposite direction, then the integral changes sign owing to the change of sign of the difference z_k-z_{k-1}.

The limit of integral sums of the form

$$\sum_1^n f(\xi_k)\,|z_k-z_{k-1}|$$

is an integral that is invariant under change of direction along the curve. This integral will be denoted by

$$\int_\Gamma f(z)\,|dz|.$$

It may be expressed in terms of real line integrals of the first kind by

$$\int_\Gamma f(z)|\,dz\,|=\int_\Gamma u\,ds+i\int_\Gamma v\,ds.$$

If the curve is piecewise smooth as well as rectifiable, then the integral reduces to the integral of a function of a real parameter t. Namely,

$$\int_\Gamma f(z)\,dz=\int_a^b f(z(t))\,z'(t)\,dt.$$

The theorem of the mean for integrals plays an important role in analysis, but does not hold for integrals of complex functions. In fact, the integral

$$\int_0^{2\pi} e^{it}\,dt=\int_0^{2\pi}\cos t\,dt+i\int_0^{2\pi}\sin t\,dt$$

equals zero, although the integrand does not vanish on the interval of integration.

The following statement to some extent takes the place of the integral theorem of the mean.

Theorem 5.1. *The modulus of the integral does not exceed the maximum of the modulus of the integrand multiplied by the length of the path of integration.*

Proof. Suppose we are given the integral

$$I=\int_{\Gamma} f(z)\,dz.$$

We denote the $\max\limits_{z\in\Gamma} |f(z)|$ by M and the length of the curve Γ by L. Let us consider an arbitrary integral sum

$$S_n=\sum_{1}^{n} f(\xi_k)(z_k-z_{k-1}).$$

As a consequence of the definition of the length of a curve (see the end of 2), we have

$$|S_n|\leqslant M\sum_{1}^{n}|z_k-z_{k-1}|\leqslant ML.$$

Thus, $|I|\leqslant ML$, which proves the theorem.

It is sometimes necessary to employ the stronger inequality

$$\left|\int_{\Gamma} f(z)\,dz\right|\leqslant\int_{\Gamma}|f(z)||dz|, \tag{5.1}$$

likewise immediately obtained by comparing integral sums.

Line integrals are usually evaluated by reduction to integrals of a function of one variable by means of the equation of the curve (according to the formula introduced above). However, it sometimes makes sense to compute the integral directly with the aid of integral sums. We shall give one example of such a calculation in order that we may then use the result so obtained.

Example 1. Let Γ be any curve beginning at point A and ending at point B. We shall show that the integral

$$\int_{\Gamma} dz$$

exists and is equal to $B-A$.

In fact, take any integral sum. We have

$$S_n=\sum_{1}^{n}(z_k-z_{k-1})=z_1-z_0+z_2-z_1+\ldots+z_n-z_{n-1}=z_n-z_0=B-A,$$

since the first point coincides with the initial point and the last with the terminal point of the curve Γ. Thus, the integral equals $B-A$.

Theorem 5.2. *Let the function f(z) be continuous in some domain D that contains the rectifiable curve Γ. Then the integral of f(z) along Γ can be approximated to within an arbitrary degree of accuracy by an integral of f(z) along some polygonal line Γ_n, also contained in D.*

Proof. We divide the curve into segments γ_k by choosing points $z_0, z_1, \ldots, z_n$, each following the other (the segment γ_k is bounded by the points z_{k-1} and z_k). Let ϱ_k denote the length of γ_k and ϱ that of Γ. We choose the values ϱ_k sufficiently small that all the circles $|z-z_{k-1}|<\varrho_k$ lie in D and such that the inequalities

$$|f(z)-f(z_{k-1})|<\frac{\varepsilon}{2\varrho} \qquad (k=1, 2, \ldots, n),$$

where $\varepsilon>0$ is some positive number, hold in these circles. Let Γ_n denote the polygonal line with vertices $z_0, z_1, \ldots, z_n$ (in that order), and γ'_k the segment of Γ_n joining z_{k-1} and z_k.

We may write

$$\int_{\Gamma} f(z)\,dz-\int_{\Gamma_n} f(z)\,dz=\sum_1^n\left\{\int_{\gamma_k} f(z)\,dz-\int_{\gamma'_k} f(z)\,dz\right\}=$$

$$=\sum_1^n\int_{\gamma_k}[f(z)-f(z_{k-1})]\,dz-\sum_1^n\int_{\gamma'_k}[f(z)-f(z_{k-1})]\,dz,$$

since, according to Example 1

$$\int_{\gamma_k} f(z_{k-1})\,dz=\int_{\gamma'_k} f(z_{k-1})\,dz=f(z_{k-1})(z_k-z_{k-1}).$$

However, because of the conditions on the choice of the values ϱ_k, the integrands cannot exceed $\varepsilon/2\varrho$, so that, after estimation of the integral with the aid of Theorem 5.1, we obtain

$$\left|\int_{\Gamma} f(z)\,dz-\int_{\Gamma_n} f(z)\,dz\right|\leqslant\sum_1^n\frac{\varepsilon}{2\varrho}\varrho_k+\sum_1^n\frac{\varepsilon}{2\varrho}\varrho_k\leqslant\varepsilon.$$

Since ε may be chosen arbitrarily small, the theorem is proved.

The most interesting of the line integrals are those taken along the boundary curves of domains.

Let D be a domain whose boundary consists of a finite number of closed, rectifiable curves.

If the function $f(z)$ is continuous in the domain D up to its boundary Γ (see 4), then we define the *integral of f(z) along in the positive sense* as the sum of the integrals along all the curves composing Γ. The direction to be taken along each of these curves must be such that the domain remains on the left under motion in this direction.

We shall introduce without proof a result analogous to Theorem 5.2, but considerably stronger.*

Theorem 5.3. *Let the function $f(z)$ be continuous in the domain D up to its boundary Γ, which consists of a finite number of rectifiable curves. Then the integral of $f(z)$ along Γ can be approximated to within an arbitrary degree of accuracy by the integral of $f(z)$ along the polygonal line Γ_n, which consists of a finite number of simple, closed polygonal lines lying in D.*

It is sometimes convenient to study the integral along the boundary of a domain of a function continuous up to the boundary of this domain as a function of the domain. Let us note one important property of the integral thus considered.

Theorem 5.4. *Let the function $f(z)$ be continuous in the domain D up to its boundary Γ, which consists of a finite number of rectifiable curves. If the domain D is divided into a finite number of nonintersecting domains D_k with boundaries Γ_k by means of rectifiable curves, then*

$$\varphi(D)=\varphi(D_1)+\ldots+\varphi(D_n),$$

where

$$\varphi(D_k)=\int_{\Gamma_k} f(z)\,dz.$$

Proof. It is sufficient to consider the case in which D is divided into two nonintersecting domains D_1 and D_2. Let Γ_1' denote that part of the boundary of D_1 which is also the boundary of D, Γ_1'' the remaining part of the boundary of D_1 (and similarly for the boundary of D_2). It is clear that Γ_1'' and Γ_2'' differ only in the direction of the path, since domain D_1 remains on the left under motion along Γ_1'', and D_2 on the right; the opposite is true under motion along Γ_2''. It is clear from these considerations that the direction of the circuit Γ_1' and Γ_2' is the same as the direction of the circuit Γ. It is also clear that Γ consists of the union of Γ_1' and Γ_2'. Thus

$$\varphi(D)=\int_{\Gamma} f(z)\,dz=\int_{\Gamma_1'} f(z)\,dz+\int_{\Gamma_2'} f(z)\,dz=$$

$$=\int_{\Gamma_1'} f(z)\,dz+\int_{\Gamma_1''} f(z)\,dz+\int_{\Gamma_2''} f(z)\,dz+\int_{\Gamma_2'} f(z)\,dz=$$

$$=\int_{\Gamma_1} f(z)\,dz+\int_{\Gamma_2} f(z)\,dz=\varphi(D_1)+\varphi(D_2),$$

which proves the theorem.

---

*Unfortunately, it is difficult to point out a book in which this theorem is proved in complete generality by elementary methods. A much more restricted theorem is proved in the book of E. Goursat, "Cours de Analyse Mathematique."

The property demonstrated is called *additivity of the integral as a function of the domain.*

Remark. The reader may readily convince himself that the property of the additivity of the integral as a function of the domain is preserved under division of D into a countable number of non-intersecting parts, if the sum of the lengths Γ_n is finite.

6. INTEGRALS DEPENDING ON A PARAMETER

We shall have to introduce the proofs of two theorems concerning integrals depending on a parameter, since they are proved in analysis only for excessively simple cases.

Theorem 6.1. *Let the function $f(z, w)$ be defined and continuous for $z \in \Gamma$, $w \in E$, where E is some set and Γ is a rectifiable curve. If*

$$f(z, w) \to \varphi(z) \qquad (w \to w_0,\ w \in E)$$

uniformly with respect to $z \in \Gamma$, then

$$\int_\Gamma f(z, w)\,dz \to \int_\Gamma \varphi(z)\,dz \qquad (w \to w_0,\ w \in E).$$

Proof. According to the definition of uniform convergence to the limit, for any $\varepsilon > 0$ we can find a $\delta > 0$ such that for all $z \in \Gamma$

$$|f(z, w) - \varphi(z)| < \frac{\varepsilon}{L} \qquad (|w - w_0| < \delta,\ w \in E)$$

(L is the length of Γ). Applying Theorem 5.1 to estimate the integral, we have

$$\left|\int_\Gamma [f(z, w) - \varphi(z)]\,dz\right| < \frac{\varepsilon}{L} \cdot L = \varepsilon \qquad (|w - w_0| < \delta,\ w \in E).$$

Since ε is arbitrary, the assertion is proved.

The following statement is a special case of the above theorem:

The series $\sum u_n(z)$ of continuous functions $u_n(z)$ can be integrated term by term along any curve on which the series converges uniformly.

Theorem 6.2. *Let the function $f(z)$ be defined and continuous for $z \in \Gamma$, $w \in C$ (Γ and C are rectifiable curves). Then the function*

$$F(w) = \int_\Gamma f(z, w)\,dz$$

is continuous for $w \in C$ and

$$\int_C \int_\Gamma f(z, w)\,dz\,dw = \int_\Gamma \int_C f(z, w)\,dw\,dz.$$

Proof. Let us note first of all that the function $f(z, w)$ is uniformly continuous as a function of both variables for $z \in \Gamma$, $w \in C$, since the curves Γ and C are closed bounded sets (this is not equivalent to the fact that they are closed curves!). This means that $|f(z_1, w_1)-f(z_2, w_2)|<\varepsilon$ whenever $|z_1-z_2|+|w_1-w_2|<\delta$ independent of the position of the points z_1 and z_2 in Γ and w_1 and w_2 in C.

Let us consider the difference $F(w)-F(\zeta)$. According to the definition of $F(w)$ we have

$$F(w)-F(\zeta)=\int_{\Gamma}[f(z, w)-f(z, \zeta)]\, dz.$$

If we choose δ such that $|f(z, w)-f(z, \zeta)|<\frac{\varepsilon}{L}$ (L is the length of Γ) for $|w-\zeta|<\delta$ and for any $z \in \Gamma$, then we obtain the inequality $|F(w)-F(\zeta)|<\varepsilon$.

This proves the continuity of $F(w)$.

Let us find the integral of $F(w)$ along C. We write the integral sum

$$S_n=\sum_1^n F(\theta_k)(w_k-w_{k-1})=\int_{\Gamma}\sum_1^n f(z, \theta_k)(w_k-w_{k-1})\, dz.$$

However, using the results of Example 5.1, we can write

$$\sum_1^n f(z, \theta_k)(w_k-w_{k-1})-\int_C f(z, w)\, dw=\sum_1^n\int_{C_k}[f(z, \theta_k)-f(z, w)]\, dw,$$

where C_k denotes the segment of the curve between w_{k-1} and w_k. We now choose a subdivision of the curve C into segments C_k so fine that for all k

$$\max_{z\in\Gamma,\, w\in C_k}|f(z, \theta_k)-f(z, w)|<\frac{\varepsilon}{LL_1}$$

(L is the length of Γ, L_1, that of C). Then according to Theorem 5.1 on the estimation of the integral, if we denote the length of C_k by ϱ_k we have

$$\left|S_n-\int_{\Gamma}\int_C f(z, w)\, dz\, dw\right|<\frac{\varepsilon}{LL_1}\cdot L\cdot\sum_1^n\varrho_k\leqslant\varepsilon.$$

However, on refinement of the subdivision

$$S_n\to\int_C F(w)\, dw=\int_C\int_{\Gamma}f(z, w)\, dz\, dw.$$

Consequently,

$$\int_C\int_{\Gamma}f(z, w)\, dz\, dw=\int_{\Gamma}\int_C f(z, w)\, dw\, dz,$$

which proves the theorem.

In conclusion, we wish to say a few words about general line integrals.

If the integrand becomes infinite at some points of the contour of integration or if the contour of integration has infinite length, then the integral, in the sense in which we have defined it, does not exist. For these cases it is necessary to introduce the concept of a generalized line integral or integral with singularities.

We shall define the generalized integral for the case in which the integrand is continuous except at a finite number of points a_1, $a_2, \ldots, a_n$, and the terminal point of the contour of integration may lie at infinity. In this case, we shall speak of an integral with singularities at the points $a_1, a_2, \ldots, a_n$ and at infinity.

It is clear that it is sufficient to define the notion of a general integral with one singularity situated at one end of the path, since an integral with several singularities can be divided into the sum of a finite number of integrals each having such a form. Thus:

Let the function $f(z)$ be continuous at all points of the finite contour C with the exception of one of its terminal points, say, a. Let C_ε denote that part of the contour C that lies outside of the circle $|z-a|<\varepsilon$. If the limit

$$\lim_{\varepsilon \to 0} \int_{C_\varepsilon} f(z)\, dz,$$

exists, then we shall call it the *generalized integral of f(z) along the contour C (with a singularity at the point a).*

The generalized integral along a contour with one end at infinity is defined analogously (an integral with a singularity at infinity).

If the generalized integral of $f(z)$ along the contour C exists, then we shall say that $f(z)$ is *integrable along the contour C.*

If the generalized integral $\int_C |f(z)|\,|dz|$ exists, then we shall say that $f(z)$ is *absolutely integrable along the contour C.*

It is not difficult to show that a function that is absolutely integrable along a contour C is integrable along this contour.

Next let the function $f(z, w)$ be continuous with respect to z at all points of the contour C for all values of the parameter $w \in E$, with the exception of the point a. If the uniform limit

$$\lim_{\varepsilon \to 0} \int_{C_\varepsilon} f(z, w)\, dz = \int_C f(z, w)\, dz$$

exists with respect to $w \in E$, then we shall say that the generalized integral *converges uniformly with respect to* $w \in E$. (An integral with several singularities is said to be uniformly convergent, if it can be presented in the form of a sum of uniformly convergent integrals with one singularity.)

Theorems 6.1 and 6.2 remain valid for uniformly convergent generalized integrals.

Let us formulate one criterion for uniform convergence of generalized integrals, analogous to Weierstrass' criterion for the uniform convergence of series.

Theorem 6.3. *If the function* $f(z, w)$, *continuous for all* $z \in C$ *and* $w \in E$, *satisfies the inequality* $|f(z, w)| \leqslant \varphi(z)$ *and the function* $\varphi(z)$ *is absolutely integrable along the contour* C, *then the integral* $\int_C f(z, w)\, dz$ *converges uniformly with respect to* $w \in E$.

CHAPTER II

Analytic Functions and Their Properties

Far from all functions of a complex variable, in fact only functions in a rather narrow class are studied in the theory of analytic functions. However, almost all the functions encountered in analysis fall into this class. This chapter has as its object the study of the simplest properties of functions of this type—analytic functions. One of the basic goals of this chapter is the demonstration of simple and convenient criteria for analyticity.

However, in the process of demonstrating these criteria we shall prove two theorems (Cauchy's theorem and the Cauchy integral formula) that are of fundamental significance for the entire theory.

1. DIFFERENTIABLE AND ANALYTIC FUNCTIONS

A function of a complex variable $f(z)$ defined in some neighborhood of the point ζ is said to be *differentiable at the point* ζ if the limit

$$f'(\zeta) = \lim_{z \to \zeta} \frac{f(z) - f(\zeta)}{z - \zeta},$$

called the *derivative* of the function $f(z)$ at the point ζ exists.

It is clear that the condition for differentiability of $f(z)$ at the point ζ may be written in the form

$$f(z) - f(\zeta) - (z - \zeta) f'(\zeta) = o(|z - \zeta|) \qquad (z \to \zeta). \tag{1.1}$$

A function $f(z)$ is said to be *differentiable in the domain D*, if it is differentiable at each point of the domain.

The following very simple properties of differentiable functions are easily proved, since they follow from the definition.

If the functions f(z) and g(z) are differentiable at the point ζ, *then so are their sum and product and*

$$(f+g)'=f'+g', \quad (fg)'=f'g+fg'.$$

If the functions f(z) and g(z) are differentiable at the point ζ *and* $g(\zeta)\neq 0$, *then the function* $F(z)=\frac{f(z)}{g(z)}$ *is also differentiable at the point* ζ *and*

$$F'=\frac{f'g-fg'}{g^2}.$$

If the function f(z) is differentiable at the point ζ *and the function* $\varphi(z)$ *is differentiable at the point* $\zeta_1=f(\zeta)$, *then the function* $F(z)=\varphi(f(z))$ *is also differentiable at the point* ζ *and*

$$F'(\zeta)=\varphi'(f(\zeta))f'(\zeta).$$

Differentiability of complex functions is a very strong requirement. In order to illustrate more clearly the meaning of this statement we shall write the function $f(z)$ in the form $f(x+iy)=u(x, y)+iv(x, y)$ and explain what conditions are imposed on the functions $u(x, y)$ and $v(x, y)$ by the requirement of differentiability of the function $f(z)$. (The initial impression that the differentiability of $f(z)$ is equivalent to the differentiability of $u(x, y)$ and $v(x, y)$ is not at all correct.)

Theorem 1.1. *For differentiability of the function f(z) at the point* $\zeta=\xi+i\eta$ *it is necessary and sufficient that the functions* $u(x, y)=\operatorname{Re} f(x+iy)$ *and u* $v(x, y)=\operatorname{Im} f(x+iy)$ *are differentiable at the point* (ξ, η) *and that their partial derivatives at this point are connected by the relations*

$$u'_x(\xi, \eta)=v'_y(\xi, \eta), \quad u'_y(\xi, \eta)=-v'_x(\xi, \eta).$$

(These relations are called the *Cauchy-Riemann equations.*)

Proof. We first prove the necessity. Differentiability of the function $f(z)$ at the point ζ is equivalent to the equality

$$f(z)-f(\zeta)=(z-\zeta)f'(\zeta)+o(|z-\zeta|) \qquad (z\to\zeta). \tag{1.2}$$

Separating the real and imaginary parts of this equality and setting $f'(\zeta)=A+iB$, we obtain as $x\to\xi$, $y\to\eta$

$$\left.\begin{aligned} u(x, y)-u(\xi, \eta)&=A(x-\xi)-B(y-\eta)+o(\varrho),\\ v(x, y)-v(\xi, \eta)&=B(x-\xi)+A(y-\eta)+o(\varrho) \end{aligned}\right\} \tag{1.3}$$

(ϱ is the distance between the points (x, y) and (ξ, η), i.e., $\varrho=|z-\zeta|$). As a consequence of equality (1.3), the functions $u(x, y)$ and $v(x, y)$ are differentiable and

$$u'_x(\xi, \eta) = A, \quad u'_y(\xi, \eta) = -B,$$

$$v'_x(\xi, \eta) = B, \quad v'_y(\xi, \eta) = A,$$

i.e., the Cauchy-Riemann conditions hold. This proves the necessity.

Next we prove the sufficiency. If the functions $u(x, y)$ and $v(x, y)$ are differentiable and satisfy the Cauchy-Riemann conditions, then, after setting $u'_x(\xi, \eta) = A$, $v'_x(\xi, \eta) = B$, we can write Eq. (1.3). If we multiply the second part of Eq. (1.3) by i and add it to the first part, then we obtain Eq. (1.2), which is equivalent to differentiability of the function $f(z)$ at the point ζ. This proves the theorem.

Thus, if the functions $u(x, y)$ and $v(x, y)$ are differentiable, then the differentiability of $f(z) = u(x, y) + iv(x, y)$ is not assured; it is still necessary that the functions $u(x, y)$ and $v(x, y)$ satisfy the system of differential equations

$$\frac{\partial u}{\partial x} = \frac{\partial v}{\partial y}, \quad \frac{\partial u}{\partial y} = -\frac{\partial v}{\partial x}$$

(the Cauchy-Riemann equation). Let us note briefly some of the interesting properties of these equations.

If one of the functions $u(x, y)$ and $v(x, y)$ is known, then the Cauchy-Riemann equations give us both partial derivatives of the second function. This allows us to reconstruct the second function to within an arbitrary constant, say, $u(x, y)$, by integration of the total derivative

$$u(x, y) = \int_{(x_0, y_0)}^{(x, y)} u'_x \, dx + u'_y \, dy + C.$$

Thus, the real and imaginary parts of a differentiable function $f(z)$ are not independent. Knowing one of them, we can reconstruct the other to within an arbitrary constant summand.

If we assume that the functions $u(x, y)$ and $v(x, y)$ are both differentiable and if we eliminate one of the functions from the Cauchy-Riemann equations (by differentiating one equation with respect to x and the other with respect to y and adding), we obtain for the functions $u(x, y)$ and $v(x, y)$ the equations

$$\frac{\partial^2 u}{\partial x^2} + \frac{\partial^2 u}{\partial y^2} = 0, \quad \frac{\partial^2 v}{\partial x^2} + \frac{\partial^2 v}{\partial y^2} = 0.$$

The differential equation

$$\frac{\partial^2 u}{\partial x^2} + \frac{\partial^2 u}{\partial y^2} = 0$$

is called *Laplace's equation* and its solutions are called *harmonic functions.* Laplace's equation is encountered in many problems of mathematical physics.

Thus, the real and imaginary parts of a differentiable function are harmonic functions (if they are both differentiable). Since they are related to one another, they are called *conjugate harmonic functions.*

It is clear from the definition of differentiability that polynomials in z are differentiable functions in the entire complex plane. Rational functions (as ratios of polynomials) are also differentiable at all points of the complex plane with the exception of those at which the denominators vanish.

We shall now define a broader class of differentiable functions.

A function $f(z)$ is said to be *analytic (regular) at the point* ζ, if it can be represented by a power series

$$f(z)=\sum_{0}^{\infty} c_n (z-\zeta)^n,$$

that converges in some neighborhood of the point (i.e., in some circle $|z-\zeta|<r$, $r>0$).

A function $f(z)$ is said to be *analytic in the domain D*, if it is defined and analytic at each of its points.

A function $f(z)$ that is analytic at the point ζ is differentiable at this point. In fact, as a consequence of the equation

$$f(z)=c_0+c_1(z-\zeta)+\ldots \qquad (|z-\zeta|<r)$$

we have $f(\zeta)=c_0$ and

$$\frac{f(z)-f(\zeta)}{z-\zeta}=c_1+c_2(z-\zeta)+\ldots \qquad (|z-\zeta|<r).$$

It is clear from this that the limit of the left-hand side exists as $z\rightarrow\zeta$ and equals c_1.

One of the fundamental criteria for analyticity which we shall prove reads as follows: a function that is differentiable in a domain is analytic (regular) in this domain. (We shall prove this statement below.) For this reason the concepts of differentiability and analyticity are often not distinguished from one another.

The concept of analyticity at infinity is often used.

A function $f(z)$ defined in some neighborhood of infinity is said to be *analytic (regular) at infinity,* if

$$f(z)=\sum_{0}^{\infty}\frac{c_n}{z^n} \qquad (|z|>R).$$

In other words, the function $f(z)$ is analytic at the point $z=\infty$ if the functions $g(\zeta)=f\left(\frac{1}{\zeta}\right)$ is analytic at the point $\zeta=0$.

2. CAUCHY'S THEOREM

The following statement is called *Cauchy's theorem*:

Let D be a finite simply connected domain and C be a closed, rectifiable curve lying in D. If the function f(z) is analytic (regular) in the domain D, then the integral of f(z) along C is zero.

This theorem has a rather simple proof. It is possible to interpret it, for example, as a special case of the Green-Ostrogradski formula. However, in spite of the simplicity of its proof, Cauchy's theorem plays a fundamental role throughout the theory of analytic functions.

To prove the equivalence of differentiability and analyticity we need to prove not Cauchy's theorem but a somewhat more refined result called Goursat's theorem.

Theorem 2.1. *Let D be a finite, simply connected domain and C be any closed, rectifiable curve contained in D. If the function f(z) is differentiable in the domain D, then the integral of f(z) along C is equal to zero.*

The basic refinement distinguishing Goursat's theorem from Cauchy's theorem lies in the fact that Goursat's theorem does not require the continuity of the derivative of the function $f(z)$ (an immediate consequence of the requirement of analyticity). Therefore it is impossible to obtain Theorem 2.1 as an immediate corollary of the Green-Ostrogradskiy formula. However, the idea of the proof of this formula, after some slight refinements, is applicable also to the proof of Theorem 2.1. The idea of the proof assumes an even simpler form, since we have only to prove a special case. Let us recall this notion.

Let the contour C be a simple, closed curve. In view of the additivity of the integral along a contour as a function of the domain (see Sect. 5, Chap. 1), if we subdivide the domain bounded by the contour C into parts, then our contour integral is equal to the sum of the integrals along the boundaries of the parts. We shall choose a sufficiently fine subdivision and replace the integrand in each of the parts by a suitable linear function. By employing the differentiability of the integrand, we shall show that under refinement of the subdivision the error engendered by this substitution tends to zero. The integral of a linear function is easily computed (we shall now show that it is zero in our case).

Lemma 1. *The integral of a linear function* $a+bz$ *along any polygonal line is zero.*

Proof. Since the integral of a linear function along any polygonal line trivially exists, it is possible to compute it by finding the limit of the integral sums arising from some method of refining the subdivision of the polygonal line and from some choice of points at which we find the values of the function. We make only one requirement concerning the points of the subdivision: all the vertices of the polygonal line must be points of the subdivision (it is evident that this condition does not hinder the degree of refinement of the subdivision). The values of the function may be taken at the points $\xi_k = \frac{z_k + z_{k-1}}{2}$. This is permissible since the segments of the polygonal line between points of the subdivision z_k and z_{k-1} are straight lines, so that the points ξ_k lie on the polygonal line. Thus

$$\int_C (a + bz)\, dz = \lim S_n,$$

where

$$S_n = \sum_1^n \left(a + b\frac{z_k + z_{k-1}}{2}\right)(z_k - z_{k-1}) =$$

$$= a\sum_1^n (z_k - z_{k-1}) + \frac{b}{2}\sum_1^n (z_k^2 - z_{k-1}^2) = a(z_n - z_0) + \frac{b}{2}(z_n^2 - z_0^2).$$

Since our polygonal line is closed, its initial and terminal points are identical and $S_n = 0$. Thus, the integral under study is equal to zero, which proves the lemma.

Proof of Theorem 2.1. Let us note first of all that it is sufficient to prove the theorem in the case that the contour C is the boundary of a triangle. In fact, in virtue of Theorem 5.2 of Chapt. I, the integral of $f(z)$ along C can be approximated to an arbitrary degree of accuracy by an integral of $f(z)$ along a polygonal line C_n lying in D. The integral along a closed polygonal line may be decomposed into the sum of a finite number of integrals along the boundaries of polygons. The polygons can be broken up into triangles and we can again make use of the additivity of the contour integral as a function of the domain. Thus we see that the integral of $f(z)$ along C can be approximated arbitrarily closely by the sum of a finite number of integrals along the boundaries of triangles. If we show that each of these integrals is zero, then we shall have shown that the integral of $f(z)$ along C is equal to zero.

Thus, let Δ be any triangle lying in D and L be its boundary. Let its area be denoted by S and its perimeter by p.

We will complete the proof by contradiction. If the theorem is false, then there exists a triangle Δ such that the integral of $f(z)$ along its boundary L is different from zero. This fact may be written in the form of an inequality

$$\left|\int_L f(z)\, dz\right| \geqslant \delta S \qquad (\delta > 0). \tag{2.1}$$

We next connect in succession the midpoints of the sides of Δ. It is then decomposed into four equal triangles $\Delta^{(1)}$, $\Delta^{(2)}$, $\Delta^{(3)}$, $\Delta^{(4)}$, which are similar to the triangle Δ. There must be at least one among these triangles (let us denote it by Δ_1) satisfying the inequality

$$\left|\int_{L_1} f(z)\,dz\right| \geqslant \delta S_1$$

(S_1 is the area and L_1 the boundary of the triangle Δ_1). In fact, as a consequence of the additivity of the contour integral as a function of the domain, we have

$$\left|\int_{L} f(z)\,dz\right| = \left|\sum_{1}^{4} \int_{L^{(k)}} f(z)\,dz\right| \leqslant \sum_{1}^{4} \left|\int_{L^{(k)}} f(z)\,dz\right|.$$

If we prove that the contrary inequality holds for all of the triangles $\Delta^{(k)}$, then we shall have arrived at a contradiction to (2.1).

Thus, we shall carry out an analogous decomposition of the triangle Δ_1 into four triangles $\Delta_1^{(1)}$, $\Delta_1^{(2)}$, $\Delta_1^{(3)}$, $\Delta_1^{(4)}$. After repeating the argument given above, we may choose a triangle Δ_2 from among these for which

$$\left|\int_{L_2} f(z)\,dz\right| \geqslant \delta S_2,$$

etc.

In this way we construct a sequence of triangles Δ_n, each contained in its predecessor and for which

$$\left|\int_{L_n} f(z)\,dz\right| \geqslant \delta S_n. \qquad (2.2)$$

All the triangles Δ_n are similar to the triangle Δ, and their area and perimeter approach 0 as $n \to \infty$. More precisely, $S_n = 4^{-n}S$ and $p_n = 2^{-n}p$. The triangles Δ_n shrink down to a point $\zeta \in D$ lying inside or on the boundary of each of them.

Now we evaluate the integral occurring in inequality (2.2) by a second method. According to lemma 1, we can add any linear function to the integrand without changing the integral. Therefore

$$\int_{L_n} f(z)\,dz = \int_{L_n} [f(z) - f(\zeta) - (z-\zeta) f'(\zeta)]\,dz.$$

However, the function $f(z)$ is differentiable at the point ζ and $|z-\zeta|$, $z \in L_n$, does not exceed half of the perimeter of the triangle Δ_n thus in virtue of (1.1)

$$\max_{z \in L_n} |f(z) - f(\zeta) - (z-\zeta) f'(\zeta)| = o(p_n).$$

Since the modulus of the integral does not exceed the product of the maximum modulus of the integrand by the length of the path of integration (see Theorem 5.2 of Chap. 1), then

$$\left|\int_{L_n} f(z)\,dz\right| = o\,(p_n^2) = o\,(S_n) \qquad (n \longrightarrow \infty) \tag{2.3}$$

(we recall that $S_n = 4^{-n}S$ and $p_n = 2^{-n}p$).

As a result of the contradiction of (2.2) by (2.3), the theorem is proved.

We wish to make a few remarks which extend and more exactly specify the nature of the theorem.

Remark 1. The theorem proved carries over to the case in which D is an arbitrary simply connected domain and the contour C is the boundary of some domain lying in D. However, it is necessary to keep in mind that by the *integral along the boundary of a domain*, bounded by a finite number of simple, rectifiable curves, we mean the sum of the integrals along all the boundary curves, where the direction along each such curve is to be chosen so that the domain remains on the left as we move along the curve in this direction.

The statement of the theorem for this case has the following form:

Let the function f(z) be differentiable in the domain D and let G be a finite domain contained, together with its boundary (which consists of a finite number of closed, rectifiable curves) in D. Then the integral of f(z) along the boundary of G is equal to zero.

This supplementary result does not require a separate proof, since by virtue of the additivity of the integral as a function of the domain we can replace the integral of $f(z)$ along the boundary of G by the sum of a finite number of integrals along the boundaries of simply connected domains.

Remark 2. It is not necessary to assume that the contour of integration is contained within the domain in which $f(z)$ is differentiable.

Let the finite domain D be bounded by a finite number of piecewise-smooth, closed curves with folds and let the function f(z) be continuous up to the boundary of D. If the function f(z) is differentiable in D, then the integral of f(z) along the boundary of D is equal to zero.

To prove this additional result we need only take note of the fact that, because of Theorem 5.3 of Chap. 1, the integral of $f(z)$ along the boundary of D can be approximated to within an arbitrary degree of accuracy by an integral of $f(z)$ along a polygonal line contained within D; this integral is, of course, zero.

Remark 3. The theorem can also be extended to infinite domains, if we impose additional conditions on $f(z)$.

Let the contour C be the boundary of the domain D where C contains the point at infinity. If the function f(z) is differentiable in the domain D, is continuous up to its boundary C and satisfies the condition

$$f(z)=o\left(\frac{1}{z}\right) \qquad (z\longrightarrow\infty,\ z\in\overline{D}), \tag{2.4}$$

then, if the generalized integral of f(z) along C converges, it is equal to zero.

Indeed, let us denote by D_R the part of the domain D inside the circle $|z|<R$, and by C_R the part of C within this circle. If the generalized integral of $f(z)$ along C exists, then it is equal to the limit

$$\lim_{R\to\infty}\int_{C_R} f(z)\,dz.$$

According to Remark 2, the integral along the total boundary of D_R is equal to zero, since the integral of $f(z)$ along C_R is equal (with change in sign) to the integral of $f(z)$ along the remainder of the boundary of D_R (which we denote L_R). But L_R is part of the circle $|z|=R$, and so L_R does not exceed $2\pi R$. If we estimate the modulus of the integral of $f(z)$ along L_R by taking the product of the maximum modulus of the integrand with the length of the path of integration, then we obtain

$$\left|\int_{C_R} f(z)\,dz\right|=\left|\int_{L_R} f(z)\,dz\right|\leqslant 2\pi R\cdot o\left(\frac{1}{R}\right)\longrightarrow 0 \qquad (R\longrightarrow\infty).$$

Consequently, the limit considered is equal to zero.

If, in addition, we have some estimate of the length of L_R whereby we may replace $2\pi R$ by a smaller number, then condition (2.4) can be considerably strengthened. Suppose, for example, that the length of L_R is bounded as $R\longrightarrow\infty$. Then condition (2.4) can be replaced by the condition

$$f(z)=o(1) \qquad (z\longrightarrow\infty,\ z\in\overline{D}).$$

3. CAUCHY'S INTEGRAL FORMULA

With the help of Cauchy's theorem it is easy to prove the so-called Cauchy integral formula. This formula allows us to express the value of an analytic function at any point of a domain in terms of the values on the boundary of this domain. Since we need this formula also for the proof of the equivalence of differentiability and analyticity, we shall prove it for differentiable functions.

Theorem 3.1. *Let the function f(z) be differentiable in the domain D. If the finite domain G together with its boundary C is* *contained in the domain D and $\zeta \in G$, then*

$$\int_C \frac{f(z)\,dz}{z-\zeta} = 2\pi i f(\zeta).$$

Proof. The function $\varphi(z) = \frac{f(z)}{z-\zeta}$ is the quotient of two differentiable functions, for which the denominator vanishes only at the point $z=\zeta$. The function $\varphi(z)$ is therefore differentiable at every point of the domain D with the exception of the point $z=\zeta$. We choose $\varrho > 0$ so small that the circle $|z-\zeta| \leqslant \varrho$ lies within the domain G; we denote by D' the domain obtained by removing the point ζ from D and by G_ρ the domain obtained by removing the circle $|z-\zeta| \leqslant \varrho$ from the domain G.

The function $\varphi(z)$ is differentiable in the domain D', and the domain G_ρ together with its boundary (which we denote by C_ρ) is contained in the domain D'. Thus, on the basis of Remark 1 to Cauchy's theorem, the integral of $f(z)$ along C_ρ is equal to zero. However, C_ρ consists of the circle $|z-\zeta| = \varrho$ and C, where integration along the circle is carried out in such a way that the domain G_ρ remains on the left (and the circle $|z-\zeta| < \varrho$ on the right). Therefore, by changing the direction of integration along the circle, we can write

$$\int_C \varphi(z)\,dz = \int_{|z-\zeta|=\varrho} \varphi(z)\,dz.$$

The left-hand integral does not depend on ϱ; thus we may arrange the value of ϱ at our discretion when we compute the integral on the right-hand side of the equality. If we denote the circle $|z-\zeta| = \varrho$ by Γ_ρ, for the sake of brevity, we have

$$\int_{\Gamma_\varrho} \varphi(z)\,dz = \int_{\Gamma_\varrho} \frac{f(z)}{z-\zeta}\,dz = f(\zeta)\int_{\Gamma_\varrho} \frac{dz}{z-\zeta} + \int_{\Gamma_\varrho} \frac{f(z)-f(\zeta)}{z-\zeta}\,dz = f(\zeta)\cdot I_1 + I_2.$$

The integrand in the integral I_2 is bounded as $z \to \zeta$: it approaches $f'(\zeta)$. Since the length of Γ_ρ is $2\pi\varrho$ and the modulus of the integral does not exceed the product of the maximum modulus of the integrand by the length of the path of integration, then $I_2 \to 0$ $(\varrho \to 0)$. The integral I_1 is easily computed. A parametric equation for the circle Γ_ρ has the form $z = \zeta + \varrho e^{i\theta}$, and so

$$\int_{\Gamma_\varrho} \frac{dz}{z-\zeta} = \int_0^{2\pi} \frac{i\varrho e^{i\theta}}{\varrho e^{i\theta}}\,d\theta = 2\pi i.$$

Thus,

$$\int_C \varphi(z)\,dz = 2\pi i f(\zeta) + o(1) \qquad (\varrho \to 0).$$

Since the left-hand side of the equality does not depend on ϱ, we obtain the statement of the theorem.

Remarks 2 and 3 to Cauchy's theorem remain valid also for Cauchy's integral formula.

We now move on to the proof of a basic criterion for analyticity.

Theorem 3.2. *If the function f(z) is differentiable in the domain D, then it is analytic in this domain.*

Proof. Let a be any point of the domain D. We choose a number r so small that the circle $|z-a|\leqslant r$ is contained in D. Then according to Cauchy's integral formula, we can write

$$f(\zeta)=\frac{1}{2\pi i}\int\limits_{|z-a|=r}\frac{f(z)\,dz}{z-\zeta}\qquad (|\zeta-a|<r).$$

We next make use of the obvious equality

$$\frac{1}{z-\zeta}=\frac{1}{z-a-(\zeta-a)}=\frac{1}{z-a}\cdot\frac{1}{1-\dfrac{\zeta-a}{z-a}}.$$

Since $z-a|=r$ and $|\zeta-a|<r$, on the contour of integration we have $\left|\frac{\zeta-a}{z-a}\right|=\theta<1$ (the point ζ lies inside the circle and the point z on its boundary). Consequently, the series

$$\frac{1}{z-\zeta}=\sum_{0}^{\infty}\frac{(\zeta-a)^n}{(z-a)^{n+1}}$$

converges uniformly on the circle $|z-a|=r$ since its terms do not exceed in absolute value the terms of the absolutely convergent numerical series $\sum\frac{1}{r}\theta^n$. Multiplication of the series by the continuous function $f(z)$ does not affect its uniform convergence, and since a uniformly convergent series can be integrated term by term, we obtain

$$f(\zeta)=\sum_{0}^{\infty}c_n(\zeta-a)^n,\qquad c_n=\frac{1}{2\pi i}\int\limits_{|z-a|=r}\frac{f(z)\,dz}{(z-a)^{n+1}}.$$

This means, of course, that the function $f(z)$ is analytic at the point a. Since a may be any point of the domain D, the theorem is proved.

Note that we can prove something a little stronger. The statement that we shall prove also has interest for analytic functions:

Theorem 3.2.* *Let the function f(z) be analytic in the domain D. If the circle $|z-a|\leqslant r$ is contained in the domain D, then the power series*

$$\sum_{0}^{\infty}c_n(z-a)^n,$$

in which

$$c_n = \frac{1}{2\pi i} \int\limits_{|z-a|=r} \frac{f(z)\,dz}{(z-a)^{n+1}},$$

converges to f(z) in this circle. (This series is called the Taylor series at $z=a$ for the function f(z).)

It is easy to obtain formulas for the derivatives of analytic functions from Cauchy's integral formula.

Theorem 3.3. *If the function f(z) is analytic in the domain D, then it has derivatives of all orders there; moreover, they are also analytic in D and are given by the formula*

$$f^{(n)}(\zeta) = \frac{n!}{2\pi i} \int\limits_C \frac{f(z)\,dz}{(z-\zeta)^{n+1}} \qquad (\zeta \in G). \tag{3.1}$$

Here G is a domain containing the point ζ and G together with its boundary C is contained in D.

Proof. We proceed by induction on n. For $n=0$ the statement of the theorem is obviously true, and formula (3.1) coincides with Cauchy's integral formula. Let us assume that we have already shown that $f^{(n-1)}(z)$ exists and is given by formula (3.1). We show that $f^{(n)}(z)$ exists and is given by formula (3.1) [the analyticity of $f^{(n-1)}(z)$ is a consequence of this].

We choose any two points ζ and $\zeta+h$, contained in G, and write

$$f^{(n)}(\zeta) = \lim_{h\to 0} \frac{f^{(n-1)}(\zeta+h) - f^{(n-1)}(\zeta)}{h} =$$

$$= \frac{(n-1)!}{2\pi i} \lim_{h\to 0} \int\limits_C \frac{1}{h}\left(\frac{1}{(z-\zeta-h)^n} - \frac{1}{(z-\zeta)^n}\right) f(z)\,dz.$$

In view of Theorem 6.1 of Chap. I concerning the possibility of interchanging the order of taking uniform limits and integrating, it is sufficient to prove that

$$\frac{1}{h}\left(\frac{1}{(z-\zeta-h)^n} - \frac{1}{(z-\zeta)^n}\right) \to \frac{n}{(z-\zeta)^{n+1}} \qquad (h\to 0)$$

uniformly with respect to $z \in G$. We now write

$$\frac{1}{(z-\zeta-h)^n} - \frac{1}{(z-\zeta)^n} = \frac{(z-\zeta)^n - (z-\zeta-h)^n}{(z-\zeta)^n (z-\zeta-h)^n} =$$

$$= (z-\zeta)^{-n} (z-\zeta-h)^{-n} \sum_1^n h^k C_n^k (z-\zeta-h)^{n-k}.$$

Since z, ζ and h are bounded above and $|z-\zeta|$ and $|z-\zeta-h|$ are bounded below for $z \in C$ (the points ζ and $\zeta+h$ are contained in G), the above expression signifies that

$$\frac{1}{(z-\zeta-h)^n}-\frac{1}{(z-\zeta)^n}=\frac{nh}{(z-\zeta)^n(z-\zeta-h)}+O(h^2) \qquad (h \to 0)$$

uniformly with respect to $z \in C$. However,

$$\frac{1}{z-\zeta-h}=\frac{1}{z-\zeta}+O(h) \qquad (h \to 0)$$

uniformly with respect to $z \in C$. Thus,

$$\frac{1}{h}\left(\frac{1}{(z-\zeta-h)^n}-\frac{1}{(z-\zeta)^n}\right)=\frac{n}{(z-\zeta)^{n+1}}+O(h) \qquad (h \to 0)$$

uniformly with respect to $z \in C$, from which it evidently follows that the left-hand side uniformly approaches the limit $n(z-\zeta)^{-n-1}$ with respect to z as $h \to 0$.

This completes the induction and proves the theorem.

We have thus proved the existence and analyticity of all the derivatives of an analytic function. Naturally, the question now arises of the existence of an antiderivative (indefinite integral) for an analytic function.

Theorem 3.4. *If a function f(z) is analytic in a finite simply connected domain D, then there exists a function F(z), analytic in the domain D and satisfying the condition* $F'(z)=f(z)$.

Proof. We first choose two points a and z of the domain D and join them by an arbitrary rectifiable curve contained in D. The integral of $f(z)$ along this curve does not depend on its shape, but only on the initial and terminal points of the curve. In fact, if we have two such curves with the same initial and terminal points, then we can join them into one closed contour (we go along the first curve from the initial to the terminal point and then back along the second). By Cauchy's theorem this integral is zero, therefore the integrals along each of our curves are the same (if we integrate along both curves from the initial to the terminal points).

Thus, we can define in the domain D the function

$$F(z)=\int_a^z f(\zeta)\,d\zeta.$$

We show that this function is differentiable and determine its derivative. Indeed

$$F(z+h)-F(z)=\int_a^{z+h} f(\zeta)\,d\zeta-\int_a^z f(\zeta)\,d\zeta=\int_z^{z+h} f(\zeta)\,d\zeta=$$

$$=f(z)\int_z^{z+h} d\zeta+\int_z^{z+h}[f(\zeta)-f(z)]\,d\zeta=f(z)\cdot I_1+I_2.$$

The integral I_1 equals h (see, for example, Example 1 of Sect. 5 in Chap. I), and we shall evaluate I_2. We assume that h is so small that the line segment joining z and $z+h$ is contained in the domain D. We can take this line segment for the contour of integration in the integral I_2. The function $f(z)$ is continuous and thus

$$\max_{\zeta} |f(z)-f(\zeta)| \longrightarrow 0 \qquad (h \longrightarrow 0)$$

(the maximum is taken along the segment joining z and $z+h$). Approximating the value of the modulus of the integral by the product of the maximum modulus of the function by the length of the path, we obtain

$$\left| \int_z^{z+h} [f(\zeta)-f(z)]\, d\zeta \right| = o(h) \qquad (h \longrightarrow 0).$$

Consequently,

$$F(z+h)-F(z) = hf(z)+o(h) \qquad (h \longrightarrow 0),$$

i.e., $F(z)$ is differentiable at any point of the domain D and its derivative equals $f(z)$. The analyticity of $F(z)$ in the domain D now follows from Theorem 3.2, which proves the theorem.

It is not difficult to show that the *antiderivative of an analytic function is uniquely determined to within an arbitrary additive constant.*

In fact, if $F_1'(z) = F_2'(z) = f(z)$, then, setting $F(z) = F_1(z) - F_2(z)$ we obtain $F'(z) = 0$. We shall employ the symbols

$$U(x, y) = \operatorname{Re} F(x+iy), \quad V(x, y) = \operatorname{Im} F(x+iy).$$

As in the derivation of the Cauchy-Riemann equations in Theorem 1.1, we find

$$U_x' = 0, \ V_x' = 0, \ U_y' = 0, \ V_y' = 0.$$

From this it is easy to see that both $U(x, y)$ and $V(x, y)$ are constants.

Another simple consequence is the Newton-Leibniz formula:

If $F(z)$ is an antiderivative of $f(z)$, then

$$\int_a^b f(z)\, dz = F(b) - F(a).$$

We should take note of the fact that a function analytic in a multiply connected domain need not have an analytic antiderivative in this domain. We will see examples of this type when we study multiple-valued functions in the following chapter.

4. CRITERIA FOR ANALYTICITY

In the preceding section we showed the equivalence of the concepts of differentiability and analyticity. This yields immediately a series of simple criteria for analyticity convenient for testing specific functions. Namely:

The sum and product of a finite number of functions analytic at the point ζ *are functions analytic at the point* ζ.

The quotient of two functions analytic at the point ζ *is also an analytic function at this point, if the denominator does not vanish at this point.*

If the function $f(z)$ *is analytic at the point* ζ, *and the function* $F(w)$ *is analytic at the point* $f(w)$, *then the function* $\varphi(z) = F(f(z))$ *is analytic at the point* ζ.

We prove next several somewhat deeper results. The following fundamental criterion is called Morera's theorem:

Theorem 4.1. *Let the function* $f(z)$ *be continuous in the domain* D *and let the integral of* $f(z)$ *along the boundary of any polygon lying in* D *be zero. Then* $f(z)$ *is analytic in the domain* D.

Proof. We denote by G any simply connected part of the domain D. Using Theorem 5.2 of Chap. I, we may readily convince ourselves that the integral of $f(z)$ along any closed, rectifiable curve contained in D is zero. By the same reasoning as in Theorem 3.4 we readily find that $f(z)$ has an antiderivative $F(z)$ which is analytic in the domain G. But $f(z) = F'(z)$, and so by Theorem 3.3 with $n = 1$ we find that $f(z)$ is also analytic in the domain G. Since G is any simply connected part of D, the theorem is proved.

The following test may be derived easily with the aid of Morera's theorem.

Theorem 4.2. *If the function* $f(z, w)$ *is analytic in* z *in the domain* G *for any* $w \in E$, *and if*

$$f(z, w) \longrightarrow \varphi(z) \qquad (w \longrightarrow w_0, \ w \in E)$$

uniformly with respect to z *in any closed subset of* G, *then the function* $\varphi(z)$ *is also analytic in the domain* G.

Proof. Let us note first of all that the function $f(z, w)$ is continuous in z in the domain G, which implies, because of Theorem 4.1 of Chap. I, that the function $\varphi(z)$ is also continuous in any closed subset of G. Let us note next that, as a consequence of Theorem 6.1 of Chap. I on the possibility of interchanging the order of integration and uniform approach to the limit, we have

$$\int_C \varphi(z)\, dz = \int_C \lim f(z, w)\, dz = \lim \int_C f(z, w)'dz,$$

in which C is any contour contained in G. If we take for C the boundary of some domain contained in G, then this last integral is zero because of Cauchy's theorem.

Thus, the function $\varphi(z)$ is continuous in the domain G and its integral along the boundary of any domain contained (along with its boundary) in G is zero. The function $\varphi(z)$ is analytic in the domain G by Morera's theorem. This proves the theorem.

The most often quoted special case of Theorem 4.2 is the following:

Corollary 1. The sum of a uniformly convergent series of analytic functions is an analytic function at all interior points of the set on which the series converges uniformly.

In particular, let us note a special case of Corollary 1:

Corollary 2. The sum of a power series is analytic within its circle of convergence.

The following criterion is also quite important.

Theorem 4.3. *Let L be any rectifiable curve in the plane of w, and $f(z, w)$ be a function analytic with respect to z in the domain G for any $w \in L$ and continuous in both variables for $z \in G$ and $w \in L$. Then the function*

$$\varphi(z) = \int_L f(z, w)\, dw$$

is analytic in the domain G.

Proof. We shall take any domain D contained together with its boundary C in G. According to Theorem 6.2 of Chap. I, the function $\varphi(z)$ is continuous in the domain G and

$$\int_C \varphi(z)\, dz = \int_C \int_L f(z, w)\, dw\, dz = \int_L \int_C f(z, w)\, dz\, dw.$$

The center integral is equal to zero by virtue of Cauchy's theorem. The function $\varphi(z)$ thus fulfills the conditions of Morera's theorem. Consequently, $\varphi(z)$ is analytic in the domain G, which proves the theorem.

Remark. We see from Theorems 4.2 and 4.3 that Theorem 4.3 remains valid also for generalized integrals, if they converge uniformly for $z \in G$.

Let us note a special case of Theorem 4.3.

Corollary 1. If the function $f(w)$ is continuous on the contour L, then the function

$$\varphi(z) = \frac{1}{2\pi i} \int_L \frac{f(w)\, dw}{w - z}$$

is analytic in any domain not containing points of the contour L.

In fact, the function $\frac{f(w)}{w-z}$ is analytic with respect to z for any $w \in L$ and continuous with respect to both variables for $z \in D$ and $w \in L$ in any domain D not containing points of the contour L. Our assertion thus immediately follows from Theorem 4.3.

Let us introduce a result of a rather different type.

Theorem 4.4. *If the function* $f(z, w)$ *is analytic in* z *in the domain* G *for any* $w \in E$ *and*

$$f(z, w) \longrightarrow \varphi(z) \qquad (w \longrightarrow w_0, \ w \in E)$$

uniformly in z *in any closed subset of the domain* G, *then*

$$f'_z(z, w) \longrightarrow \varphi'(z) \qquad (w \longrightarrow w_0, \ w \in E)$$

uniformly with respect to z *also in any closed subset of the domain* G.

Proof. Let $\overline{B}$ denote any closed subset of G, and D denote any domain containing $\overline{B}$ and contained together with its boundary C in G. Then for $z \in \overline{B}$, $\zeta \in C$

$$\frac{f(\zeta, w)}{(\zeta-z)^2} \longrightarrow \frac{\varphi(\zeta)}{(\zeta-z)^2} \qquad (w \longrightarrow w_0, \ w \in E)$$

uniformly with respect to $z \in \overline{B}$ and $\zeta \in C$. Because of Theorem 6.1 of Chap. I on the possibility of interchanging the order of integration and uniform approach to the limit, we have

$$\frac{1}{2\pi i} \int_C \frac{f(\zeta, w)}{(\zeta-z)^2} dz \longrightarrow \frac{1}{2\pi i} \int_C \frac{\varphi(\zeta)}{(\zeta-z)^2} d\zeta \qquad (w \longrightarrow w_0, \ w \in E).$$

The left-hand side is equal to $f'_z(z, w)$ because of Theorem 3.3, and the right-hand side is equal to $\varphi'(z)$ because of Theorems 4.2 and 3.3. The assertion of the theorem follows from this.

In particular:

Corollary 1. A series of analytic functions converging uniformly in any closed subset of the domain G can be differentiated term by term, and the resulting series will converge uniformly in any closed subset of the domain G.

The following result is proved in a fashion completely analogous to that of Theorem 4.4.

Theorem 4.5. *If* $f(z, w)$ *is a function analytic in* z *in the domain* G *for any* $w \in L$ *and continuous in both variables for* $z \in G$, $w \in L$, *and*

$$\varphi(z) = \int_L f(z, w)\, dw,$$

then

$$\varphi'(z) = \int_L f'_z(z, w)\, dw.$$

Remark. It is clear that the statement of Theorem 4.5 remains valid also for uniformly convergent generalized integrals.

In conclusion we prove one more theorem: *the compactness principle for analytic functions.*

Theorem 4.6. *Given a uniformly bounded sequence of functions* $\{f_n(z)\}$, *analytic in the domain G, it is always possible to select a subsequence* $\{f_{n_k}(z)\}$ *that converges uniformly in any closed subset of the domain G.*

Proof. Let $\overline{B}$ denote any closed subset of the domain G, and D be a domain containing $\overline{B}$ and contained together with its boundary C in G. According to Theorem 3.3

$$f'_n(z) = \frac{1}{2\pi i}\int\limits_C \frac{f_n(\zeta)}{(\zeta - z)^2}\, d\zeta \qquad (z \in D).$$

Uniform boundedness for the sequence $\{f_n(z)\}$ means that

$$|f_n(z)| \leqslant M \qquad (z \in G).$$

Therefore, if we estimate the modulus of the integral by the product of the maximum modulus of the integrand by the length of the path of integration, we obtain

$$|f'_n(z)| \leqslant M \cdot L \cdot \frac{1}{2\pi\varrho^2} \qquad (z \in \overline{B}),$$

in which L is the length and ϱ is the distance from $\overline{B}$ to C.

Thus, the sequence of these same functions as well as the sequence of their derivatives are also uniformly bounded on the set $\overline{B}$. As a consequence of the uniform boundedness of the sequence of derivatives, however, we have equicontinuity for the sequence $\{f_n(z)\}$. Applying Arzéla's theorem (see Sect. 4, Chap. I), we may therefore choose a subsequence of the sequence $\{f_n(z)\}$ that converges uniformly on the set $\overline{B}$.

Thus, for each closed subset of the domain G we may select a subsequence of the sequence $\{f_n(z)\}$ that converges uniformly on this subset (the subsequence will be different in general for each subset). Let us show also that it is possible to choose a subsequence that converges uniformly on any closed subset of the domain G. We find such a uniformly convergent subsequence for each closed subset $\overline{B}$. Then we construct an increasing sequence of closed sets $\overline{B}_k$, whose union covers all of G. After that, we choose the first function from the sequence for $\overline{B}$, the second from the sequence for $\overline{B}_k$, etc. This sequence will be the one we seek.

5. A UNIQUENESS THEOREM

We prove now one of the most important properties of analytic functions: *the uniqueness theorem.*

Theorem 5.1. *Let the function f(z) be analytic in the domain D and let* $z_1, z_2, z_3, \ldots$ *be an infinite sequence of points in D and having a limit point in the domain D. If* $f(z_n)=0$ $(n=1, 2, 3, \ldots)$*, then the function f(z) vanishes on the entire domain D.*

Proof. Let a be a limit point in D of the sequence $\{z_n\}$. We show first that the function $f(z)$ is zero in some neighborhood of the point a. We know that the function is analytic at the point a, i.e.,

$$f(z)=\sum_0^\infty c_n(z-a)^n \qquad (|z-a|<r).$$

We may assume without loss of generality that $z_n \to a$ and that we have $|z_n-a|<r$ for all n. Setting $z=z_n$ and recalling that $f(z_n)=0$, we obtain

$$0=c_0+c_1(z_n-a)+\ldots .$$

Taking the limit as $n\to\infty$, we find that $c_0=0$. Because of this we can write

$$\frac{f(z)}{z-a}=c_1+c_2(z-a)+\ldots \qquad (|z-a|<r).$$

Again putting $z=z_n$ and allowing n to approach ∞, we find that $c_1=0$. Continuing in this fashion, we may show that all c_n are zero, i.e., that the function $f(z)$ vanishes for $|z-a|<r$.

Next we show that the function $f(z)$ vanishes at each point of the domain D. To do this, we take any point $\zeta\in D$ and join it to the point a by a simple polygonal line lying in D (this is possible because the domain D is a connected set). Now suppose that $f(\zeta)\neq 0$. Then we can find a point a' on the polygonal line L with the following properties:

The function $f(z)$ vanishes on the segment of L between the points a and a'.

We can find at least one point in the circle $|z-a'|<\varrho$ for any $\varrho>0$ such that $f(z)$ is different from zero at this point.

Thus we can find a sequence of points $\{z'_n\}$ of L for which $z'_n\to a'$ and $f(z'_n)=0$. Then we take the point a' in place of a and the sequence $\{z_n\}$ in place of the sequence $\{z'_n\}$ and repeat the argument carried out above. We find that $f(z)=0$ for $|z-a'|<r'$. This contradicts the second property of the point a'.

The assumption that there exists a point $\zeta\in D$ such that $f(\zeta)\neq 0$ leads to a contradiction, which proves the theorem.

The concept of analytic continuation plays an important role in the applications of the uniqueness theorem.

Suppose we are given a set E, a function $f(z)$ defined on E and a domain D containing the set E. A function $F(z)$ which is analytic (regular) in the domain D and coincides with $f(z)$ on the set E is called an *analytic continuation of the function f(z) to the domain D.*

The *principle of analytic continuation* is an immediate consequence of the uniqueness theorem.

If the set E has at least one limit point contained within the domain D, then the function f(z) has at most one analytic continuation to the domain D.

In fact, if there are two distinct analytic continuations to the domain D of the function $f(z)$, then their difference constitutes a contradiction to the uniqueness theorem.

We show how it is possible with the help of the principle of analytic continuation to obtain extensions of some of the elementary functions for complex values of the variable and to study their properties in the complex plane.

It is known from analysis that the functions e^x, $\sin x$, $\cos x$ can be expanded in power series

$$e^x = \sum_0^\infty \frac{x^n}{n!}, \quad \sin x = \sum_0^\infty (-1)^n \frac{x^{2n+1}}{(2n+1)!}, \quad \cos x = \sum_0^\infty (-1)^n \frac{x^{2n}}{(2n)!},$$

which converge for all real x. These series also converge for all complex values of the variable. It is therefore natural to define the functions e^z, $\sin z$, $\cos z$ for complex values of z by means of series. According to Corollary 2 of Theorem 4.2, the sums of these series are functions that are analytic in the entire complex plane, i.e., they give us analytic continuations of the functions e^x, $\sin x$, $\cos x$ to the entire complex plane. There can be no other extensions because of the principle of analytic continuation.

Now we show how to investigate functions of a complex variable arising as analytic continuations. In particular, we show how to transfer the formulas (known for real values) to the complex plane. Since the reasoning involved is almost the same for the various formulas, we limit ourselves to one formula.

Example 1. Let us show that for any complex numbers z and ζ we have the formula

$$e^{z+\zeta} = e^z e^\zeta. \tag{5.1}$$

The functions in both sides of formula (5.1) are analytic in z for any fixed ζ and in ζ for any fixed z. We must show that these functions coincide for all z and ζ. Let us first consider real values of ζ. If z is also real, then the formula obviously holds. But because of the uniqueness theorem, two functions of the complex variable z that are analytic in the entire complex plane and coincide for all real values of z are identical. Thus we have proved formula (5.1) for any complex z and any real ζ.

Next taking any complex value of z and carrying out analogous reasoning with our functions as functions of ζ, we may easily verify that formula (5.1) is valid for all complex z and ζ.

It is clear that formula (5.1) could also be proved directly and easily by multiplying out series, but the method of reasoning used is noteworthy not only for (and not so much for) its simplicity but also for its generality.

It is easy to obtain a simple formula for the computation of values of the function e^z for any complex z with the aid of formula

(5.1). In fact, set $z=x+iy$. Then, according to formula (5.1), we have $e^z=e^x e^{iy}$. To compute e^{iy} we replace z by iy in the series e^z and separate the real and imaginary parts. This gives us Euler's formula

$$e^{iy}=\cos y+i\sin y.$$

With its aid we find

$$e^{x+iy}=e^x\cos y+ie^x\sin y. \tag{5.2}$$

It follows from formula (5.2), in particular, that

$$|e^z|=e^{\operatorname{Re} z}. \tag{5.3}$$

The majority of functions arising in analysis can be continued analytically to complex values of the variable. This can be done quite simply for the exponential and trigonometric functions; it is more complicated for others. Thus, for example, the analytic continuation of the function $\ln x$, which we shall take up in the following chapter, gives us considerable trouble. Now we study one more example of the analytic continuation of a function defined for real values to the complex plane; here the definition will be in terms of an integral rather than a series.

Example 2. We find the analytic continuation to the entire complex plane of Euler's gamma function $\Gamma(z)$, which is defined for positive real z by the integral

$$\Gamma(z)=\int_0^\infty t^{z-1}e^{-t}\,dt.$$

The function t^{z-1} occurring in the integrand is easy to continue analytically to the entire complex plane, since

$$t^{z-1}=e^{(z-1)\ln t},$$

and we already know the analytic continuation of the exponential function. Thus, applying Theorem 4.3, we see that the integral

$$\int_a^b t^{z-1}e^{-t}\,dt$$

for $a>0$ and $b<\infty$ is an analytic function of z in the entire complex plane. However, it is a generalized integral for $a=0$ and $b=\infty$, and so we need to show that it converges uniformly for any z. Since the integral defining $\Gamma(z)$ has two singularities (at zero and infinity), it is simpler to split it into the sum of two integrals and investigate the convergence of each of these.

We put

$$\Gamma(z)=\alpha(z)+\beta(z),$$

where

$$\alpha(z)=\int_0^1 t^{z-1}e^{-t}\,dt,\qquad \beta(z)=\int_1^\infty t^{z-1}e^{-t}\,dt.$$

First we study the integral $\beta(z)$. In view of formula (5.3), for $\operatorname{Re} z\leqslant R$ we have the following inequality for the integrand:

$$|t^{z-1}e^{-t}|\leqslant t^{R-1}e^{-t},$$

since $t\geqslant 1$ and $\ln t>0$ on the integral of integration. However,

$$\int_1^\infty t^{R-1}e^{-t}\,dt<\infty,$$

since the function e^{-t} approaches zero faster than any power of t as $t\to+\infty$. It follows from the criterion for uniform convergence of integrals (see the end of Sect. 6, Chap. I) that the integral defining the function $\beta(z)$ converges uniformly with respect to z in the half-plane $\operatorname{Re} z\leqslant R$ for any R. Using the remark to Theorem 4.3, we next obtain the analyticity of the function $\beta(z)$ in the entire complex plane.

Let us now consider the integral for $\alpha(z)$. We have the following inequality for the integrand for $\operatorname{Re} z\geqslant\delta$:

$$|t^{z-1}e^{-t}|\leqslant t^{\delta-1}e^{-t}<t^{\delta-1},$$

since $0<t<1$ and $\ln t\leqslant 0$ on the integral of integration. But for $\delta>0$ we have

$$\int_0^1 t^{\delta-1}\,dt=\frac{1}{\delta}<\infty.$$

From this and from the above considerations, we obtain analyticity for the function $\alpha(z)$ in the half-plane $\operatorname{Re} z>0$.

We can thus continue the function $\Gamma(z)=\alpha(z)+\beta(z)$ analytically to the half-plane $\operatorname{Re} z>0$. It is possible to show that the integral defining the function $\Gamma(z)$ diverges outside the limits of this half-plane. Thus, the following reasoning is completely atypical.

Since the function $\beta(z)$ is analytic in the entire complex plane, we need only to continue the function $\alpha(z)$. We expand the function e^{-t} in a power series

$$e^{-t}=\sum_0^\infty(-1)^n\frac{t^n}{n!},$$

which converges uniformly on the interval (0, 1). The function t^{z-1} is continuous on this interval for $z>1$ and multiplying the series by t^{z-1} does not affect its uniform convergence. Integrating term by term, we obtain

$$\alpha(z)=\int_0^1 t^{z-1}\sum_0^\infty(-1)^n\frac{t^n}{n!}\,dt=\sum_0^\infty\frac{(-1)^n}{n+z}\cdot\frac{1}{n!}\qquad(z>1).$$

The terms of the series $\sum_{0}^{\infty}\frac{(-1)^n}{n+z}\cdot\frac{1}{n!}$ are functions analytic in the entire plane with the exception of the points $z=0, -1, -2, \ldots,$ and the series converges uniformly in any finite region of the plane that does not contain these points (all terms of the series starting at some point do not exceed the terms of the convergent numerical series $\sum_{0}^{\infty}\frac{c}{n!}$). Consequently, the sum of the series $\sum_{0}^{\infty}\frac{(-1)^n}{n+z}\cdot\frac{1}{n!}$ is analytic in the entire complex plane with the exception of the points $z=0, -1, -2, \ldots$. Since this sum coincides with the function $\alpha(z)$ for $z>1$, it gives us the analytic continuation of the function $\alpha(z)$.

The formula

$$\Gamma(z)=\sum_{0}^{\infty}\frac{(-1)^n}{n+z}\cdot\frac{1}{n!}+\int_{1}^{\infty}t^{z-1}e^{-t}\,dt$$

gives us the analytic continuation we seek for the function $\Gamma(z)$ to the entire complex plane with the exception of the points $z=0, -1, -2, \ldots$. We may readily convince ourselves that the function $\Gamma(z)$ approaches infinity as z approaches any of these points.

6. THE BEHAVIOR OF THE BASIC ELEMENTARY FUNCTIONS

We now have a sufficiently large stock of analytic functions. We observed in Sect. 1 that polynomials and rational functions are analytic in the entire complex (with the possible exception of the zeros of the denominator for rational functions). We showed in the preceding section that the functions e^z, $\sin z$, $\cos z$ are also analytic in the entire complex plane. This allows us to speak of any trigonometric function as a complex function. We can greatly extend our stock of analytic functions with the help of the theorem on the analyticity of a composite function (see the beginning of Sect. 4). These methods of enlarging the stock of analytic functions do not require any discussion of the behavior of the functions. However, it is still necessary in the study of series and integrals to know how to estimate integrands and terms of the series. We were faced with this necessity in Example 2 of the preceding section. Therefore we set forth at this point some properties of the basic elementary functions that are helpful in a variety of approximations.

1. *The power function* cz^n (n is a positive integer). We set $z=re^{i\varphi}$ and denote $\arg c$ by α. Then we have

$$|cz^n|=|c|r^n, \qquad \arg(cz^n)=\alpha+n\varphi,$$

$$\operatorname{Re}(cz^n)=|c|r^n\cos(n\varphi+\alpha), \qquad \operatorname{Im}(cz^n)=|c|r^n\sin(n\varphi+\alpha).$$

We need only direct our attention to the properties of $\operatorname{Re}(cz^n)$. The function $\cos(n\varphi+\alpha)$ is positive for angles

$$-\alpha-\frac{\pi}{2n}+\frac{2k\pi}{n}<\arg z<-\alpha+\frac{\pi}{2n}+\frac{2\pi k}{n} \qquad (6.1)$$
$$(k=0, 1, \ldots, n-1)$$

and negative for angles

$$-\alpha+\frac{\pi}{2n}+\frac{2\pi k}{n}<\arg z<-\alpha+\frac{3\pi}{2n}+\frac{2\pi k}{n} \tag{6.2}$$
$$(k=0,\ 1,\ \ldots,\ n-1).$$

Thus, the function cz^n has a positive real part for angles satisfying the inequalities (6.1) and a negative real part for angles satisfying the inequalities (6.2). These angles divide the plane into $2n$ equal parts over which the sign of $\operatorname{Re}(cz^n)$ alternates.

Let D denote any one of the sectors determined by the inequalities (6.1), and let D' be a sector whose ray is contained within D. Then in D' we have $\cos(n\varphi+\alpha)>\eta>0$ and

$$\operatorname{Re}(cz^n)>|c|\,\eta r^n,$$

i.e., as $z\to\infty$, $z\in D'$, the real part of the function cz^n approaches $+\infty$. Analogously, within a sector D'' contained within a sector determined by the inequalities (6.2), $\operatorname{Re}(cz^n)\to-\infty$, $(z\to\infty,\ z\in D'')$.

Note that by knowing the behavior of the function cz^n we can forecast the behavior as $z\to\infty$ of any polynomial (and even any rational function), since if

$$P(z)=c_0z^n+c_1z^{n-1}+\ldots+c_n,$$

then

$$P(z)\sim c_0z^n \qquad (z\to\infty).$$

2. *The function* e^z. Let us recall first of all an identity proved in the preceding section:

$$|e^z|=e^{\operatorname{Re} z}. \tag{6.3}$$

It is evident from this identity that the function e^z does not vanish for any value of z.

Moreover, it is clear from (6.3) that $|e^z|<1$ in the left half-plane and that $e^z\to 0$ as $\operatorname{Re} z\to-\infty$ uniformly with respect to $\operatorname{Im} z$.

Note further that the equation $e^z=A$ has infinitely many solutions for any $A\neq 0$. Indeed, writing $z=x+iy$, we deduce from the equation $e^z=A$ that

$$e^x=|A|,\quad e^{iy}=e^{i\arg A},$$

from which

$$x=\ln|A|,\qquad y=\arg A+2\pi k.$$

The function e^z is periodic with period $2\pi i$. In fact,

$$e^{z+2\pi i}=e^ze^{2\pi i}=e^z,$$

since it is immediately obvious from Euler's formula that $e^{2\pi i}=1$.

Combining this with the information we have obtained on the power function, it is not difficult to determine the properties of the function e^{cz^n}.

3. *The function* sin z. The study of the function sin z simply reduces to the study of the exponential function. In fact, in the preceding section we proved the formula

$$e^{iz} = \cos z + i \sin z.$$

(We demonstrated it only for real z, but it applies for all z because of the principle of analytic continuation.) If we replace z in this formula by $-z$ and solve the resulting two formulas for sin z and cos z, we find

$$\sin z = \frac{e^{iz} - e^{-iz}}{2i}, \qquad \cos z = \frac{e^{iz} + e^{-iz}}{2}.$$

Now we set $z = x + iy$ and study $|\sin z|$. It follows from the inequalities of Theorem 1.1 of Chap. I that

$$||e^{iz}| - |e^{-iz}|| \leqslant |e^{iz} - e^{-iz}| \leqslant |e^{iz}| + |e^{-iz}|,$$

and in view of (6.3),

$$|e^{iz}| = e^{-y}, \qquad |e^{-iz}| = e^{y}.$$

Therefore,

$$\frac{e^{|y|} - e^{-|y|}}{2} \leqslant |\sin(x + iy)| \leqslant \frac{e^{y} + e^{-y}}{2}. \tag{6.4}$$

It is immediately obvious from this formula that the function sin z vanishes only for real z, i.e., for $z = \pi n$ (n a whole number), since we already know the real roots of sin z.

Furthermore, it is easy to deduce from formula (6.4) that

$$|\sin(x + iy)| \sim \frac{1}{2} e^{|y|} \qquad (y \to \pm\infty)$$

uniformly in x.

It is an immediate consequence of the principle of analytic continuation that the function sin z is periodic with period 2π.

The equation sin $z = A$ has infinitely many solutions for any A. In fact, we can write this equation in the form

$$\frac{1}{2i}(e^{iz} - e^{-iz}) = A,$$

which, if we set $e^{iz} = \zeta$, reduces to the equation in ζ:

$$\zeta^2 - 2iA\zeta - 1 = 0.$$

This equation has two roots ζ_1 and ζ_2 for any A (a result of the fundamental theorem of algebra), and these roots are different from zero (their product is -1 by Viète's theorem). Consequently, the equations $e^{iz}=\zeta_1$ and $e^{-iz}=\zeta_2$ have infinitely many roots.

The function cos z also has the properties enumerated above: this is most easily verified by using the formula $\cos z=\sin\left(\frac{\pi}{2}-z\right)$.

4. *The functions* tan z and cot z. The functions tan π and cot z are defined for complex values of z by the equations

$$\tan z=\frac{\sin z}{\cos z}, \qquad \cot z=\frac{\cos z}{\sin z}.$$

Since sin z and cos z vanish only for real z, tan z is an analytic function in the entire plane with the exception of the points $z=\frac{\pi}{2}+\pi n$ (n an integer), and cot z in the entire plane with the exception of the points $z=\pi n$.

The functions tan z and cot z are readily seen on the basis of the principle of analytic continuation to be periodic with period z.

If we express tan z and cot z in terms of exponential functions, then we arrive at the formulas

$$\tan z=-i\frac{e^{iz}-e^{-iz}}{e^{iz}+e^{-iz}},$$

$$\cot z=i\frac{e^{iz}+e^{-iz}}{e^{iz}-e^{-iz}}.$$

In the same way as in the estimation of $|\sin z|$, we deduce from these formulas the following inequalities:

$$\frac{e^{-2y}}{1+e^{-2y}}<|\tan(x+iy)-i|<\frac{e^{-2y}}{1-e^{-2y}} \qquad (y>0),$$

$$\frac{e^{-2y}}{1+e^{-2y}}<|\cot(x+iy)+i|<\frac{e^{-2y}}{1-e^{-2y}} \qquad (y>0)$$

and

$$\frac{e^{2y}}{1+e^{2y}}<|\tan(x+iy)+i|<\frac{e^{2y}}{1-e^{2y}} \qquad (y<0),$$

$$\frac{e^{2y}}{1+e^{2y}}<|\cot(x+iy)-i|<\frac{e^{2y}}{1-e^{2y}} \qquad (y<0).$$

In particular, it is a consequence of these inequalities that

$$\tan z\to i, \qquad \cot z\to -i \qquad (\operatorname{Im} z\to+\infty)$$

uniformly with respect to $\operatorname{Re} z$ and

$$\tan z\to -i, \quad \cot z\to i \qquad (\operatorname{Im} z\to-\infty)$$

uniformly with respect to $\operatorname{Re} z$.

CHAPTER III

Multiple-Valued Analytic Functions

The natural logical development of the principle of analytic continuation is the concept of analytic function. This concept cannot be confined within the usual framework of the concept of function. One of the basic peculiarities distinguishing the concept of analytic function is that of being multiple-valued. The introduction of the conception of analytic function cannot simply be explained as a logician's whim—without this concept it would be difficult to operate with even the simplest elementary functions, for example, with logarithms. From here on we shall replace the term analytic in its earlier meaning by the term regular.

1. THE CONCEPT OF A COMPLETE ANALYTIC FUNCTION

Let us try to examine critically the general notion of function from the point of view of the reasonableness of its application to regular functions. As is well known, a function is given in terms of a domain of definition and a law, according to which each point of the domain of definition is placed in correspondence with a value of the function. It is clearly necessary that such a law be given. But is it also necessary to give a domain of definition? Naturally, when we are discussing continuous functions, we cannot manage without knowing the domain of definition, since it is possible to extend a continuous function while preserving continuity in an infinite number of ways. But the situation is different with regular functions; according to the uniqueness theorem it is possible in only one way to extend a regular function to the limits of the domain while preserving regularity. This means that by giving a regular function in however small a domain is to define this function, albeit implicitly, at every point at which it can be defined.

It is thus more natural not to give a domain of definition for regular function. It is possible to define it in terms of a law which permits us to find its values in any domain (element of the function) and to assume that the function is obtained from the given element by analytic continuation as far as possible.

Further development of this natural idea leads to the concept of a complete analytic function, first rigorously introduced into mathematics by Weierstrass.

We need some preparation in order to define this concept.

The principal difficulty consists in giving meaning to our requirement of analytic continuation "as far as possible." The trouble is that the points of the plane are not ordered. However, it is necessary to define the extension from the domain to some point lying outside in such a way that the concept has a precise meaning. We proceed according to the following plan: first we define the notion of analytic continuation along a curve, then we study continuation along all possible curves. Moreover, we resign ourselves to the idea that the result of continuation from the domain to a new point may not, generally speaking, be single-valued.

Analytic continuation along a curve is a comparatively simple concept, since the points of a curve are ordered.

Suppose that we are given a function $\varphi(\zeta)$, defined on some continuous curve Γ. The curve Γ may intersect itself (see Sect 2, Chap. I), and the function is assumed to be given on the curve, and not on the points of the plane through which the curve passes. This means that the function $\varphi(\zeta)$ may take on several different values at the same point of the plane, if the curve Γ passes through this point several times.

We define the concept of *regular function* $\varphi(\zeta)$ *on the curve* Γ. The definition is intuitive in the case of a simple curve:

A function $\varphi(\zeta)$ defined on a simple curve Γ is said to be regular on Γ, if there exists some regular function $f(z)$ coinciding with $\varphi(\zeta)$ on the curve Γ and regular in a domain containing Γ.

If the curve Γ intersects itself, then it is necessary to adopt a more complicated definition:

The function $\varphi(\zeta)$ defined on the curve Γ is regular on the curve, if there exists a family of functions $f_\zeta(z)$ (ζ any point of Γ) with the properties:

1. For any $\zeta \in \Gamma$ the function $f_\zeta(z)$ is regular in z in some neighborhood of the point $z = \zeta$.
2. For any $\zeta \in \Gamma$ there exists a segment γ_ζ of the curve Γ, containing the point ζ and such that $f_\zeta(t) = \varphi(t)$ $(t \in \gamma_\zeta)$.

We call the function $f_\zeta(z)$ appearing in the definition of the function and regular on the curve, an *element of the function regular on the curve at the point* ζ.

We can thus study a function regular on a curve in terms of the totality of its elements $\{f_\zeta(z)\}$, $\zeta \in \Gamma$.

We now introduce the concept of analytic continuation. Let the function $\Phi(\zeta)$ be regular on the curve Γ and let the function $\varphi(\zeta)$ be regular on the curve γ, which is part of Γ. If

$$\Phi(\zeta) = \varphi(\zeta) \qquad (\zeta \in \gamma),$$

then we say that the function $\Phi(\zeta)$ is the analytic continuation of the function $\varphi(\zeta)$ to the entire curve Γ.

An immediate consequence of the uniqueness theorem is:

There exists at most one analytic continuation of the function to the same curve.

We shall be interested in the following problem:

Given a curve Γ beginning at ζ_0 and an element $f_{\zeta_0}(z)$, analytically continue this element as far as possible along the curve Γ.

It is possible to put forward a completely general (but only theoretically suitable) solution for this problem of the construction of a maximal analytic continuation:

We expand the function $f_{\zeta_0}(z)$ in the series

$$\sum_0^\infty c_n^{(0)} (z-\zeta_0)^n.$$

This series has a circle of convergence $|z-\zeta_0| < R_0$, and its sum (which we denote as above by $f_{\zeta_0}(z)$ is analytic in this circle because of Corollary 2 of Theorem 4.2 of Chap. II. We denote by γ_0 the segment of the curve Γ from the point ζ_0 to the first intersection with the circle $|z-\zeta_0| = R_0$. For $\zeta \in \gamma_0$ we put $f_\zeta(z) = f_{\zeta_0}(z)$. Moreover, if we take any point $\zeta_1 \in \gamma_0$, the function $f_{\zeta_0}(z)$ is regular at this point, since we can expand it in a series

$$\sum_0^\infty c_n^{(1)} (z-\zeta_1)^n \qquad (|z-\zeta_1| < R_1).$$

We denote the sum of this series by $f_{\zeta_1}(z)$ and the connected segment of the curve Γ contained in the circle $|z-\zeta_1| < R_1$, and containing the point ζ_1 by γ_1. It is clear that we have $f_{\zeta_0}(z) = f_{\zeta_1}(z)$ on the common part of γ_0 and γ_1. If γ_1 has points different from those of γ_0, then we obtain an analytic continuation of $f_{\zeta_0}(z)$ to the segment of Γ consisting of the union of γ_0 and γ_1. Without fear of contradicting the previous definition, we can put $f_\zeta(z) = f_{\zeta_1}(z)$ $(\zeta \in \gamma_1)$. Choosing a point ζ_2 etc., we find step by step the analytic continuation in question.

This method of analytic continuation is completely valid theoretically, but it requires such enormous computations that it is difficult to use even in the simplest examples.

We have thus become acquainted with the concept of the analytic continuation of a given element to some curve. However, we will be interested in the analytic continuation of a given element to a point of the plane. Therefore the following problem arises naturally:

Suppose that we have two curves Γ_1 and Γ_2 connecting the points t and w. Suppose in addition that the element $f_t(z)$ can be continued analytically along both curves. Will the result of the continuation depend on the choice of curves?

Theorem 1.1. *Let the element $f_t(z)$ coincide with the function $F(z)$, analytic in the domain D, in a neighborhood of the point t. If* *the curve Γ is contained in D, then the result of the continuation of the element $f_t(z)$ along Γ does not depend on the nature of Γ, but only depends on its end point. The result of the continuation coincides with $F(z)$ in some neighborhood of the end point of Γ.*

Proof. The function $F(z)$ gives us an analytic continuation of the element $f_t(z)$ to the entire curve Γ. Since the analytic continuation is unique, we obtain the statement of the theorem.

It is possible to extract an important corollary from Theorem 1.1 which bears on the general case in which there is not a single function $F(z)$ for all curves Γ.

Corollary. The result of the continuation along Γ does not change if the deformation of the curve Γ (leaving its end point fixed) is sufficiently small.

In fact, we can partition the curve Γ into segments $\gamma_0, \ldots, \gamma_n$ by means of the points $\zeta_1, \ldots, \zeta_{n-1}$, succeeding one another along the curve in such a way that the element $f_t(z)$ will be a regular function in a domain containing γ_k. The analytic continuation of the function $f_t(z)$ along the curve Γ is the union of the analytic continuations of the elements $f_{\zeta_k}(z)$ along the curves γ_k. Each of these analytic continuations is carried out within the domain of regularity of the element $f_{\zeta_k}(z)$, so that its result does not depend on the form of γ_k. Since the points ζ_k can be varied slightly, we obtain the assertion of our theorem.

In particular: *for analytic continuation along the curve Γ it is possible without loss of generality to assume that it is a polygonal line.*

We can now go on to define the notion of a complete analytic function. (For the sake of brevity, we shall use the terms "complete analytic function" and "analytic function" interchangeably. This should not give rise to any misunderstanding.)

Let there be given some element $f_t(z)$ at the point $z = t$. By analytic continuation of this element along the curve Γ we obtain a class of elements $\{f_\zeta(z, \Gamma)\}$, $\zeta \in \Gamma$. This class of elements obtained by analytic continuation of $f_t(z)$ along all possible curves Γ for each element (the curve along which it was obtained must be given) will be called an *analytic function.*

In other words, an *analytic function is given,* if:

1. we are given an initial element;
2. we know all the curves along which the initial element can be continued analytically.

From a first glance at the definition it would appear that the multivalence of an analytic function is enormous. However, it is already clear from the corollary to Theorem 1.1 that this is not the case, since small deformations of the curve do not change the result of continuation along the given curve.

Theorem 1.2. *The number of different elements of an analytic function at the same point is at most denumerable.*

Proof. According to the definition, all elements of an analytic function are obtained by some particular analytic continuation along all possible closed curves (closed since we are dealing with only one point). According to the corollary to Theorem 1.1, this curve can be assumed to be a polygonal line with vertices at points with rational coordinates. Since such polygonal lines are countable in number, the theorem is proved.

In order to master the new concepts we must examine some examples of multiple-valued analytic functions. These will be carried out in the following section. In concluding this section we wish to introduce one geometric concept that has primary importance in all questions concerning multiple-valued analytic functions: the number of circuits made by a closed curve around a given point in the positive direction.

The intuitive meaning of this concept is rather simple. Imagine a closed curve to be a thread lying on the table and the point to be a needle sticking into the table. If we stretch the thread along the table, then the thread catches on the needle and stretches around it. The number of loops of thread on the needle is the number of interest to us (if we attach the appropriate sign to it).

Let us go on to the exact definition.

Suppose we are given: a simply connected domain D, a point $\zeta \in D$ and a closed polygonal line C, contained in D and not passing through the point ζ. The number defined below of circuits around the point ζ by the polygonal line C in the positive direction will be denoted by $\nu(C, \zeta)$.

Let us first define the number $\nu(C, \zeta)$ in the case in which C is a simple closed curve. To do this we denote by G that one of the two bounded by the curve C which is contained in D. If G does not contain the point ζ, then we say that $\nu(C, \zeta)=0$. If G contains the point ζ, then two possibilities arise: the domain G lies on the left or on the right as we move along C. In the first case we say that $\nu(C, \zeta)=1$, in the second that $\nu(C, \zeta)=-1$.

In order to define $\nu(C, \zeta)$ for a polygonal line C with any number of self-intersections, we devide this polygonal line into simple closed polygonal lines $C_1, C_2, \ldots, C_n$ (loops). We do this as follows: we move along C until we reach a point of the plane which we have traversed before; the part of C from the first meeting with this point to the second will be called C_1; moving further along C, we define C_2 analogously, etc.

After completing such an operation, we put

$$\nu(C, \zeta)=\sum_1^n \nu(C_k, \zeta).$$

We present one simple geometrical result concerning the number of circuits.

Lemma. *We construct a cross cut joining the point ζ with the boundary of the simply connected domain D (the direction of the* *cross cut is from the point to the boundary). If the polygonal line crosses over the cross cut* ν^+ *times from right to left and* ν^- *times from left to right, then* $\nu^+ - \nu^- = \nu(C, \zeta)$.

We shall not carry out the proof of this proposition. The reader may easily verify it himself if he wishes.

Ordinarily the domain D will be taken to be the entire finite plane.

2. THE ANALYTIC FUNCTION ln z

We first illustrate the concepts introduced in the preceding section by the example of the analytic continuation of the function ln z, and after this example we lay the groundwork for further investigations.

Among all the properties of the function $\ln x$, defined for real positive x, the most convenient for analytic continuation to complex values of the variable is the relation

$$\ln x = \int_1^x \frac{dt}{t}.$$

We take some finite simply connected domain D that contains the point $z=1$ and does not contain the point $z=0$. The function $1/z$ is regular in D since it is the ratio of two regular functions (the denominator does not vanish). According to Theorem 3.4 of Chap. II, the function $1/z$ has the antiderivative

$$\psi(z) = \int_1^z \frac{dt}{t},$$

which is regular in the domain D (the integration is carried out along any rectifiable curve contained in D and going from the point $t=1$ to the point $t=z$). The function $\psi(z)$ coincides with the function ln z for real z contained in some neighborhood of the point $z=1$. Consequently, the function $\psi(z)$ gives us the analytic continuation of the function $\ln z$ to the domain D. We naturally wish to choose D to be as large as possible. Here we immediately encounter the problem that there is no largest domain among those satisfying the required conditions (finite, simply connected and not containing the point $z=0$). In fact, the plane with a cross cut along the negative part of the real axis is no better than the plane with a cross cut along any other ray. It remains to decide whether the requirement of simple connectedness for the domain D is really necessary. For this purpose we take as our domain D the plane with a cross cut along the negative part of the real axis and see if it is possible remove the cross cut, leaving only the point $z=0$. In other words, to decide if there exists a function

$$\psi(z)=\int_1^z \frac{dt}{t} \qquad (|\arg z|<\pi)$$

that is regular in the entire finite plane with the exception of the point $z=0$.

Let us find the values of the function $\psi(z)$. We choose our path of integration as follows: from the point $t=1$ to the point $t=|z|$ along the line segment; from the point $t=z$ to the point $t=|z|$ along the circle $|t|=|z|$ (along that one of the two arcs which does not intersect the negative part of the real axis). On the first segment we have $t=x$, $dt=dx$, on the second

$$t=|z|e^{i\theta}, \quad dt=i|z|e^{i\theta}d\theta,$$

varies from θ to $\arg z$, where we must take for $\arg z$ the value between $-\pi$ and π. Therefore

$$\psi(z)=\int_1^{|z|}\frac{dx}{x}+i\int_0^{\arg z} d\theta,$$

i.e.,

$$\psi(z)=\ln|z|+i\arg z \qquad (|\arg z|<\pi). \tag{2.1}$$

The function $\psi(z)$ is frequently called the *principal value* of $\ln z$.

It is easy to see with the help of formula (2.1) that the function $\psi(z)$ is not analytic in the entire plane with the exception of the points $z=0$ and $z=\infty$. Indeed, a regular function would have to be continuous, i.e., the limits at points of the negative part of the real axis should coincide under approach from above or from below. But it is clear from formula (2.1) that the limit as $z\to -x$ from above is $\ln x+\pi i$, while as $z\to -x$ from below it equals $\ln x-\pi i$.

Thus there is no largest domain of regularity for the analytic continuation of $\ln z$. Therefore we must understand by the function $\ln z$ in the complex plane an analytic function in the sense of the definition of Sect. 1. Sometimes the designation $\mathrm{Ln}\, z$ is taken for the analytic function and the designation $\ln z$ is reserved for the principal value. This symbolism is not too convenient and we shall not use it here.

Therefore, let us go on to the study of $\ln z$ as an analytic function. To specify an analytic function we must give its initial element and describe all the paths along which it can be continued. As our initial element we can take the principal of $\ln z$, by basing it on the point $z=1$. We now point out the possible continuations of the initial element.

Lemma 1. *The initial element of the analytic function in z can be analytically continued along any path not passing through the points $z=0$ and $z=\infty$.*

Proof. Let us note first of all that, according to the corollary to Theorem 1.1, the path for the continuation can be assumed to be a polygonal line.

Thus, suppose we are given any polygonal line Γ starting at the point $t=1$ and not passing through the points $t=0$ and $t=\infty$. Denote the segment of the polygonal line Γ from the point $t=1$ to the point $t=\zeta$ by Γ_ζ and set

$$\varphi(\zeta)=\int_{\Gamma_\zeta}\frac{dt}{t} \qquad (\zeta\in\Gamma).$$

For ζ sufficiently close to the beginning of the polygonal line Γ, i.e., to the point $t=1$, the polygonal line Γ_ζ is small and does not reach the cross cut along the negative part of the real axis. Thus

$$\varphi(\zeta)=\int_{\Gamma_\zeta}\frac{dt}{t}=\int_1^\zeta\frac{dt}{t}=\psi(\zeta).$$

This means that the function $\varphi(\zeta)$ coincides with the initial element of the function $\ln z$ in some neighborhood of the initial point of the curve Γ. We show that the function $\varphi(\zeta)$ is regular on the curve Γ. (See the beginning of Sect. 1.) For this we need to construct a family of functions $f_\zeta(z;\ \Gamma)$ (ζ is any point of Γ), satisfying the conditions:

1. For any $\zeta\in\Gamma$ the function $f_\zeta(z;\ \Gamma)$ is analytic in z in some neighborhood of the point $z=\zeta$.

2. For any $\zeta\in\Gamma$ we have a segment γ_ζ fo the polygonal line Γ, containing the point ζ and such that $f_\zeta(w;\ \Gamma)=\varphi(w)$ $(w\in\gamma_\zeta)$.

Let G_ζ denote some simply connected domain containing the point $t=\zeta$ and not the point $t=0$ (for example, we might take for G_ζ the circle $|t-\zeta|<|\zeta|$); we put

$$f_\zeta(z;\ \Gamma)=\int_{\Gamma_\zeta}\frac{dt}{t}+\int_\zeta^z\frac{dt}{t} \qquad (z\in G_\zeta)$$

(the integration from ζ to z is carried out along any path contained in G_ζ).

Condition 1 holds, since the function $f_\zeta(z;\ \Gamma)$ is regular in the domain G_ζ because of the theorem on the regularity of the antiderivative.

Let γ_ζ denote a connected part of the polygonal line Γ contained in G_ζ and containing the point ζ; let $\Gamma_{\zeta,w}$ denote the part of Γ between the points $\zeta \in \Gamma$ and $w \in \Gamma$ (the direction of $\Gamma_{\zeta, w}$ is from ζ to w). Then for $w \in \gamma_\zeta$ we have

$$f_\zeta(w, \Gamma) = \int_{\Gamma_\zeta} \frac{dt}{t} + \int_\zeta^w \frac{dt}{t} = \int_{\Gamma_\zeta} \frac{dt}{t} + \int_{\Gamma_{\zeta, w}} \frac{dt}{t} = \int_{\Gamma_w} \frac{dt}{t} = \varphi(w),$$

i.e., condition 2 is also fulfilled.

Consequently, the function $\varphi(\zeta)$ that we have constructed is analytic on the polygonal line Γ and gives the analytic continuation of the initial element of the function $\ln z$ to the whole polygonal line Γ. This proves the lemma.

Remark. The function

$$f_\zeta(z, \Gamma) = \int_{\Gamma_\zeta} \frac{dt}{t} + \int_\zeta^z \frac{dt}{t} \qquad (z \in G_\zeta) \tag{2.2}$$

is none other than the element at the point ζ of the analytic function $\ln z$, obtained by analytic continuation of the initial element along the path Γ, going from the point $t=1$ to the point $t=\zeta$ and not passing through the points $t=0, \infty$. Up to now we have not proved that it is impossible to continue the initial element analytically along some path passing through the points $t=0$ or $t=\infty$. Therefore we can not yet assert that the analytic function $\ln z$ coincides with the totality of elements of the form (2.2).

Lemma 2. *Let $f_\zeta(z, \Gamma)$ and $f_\zeta(z, L)$ be two elements of the form (2.2) of the analytic function $\ln z$. Let C denote the closed polygonal line consisting of the segment of the polygonal line L that goes from the point $t=\zeta$ to the point $t=1$, and of the segment of Γ that goes from the point $t=1$ to the point $t=\zeta$. Then*

$$f_\zeta(z, \Gamma) - f_\zeta(z, L) = 2\pi i \nu(C, 0),$$

where $\nu(C, 0)$ is the number of circuits made by the polygonal line C around the point $t=0$ in the positive direction (see the end of Sect. 1).

Proof. We readily obtain from formula (2.2) that

$$f_\zeta(z, \Gamma) - f_\zeta(z, L) = \int_{\Gamma_\zeta} \frac{dt}{t} - \int_{L_\zeta} \frac{dt}{t} = \int_C \frac{dt}{t}.$$

We still have to evaluate the integral of $1/t$ along C. For this purpose we divide the polygonal line C into loops $C_1, C_2, \ldots, C_n$ (see the end of Sect. 1). The integral along C equals the sum of the integrals along C_k. Let G_k be the finite domain bounded by the simple closed polygonal line C_k. We may readily establish that

$$\int_{C_k} \frac{dt}{t} = 2\pi i \nu (C_k, 0).$$

In fact, if the point $t = 0$ is not contained in G_k, then the integral along the boundary of G_k equals zero by Cauchy's theorem. If the point $t = 0$ lies in G_k, then the integral of $1/t$ along the boundary of G_k equals $2\pi i$ by Cauchy's integral formula (with $f(t) = 1$ and $\zeta = 0$). If we now take the direction of C_k into account, we then obtain our assertion. Using the definition of the notion of circuit number, we then obtain the statement of the lemma.

Theorem 2.1. *Any element of the analytic function* $\ln z$ *can be analytically continued along any path not passing through the points* $z = 0$ *and* $z = \infty$.

If $(\ln z)_1$ *and* $(\ln z)_2$ *are the values of two elements of* $\ln z$ *at the point* z *and the second element is obtained from the first by analytic continuation along the closed polygonal line C (not passing through the points* $z = 0$ *and* $z = \infty$*), then*

$$(\ln z)_2 - (\ln z)_1 = 2\pi i \nu (C, 0),$$

in which $\nu(C, 0)$ *is the number of circuits made by the polygonal line C around the point* $z = 0$ *in the positive direction.*

No element of the analytic function $\ln z$ *can be continued analytically along any path passing through either of the points* $z = 0$, $z = \infty$.

Proof. The first two assertions of the theorem follow from the third in virtue of lemmas 1 and 2. To prove the third statement it is sufficient to show that no initial element of $\ln z$ can be continued analytically along a path passing through either of the points $z = 0$, $z = \infty$.

Let us assume the contrary. Then there exists a polygonal line Γ beginning at the point $t = 1$ and ending at the point $t = 0$ (or $t = \infty$) not passing through the points $t = 0$ and $t = \infty$, along which the initial element of $\ln z$ can be continued analytically to the point $t = 0$. The element obtained $f_0(z, \Gamma)$ is analytic in some circle $|z| < \varrho$. We choose an element $f_\zeta(z, \Gamma)$, where ζ is some point of Γ and sufficiently close to the point $t = 0$. According to Theorem 1.1, this element is not changed by analytic continuation along some closed path contained in the circle $|z| < \varrho$. But the element $f_\zeta(z, \Gamma)$ has the form (2.2), since it was obtained by analytic continuation of the initial element of $\ln z$ along the polygonal line Γ which does not pass through either of the points $t = 0$, $t = \infty$. Consequently, according to Lemma 2, the analytic continuation of $f_\zeta(z, \Gamma)$ along the circle $|z| = |\zeta| < \varrho$, circles the point $z = 0$ once in the positive direction and thus differs from $f_\zeta(z, \Gamma)$ by the term $2\pi i$. This contradiction proves the theorem.

We shall make a few closing remarks about the analytic function $\ln z$. It is clear that all the formulas satisfied by $\ln x$ can be carried over for complex values of the variable. Thus, for example, with the help of the principle of analytic continuation we can easily obtain

$$e^{\ln z} = z.$$

It is obvious that we must employ caution in using formulas involving multiple-valued analytic functions. An equality of multiple-valued analytic functions means the equality of the corresponding elements (by no means taken arbitrarily) of these functions. Thus, for example, the formula

$$\ln (z\zeta) = \ln z + \ln \zeta,$$

holding for the analytic functions found on both sides of the equality, ceases to be true if we do not assume that by $\ln z$, $\ln \zeta$ and $\ln (z\,\zeta)$ are understood the principal values. (This is one of the basic reasons why we deem it inadvisable to introduce the notation $\operatorname{Ln} z$ for the analytic function and reserving the notation $\ln z$ for the principal value of the logarithm.)

Still another hazard is that an expression involving multiple-valued analytic functions may itself not be an analytic function. Thus, for example, the expression $\ln e^z$ is not an analytic function, but consists of a collection of unrelated functions $z + 2\pi ik$ (k any integer). We must avoid allowing expressions of this type to appear in our equalities.

It is not necessary to investigate the remaining elementary multiple-valued functions in such detail as in the case of $\ln z$. In fact, it is always possible to reduce their study to that of $\ln z$.

We shall present two examples.

Example 1. The function z^α (α—any complex number).

This function is defined by means of the equality

$$z^\alpha = e^{\alpha \ln z}.$$

Since the properties of the exponential function and the logarithm are known to us, we can immediately make the statement:

The function z^α is a multiple-valued analytic function. Any of the elements can be continued analytically along any path not passing through the points $z = 0$ and $z = \infty$.

The analytic continuation of any element of the function z^α along the closed curve C reduces to multiplication of this element by the factor $e^{2\pi i\alpha\nu}$, where $\nu = \nu(C, 0)$ is the number of circuits made by the polygonal line C around the point $z = 0$ in the positive direction.

If $e^{2\pi i\alpha} \neq 1$, i.e., if α is not a real integer, then by employing the same arguments as in the proof of Theorem 2.1, we obtain:

If α is not a real integer, then no element of the analytic function z^α can be continued analytically along any path to the point $z = 0$ or to the point $z = \infty$.

The case in which $\alpha = m/n$ is of interest (m and n are real integers). In this case, after n circuits of the point $z = 0$ the initial element of the function z^{α} is multiplied by $e^{2\pi i m} = 1$, i.e., returns to its original value. Thus, the function $z^{m/n}$ has only n different elements at each point. Such functions are called n-valued. Thus, for example, $\sqrt{z}$ – is a two-valued function.

If α is a real number, then it is easy to obtain the formulas

$$|z^{\alpha}| = |z|^{\alpha}, \qquad \arg(z^{\alpha}) = \alpha \arg z, \tag{2.3}$$

from formula (2.1). These formulas permit us to find the values of the function z^{α} for any complex value of z. The arbitrariness in the choice of the value of $\arg z$ gives rise to a corresponding arbitrariness in the choice of the element of the analytic function z^{α}. If $\arg z$ is taken between $-\pi$ and π, then we speak of the principal value of the function z^{α}.

Let us note one important consequence of the formulas (2.3), which it will be necessary to employ frequently:

Under analytic continuation of any element of the function z^{α} *(α- any real number) from the point* $re^{i\varphi}$ *to the point* $re^{i\theta}$ *along an arc of the circle* $|z| = r$, $\varphi < \arg z < \theta$, *the modulus of the function* z^{α} *does not change and the argument varies continuously, increasing by the amount* $\alpha(\theta - \varphi)$.

Example 2. The function arc tan z. We may easily analytically continue the function arctan z from the real axis to any simply connected domain not containing the points $z = i$, $z = -i$, with the aid of Theorem 3.4 of Chap. II on the analyticity of the antiderivative. For example, in the circle $|z| < 1$ the formula is

$$\arctan z = \int_0^z \frac{dt}{1+t^2}.$$

We shall express arctan z in terms of the logarithm. For $z = iy$ we have

$$\arctan(iy) = \int_0^{iy} \frac{dt}{1+t^2} = i\int_0^{y} \frac{du}{1-u^2} = \frac{i}{2}\ln\frac{1+y}{1-y}.$$

Consequently,

$$\arctan z = \frac{i}{2}\ln\frac{1+iz}{1-iz} = \frac{i}{2}\ln\frac{i-z}{i+z}.$$

The properties of ln z are known to us; therefore:

The function arctan z *is a multiple-valued analytic function. Any one of its elements can be continued analytically along any path not passing through the points* $z = i$ *or* $z = -i$.

It is easy to see from the formulas

$$\arctan z = \frac{i}{2}\ln\left(-1+\frac{i}{z}\right)-\frac{i}{2}\ln\left(1+\frac{i}{z}\right)$$

that the function arctan z cannot be analytically continued to the points $z = i$ or $z = -i$, but can be analytically continued to $z = \infty$.

On analytic continuation of any element of arctan z along the closed path C the term

$$\pi\{\nu(C, -i)-\nu(C, i)\},$$

is added to the element, where $\nu(C, \zeta)$ is the number of circuits of the point ζ made by the polygonal line C in the positive direction.

3. MONODROMY THEOREM

Our acquaintance with the analytic function ln z suggests that analytic continuation along a closed curve leads to a change in the element only in the case that this curve makes a circuit around a point to which analytic continuation is impossible. In the present section we shall prove a general result which approximately amounts to that. We shall need to introduce some new notions in order to facilitate the formulation of this result.

Let some element $f_\zeta(z)$ be given in a neighborhood of the point ζ of the domain D, and suppose that this element can be continued analytically along any path not crossing the boundary of the domain D. Then the totality of all elements $f_\xi(z)$ obtained by such analytic continuation (the path along which they are obtained is to be indicated) is called an *analytic function in the domain D.*

Thus, a function analytic in the domain D is a part (or, as it is usually called, a branch) of the complete analytic function obtained from the element $f_\xi(z)$.

If $F(z)$ is a function analytic in the domain D, then to each point of D there corresponds, generally speaking, an infinite number of distinct elements of the function. If to each point of the domain D there corresponds exactly one element of the function $F(z)$, analytic in the domain D, then $F(z)$ is single-valued in D, and thus is also regular in D. In this case it is said that $F(z)$ is a *regular branch* of the complete analytic function.

The following result, the monodromy theorem, plays a fundamental role throughout the theory of analytic functions.

Theorem 3.1. A function analytic in a simply connected domain is regular in this domain.

Proof. We must show that to each point of the domain (let us say D) there corresponds only one element. In other words, if we analytically continue any element along any closed curve in D, we obtain the same element.

Suppose that the theorem is false. Then there exists a closed polygonal line C_0 and an element $f_{\zeta_0}(z)$ at the point $\zeta_0 \in D$ such that analytic continuation of the element $f_{\zeta_0}(z)$ along C_0 leads to an element $f^{(1)}_{\zeta_0}(z)$ different from $f_{\zeta_0}(z)$.

Let us show that C_0 can be assumed to be a *simple* closed polygonal line. We continue the element $f_{\zeta_0}(z)$ along C_0 until we come to a point ζ_1 previously reached. If the element $f_{\zeta_1}(z)$ obtained when the point ζ_1 was reached the first time coincides with the element $f^{(1)}_{\zeta_1}(z)$, obtained the second time we reach this point, then we can eliminate the segment of C_0 between the first arrival at ζ_1 and the second. If $f^{(1)}_{\zeta_1}(z)$ does not coincide with $f_{\zeta_1}(z)$, then we choose $f_{\zeta_1}(z)$ in place of $f_{\zeta_0}(z)$ and replace the polygonal line C_0 by the segment mentioned. Continuing in this manner, we eventually replace C_0 by a simple closed polygonal line.

Let us now study the totality $S(C_0)$ of all elements obtained by the analytic continuation of the element $f_{\zeta_0}(z)$ along C_0. It is clear that this collection can be obtained by the analytic continuation along C_0 of any element of $S(C_0)$. Thus, our assumption means that to any point $\zeta \in C_0$ there corresponds at least two distinct elements $f_\zeta(z)$ and $f^{(1)}_\zeta(z)$ in $S(C_0)$, obtained from one another by analytic continuation along C_0.

We introduce some auxiliary constructions necessary for the proof.

Since the domain D is simply connected and C_0 is a simple closed polygonal line contained in D, then C_0 is the boundary of some domain G_0 contained in D. Let us divide the domain G_0 into two parts G_0' and G_0'' by means of some simple polygonal line L joining the points ζ_0' and ζ_0'' contained in C_0. We denote the boundaries of the domains G_0' and G_0'' by C_0' and C_0''. Let $S(C_0')$ and $S(C_0'')$ denote the totalities of elements obtained by analytic continuation along C_0' and C_0'', respectively, from the element $f_{\zeta_0'}(z)$ [the point ζ_0' is contained in both C_0' and C_0''].

Let us show that either $S(C_0')$ or $S(C_0'')$ have the same property as $S(C_0)$, i.e., that any element of S changes under continuation along the corresponding polygonal line. For this purpose let us study the analytic continuation of the element $f_{\zeta_0'}(z)$ along the following closed path: we go along C_0 from ζ_0' to ζ_0''; then stop there and continue our excursion along L to ζ_0' and back; having returned to ζ_0'', we continue our interrupted path along C_0 to ζ_0' (Fig. 2).

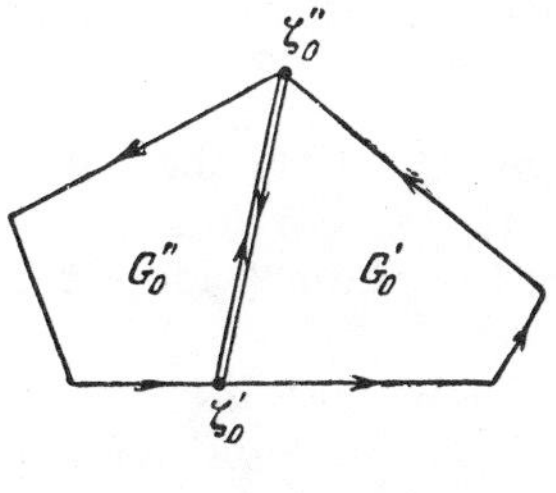

Fig. 2.

On the one hand, the result of continuation along the described path is the same as that under continuation along C_0, since the excursion along L does not change the element at the point ζ_0''. On the other hand, the continuation along the described path can be considered as the continuation of the element $f_{\zeta_0'}(z)$ first along C_0', then along C_0''. Since continuation along C_0 changes the element $f_{\zeta_0'}(z)$, then either continuation along C_0', or continuation along C_0'' must also change this element.

We shall denote that one of the polygonal lines C_0', C_0'' whose collection S possesses the required property by C_1 and the domain bounded by it by G_1.

We again choose points ζ_1' and ζ_1'' on the polygonal line C_1 and divide the domain G_1 into two parts G_1' and G_1''. We choose the domain G_2 from one of these by an analogous procedure, etc. We carry out the subdivision process in such a way that we obtain a descending sequence of domains G_n that contract to some point $\zeta^* \in D$. Moreover, all the collections $S(C_n)$ possess the property, i.e., an element $f_{\zeta_n'}(z)$ occurring in $S(C_n)$, occurs in $S(C_{n+1})$ and changes under continuation along C_n.

We now construct a path consisting of the segments of the polygonal lines C_n from ζ_{n-1}' to ζ_n'. The initial point of this path is the point ζ_0' and its terminal point is ζ^*. The element $f_{\zeta_0'}(z)$ can be continued analytically along this path to the point ζ^*, since our function is analytic in the domain D. As a result of continuation, we obtain element $f_{\zeta^*}(z)$ which is regular in some neighborhood of the point ζ^*. All the polygonal lines C_n, beginning with some n, are contained in this neighborhood. According to Theorem 1.1, an element at some point ζ, sufficiently close to ζ^*, is not changed by continuation along any closed path continued in this neighborhood. This is true in particular for the element $f_{\zeta_n'}(z)$ for sufficiently large n. We thus arrive at a contradiction to the property of the collection $S(C_n)$, which proves the theorem.

We shall encounter very frequently applications of the monodromy theorem later on. We now study two of the simplest examples.

Example 1. Let us show that the analytic function

$$F(z) = \frac{\ln\left(z + \sqrt{z^2+1}\right)}{z^2-1}$$

admits a division into regular branches in the domain D obtained by removing the rays $(i, +i\infty)$ and $i, -i\infty)$ and the points $z = 1$ and $z = -1$ from the entire plane (independent of the choice of the initial element of the function).

It is necessary to show that the analytic continuation of any element of the function $F(z)$ gives us a function analytic in the domain D, and then show that this function is regular (i.e., single-valued).

Let us first study the analytic function $\ln(z+\sqrt{z^2+1})$ and show that it admits a division into regular branches in the plane with the cuts $(i, +i\infty)$ and $(-i, -i\infty)$ (we shall call this domain D_0). It may be established that any element of the analytic function $\ln(z+\sqrt{z^2+1})$ can be analytically continued along any path contained in D_0. We know that the analytic function ln w can be continued analytically along any path not passing through the points $w=0$ and $w=\infty$. Therefore, the analytic function $\ln(z+\sqrt{z^2+1})$ can be continued analytically along any path along which we can analytically continue the analytic function $w(z)=z+\sqrt{z^2+1}$, and on which the element obtained for the function $w(z)$ does not vanish. However, $\sqrt{z^2+1}$ can be continued analytically along any path on which z^2+1 does not vanish (see the properties of the function z^α, Example 1, Sect. 2). Moreover, no element of the analytic function $z+\sqrt{z^2+1}$ vanishes for any finite z. Thus, any element of the analytic function $\ln(z+\sqrt{z^2+1})$ can be continued analytically along any path which does not pass through the points $z=i$, $z=-i$, $z=\infty$. This means, in particular, that any element of the analytic function $\ln(z+\sqrt{z^2+1})$ can be continued analytically along any path contained in the domain D_0.

Consequently, the totality of all continuations of any element of $\ln(z+\sqrt{z^2+1})$ along paths contained in D is a function analytic in the domain D_0. But the domain D_0 is simply connected, thus this analytic function is regular in D according to the monodromy theorem; in other words, a partition of $\ln(z+\sqrt{z^2+1})$ into regular branches is possible in D_0.

The ratio of a single regular branch of $\ln(z+\sqrt{z^2+1})$ and the function z^2-1 regular in the whole plane is a regular branch of the analytic function $F(z)$ in the domain D (obtained from D_0 by removing the points $z=1$ and $z=-1$).

Example 2. The element $f(z)$ of the analytic function

$$F(z)=\sqrt[3]{(z^2-1)(z^2-4)}$$

at the point $z=3$ is selected to satisfy the condition $f(3)=\sqrt[3]{40}$. We find the value at the point $z=i$ of the element of $F(z)$ obtained by analytic continuation of $f(z)$ along the line segment joining the points $z=3$ and $z=i$.

Any element of the analytic function $F(z)$ can be continued analytically along any path on which the function $(z^2-1)(z^2-4)$ does not vanish or become infinite, i.e., along any path not passing through the points $z=\pm 1$, $z=\pm 2$ and $z=\infty$. Consequently, according to the monodromy theorem, the analytic continuation of the element $f(z)$ to the entire plane with a cross cut along the ray $(-\infty, 2)$ is a regular function. This means that the result of the continuation does not depend on the path from the point $z=3$ to the point $z=i$ (according to Theorem 1.1), if this path does not intersect the cross cut $(-\infty, 2)$. We make use of this in order to replace the line segment $(3, i)$, along which the continuation is rather complicated, by a more convenient path. It is easier to carry out the required continuation along the polygonal line consisting of the segments (3, 0) and (0, i) (we bypass the points $z = 2$ and $z = 1$, through which continuation is impossible, by moving along small semicircles in the upper half-plane).

Let us make clear that our path is well chosen. In fact it follows immediately from the form of the analytic function $F(z) = \sqrt[3]{(z^2-1)(z^2-4)}$ that $f(i)$ can have only one of the three values

$$\sqrt[3]{10},\ \sqrt[3]{10}\cdot e^{\frac{2\pi i}{3}},\ \sqrt[3]{10}\cdot e^{-\frac{2\pi i}{3}}.$$

Therefore we need only concern ourselves with the value of arg $f(i)$. However, arg $f(z)$ can be assumed to be a continuous function on any curve on which $f(z)$ does not vanish. Therefore, on the path we have chosen, arg $f(z)$ changes only on the small semicircles, by means of which we avoid the points $z = 2$ and $z = 1$. It is much easier to observe this change than to follow the change of arg $f(z)$ along the entire straight line segment joining the points $z = 3$ and $z = i$.

To find the magnitude of the change of arg $f(z)$ as we follow the semicircle $|z-2| = \varepsilon$, $\operatorname{Im} z > 0$, we write

$$\arg f(z) = \arg \sqrt[3]{(z^2-1)(z+2)} + \arg \sqrt[3]{z-2}.$$

(We choose some regular branch in the plane with the cross cut $(-\infty, 2)$ for each of the functions $\sqrt[3]{(z^2-1)(z+2)}$ and $\sqrt[3]{z-2}$. This is possible because of the monodromy theorem.) An arbitrary element of the analytic function $\sqrt[3]{(z^2-1)(z+2)}$ is analytically continued to the point $z = 2$ and we can replace continuation of the first summand along the small semicircle by continuation along the real axis. The first summand therefore does not change. The second summand is increased by $\pi/3$ during the circuit of the semicircle (see the end of Example 1, Sect. 2).

For the circuit of the semicircle $|z-1| = \varepsilon$, $\operatorname{Im} z > 0$, we write

$$\arg f(z) = \arg \sqrt[3]{(z+1)(z^2-4)} + \arg \sqrt[3]{z-1}$$

and then use these expressions. As a result we find that arg $f(z)$ again increases by $\pi/3$ in the circuit of this semicircle.

Consequently, assuming that arg $f(3) = 0$, we find that arg $f(i)$ $= \frac{2\pi}{3}$ and $f(i) = \sqrt[3]{10}\cdot e^{\frac{2\pi i}{3}}$.

It is clear that a function analytic in a multiply connected domain does not have to be regular in this domain. This is shown by the example of the function ln z which is analytic in the annulus $0 < |z| < \infty$, but is not regular in this annulus.

The following problem arises naturally for functions analytic in multiply connected domains:

Let $f_\zeta(z)$ be an element of a function analytic in the domain D (at the point $\zeta \in D$) and suppose that we are given two closed curves

C_1 and C_2, lying in D and passing through the point ζ. Under what conditions on the curves C_1 and C_2 does the result of continuations of $f_\zeta(z)$ along the curve C_1 coincide with the result of continuation along C_2?

It is not difficult to obtain a solution of this problem for any multiply connected domain with the help of the monodromy theorem. We shall carry out the proof of this result only for doubly connected domains, since its formulation does not require the introduction of any new concepts in this case. New concepts are even less necessary in the investigation of the nature of multiple-valued functions which are analytic in a neighborhood of some point (with the exception of the point itself).

We shall introduce some new notations necessary for the formulation of the theorem:

Let D_1 be a doubly connected domain obtained by removing some connected closed set E from the simply connected domain D, and let P be any point of the set E.

Let $\nu(C, E)$ (the circuit number of the hole E) denote the number of circuits of the point P in the positive direction made by the closed polygonal line C contained in D_1. (It is clear that $\nu(C, E)$ does not depend on the choice of the point P in the set E.)

Theorem 3.2. *Let $F(z)$ be a function analytic in the domain D_1, and let $\varphi_\zeta(z)$ be its element at some point $\zeta \in D_1$. If C_1 and C_2 are two closed polygonal lines contained in the domain D_1 and passing through the point ζ, and if*

$$\nu(C_1, E) = \nu(C_2, E),$$

then the result of analytic continuation of $\varphi_\zeta(z)$ along C_1 coincides with the result of analytic continuation of $\varphi_\zeta(z)$ along C_2.

Proof. We shall introduce into the domain D_1 the cross cut L joining the set E with the boundary of the simply connected domain D. After the introduction of the cross cut, the domain D_1 is converted into a simply connected domain, which we shall denote by G. If we choose in G some element of the function $F(z)$, analytic in the domain D_1, and continue it along all paths contained in G, then, in accord with the monodromy theorem, we shall obtain a regular branch of the function $F(z)$. Generally speaking, these regular branches form a countably infinite set, since by continuing distinct elements we arrive at distinct regular branches.

Thus, after the introduction of the cross cut, our function $F(z)$, analytic in the domain D_1, is broken up in some way into separate regular branches $f_n(z)$ $(n = 0, \pm 1, \pm 2, \ldots)$. Each of the functions $f_n(z)$, regular in G, can be continued analytically across the cross cut. Moreover, in this process they are permitted among themselves. We can assume without loss of generality that the functions $f_n(z)$ are numbered in such a way that $f_n(z)$ turns into $f_{n+1}(z)$ under continuation across the cross cut from right to left and that $f_n(z)$ turns into $f_{n-1}(z)$ under continuation from left to right.

Let us assume that we obtain the regular branch $f_k(z)$ under continuation of the element $\varphi_\zeta(z)$ in the domain G. We shall indicate which branch is obtained from the element obtained by analytic continuation of the element $\varphi_\zeta(z)$ along the closed polygonal line C contained in D_1. The polygonal line C intersects the cross cut a certain number of times. Suppose that it intersects it ν^+ times from right to left and ν^- from left to right. Each crossing from right to left corresponds to crossing over to the branch with index greater by one, and each crossing from left to right is a crossing to the branch with index less by one. Therefore, under continuation along C we arrive at an element that generates the branch with index $k+\nu^+-\nu^-$.

If we apply the lemma of Sect. 1 on the circuit number, we arrive at the statement of the theorem, since according to this lemma $\nu^+-\nu^-=\nu$ (C, E), i.e., the change of the number of the branch depends only on the number of circuits of the hole E made by the polygonal line C.

In the case of an m-connected domain with $m>2$, the index of branches generated by the new element depends not only on the number of circuits of all $m-1$ holes, but also on the order in which the circuits are made.

4. RIEMANN SURFACES

Up to this point we have not associated any descriptive geometric representation with analytic functions. This may be explained by the fact that the "graph" of a complex-valued function of a complex variable is a two-dimensional surface in a four-dimensional space. Such a representation can hardly be called intuitive. However, some kind of intuitive geometric picture would be very useful in the study of the multiple-valued nature of analytic functions. The concept of a Riemann surface serves this purpose. Before defining this concept, we shall introduce some analogs and study the simplest special cases.

Suppose that we have a planar curve given by the equation $F(x, y)=0$. If we solve this implicit equation with respect to y, then, generally speaking, we obtain a multiple-valued function $y = y(x)$. It is very easy to depict the nature of this multiple-valuedness by mapping the curve on the plane. Moreover, we do not even need to have an exact representation of the curve. It is sufficient to have a scheme showing how many sections of the curve are situated above any given point of the x-axis, where these sections are joined together and in what order. We can represent such a scheme by replacing the sections of the curve by straight line segments parallel to the x-axis and situated one above the other. Of course, such a scheme is not as descriptive as the plotting of the curve itself. The situation is similar for functions of a complex variable. There the surface lies in a four-dimensional space, but a scheme of representation is possible in a three-dimensional space.

Let us describe such a procedure for the analytic function ln z.

We take an infinite number of copies of the plane cut along the negative half of the real axis. Each of these copies corresponds to a regular branch of ln z. These branches turn into one another under continuation across the negative half of the real axis. This can be represented by gluing one edge of the cut in one plane to the other edge of the cut in another. Since each circuit of the point $z = 0$ in the positive direction leads us to a new regular branch of ln z, it is therefore necessary that all the copies be glued together This can be done most naturally in the following way.

We choose some example of the plane with the cross cut. We call the side of the cross cut adjoining the lower half-plane the lower edge and the other the upper edge of the cross cut. We next number the copies and use for this the integers from $-\infty$ to $+\infty$. The lower of the nth copy is glued to the upper edge of the $(n + 1)$st copy. After carrying out this procedure, we obtain a surface reminiscent of a spiral ramp. This is the intuitive representation we sought for depicting the character of the multiple-valued function ln z (the Riemann surface of ln z).

Unfortunately, it is often necessary in the construction of these representations to carry out procedures which contradict our ordinary geometric intuition. For example, let us construct the Riemann surface of $\sqrt[n]{z}$. The function $\sqrt[n]{z}$ is n-valued, thus we need n copies of a slit plane. We number them from 1 to n and carry out the same procedure of pasting together as was done for ln z. Thus, the upper edge of the cut of the first copy and the lower edge of the cut of the nth copy will remain free. We have to glue these together, for after n circuits of the point $z = 0$ in the positive direction we return to the original value of the element (see Example 1 of Sect. 2). The existence of such an arrangement is impossible in three-dimensional space. This is explained by the fact that we are carrying out a procedure in three-dimensional space for representing a surface in four-dimensional space. Such a procedure is, of course, possible in four-dimensional space. In what follows, we shall always speak of the gluing procedure without being concerned about whether or not it can be carried out in three-dimensional space.

Let us now turn to the definitions.

Let $F(z)$ be an analytic function and let $f_\zeta(z)$ be an element of the analytic function $F(z)$ at the point ζ.

We shall call the set consisting of the point ζ and the element $f_\zeta(z)$, i.e., the pair $(\zeta, f_\zeta(z))$, a *point of the abstract Riemann surface of the analytic function* $F(z)$.

We shall say that two points $(\zeta, f_\zeta(z))$ and $(w, f_w(z))$ of the Riemann surface are identical if $\zeta = w$ and $f_\zeta(z) = f_w(z)$.

We shall call the set $G_\varrho(P)$ (where ϱ is any positive number), consisting of the points $(w, f_w(z))$ such that the element $f_w(z)$ can be obtained by analytic continuation of the element $f_\zeta(z)$ along any path of length less than ϱ, a neighborhood of the point $P = (\zeta, f_\zeta(z))$ of the abstract Riemann surface.

Thus, an abstract Riemann surface is a set of pairs $(\zeta, f_\zeta(z))$ in which we have defined a notion of "nearness" for the pairs. Sets in which a notion of nearness is defined in terms of the notion of neighborhood are called topological spaces.

The set of pairs $(\zeta, f_\zeta(z))$ can be represented in the four dimensional (i.e., two dimensional complex) space (ζ, w) as the "graph" of the multiple-valued function $w = F(\zeta)$. This means that the abstract Riemann surface is the "graph" of the analytic function, in which all of its properties are missing except those which can be defined in terms of the notion of neighborhood. Of course, the number of such properties is not small (they are called topological properties). It is easy to define the concepts of limit point, open and closed set with the aid of the notion of neighborhood. It is also possible to define the notion of connectedness for open sets.

We shall now introduce the notion of connectedness for open sets.

We shall say that the open set E is connected, if for any two points $P \in E$ and $P' \in E$ we can construct a sequence of points P_k $(k = 1, 2, \ldots, n)$, $P_1 = P$ and $P_n = P'$ contained in neighborhoods G_1, G_2, ..., G_n which lie in E such that the intersection of G_{k+1} and G_k is never empty.

If we recall the definition of neighborhood, we see that the set E of points of the abstract Riemann surface is connected, if any two of its points $(\zeta, f_\zeta(z))$ and $(w, f_w(z))$ are such that the element $f_w(z)$ can be obtained from the element $f_\zeta(z)$ by analytic continuation through a sequence of points $\zeta_1, \zeta_2, \ldots, \zeta_n$ such that $(\zeta_k, f_{\zeta_k}(z)) \in E$ $(k = 1, 2, \ldots, n)$.

In particular, it is clear from the definition of connectedness that the abstract Riemann surface is a connected open set.

An abstract Riemann surface can be realized in the form of one or another concrete surface. To do this we establish a one-one correspondence between the points of this concrete surface and the points of the abstract Riemann surface, and establish that points which are near on the abstract Riemann surface remain near when mapped into the concrete surface (in the sense of the distance between them along the surface). The reader may verify that the schemes we have constructed for $\ln z$ and $\sqrt[n]{z}$ actually afford us realizations of the abstract Riemann surfaces of these functions. In what follows, when we speak of the Riemann surface of analytic functions we shall mean the realization of the abstract Riemann surface in terms of such a scheme.

What we relaize an abstract Riemann surface by a scheme, then not all points of the scheme correspond to points of the abstract Riemann surface. For example, in the scheme we constructed for the function $\ln z$, the points $z = 0$ and $z = \infty$ of each copy of the slit plane do not correspond to any point of the surface of the abstract Riemann surface of the analytic function $\ln z$. More generally, points of the abstract Riemann surface correspond to some open connected set of the scheme. The boundary points of this set are called *singular points of the analytic function.*

Many terms in the theory of analytic functions arise from the geometric representation related to Riemann surfaces. We shall now introduce some of these terms.

On the Riemann surface, points corresponding to the same point ζ are called *points situated above the point* ζ. (This term is sometimes employed also for elements of the analytic function.)

A set of points of the Riemann surface is called *one-sheeted*, if distinct points of this set are situated above distinct points of the plane.

Let us study the part of the Riemann surface consisting of the points situated above some domain D of the complex plane. This part will be divided into several connected components. If some connected component does not contain any singular points, then we shall call it a *branch* of the analytic function in the domain D or a *function analytic in the domain* D. If in addition this component is one-sheeted, then we shall call it a *regular branch* of the analytic function.

The monodromy theorem may be translated into these terms as follows:

If the domain D *is simply connected, then any connected component of the Riemann surface situated above* D *and not containing any singular points is one-sheeted.*

5. EXAMPLES OF THE CONSTRUCTION OF RIEMANN SURFACES

In this section we shall present a series of examples of the construction of schemes similar to the one constructed for the analytic function $\ln z$ at the beginning of Sect. 4. In what follows we shall call these schemes the Riemann surfaces corresponding to the analytic functions.

Let us begin by making some general remarks about the method of construction.

Suppose that we are given an analytic function $F(z)$. We make cross cuts L_1, L_2, ... in the complex plane so that the analytic function $F(z)$ admits division into regular branches for any initial element in the cut plane. Then the Riemann surface of the analytic function $F(z)$ is divided into one-sheeted parts corresponding to these regular branches. These pieces are copies of the cut plane. We then take as many copies for the cut plane as there are distinct regular branches. These are then numbered after we have numbered the regular branches $f_1(z), f_2(z), \ldots$, as $A_1, A_2, \ldots$.

Thus, we have the Riemann surface of the analytic function in the form of a collection of sheets $A_1, A_2, \ldots$, to be pasted together. Of course, we know where the pasting together is to be carried out — it is along the cross cuts $L_1, L_2, \ldots$. We need to determine how the sheets are to be pasted together along each cross cut. This is done in the following way.

Each cross cut L_k has two sides, which we denote L_k^+ and L_k^-. Let us study the analytic continuation of the regular branch $f_s(z)$ across the side L_k^+ of the cut L_k. As a result of analytic continuation, we arrive at some other regular branch of the analytic function

$F(z)$. Since all possible analytic branches have been numbered, this will be the regular branch $f_m(z)$. Then we glue the edge L_k^+ of the cut L_k on the sheet A_s to the edge L_k^- of the cut L_k on the sheet A_m.

After completing all the pasting together according to this rule, we obtain the Riemann surface we sought.

We now illustrate these remarks by examples.

Example 1. Let us construct the Riemann surface of the analytic function

$$F(z) = \sqrt{1+z} + \sqrt{1-z}.$$

We first make cross cuts along the rays $(-\infty, -1)$ and $(1, +\infty)$ in the z-plane. According to the monodromy theorem, the analytic function $F(z)$ admits a division into regular branches in the cut plane. It is clear that there are four distinct regular branches. We can distinguish them most easily on the interval $(-1, 1)$. We shall number them thus:

$$\begin{aligned}
f_1(x) &= \sqrt{1+x} + \sqrt{1-x} \qquad (-1 < x < 1),\\
f_2(x) &= \sqrt{1+x} - \sqrt{1-x} \qquad (-1 < x < 1),\\
f_3(x) &= -\sqrt{1+x} + \sqrt{1-x} \qquad (-1 < x < 1),\\
f_4(x) &= -\sqrt{1+x} - \sqrt{1-x} \qquad (-1 < x < 1).
\end{aligned}$$

We denote the cut $(-\infty, -1)$ by L_1, its lower edge by L_1^+ and its upper edge by L_1^-. Analogously, we denote the cut $(1, +\infty)$ by L_2, its lower edge by L_2^+ and its upper edge by L_2^-.

It is easy to see that we have the following changes under analytic continuation across L_1^+: $f_1(z)$ goes into $f_3(z)$, $f_2(z)$ into $f_4(z)$ $f_3(z)$ into $f_1(z)$ and $f_4(z)$ into $f_2(z)$. Under analytic continuation across L_2^+ we find: $f_1(z)$ goes into $f_2(z)$, $f_2(z)$ into $f_1(z)$, $f_3(z)$ into $f_4(z)$ and $f_4(z)$ into $f_3(z)$.

Consequently, we obtain the Riemann surface we seekby gluing: $(L_1^+, A_1)+(L_1^-, A_3)$, $(L_1^+, A_2)+(L_1^-, A_4)$, $(L_1^+, A_3)+(L_1^-, A_1)$, $(L_1^+, A_4)+(L_1^-, A_2)$ etc.

Example 2. We shall construct the Riemann surface of the analytic function arc sin z. We shall express arc sin z in terms of the logarithm. It readily follows from the formula

$$\operatorname{arc\,sin} z = \int_0^z \frac{dt}{\sqrt{1-t^2}} \qquad (|z| < 1)$$

that

$$\operatorname{arc\,sin} z = i \ln (\sqrt{1-z^2} - iz).$$

Now we shall indicate where the singular points of the function arc sin z are situated. It is immediately clear that the point $z = 1$

and $z = -1$ are singular points through which it is impossible to analytically continue $\sqrt{1-z^2}$. In addition to these we have the singular points at which the expression $\sqrt{1-z^2}-iz$ vanishes or becomes infinite. On checking we find that this occurs only at the point $z = \infty$. Consequently, the only singular points of the analytic function arc sin z are the points on the Riemann surface situated above the points $z = 1$, $z = -1$, $z = \infty$.

It is sufficient to make cuts along the rays $(-\infty, -1)$ and $(1, +\infty)$ in order to obtain a simply connected domain above which no singular points are situated. According to the monodromy theorem, the analytic function arc sin z admits a division in this domain into regular branches with any element in the role of initial element.

There are infinitely many regular branches. It is most convenient to distinguish them by their behavior on the interval $(-1, 1)$ of the real axis. We shall number them in the following way:

$$-\frac{\pi}{2}+\pi k<f_k(x)<\frac{\pi}{2}+\pi k \qquad (-1<x<1),$$
$$k=0,\ \pm 1,\ \pm 2,\ \ldots .$$

We denote the cut $(-\infty, -1)$ by L_1, its lower edge by L_1^+ and its upper edge by L_1^-. Analogously, the cut $(1, +\infty)$ is denoted by L_2, its lower edge by L_2^+ and its upper edge by L_2^-.

We now point out into what branch $f_n(z)$ changes under analytic continuation across L_1^+. In order to do this we must continue arc sin z analytically along a small circle $|z+1|=\varepsilon$ in the clockwise sense and observe which branch corresponds to the value obtained.

It is clear that the possible values of $f_k(z)$ have the form

$$f_k(z)=i\ln(\pm\sqrt{1-z^2}-iz)+2\pi m.$$

Since the expression $\sqrt{1-z^2}-iz$ differs slightly from i for z near -1, we can choose some branch (not regular, since $\sqrt{1-z^2}$ has a singular point at $z = -1$) in the annulus $0<|z+1|<\varepsilon$ for $\ln(\sqrt{1-z^2}-iz)$. For example, we can choose the one whose value $\ln(\sqrt{1-z^2}-iz)$ is close to $\frac{\pi i}{2}$. Then for $-1<x<-1+\varepsilon$ we have

$$0>i\ln(\sqrt{1-x^2}-ix)>-\frac{\pi}{2},$$
$$\frac{\pi}{2}>i\ln(-\sqrt{1-x^2}-ix)>\pi,$$

since the point $\sqrt{1-x^2}-ix=w_1$ is found in the right and the point $w_2=-\sqrt{1-x^2}-ix$ in the left half plane. This means that for this choice of the branch of the logarithm we have for $-1<x<-1+\varepsilon$:

$$f_{2n}(x)=i\ln(\sqrt{1-x^2}-ix)+2\pi n,$$
$$f_{2n-1}(x)=i\ln(-\sqrt{1-x^2}-ix)+2\pi n.$$

$\sqrt{1-z^2}$ changes sign after a circuit of the point $z=-1$ along a small circle. Therefore, on continuation across L_1^+ the regular branch $f_{2n}(z)$ becomes $f_{2n-1}(z)$ and $f_{2n-1}(z)$ becomes $f_{2n}(z)$. Thus, we have to perform the gluings:

$$(L_1^+,\ A_{2n})+(L_1^-,\ A_{2n-1}),\ (L_1^+,\ A_{2n-1})+(L_1^-,\ A_{2n})$$
$$(n=0,\ \pm 1,\ \pm 2,\ \ldots).$$

By analogous reasoning we may readily verify that under continuation across L_2^+ the branch $f_{2n}(z)$ becomes $f_{2n+1}(z)$ and the branch $f_{2n+1}(z)$ becomes $f_{2n}(z)$. We thus must glue together:

$$(L_2^+,\ A_{2n})+(L_2^-,\ A_{2n+1}),\quad (L_2^+,\ A_{2n+1})+(L_2^-,\ A_{2n}),$$

in order to obtain the desired Riemann surface.

Example 3. We shall construct the Riemann surface of the analytic function $F(z)=\sqrt{1+\sqrt{z}}$.

The singular points of the analytic function $F(z)$ can be only points situated above the points $z = 0$, $z=\infty$ and $z = 1$. Thus, we make cuts along the rays $(-\infty,\ 0)$ and $(1,\ +\infty)$. We obtain four regular branches which may most easily be distinguished by the values along the interval $(0,\ 1)$:

$$f_1(x)=\sqrt{1+\sqrt{x}},\qquad f_2(x)=-\sqrt{1+\sqrt{x}},$$
$$f_3(x)=\sqrt{1-\sqrt{x}},\qquad f_4(x)=-\sqrt{1-\sqrt{x}}.$$

We denote the cut $(-\infty,\ 0)$ by L_1, its lower edge by L_1^+ and its upper edge by L_1^-; the cut $(1,\ +\infty)$ by L_2, its lower edge by L_2^+ and its upper edge by L_2^-.

It is clear that we have the following transitions under continuation across L_2^+: $f_3(z)$ into $f_4(z)$ and $f_4(z)$ into $f_3(z)$. On crossing L_1^+ we find: $f_1(z)$ becomes $f_3(z)$, $f_2(z)$ becomes $f_4(z)$, $f_3(z)$ becomes $f_1(z)$ and $f_4(z)$ becomes $f_2(z)$. It is clear that $f_1(z)$ and $f_2(z)$ do not change under continuation across L_2^+. After completing the corresponding gluings, we obtain the desired Riemann surface. The Riemann surface constructed in this example is interesting in that both singular and nonsingular points are situated above the point $z = 1$.

CHAPTER IV

Singular Points and Expansion in Series

Many of the problems of the theory of analytic functions reduce to the investigation of the behavior of the function near its singular points. In the present chapter we give a classification and present general methods of study. The basic tools of the theory of analytic functions are developed in this chapter.

1. THE NOTATION OF A SINGULAR POINT OF REGULAR FUNCTION

We introduced the notion of singular point of an analytic function at the end of Sect. 4 of Chapter III. We shall have relatively little need to use it. The notion of singular point of a regular function will be used much more often. Clearly, a singular point of a regular function must be a boundary point of the domain of regularity. Unfortunately, the same point of the boundary of a domain with cross cuts can be both a singular and a nonsingular point (depending on how the approach to it is made). We shall therefore first introduce an auxiliary notion.

Let ζ be a boundary point of the domain D, and let L be a simple curve contained in D with the exception of its end point ζ. We shall call the pair (ζ, L) consisting of the point ζ and the curve L leading to it, an *accessible boundary point of the domain D.*

The intersection of the domain D with the circle $|z-\zeta|<\varrho$ may break up into several connected components. If the curves L_1 and L_2, ending at the point ζ, are such that the parts of them contained in the circle $|z-\zeta|<\varrho$, fall in the same connected component of the above-mentioned intersection (for all sufficiently small ϱ), then we shall say that the *accessible boundary points* (ζ, L_1) *and* (ζ, L_2) *coincide.*

If the domain D is bounded by a *simple* piecewise-smooth closed curve, then for sufficiently small ϱ the intersection of the domain D with the circle $|z-\zeta|<\varrho$ consists of one connected component. For such domains there is no distinction between accessible boundary points and points of the boundary.

It is easy to verify that for domains bounded by piecewise-smooth curves with folds the accessible boundary points of the domain are no longer the points of the boundary of the domain, but the points of the boundary curve. In other words, for domains with cross cuts points on different sides of the cut correspond to distinct accessible boundary points.

We shall call an accessible boundary point (ζ, L) of the domain D a *singular point of the function* $f(z)$, regular in the domain D, if the function cannot be analytically continued along the curve L to the point ζ.

In justification of the given definition, we may readily convince ourselves that the possibility of analytic continuation does not depend on the choice of the curve L (determined by the given accessible boundary point). Indeed, if the function $f(z)$ can be continued along the curve L to the point ζ, then there exists a function $f_1(z)$ that is regular in the circle $|z-\zeta|<\varrho$ and coincides with $f(z)$ on L. According to the principle of analytic continuation, $f_1(z)=f(z)$ in the entire connected component of the intersection of the circle $|z-\zeta|<\varrho$ with the domain D in which L occurs. Consequently, the function $f(z)$ can be continued analytically to the point ζ along any other path which is contained in the same connected component.

We shall give an example of a domain with cross cuts and two accessible points (corresponding to the same point of the cross cut) one of which is a singular point and the other is not.

Example 1. Let D be the z-plane with a cross cut along the negative part of the real axis. Let $f(z)=\frac{1}{1+i\sqrt{z}}$ (we shall choose the principal value for $\sqrt{z}$).

The cross cut divides every sufficiently small circle of the form $|z+x|<\varrho$, $0<x<\infty$, into two halves—an upper and a lower. This means that every point of the cross cut $(-\infty, 0)$ with the exception of its end point corresponds to two accessible points of the domain D (from above and from below). Therefore, for the sake of brevity, we shall speak of points on the upper and lower edges of the cross cut and we shall drop the word "accessible."

We know (see Example 1, Sect. 2, Chap. III) that the function $\sqrt{z}$ cannot be continued analytically along any path leading to the points $z=0$ and $z=\infty$. Since $\sqrt{z}=\frac{1}{i}\left(\frac{1}{f(z)}-1\right)$ and $f(0)=1\neq 0$, then continuation of the function $f(z)$ to the point $z=0$ would imply that $\sqrt{z}$ could also be continued to the point $z=0$, which is impossible. Consequently, the point $z=0$ is a singular point of the function $f(z)$.

Moreover, the function $1+i\sqrt{z}$ can be continued analytically along any path not passing through the points $z=0$ and $z=\infty$, in particular, across the points of the cross cut. Thus, the function $f(z)=\frac{1}{1+i\sqrt{z}}$ can be continued analytically through all the points at which $1+i\sqrt{z}$ does not vanish. At the point $z=-x$ on the upper edge of the crosscut, the function $\sqrt{z}$ takes on the value $i\sqrt{x}$, and at the lower edge the value $-i\sqrt{x}$. Thus, the function $f(z)$ can be continued analytically through all the points of the cross cut with the possible exception of the point $z=-1$ on its upper boundary. It is quite easy to see that this point is a singular point, for $f(z)\to\infty$ as this point is approached. (See below, Theorem 1.2.)

Let the function $F(z)$ be regular in some circle, let us say, the circle $|z|<R$. According to Theorem 3.2* of Chap. II, the function $F(z)$ can be expanded in a Taylor series

$$F(z)=\sum_0^\infty c_n z^n, \qquad c_n=\frac{1}{n!}F^{(n)}(0),$$

which converges in this circle. This series has a definite radius of convergence R_0, which can be determined in terms of the coefficients c_n with the aid of the Cauchy-Hadamard formula, $1/R_0 = \overline{\lim\limits_{n\to\infty}}\sqrt[n]{|c_n|}$ (see Sect. 3, Chap. II). From Theorem 3.2 of Chap. II we obtain the inequality $R\leqslant R_0$. It is natural to try to find out which properties of the sum of the series are connected with the magnitude of the radius of convergence.

Theorem 1.1. *At least one singular point of the sum of the series lies on the boundary of the circle of convergence.*

Proof. Without loss of generality, we may assume that we are dealing with a series of the form $\sum\limits_0^\infty c_n z^n$ and that its radius of convergence is one. The sum of the series (which we denote by $f(z)$) is regular within the circle of convergence $|z|=1$. Each point on the boundary is an accessible singular point. We shall denote by $\varrho(\varphi)$ the least upper bound of the values of ϱ for which the function $f(z)$ can be continued analytically in the circle $|z-e^{i\varphi}|<\varrho$. It is clear that $\varrho(\varphi_0)=0$ if and only if the point $z=e^{i\varphi_0}$ is a singular point of the function $f(z)$.

Let us note that the circle $|z-a|<r$ contains the circle $|z-b|<r-|a-b|$. If we set $a=e^{i\varphi_1}$, $b=e^{i\varphi_2}$, $r=\varrho(\varphi_1)$, then we obtain the inequality

$$\varrho(\varphi_2)\geqslant\varrho(\varphi_1)-|e^{i\varphi_1}-e^{i\varphi_2}|.$$

However, φ_1 and φ_2 may be interchanged and thus we obtain the inequality

$$\varrho(\varphi_1)\geqslant\varrho(\varphi_2)-|e^{i\varphi_1}-e^{i\varphi_2}|.$$

We find from these two inequalities that

$$|\varrho(\varphi_1)-\varrho(\varphi_2)|\leqslant 2\left|\sin\frac{(\varphi_1-\varphi_2)}{2}\right|.$$

The last inequality shows that $\varrho(\varphi)$ is a continuous function. Let $\varrho_0=\min\limits_\varphi\varrho(\varphi)$. The function $f(z)$ can evidently be continued analytically throughout the circle $|z|<1+\varrho_0$, and the analytic continuation will be a regular function in this circle. Its series coincides with the series for $f(z)$; however, according to Theorem 3.2*, it must converge in the circle $|z|<1+\varrho_0$. In view of the definition of radius of convergence (the radius of convergence is one for our series), we have $\varrho(\varphi_0)=0$. The continuous function $\varrho(\varphi)$ must assume its minimum value, thus there exists a φ_0 such that $\varrho(\varphi_0)=0$. Consequently, the point $z=e^{i\varphi_0}$ is a singular point of the function $f(z)$, which proves the theorem.

The theorem proved is sometimes more convenient to use in the following form:

The radius of convergence of the Taylor series

$$F(z)=\sum_0^\infty c_n(z-a)^n$$

equals the distance from the point a to the nearest singular point of F(z).

We now direct our attention to the following problem:

Suppose that we are given a function $f(z)$ that is regular in some domain and an accessible boundary point of this domain. We wish to determine whether or not this point is a singular point of the function $f(z)$.

This problem is very complex and we shall not speak of its solution in general form. We shall discuss simple sufficient criteria. A considerable number of mathematicians have occupied themselves with this problem in the case that the function is given in terms of a power series and it is a question of writing down conditions on the coefficients of the series. We shall present three of the most elegant results (without proof).*

Pringsheim's theorem. If $\overline{\lim\limits_{n\to\infty}}\sqrt[\lambda_n]{|c_n|}=1$ *and* $\operatorname{Re} c_n\geqslant 0$, *then the sum of the series* $\sum\limits_0^\infty c_n z^{\lambda_n}$ *will have the point* $z=1$ *as a singular point.*

Fabry's theorem. If $\overline{\lim\limits_{n\to\infty}}\sqrt[n]{|c_n|}=1$ *then the sum of the series* $\sum\limits_0^\infty c_n z^{\lambda_n}$ *has* $z=1$ *as a singular point.*

Polya's theorem. If $0<\lambda_0<\lambda_1<\lambda_2<\ldots$, $\overline{\lim\limits_{n\to\infty}}\sqrt[\lambda_n]{|c_n|}=1$ *and* $\lim\limits_{n\to\infty}\frac{n}{\lambda_n}=\sigma$, *then the series* $\sum\limits_0^\infty c_n z^{\lambda_n}$ *has at least one singular point on any arc of the circle* $|z|=1$ *of length greater than* $2\pi\sigma$.

(We still have to examine what can be obtained from the statement of Polya's theorem for $\sigma=1$ and $\sigma=0$.)

---

*The proof of this theorem can be found in various monographs: P. Dienes, The Taylor Series, Oxford, 1931; L. Bieberbach, Analytische Fortsetzung, Berlin, 1955.

We now prove one considerably simpler sufficient criterion whose application is not restricted to power series.

Theorem 1.2. Let (ζ, L) be an accessible boundary point of domain D. If the function $f(z)$ is regular in D and for some k we have

$$\overline{\lim_{z\to\zeta,\ z\in L}}\ |f^{(k)}(z)| = \infty,$$

then (ζ, L) is a singular point of the function $f(z)$.

Proof. If the function $f(z)$ can be continued analytically to the point ζ along the path L, then there exists a function $f_\zeta(z)$ that is regular in some circle $|z-\zeta|<\varrho$ and coincides with $f(z)$ in the part of L contained within the circle. But then $f^{(k)}(z) \to f_\zeta^{(k)}(\zeta)$ as $z \to \zeta$, $z\in L$. As a result of this contradiction, the theorem is proved.

It is easy to verify with the help of Theorem 1.2 that the point $z=-1$ on the upper edge of the cross cut is a singular point of the function studied in Example 1. After applying Theorem 1.2 with $k=1$, we see that the point $z=0$ is also a singular point of this function.

We present one more example.

Example 2. Let us show that all points of the circle $|z|=1$ are singular points of the sum of the series $f(z)=\sum_0^\infty z^{2^n}$.

Let us first verify that the point $z=1$ is a singular point of the function $f(z)$. For this purpose we use Theorem 1.2, where L is the radius from $z=0$ to $z=1$ and where $k=0$.

$$\overline{\lim_{x\to 1-0}}\ f(x) \geqslant \lim_{x\to 1-0} \sum_0^N x^{2^n} = N+1,$$

and since N is arbitrary, our limit equals infinity, i.e., the point $z=1$ is a singular point of $f(z)$.

Furthermore, let us note that the function $f(z)$ satisfies the functional relation $f(z)=z+f(z^2)$. Since $z=1$ is a singular point of the function $f(z)$, then the points at which $z^2=1$ must be singular points of the function $f(z^2)$. But in view of the functional relation, these points must also be singular points of the function $f(z)$. Following this line of attack further, we see that all points z for which $z^{2^k}=1$ (for some integer k) must be singular points of the function $f(z)$. These points constitute an everywhere dense set of points on the circle $|z|=1$. Furthermore, it is evident that limit points of the set of singular points are themselves singular points. Consequently, all points of the circle $|z|=1$ are singular points of $f(z)$.

It must be stressed that Theorem 1.2 gives only a sufficient condition which is by no means necessary. To convince ourselves of this, we study the function $f(z)=\sum_0^\infty e^{-\sqrt{n}} z^n$. It, together with all its derivatives, is continuous in the circle $|z|\leqslant 1$. Nevertheless, this function must have at least one singular point on the circle $|z|=1$, since the radius of convergence of the series is one. (It may be seen right away from either Pringsheim's or Fabry's theorem that the singular point is the point $z=1$.) By methods with which we shall become acquainted in Chap. VI this function can be analytically continued and a detailed study can be made of this singular point.

2. REMOVAL OF SINGULARITIES

We shall now consider a problem in some sense opposite to the problem studied in the preceding section. Namely:

Suppose that we are given an accessible boundary point of the domain D. Do there exist simple conditions sufficient to ensure that (ζ, L) is not a singular point of the function $f(z)$ regular in the domain D?

We have to solve this problem when we have a regular function given by means of some formula and the fomula does not represent the function at isolated points. Let us study one typical example of this type.

Example 1. Let the functions $f(z)$ and $g(z)$ be regular in a neighborhood of the point $z=a$, where $f(a)=g(a)=0$ and $g'(a)\neq 0$. We will show that the function $\varphi(z)=\frac{f(z)}{g(z)}$ can be analytically continued to the point $z=a$.

The formula $\varphi(z)=\frac{f(z)}{g(z)}$, which defines the function $\varphi(z)$, ceases to be valid at the point $z=a$, since the denominator vanishes. To fill in this gap in the formula, we write

$$f(z)=f(a)+(z-a)f'(a)+\ldots =(z-a)f_1(z),$$

$$g(z)=g(a)+(z-a)g'(a)+\ldots =(z-a)g_1(z).$$

It is clear that the functions $f_1(z)$ and $g_1(z)$ are regular at the point $z=a$; here $g_1(a)=g'(a)\neq 0$. For $z\neq a$ we have

$$\varphi(z)=\frac{(z-a)f_1(z)}{(z-a)g_1(z)}=\frac{f_1(z)}{g_1(z)},$$

and this formula is valid also at the point $z=a$, since the denominator does not vanish at this point. Thus, this formula gives an analytic continuation of the function $\varphi(z)$ to the point $z=a$. Moreover, it is clear that

$$\varphi(a)=\frac{f_1(a)}{g_1(a)}=\frac{f'(a)}{g'(a)}.$$

If analytic continuation to a boundary point can be accomplished, we shall say that it is a removable singular point or removable singularity.

Theorem 2.1. *Let the function $f(z)$ be regular in the domain D_0, obtained from the domain D by removal of the point $a\in D$. If*

$$\lim_{\varepsilon \to 0} \varepsilon M(\varepsilon) = 0, \qquad M(\varepsilon) = \max_{|z-a| = \varepsilon} |f(z)|, \tag{2.1}$$

then the function $f(z)$ can be continued analytically to the point $z = a$.

Proof. Without loss of generality we may assume that the domain D is bounded by a simple closed curve C and that $f(z)$ is continuous in $\overline{D}$, except at the point $z = a$. We choose a number $\varepsilon > 0$ so small that the circle $|z-a| \leqslant \varepsilon$ is contained in D, and then denote by D_ε the domain obtained by removing this circle from D. Let C_ε denote the boundary of D_ε. Since the function $f(z)$ is regular in D and continuous up to its boundary, the Cauchy integral formula gives us

$$f(z) = \frac{1}{2\pi i} \int_{C_\varepsilon} \frac{f(\zeta)\, d\zeta}{\zeta - z} \qquad (z \in D_\varepsilon)$$

or

$$f(z) = \frac{1}{2\pi i} \int_{C} \frac{f(\zeta)\, d\zeta}{\zeta - z} - \frac{1}{2\pi i} \int_{|\zeta - a| = \varepsilon} \frac{f(\zeta)\, d\zeta}{\zeta - z} \qquad (z \in D_\varepsilon). \tag{2.2}$$

We take $\varepsilon = \varepsilon_k$ in this formula so that $\varepsilon_k M(\varepsilon_k) \to 0$ as $k \to \infty$ [this is possible in view of condition (2.1)]. Since the modulus of the integral does not exceed the value $2\pi\varepsilon_k M(\varepsilon_k) \dfrac{1}{|z-a| - \varepsilon_k}$ on the circle $|\zeta - a| = \varepsilon_k$, then, taking limits as $k \to \infty$, we obtain

$$f(z) = \frac{1}{2\pi i} \int_{C} \frac{f(\zeta)\, d\zeta}{\zeta - z} \qquad (z \in D_0).$$

According to Corollary 1 of Theorem 4.3 of Chap. II, the integral on the right-hand side of the equality is a regular function in the domain D. Since $f(z)$ coincides with this integral for $z \in D_0$, we thus obtain the desired analytic continuation, which proves the theorem.

The example of the function $f(z) = \dfrac{1}{z-a}$ shows that condition (2.1) cannot be weakened.

The following theorem concerns the removal of singularities on curves.

Theorem 2.2. *If the function $f(z)$ is continuous in the domain D and is regular at all points of the domain with the exception of the points of a simple rectifiable curve L, then the function is regular in the entire domain D.*

Proof. In virtue of Morera's theorem (Theorem 4.1 of Chap. II), we need only show that the integral of $f(z)$ along any polygon contained in the domain D is zero.

Let G be any polygonal domain contained in D and let Γ be its boundary. The curve L divides G into a countable number of parts G_n with boundaries Γ_n. The sum of the lengths of the Γ_n is finite; it cannot exceed $Q + 2b$ where a is the length of Γ and b is the length of L. The integral along Γ equals the sum of the integrals along Γ_n (see the remark to Theorem 5.4 of Chap. 1). The function $f(z)$ is regular in the domains G_n (they do not contain points of L) and continuous in $\overline{G}_n$. According to Cauchy's theorem, the integral of $f(z)$ along Γ_n is equal to zero. Consequently, the integral of $f(z)$ along Γ also equals zero, which proves the theorem.

Note that the requirement of the continuity of $f(z)$ at points of the curve L cannot be replaced by the requirement of boundedness for $f(z)$ in the domain D (allowing discontinuities on L). This is shown by the example of a function $f(z)$, that is regular and bounded in the circle with a cross cut along the radius from $z=0$ to $z=\infty$, but is not regular in the entire circle $|z|<1$.

There exists still another type of theorem on the removal of singularities. In theorems of this type it is asserted that if the conditions of the theorem are fulfilled the function cannot only be continued analytically, but is a constant or a polynomial. The following result is customarily called Liouville's theorem.

Theorem 2.3. *Let the function f(z) be regular in the entire finite plane. If*

$$\lim_{R \to \infty} \frac{M(R)}{R^n} = 0, \qquad M(R) = \max_{|z|=R} |f(z)|,$$

then f(z) is a polynomial of degree not exceeding $n-1$.

Proof. According to the formula for higher derivatives of a regular function (see Sect. 3, Chap. II), we have

$$f^{(n)}(z) = \frac{n!}{2\pi i} \int_{|\zeta|=R} \frac{f(\zeta)\,d\zeta}{(\zeta - z)^{n+1}} \qquad (|z|<R).$$

In accord with the condition of the theorem, there exists a sequence R_k such that

$$M(R_k) = o(R_k^n) \qquad (k \longrightarrow \infty).$$

Thus, if we estimate the modulus of the integral by taking the product of the maximum modulus of the integrand by the length of the path, we obtain

$$|f^{(n)}(z)| = o(R_k^n) \frac{R_k}{(R_k - |z|)^{n+1}} = o(1) \qquad (R_k \longrightarrow \infty).$$

Taking the limit as $k \longrightarrow \infty$, we find $f^{(n)}(z) = 0$. Since z is any point of the plane, then $f^{(n)}(z) \equiv 0$. Consequently, $f(z)$ is a polynomial of degree not exceeding $n-1$, which proves the theorem.

We may conclude from the theorem proved that an analytic function is the more complicated, the more singularities it has and the faster it increases on approaching these singularities. The only functions not having any singularities (in the finite plane as well as at infinity) are the constant functions.

We shall prove one more theorem of this type.

Theorem 2.4. *Suppose that any element of the analytic function F(z) can be continued analytically along any path not passing through the points $z=0$ and $z=\infty$. If in addition the values of all the elements of F(z) are bounded by the same constant, then the function is a constant function.*

Proof. Let us consider the analytic function $f(z)=F(e^z)$. Since e^z does not vanish at any point in the extended complex plane, then any element of the analytic function $f(z)$ can be continued analytically along any finite path. The entire finite plane is a simply connected domain; thus, according to the monodromy theorem, the function $f(z)$, analytic in the entire finite plane, is also regular there. Moreover, it follows from the conditions of the theorem that $f(z)$ is bounded. According to Liouville's theorem, it must be a constant. Thus, $F(z)$ is also a constant, which proves the theorem.

It is interesting to note that the theorem becomes false as soon as we assume that the analytic function $F(z)$ has even one singularity other than at $z=0$ or $z=\infty$. We shall introduce an example of a bounded, many-valued analytic function having three singular points in Chap. IX.

3. ISOLATED SINGULAR POINTS

The most important class of singular points is the class of so-called isolated singular points. All elementary functions as well as the great majority of special functions have only such singularities. Singular points of both single-valued and multiple-valued functions are called isolated singular points.

If the function $f(z)$ is regular in some annulus

$$0<|z-a|<r$$

and the point $z=a$ is a singular point of the function $f(z)$, then we say that the point $z=a$ is an *isolated singular point of single-valued character of the function f(z).*

We call a singular point of single-valued character $z=a$ a pole, if $f(z)\to\infty$ as $z\to a$; otherwise we call the point $z=a$ an *essential singular point.*

Poles are especially simple types of singularities. In many problems poles cannot be distinguished from regular points. The reason for this is the following property of poles.

Theorem 3.1. *Let the function f(z) have a pole at the point $z=a$ and let the function $F(w)$ be regular at the point $w=\infty$. The function $\varphi(z)=F(f(z))$ is then regular at the point $z=a$. If the function $F(w)$*

has a pole at the point $z=a$, *then* $\varphi(z)$ *also has a pole at the point* $z=a$.

Proof. We only need to prove the first assertion of the theorem, since the second follows immediately from the definition of pole.

We can assume without loss of generality that $a\neq\infty$. Since the function $f(z)$ has a pole at the point $z=a$, then it is regular in some annulus $0<|z-a|<r$ and the values it assumes in this annulus lie outside the circle $|w|\leqslant R(r)$, where $R(r)\to\infty$ as $r\to 0$. For sufficiently small r the domain $|w|\geqslant R(r)$ falls within the domain of regularity of the function $F(w)$. Thus, the function $\varphi(z)$ is regular in the annulus $0<|z-a|<r_0$ for sufficiently small r_0. Since $f(z)\to\infty$ as $z\to a$, then $\varphi(z)\to F(\infty)$. If we put $M(\varepsilon)=\max\limits_{|z-a|=\varepsilon}|\varphi(z)|$, we see that $M(\varepsilon)\to|F(\infty)|$ $(\varepsilon\to 0)$, i.e., $\lim\limits_{\varepsilon\to 0}\varepsilon M(\varepsilon)=0$. According to Theorem 2.1, therefore, the function $\varphi(z)$ can be continued analytically to the point $z=a$, which proves the theorem.

Corollary. If the function $f(z)$ has a pole at the point $z=a$, then the function $g(z)=\frac{1}{f(z)}$ is regular at the point $z=a$ and $g(a)=0$.

Let n be a positive integer.

We call the point $z=a$, a *zero of multiplicity n* (or a zero of *order n*) of the function $f(z)$, if $f(z)$ can be written in the form $f(z)=(z-a)^n f_1(z)$, where the function $f_1(z)$ is regular at the point $z=a$ and $f_1(a)\neq 0$.

The point $z=\infty$ is called a *zero of multiplicity n* (or *zero of order n*) of the function $f(z)$, if $f(z)$ can be written in the form $f(z)=z^{-n}f_1(z)$, where the function $f_1(z)$ is regular at the point $z=\infty$ and $f_1(\infty)\neq 0$.

We say that the *multiplicity* (or *order*) *of a pole* of the function $f(z)$ at the point $z=a$ is the multiplicity of the zero of the function $g(z)=1/f(z)$ at this point. Zeros and poles of first order are called *simple*.

We see from the definition of the order of a zero that a pole of order n can be considered as a zero of order $-n$.

If $a\neq\infty$, then we have a simple criterion for the determination of the order of a zero at the point $z=a$:

Let $f(a)=f'(a)=\ldots=f^{(n-1)}(a)=0$, and let $f^{(n)}(a)\neq 0$. Then the point $z=a$ is a zero of multiplicity n of the function $f(z)$ (regular at the point $z=a$).

The reader can easily verify this criterion for himself.

We also leave it to the reader to prove the following obvious result, to which we shall frequently refer:

Lemma. *If the functions f(z) and g(z) are regular at the point* $z=a$, *then the function* $F(z)=f(z)/g(z)$ *is regular at the point* $z=a$ *or has a pole at this point.*

We introduce one more frequently encountered term.

We call a function that is regular in any closed region of the domain D, with the exception of a finite number of poles (they may be situated on the boundary of $\bar{D}$), a *meromorphic function in the domain D.*

We shall now consider essential singular points. Let us recall that an essential singular point is a singularity, single-valued character, and not a pole. One fact is clear from this definition: if $z=a$ is an essential singular point of the function $f(z)$ then $f(z)$ does not approach infinity as $z \longrightarrow a$. This does not imply at all that $f(z)$ is bounded in some neighborhood of the point a.

Theorem 3.2. *Let the point $z=a$ be an essential singular point of the function f(z). We set*

$$M(\varepsilon) = \max_{|z-a|=\varepsilon} |f(z)|.$$

Then for any k

$$\lim_{\varepsilon \to 0} \varepsilon^k M(\varepsilon) = \infty.$$

Proof. Let us assume the contrary. Then there exists a k such that

$$\lim_{\varepsilon \to 0} \varepsilon^k M(\varepsilon) < \infty.$$

We choose some integer $m > k$ and set

$$g(z) = (z-a)^m f(z), \qquad M_g(\varepsilon) = \max_{|z-a|=\varepsilon} |g(z)|.$$

It is clear that the function $g(z)$ is regular in the annulus and that

$$\lim_{\varepsilon \to 0} \varepsilon M_g(\varepsilon) = \lim_{\varepsilon \to 0} \varepsilon^{m+1} M(\varepsilon) = 0.$$

According to Theorem 2.1, the function $g(z)$ is regular at the point $z=a$ and, consequently, the function $f(z) = g(z)/(z-a)^m$, as we see from the lemma, has a pole at the point $z=a$ (or is regular there), contrary to hypothesis. This contradiction proves the theorem.

Thus, a function having an essential singularity at the point $z=a$ must approach infinity along *some* path leading to this point; however, the approach to infinity is not uniform along all paths, as in the case of a pole. A typical example is the point $z=\infty$ for the function e^z.

The behavior of a function in the neighborhood of an essential singularity can be very complicated. A special branch of the theory of analytic functions—the theory of entire functions—deals with problems involving functions having essential singularities.

Singular points that are limits of poles are very similar in their properties to essential singular points.

If the function $f(z)$ is meromorphic in the annulus $0 < |z-a| < r$ and has infinitely many poles in any neighborhood of the point $z=a$, then we call the point $z=a$ a singular point [of the function $f(z)$] that is, a *limit of poles.*

The following result is called Sokhotski's theorem.

Theorem 3.3. *If the point $z=a$ is an essential singular point of the function f(z) limit (in particular, a point of poles of the function f(z)) then in any neighborhood of the point $z=a$ the function f(z) assumes values arbitrarily close to any given number A.*

Proof. Let us assume the contrary. Then there exist numbers $\delta>0$, $\varrho>0$ and A such that $|f(z)-A|>\delta$ for all z satisfying the condition $|z-a|<\varrho$. Then the function $g(z)=1/f(z)-A$ is regular and bounded in the annulus $0<|z-a|<\varrho$. According to Theorem 2.1, the function $g(z)$ is regular in the circle $|z-a|<\varrho$ and, on the other hand:

$$f(z)=A+\frac{1}{g(z)}.$$

It follows from the lemma that the function $f(z)$ either has a pole at $z=a$ or is regular there. This contradicts the hypothesis that $z=a$ is an essential singular point, and thus proves the theorem.

Let us now consider isolated singular points of a many-valued character. They are also called isolated branch points.

Let $F(z)$ be a function that is analytic in the annulus $<|z-a|<r$. If $F(z)$ is not a regular function in this annulus (i.e., if $F(z)$ is many-valued), then we shall say that the point $z=a$ is an *isolated branch point.*

If the number of distinct elements of $F(z)$ at each point of the annulus $0<|z-a|<r$ is finite and equals n, then we shall call the isolated branch point $z=a$ a *branch point of order n.* If the number of distinct elements of $F(z)$ at each point of the annulus is infinite, then we shall call the isolated branch point a *logarithmic branch point.*

The study of branch points of finite order may be reduced to the study of isolated singular points of single-valued character by means of the following theorem:

Theorem 3.4. *Let F(z) be an analytic function in the annulus $r<|z-a|<R$. If F(z) has n distinct elements at each point of the annulus, then $F(z)=\varphi(\sqrt[n]{z-a})$, where $\varphi(\zeta)$ is a regular function in the annulus $\sqrt[n]{r}<|\zeta|<\sqrt[n]{R}$.*

Proof. We first introduce a cross cut along some radius into the annulus $r<|z-a|<R$. Then the analytic function $F(z)$ may be divided into n regular branches

$$F_1(z), \dots, F_n(z).$$

We next index these branches in such a way that analytic continuation across the cut from right to left changes $F_k(z)$ into $F_{k+1}(z)$ (for $1\leqslant k\leqslant n-1$). Thus, $F_n(z)$ must turn into $F_1(z)$ under continuation.

Let us now study the function $\varphi(\zeta)=F(a+\zeta^n)$. It is an analytic function in the annulus $\sqrt[n]{r}<|\zeta|<\sqrt[n]{R}$, since any point ζ in this annulus corresponds to a point $z=a+\zeta^n$ contained in the annulus

$r<|z-a|<R$. We wish to prove that the function $\varphi(\zeta)$ is regular in its own annulus. To do this we must verify that analytic continuation of any element $\varphi(\zeta)$ along any path contained in the annulus leads back to the original element. According to Theorem 3.2 of Chap. III, the result of analytic continuation along two closed curves starting from point ζ_0 is the same, if the two curves make the same number of circuits in the positive direction around the hole in the annulus. Therefore, we may carry out the continuation along the most convenient closed curve. It is most simple to carry out the continuation along the circle $|\zeta|=|\zeta_0|$. Let us determine the behavior of the point $z=a+\zeta^n$ as the point ζ traces out the circle $|\zeta|=|\zeta_0|$ in the positive direction. We set $\zeta=|\zeta_0|e^{i\theta}$. During the circuit, θ increases monotonically from 0 to 2π. Moreover, $z-a=|\zeta_0|^n e^{in\theta}$. As θ increases monotonically from 0 to 2π, the point z makes a circuit of the circle $|z-a|=|\zeta_0|^n$ in the positive direction n times. Thus, one circuit by the point ζ along the circle $|\zeta|=|\zeta_0|$ corresponds to n circuits by the point z around the circle $|z-a|=|\zeta_0|^n$. However, we know that after n circuits by the point z of the circle $|z-a|=\varrho$, the element of the function $F(z)$ returns to its original value. Consequently, the element of the function $\varphi(\zeta)$ returns to its original value after one circuit. This means that the function $\varphi(\zeta)$ is single-valued and therefore regular in its annulus, which proves the theorem.

If the point $z=a$ is a branch point of order n of the analytic function $F(z)$ in the annulus $0<|z-a|<r$ and if the function $\varphi(\zeta)=F(a+\zeta^n)$ is regular at the point $\zeta=0$ or has a pole there, then we say that the point $z=a$ is an *algebraic singular point* of the function $F(z)$ analytic in the annulus.

This name is explained by the fact that algebraic functions, i.e., roots of polynomials whose coefficients are rational functions, have only such singularities.

Let us enumerate the singular points of the elementary functions.

The functions e^z, $\sin z$, $\cos z$ are regular in the entire finite plane. The point $z=\infty$ is an essential singularity for these functions. In fact, none of these functions approaches ∞ as $z\to\infty$ ($\sin z$ and $\cos z$ are bounded along the real axis, e^z along the imaginary axis).

The functions $\tan z$, $\cot z$, $\sec z$, $\operatorname{cosec} z$ are meromorphic in the entire finite plane, since they are ratios of functions that are regular in the entire finite plane. The point $z=\infty$ is a limit point of poles for these functions.

The function $\ln z$ has logarithmic branch points at $z=0$ and $z=\infty$. The function $\sqrt[n]{z}$ has branch points of order n at the points $z=0$ and $z=\infty$.

The function z^α has branch points of finite order at the points $z=0$ and $z=\infty$ for real rational α, and for all other values of α has logarithmic branch points there.

The function $\arctan z$ has logarithmic branch points at the points $z=i$ and $z=-i$ (see Example 2, Sect. 2, Chap. III).

The function $\arcsin z$ has branch points of second order at $z=1$ and $z=-1$, and has a logarithmic branch point at $z=\infty$ (see Example 2, Sect. 5, Chap. III).

Euler's gamma function $\Gamma(z)$ is meromorphic in the entire finite plane. The point $z=\infty$ is a limit point of poles (see Example 2, Sect. 5, Chap. II).

4. RESIDUES AND LAURENT SERIES

The first problem that gave rise to the theory of analytic functions as a separate branch of analysis was the problem of evaluation of the integral along any closed contour of a function regular inside the contour except at a finite number of poles. The advantages of the study of the properties of regular functions became fully apparent in treating this problem. The complicated process of evaluating integrals with the help of these properties was reduced to finding so-called residues. In their turn the residues were easily calculated by means of differentiation. For this reason a great deal of attention was devoted to methods of reduction of various problems to contour integration. The collection of these methods received the name of the theory of residues.

Before we define the notion of residue, let us prove one rather simple lemma.

Lemma 1. *If the function F(z) is regular in the annulus*

$$r<|z-a|<R,$$

then the integral

$$\int_{|z-a|=\varrho} F(z)\,dz, \qquad r<\varrho<R,$$

does not depend on ϱ.

Proof. Let $r<\varrho_1<\varrho_2<R$. The difference of the integrals of $F(z)$ along the circles $|z-a|=\varrho_1$ and $|z-a|=\varrho_2$ can be studied as the integral of $F(z)$ along the boundary of the annulus contained between these two circles. According to Cauchy's theorem, this integral is zero, since this annulus lies within the annulus of regularity of the function $F(z)$. This proves the lemma.

Now it is possible to give the definition of residue.

Let the function $f(z)$ have an isolated singular point of single-valued character at the point $z=a$ (or be regular at the point $z=a$). If a is finite, we shall say that the *residue of the function f(z) at the point* $z=a$ is the quantity*

$$\operatorname*{res}_{z=a} f(z)=\frac{1}{2\pi i}\int_{|z-a|=\varrho} f(z)\,dz$$

(ϱ is any sufficiently small positive number). If $a=\infty$,

---

*The notation res is taken from the french word residu.

$$\operatorname*{res}_{z=\infty} f(z) = -\frac{1}{2\pi i} \int_{|z|=R} f(z)\, dz$$

(R is any sufficiently large positive number).

The independence of the integral from ϱ (or from R) follows from Lemma 1. If $a \neq \infty$ and $f(z)$ is regular at the point $z=a$, then by Cauchy's theorem $\operatorname*{res}_{z=a} f(z)=0$. However, the residue at the point at infinity may turn out to be different from zero even for a function which is regular at infinity (example: $f(z)=1/z$).

It is not difficult to modify the definition of residue so that the point $z=\infty$ does not play a special role:

We say that the residue of the function $f(z)$ at the point $z=a$ is the integral (divided by $2\pi i$) of $f(z)$ along the boundary of some sufficiently small neighborhood of the point $z=a$. (The function is assumed to be regular in some neighborhood of the point $z=a$, except perhaps at the point itself.)

The equivalence of the two definitions becomes immediately clear, if we recall that we agreed to choose the direction of integration along the boundary of a domain so that the domain remained on the left and the circumference $|z|=R$ is taken as the boundary of the circle $|z|<R$ (unless otherwise stipulated).

The following statement is called the *residue theorem*

Theorem 4.1. *Let the function f(z) be regular in the domain D and continuous up to its boundary, with the exception of a finite number of points* $z_k \in D$ $(k=1, 2, \ldots, n)$, *that are isolated singular points of single-valued character. Then (C is the boundary of the domain D)*

$$\int_C f(z)\, dz = 2\pi i \sum_{k=1}^{n} \operatorname*{res}_{z=z_k} f(z).$$

(We assume that the point $z=\infty$ does not lie in the domain D. If the point $z=\infty$ does lie in D, then it must be one of the points z_k.)

Proof. Let $G_\varepsilon(z_k)$ denote the circle $|z-z_k|<\varepsilon$ for $z_k \neq \infty$, and the set $|z|>1/\varepsilon$ for $z_k=\infty$. Let Γ_k be the boundary of $G_\varepsilon(z_k)$. According to the definition of residue, for sufficiently small ε we have

$$\int_{\Gamma_k} f(z)\, dz = 2\pi i \operatorname*{res}_{z=z_k} f(z). \tag{4.1}$$

We choose $\varepsilon>0$ so small that all $G_\varepsilon(z_k)$ are contained within the domain D and we let D_ε denote the domain obtained from D by removing all the $G_\varepsilon(z_k)$. The domain D_ε is finite and the function $f(z)$ is regular in D_ε and continuous up to its boundary. According to Cauchy's theorem, the integral of $f(z)$ along the boundary of D_ε is zero. However, the boundary of D_ε consists of the boundary of the domain D and the boundaries of the domains $G_\varepsilon(z_k)$, traversed in the positive direction. Thus,

$$\int_C f(z)\, dz - \sum_{1}^{n} \int_{\Gamma_k} f(z)\, dz = 0.$$

If we now insert (4.1), we obtain the statement of the theorem.

Thus, the problem of evaluating integrals reduces to the problem of finding residues. Now we shall prove that if all the singular points of $f(z)$ are poles, then finding the residues simply reduces to differentiation.

Theorem 4.2. Let $F(z)=\frac{f(z)}{g(z)}$, *where the functions* $f(z)$ *and* $g(z)$ *are regular at the point* $z=a$ *and* $g(z)$ *has a zero of order* n *at the point* $z=a$. *Then*

$$\operatorname*{res}_{z=a} F(z)=\lim_{z\to a}\left\{\frac{1}{(n-1)!}\frac{d^{n-1}}{dz^{n-1}}[(z-a)^n F(z)]\right\}.$$

Proof. Since the function $g(z)$ has a zero of order n at the point $z=a$, then it can be presented in the form $g(z)=(z-a)^n g_1(z)$ where $g_1(a)\neq 0$. Thus, $F(z)=\frac{\varphi(z)}{(z-a)^n}$, where the function $\varphi(z)=\frac{f(z)}{g_1(z)}$ is regular at the point $z=a$. According to the definition of residue

$$\operatorname*{res}_{z=a} F(z)=\frac{1}{2\pi i}\int_{|z-a|=\rho} F(z)\,dz=\frac{1}{2\pi i}\int_{|z-a|=\rho}\frac{\varphi(z)}{(z-a)^n}\,dz,$$

and the last integral equals $\frac{1}{(n-1)!}\varphi^{(n-1)}(a)$ on the basis of the formula for higher derivatives (see Sect. 3 of Chap. II). Since $\varphi(z)=(z-a)^n F(z)$ for $z\neq a$, we arrive at the statement of the theorem.

Remark. If the function $g(z)$ has a zero of first order at the point $z=a$, then the formula for the residue acquires the especially simple form

$$\operatorname*{res}_{z=a}\frac{f(z)}{g(z)}=\frac{f(a)}{g'(a)}.$$

The above formula is not suitable for finding the residue at the point at infinity. It is also not valid when the point $z=a$ is an essential singularity of the function $F(z)$. We must use an expansion in Laurent series in these cases. Moreover, it is often convenient to use an expansion in a Laurent series for finding the residues at poles located at points in the finite plane.

First, we must prove a general theorem on the expansion of functions in a Laurent series:

Theorem 4.3. *The function* $f(z)$, *regular in the annulus* $r<|z-a|<R$, *can be expanded in the series*

$$f(z)=\sum_{-\infty}^{\infty} c_n(z-a)^n,$$

where

$$c_n=\frac{1}{2\pi i}\int_{|z-a|=\rho} f(z)(z-a)^{-n-1}\,dz \qquad (r<\rho<R),$$

which converges uniformly in z *in any interior annulus.*

Proof. Let $r_1 \leqslant |z-a| \leqslant R_1$, $r_1 > r$, $R_1 < R$. We take $r < r_2 < r_1$, $R_1 < R_2 < R$ and let C denote the boundary of the annulus $r_2 < |\zeta - a| < R_2$. According to Cauchy's integral formula,

$$f(z) = \frac{1}{2\pi i} \int\limits_C \frac{f(\zeta)\, d\zeta}{\zeta - z} \qquad (r_2 < |z-a| < R_2),$$

or

$$f(z) = \frac{1}{2\pi i} \int\limits_{|\zeta - a| = R_2} \frac{f(\zeta)\, d\zeta}{\zeta - z} - \frac{1}{2\pi i} \int\limits_{|\zeta - a| = r_2} \frac{f(\zeta)\, d\zeta}{\zeta - z}. \tag{4.2}$$

The series

$$\frac{1}{\zeta - z} = \sum_0^{\infty} \frac{(z-a)^n}{(\zeta - a)^{n+1}} \qquad (|\zeta - a| = R_2, \quad |z-a| \leqslant R_1)$$

and

$$\frac{1}{\zeta - z} = -\sum_0^{\infty} \frac{(\zeta - a)^n}{(z-a)^{n+1}} \qquad (|\zeta - a| = r_2, \quad |z-a| \geqslant r_1)$$

are uniformly convergent in z and ζ under the conditions indicated in parentheses. If we substitute the first series in the first integral formula, the second series in the second integral formula and integrate term by term, we obtain

$$f(z) = \sum_0^{\infty} c_n (z-a)^n + \sum_0^{\infty} c_n' (z-a)^{-n-1},$$

where

$$c_n = \frac{1}{2\pi i} \int\limits_{|\zeta - a| = R_2} f(\zeta) (\zeta - a)^{-n-1}\, d\zeta,$$

$$c_n' = \frac{1}{2\pi i} \int\limits_{|\zeta - a| = r_2} f(\zeta) (\zeta - a)^n\, d\zeta.$$

Setting $c_n' = c_{-n-1}$, we combine the two sums. According to Lemma 1, the integrals in the formulas for the coefficients can be taken along any circumference $|\zeta - a| = \varrho$, $r < \varrho < R$. This proves the theorem.

If the point $z = a$ is an isolated singular point of single-valued character for the function $f(z)$, then $f(z)$ is regular in some annulus $0 < |z-a| < r$ and can be expanded in a Laurent series that converges in this annulus. This series is called a *Laurent series for the function f(z) in a neighborhood of the point* $z = a$.

We say that a *Laurent series for the function f(z) at the point at infinity* is a series of the form

$$f(z) = \sum_{-\infty}^{\infty} c_n z^n \qquad (R < |z| < \infty).$$

The Laurent series consists of two series similar to the Taylor series; one in powers of $(z-a)$ and the other in powers of $1/z-a$.

If we have a Laurent series for the function $f(z)$ in a neighborhood of a finite point

$$f(z)=\sum_{-\infty}^{\infty} c_n(z-a)^n \qquad (0<|z-a|<r),$$

then the series

$$\sum_{-\infty}^{-1} c_n(z-a)^n \quad (|z-a|>0), \quad \sum_{0}^{\infty} c_n(z-a)^n \quad (|z-a|<r)$$

are called, respectively, the *principal part and the regular part of the Laurent series* for $f(z)$ in a neighborhood of the point $z=a$.

For a Laurent series in a neighborhood of the point at infinity the part of the series consisting of the terms with positive powers of z is called the *principal part.*

The principal part of the Laurent series for the function $f(z)$ in a neighborhood of the point $z=a$ is an elementary function having the same singularity as $f(z)$ at the point $z=a$. The principal part is regular in the entire plane with the exception of the point $z=a$, and the difference between $f(z)$ and its principal part is regular at the point $z=a$.

The application of expansion in Laurent series to finding residues is based on the following theorem:

Theorem 4.4. *If $z=a$ $(a\neq\infty)$ is an isolated singular point of single-valued character for the function f(z) and $\sum_{-\infty}^{\infty} c_n(z-a)^n$ is the expansion of f(z) in a Laurent series in a neighborhood of the point $z=a$, then*

$$\operatorname*{res}_{z=a} f(z)=c_{-1}.$$

If $\sum_{-\infty}^{\infty} c_n z^n$-is the expansion of f(z) in a Laurent series in a neighborhood of the point at infinity, then res $f(z)=-c_{-1}$.

Proof: Suppose that $a\neq\infty$. Integrating term by term, we find

$$\operatorname*{res}_{z=a} f(z)=\frac{1}{2\pi i}\int_{|z-a|=\varrho} f(z)\,dz=\sum_{-\infty}^{\infty}\frac{c_n}{2\pi i}\int_{|z-a|=\varrho}(z-a)^n\,dz.$$

To evaluate the integrals under the summation sign, we put $z=a+\varrho e^{i\theta}$, $0\leqslant\theta<2\pi$. Then $dz=i\varrho e^{i\theta}$ and we obtain

$$\int_{|z-a|=\varrho}(z-a)^n\,dz=i\varrho^{n+1}\int_0^{2\pi} e^{i(n+1)\theta}\,d\theta.$$

This last integral is 0 for $n \neq -1$ and 2π for $n = -1$. Thus, only one term remains from the entire summation and we obtain the statement of the theorem. The proof in the case $a = \infty$ is completely analogous.

If the expansion in a Laurent series can be obtained only with the aid of formulas for the coefficients, then Theorem 4.4 does not give us a method for finding residues. However, the expansion of a function in a Laurent series can be obtained from specially constructed expressions, for examples, with the aid of various operations on the Taylor series. For this it is necessary to use the following statement:

If the series $\sum_{-\infty}^{\infty} a_n (z-a)^n$ *and* $\sum_{-\infty}^{\infty} b_n (z-a)^n$ *converge uniformly on the circle* $|z-a| = \varrho$ *and converge there to the same sum, then the corresponding coefficients of these series are identical.*

In fact, after taking the difference between the two series, we obtain

$$\sum_{-\infty}^{\infty} (a_n - b_n)(z-a)^n = 0 \qquad (|z-a| = \varrho).$$

If we multiply this equality by $(z-a)^{-m-1}$ and integrate term by term, then on the basis of the same reasoning as that used in the proof of Theorem 4.4 we arrive at the equality $a_m - b_m = 0$.

Frequently, isolated singular points of single-valued character are classified according to the properties of the expansion of the function in a Laurent series in neighborhoods of these points. We suggest that the reader prove the following statement allowing us to arrive at this classification:

For the point $z = a$ *to be a pole of the function f(z) it is necessary and sufficient that the principal part of the Laurent series for the function f(z) in a neighborhood of the point* $z = a$ *be different from zero and consist of a finite number of terms.*

5. EXPANSION OF MEROMORPHIC FUNCTIONS IN SERIES OF PARTIAL FRACTIONS

We have already said that the theory of residues is the totality of methods for the reduction of various types of problems involving contour integration. In what follows we shall devote an entire chapter to the presentation of these methods, and here we shall restrict ourselves to the demonstration of one of them.

We shall speak of the problem of the expansion in a series of partial fractions of functions that are meromorphic in the entire finite plane. This problem has two aspects. The first aspect is the demonstration of the possibility of constructing functions that are meromorphic in the entire finite plane (or even in some domain) and that have poles at preassigned points and with preassigned principal parts of the Laurent series (in neighborhoods of these points). The theory of residues is not necessary for the solution of this problem. The second aspect is the determination of the expansion in series of partial fractions for the given meromorphic function. The solution of this problem gives us many new formulas for the elementary functions and these will also be of interest to us.

Let $P(z)$ be a proper rational function (the degree of the numerator is less than that of the denominator). It is proved in analysis that a rational function of this type can be written as a sum of partial fractions, i.e., fractions of the form

$$\frac{A_{m,k}}{(z-a_k)^m}.$$

The numbers a_k are the zeros of the denominator of the rational function.

If we use the terminology we introduced in the preceding section, then such an expansion takes on a very simple form. Each zero of the denominator is a pole of the rational function. Let us expand the functions in a Laurent series in a neighborhood of this pole and take the principal part of this expansion, which we shall denote $G(z;\ a_k)$. We have

$$G(z;\ a_k)=\sum_{m=1}^{m_k}\frac{A_{m,k}}{(z-a_k)^m}.$$

Expansion of the rational function $P(z)$ in partial fractions means that

$$P(z)=\sum_{k=1}^{n} G(z;\ a_k).$$

We will show that this statement can be carried over to many functions that are meromorphic in the entire plane. To make clear what requirement is to replace the requirement of proper rationality, let us note that a proper rational function approaches zero as $z\to\infty$.

Theorem 5.1. *Let the function f(z) be meromorphic in the entire finite plane, let the points* a_k $(k=1,2,\ldots)$ *be its poles, let* $G(z;\ a_k)$ *be the principal part of f(z) at the pole* $z=a_k$. *If there exists a sequence* $r_\nu\to+\infty$ *for which*

$$M(r_\nu)\to 0\ \ (\nu\to\infty),\quad M(r)=\max_{|z|=r}|f(z)|,$$

then

$$f(z)=\lim_{\nu\to\infty}\sum_{|a_k|<r_\nu} G(z;\ a_k).$$

The convergence to the limit is uniform in any finite domain not containing the point $z=a_k$.

Proof: Let us consider the integral

$$I_\nu(z)=\frac{1}{2\pi i}\int\limits_{|\zeta|=r_\nu}\frac{f(\zeta)\,d\zeta}{\zeta-z}\qquad (|z|<r_\nu).$$

If we estimate the modulus of the integral by the product of the maximum modulus of the integrand and the length of the path of integration, then we obtain

$$|I_\nu(z)|\leqslant\frac{r_\nu}{r_\nu-|z|}\cdot M(r_\nu),$$

from which it is clear that $I_\nu(z)\to 0$ as $\nu\to\infty$ uniformly in z in any finite domain.

On the other hand, the integral $I_\nu(z)$ can be evaluated with the help of the residue theorem. The integrand has poles in the circle $|\zeta|<r_\nu$ at the points $\zeta=a_k$ (for $|a_k|<r_\nu$) as well as at the point $\zeta=z$, so that

$$I_\nu(z)=\operatorname*{res}_{\zeta=z}\frac{f(\zeta)}{\zeta-z}+\sum_{|a_k|<r_\nu}\operatorname*{res}_{\zeta=a_k}\frac{f(\zeta)}{\zeta-z}.$$

It is clear that the residue at the point $\zeta=z$ equals $f(z)$ if $z\neq a_k$. We find the residue at the points $\zeta=a_k$. First,

$$\operatorname*{res}_{\zeta=a_k}\frac{f(\zeta)}{\zeta-z}=\operatorname*{res}_{\zeta=a_k}\frac{G(\zeta;\ a_k)}{\zeta-z}\qquad (z\neq a_k),$$

since according to the definition of the principal part the difference $f(\zeta)-G(\zeta,a_k)$ is regular at the point $\zeta=a_k$. To find the latter residue we consider the integral

$$U_R(z)=\frac{1}{2\pi i}\int\limits_{|\zeta|=R}G(\zeta;\ a_k)\frac{d\zeta}{\zeta-z}$$

for sufficiently large R (so large that both the points $\zeta=a_k$ and $\zeta=z$ lie within the circle $|\zeta|<R$). Since we have

$$G(\zeta;\ a_k)=O\left(\frac{1}{\zeta}\right),\qquad \frac{1}{\zeta-z}=O\left(\frac{1}{\zeta}\right),$$

as $U_R(z)$, then, again estimating the modulus of the integral by the product of the maximum modulus of the integrand and the length of the path of integration, we find that $U_R(z)=O(1/R)\to 0$ $(R\to\infty)$.

On the other hand, according to the residue theorem,

$$U_R(z)=\operatorname*{res}_{\zeta=z}\frac{G(\zeta;\ a_k)}{\zeta-z}+\operatorname*{res}_{\zeta=a_k}\frac{G(\zeta;\ a_k)}{\zeta-z}=G(z;\ a_k)+\operatorname*{res}_{\zeta=a_k}\frac{G(\zeta;\ a_k)}{\zeta-z}$$

and the rightmost term of the inequality does not depend on R. Thus,

$U_R(z)=0$ for sufficiently large R and

$$\operatorname*{res}_{\zeta=a_k} \frac{G(\zeta;\ a_k)}{\zeta - z} = -G(z,\ a_k) \qquad (z \neq a_k).$$

Thus,

$$I_\nu(z) = f(z) - \sum_{|a_k| < r_\nu} G(z;\ a_k) \qquad (z \neq a_k,\ |z| < r_\nu).$$

Since we showed that $I_\nu(z) \to 0$ uniformly in z as $\nu \to \infty$ in any finite domain, the theorem is proved.

The theorem just proved can be generalized to the case in which $f(z)$ does not approach zero on the sequence of circles $|z| = r_\nu$, but does not increase more quickly than some power of $|z|$. We shall not carry out this generalization, but shall restrict ourselves to the study of one specific example.

Example 1. We expand $\cot z$ in a series of partial fractions.

We studied the behavior of the function $\cot z$ for large z in article 4, Sect. 6, Chap. II. There we pointed out that the function $\cot z$ is bounded in the entire plane after removal of neighborhoods of the points $z = \pi k$ (k any integer), but that $\cot z$ does not converge to zero as $z \to \infty$. Therefore, we can apply Theorem 4.1, not to the function $\cot z$ itself, but to the function $\cot z/z$. For the sequence r_ν we can take $r_\nu = \pi(\nu + 1/2)$ $(\nu = 0, 1, 2, \ldots)$. Then Theorem 4.1 yields

$$\frac{\cot z}{z} = \lim_{\nu \to \infty} \sum_{-\nu}^{\nu} G(z;\ \pi k),$$

since the function $\cot z/z$ has poles at the points $a_k = k\pi$, $k = 0$, ± 1. We find now the principal parts $G(z;\ \pi k)$.

In a neighborhood of the point $z = 0$, we have

$$\frac{\cot z}{z} = \frac{\cos z}{z \sin z} = \frac{1 - \frac{z^2}{2} + \ldots}{z^2\left(1 - \frac{z^2}{6} + \ldots\right)} = \frac{1}{z^2} - \frac{1}{3} + \ldots,$$

i.e.,

$$G(z;\ 0) = \frac{1}{z^2}.$$

If for convenience we set $t = z - \pi k$, then in a neighborhood of the point $z = \pi k$, $k \neq 0$, we have

$$\frac{\cot z}{z} = \frac{\cos t}{(\pi k + t)\sin t} = \frac{1 - \frac{t^2}{2} + \ldots}{(\pi k + t)\left(t - \frac{t^3}{6} + \ldots\right)} = \frac{1}{\pi k t} - \frac{1}{\pi^2 k^2} + \ldots,$$

i.e.,

$$G(z;\ \pi k)=\frac{1}{\pi k\,(z-\pi k)} \qquad (k\neq 0).$$

Consequently,

$$\cot z = z \lim_{\nu\to\infty}\left\{\frac{1}{z^2}+\sum_{1}^{\nu}\frac{1}{\pi k\,(z-\pi k)}+\sum_{-1}^{-\nu}\frac{1}{\pi k\,(z-\pi k)}\right\},$$

or, combining the terms containing the numbers k and $-k$, we obtain

$$\cot z=\frac{1}{z}+\sum_{1}^{\infty}\frac{2z}{z^2-\pi^2k^2} \qquad (z\neq\pi k). \tag{5.1}$$

In addition, let us note that

$$\cot z=\frac{d}{dz}\ln\sin z$$

and

$$\ln\frac{\sin z}{z}=\int_0^z\left(\cot t-\frac{1}{t}\right)dt.$$

If we integrate the series (5.1) term by term (which is completely legitimate in view of its uniform convergence), we arrive at the formula

$$\sin z = z\prod_{1}^{\infty}\left(1-\frac{z^2}{\pi^2k^2}\right). \tag{5.2}$$

Analogous expansions in series of partial fractions and in infinite products can also be obtained for many other elementary functions.

6. THE ARGUMENT PRINCIPLE AND ROUCHE'S THEOREM

It is necessary in many cases to count the number of zeros of a regular function in a given domain. The general formula customarily used for this purpose is easily proved with the aid of the residue theorem.

Theorem 6.1. *Let the function f(z) be regular in the domain D and continuous up to its boundary C, with the exception of a finite number of poles. If the function f(z) does not vanish on C nor becomes infinite there, then*

$$\frac{1}{2\pi i}\int_C\frac{f'(z)}{f(z)}\,dz=\nu_f^{+}-\nu_f^{-}, \tag{6.1}$$

where ν_f^+ is the number of zeros and ν_f^- is the number of poles of the function f(z) in the domain D (both zeros and poles are counted as many times as their multiplicities).

Proof. The function $F(z) = f'(z)/f(z)$ is regular at all points of the domain D at which $f(z)$ is regular and different from zero. Thus, the function $F(z)$ has only isolated singular points in the domain D; moreover, they can only be at points where $f(z)$ has zeros or poles. It is even clear that the singular points of $F(z)$ must be poles, since $F(z)$ is the ratio of two meromorphic functions. The integral of interest to us equals the sum of the residues of $F(z)$ at these poles. We now find the residues.

Let us find the value of the residue $\operatorname*{res}_{z=a} \frac{f'(z)}{f(z)}$ when the function $f(z)$ has a zero of order n at the point $z = a$ (to avoid speaking separately about zeros and poles let us recall that a pole of order n is a zero of order $-n$). According to the definition of the order of a zero, we have

$$f(z) = (z-a)^n f_1(z),$$

where the function $f_1(z)$ is regular at the point $z = a$ and $f_1(a) \neq 0$. Consequently,

$$\frac{f'(z)}{f(z)} = \frac{n}{z-a} + \frac{f_1'(z)}{f_1(z)},$$

and the function $f_1'(z)/f_1(z)$ is regular at the point $z = a$. Thus the residue we seek is n.

If we now sum over all zeros and poles, we obtain the statement of the theorem.

Remark. We can use one of the two following formulas:

$$\nu_f^+ - \nu_f^- = \frac{1}{2\pi i} \operatorname*{var}_C \ln f(z), \tag{6.2}$$

$$\nu_f^+ - \nu_f^- = \frac{1}{2\pi} \operatorname*{var}_C \arg f(z) \tag{6.3}$$

in place of formula (6.1). Here var $F(z)$ means the variation of the function $F(z)$ (not necessarily single-valued in the domain D) under a single circuit of the boundary C of domain D in the positive direction. If the domain D is multiply connected, then C consists of several connected components; we then understand by var $F(z)$ the sum of the variations along each of these components.

To prove formulas (6.2) and (6.3), let us note that $\frac{f'(z)}{f(z)} = (\ln f(z))'$ and $\int_C (\ln f(z))'$ is exactly equal to the variation of the element of the analytic function $\ln f(z)$ under analytic continuation along the curve

C. Formula (6.3) is an immediate consequence of formula (6.2), if we recall that $\ln w = \ln|w| + i \arg w$ and note that the variation of $\ln|f(z)|$ along a closed contour equals zero, since the different values of $\ln w$ differ only by the pure imaginary term $2\pi i k$.

Formula (6.3) is called the *argument principle*.

We shall prove two more simple but useful theorems about the zeros of regular functions.

The following theorem is called *Rouché's theorem*.

Theorem 6.2. *Let the functions $F(z)$ and $f(z)$ be regular in the domain D and continuous up to its boundary C. If the inequality $|f(z)| < |F(z)|$ holds on the boundary of D; then the functions $F(z) + f(z)$ and $F(z)$ have the same number of zeros in the domain D. (Each zero is counted as many times as its multiplicity.)*

Proof. Since the functions $F(z)$ and $f(z)$ are regular in the domain D, they do not have poles there. It is clear from the inequality $|f(z)| < |F(z)|$, satisfied on C, that the functions $F(z)$ and $F(z)+f(z)$ do not vanish on C. Thus, applying formula (6.2), we can write

$$\nu_{F+f} = \frac{1}{2\pi i} \operatorname*{var}_{C} \ln [F(z) + f(z)] =$$
$$= \frac{1}{2\pi i} \operatorname*{var}_{C} \ln F(z) + \frac{1}{2\pi i} \operatorname*{var}_{C} \ln \left[1 + \frac{f(z)}{F(z)}\right] =$$
$$= \nu_F + \frac{1}{2\pi i} \operatorname*{var}_{C} \ln \left[1 + \frac{f(z)}{F(z)}\right].$$

When the point z makes a circuit of the curve C, the point $\zeta = 1 + f(z)/F(z)$ makes a circuit of some curve Γ contained in the circle $|\zeta - 1| < 1$ (since the condition $\left|\frac{f(z)}{F(z)}\right| < 1$) holds on C), and

$$\frac{1}{2\pi i} \operatorname*{var}_{C} \ln \left[1 + \frac{f(z)}{F(z)}\right] = \frac{1}{2\pi i} \operatorname*{var}_{\Gamma} \ln \zeta.$$

But the curve Γ is contained in the circle $|\zeta - 1| < 1$, so that it cannot make a circuit around the point $\zeta = 0$. Therefore, continuation of $\ln \zeta$ along Γ leads back to the original value, i.e., $\operatorname{var} \ln \zeta = 0$. Thus,

$\nu_{F+f} = \nu_F$, which proves the theorem.

Rouché's theorem plays approximately the same role in the theory of analytic functions as the theorem asserting that a continuous function having different signs at the endpoints of an interval must vanish on the interval, plays in analysis. We illustrate the use of Rouché's theorem by means of one well-known example.

Example 1. Let us show that the polynomial $P(z) = z^n + a_1 z^{n-1} + \ldots + a_n$ has exactly n zeros in the complex plane (the fundamental theorem of algebra).

The polynomial z^n has n zeros in the complex plane (the point $z=0$ is a zero multiplicity of n). Let us set $P(z) = F(z) + f(z)$, where $F(z) = z^n$, and $f(z) = a_1 z^{n-1} + \ldots + a_n$. As the domain D we choose the circle $|z| < R$, where R is taken so large that

$$|F(z)| > |f(z)| \qquad (|z| = R).$$

For example, it is sufficient to take

$$R = 1 + |a_1| + \ldots + |a_n|.$$

Then, according to Rouché's theorem, the number of zeros of $F(z)$ and $P(z)$ in the circle $|z| < R$ is the same, i.e., $P(z)$ has n roots.

Theorem 6.3. *Let the sequence of functions $f_n(z)$, regular in the domain G, converge uniformly to the nonconstant function f(z) in some closed subset of G. If each of the functions $f_n(z)$ is such that the function $f_n(z) - w$ has at most m zeros in the domain G for any w, then the limit function f(z) also enjoys this property.*

Proof. Let us assume the contrary. Then there exists an a such that the number of zeros of the function $f(z) - a$ in the domain G is at least $m+1$. Let us choose a domain D such that:

1. the domain D along with its boundary C is contained in the domain G;
2. the function $f(z) - a$ has no fewer than $m+1$ zeros in the domain D; and
3. the function $f(z) - a$ does not vanish on C.

Such a choice is possible since we assumed that the function $f(z)$ was not a constant.

According to Theorem 4.4 of Chap. II, it follows from the uniform convergence of the sequence $f_n(z)$ in any closed subset of G that the sequence $f'_n(z)$ converges uniformly on any closed subset of the domain G. The curve C is a closed subset of domain G; thus,

$$f_n(z) - a \longrightarrow f(z) - a, \qquad f'_n(z) \longrightarrow f'(z) \qquad (z \in C).$$

Therefore, all the functions $f_n(z) - a$, starting with some n, are nonzero on C and

$$\frac{1}{2\pi i}\int\limits_C \frac{f'_n(z)}{f_n(z) - a}\,dz \longrightarrow \frac{1}{2\pi i}\int\limits_C \frac{f'(z)}{f(z) - a}\,dz.$$

This means that $\nu_{f_n - a} \longrightarrow \nu_{f-a}$ as $n \longrightarrow \infty$. Since ν_{f_n-a} and ν_{f-a} are integers, it follows from this that $\nu_{f_n-a} = \nu_{f-a} > m$ for $n > N$, which contradicts the property of the functions $f_n(z)$ and thus proves the theorem.

7. IMPLICIT FUNCTIONS AND INVERSE FUNCTIONS

We said nothing in Chapter II about formulas for the differentiation of implicit and inverse functions. The reason for this was that we were not yet prepared for the study of the question of their existence. We are now able to take up this question.

First of all, we prove a general theorem on the existence of implicit functions.

Theorem 7.1. *Let the function $F(z, w)$ be defined in the domain $|z-a|<r$, $|w-b|<R$ and continuous as a function of two variables in this domain. Moreover, let the function $F(z, w)$ be regular in z in the circle $|z-a|<r$ for any w, $|w-b|<R$, and regular in w in the circle $|w-b|<R$ for any z, $|z-a|<r$. If $F(a, b)=0$ and $F'(a, b)\neq 0$, then there exists a unique function $w(z)$, continuous at the point $z=a$ and satisfying the conditions*

$$F(z, w(z))\equiv 0, \qquad w(a)=b.$$

This function $w(z)$ is regular at the point $z=a$ and

$$w'(z)=-\frac{F'_z(z, w(z))}{F'_w(z, w(z))}$$

for all z in some neighborhood of the point $z=a$.

Proof. We shall break up the proof into several steps.

1) Let us show that the function $F(z, w)$ is locally linear, i.e., that

$$F(z, w)=A(z-a)+B(w-b)+\varepsilon(z, w), \tag{7.1}$$

where A and B are some numbers and the function $\varepsilon(z, w)$ satisfies the condition

$$\varepsilon(z, w)=o(|z-a|+|w-b|) \qquad (z\to a,\ w\to b). \tag{7.2}$$

It is clear that $\varepsilon(z, w)$ is regular in w and z wherever $F(z, w)$ is.

Since the function $F(z, w)$ is regular in z in the circle $|z-a|<r$ for any w, then $(r_1<r)$

$$F(z, w)=\sum_{n=0}^{\infty} C_n(w)(z-a)^n, \quad C_n(w)=\frac{1}{2\pi i}\int\limits_{|z-a|=r_1}\frac{F(z, w)}{(z-a)^{n+1}}dz.$$

According to Theorem 4.3 of Chap. II, the coefficients $C_n(w)$ are regular functions of w in the circle $|w-b|<R$, since $F(z, w)$, is regular in w in this circle. Expanding the function $C_n(w)$ in a series of powers $w-b$, we obtain the double series

$$F(z, w)=\sum_{n=0}^{\infty}\sum_{k=0}^{\infty} c_{n,k}(z-a)^n(w-b)^k,$$

which is absolutely and uniformly convergent of r $|z-a|\leqslant r_1$, $|w-b|\leqslant R_1$, $r_1<r$, $R_1<R$. It is clear that the sum of all the terms of this series obtained by summing those of index greater than one is equal to

$$o(|z-a|+|z-b|) \qquad (z\to a,\ w\to b).$$

The constant term is zero, since $F(a, b) = 0$. Moreover, it is clear that

$$A = F'_z(a, b), \qquad B = F'_w(a, b).$$

2) Now we show that there exists numbers r_1, $0 < r_1 < r$ and R_1, $0 < R_1 < R$, such that for any z from the circle $|z - a| < r_1$ the equation $F(z, w) = 0$ has exactly one solution satisfying the inequality

$$|w(z) - b| < R_1. \tag{7.3}$$

We shall employ Rouché's theorem for this purpose (Theorem 6.2). We choose r_1 and R_1 in such a way that the summand $B(w - b)$ on the right-hand side of equality (7.1) has a greater modulus than the sum of the two others on the circle $|w - b| = R_1$ (for any z, $|z - a| < r_1$). To do this we choose r_1 and R_1 so that the conditions

$$\begin{aligned} & r_1 < R_1 \min\left(\frac{|B|}{2|A|},\ 1\right), \\ & \max_{|z-a| \leq r_1,\ |w-b| \leq R_1} |\varepsilon(z, w)| < \frac{|B|}{2} R_1 \end{aligned} \tag{7.4}$$

are satisfied. It is possible to satisfy these conditions because of (7.2) [recall that $B \neq 0$ according to the hypotheses of the theorem, since $B = F'_w(a, b)$].

We choose z in the circle $|z - a| < r_1$ and consider $F(z, w)$ as a function of w in the circle $|w - b| \leq R_1$. According to Rouché's theorem, the function $F(z, w)$ has as many roots in this circle as the summand $B(w - b)$, which, on the circumference of this circle, has a modulus greater than the sum of the two other terms. But the function $B(w - b)$ has in all one root: $w = b$. This means that the function $F(z, w)$ has exactly one root in the circle $|w - b| < R_1$. However, this root also satisfies the inequality (7.3). We shall denote this root by $w(z)$.

3) Next we prove the differentiability of the function $w(z)$ at the point $z = a$.

For this we have to estimate $w(z)$ somewhat more exactly. We again employ Rouché's theorem, first breaking up the function $F(z, w)$ into several different terms. It is clear that we obtain a sufficiently good approximation to the function $w(z)$ by equating the linear part of $F(z, w)$ to zero. Therefore, we set

$$w_0(z) = b - \frac{A}{B}(z - a)$$

($w = w_0(z)$ and is the root of the linear part of $F(z, w)$) and write $F(z, w)$ in the form

$$F(z, w) = B(w - w_0(z)) + \varepsilon(z, w).$$

We study $F(z, w)$ as a function of w on the circumference $C = C(z, \varepsilon)$ (in the w-plane), which has the equation

$$|w - w_0(z)| = \varepsilon |z-a|$$

(ε is a given positive number). We show that for z sufficiently close to a the term $B(w-w_0(z))$ has a modulus greater than that of the term $\varepsilon(z, w)$ on the circle C. According to (7.2), $\varepsilon(z, w) = o(|z-a| + |w-b|)$, and on the circle C we have $|w-b| < M|z-a|$ (M is any number). Therefore,

$$\varepsilon(z, w) = o(|z-a|) \quad (z \to a, \ w \in C(z, \varepsilon)).$$

We can thus find a $\delta > 0$ such that for $|z-a| < \delta$ and $w \in C$ we have

$$|\varepsilon(z, w)| < \varepsilon |B| |z-a|.$$

However, $|B(w-w_0(z))| = \varepsilon|B||z-a|$ for $w \in C$ and any z. Thus, the summand $B(w-w_0(z))$ has a greater modulus than the summand $\varepsilon(z, w)$ on the circumference C. According to Rouché's theorem, the function $F(z, w)$ has as many zeros inside C as the summand $B(w-w_0(z))$, i.e., exactly one zero. It is evident that this zero must approach b as $z \to a$, since for z sufficiently close to a the zero must coincide with $w(z)$ in view of the statement proved in the second step. In other words, the point $w = w(z)$ lies within the circumference C, which gives us the inequality

$$|w(z) - w_0(z)| < \varepsilon |z-a| \qquad (|z-a| < \delta)$$

or, upon replacing $w_0(z)$ by the expression it denotes, we find

$$\left| \frac{w(z)-b}{z-a} + \frac{A}{B} \right| < \varepsilon \qquad (|z-a| < \delta).$$

Since $\varepsilon > 0$ is arbitrary, this inequality means that the function $w(z)$ is differentiable at the point $z = a$ and that

$$w'(a) = -\frac{A}{B} = -\frac{F'_z(a, b)}{F'_w(a, b)}.$$

4) We prove next that $w(z)$ is regular at the point $z = a$.

To do this we prove that the function $w(z)$ is differentiable not only at the point $z = a$, but in an entire neighborhood of this point. Since the function $w(z)$ is continuous at the point $z = a$, we can choose a_1 so close to a that $b_1 = w(a_1)$ is so close to b that for all z in the circle $|z-a| < 2|a_1 - a|$ the equation $F(z, w) = 0$ has exactly one root contained in the circle $|w-b| < 2|b_1 - b|$ (see the second step of the proof) and, moreover, the inequality

$$F'_w(a_1, b_1) \neq 0$$

is satisfied. Thus, the conditions of the theorem are satisfied after replacement of (a, b) by (a_1, b_1), and the solution of the equation $F(z, w) = 0$, satisfying the condition $w(a_1) = b_1$, is always the function

$w(z)$. We may deduce from this that the function $w(z)$ is differentiable at the point $z = a_1$. Since $z = a_1$ is any point sufficiently close to the point $z = a$, the function $w(z)$ is regular at the point $z = a$ (in view of the equivalence of regularity and differentiability in a domain).

The theorem is now completely proved.

Applying Theorem 7.1 to a special form of the equation, in which

$$F(z, w) = \varphi(w) - z,$$

we immediately obtain a theorem about the inverse function:

Theorem 7.2. *Let the function* $\varphi(w)$ *be regular at the point* $w = b$. *If* $\varphi'(b) \neq 0$, *then there exists a unique function* $w(z)$, *continuous at the point* $a = \varphi(b)$ *and satisfying the conditions*

$$\varphi(w(z)) \equiv z, \qquad w(a) = b.$$

The function $w(z)$ is regular at the point $z = a$ and $w'(a) = 1/\varphi'(b)$.

Thus, we have solved locally the question of the existence of an implicit function. Naturally, the question arises of how to represent the totality of solutions of the equation $F(z, w) = 0$. In the case of the equation of general form, this totality may consist of a collection of unrelated analytic functions, as is shown by the example of the equation $w^2 - z^2 = 0$. The situation is the same for the equation $\varphi(w) = z$.

Let $\varphi(w)$ be an analytic function. Each of its elements $\varphi_b(w)$ for which $\varphi_b'(b) \neq 0$ corresponds, according to Theorem 7.2, to a function $w_a(z)$, is regular in a neighborhood of the point $z = a$, where $a = \varphi_b(b)$. The class of functions $w_a(z)$ coincides, as we now show, with the collection of all elements of some analytic function $w(z)$, which we naturally call the analytic function inverse to the analytic function $\varphi(w)$.

In order to determine an analytic function we must:

1. give the initial element;
2. describe all paths along which the initial element can be analytically continued.

The intial element given to us is $w_a(z)$. As the point z moves along the path C, the point $w = w_a(z)$ describes the path Γ. For each point $c \in \Gamma$ we have an element $\varphi_c(w)$ and an element $w_{\varphi(c)}(z)$ corresponding to it. It is clear that if the points c and c' are sufficiently close, then the elements $w_{\varphi(c)}(z)$ and $w_{\varphi(c')}(z)$ will coincide. This makes it possible for us to construct the analytic continuation of the initial element along the curve. Clearly, the curve C must satisfy the following conditions:

It must be possible to continue the function $\varphi(w)$ analytically along the curve Γ and the curve Γ must not contain any points c at which $\varphi_c'(c) = 0$.

Thus, we have obtained a description of all the curves along which it is possible to continue the initial element $w_a(z)$ analytically.

Since it is possible to obtain a curve C by giving the curve Γ, and the curve Γ can be chosen so that we can reach any element of the analytic function $\varphi(w)$, then any element $w_{a'}(z)$ can be obtained from the element $w_a(z)$ by analytic continuation along some curve.

We can also obtain a representation of the inverse function in a neighborhood of the point $z=a$, $a=\varphi(b)$, where $\varphi'(b)=0$.

Theorem 7.3. *Let the function $\varphi(w)$ be regular at the point $w=b$, and let the function $\varphi'(w)$ have a zero of order $n-1$ at the point $w=b$. Moreover, let $w_1(z)$ be a solution of the equation $\varphi(w)=z$ which is regular at the point a_1, close to $a=\varphi(b)$. If under continuation along the curve C starting from the point a_1 to the point a we have $w_1(z)\to b$ $(z\to a,\ z\in C)$, then analytic continuation of the solution $w_1(z)$ gives us an analytic function $w(z)=g(\sqrt[n]{z-a})$ in this neighborhood. Here the function $g(\zeta)$ is regular in a neighborhood of the point $\zeta=0$ and $g'(0)\neq 0$.*

Proof. Since the function $\varphi'(w)$ has a zero of order $n-1$ at the point $w=b$, the function $\varphi(w)-a$ $(a=\varphi(b))$ has a zero of order n at the point $w=b$ and it can be written in the form

$$\varphi(w)-a=(w-b)^n\psi(w), \qquad \psi(b)\neq 0,\ \infty.$$

Therefore, we can write the equation $\varphi(w)=z$ in the form

$$(w-b)^n\psi(w)=z-a$$

or, taking nth roots of both sides, in the form

$$\theta(w)=\sqrt[n]{z-a} \qquad (\theta(w)=(w-b)\sqrt[n]{\psi(w)})$$

(we choose the branch of the root so that the function $w_1(z)$ satisfies the new equation for $z\in C$). We put

$$\zeta=\sqrt[n]{z-a}$$

and apply Theorem 7.2 to the equation $\theta(w)=\zeta$ with $a'=\theta(b)=0$. This is possible because $\theta'(b)=\psi(b)\neq 0,\infty$. We find that the solution has the form $w=g(\zeta)$, where the function $g(\zeta)$ is regular at the point $\zeta=0$ and $g'(0)=1/\theta'(0)\neq 0$. Thus, $w=g(\sqrt[n]{z-a})$. For points of the curve C that are sufficiently close to the point $z=a$ the solution must coincide with the solution $w_1(z)$. This proves the theorem.

It is clear from the theorem just proved that the points $a=\varphi(b)$ are singular points of the inverse function, if $\varphi'(b)=0$. According to our classification, these singular points are branch points of finite order n, if the point $w=b$ is a zero of order $n-1$ for the function $\varphi'(w)$.

Corollary. Let the function $\varphi(w)$ be regular at the point $w=b$ and let the function $\varphi'(w)$ have a zero of order $w=b$ at the point $n-1$. Then for all z sufficiently close to $a=\varphi(b)$ the equation $\varphi(w)=z$ has exactly n solutions contained in any given neighborhood of the point $w=b$.

We can carry out an investigation of the singular points of the function $w(z)$, defined by some other implicit equation, in an analogous way. It is evident that the singular points must be sought among the solutions of the system of equations

$$F(z, w) = 0, \qquad F'_w(z, w) = 0.$$

Solutions of such a system are pairs of numbers (z_k, w_k). The first denotes the point of the plane, the second selects the branch of the analytic function for which this point may turn out to be a singular point. Both singular points and nonsingular points may be situated above the same point of the plane (see Example 3, Sect 5, Chap. III).

CHAPTER V

Conformal Mappings

We have already pointed out that any function of a complex variable can be considered as a mapping of one complex plane into another. A great deal of attention is devoted to the study of completely regular functions. The reason for this is that many problems from the theory of analytic functions can be solved according to the following procedure: first, solve the problem for the simplest possible type of domain; then express the desired solution in terms of the one already found with the aid of a mapping. It is necessary that the function to be mapped be regular so that the character of the problem will not be changed under the mapping. We shall make use of this method in Chapter VIII and again after that; in the present chapter we shall discuss the basic properties of mappings.

1. GENERAL INFORMATION ABOUT MAPPINGS

Let us begin by recalling some terminology.

Let the function of a complex variable $f(z)$ be defined in the domain D, and let E be some subset of D. We call the set E' consisting of the values w taken on by the function $f(z)$ in the set E, the *image of the set* E under the mapping $w=f(z)$ and we denote it by $E'=f(E)$. The set E is called a *preimage of the set* E' under the mapping $w=f(z)$.

In the sequel we shall study only *continuous mappings*, i.e., the function $f(z)$ will be assumed to be continuous. Moreover, the continuity is understood to be on the Riemann sphere, i.e., points z_1 and z_2 that are close to one another on the Riemann sphere must correspond to values of the function $f(z_1)$ and $f(z_2)$ that are also close to one another on the Riemann sphere. In particular we assume that the function $f(z)$ is defined at infinity.

The image of a closed set E under a continuous mapping is again a closed set [since a closed set on the Riemann sphere is compact (Ed.)]; however, the image of an open set does not have to be an open set, as is shown by the example of the mapping of the circle $|z| < 1$ by the function which equals z for $\operatorname{Im} z > 0$ and equals $\bar{z}$ for $\operatorname{Im} z < 0$. We shall be most interested in one-to-one mappings.

If the function $f(z)$ takes on different values at distinct points of the set E, then we say that the function $f(z)$ is *univalent on the set E* and that the mapping $w = f(z)$ is *one-to-one mapping* from the set E to the set $E' = f(E)$.

We shall frequently employ the following two obvious criteria in order to show that a function $f(z)$ is univalent:

In order that the function f(z) be univalent in the domain E it is necessary and sufficient that there exist a function $\varphi(w)$ *which is continuous on the set E' = F(E) and is inverse to f(z), i.e., is such that*

$$\varphi(f(z)) = z \qquad (z \in E) \text{ and } f(\varphi(w)) = w \qquad (w \in E').$$

If the function $F(z)$ is univalent on the set E and the function $f(z)$ is univalent on the set $f(E)$, then the function $F(f(z))$ is univalent on the set E.

Let us now turn to the mappings of regular functions.

Theorem 1.1. *Let the function* $f(z)$ *be regular in the domain D. Let* G_m *denote the set of its values w for which the equation* $f(z) = w$ *has no fewer than m solutions in the domain D. Then* G_m *is an open set.*

Proof. We must show that all points sufficiently close to a point $w_0 \in G_m$ also lie in G_m. Let the function $f(z)$ take on the value w_0 at the points $z_s \in D$ with multiplicity m_s $(s = 1, 2, \ldots, k)$ and $\sum_1^k m_s \geqslant m$. The function $f(z) - w_0$ has a zero of multiplicity m_s at the point $z = z_s$ so that the function $f'(z)$ will have a zero of mulitplicity $m_s - 1$ at the point $z = z_s$. If we apply the corollary to Theorem 7.3 of Chapt. IV, the we see that the function $f(z) - w$ has m_s zeros in a given neighborhood of the point z_s for all w sufficiently close to w_0. If we choose a neighborhood (of the point z_s) that is completely contained in D, then it is clear that the function $f(z) - w$ has not less than $\sum_1^k m_s \geqslant m$ zeros in D (for w sufficiently close to w_0). Thus, all the values of w sufficiently close to w_0 lie in G_m, which proves the theorem.

Corollary. The image of a domain under a mapping by a regular function is again a domain.

First of all, it follows from the theorem just proved that the image of the domain is an open set. The connectedness of the image is an easy consequence of the continuity of the mapping.

Let us now turn to the properties of one-to-one mappings given in terms of regular functions. In addition to mappings given by regular functions, we intend to study mappings given by meromorphic functions (i.e., we shall allow the function to have poles). It will be assumed that the image under the mapping $w=f(z)$ of the point $z=a$ at which $f(z)$ has a pole will be the point $w=\infty$.

We say that the function $f(z)$ is *univalent at the point* $z=a$, if there exists a domain D containing the point $z=a$ and in which $f(z)$ is univalent.

Theorem 1.2. *For the function f(z) that is regular at the point* $z=a\ (a\neq\infty)$ *to be univalent at this point it is necessary and sufficient that* $f'(a)\neq 0$.

The proof is an immediate consequence of the corollary to Theorem 7.3 of Chap. IV.

This criterion may be easily converted to one applying in the cases in which $a=\infty$ or the function $f(z)$ has a pole at the point $z=a$. To do this it is sufficient to note that the function $\zeta=\frac{1}{z}$ represents a one-to-one mapping of a neighborhood of the point $z=a$, into a neighborhood of the point $\zeta=0$. Applying the transformation to the independent variable and to the function, respectively, we find:

Corollary 1. For the function

$$f(z)=c_0+\frac{c_1}{z}+\frac{c_2}{z^2}+\dots \qquad (|z|>R),$$

which is regular at the point $z=\infty$, *to be univalent at this point it is necessary and sufficient that* $c_1\neq 0$.

Corollary 2. For the function f(z) having a pole at the point z = a to be univalent at this point it is necessary and sufficient that this pole be a pole of first order.

Remark. For the function $f(z)$ to be univalent in the domain D it is necessary (but not sufficient!) that the function $f(z)$ be univalent at each point of the domain.

The function $f(z)=e^z$ serves as an example of a function that is univalent at each point of the finite plane but is not univalent in the entire finite plane.

It is considerably more dificult to test for the univalence of a function in a domain than to test for it at a point. For regular functions, in addition to the criteria presented at the beginning of the section, there is one more criterion, called the *principle of corresponding boundaries*.

Theorem 1.3. *Let D and G be finite, simply connected domains bounded by the closed, piecewises smooth curves C and Γ, respectively. Furthermore, let the function f(z) be regular in the domain D and continuous up to its boundary. If, as the point z moves in the positive direction along the curve C, the point w = f(z) moves in the positive direction along the curve Γ, and if one circuit of C* *corresponds to one circuit of* Γ, *then the mapping* $w=f(z)$ *is a one-to-one mapping of the domain D onto the domain G.*

Proof. We have to show that the function $f(z)$ is univalent in the domain D and that $f(D)=G$.

Let $\nu(\zeta)$ denote the number of zeros of the function $f(z)-\zeta$ in the domain D. Univalence of $f(z)$ in D means that $\nu(\zeta)\leqslant 1$ for all ζ. We single out three possibilities for ζ: $\zeta\in G$, $\zeta\bar{\in}\bar{G}$ and $\zeta\in\Gamma$. We do not need to consider the possibility $\zeta\in\Gamma$, since the set of values of ζ for which $\nu(\zeta)\geqslant 2$, according to Theorem 1.1, is an open set, i.e., consists only of interior points, whereas the curve Γ is a closed set none of whose points are interior points. According to the hypothesis of the theorem, the set of values ζ assumed by the function $f(z)$ on the curve C coincides with the curve Γ. Therefore, if $\zeta\bar{\in}\Gamma$, then the function $f(z)-\zeta$ does not vanish on C. Applying the argument principle (see formula (6.3), Chap. IV), we find:

$$\nu(\zeta)=\frac{1}{2\pi}\operatorname*{var}_{C}\arg[f(z)-\zeta].$$

According to the hypothesis of the theorem, the point $w=f(z)$ makes one circuit of the curve Γ in the positive direction as the point z makes one circuit of the curve C in the positive direction. This means that

$$\nu(\zeta)=\frac{1}{2\pi}\operatorname*{var}_{C}\arg[f(z)-\zeta]=\frac{1}{2\pi}\operatorname*{var}_{\Gamma}\arg(w-\zeta).$$

According to the argument principle, this last expression equals the number of zeros of the function $w-\zeta$ in the domain G. This number is zero if $\zeta\bar{\in}\bar{G}$ and one if $\zeta\in G$. Thus, $\nu(\zeta)\leqslant 1$ for $\zeta\bar{\in}\Gamma$, and, thus, on the basis of what was said at the beginning of the proof, for all ζ.

Note that in addition to the univalence of the function $f(z)$ in the domain D, we have also proved that $\nu(\zeta)=0$ for $\zeta\bar{\in}\bar{G}$. This means that the set $f(D)$ is contained in $\bar{G}$. However, since $f(C)=\Gamma$, all points of the boundary of G are images under $f(z)$ of points of the boundary of D. It is easy to show that the values assumed by a univalent function inside a domain are not assumed by it on the boundary of the domain. Indeed, if the function $f(z)$ assumes the value w_0 at the point $z_0\in D$, then all values w that are sufficiently close to w_0 will be assumed by the function $f(z)$ in some neighborhood of the point z_0; and, in view of the univalence, only in this neighborhood. Thus, the values of $f(z)$ at the remaining points cannot be close to w_0. We now see that points of the boundary of G cannot lie in $f(D)$ and that $f(D)=G$, which proves the theorem.

Let us now explain how mappings effected by regular functions differ geometrically from those of arbitrary functions. We study the principal linear part of the mapping $w=f(z)$ (see Sect. 2, Chap. 1). If the function $f(z)$ is regular at the point $z=z_0$, then the principal linear part of the mapping is the linear mapping

$$w-w_0=A(z-z_0), \tag{1.1}$$

where $w_0 = f(z_0)$, $A = f'(z_0)$. The linear mapping (1.1) is a combination of a rotation and a similarity transformation (if $A \neq 0$). The coefficient of dilation is $|A|$ and the angle of rotation is $\arg A$. The similarity transformation and the rotation preserve the shape of a figure. The condition $A \neq 0$ arises since the function $f(z)$ is univalent at the point $z = z_0$. Therefore, mappings effected by regular, univalent functions have received the name of conformal mappings (i.e., mappings that preserve the form).

Mappings effected by univalent meromorphic functions are also called *conformal mappings* (they preserve the form of sufficiently small figures on the Riemann sphere).

An obvious consequence of these geometric considerations that will be frequently employed is the following:

Under conformal mapping the angle between two curves (at the point of intersection) equals the angle between the images of these curves.

It is customary to introduce the concept of the angle between two curves intersecting at the point at infinity in such a way that the above statement is valid also for mappings effected by meromorphic functions. Namely:

Suppose that we have two curves that diverge to infinity. If their images under the mapping $\zeta = \frac{1}{z}$ have tangents at the point $\zeta = 0$, then we say that the original curves intersect at the point at infinity with an angle equal to that between their images.

Starting from this definition, we can easily verify that *the angle between two lines at the point at infinity* equals the angle between the two lines at their finite point of intersection, but taken with the opposite sign.

We state two more formulas that are easy consequences of the foregoing geometric considerations:

Let $w=f(z)$ be a conformal mapping of the domain D onto the domain D'. If L is a curve contained in the domain D, L' is its image and S' is the length of L', then

$$S' = \int_L |f'(z)|\,|dz|. \tag{1.2}$$

If G is a domain contained in D, G' is its image and σ' is the area of G', then

$$\sigma' = \iint_D |f'(z)|^2\,dx\,dy. \tag{1.3}$$

Both these formulas are easily proved with the aid of the following geometric arguments: a sufficiently small element of length and a sufficiently small element of area are not changed under rotation; under a similarity transformation the element of length is multiplied by the coefficient of dilation and the element of area by its square. We shall not give the details of the proofs of the formulas. The reader familiar with the concept of the integral will have no difficulty in proving it himself.

Let us note in addition that the Jacobian of the mapping $w = f(z)$ is equal to $|f'(z)|^2$. Indeed, the mapping $w = f(z)$ can be written in the form

$$u = u(x, y), \qquad v = v(x, y),$$

where

$$w = u + iv, \qquad z = x + iy;$$
$$u(x, y) = \operatorname{Re} f(x + iy), \qquad v(x, y) = \operatorname{Im} f(x + iy).$$

Thus,

$$\frac{\partial(u, v)}{\partial(x, y)} = \frac{\partial u}{\partial x}\frac{\partial v}{\partial y} - \frac{\partial v}{\partial x}\frac{\partial u}{\partial y},$$

which, as a consequence of the Cauchy-Riemann equations (see Sect. 1, Chap. II) is equal to $|f'(z)|^2$.

In conclusion we wish to state two results fundamental for the entire theory of conformal mapping.

Riemann's theorem. For a simply connected domain whose boundary consists of more than one point, there exists a function f(z) that is meromorphic in this domain and that maps it conformally onto the circle $|w| < 1$. *The function f(z) is uniquely determined by the conditions* $f(a) = 0$, $\arg f'(a) = \theta$ *(a is any point of the domain,* θ *is any positive real number).*

We shall prove this theorem in a more general form in Chap. IX, where we shall study questions involving the informal mapping of multiply connected domains.

The corresponding boundaries theorem. Let D be any finite, simply connected domain bounded by a piecewise smooth curve, and let f(z) be any function that maps the domain D conformally onto the circle $|w| < 1$. *Then the function f(z) is continuous up to the boundary of S and its inverse function* $\varphi(w)$ *is uniformly continuous in the circle* $|w| < 1$.

We shall also prove this theorem in Chap. IX.

2. LINEAR FRACTIONAL TRANSFORMATIONS

Mappings effected by functions of the form (linear fractional functions)

$$w(z)=\frac{az+b}{cz+d} \qquad (ad-bc\neq 0) \tag{2.1}$$

are called *linear fractional transformations*. The condition $ad-bc\neq 0$ means that the function $w(z)$ cannot be a constant. The formula does not define the function at $z=\infty$ and $z=-\frac{d}{c}$. We may extend the definition while preserving continuity by setting

$$w(\infty)=\frac{a}{c}, \quad w\left(-\frac{d}{c}\right)=\infty$$

(if $c=0$ then $w(\infty)=\infty$).

The linear fractional function thus defined on the entire extended complex plane is evidently meromorphic there. Equality (2.1) can be solved for z; this yields

$$z(w)=\frac{dw-b}{-cw+a}.$$

Thus, the inverse of a linear fractional function is also a linear fractional function. As a consequence of this, linear fractional functions are univalent in the entire extended complex plane. Hence:

Property 1. Linear fractional transformations are conformal mappings of the extended complex plane z onto the extended complex plane w.

Let us demonstrate yet another property of linear fractional transformations.

Property 2. The resultant of two successive linear fractional transformations is again a linear fractional transformation. The inverse of a linear fractional transformation is also a linear fractional transformation.

(This property is sometimes formulated as follows: *the set of linear fractional transformations forms a group.)*

The second part of the assertion has already been proved. In order to prove the first part we write

$$\zeta=\frac{a_1z+b_1}{c_1z+d_1}, \quad w=\frac{a_2\zeta+b_2}{c_2\zeta+d_2}.$$

Substituting the expression for ζ into the formula for w, we find

$$w=\frac{az+b}{cz+d},$$

where

$$a = a_1 a_2 + b_2 c_1, \quad b = a_2 b_1 + b_2 d_1,$$
$$c = a_1 c_2 + c_1 d_2, \quad d = b_1 c_2 + d_1 d_2.$$

It is easy to verify that $ad - bc = (a_1 d_1 - b_1 c_1)(a_2 d_2 - b_2 c_2)$, from which it is clear that $ad - bc \neq 0$, if $a_1 d_1 - b_1 c_1 \neq 0$ and $a_2 d_2 - b_2 c_2 \neq 0$.

Let us note that if we let the linear fractional transformation $w = \frac{az+b}{cz+d}$ correspond to the matrix $\begin{pmatrix} a & b \\ c & d \end{pmatrix}$, then the inverse transformation corresponds to the inverse matrix and the resultant of two transformations corresponds to the product of the matrices.

Property 3. Under linear fractional transformation the image of any circle or line is again a circle or a line.

Let us prove this property directly. We take some circle $|z - z_0| = R$ and study how it is affected by linear fractional tranformation. The case of a line does not need to be studied separately, since a line is a limiting case of a circle. Let the mapping have the form $z = \frac{aw+b}{cw+d}$. After substituting the expression for z into the equation of the circle, we find

$$|(a - cz_0) w + (b - dz_0)| = R \, |cw + d|$$

or

$$|a'w + b'|^2 = R^2 \, |cw + d|^2.$$

The square of the modulus of a complex number equals the product of this number by its complex conjugate; therefore we can put the above equation into the form

$$(a'w + b')(\overline{a'}\bar{w} + \overline{b'}) = R^2 (\bar{c}\bar{w} + \bar{d})(cw + d)$$

or

$$|a'|^2 |w|^2 + |b'|^2 + a'\overline{b'}w + \overline{a'}b'\bar{w} =$$
$$= R^2 (|c|^2 |w|^2 + |d|^2 + c\bar{d}w + \bar{c}d\bar{w}).$$

If we set $w = u + iv$ and write the equation in terms of Cartesian coordinates in the u, v-plane, we obtain the equation

$$A(u^2 + v^2) + Bu + Cv + D = 0,$$

which is the equation of a circle or of a line. This completes the proof.

To formulate the next property we need to introduce the concept of symmetry with respect to a circle.

The points z and ζ are said to be *symmetric with respect to the circle* Γ, if they both lie on the same ray issuing from the center of

Γ and the product to their distances from the center equals the square of the radius of Γ. The center of Γ is taken to be symmetric with the point at infinity.

We understand symmetry with respect to a line in the usual sense:

The points z and ζ are said to be *symmetric with respect to the line* Γ, if they lie on opposite sides of Γ, and Γ is the perpedicular bisector of the segment joining them.

We next introduce some typical examples of symmetric points.

The points z and $\bar{z}$ are symmetric with respect to the real axis.

The points z and $\bar{z}$ are symmetric with respect to the imaginary axis.

The points z and $\frac{1}{\bar{z}}$ are symmetric with respect to the circle $|z|=1$.

The notion of sets symmetric with respect to a circle is introduced in the obvious way.

We can study symmetry with respect to a circle in terms of a mapping of the extended complex plane onto the extended complex plane. The formula for this mapping is easily found:

If $\zeta(z)$ is the symmetric point of z with respect to the circle $|z-a|=R$, then $\zeta(z)=a+\frac{R^2}{\bar{z}-\bar{a}}$.

Thus, a symmetry transformation with respect to a circle differs from a linear fractional transformation only in the presence of complex conjugates.

The properties of symmetry transformations are closely connected with those of the linear fractional transformations. Thus, for example, property 3 becomes:

The set symmetric to a circle with respect to a circle is a circle or a line.

Lemma. For the points z and ζ to be symmetric to the circle Γ it is necessary and sufficient that any circle passing through these points intersect Γ in a right angle.

Proof. We can assume without loss of generality that the center of the circle Γ is located at the origin.

Let us first show the sufficiency. Since any circle passing through the points z and ζ intersects Γ in a right angle, the same is true of the line joining these points. Thus, the line joining the points z and ζ must pass through the origin. The points z and ζ must both be on one ray issuing from the origin and on opposite sides of Γ; otherwise the circle passing through z and ζ and having the segment (z, ζ) as a diameter would not intersect Γ in a right angle. Thus, the origin is exterior to any circle C passing through z and ζ and the ray passing through these points is a secant of this circle. The radius from the origin to the nearer of the two points z and ζ is the exterior part of the secant and from there to the farther point is the length of the secant (in the terminology of textbooks of elementary geometry). A well-known theorem of elementary geometry states that the product of the sector by its exterior part equals the square of the tangent from that point. The tangent to C from the origin has the same length as the radius of Γ, since according to hypothesis C and Γ intersect in a right angle. This proves the sufficiency.

The necessity is proved by means of the same construction, since the product of the secant by its exterior part can equal the square of the external part of another secant only in the case that this second secant is a tangent. This proves the lemma.

Property 4. If the points z_1 and z_2 are symmetric with respect to a line or circle Γ and if w_1, w_2 and L are the images of z_1, z_2 and under a linear fractional transformation, then the points w_1 and w_2 are symmetric with respect to the circle (or line) L.

On the basis of the lemma, it is sufficient for the proof of the symmetry of the points w_1 and w_2 relative to the circle L to show that all circles passing through these points intersect L in a right angle. But a circle passing through the points w_1 and w_2 is the image of a circle passing through z_1 and z_2. Since the points z_1 and z_2 are symmetric with respect to Γ, then a circle passing through z_1 and z_2 must intersect Γ in a right angle.

Since a linear fractional transformation is conformal, the angle between the curves equals the angle between their images. Our assertion follows from this.

We prove next some formulas relating to linear fractional transformations.

Theorem 2.1. *Suppose that no two of the points z_1, z_2, z_3, nor of the points w_1, w_2, w_3 are equal. Then there exists a unique linear fractional transformation $w = w(z)$ carrying the points z_k into the point w_k. This transformation is given by the formula*

$$\frac{w-w_1}{w-w_2}\cdot\frac{w_3-w_2}{w_3-w_1}=\frac{z-z_1}{z-z_2}\cdot\frac{z_3-z_2}{z_3-z_1}. \tag{2.2}$$

Proof. It is clear that the function $w(z)$ defined by the equality (2.2) is a linear fractional function and that it carries the point z_k into the point w_k. Therefore, we need only to show that $w(z)$ is the only such linear fractional function. Let there be two such functions $w_1(z)$ and $w_2(z)$, and let $\zeta_2(w)$ be the inverse of $w_2(z)$. It is clear that the mapping effected by the function $\zeta_2(w_1(z))$ has z_k as a fixed point, for $w_1(z_k)=w_k$ and $\zeta_2(w_k)=z_k$. $\zeta_2(w_1(z))$ is a linear fractional function because of property 2. We set

$$\zeta_2(w_1(z))=\frac{az+b}{cz+d}.$$

If we write down the conditions under which z_k is a fixed point under the mapping effected by $\zeta_2(w_1(z))$, we find the system of equations

$$\frac{az_k+b}{cz_k+d}=z_k \qquad (k=1,\ 2,\ 3)$$

or

$$cz_k^2+(d-a)z_k+b=0 \qquad (k=1,\ 2,\ 3).$$

The second-degree polynomial $cz^2+(d-a)z+b$ may have three distinct roots only when all its coefficients vanish. Therefore, $\zeta_2(w_1(z))\equiv z$ and $w_2(z)=w_1(z)$, which proves the theorem.

Theorem 2.2. *A conformal mapping of the circle* $|z|<1$ *onto the circle* $|w|<1$ *must have the form*

$$w(z)=e^{i\theta}\frac{z-a}{1-z\bar{a}}, \tag{2.3}$$

in which a is any point of the circle $|z|<1$ *and* θ *is any real number.*

Proof. Let us show first that the function defined by (2.3) actually maps the circle $|z|<1$ onto the circle $|w|<1$. In view of the one-to-oneness of a linear fractional transformation, it is sufficient for this to show that the circle $|z|=1$ is taken into the circle $|w|=1$ (since the point $z=a$ from the circle $|z|<1$ is mapped into the point $w=0$ of the $|w|<1$). We set $z=e^{i\varphi}$. Then $|z|=1$, $\bar{z}=e^{-i\varphi}$, and we obtain

$$w=\frac{e^{i\theta}}{e^{i\varphi}}\cdot\frac{e^{i\varphi}-a}{e^{-i\varphi}-\bar{a}}=e^{i(\theta-\varphi)}\cdot\frac{z-a}{\overline{z-a}}, \qquad |w|=1,$$

since the complex conjugate has the same modulus as the number itself. Thus we have shown that the function defined by equality (2.3) maps the circle $|z|<1$ onto the circle $|w|<1$. Let us show that there are no other conformal mappings. According to Riemann's theorem (see the end of Sect. 1), the conformal mapping of any simply connected domain onto the circle $|w|<1$ is uniquely determined if the point $z=a$ of the reimage which maps into the point $w=0$ and the argument of the value of the derivative of the mapping function at the point $z=a$ are given. For the function defined by equality (2.3) $w(a)=0$ and $\arg w'(a)=\theta$. Thus there is no other mapping, which proves the theorem.

The following statements are proved analogously:

A conformal mapping of the circle $|z|<R$ *onto the circle* $|w|<1$ *must have the form*

$$w=Re^{i\theta}\frac{z-a}{R^2-z\bar{a}} \qquad (|a|<R). \tag{2.4}$$

Any conformal mapping of the half-plane $\operatorname{Im} z>0$ *onto the circle* $|w|<1$ *must have the form*

$$w=e^{i\theta}\frac{z-a}{z-\bar{a}} \qquad (\operatorname{Im} a>0). \tag{2.5}$$

A conformal mapping of the half-plane $\operatorname{Im} z > 0$ *onto the half-plane* $\operatorname{Im} w > 0$ *must have the form*

$$w = \frac{az+b}{cz+d}, \qquad (2.6)$$

where a, b, c, d are real numbers and ad - bc > 0.

3. CONFORMAL MAPPING OF THE ELEMENTARY FUNCTIONS

If we are given a domain and a function $f(z)$ regular therein, it is not immediately clear that there exists an algorithm that permits us to find the image of the given domain under the mapping $w = f(z)$. The situation is simpler for curves. If $z = z(t)$ is the equation of a curve in the z-plane, then the equation of its image is $w = f(z(t))$. The study of the mapping effected by the given function is best carried out as follows: choose a family of curves that cover the domain under study: next find the images of the curves of this family. The choice of the family is naturally determined by the concrete form of the mapping function.

We now show how to carry out the investigation of the basic mappings effected by the elementary functions. This will yield us a collection of the simplest mappings; we shall make frequent use of them in the sequel.

1 . *The functions* $w = e^z$ *and* $z = \ln w$.

For the investigation of the mapping $w = e^z$ it is convenient to study the family of lines parallel to the real axis. The parametric equation of these lines has the form $z = x + iC$, where C is any real number and the parameter x varies from $-\infty$ to $+\infty$. As the parameter z increases from $-\infty$ to $+\infty$, the point x traces out the line $\operatorname{Im} z = C$ from left to right. The equation of the image under the mapping $w = e^z$ has the form $w = e^x \cdot e^{iC}$, $-\infty < x < \infty$, or $w = te^{iC}$, $0 < t < \infty$. Thus, the image of the line $\operatorname{Im} z = C$ under the mapping $w = e^z$ is the ray $\arg w = C$.

The line is next translated by continuously increasing C, say, from a to b. The ray that is the image of the line is then rotated continuously in the counterclockwise direction. Under this type of movement the line describes the strip $a < \operatorname{Im} z < b$, while its image, the ray, describes the angle $a < \arg w < b$, if b does not exceed $a + 2\pi$. For $b > a + 2\pi$ the ray completes a full revolution and describes the entire w plane except for the deleted point $w = 0$. Thus, the image of the strip $a < \operatorname{Im} z < b$ under the mapping given by the function $w = e^z$ is the angle $a < \arg w < b$, if $b - a \leqslant 2\pi$, and is the entire finite plane except for the (deleted) point $w = 0$, if $b - a > 2\pi$.

We now determine the conditions making the mapping one-to-one, i.e., under which the function e^z is univalent. We remarked at the beginning of Sect. 1 that a necessary and sufficient condition for the univalence of a function in a domain D is the existence of an inverse function in the image of this domain. The analytic function $\ln w$ is inverse to the function e^z. An inverse function to e^z is defined (i.e., single-valued) in the domain if the analytic function $\ln w$ admits a partition into regular branches in this domain. If $b-a \leqslant 2\pi$, then we know that the function $\ln w$ admits a partition into regular branches in the angle $a < \arg w < b$. It is impossible to partition the function $\ln w$ into regular branches in the w-plane with the point $w=0$ deleted. Thus, we have arrived at the following result:

The strip

$$a+2\pi k < \operatorname{Im} z < b+2\pi k \qquad (b-a \leqslant 2\pi) \tag{3.1}$$

for any integer k is mapped conformally by the function w = e onto the angle

$$a < \arg w < b. \tag{3.2}$$

The function ln w maps the angle (3.2) conformally onto one of the strips (3.1) (the number k is determined by the choice of the regular branch of the analytic function $\ln w$ in this angle).

The mapping effected by the function $w=e^z$ *of a strip* $a < \operatorname{Im} z < b$ *of width greater than* 2π *onto the annulus* $0 < |w| < \infty$ *is no longer one-to-one.*

Note that the last statement is an immediate consequence of the periodicity of the function e^z (its period is $2\pi i$).

It is useful to know how lines parallel to the imaginary axis are transformed under mapping by the function $w=e^z$. After writing the equation of such a line in the form $z=C+iy$, $-\infty < y < \infty$, we find that the image has the equation $w=e^C e^{iy}$, $-\infty < y < \infty$. It is clear that this equation is that of the circle $|w|=e^C$, traced out infinitely many times. Each line segment of length 2π corresponds to a complete circuit of the circle.

The rectangle

$$c < \operatorname{Re} z < d,\ a+2\pi k < \operatorname{Im} z < b+2\pi k\ (b-a < 2\pi) \tag{3.3}$$

for any integer k is mapped conformally by the function $w=e^z$ *onto the annular sector*

$$e^c < |w| < e^d,\ a < \arg w < b. \tag{3.4}$$

The function $z=\ln w$ maps the annular sector (3.4) conformally onto *one of the rectangles (3.3)* (the number k is determined by the choice of the regular branch of the analytic function $\ln w$ in the sector).

2 . *Zhukovskiy's function* $w=\frac{1}{2}\left(z+\frac{1}{z}\right)$ *and the function* $z=w+\sqrt{w^2-1}$.

We shall study these two functions together since they are inverse to one another.

It will be convenient to take for our family of curves the rays $\arg z=\varphi$ or the circles $|z|=r$. Both families are needed for the study. Let us begin by considering the family of circles.

The equation of the circle $|z|=r$ will be written in the form $z=re^{i\varphi}$, $0\leqslant\varphi<2\pi$. Then the equation of the image of this circle under the mapping $w=\frac{1}{2}\left(z+\frac{1}{z}\right)$ is obtained in the form

$$w=\frac{1}{2}\left(re^{i\varphi}+\frac{1}{r}e^{-i\varphi}\right),\quad 0\leqslant\varphi<2\pi.$$

Since we are not yet acquainted with this equation, it is worthwhile to study the equations for its real and imaginary parts. Setting $w=u+iv$ we see

$$u=\frac{1}{2}\left(r+\frac{1}{r}\right)\cos\varphi,\quad v=\frac{1}{2}\left(r-\frac{1}{r}\right)\sin\varphi. \tag{3.5}$$

After eliminating the parameter φ from this system of equations, we arrive at the equation of the ellipse

$$\frac{u^2}{a_r^2}+\frac{v^2}{b_r^2}=1\quad\left(a_r=\frac{1}{2}\left(r+\frac{1}{r}\right),\ b_r=\frac{1}{2}\left(r-\frac{1}{r}\right)\right),$$

which has foci at the points $w = 1$ and $w = -1$. Therefore, the image of the circle $|z|=r$ under the mapping $w=\frac{1}{2}\left(z+\frac{1}{z}\right)$ is this ellipse (or part of it). It is clear from Eq. (3.5) that the point w makes a complete circuit of the ellipse as φ varies from 0 to 2π; here the motion is in the clockwise direction for $r<1$ and in the counter-clockwise direction for $r>1$.

Let us study the variation of the ellipse as r increases monotonically and continuously from one to infinity. For $r=1$ the minor axis of the ellipse is zero and the ellipse degenerates into the line segment (-1, 1) which is traversed twice. As r increases, both axes do likewise; as $r\to+\infty$ so do the axes of the ellipse. Consequently, the image of the domain $|z|>1$ regarded as covered by the circles $|z|=r$, $r>1$, is the entire w-plane with a cross cut along the segment (-1, 1). The mapping is one-to-one since the inverse function $w+\sqrt{w^2-1}$ admits a partition into regular branches in the w-plane with a cross cut along the segment (-1, 1). (To see this, write the function in the form $w\left(1+\sqrt{1-\frac{1}{w^2}}\right)$, after which the monodromy theorem, applied to the second factor in the extended plane with a cross cut along the segment (-1, 1), yields the result.)

Let us point out one additional method of studying the univalence of the function $w=\frac{1}{2}\left(z+\frac{1}{z}\right)$. The value of this function is not changed by replacing z by $1/z$. Since the inverse function is double-valued, we then see that each value is assumed by Zhukovskiy's function at the two points z and $1/z$ (and only there). Therefore, for the univalence of Zhukovskiy's function in the domain D it is necessary and sufficient that the domain D and its image D' under the mapping $\zeta = 1/z$ do not have any points in common.

It follows from this reasoning that Zhukovskiy's function is univalent in the domains $|z|<1$ and $|z|>1$, and that the image of each of these domains under mapping by Zhukovskiy's function is the entire w-plane with a cross cut along the segment $(-1, 1)$.

A study of the images of the rays $\arg z=\varphi$ under mapping by the function $w=\frac{1}{2}\left(z+\frac{1}{z}\right)$ may be carried out in a completely analogous manner. After eliminating r from Eqs. (3.5), we arrive at the equation of the hyperbola

$$\frac{u^2}{\cos^2\varphi}-\frac{v^2}{\sin^2\varphi}=1$$

with foci at the points $w = 1$ and $w = -1$. It is easy to verify that the image of the ray $\arg z=\varphi$ is one of the branches of the hyperbola. The branch corresponding to $\varphi=0$ degenerates into the ray $(1,+\infty)$ which is traversed twice, the branch corresponding to $\varphi=\frac{\pi}{2}$ degenerates into the entire imaginary axis, the one corresponding to $\varphi=\pi$ into the ray $(-\infty, -1)$ traversed twice.

The study we have just carried out allows us to describe a whole series of conformal mappings effected by Zhukovskiy's function $w=\frac{1}{2}\left(z+\frac{1}{z}\right)$.

The circle $|z|<1$ *is mapped onto the w-plane with a cross cut along the segment* $(-1, 1)$.

The half-plane Im $z>0$ *is mapped onto the w-plane with cross cuts along the rays* $(-\infty, -1)$ *and* $(1, +\infty)$.

The semicircle $|z|<1$, *Im* $z>0$ *is mapped onto the half-plane Im* $w<0$.

The circle $|z|<1$ *with a cross cut along the segments* $(b, 1), 0<b<1$ *and* $(-1, -a)$, $0<a<1$, *is mapped onto the w-plane with a cross cut along the segment* $(-\alpha, \beta)$ *where* $\alpha=\frac{1}{2}\left(a+\frac{1}{a}\right)$, $\beta=\frac{1}{2}\left(b+\frac{1}{b}\right)$.

A domain in the z-plane may be interchanged with its image by applying the mapping $\zeta=\frac{1}{z}$, which does not change the domains obtained in the w-plane.

The function $z=w+\sqrt{w^2-1}$ effects mappings inverse to those discussed above.

The mappings described in 1 and 2 of this section together with the linear fractional transformations, afford us an abundant supply of fundamental mappings. We can construct mappings of other elementary functions with their help. The basis for this is that, knowing the mappings effected by the functions $f(z)$ and $F(z)$, we can also determine the mapping effected by the function $F(f(z))$ (the compostion of the first two mappings). A mapping by any of the basic elementary functions can be presented in the form of a composition of a number of the mappings already studied. For example, the mapping $w = \tan z$ can be written in the form

$$w_1 = 2iz, \quad w_2 = e^{w_1}, \quad w = -i\frac{w_2 - 1}{w_2 + 1},$$

and the mapping $w = \cos z$ in the form

$$w_1 = iz, \quad w_2 = e^{w_1}, \quad w = \frac{1}{2}\left(w_2 + \frac{1}{w_2}\right).$$

We shall make a detailed study of one of the simplest examples.

3. *The function* $w = z^\alpha$ (α a positive real number).

We have $z^\alpha = e^{\alpha \ln z}$. We may present the mapping effected by the function z^α in the form of a composition of mappings as follows:

$$w_1 = \ln z, \quad w_2 = \alpha w_1, \quad w = e^{w_2}$$

and then study the mapping of the angle $a < \arg z < b$ $(b - a \leqslant 2\pi)$. According to 1, we have: the angle

$$a < \arg z < b \qquad (b - a \leqslant 2\pi)$$

is transformed into one of the strips

$$a + 2\pi k < \operatorname{Im} w_1 < b + 2\pi k \tag{3.6}$$

(the integer k is determined by the choice of the branch of $\ln z$ in the angle).

The strip (3.6) is transformed into the strip

$$\alpha a + 2\pi\alpha k < \operatorname{Im} w_2 < \alpha b + 2\pi\alpha k. \tag{3.7}$$

The strip (3.7) for $\alpha(b - a) \leqslant 2\pi$ is transformed into the angle

$$\alpha a + 2\pi\alpha k < \arg w < \alpha b + 2\pi\alpha k, \tag{3.8}$$

and for $\alpha(b - a) > 2\pi$ into the entire w-plane with the point $w = 0$ deleted.

Thus:

If $0 < b - a \leqslant 2\pi$ *and* $\alpha(b - a) \leqslant 2\pi$, *then the angle*

$$a < \arg z < b$$

is mapped conformally by the function $w = z^\alpha$ *onto one of the angles*

$$\alpha a + 2\pi\alpha k < \operatorname{Im} w < \alpha b + 2\pi\alpha k$$

(the integer k is determined by the choice of the regular branch of the function in the original angle).

It is clear that, if we replace the original angle by an annular sector, the result of the mapping will also be an annular sector.

If we are given the problem of finding a function that maps a given domain conformally onto another given domain, then we proceed in roughly the same way as we do when we seek to carry out an integration. The mappings described above play roughly the same role in this procedure as tables of integrals play in the problem of integration.

4. THE RIEMANN-SCHWARZ SYMMETRY PRINCIPLE

The Riemann-Schwarz symmetry principle is a method, noted for its simplicity, of analytic continuation. It has great importance for the theory of conformal mapping.

We first prove a simple result.

Theorem 4.1. *Let the function $f(z)$ be regular in the domain D, part of whose real boundary is a segment L of the real axis, and let it be continuous up to the boundary of D. If the function assumes real values on the segment L, then it can be continued analytically across the segment L to the domain D', symmetric with D with respect to the real axis. The continuation may be carried out by means of the formula*

$$F(z) = \overline{f(\bar{z})}. \tag{4.1}$$

(If D and D' have common points, then the values of $F(z)$ and $f(z)$ need not coincide at these points.)

Proof. Let us show first of all that the function $F(z)$, defined by (4.1), is regular in the domain D' and is continuous up to its boundary. Continuity follows from the obvious relation

$$|F(z_1) - F(z_2)| = |f(\bar{z}_1) - f(\bar{z}_2)|.$$

To prove that $F(z)$ is differentiable we put

$$A = \frac{F(z) - F(a)}{z - a}.$$

Then

$$\bar{A} = \frac{\overline{F(z)} - \overline{F(a)}}{\bar{z} - \bar{a}} = \frac{f(\bar{z}) - f(\bar{a})}{\bar{z} - \bar{a}}$$

and $\lim_{z \to a} \overline{A} = f'(\bar{a})$. Thus, the limit $\lim_{z \to a} \frac{F(z) - F(a)}{z - a}$ exists and equals $\overline{f'(\bar{a})}$, i.e., $F(z)$ is differentiable in D' and therefore regular there.

We next choose some sufficiently small neighborhood of a point of the segment L. Half of this neighborhood lies in D and the other half in D'. Let us consider the function $\varphi(z)$, equal to $f(z)$ in the first half and to $F(z)$ in the second half. If we are able to prove that $\varphi(z)$ is regular in the entire neighborhood, this will show that the function $f(z)$ can be continued analytically across L, and we shall have proved the theorem. For this we note that $\varphi(z)$ is continuous at the points of the segment L (and this means that it is true for the entire neighborhood), since $\lim_{z \to x} f(z) = f(x)$, $\lim_{z \to x} F(z) = \overline{f(x)}$ and $f(x) = \overline{f(x)}$ since $f(x)$ is real for $x \in L$. Applying Theorem 2.2 of Chap. IV on the removal of singularities, we obtain the regularity of $\varphi(z)$. This proves the theorem.

Remark. If the function $f(z)$ maps the domain D conformally onto another domain B, then it readily follows from formula (4.1) that the function $F(z)$ maps the domain D' conformally on the domain B', symmetric to the domain B with respect to the real axis.

Using linear fractional transformations, we can give Theorem 4.1 a significantly more general form.

Theorem 4.2. *Let the function f(z) be regular in the domain D, whose boundary contains an arc L of a circle, and let it be continuous up to the boundary of D. If the values assumed by the function f(z) on the arc L lie on the circle L, then the function f(z) can be continued across the arc L analytically into the domain D′, symmetric to the domain D with respect to the circle which contains the arc L. The function F(z) that continues f(z) analytically into the domain D′ is determined in the following way: the values of F(z′) and f(z) are symmetric with respect to the circle L, if the points z′ and z are symmetric with respect to the circle that contains the arc L.*

Proof. Let

$$z(\zeta) = \frac{a\zeta + b}{c\zeta + d}, \quad t(w) = \frac{a'w + b'}{c'w + d'},$$

and let $\zeta(z)$ and $w(t)$ be the linear fractional transformations inverse to these. We select the functions $z(\zeta)$ and $t(w)$ so that the real axis of the ζ-plane is mapped by the function $z = z(\zeta)$ into the circle in the z-plane which contains the arc L, and so that the circle Γ in the w-plane is mapped by the function $t = t(w)$ into the real axis of the t-plane. We assert that this can always be done with the aid of the formula of Theorem 2.1, after the triple of points has been assigned.

Let D_1 denote the image in the ζ-plane of the domain D under the mapping $z = z(\zeta)$, and let L_1 denote the preimage of the arc L under this mapping. It follows from the choice of the function $z(\zeta)$ that this preimage is a segment of the real axis. Thus, the function $f_1(\zeta)=f(z(\zeta))$ is regular in the domain D_1 and continuous up to its boundary, and the function $f_1(\zeta)$ assumes values on the segment of the real axis L_1 which are contained in the circle Γ.

Next, let us study the function

$$g(\zeta)=t(f_1(\zeta))=t(f(z(\zeta))).$$

Since the circle Γ is mapped into the real axis under the mapping $t=t(w)$, the function $g(\zeta)$ satisfies all the requirements of Theorem 4.1 and so can be continued analytically into the domain D_1, symmetric to D_1 with respect to the real axis. Consequently, the function $f(z)$ which may be expressed in terms of $g(\zeta)$with the aid of the linear fractional transformation

$$f(z)=w(g(\zeta(z))),$$

can be continued analytically into the domain D', the image if D_1' under the mapping $z=z(\zeta)$. But linear fractional transformations preserve symmetry of points with respect to lines and circles. Thus, the domain D' is symmetric to the domain D with respect to the image of the real axis under the mapping $z=z(\zeta)$, i.e., relative to the circle containing the arc L. We have thus obtained the statement of the theorem on the possibility of continuing the function $f(z)$ analytically across the arc L into the domain D'. The formula for the continuation is obtained by the same argument. This completes the proof.

It is clear that the remark to Theorem 4.1 also applied here. Since this remark will be frequently used, we formulate it here:

Corollary. Let the function f(z) be regular in the domain Dand continuous up to its boundary. Suppose that it maps the domain D conformally onto the domain B. Suppose, in addition, that the arc L of a circle forms part of the boundary of D and is mapped by w =f(z) into an arc (of the circle Γ) that forms part of the boundary of B. Let D′ denote the domain symmetric to the domain D with respect to the circle containing the arc of L, and let B′ denote the domain symmetric to the domain B with respect to the circle containing the arc of Γ. We assume that the domains D andD′, B and B′ have no common points. LetG denote the domain consisting of the union of D, D′and thearc of L contained in both their boundaries; let K denote the domain consisting of the union of B, B′ and the corresponding arc of Γ. Then the function f(z) can be continued analytically into the domain G and maps it conformally onto the domain K.

Let us show how to apply the symmetry principle to find conformal mappings of given domains.

Example 1. We find a function that maps the z-plane with cross cuts along the segments$\left(0,\ e^{\frac{k\pi i}{n}}\right)$ $(k=1,\ 2,\ \ldots,\ 2n)$ confromally onto the circle $|w|<1$.

Both the plane with cross cuts and the circle may be divided into $2n$ symmetric parts: the angles

$$\frac{k-1}{n}\pi < \arg z < \frac{k}{n}\pi \qquad (k = 1, 2, \ldots, 2n)$$

and the sectors

$$|w| < 1, \quad \frac{k-1}{n}\pi < \arg w < \frac{k}{n}\pi \quad (k = 1, 2, \ldots, 2n).$$

It is natural to expect that among the functions that map our domain conformally on the circle one may be found that maps each of the angles onto the corresponding sectors.

In fact, we are now in a position to show that the function $f(z)$ maps the angle

$$0 < \arg z < \frac{\pi}{n} \tag{4.2}$$

conformally onto the sector

$$|w| < 1, \qquad 0 < \arg w < \frac{\pi}{n}, \tag{4.3}$$

and transforms the rays $(1, +\infty)$ and $\left(e^{\frac{\pi i}{n}}, +\infty e^{\frac{\pi i}{n}}\right)$ into the radii (0, 1) and $\left(0, e^{\frac{\pi i}{n}}\right)$ of the sector. The function $f(z)$ can be continued analytically to the plane with crosscuts $\left(0, e^{\frac{k}{n}\pi i}\right)$ $(k = 1, 2, \ldots, 2n)$ and the continuation maps the plane with crosscuts onto the circle $|w| < 1$.

We shall employ the symmetry principle for the proof. We take as our domain the angle (4.2), as B we take the sector (4.3), and as L and Γ we take the rays $\left(e^{\frac{\pi i}{n}}, +\infty e^{\frac{\pi i}{n}}\right)$ and the radius $\left(0, e^{\frac{\pi i}{n}}\right)$ respectively. Then, applying the corollary to Theorem 4.2, we find that the function $f(z)$ can be continued analytically across the ray L to the domain G, that is, the angular sector $0 < \arg z < \frac{2\pi}{n}$ with a cross cut along the segment $\left(0, e^{\frac{\pi i}{n}}\right)$. The image of the domain G under the mapping effected by the continuation is the sector $|w| < 1, 0 < \arg w < \frac{2\pi}{n}$.

The above reasoning can be repeated, by applying it to the domain G and to the continuation, and by using the ray $\left(e^{\frac{2\pi i}{n}}, +\infty e^{\frac{2\pi i}{n}}\right)$ for the new arc L, etc. Following this line of argument, we arrive at the continuation of the function $f(z)$ to the entire plane with cross cuts.

Thus, it remains only to find the mapping of the angular sector onto the sector satisfying the indicated conditions, i.e., the function $f(z)$. Note that we do not in fact have to carry out any analytic continuations. The argument involving analytic continuation was necessary only for the justification of the conditions determining the mapping of the angular sector onto the sector.

We adopt the following procedure to find the function $f(z)$:

The mapping $w_1 = z^n$ transforms the angular sector $0 < \arg z < \frac{\pi}{n}$ into the half-plane $\operatorname{Im} w_1 > 0$ and the rays $(1, +\infty)$ and $\left(e^{\frac{\pi i}{n}}, +\infty\, e^{\frac{\pi i}{n}}\right)$ into the rays $(1, +\infty)$ and $(-1, -\infty)$, respectively.

The mapping $w_2 = w_1 - \sqrt{w_1^2 - 1}$ (the inverse to Zhukovskiy's function) transforms the half-plane $\operatorname{Im} w_1 > 0$ into the semicircle $|w_2| < 1$, $\operatorname{Im} w_2 < 0$, here the ray $(1, +\infty)$ is transformed into the radius $(0, 1)$ and the ray $(-1, -\infty)$ into the radius $(-1, 0)$.

The mapping $w_3 = -w_2$ is a rotation of angle π around the origin in the counterclockwise direction.

The mapping $w = \sqrt[n]{w_3}$ transforms the semicircle $|w_3| < 1$, $\operatorname{Im} w_3 > 0$ into the sector $|w| < 1, 0 < \arg w < \frac{\pi}{n}$, and here radii go into radii.

We now have the mapping we sought. If we express w directly in terms of z, we find

$$w(z) = \sqrt[n]{z^n - \sqrt{z^{2n} - 1}}.$$

We choose the branch of the function $\left(z^n - \sqrt{z^{2n} - 1}\right)^{\frac{1}{n}}$ that is regular in our plane with cross cuts and that takes on positive values for $z > 1$.

It should not be thought that the symmetry principle facilitates the construction of mapping functions only in the case of domains with a large number of symmetries.

Example 2. We next find a function that maps the domain D in the x-plane $z = z + iy$ and defined by the equations

$$x^2 - y^2 > \frac{1}{2}, \quad x > 0,$$

conformally onto the half-plane $\operatorname{Re} w > 0$.

When we studied Zhukovskiy's function in Sect. 3 we saw that the boundary of the domain D (i.e., the branch of the hyperbola $x^2 - y^2 = \frac{1}{2}$, $x > 0$) is mapped by the function $w = z + \sqrt{z^2 - 1}$ into the ray $\arg w = \frac{\pi}{4}$. However, we cannot apply the function of the entire domain D, since it has a singular point at $z = 1$. Nevertheless, we may employ this mapping in our search for a mapping of the upper half of domain D, i.e., the domain defined by the inequalities

$$x^2 - y^2 > \frac{1}{2}, \quad x > 0, \quad y > 0. \tag{4.4}$$

We can easily find the desired mapping with the help of the symmetry principle.

The same argument as that employed in Example 1 shows that we obtain the desired mapping if we can find a mapping of the upper half of domain D onto the angular sector $0 < \arg w < \frac{\pi}{2}$. It is only necessary for this to require that the additional cross cut in domain D, i.e., the ray $\left(\frac{1}{\sqrt{2}}, +\infty\right)$, is mapped into the additional cross cut in the half-plane Re $w > 0$, i.e., the ray $\arg w = 0$; in other words, that the part of the hyperbola given by $x^2 - y^2 = \frac{1}{2}$, $x > 0$, $y > 0$, becomes the positive half of the real axis. This mapping may be constucted as follows:

The function $w_1 = z + \sqrt{z^2 - 1}$ maps the domain defined by inequality (4.4) onto the sector $|w_1| < 1$, $0 < \arg w_1 < \frac{\pi}{4}$, and here the part of the hyperbola that bounds the domain is mapped into the radius $\left(0, e^{\frac{\pi i}{4}}\right)$.

The function $w_2 = w_1^4$ maps the sector $|w_1| < 1$, $0 < \arg w_1 < \frac{\pi}{4}$, into the half-circle $|w_2| < 1$, Im $w_2 > 0$, and here the radius $\left(0, e^{\frac{\pi i}{4}}\right)$ is mapped into the radius $(0, -1)$.

The function $\zeta = \frac{1}{2}\left(w_2 + \frac{1}{w_2}\right)$ maps the semicircle $|w_2| < 1$, Im $w_2 > 0$, into the half-plane Im $\zeta < 0$, and here the radius $(0, -1)$ is mapped into the ray $(-1, -\infty)$.

Thus, the mapping $\zeta = \zeta(z)$ maps the upper half of domain D into the half-plane Im $\zeta < 0$, here that part of the hyperbola occurring in the boundary of this half is transformed into the ray $(-1, -\infty)$ and the ray $\left(\frac{1}{\sqrt{2}}, +\infty\right)$ into the remaining part of the boundary, i.e., into the ray $(-1, +\infty)$. By virtue of the symmetry principle, the function $\zeta(z)$ can be continued analytically across the ray $\left(\frac{1}{\sqrt{2}}, +\infty\right)$ into the domain D and the continuation maps the domain D onto the ζ-plane with a cross cut along the ray $(-1, -\infty)$. To obtain the final result, we still have to carry out the mapping $w = \sqrt{2\zeta + 2}$, which sends the plane with a cross cut into the half-plane Re $w > 0$.

Expressing w in terms of z, we find the final expression for the desired mapping function

$$w = \sqrt{2 + (z + \sqrt{z^2 - 1})^4 + (z - \sqrt{z^2 - 1})^4}.$$

5. THE SCHWARZ-CHRISTOFFEL INTEGRAL

We now apply the symmetry principle to derive a formula giving an analytic expression for a function that maps the circle or the half-plane conformally onto a polygon. This formula is well known under the name of the Schwarz-Christoffel formula or the Schwarz-Christoffel transformation. We give a complete proof only for the simplest case.

Theorem 5.1. *Let D be a finite polygon (simply connected) with vertices at the points $w = A$ $(k=1, 2, \ldots, n)$ and with interior angles at these vertices equal to $\pi\alpha_k$ $(0 < \alpha_k \leqslant 2)$. If the function f(z) maps the circle $|z| < 1$ conformally onto the polygon D in the w-plane where the preimages of the vertices A_k are the points a_k situated on the circle $|z| = 1$, then*

$$f(z) = C\int_0^z (\zeta - a_1)^{\alpha_1 - 1} \ldots (\zeta - a_n)^{\alpha_n - 1}\, d\zeta + C_1 \quad (|z| < 1), \tag{5.1}$$

where C and C_1 are constants.

Proof. In view of the complexity of the theorem, we split up the proof into several parts.

1) According to Riemann's theorem (see the end of Sect. 1), there exists a function $f(z)$ that maps the circle $|z| < 1$ conformally onto the polygon D. Let us show that the function $f(z)$ can be continued analytically along any path that does not intersect the points $a_1, a_2, \ldots, a_n$, and that any element of the analytic function thus obtained is univalent in the extended complex plane with the exception of the points a_k, $\kappa = 1, 2, \ldots, n$.

The points a_k divide the circle $|z| = 1$ into n arcs, which we denote $L_1, L_2, \ldots, L_n$. According to the theorem of corresponding boundaries (see the end of Sect. 1), the function $f(z)$ is continuous in the circle $|z| \leqslant 1$ and maps the arcs L_k into the corresponding sides of the polygon D; we designate these by Γ_k. According to the symmetry principle (see Theorem 4.2 and its corollary), the function $f(z)$ can be continued analytically into the domain $|z| > 1$ across any of the arcs L_k. As a result of this continuation, we obtain a function $F_k(z)$ that is regular in the domain $|z| > 1$ and that maps this domain conformally onto the polygon D_k, symmetric to the polygon D with respect to the side Γ_k.

Each of the functions $F_k(z)$ enjoys the same properties as the function $f(z)$. Each is regular in the domain $|z| > 1$ and maps this domain conformally onto the polygon D_k, and here the points a_s are sent into the vertices of the polygon and the arcs L_s into its sides. Therefore, each of the functions may be continued analytically across the arc L_s into the circle $|z| < 1$. As a result of this continuation, we obtain functions $F_{k,s}(z)$ to which the same argument can be applied, etc.

The argument just developed shows that the function $f(z)$ can be continued analytically along any path that does not intersect the points a_k, the endpoints of the arcs L_k.

We now study the univalence properties of the elements of the analytic function thus obtained (we denote it by $F(z)$).

It is evident that any element of the function $F(z)$ is univalent at any point not on the circle $|z| = 1$. In fact, if, in the circle $|z| < 1$ (or in the domain $|z| > 1$) we choose in the circle $|z| < 1$ a regular branch of the analytic function $F(z)$ for this element we then obtain a function that maps this domain conformally onto a polygon obtained from the polygon D by some type of symmetry operation. It follows from this by definition that the element is univalent at any point of the circle $|z|<1$ (or of the domain $|z|>1$).

If the point $z=a$ is situated on the arc L_k, then we choose a regular branch in the plane with a cross cut along the entire circle $|z|=1$ with the exception of the arc L_k. Thus, the regular branch chosen maps the circle $|z|<1$ conformally onto some polygon and the domain $|z|>1$ onto a polygon symmetric to it with respect to the corresponding side. It is clear that some circle containing an arc L_k is mapped onto some domain that contains the corresponding side common to both of the polygons referred to. From this follows the univalence of all of the elements of $F(z)$ at all points of the circle $|z|=1$ with the exception of the points a_k.

It must be stressed, in particular, that the point at infinity is not an exception — all the elements of $F(z)$ are regular and univalent at the point ∞.

2) We now study the multiple-valued character of the analytic function $F(z)$ in more detail and show that the function $g(z)=\frac{F''(z)}{F'(z)}$ is regular in the entire plane with the exception, perhaps, of the points a_k and the point $z=\infty$.

To obtain another regular branch of $f(z)$ from the original function $F(z)$ in the circle $|z|<1$ (or in the domain $|z|>1$), we select a sequence of numbers $k_1, k_2, \ldots, k_m$ indexing arcs L_k across which we carry out the analytic continuation. Generally speaking, for different sequences of numbers we obtain different regular branches of $F(z)$. We now show how they differ from one another. It is sufficient to indicate the difference between the functions $F_k(z)$ and $F_s(z)$, which we constructed in the first part of the proof.

For the sake of brevity, we denote by $(A)_\Gamma$ the point symmetric to the point A with respect to the line Γ. It is clear that $((A)_\Gamma)_\Gamma = A$.

According to the symmetry principle, we have

$$F_k(z)=\left(f\left(\frac{1}{\bar z}\right)\right)_{\Gamma_k}, \quad f\left(\frac{1}{\bar z}\right)=(F_s(z))_{\Gamma_s},$$

since the points z and $1/\bar z$ are symmetric with respect to the circle $|z|=1$. From this we find

$$F_k(z)=((F_s(z))_{\Gamma_s})_{\Gamma_k}=e^{i\varphi_{k,s}}F_s(z)+\gamma_{k,s}$$

($\varphi_{k,s}$ and $\gamma_{k,s}$ are constants), since two consecutive symmetries carried out with respect to lines are equivalent to a translation and a rotation. We put $T_{k,s}(w)=e^{i\varphi_{k,s}}w+\gamma_{k,s}$. Then the relation we have obtained can be written in the form

$$F_k(z)=T_{k,s}(F_s(z)).$$

From this relation it readily follows that

$$F_{k,m}(z)=T_{m,p}(T_{k,s}(F_{s,p}(z))),$$

with an anlogous result for any number of indices.

Since the compostion of two linear functions is again a linear function, we see that any two branches of the analytic function $F(z)$, let us say, $f_1(z)$ and $f_2(z)$, are connected by the relation

$$f_2(z) = e^{i\varphi} f_1(z) + \gamma,$$

where φ and γ are constants. Thus, $\dfrac{f_1''(z)}{f_1'(z)} = \dfrac{f_2''(z)}{f_2'(z)}$.

The last equality shows that the expression $g(z) = \frac{F''(z)}{F'(z)}$ does not depend on the choice of the branch of $F(z)$. This means that the function $g(z)$ is single-valued in the entire plane. In view of the proof (which we carried out in the first part) of the univalence of all elements of $F(z)$ at points distinct from $z = a_k$, according to Theorem 1.2, we find that $F'(z) \neq 0$ for $z \neq a_k$ and $z \neq \infty$. Thus the function $g(z)$ is regular in the entire plane with the possible exception of the points a_k and the point ∞.

3) We show next the function $g(z) = \frac{F''(z)}{F'(z)}$ we have constructed satisfies the relation

$$g(z) = \sum_{k=1}^{n} \frac{\alpha_k - 1}{z - a_k}.$$

Let us study the behavior of the function $g(z) = \frac{F''(z)}{F'(z)}$ in a neighborhood of the point at infinity and in a neighborhood of the point a_k (as we proved in the first step, each of these points may be an isolated singular point of single-valued character for $g(z)$). In this study, we shall employ some regular branch of the analytic function $F(z)$, perhaps the original function $f(z)$.

As we showed in the first part, the function $f(z)$ can be continued analytically in a neighborhood of the point at infinity and is univalent there. According to Corollary 1 of Theorem 1.2, we have

$$f(z) = c_0 + \frac{c_1}{z} + \frac{c^2}{z^2} + \dots \qquad (c_1 \neq 0).$$

From this we find

$$f'(z) = -\frac{c_1}{z^2} - \frac{2c_2}{z^3} - \dots,$$

$$f''(z) = \frac{2c_1}{z^3} + \frac{6c_3}{z^4} + \dots .$$

Thus,

$$g(z) = -\frac{2}{z} + \frac{c_2'}{z^2} + \dots .$$

It follows that the function $g(z)$ is regular at the point ∞.

To study the function $g(z)$ in a neighborhood of the point a_k we consider the function

$$h_k(z) = [f(z) - A_k]^{\frac{1}{\alpha_k}}$$

in a sufficiently small "semicircle" $|z-a_k| < \varrho$, $|z| < 1$. The function $f(z)$ maps this "semicircle" conformally onto a domain bounded by the two sides of the polygon D that meet at the point A_k and some curve (the image of the "semicircumference" $|z-a_k| = \varrho$, $|z| < 1$). However, the function $w = (\zeta - A)^{\frac{1}{\alpha}}$ maps the angular sector of size $\pi\alpha$ with its vertex at the point $\zeta = A$ conformally onto the angular sector of size π with its vertex at the point $w = 0$, i.e., onto the half-plane. Thus, the function $h_k(z)$ maps our semicircle conformally onto the domain bounded by a line segment (the image of a "diameter") and some curve (the image of the "semicircumference"). According to the symmetry principle, $h_k(z)$ can be continued analytically across the diameter of the semicircle and the analytic continuation (we denote it as before by $h_k(z)$) thus obtained will map the circle $|z-a_k| < \varrho$ conformally onto some domain containing the point $w = 0$. Therefore the function $h_k(z)$ is regular and univalent at the point a_k. As a consequence of this, according to Theorem 1.2, we have $h_k'(a_k) \neq 0$ and we can write

$$h_k(z) = (z - a_k)\,\varphi_k(z),$$

where $\varphi_k(z)$ is regular at the point a_k and $\varphi_k(a_k) \neq 0$. From this it follows that

$$f(z) = A_k + (z - a_k)^{\alpha_k}\psi_k(z), \qquad g(z) = \frac{\alpha_k - 1}{z - a_k} + \theta_k(z),$$

where $\theta_k(z)$ is regular at the point a_k.

We now consider the function

$$\delta(z) = g(z) - \sum_{k=1}^{n} \frac{\alpha_k - 1}{z - a_k}.$$

This function is regular in the entire extended plane, since according to Liouville's theorem (see Theorem 2.3, Chap. IV), we have $\delta(z) \equiv \text{const}$. Moreover, we showed that $g(z) \sim -\frac{2}{z}$ as $z \to \infty$, which means that $\delta(z) \to 0$ as $z \to \infty$. Thus, $\delta(z) \equiv 0$ and our assertion is proved.

4) We proved that

$$\frac{f''(z)}{f'(z)} = \sum_{k=1}^{n} \frac{\alpha_k - 1}{z - a_k}.$$

Integrating this equation, we find

$$\ln f'(z)=\sum_{k=1}^{\infty}(\alpha_k-1)\ln(z-a_k)+\ln C,$$

or

$$f'(z)=C(z-a_1)^{\alpha_1-1}\dots(z-a_n)^{\alpha_n-1}.$$

Integrating once more, we obtain the statement of the theorem.

Let us take note of some modifications of formula (5.1).

First of all we remark that the same formula (5.1) is suitable for the determination of a function that maps any half-plane or circle onto the polygon D. It is only necessary to assume that the points a_k are distributed on the appropriate circumference or line.

If one of the points a_k is the point at infinity, then formula (5.1) becomes even simpler. Indeed, if $a_n=\infty$, then

$$f(z)=C\int_0^z(\zeta-a_1)^{\alpha_1-1}\dots(\zeta-a_{n-1})^{\alpha_{n-1}-1}\,d\zeta+C_1. \tag{5.2}$$

The proof of formula (5.2) is unchanged except for the necessity of taking the point ∞ for one of the points a_k in the third part.

Formulas (5.1) and (5.2) remain unchanged if one or several of the vertices of the polygon D are situated at infinity. It is only necessary to employ the definition of the angle at the point at infinity, mentioned in Sect. 1, in the definition of the corresponding angles of sizes $\pi\alpha_k$. The value of $\pi\alpha_k$ may equal zero (in general, it is negative). The proof remains unchanged.

If the point at infinity lies within the polygon, then the formula takes the form

$$f(z)=\int_0^z(\zeta-a_1)^{\alpha_1-1}\dots(\zeta-a_n)^{\alpha_n-1}\frac{d\zeta}{(\zeta-a)^2}+C_1, \tag{5.3}$$

where a is the point transformed into infinity. The proof differs only in that we must also study the point $z=a$ in the third part.

By analogous methods we can obtain formulas for functions that map the half-plane or the circle conformally onto a polygon bounded by arcs of circles. The plan of the proof is as before, but all the steps except the first undergo significant changes. In the second part, we have to prove the univalence not of the function $g(z;\,f)=\frac{f''(z)}{f'(z)}$, but of the more complicated function

$$S(z;\,f)=\frac{f'''(z)}{f'(z)}-\frac{3}{2}\left(\frac{f''(z)}{f'(z)}\right)^2=\sqrt{f'(z)}\cdot\frac{d^2}{dz^2}\left(\frac{1}{\sqrt{f'(z)}}\right),$$

which is invariant not only under linear, but also under linear fractional transformations carried out on the function $f(z)$, i.e., it satisfies the relation

$$S(z;\ f) \equiv S(z,\ T(f)), \quad T(f) = \frac{af+b}{cf+d}.$$

(The expression $S(z; f)$ is called *Schwarz's invariant.)* The change in the third step is comparatively small. Using the same arguments, we prove the equality

$$S(z;\ f) = \frac{1}{2}\sum_{k=1}^{n}\frac{1-\alpha_k^2}{(z-a_k)^2} + \sum_{k=1}^{n}\frac{C_k}{z-a_k},$$

where the constants C_k are selected so that $S(z; f) = O(z^{-4})\ (z \to \infty)$. The proof of the fourth part becomes the most complicated of all. In place of the easily integrated equality

$$g(z;\ f) = \frac{f''(z)}{f'(z)}$$

we find the differential equation

$$q'' = S(z;\ f)\,q,$$

where

$$q(z) = \frac{1}{\sqrt{f'(z)}}.$$

The integrals arising from the Schwarz-Christoffel formula do not as a rule turn out to be elementary functions. However, this is not the main difficulty. The greatest problem is the determination of the constants a_k (and in the case of polygons bounded by arcs of circles, the constants C_k). Only three constants a_k can be assigned arbitrarily. The mapping is completely determined by these, and therefore so are the remaining constants. It is possible to write down a system of equations for these, but it is usually not possible to solve this system exactly. Explicit formulas for the mapping function are therefore given by the Schwarz-Christoffel transformation only for triangles and for polygons that can be reduced to triangles with the aid of the symmetry principle. In the case of a right triangle, the mapping function is expressed in terms of elliptic functions; in the case of a triangle bounded by arcs of circles, in terms of hypergeometric functions. In the case of very special triangles, it is possible to find integrals in terms of the elementary functions.

6. APPROXIMATION OF CONFORMAL MAPPINGS NEAR THE BOUNDARY

In many cases it is not necessary to know the exact mapping function. It is sometimes sufficient to have a knowledge of the behavior of this function near this or that boundary point. In the present section, we intend to introduce inequalities allowing the approximation of a function that maps a given domain G onto some canonical domain. The approximation is given in terms of simple geometric characteristics of the boundary of the domain ζ in the neighborhood of points of interest to us.

First, let us clarify the significance of the inequalities we are about to prove by means of a simple example.

Let the part of the domain G contained in the neighborhood of the boundary point ζ be an angular sector of size $\frac{\pi}{\alpha}$. Then the function $w(z)$ that maps the domain G conformally onto the circle $|w|<1$ has the form

$$w(z)=w(\zeta)+(z-\zeta)^{\alpha}g(z), \tag{6.1}$$

where the function $g(z)$ is regular at the point ζ and $g(\zeta)\neq 0$. (We proved a similar statement with the help of the symmetry principle in the third part of the proof of Theorem 5.1.)

It follows from formula (6.1) that

$$C|z-\zeta|^{\alpha}<|w(z)-w(\zeta)|<C'|z-\zeta|^{\alpha}.$$

Our fundamental purpose is to prove an analogous inequality for cases in which the point ζ joins not two lines, but two more or less arbitrary curves. For this, of course, the function $|z-\zeta|^{\alpha}$ will have to be replaced by some other function determined by the distance between the curves to be joined.

To make greater simplification of the formulation of the result possible, the problem is usually considered in the following canonical form.

In the sequel we shall assume that:

The domain D is simply connected and has a finite nonempty intersection with any line Re $z=x$, $-\infty<x<\infty$.

The function $w(z)$ maps the domain D conformally onto the strip $|\text{Im}\, w|<\frac{\pi}{2}$, in such a way that Re $w\to\pm\infty$ as Re $z\to\pm\infty$. We denote the inverse to $w(z)$ by $z(w)$.

It is easy to verify that the function $w(z)$ is determined to within an additive constant by the requirements set forth.

The boundary of the domain D is split up into two parts, united only at infinity. We denote the upper boundary curve by C^+, and the lower by C^-. It is clear that under the mapping by $w=w(z)$ the curve C^+ is sent into the line Im $w=\frac{\pi}{2}$, and the curve C^- int the line Im $w=-\frac{\pi}{2}$.

Let us study the intersection of the domain D with the line $\operatorname{Re} z = x$. In general, this intersection consists of a countable number of segments. We select from among these segments those that join C^+ and C^- (even if there is only one of these or if their number is finite). The segment which is first encountered as we move in the domain D from $\operatorname{Re} z = -\infty$ to $\operatorname{Re} z = +\infty$ is denoted θ_x (Fig. 3), and its length is denoted $\theta(x)$.

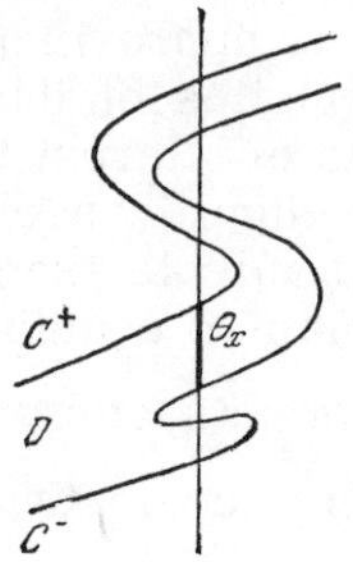

Fig. 3

The problem is to find an approximation of the values of $\operatorname{Re}[w(z) - w(\zeta)]$ in terms of $\theta(x)$ for large values of $\operatorname{Re}(z-\zeta)$.

Any problem can be reduced to essentially the formulation already presented. For example, in studying the mapping $t = t(\zeta)$ of the domain G onto the circle $|t| < 1$ in a neighborhood of the finite point a, we can reduce the problem to the canonical form after substituting for the variables $z = \ln \frac{\zeta - a'}{\zeta - a}$, $w = \ln \frac{t - t(a')}{t - t(a)}$ where a and a' are boundary points of the domain G. This substitution transforms the domain G into a strip domain D and the circle into a strip.

The following result is called Ahlfors' theorem.

Theorem 6.1. *If* $z \in \theta_a$, $\zeta \in \theta_b$, *and*

$$\int_a^b \frac{dx}{\theta(x)} > 2,$$

then

$$\operatorname{Re}[w(\zeta) - w(z)] > \pi \int_a^b \frac{dx}{\theta(x)} - 4\pi.$$

Before we undertake the proof of the theorem, let us prove an elementary lemma on an integral inequality that will be needed in the sequel.

Lemma 1. *Let* $\theta(x)$ *and* $\omega(x)$ *be arbitrary positive functions. If* $\int_a^b \frac{dx}{\theta(x)} > 2$, *then we can find* ξ *and* η *satisfying the conditions* $a < \xi < \eta < b$, *such that*

$$\int_a^{\xi} \frac{dx}{\theta(x)} < 1, \quad \int_{\eta}^{b} \frac{dx}{\theta(x)} < 1$$

and

$$\frac{1}{\pi} \int_{\xi}^{\eta} \frac{\omega^2(t)}{\theta(t)} dt - \omega(\xi) - \omega(\eta) > -2\pi.$$

Proof of the lemma. Let us first reduce the statement to a form much easier to prove.

Let c, a', b' denote numbers satisfying the condition $a < a' < c < b' < b$, and such that

$$\int_a^c \frac{dt}{\theta(t)} = \int_c^b \frac{dt}{\theta(t)} = \frac{1}{2} \int_a^b \frac{dt}{\theta(t)} > 1, \quad \int_a^{a'} \frac{dt}{\theta(t)} = \int_{b'}^{b} \frac{dt}{\theta(t)} = 1.$$

In addition, we set

$$\varphi(x) = \left| \int_c^x \frac{\omega^2(t)}{\theta(t)} dt \right| \qquad (a < x < b).$$

The statement of the lemma trivially follows from the following statement:

There exist points ξ *and* η, $a < \xi < a'$, $b' < \eta < b$, *for which*

$$\frac{1}{\pi} \varphi(\xi) > \omega(\xi) - \pi, \quad \frac{1}{\pi} \varphi(\eta) > \omega(\eta) - \pi.$$

We prove the existence of η. Suppose the contrary. Then on any segment (b', b) we have the inequality $\frac{1}{\pi} \varphi(x) < \omega(x) - \pi$ which can be written in the form

$$\omega^2(x) > \left[\frac{1}{\pi} \varphi(x) + \pi\right]^2 \qquad (b' < x < b).$$

If we differentiate the formula for $\varphi(x)$ for $x > c$, we easily obtain $\omega^2(x) = \varphi'(x)\,\theta(x)$. Thus, we find

$$\frac{1}{\theta(x)} < \frac{\pi^2 \varphi'(x)}{[\varphi(x) + \pi^2]^2} \qquad (b' < x < b).$$

Integrating this inequaity from b' to b, we obtain

$$\int_{b'}^{b} \frac{dx}{\theta(x)} < \pi^2 \int_{\varphi(b')}^{\varphi(b)} \frac{d\varphi}{(\varphi+\pi^2)^2} < \pi^2 \int_{0}^{\infty} \frac{d\varphi}{(\varphi+\pi^2)^2} = 1.$$

However, according to the definition of the number b', the left-hand integral equals one. This contradiction proves the existence of the number η.

The existence of ξ is proved analogously.

Proof of the theorem. Let L_x denote the image of the segment under the mapping $w = w(z)$ and set (Fig. 4)

$$u^+(x) = \sup_{w \in L_x} \operatorname{Re} w,$$
$$u^-(x) = \inf_{w \in L_x} \operatorname{Re} w,$$
$$\omega(x) = u^+(x) - u^-(x).$$

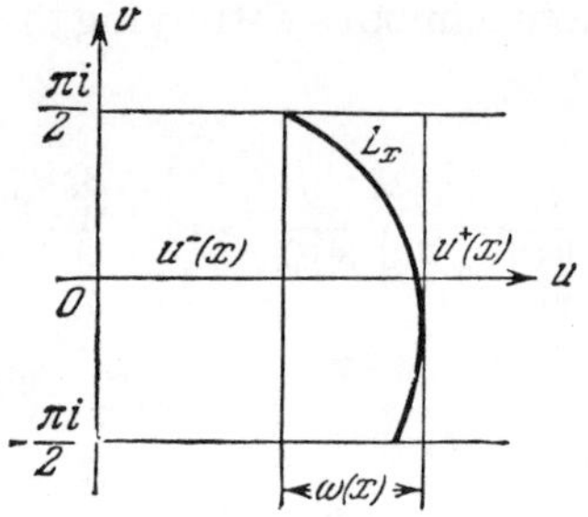

Fig. 4

Since the segment θ_x joins the curves C^+ and C^-, the curve L_x joins the lines $\operatorname{Im} w = \frac{\pi}{2}$ and $\operatorname{Im} w = -\frac{\pi}{2}$. This curve is contained in the rectangle $|\operatorname{Im} w| < \frac{\pi}{2}$, $u^-(x) < \operatorname{Re} w < u^+(x)$, and has points in common with each of its sides (possibly at its endpoints). Thus the length of the curve L_x is not less than the length of the diagonal of the rectangle, which equals $\sqrt{\pi^2 + \omega^2(x)}$. On the other hand, the length of the curve can be written in the form of the integral

$$\int_{L_x} |dw| = \int_{\theta_x} |dw(z)| = \int_{\theta_x} |w'(z)|\,|dz| = \int_{\theta_x} |w'(z)|\, dy.$$

Thus, we obtain the inequality

$$\pi^2 + \omega^2(x) \leqslant \left\{ \int_{\theta_x} |w'(z)|\, dy \right\}^2.$$

But in view of the Cauchy-Schwarz inequality

$$\left[\int fg\,dy\right]^2 \leqslant \int f^2\,dy \int g^2\,dy. \tag{6.2}$$

Hence, if we set $f=1$, $g=|w'(z)|$, and keep in mind that $\int\limits_{\theta_x} dy=\theta(x)$ we arrive at the inequality

$$\pi^2+\omega^2(x)\leqslant\theta(x)\int\limits_{\theta_x}|w'(z)|^2\,dy.$$

Dividing both sides of the inequality by $\theta(x)$ and integrating with respect to x from a to b, we obtain

$$\int\limits_a^b\int\limits_{\theta_x}|w'(x+iy)|^2\,dx\,dy\geqslant\pi^2\int\limits_a^b\frac{dx}{\theta(x)}+\int\limits_a^b\frac{\omega^2(x)}{\theta(x)}\,dx.$$

The integral on the left side of the inequality is none other than the area of the image of the part of the domain D contained between θ_a and θ_b under the mapping $w=w(z)$ (see Sect. 1, formula (1.3)). This image is the part of the strip $|\operatorname{Im} w|<\frac{\pi}{2}$ contained between the curves L_a and L_b, thus it obviously is contained inside the rectangle

$$|\operatorname{Im} w|<\frac{\pi}{2},\quad u^-(a)<\operatorname{Re} w<u^+(b)$$

and its area does not exceed the area of this rectangle. Since the area of the rectangle is equal to

$$\pi[u^+(b)-u^-(a)]=\pi[u^-(b)-u^+(a)]+\pi[\omega(b)+\omega(a)],$$

we obtain the inequality

$$u^-(b)-u^+(a)\geqslant\pi\int\limits_a^b\frac{dx}{\theta(x)}+\frac{1}{\pi}\int\limits_a^b\frac{\omega^2(x)}{\theta(x)}\,dx-\omega(a)-\omega(b).$$

However, $u^+(x)$ and $u^-(x)$ are increasing functions; therefore if $a<\xi<\eta<b$, we have $u^-(b)-u^+(a)>u^-(\eta)-u^+(\xi)$. If we choose ξ and η to satisfy the conditions of the lemma, we find that

$$u^-(b)-u^+(a)>\pi\int\limits_\xi^\eta\frac{dx}{\theta(x)}-2\pi>\pi\int\limits_a^b\frac{dx}{\theta(x)}-4\pi.$$

This gives us the statement of the theorem, for $\operatorname{Re} w(\zeta)>u^-(b)$ when $\zeta\in\theta_b$ and $\operatorname{Re} w(z)<u^+(a)$ when $z\in\theta_a$.

The following result, due to Warschawskiy, allows us to estimate the value of $\operatorname{Re}[w(\zeta)-w(z)]$ from the other side. Here more rigid conditions must be imposed on the curves C^+ and C^-.

We suppose that the equations of the curves C^+ and C^- have the form

$$y=\varphi^+(x),\quad y=\varphi^-(x).$$

It is clear that $\theta(x)=\varphi^{+}(x)-\varphi^{-}(x)$. Moreover, we set $\varphi(x)=\frac{1}{2}[\varphi^{+}(x)+\varphi^{-}(x)]$. Then $\varphi^{\pm}(x)=\varphi(x)\pm\frac{1}{2}\theta(x)$.

Theorem 6.2. *Suppose that for all x we have $|\varphi'(x)|<M$, $|\theta'(x)|<M$. If $a<b$, $z\in\theta_a$, $\zeta\in\theta_b$, then*

$$\operatorname{Re}[w(\zeta)-w(z)]<\pi\int_a^b\frac{1+\varphi'^2(x)}{\theta(x)}dx+\frac{\pi}{12}\int_a^b\frac{\theta'^2(x)}{\theta(x)}dx+12\pi(1+M^2).$$

Proof. Let P_u denote the image of the segment $\operatorname{Re}w=u$, $|\operatorname{Im}w|<\frac{\pi}{2}$, under the mapping $z=z(w)$. It is clear that the curve P_u connects the curves C^+ and C^-. We put

$$x^+(u)=\sup_{z\in P_u}\operatorname{Re}z,\quad x^-(u)=\inf_{z\in P_u}\operatorname{Re}z.$$

Note first that

$$\int_{x^-(u}^{x^+(u)}\frac{dx}{\theta(x)}<4. \tag{6.3}$$

In fact, if the integral of interest is less that two, then nothing more needs to be said. If it is greater than two, then, after taking values $y^{\pm}$ such that $\operatorname{Re}w(x^++iy^+)=\operatorname{Re}w(x^-+iy^-)=u$, according to Theorem 6.1, we obtain

$$0=u-u>\pi\int_{x^-}^{x^+}\frac{dx}{\theta(x)}-4\pi\qquad(x^{\pm}=x^{\pm}(u)).$$

Inequality (6.3) follows from this.

Let us turn our attention to the main part of the proof. Let $w=u+iv$ be any point of the strip $|\operatorname{Im}w|<\frac{\pi}{2}$. We put

$$\xi(v)=\xi_u(v)=\tau(x(u,v),\,y(u,v)),\quad\tau(x,y)=\frac{y-\varphi(x)}{\theta(x)},$$

where

$$x(u,v)=\operatorname{Re}z(u+iv),\quad y(u,v)=\operatorname{Im}z(u+iv).$$

Since the point $z(w)=x(u,v)+iy(u,v)$ is contained in the domain D, and this domain is defined by the inequalities $\varphi^-(x)<y<\varphi^+(x)$, where $\varphi^{\pm}(x)=\varphi(x)\pm\frac{1}{2}\theta(x)$, then $-\frac{1}{2}<\xi(v)<\frac{1}{2}$ for $-\frac{\pi}{2}<v<\frac{\pi}{2}$ for any u, and $\xi\left(\pm\frac{\pi}{2}\right)=\pm\frac{1}{2}$. Therefore

$$1=\xi\left(\frac{\pi}{2}\right)-\xi\left(-\frac{\pi}{2}\right)=$$

$$=\int_{-\frac{\pi}{2}}^{\frac{\pi}{2}}\xi'(v)\,dv\leqslant\int_{-\frac{\pi}{2}}^{\frac{\pi}{2}}|\xi'(v)|\,dv=\int_{-\frac{\pi}{2}}^{\frac{\pi}{2}}\left|\frac{\partial\tau}{\partial x}\frac{\partial x}{\partial v}+\frac{\partial\tau}{\partial y}\frac{\partial y}{\partial v}\right|dv$$

or

$$1\leqslant\left\{\int_{-\frac{\pi}{2}}^{\frac{\pi}{2}}\left|\frac{\partial\tau}{\partial x}\frac{\partial x}{\partial v}+\frac{\partial\tau}{\partial y}\frac{\partial y}{\partial v}\right|dv\right\}^2.$$

We apply the Cauchy-Schwarz inequality to this last integral (see (6.2)) after setting $f=1, g=\left|\frac{\partial\tau}{\partial x}\frac{\partial x}{\partial v}+\frac{\partial\tau}{\partial y}\frac{\partial y}{\partial v}\right|$. This gives us

$$1\leqslant\pi\int_{-\frac{\pi}{2}}^{\frac{\pi}{2}}\left|\frac{\partial\tau}{\partial x}\frac{\partial x}{\partial v}+\frac{\partial\tau}{\partial y}\frac{\partial y}{\partial v}\right|^2dv.$$

However,

$$\left|\frac{\partial\tau}{\partial x}\frac{\partial x}{\partial v}+\frac{\partial\tau}{\partial y}\frac{\partial y}{\partial v}\right|^2\leqslant\left[\left(\frac{\partial\tau}{\partial x}\right)^2+\left(\frac{\partial\tau}{\partial y}\right)^2\right]\left[\left(\frac{\partial x}{\partial v}\right)^2+\left(\frac{\partial y}{\partial v}\right)^2\right].$$

Therefore

$$1\leqslant\int_{-\frac{\pi}{2}}^{\frac{\pi}{2}}\left[\left(\frac{\partial\tau}{\partial x}\right)^2+\left(\frac{\partial\tau}{\partial y}\right)^2\right]\left[\left(\frac{\partial x}{\partial v}\right)^2+\left(\frac{\partial y}{\partial v}\right)^2\right]dv.$$

Integrating this last inequality with respect to u from $u_1=\operatorname{Re} w(z)$ to $u_2=\operatorname{Re} w(\zeta)$, we obtain

$$u_2-u_1\leqslant\pi\int_{u_1}^{u_2}\int_{-\frac{\pi}{2}}^{\frac{\pi}{2}}\left[\left(\frac{\partial\tau}{\partial x}\right)^2+\left(\frac{\partial\tau}{\partial y}\right)^2\right]\left[\left(\frac{\partial x}{\partial v}\right)^2+\left(\frac{\partial y}{\partial v}\right)^2\right]du\,dv.$$

We now make the substitution $x=x(u,\ v)$, $y=y(u,\ v)$ in the integral (i.e., in the mapping $z=z(u+iv)$). In view of the Cauchy-Riemann equations, the Jacobian of this substitution equals $\left(\frac{\partial x}{\partial v}\right)^2+\left(\frac{\partial y}{\partial v}\right)^2$, so that

$$\left[\left(\frac{\partial x}{\partial v}\right)^2+\left(\frac{\partial y}{\partial v}\right)^2\right]du\,dv=dx\,dy,$$

and the inequality is brought into the form

$$u_2-u_1\leqslant\pi\iint\limits_{D_{1,2}}\left[\left(\frac{\partial\tau}{\partial x}\right)^2+\left(\frac{\partial\tau}{\partial y}\right)^2\right]dx\,dy.$$

Here $D_{1,2}$ is the image of the rectangle $|\operatorname{Im} w|<\frac{\pi}{2}$, $u_1<\operatorname{Re} w<u_2$, under the mapping $z=z(w)$.

Note that the domain $D_{1,2}$ is trivially contained in the domain

$$\varphi^-(x)<y<\varphi^+(x),\quad a^-<x<b^+,$$

where $a^-=x^-(u_1)$, $b^+=x^+(u_2)$. Therefore

$$u_2-u_1\leqslant\pi\int\limits_{a-}^{b+}\left\{\int\limits_{\varphi-(x)}^{\varphi+(x)}\left[\left(\frac{\partial\tau}{\partial x}\right)^2+\left(\frac{\partial\tau}{\partial y}\right)^2\right]dy\right\}dx. \tag{6.4}$$

We now find $\left(\frac{\partial\tau}{\partial x}\right)^2+\left(\frac{\partial\tau}{\partial y}\right)^2$. Since $\tau(x,y)=\frac{y-\varphi(x)}{\theta(x)}$, then

$$\frac{\partial\tau}{\partial x}=-\frac{\varphi'(x)}{\theta(x)}-\frac{y-\varphi(x)}{\theta^2(x)}\theta'(x),\quad \frac{\partial\tau}{\partial y}=\frac{1}{\theta(x)}$$

and

$$\left(\frac{\partial\tau}{\partial x}\right)^2+\left(\frac{\partial\tau}{\partial y}\right)^2=\frac{1+\varphi'^2(x)}{\theta^2(x)}-\frac{y-\varphi(x)}{\theta^3(x)}\varphi'(x)\theta'(x)+\frac{[y-\varphi(x)]^2}{\theta^4(x)}\theta'^2(x).$$

We substitute this expression into (6.4) and carry out integration with respect to y. After some simple rearrangements, we obtain

$$u_2-u_1\leqslant\pi\int\limits_{a-}^{b+}\left\{1+\varphi'^2(x)+\frac{1}{12}\theta'^2(x)\right\}\frac{dx}{\theta(x)}.$$

Since according to the conditions of the theorem we have $1+\varphi'^2(x)+\frac{1}{12}\theta'^2(x)<\frac{13}{12}(1+M^2)$, and since according to inequality (6.3)

$$\int\limits_{a-}^{a}\frac{dx}{\theta(x)}+\int\limits_{b}^{b+}\frac{dx}{\theta(x)}<8,$$

we arrive at the statement of the theorem.

Under the same assumptions as in Theorem 6.2, we can also prove the inequality

$$\operatorname{Re}[w(\zeta)-w(z)] > \pi\int_a^b \frac{1+\varphi'^2(x)}{\theta(x)}\,dx - \frac{\pi}{4}\int_a^b \frac{\theta'^2(x)}{\theta(x)}\,dx + C$$

$$(z\in\theta_a,\ \zeta\in\theta_b),$$

which is a refinement of Ahlfors' inequality.

If we suppose that $\varphi'(x)\to 0$ as $x\to+\infty$ and that $\int_0^\infty \frac{\theta'^2(x)}{\theta(x)}\,dx<\infty$, we can obtain the formula*

$$w(x+iy) = C+\pi\int_0^x \frac{1+\varphi'^2(t)}{\theta(t)}\,dt + \pi i\,\frac{y-\varphi(x)}{\theta(x)} + o(1)$$

$$(x\to+\infty,\ x+iy\in D).$$

---

*) The proof of these facts (in an even stronger formulation) can be found in the article of Warschawskiy appearing in Russian translation in: Sbornik perevodov "Matematika," 2:4, 1958.

CHAPTER VI

The Theory of Residues

Cauchy's theorem and the theory of residues give rise to a wide variety of procedures for the transformation of integrals and sums. The collection of these procedures has received the name of the theory of residues. The basic purpose of the present chapter is to acquaint the reader with the basic methods of the theory by means of a series of concrete examples.

1. GENERALIZED CONTOUR INTEGRALS

The theory of residues has to do mainly with generalized integrals of regular functions, i.e., with integrals along paths whose ends are situated at singular points of the integrand. This somewhat complicates the application of Cauchy's theorem or the theory of residues to such integrals. Let us examine a simple example in order to make clear how the complication can arise:

The integral

$$I = \int_{-\infty}^{\infty} e^{-x^2}\,dx$$

can be studied as an integral along the boundary of the half-plane $\operatorname{Im} z > 0$ (or $\operatorname{Im} z < 0$) of the function $f(z) = e^{-z^2}$, which is regular in this half-plane and has an essential singular point at the point $z = \infty$ (which is situated on the boundary of this half-plane). If Cauchy's theorem were applicable, the integral would equal zero. But it is clearly positive (it is known from analysis that it equals $\sqrt{\pi}$).

It is natural to ask the question: how can the residue theorem (in particular, Cauchy's theorem) be applied to integrals along contours that pass through singular points of the integrand?

We now present several criteria that permit us to answer this question. However, before formulating these criteria, we clarify the nature of the phenomenon by means of an example.

Let us examine the behavior of the modulus of the function e^{-z^2} in a neighborhood of the point at infinity. Setting $z=re^{i\varphi}$, we have

$$|e^{-z^2}|=e^{-r^2\cos 2\varphi}.$$

Since $\cos 2\varphi>0$ for $-\pi/4<\varphi<\pi/4$ and for $3\pi/4<\varphi<5\pi/4$, and we have $\cos 2\varphi<0$ for the remaining values of φ, the neighborhood of the point at infinity may be split up into four equal sectors. In two sectors

$$|z|>R, \quad -\frac{\pi}{4}<\arg z<\frac{\pi}{4},$$

and

$$|z|>R, \quad \frac{3\pi}{4}<\arg z<\frac{5\pi}{4},$$

the modulus of the function e^{-z^2} is small, and in the other two sectors

$$|z|>R, \quad \frac{\pi}{4}<\arg z<\frac{3\pi}{4},$$

and

$$|z|>R, \quad -\frac{3\pi}{4}<\arg z<-\frac{\pi}{4},$$

it is large. The endpoints of our contour (the real axis) lie in those sectors where the modulus of the function e^{-z^2} is small, which would naturally be the case since the integral must converge. However, the endpoints of the contour could both lie in one sector or they might lie in different sectors. They do, in fact, lie in different sectors so that the integral is not zero. This suggests that a regularity of this type is a general phenomenon. Such regularity is indeed found for all the simple functions that are usually encountered in concrete examples. Unfortunately, any attempt to describe the class of functions exhibiting this regularity must lead to very complicated problems of formulation. It is therefore wiser to demonstrate simply formulated sufficient conditions, which arise in rather simple special cases, and at the same time to keep in mind the possibility of a general formulation, while not requiring its rigorous statement. This regularity may be expressed as follows:

Any sufficiently small neighborhood of a singular point of the function f(z) may be split up into some number of connected parts. In some of these regions the modulus of the function $f(z)$ is small while in the others it is large. If both endpoints of the contour C *fall in one connected part where* $|f(z)|$ *is small, then the residue theorem applies to the integral of f(z) along C, otherwise not.*

Thus, if the integral of the function $f(z)$ of interest to us is taken along a path C that passes through a singular point a, our first step must be to examine the behavior of the modulus of $f(z)$ in a neighborhood of this singular point and find the parts of this neighborhood in which it is small. If both endpoints of the contour lie in a single connected part of the neighborhood, then the applicability of the theorem of residues is easily proved with the aid of one of the criteria that we present next.

We first discuss some symbolism to simplify the formulation.

Let the domain D be bounded by a piecewise-smooth curve C and let a be some point of C.

K_ρ will denote the circle $|z-a|<\varrho$ for $a\neq\infty$ and the domain $|z|>1/\varrho$ for $a=\infty$.

Let D_ρ denote the part of D lying outside K_ρ, let C_ρ be the part of C lying outside K_ρ and let γ_ρ be the part of the boundary of K_ρ contained in D. (It is clear that the boundary of D_ρ consists of C_ρ and γ_ρ.)

Theorem 1.1. *Let the function f(z) be regular in the domain D except at a finite number of poles* $z_1, z_2, \ldots, z_n$, *and continuous up to its boundary except at the point a. If*

$$\left|\int_{\gamma_\rho} f(z)\,dz\right| \to 0 \qquad (\varrho\to 0) \tag{1.1}$$

and if the generalized integral of f(z) along C exists, then

$$\int_C f(z)\,dz = 2\pi i \sum_1^n \operatorname*{res}_{z=z_k} f(z).$$

Proof. If the generalized integral of $f(z)$ along C exists, then (see Sect. 6, Chap. I)

$$\int_C f(z)\,dz = \lim_{\rho\to 0}\int_{C_\rho} f(z)\,dz.$$

On the other hand, according to the residue theorem, the integral along the boundary of the domain D_ρ of the function $f(z)$ for ϱ sufficiently small (so small that all poles of $f(z)$ are in D_ρ) equals

$$2\pi i \sum_1^n \operatorname*{res}_{z=z_k} f(z).$$

Since the boundary of D_ρ consists of C_ρ and γ_ρ, this means that

$$\int_{C_\rho} f(z)\,dz = 2\pi i \sum_1^n \operatorname*{res}_{z=z_k} f(z) - \int_{\gamma_\rho} f(z)\,dz.$$

Taking the limit as $\varrho \to 0$, we obtain the statement of the theorem.

Remark. Let $\gamma(\varrho)$ denote the length of γ_ρ, and let

$$M(\varrho) = \max_{z \in \gamma_\rho} |f(z)|.$$

Then the fulfillment of condition (1.1) is trivially guaranteed, if

$$M(\varrho)\,\gamma(\varrho) \to 0 \qquad (\varrho \to 0). \tag{1.2}$$

It is clear that for $a \neq \infty$ we have $\gamma(\varrho) \leqslant 2\pi\varrho$ and for $a = \infty$ we have $\gamma(\varrho) \leqslant 2\pi/\varrho$. Therefore, condition (1.2) can be replaced by the still simpler conditions:

$$\lim_{\rho \to 0} \varrho M(\varrho) = 0 \qquad (a \neq \infty), \tag{1.3}$$

$$\lim_{\rho \to 0} \frac{M(\varrho)}{\varrho} = 0 \qquad (a = \infty). \tag{1.4}$$

These simple conditions may sometimes prove too restrictive. The following result gives a more refined condition sufficient for the fulfillment of condition (1.1); it is called *Jordan's lemma.*

Lemma 1. *Let Γ_R be the arc of the circle $|z| = R$, $|\arg z - \varphi_0| < \pi/2\nu$, and let the function f(z) satisfy the inequality*

$$|f(Re^{i\varphi})| \leqslant \varepsilon(R)\, e^{-R^\nu \cos \nu(\varphi - \varphi_0)}$$

on this arc. If $\varepsilon(R) R^{1-\nu} \to 0 \quad (R \to \infty)$, then

$$\lim_{R \to \infty} \int_{\Gamma_R} |f(z)|\,|dz| = 0.$$

Proof. The equation of the arc Γ_R has the form $z = Re^{i\varphi}$, $|\varphi - \varphi_0| < \pi/2\nu$. Therefore $|dz| = R\,d\varphi$ and

$$\int_{\Gamma_R} |f(z)|\,|dz| \leqslant R\varepsilon(R) \int_{\varphi_0 - \frac{\pi}{2\nu}}^{\varphi_0 + \frac{\pi}{2\nu}} e^{-R^\nu \cos \nu(\varphi - \varphi_0)}\, d\varphi =$$

$$= \frac{2}{\nu} R\varepsilon(R) \int_0^{\frac{\pi}{2}} e^{-R^\nu \sin\theta}\, d\theta.$$

Since $\sin\theta > 2/\pi\,\theta$ for $0 < \theta < \pi/2$, then as $R \to \infty$

$$\int_{\Gamma_R} |f(z)|\,|dz| \leqslant \frac{2}{\nu} R\varepsilon(R) \int_0^\infty e^{-\frac{2}{\pi}\theta R^\nu}\, d\theta = \frac{\pi}{\nu} R^{1-\nu} \varepsilon(R) \to 0,$$

which proves the lemma.

Contours C_1 and C_2 for which

$$\int_{C_1} f(z)\,dz = \int_{C_2} f(z)\,dz,$$

will frequently be called *equivalent* for the sake of brevity.

The problem of the equivalence of two contours with the same initial and terminal points may be solved by reduction to an integral along a closed contour.

We now present a typical specimen of the reasoning involved in proving two contours equivalent.

Example 1. Let us show that

$$\int_0^\infty \sin x^2\,dx = \int_0^\infty \cos x^2\,dx = \sqrt{\frac{\pi}{2}}.$$

It is known from analysis that

$$\int_0^\infty e^{-z^2}\,dz = \frac{1}{2}\sqrt{\pi}.$$

We have already studied the behavior of the modulus of the function e^{-z^2} in a neighborhood of the point at infinity and showed that it is small in the angle $|\arg z| < \pi/4$. Let us show that all the rays $\arg z = \varphi$, $|\varphi| \leqslant \pi/4$ are equivalent contours. We take $-\pi/4 \leqslant \alpha < \beta \leqslant \pi/4$ and consider the integral e^{-z^2} along the boundary of the sector $|z| < R$, $\alpha < \arg z < \beta$. According to Cauchy's theorem, this integral is zero. If $L_{R\varphi}$ denotes the segment $(0,\ Re^{i\varphi})$, and $\Gamma_{R_{\alpha\beta}}$ denotes the arc $|z| = R$, $\alpha \leqslant \arg z \leqslant \beta$, then this fact may be indicated by means of the formula

$$\int_{L_{R\alpha}} e^{-z^2}\,dz + \int_{\Gamma_{R\alpha\beta}} e^{-z^2}\,dz - \int_{L_{R\beta}} e^{-z^2}\,dz = 0.$$

It is clear that as $R \to \infty$ the integral $L_{R\varphi}$ approaches the integral along the ray $\arg z = \varphi$ (if it exists). We must evaluate the integral along the ray $\Gamma_{R_{\alpha\beta}}$. If $\alpha > -\pi/4, \beta < \pi/4$, then the fact that the integral along $\Gamma_{R_{\alpha\beta}}$ approaches zero as $R \to \infty$ is an easy consequence of the remark to Theorem 1.1. However, this argument fails for $\alpha = -\pi/4$ or $\beta = \pi/4$. Therefore, it is better to apply Jordan's lemma immediately. It is obvious that

$$|e^{-z^2}| = e^{-R^2 \cos 2\varphi} \qquad (|z| = R,\ \arg z = \varphi),$$

i.e., $\nu = 2$, $\varepsilon(R) = 1$ and $\varepsilon(R) R^{1-\nu} = \frac{1}{R} \to 0$. Thus,

$$\int_{\Gamma_{R\alpha\beta}} |e^{-z^2}|\,|dz| \leqslant \int_{\Gamma_{R,\,-\frac{\pi}{4},\,\frac{\pi}{4}}} |e^{-z^2}|\,|dz| \to 0 \qquad (R \to \infty).$$

From this we see that

$$\int_0^{\infty e^{i\alpha}} e^{-z^2}\,dz = \int_0^{\infty e^{i\beta}} e^{-z^2}\,dz \qquad \left(-\frac{\pi}{4} \leqslant \alpha < \beta \leqslant \frac{\pi}{4}\right).$$

If, in particular, we set $\alpha = 0$, and $\beta = \pi/4$, we find

$$\frac{1}{2}\sqrt{\pi} = \int_0^{\infty} e^{-z^2}\,dz = \int_0^{\infty e^{\frac{\pi i}{4}}} e^{-z^2}\,dz.$$

Making the change of variables $z = xe^{\frac{\pi i}{4}}$ in the second integral $0 < x < \infty$, we obtain

$$\frac{1}{2}\sqrt{\pi} = e^{\frac{\pi i}{4}} \int_0^{\infty} e^{-ix^2}\,dx.$$

Equating real and imaginary parts, we find the required formula.

2. ANALYTIC CONTINUATION OF CONTOUR INTEGRALS

The great majority of the functions with which we have to deal in analysis can be presented in the form of generalized contour integrals. The considerations adduced in Sect. 1 play a significant role in their investigation. The possibility of replacement of the contour of integration by an equivalent one frequently opens up opportunities for the analytic continuation of functions given in terms of integrals as well as for obtaining estimates of these functions. We now prove two theorems on the analytic continuation of integrals on which we shall frequently have to rely in future discussions.

Theorem 2.1. *Let the function* $f(\zeta)$ *be regular and bounded in the angle* $|\arg \zeta - \varphi| < \alpha$, $\alpha \leqslant \pi/2$. *Then, the function*

$$F(z) = \int_0^{\infty e^{i\varphi}} f(\zeta)\, e^{-z\zeta}\, d\zeta$$

can be continued analytically in the angle $|\arg z + \varphi| < \frac{\pi}{2} + \alpha$.

Proof. The integral giving $F(z)$ converges uniformly in z in the half-plane $\operatorname{Re}(ze^{i\varphi}) \geqslant \delta > 0$. In fact, for $\operatorname{Re}(ze^{i\varphi}) \geqslant \delta$ and $\arg \zeta = \varphi$ we have

$$|f(\zeta)| \leqslant M, \qquad |e^{-z\zeta}| \leqslant e^{-\delta|\zeta|},$$

i.e., that the modulus of the integrand does not exceed that of the absolutely integrable function $Me^{-\delta|\zeta|}$. Applying Weierstrass' test (see Sect. 6, Chap. I), we readily verify the uniform convergence of the integral. Thus, the function $F(z)$ is regular in the half-plane $\operatorname{Re}(ze^{i\varphi}) > 0$.

We next set $z = re^{-i\varphi}$, $r > 0$, and determine the contours of integration that are equivalent to $\arg\zeta = \varphi$. If $\arg\zeta = \theta$, then

$$|e^{-z\zeta}| = e^{-r\cos(\varphi-\theta)},$$

i.e., the integrand approaches zero more rapidly than any power of ζ in the angle $|\arg\zeta - \varphi| < \varphi$. This means that all rays $\arg\zeta = \theta$, $|\theta - \varphi| < \alpha$ are equivalent contours, i.e.,

$$F(z) = \int_0^{\infty e^{i\theta}} f(\zeta)\, e^{-z\zeta}\, d\zeta \qquad (\arg z = -\varphi,\ |\theta - \varphi| < \alpha).$$

But by the same reasoning as that above this last integral also represents a function that is regular in the half-plane $\operatorname{Re}(ze^{i\theta}) > 0$. We thus are able to obtain an analytic continuation of $F(z)$ into all half-planes of the form $\operatorname{Re}(ze^{i\theta}) > \theta$, $|\theta - \varphi| < \alpha$. It is easy to verify that the set of these half-planes describes that angle $|\arg z + \varphi| < \pi/2 + \alpha$. This proves the theorem.

Remark 1. It is clear that the requirement of boundedness for the function $f(\zeta)$ in the angle $|\arg\zeta - \varphi| < \alpha$ is often not essential for analytic continuation. If we require that the function $\varphi(\zeta)$ be regular in the angle $|\arg\zeta - \varphi| < \alpha$ and satisfy the condition

$$|f(re^{i\theta})| < g(r)\, e^{r\nu(\theta)}, \qquad \int_0^\infty g(r)\, dr < \infty$$

$$\left(|\theta - \varphi| < \alpha < \frac{\pi}{2}\right),$$

then by the same arguments we may arrive at the conclusion that the function $F(z)$ can be continued analytically in the domain obtained by taking the union of the half-planes $\operatorname{Re}(ze^{i\theta}) > \nu(\theta)$, $|\theta - \varphi| < \alpha$.

Remark 2. This particular form of the integrand is not strictly necessary. For instance, we can prove an analogous theorem for integrals of the form

$$F(z) = \int_0^{\infty e^{i\varphi}} f(\zeta) \frac{d\zeta}{1 - e^{z\zeta}} \qquad (\operatorname{Re}(ze^{i\varphi}) > 0).$$

Applying the same idea, we can carry the analytic continuation even farther, even by-passing the point $z = 0$, which is, generally speaking, a singlular point of the function $F(z)$. We now present an example in which such an investivation is carried out.

Example 1. Let the function $F(z)$ be given for real positive z by the equation

$$F(z) = \int_0^\infty \frac{e^{-z\zeta}}{\sqrt{1+\zeta^2}}\, d\zeta \qquad (\sqrt{1+\zeta^2} > 0).$$

We determine the analytic function obtained by analytic continuation of the function $F(z)$.

Since the function $f(\zeta)=\frac{1}{\sqrt{1+\zeta^2}}$ is regular and bounded in the half-plane $\operatorname{Re}\zeta>0$, then according to Theorem 2.1, we may obtain an analytic continuation of the function $F(z)$ into the z-plane with a cross cut along the negative half of the real axis.

We associate with each value of θ a function $F_\theta(z)$ that is regular in the half-plane $\operatorname{Re}(ze^{-i\theta})>0$ and obtained by analytic continuation of the function $F_0(z)=F(z)$ from the point t $(\operatorname{Re} t>0)$ to the point $te^{i\theta}$ along the arc of the circle $|z|=|t|, 0<\arg z/t<\theta$. It follows from Theorem 2.1 that

$$F_\theta(z)=\int_0^{\infty e^{-i\theta}} \frac{e^{-z\zeta}}{\sqrt{1+\zeta^2}}\,d\zeta \qquad \left(|\theta|<\frac{\pi}{2}\right).$$

We next construct a function $F_\theta(z)$ for each θ. To do this we let L_θ designate the following contour:

For $0<\theta<\pi/2$, the ray $\arg\zeta=-\theta$.

For $\pi/2<\theta<3\pi/2$, we make a cut in the plane along the segment $(-i, i)$ and form the contour L_θ from the segment $(0, -i)$ of the right edge of the cut, the segment $(-i, i)$ of the left edge of the cut and the ray $\arg\zeta=-\theta$.

For $3\pi/2<\theta<5\pi/2$, we form the contour from the segment $(0, -i)$ of the right edge of the cut, the segment $(-i, i)$ of the left edge of the cut, the segment $(i, 0)$ of the right edge of the cut and the ray $\arg\zeta=-\theta$. We set

$$F_\theta(z)=\int_{L_\theta} \frac{e^{-z\zeta}}{\sqrt{1+\zeta^2}}\,d\zeta \qquad (\operatorname{Re}(ze^{-i\theta})>0).$$

It is easy to verify that if θ, θ' and $\arg z$ are close to one another, the contours L_θ and $L_{\theta'}$ are equivalent, i.e.,

$$F_\theta(z)=F_{\theta'}(z)$$

for θ, θ' and $\arg z$ close to one another. Therefore the collection of functions $F_\theta(z)$ realizes an analytic continuation of the function $F(z)$. Each function $F_\theta(z)$ is a regular in the half-plane $\operatorname{Re}(ze^{-i\theta})>0$. If the value of θ exceeds 2π, we return to the starting point after carrying out analytic continuation along a circle that makes a circuit around the origin in the counterclockwise direction. In this operation, we add to the original integral an integral along both sides of the cross cut $(-i, i)$, taken in the direction: $(0, -i)$ along the right side of the cut, $(-i, i)$ along the left side of the cut and $(i, 0)$ along the right side of the cut. The function $\sqrt{1+\zeta^2}$ is taken to be positive for $\zeta>0$, so that it will also be positive along the right side of the cut. Therefore, computing the additional integral, we find

$$F_{\theta+2\pi}(z)=F_\theta(z)-2i\int_{-1}^{1} \frac{e^{-iyz}}{\sqrt{1-y^2}}\,dy.$$

This resolves the question of the analytic continuation of $F(z)$.

The following theorem is related to the problem of analytic continuation of integrals of the Cauchy type

$$F(z)=\frac{1}{2\pi i}\int_C \frac{f(\zeta)}{\zeta-z}\,d\zeta. \qquad (2.1)$$

We first show that the function represented by this integral is regular.

Lemma. If

$$\int_C \frac{|f(\zeta)|}{1+|\zeta|}\,|d\zeta|<\infty,$$

then the integral (2.1) uniformly converges in z in any closed set that does not contain points of the contour C.

Proof. Let E be a finite closed set that does not contain points of the contour C. Let R denote the radius of a circle with center at the origin and that contains the set E, and let ϱ be the distance from E to C. If $\zeta\in C$ and $z\in E$, then $|\zeta-z|\geqslant\varrho$ for all ζ, and for $|\zeta|\geqslant 2R$ we have $|\zeta-z|\geqslant|\zeta|-|z|\geqslant 1/2|\zeta|$. Thus, for some $M=M(R,\varrho)$ we have the inequality

$$\left|\frac{f(\zeta)}{\zeta-z}\right|\leqslant M\frac{|f(\zeta)|}{1+|\zeta|} \qquad (\zeta\in C,\ z\in E).$$

In view of the hypothesis of the lemma, we obtain the uniform convergence of the integral under consideration by the use of Weierstrass' test.

Corollary. The integral (2.1) represents a function that is regular in any domain not containing points of the contour C.

If the contour C divides the plane into regions, then a regular function will be associated with each region. In any case, the points of the contour form the boundary of the domain of regularity of the function.

The following theorem affords a complete solution of the problem of analytic continuation of an integral of the Cauchy type through points of the contour of integration.

Theorem 2.2. *Let the function $f(\zeta)$ be regular in a domain D that contains a segment C_0 (not all) of the contour C. Furthermore, let C_0 divide the domain D into two parts D^+ and D^-, situated on the left and right of C_0 respectively; let $F^+(z)$ and $F^-(z)$ be the functions represented by the integral (2.1) in D^+ and D^- respectively. Then the function $F^-(z)+f(z)$ gives an analytic continuation of the function $F^+(z)$ across the arc C_0 into the domain D^-.*

Proof. Let C^* denote the contour obtained from C by replacing C_0 by a part of the boundary of D (the part whose positive direction coincides with the direction of C^*). It is clear that this part of the boundary is also part of the boundary of D^- (Fig. 5). Let L^- denote the complete boundary of D^-. In addition to the part of the boundary of D already mentioned, L^- contains the curve C_0 traversed in the opposite direction. Thus, for any z from the domain D and not on C_0, we have

$$\frac{1}{2\pi i}\int_{C^*}\frac{f(\zeta)}{\zeta-z}\,d\zeta=\frac{1}{2\pi i}\int_{C}\frac{f(\zeta)}{\zeta-z}\,d\zeta+\frac{1}{2\pi i}\int_{L^-}\frac{f(\zeta)}{\zeta-z}\,d\zeta. \qquad (2.2)$$

Let $F(z)$ denote the integral occurring in the left side of the equation. Since there are no points of the contour C^* in the domain D $F(z)$ is a function regular in this domain.

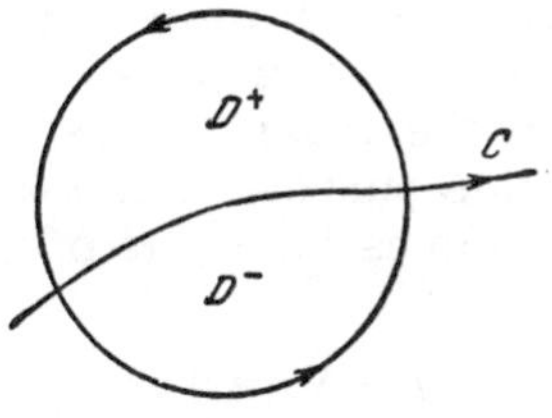

Fig. 5.

For $z\in D^+$ we have $F(z)=F^+(z)$, since the first integral on the right side of the equation equals $F^+(z)$ by definition and the second is zero by Cauchy's theorem.

For $z\in D^-$ we have $F(z)=F^-(z)+f(z)$, since by definition the first integral equals $F^-(z)$ and the second equals $f(z)$ because of Cauchy's integral formula.

Thus, the function $F^+(z)$ continues the function $F(z)$ analytically to the entire domain D, which proves the theorem.

Integrals of the Cauchy type arise in many problems of the theory of analytic functions. For example, we have already used integrals of the Cauchy type in obtaining Laurent expansions of a function.

One of the typical applications of an integral of the Cauchy type arises in the problem of splitting up a function given on the boundary of a domain into a sum of two functions, one of which is regular inside the domain and the other outside the domain. This problem can be solved even in the absence of regularity of the function $f(\zeta)$ on the contour C (the boundary of the domain). In this case the function is usually assumed to satisfy a Lipschitz condition of some positive order α on the contour, i.e., it satisfies the condition

$$|f(\zeta)-f(\zeta')|<M|\zeta-\zeta'|^{\alpha} \qquad (\zeta\in C,\ \zeta'\in C).$$

No further discussion of the analytic continuation of Cauchy integrals of this type is necessary. The theorem now reduces to the statement):*

---

*Further details concerning integrals of the Cauchy type (without the hypothesis of regularity for the function $f(\zeta)$) can be found in the book of I. I. Privalov, Boundary Conditions of Analytic Functions (in Russian), Gostekhizdat, Moscow, 1950.

The functions $F^+(z)$ *and* $F^-(z)$ *are uniformly continuous in the domains* D^+ *and* D^-, *respectively, and*

$$F^+(\zeta)-F^-(\zeta)=f(\zeta) \qquad (\zeta \in C).$$

3. EVALUATION OF DEFINITE INTEGRALS

The oldest problem to which the theory of residues has been applied is that of evaluation in finite form of (usually improper) integrals of real functions. It is possible to solve many such integrals with the aid of the theory of residues, but the number of methods employed for this purpose is not large.

The first method concerns integrals of the form

$$I=\int_{-\infty}^{\infty} \varphi(x)\,dx, \tag{3.1}$$

in which the function $\varphi(z)$ is regular in the half-plane $\operatorname{Im} z>0$ except at the finite set of poles $z_1, z_2, \ldots, z_n$ (contained in this half-plane), is continuous in the half-plane $\operatorname{Im} z \geqslant 0$ (except at the above-mentioned poles) and satisfies the condition

$$\int_{\Gamma_R} \varphi(z)\,dz \longrightarrow 0 \quad (R \longrightarrow \infty) \tag{3.2}$$

(Γ_R is the semicircle $|z|=R$, $\operatorname{Im} z>0$).

The conditions of Theorem 1.1 are satisfied if we take the half-plane $\operatorname{Im} z>0$ as our domain. This means that the integral (3.1) can be considered to be an integral along the boundary of the half-plane $\operatorname{Im} z>0$ and the theory of residues can be applied to it. This gives us the formula

$$\int_{-\infty}^{\infty} \varphi(x)\,dx=2\pi i \sum_{k=1}^{n} \operatorname*{res}_{z=z_k} \varphi(z). \tag{3.3}$$

Let us examine the possibilities of this method for the evaluation of integrals of real functions. It is clear that we can take for $\varphi(z)$ any rational function the degree of whose denominator exceeds that of the numerator by at least two (this is necessary both for the convergence of the integral and for the fulfillment of condition (3.2)). On the other hand, if we assume that the function $\varphi(x)$ is real for real x, then it is not difficult to show with the aid of the symmetry principle that there are no other possibilities.

However, it is not necessary to assume that the function $\varphi(x)$ is real for real x in order to obtain integrals of functions of a real variable. We can write

$$\int_{-\infty}^{\infty} u(x)\,dx=\operatorname{Re}\left\{2\pi i \sum_{k=1}^{n} \operatorname*{res}_{z=z_k} \varphi(z)\right\}, \quad u(x)=\operatorname{Re} \varphi(x). \tag{3.4}$$

The use of this expression enables us to extend considerably the class of integrals that can be evaluated with the aid of the theory of residues, but it makes the evaluation much more complicated. The reason for this is that in formula (3.4) we integrate the function $u(x) = \operatorname{Re}\varphi(x)$, but we compute the residues from the function $\varphi(z)$. Thus, when we are given an integral, we then know only the function $u(x) = \operatorname{Re}\varphi(x)$ for real x, although we need to know the values of the function $\varphi(z)$ for all z. It is no simpler to solve this problem (generally speaking) than it is to evaluate the integral. However, it is frequently possible to solve this problem by a combination of inspection and conjecture (similar to the determination of an antiderivative).

We mention two further types of integrals that can be evaluated with the aid of the arguments already presented.

Let R(z) be a rational function the degree of whose denominator exceeds that of its numerator. If the function $R(x)$ is real for real x, does not have poles along the real axis, and $R(z)$ has poles $z_1, z_2, \ldots, z_n$, in the half-plane $\operatorname{Im} z > 0$, then for any $a > 0$

$$\int_{-\infty}^{\infty} R(x) \cos ax \, dx = -2\pi \operatorname{Im} \sum_{1}^{n} \operatorname*{res}_{z=z_k} R(z) e^{iaz} \tag{3.5}$$

and

$$\int_{-\infty}^{\infty} R(x) \sin ax \, dx = 2\pi \operatorname{Re} \sum_{k=1}^{n} \operatorname*{res}_{z=z_k} R(z) e^{iaz}. \tag{3.6}$$

If we make the additional assumption that the degree of the denominator of $R(z)$ exceeds that of the numerator by at least two, then for any $a > 0$ we have

$$\int_{-\infty}^{\infty} R(x) \ln(x^2 + a^2) \, dx = -4\pi \operatorname{Im} \sum_{k=1}^{n} \operatorname*{res}_{z=z_k} R(z) \ln(z + ia) \tag{3.7}$$

(we choose any branch of $\ln(z + ia)$ that is regular in the half-plane $\operatorname{Im} z > 0$).

The proof of this formula follows in an obvious way from the arguments given above. We may use Jordan's lemma (see Sect. 1) as a test for the fulfillment of conditions (3.2) in the first two formulas, and the remark to Theorem 1.1 in the third.

The second method is only a little more complicated. The following lemma is needed in order to establish it:

Lemma 1. *Let the functions $f(z)$ and $g(z)$ be regular inside the strip $a < \operatorname{Im} z < b$ except at the finite set of poles $z_1, z_2, \ldots, z_n$, and continuous in the closed strip (at these same poles). If f(z) is a* *periodic function with period* $i(b-a)$ *and satisfies the condition*

$$\int_{\Gamma_R} f(z)\,g(z)\,dz \to 0 \qquad (R \to \pm\infty) \tag{3.8}$$

(Γ_R is a segment of $\operatorname{Re} z = R$, $a < \operatorname{Im} z < b$), then

$$\int_{-\infty}^{\infty} f(x)\,[g(x+ai) - g(x+bi)]\,dx = 2\pi i \sum_{k=1}^{n} \operatorname*{res}_{z=z_k} f(z)\,g(z).$$

Proof. In view of condition (3.8), the difference of the integrals

$$\int_{ia-\infty}^{ia+\infty} f(z)\,g(z)\,dz - \int_{ib-\infty}^{ib+\infty} f(z)\,g(z)\,dz =$$

$$= \int_{-\infty}^{\infty} f(x)\,[g(x+ai) - g(x+bi)]\,dx$$

can be studied as an integral along the boundary of the strip $a < \operatorname{Im} z < b$. Applying Theorem 1.1, we obtain the statement of the lemma.

We now introduce two types of integrals that can be evaluated by the use of this method.

Let R(z) be a rational function with poles $z_1, z_2, \ldots, z_n$, *and such that the degree of its denominator exceeds that of its numerator by m; we assume also that R(z) has no poles along the negative half of the real axis nor at* $z=0$.

Setting $f(z) = R(-e^z)$, $g(z) = e^{\alpha z}$, $a = -\pi$, $b = \pi$, *we find*

$$\int_{-\infty}^{\infty} R(-e^x)\,e^{\alpha x}\,dx = -\frac{\pi}{\sin \alpha\pi} \sum_{1}^{n} \operatorname*{res}_{z=\ln z_k} R(e^z)\,e^{\alpha z} \tag{3.9}$$

$$(0 < \alpha < m).$$

The condition $0 < \alpha < m$ ensures that the integral converges and that condition (3.8) is satisfied.

Setting $f(z) = R(-e^z)$, $g(z) = \frac{1}{z}$, $a = -\pi$, $b = \pi$ *and assuming that* $m \geqslant 2$, *we find*

$$\int_{-\infty}^{\infty} \frac{R(-e^x)}{x^2+\pi^2}\,dx = \frac{1}{2} \sum_{1}^{n} \operatorname*{res}_{z=\ln z_k} \frac{R(e^z)}{z}. \tag{3.10}$$

We must take the principle value of $\ln z_k$ *in both formulas.*

Approximately the same difficulties are connected with the application of the second method as with the application of the first. The function to be integrated is $f(x)\,[g(x+ai) - g(x+bi)]$, but we have to compute the residues from the function $f(z)\,g(z)$.

A third method concerns integrals of the form

$$\int_0^{2\pi} \varphi(e^{ix})\,dx, \tag{3.11}$$

where the function $\varphi(z)$ is regular in the circle $|z|<1$, except at a finite number of poles. The method consists in making the substitution $z=e^{ix}$, which converts integral (3.11) into

$$\frac{1}{i}\int_{|z|=1} \varphi(z)\frac{dz}{z},$$

which can be evaluated with the aid of the theory of residues. The third method differs little from the first.

We have discussed evaluation using the theory of residues of integrals presented in one or another canonical form. In practice it is always necessary to transform the integrals into this form or to apply analogous methods to the integrals in the form in which they are given. Let us consider several examples.

Example 1. We show that

$$\int_0^{\infty} \frac{\sin x}{x}\,dx=\frac{\pi}{2}.$$

Even after writing the integral in the form of an integral along the entire axis, we cannot apply formula (3.6), since the function $R(z)=1/z$ has a pole on the real axis. But if $a>0$, we have

$$\left|\int_0^{\infty}\frac{\sin x}{x}dx-\int_0^{\infty}\frac{x\sin x}{x^2+a^2}dx\right|=\left|a^2\int_0^{\infty}\frac{\sin x}{x}\,\frac{dx}{x^2+a^2}\right|\leqslant a\int_0^{\infty}\frac{dx}{x^2+a^2}=\frac{\pi a}{2},$$

so that

$$\int_0^{\infty}\frac{\sin x}{x}dx=\lim_{a\to 0}\int_0^{\infty}\frac{x\sin x}{x^2+a^2}=\frac{1}{2}\lim_{a\to 0}\int_{-\infty}^{\infty}\frac{x\sin x}{x^2+a^2}.$$

This last integral is easy to evaluate by using formula (3.6). We find

$$\int_{-\infty}^{\infty}\frac{x\sin x}{x^2+a^2}dx=2\pi\,\mathrm{Re}\,\operatorname*{res}_{z=ia}\frac{ze^{iz}}{z^2+a^2}=\pi e^{-a}\qquad (a>0)$$

and

$$\int_0^{\infty}\frac{\sin x}{x}dx=\lim_{a\to 0}\frac{\pi}{2}e^{-a}=\frac{\pi}{2}.$$

Example 2. We now evaluate the integral

$$I=\int_0^\infty \frac{x^{\alpha-1}\ln x}{x+1}\,dx \qquad (0<\alpha<1).$$

We make the substitution $\ln x=t$. This gives us

$$I=\int_{-\infty}^{\infty}\frac{te^{\alpha t}}{1+e^t}\,dt=\frac{d}{d\alpha}\int_{-\infty}^{\infty}\frac{e^{\alpha t}}{1+e^t}\,dt.$$

Now, using formula (3.9), we obtain $\left(R(z)=\frac{1}{1-z}\right)$

$$\int_{-\infty}^{\infty}\frac{e^{\alpha t}}{1+e^t}\,dt=-\frac{\pi}{\sin\alpha\pi}\operatorname*{res}_{z=0}\frac{e^{\alpha z}}{1-e^z}=\frac{\pi}{\sin\alpha\pi}.$$

Thus,

$$I=-\frac{\pi^2\cos\alpha\pi}{\sin^2\alpha\pi}.$$

Example 3. We now evaluate the integral

$$I=\int_0^1 x^\alpha(1-x)^{1-\alpha}\,dx \qquad (-1<\alpha<2).$$

The integral I can be expressed in terms of an integral of the function

$$f(z)=z^\alpha(1-z)^{1-\alpha}$$

along the boundary C of the domain D, the extended plane with a cross cut along the segment $(0, 1)$. Indeed, the function $f(z)$ admits a partition into single-valued branches in the domain D (to see this we have only to write it in the form

$$f(z)=z\left(\frac{1}{z}-1\right)^{1-\alpha}$$

and apply the monodromy theorem to the second factor). We choose the branch that is positive on the upper edge of the cross cut. Then the function $f(z)$ equals $e^{2\pi i\alpha}z^\alpha(1-z)^{1-\alpha}$ on the lower edge of the cross cut (as it makes a circuit of the point $z=0$ along a small circle in the counterclockwise direction, the argument of z^α increases by $2\pi\alpha$, while the factor $(1-z)^{1-\alpha}$ is not changed). Therefore,

$$\int_C f(z)\,dz=I-e^{2\pi i\alpha}I=I(1-e^{2\pi i\alpha}).$$

On the other hand, according to the residue theorem $\int_C f(z)\,dz = 2\pi i \operatorname*{res}_{z=\infty} f(z)$. To find the residue we find the values of $f(z)$ for large z. For $z > 1$ we have $f(z) = -e^{\pi i\alpha} z^{\alpha}(z-1)^{1-\alpha}$, since $f(z) > 0$ on the upper edge of the cross cut (0, 1) and as we make a circuit of the point along the upper half of a small circle, we decrease the $\arg(1-z)^{1-\alpha}$ by $\pi(1-\alpha)$ (arg z^{α} does not change). Thus, $f(z) = -e^{\pi i\alpha} z\left(1-\frac{1}{z}\right)^{1-\alpha}$, and expanding the last factor in a series of powers of $1/z$, we find

$$f(z) = -e^{\pi i\alpha} z\left(1-\frac{c_1}{z}+\frac{c_2}{z^2}-\dots\right),$$

$$c_1 = 1-\alpha, \quad c_2 = \frac{(1-\alpha)(-\alpha)}{1\cdot 2}, \quad \dots .$$

From this we easily obtain $\operatorname*{res}_{z=\infty} f(z) = -e^{\pi i\alpha}\frac{\alpha(1-\alpha)}{2}$ and

$$I = -\frac{2\pi i}{1-e^{2\pi i\alpha}} \cdot e^{\pi i\alpha}\frac{\alpha(1-\alpha)}{2} = \frac{\pi\alpha(1-\alpha)}{2\sin\alpha\pi}.$$

Example 4. Finally, we evaluate the integral

$$I = \int_{-\pi}^{\pi} \frac{\ln|\sin x|}{1+a\cos x}\,dx \qquad (0 < a < 1).$$

Note that

$$\ln|\sin x| = \ln\left|\frac{e^{ix}-e^{-ix}}{2i}\right| = \ln\left|\frac{1-e^{2ix}}{2}\right| = \operatorname{Re}\ln\frac{1-e^{2ix}}{2}.$$

If we make the substitution $z = e^{ix}$ and take into account that

$$\cos x = \frac{1}{2}\left(z+\frac{1}{z}\right), \quad dx = \frac{dz}{iz}, \quad \ln|\sin x| = \operatorname{Re}\ln\frac{1-z^2}{2},$$

we find

$$I = \operatorname{Re}\frac{2}{i}\int_{|z|=1} \ln\frac{1-z^2}{2}\cdot\frac{dz}{2z+az^2+a}.$$

The integrand has a simple pole in the circle $|z| < 1$ at the point $z = \frac{\sqrt{1-a^2}-1}{a}$. The residue at this pole is

$$I = \frac{2\pi}{\sqrt{1-a^2}}\cdot\left[\ln\frac{\sqrt{1-a^2}-1+a^2}{a^2}+\ln 2\right].$$

4. ASYMPTOTIC FORMULAS FOR INTEGRALS

The theory of residues certainly plays a role in the evaluation of integrals, but it has not had great importance for the development of mathematics in recent years. The reason for this is that only a few of the integrals with which we have to deal can be evaluated in finite form. Such, for example, are the integrals representing special functions. However, the evaluation of integrals does not exhaust the use of the theory of residues. Using this theory, we can find so-called asymptotic formulas for integrals.

By an *asymptotic formula* for the function $f(z)$ as $z \to \infty$ in the domain D we mean the limit relation

$$f(z) \sim \varphi(z) \qquad (z \to \infty,\ z \in D).$$

Some slight distinctions exist between asymptotic formulas and all other limit formulas of this form. The numbers of an asymptotic formula are not equivalent. The formula signifies that the complicated function $f(z)$ is to be replaced by the simple function $\varphi(z)$ (this complexity can be understood from several points of view, for example, from the point of view of computing its values). Stated in words, the function $f(z)$ becomes more complicated as z increases, while the asymptotic formula becomes more exact.

We present two examples of the use of the theory of residues in finding asymptotic formulas.

Example 1. Let the function $E(z)$ (the Mittag-Leffler function) be defined for z outside the half-strip $\operatorname{Re} z > 0\ |\operatorname{Im} z| < \pi$ (let G denote the strip and L its boundary), by the equation

$$E(z) = \frac{1}{2\pi i} \int\limits_L \frac{e^{e^\zeta}}{\zeta - z}\, d\zeta.$$

We next find an analytic continuation of the function $E(z)$ to the entire plane and obtain an asymptotic formula for $E(z)$ as $z \to \infty$.

We can continue the function $E(z)$ analytically to the entire plane with the aid of Theorem 2.2 on the analytic continuation of integrals of the Cauchy type. If $I(z)$ denotes the values of the Cauchy integral (which determines the function $E(z)$ for $z \overline{\in} \overline{G}$), then an analytic continuation of the function $E(z)$ to the half-plane G is given by the formula

$$E(z) = I(z) - e^{e^z} \qquad (z \in G).$$

Thus, in order to obtain an asymptotic formula for the function $E(z)$ it is sufficient to find an asymptotic formula for an integral of the Cauchy type $I(z)$.

Using the equality

$$\frac{1}{\zeta - z} = -\frac{1}{z} - \frac{\zeta}{z^2} + \frac{\zeta^2}{z^2(\zeta - z)}$$

we obtain easily

$$I(z) = \frac{c_0}{z} + \frac{c_1}{z^2} + \frac{1}{z^2}\psi(z),$$

where

$$c_0 = -\frac{1}{2\pi i}\int\limits_L e^{e^\zeta}d\zeta, \quad c_1 = -\frac{1}{2\pi i}\int\limits_L \zeta e^{e^\zeta}d\zeta, \quad \psi(z) = \frac{1}{2\pi i}\int\limits_L \frac{\zeta^2 e^{e^\zeta}}{\zeta - z}\,d\zeta.$$

We now show that $c_0 = 1$ and that $\psi(z) = O(1)$ $(z \to \infty)$. This gives us the asymptotic formula

$$I(z) = \frac{1}{z} + O\left(\frac{1}{z^2}\right),$$

from which we obtain the asymptotic formulas of interest

$$E(z) = \frac{1}{z} + O\left(\frac{1}{z^2}\right) \quad (z \to \infty,\ z \,\overline{\in}\, G),$$

$$E(z) = \frac{1}{z} - e^{e^z} + O\left(\frac{1}{z^2}\right) \quad (z \to \infty,\ z \in G).$$

We first show that $\psi(z) = O(1)$ $(z \to \infty)$. For this purpose let L_1 denote the part of the contour L lying inside the circle $|\zeta - z| < 1$ and let L_2 denote the remainder of L. It is clear that

$$\psi(z) = \frac{1}{2\pi i}\int\limits_{L_1} \frac{\zeta^2 e^{e^\zeta}}{\zeta - z}\,d\zeta + \frac{1}{2\pi i}\int\limits_{L_2} \frac{\zeta^2 e^{e^\zeta}}{\zeta - z}\,d\zeta = \psi_1(z) + \psi_2(z).$$

It follows immediately that

$$|\psi_2(z)| \leqslant \frac{1}{2\pi}\int\limits_L |\zeta|^2\, |e^{e^\zeta}|\, |d\zeta| < \infty.$$

To estimate $|\psi_1(z)|$ let ξ denote the point of L_1 nearest z. We write

$$\psi_1(z) = \frac{e^{e^\xi}}{2\pi i}\left\{\int\limits_{L_1} \frac{d\zeta}{\zeta - z} + \int\limits_{L_1} \frac{e^{e^\zeta - e^\xi} - 1}{\zeta - z}\,d\zeta\right\}.$$

Note that

$$\left|\frac{e^{e^\zeta - e^\xi} - 1}{\zeta - z}\right| \leqslant M \quad (|\zeta - z| < 1), \qquad \frac{1}{2\pi i}\int\limits_{L_1} \frac{d\zeta}{\zeta - z} = \frac{1}{2\pi i}\ln\frac{z - b}{z - a},$$

where a and b are the endpoints of L_1, i.e., the points of intersection of L_1 with the circle $|\zeta - z| = 1$. Since $|z - a| = |z - b| = 1$, then $\left|\frac{1}{2\pi i}\int\limits_{L_1} \frac{d\zeta}{\zeta - z}\right| \leqslant 1$. It is also clear that $e^{e^\xi} \leqslant 1$, since ξ is on L. Therefore $|\psi_1(z)| \leqslant M_1$, i.e., $\psi(z) = O(1)$ $(z \to \infty)$.

We still have to show that $c_0 = 1$. For this we write

$$-c_0 = \frac{1}{2\pi i}\int\limits_L e^{e^\zeta}\,d\zeta = \frac{1}{2\pi i}\int\limits_{\pi i + \infty}^{\pi i} e^{e^\zeta}\,d\zeta +$$

$$+ \frac{1}{2\pi i}\int\limits_{\pi i}^{-\pi i} e^{e^\zeta}\,d\zeta + \frac{1}{2\pi i}\int\limits_{-\pi i}^{-\pi i + \infty} e^{e^\zeta}\,d\zeta.$$

The first and third integrals on the right side cancel one another because of the periodicity of the function $e^{e^{\zeta}}$ (its period is $2\pi i$). We make the substitution $e^{\zeta}=w$ (third method of Sect. 3) in the second integral. This gives us

$$-c_0=-\frac{1}{2\pi i}\int\limits_{|w|=1}\frac{e^w}{w}\,dw=-1.$$

This completes the proof of the asymptotic formulas for $E(z)$.

It is clear that if we had wished we could have obtained the more exact asymptotic formulas:

$$I(z)=\frac{c_0}{z}+\frac{c_1}{z^2}+\ldots+\frac{c_n}{z^{n+1}}+O\left(\frac{1}{z^{n+2}}\right)\qquad(z\to\infty),$$

where

$$c_n=-\frac{1}{2\pi i}\int\limits_L\zeta^n e^{e^{\zeta}}\,d\zeta.$$

Example 2. We now find an asymptotic formula for $\Gamma(z+1)$ ($\Gamma(z)$ is Euler's gamma function) as $z\to+\infty$.

The function $\Gamma(z+1)$ is defined for $z>-1$ by the formula

$$\Gamma(z+1)=\int\limits_0^\infty t^z e^{-t}\,dt.$$

Making the substitution $t=\xi z$, we obtain

$$\Gamma(z+1)=z^{z+1}\int\limits_0^\infty e^{-z(\xi-\ln\xi)}\,d\xi.$$

We next make still another substitution $\xi-\ln\xi=w$. Then, letting C denote the image of the ray $\arg\xi=0$ under the conformal mapping $w=\xi-\ln\xi$, we obtain

$$z^{-z-1}\Gamma(z+1)=\int\limits_C\xi'(w)\,e^{-zw}\,dw,$$

where $\xi(w)$ is some branch of the analytic function inverse to the function $w=\xi-\ln\xi$. We now determine this C and also which branch of the analytic function should appear in the integral.

As ξ increases from 0 to 1, w decreases from $+\infty$ to 1. This means that

$$\int\limits_0^1 e^{-z(\xi-\ln\xi)}\,d\xi=\int\limits_{+\infty}^1 e^{-zw}\xi_1'(w)\,dw,$$

where $\xi_1(w)$ is the inverse of $\xi-\ln\xi$ that is positive and does not exceed one for $w>1$ (as $w\to+\infty$, we have $\xi_1(w)\to 0$).

As ξ increases from 1 to $+\infty$, w also increases from 1 to $+\infty$. Thus,

$$\int_1^{+\infty} e^{-z(\xi-\ln\xi)}\,d\xi = \int_1^{+\infty} e^{-zw}\xi_2'(w)\,dw,$$

where $\xi_2'(w)$ is the branch of the inverse to $\xi - \ln\xi$ that is positive and greater than one for $w > 1$ (as $w \to +\infty$, we have $\xi_2(w) \to +\infty$).

Thus, the contour C, the ray $(1, +\infty)$, is traversed twice, so that we can write

$$z^{-z-1}\Gamma(z+1) = \int_1^{\infty} e^{-zw}[\xi_2'(w) - \xi_2'(w)]\,dw.$$

Let us now examine the behavior of the functions $\xi_1'(w)$ and $\xi_2'(w)$ on the entire ray $(1, +\infty)$ and in a neighborhood of the point 1. According to the formula for the differentiation of the inverse function (see Theorem 7.2, Chap. IV), we have

$$\xi_1'(w) = \frac{\xi_1(w)}{\xi_1(w)-1}, \qquad \xi_2'(w) = \frac{\xi_2(w)}{\xi_2(w)-1},$$

from which it is clear that $\xi_1'(w)$ and $\xi_2'(w)$ are bounded as $w \to +\infty$ and become infinite as $w \to 1$. Since the derivative of the function $w = \xi - \ln\xi$ has a simple zero when $\xi = 1$ (whence $w = 1$) then, according to Theorem 7.3 of Chap. IV, the function $\xi(w)$ can be represented in a neighborhood of the point 1 in the form $\xi(w) = g(\sqrt{w-1})$, where $g(\zeta)$ is a regular function in a neighborhood of the point $\zeta = 0$, $g(0) = 1$ and $g'(0) = \frac{\sqrt{2}}{\sqrt{w''(1)}} = \sqrt{2}$. This means that for $w > 1$

$$\xi_1(w) = 1 - \sqrt{2}\sqrt{w-1} + \ldots, \quad \xi_2(w) = 1 + \sqrt{2}\sqrt{w-1} + \ldots$$

and

$$\xi_2'(w) - \xi_1'(w) = \frac{\sqrt{2}}{\sqrt{w-1}} + \psi(w).$$

Here the function $\psi(w)$ satisfies the inequality

$$|\psi(w)| \leqslant M\sqrt{|w-1|} \qquad (w > 1).$$

Therefore,

$$z^{-z-1}\Gamma(z+1) = \sqrt{2}\int_1^{\infty}(w-1)^{-\frac{1}{2}}e^{-zw}\,dw + \int_1^{\infty}\psi(w)\,e^{-zw}\,dw.$$

However,

$$\int_1^{\infty}(w-1)^{-\frac{1}{2}}e^{-zw}\,dw = \frac{e^{-z}}{\sqrt{z}}\int_0^{\infty}t^{-\frac{1}{2}}e^{-t}\,dt = 2\frac{e^{-z}}{\sqrt{z}}\int_0^{\infty}e^{-x^2}\,dx = \sqrt{\frac{\pi}{z}}\,e^{-z}$$

(it is known from analysis that this last integral equals $\sqrt{\pi}/2$, and

$$\left|\int_1^\infty \psi(w)\, e^{-zw}\,dw\right| \leqslant M\int_1^\infty (w-1)^{\frac{1}{2}}\, e^{-zw}\,dw = \frac{Me^{-z}}{z^{\frac{3}{2}}}\int_1^\infty t^{\frac{1}{2}} e^{-t}\,dt = M_1\frac{e^{-z}}{z^{\frac{3}{2}}}.$$

We thus obtain the asymptotic formula

$$\Gamma(z+1) = \sqrt{2\pi}\, z^{z+\frac{1}{2}} e^{-z}\left(1 + O\left(\frac{1}{z}\right)\right),$$

well known under the name of Stirling's formula

It is not difficult to show that Stirling's formula remains valid as $\operatorname{Re} z \to +\infty$ [replacing $O(1/z)$ by $O(1/\operatorname{Re} z)$].

We now wish to make a few remarks of a general nature about the methods we have employed in the derivation of Stirling's formula.

We used two ideas. One was that of a substitution, which brought the integral into the form

$$\int_a^\infty \left\{\frac{c}{\sqrt{w-a}} + \psi(w)\right\} e^{-wz}\,dz,$$

where the function $\psi(w)$ satisfies the inequality $|\psi(w)| \leqslant M\sqrt{|w-a|}$, and the other was that of obtaining an asymptotic formula for the latter integral. Each of these ideas can be developed further and generalized.

To obtain asymptotic formulas for integrals of the form

$$F(z) = \int_a^{a+\infty} \varphi(w)\, e^{-wz}\,dw \qquad (\operatorname{Re} z \to +\infty) \tag{4.1}$$

we use the following result:

Theorem 4.1. *If the function $\varphi(w)$ satisfies the conditions*

$$|\varphi(w)| < M \qquad (w-a \geqslant \varrho > 0)$$

and

$$\varphi(w) = \sum_{k=0}^{\infty} c_k (w-a)^{\alpha+\beta k} \qquad (0 < w-a < \varrho),$$

then we have the following asymptotic formula for integral (4.1):

$$F(z) = \sum_{k=0}^{n-1} c_k \Gamma(\alpha+\beta k)\, z^{-\alpha-\beta k-1} + O\left((\operatorname{Re} z)^{-\alpha-\beta n-1}\right)$$
$$(\operatorname{Re} z \to +\infty),$$

where n is any positive integer. ($\Gamma(x)$ *is Euler's gamma function.*)

This theorem can also be proved by the same reasoning as we employed in Example 2.

A change of variables is applied to integrals of the form

$$F(z) = \int_\Gamma f(\xi)\, e^{-zh(\xi)}\,d\xi,$$

in order to turn these integrals into integrals of the form (4.1). Making the substitution $w = h(\xi)$, the integral takes on the form

$$F(z) = \int_{\Gamma_1} \varphi(w)\, e^{-zw} dw,$$

where $\varphi(w) = f(\xi(w))\, \xi'(w)$ and the contour Γ_1 is the image of the contour Γ under the mapping $w = h(\xi)$. We deform the contour Γ_1 by moving it as far to the right as possible (this decreases the factor e^{-zw}, which is essential if Re z is large). Under such deformation endpoints of the contour and singular points of the function $\varphi(w)$ may coincide. Then the contour is broken up into a sum of contours, each of which is a ray issuing from a singular point and parallel to the positive part of the real axis. Rays issuing from endpoints of a contour are gone around once and those issuing from singular points twice. The integral along each of these rays is also an integral of the form (4.1).

It is very difficult to justify the procedure described in the general case, but this is not often necessary. What has been said is only to be taken as an indication of the procedure to be followed in concrete examples.

The method described turns out to be closely connected with the so-called saddle-point method.*

5. THE SUMMATION OF SERIES

The methods of the theory of residues can be applied also to the study of sums of series. For this purpose, the sum of the series must be expressed in terms of a contour integral. We shall now undertake a brief discussion of the methods that may be applied for this purpose.

We first present one of the few cases in which it is possible to find the sum of the series in finite form with the aid of the theory of residues. In addition to the fact that these cases have interest in their own right, they serve as preparation for what is to follow.

Theorem 5.1. *Let* $Q(z)$ *be a rational function with poles* z_1, z_2, $\ldots$, z_p, *and let the degree of the numerator be at least two less than that of the denominator. Then*

$$\sum_{-\infty}^{\infty} Q(k) = -\pi \sum_{1}^{p} \operatorname*{res}_{z=z_s} Q(z) \cot \pi z.$$

Proof. Let us consider the integral

---

*We refer readers seeking a more detailed knowledge of the methods of obtaining asymptotic formulas to the books: N. G. de Bruijn, Asymptotic Methods in Analysis, Interscience, Wiley, N.Y., 1958; and M. A. Evgrafov, Asymptotic Estimates and Entire Functions, Gordon and Breach, N.Y., 1962.

$$J_n = \int\limits_{|z|=n+\frac{1}{2}} Q(z) \text{ cotan } \pi z \, dz \qquad (n=0,\ 1,\ 2,\ \ldots).$$

Since the degree of the numerator of $Q(z)$ is at least two less than the degree of its denominator, we have

$$\max_{|z|=R} |Q(z)| \leqslant \frac{M}{R^2} \qquad (R > R_0).$$

We showed in Sect. 6 of Chap. II that the function cos πz is bounded in the z-plane after removal of the circles $|z-k| < \varepsilon (k=0,\ \pm 1,\ \pm 2,\ \ldots)$. Therefore,

$$\max_{|z|=n+\frac{1}{2}} |\text{ cotan } \pi z| \leqslant M_1.$$

Thus, bounding the integral J_n by the product of the maximum modulus of the integrand by the length of the path of integration, we find

$$|J_n| \leqslant 2\pi \left(n+\frac{1}{2}\right) \frac{M}{\left(n+\frac{1}{2}\right)^2} \cdot M_1 \to 0 \qquad (n \to \infty).$$

On the other hand, the integral J_n can be evaluated with the aid of the residue theorem. The poles $z_1,\ z_2,\ \ldots,\ z_p$ of the function $Q(z)$ are contained in the circle $|z| < n+1/2$ for n sufficiently large; this circle also contains the poles $0,\ \pm 1,\ \ldots,\ \pm n$ of the function cotan πz. The residue of the pole k equals $1/\pi Q(k)$. Therefore

$$J_n = 2\pi i \left\{ \frac{1}{\pi} \sum_{-n}^{n} Q(k) + \sum_{1}^{p} \operatorname*{res}_{z=z_s} Q(z) \text{ cotan } \pi z \right\}.$$

Taking limits as $n \to \infty$, we obtain the statement of the theorem.

In a completely analogous way we can prove the formula

$$\sum_{-\infty}^{\infty} (-1)^k Q(k) = -\pi \sum_{1}^{p} \operatorname*{res}_{z=z_s} \frac{Q(z)}{\sin \pi z}.$$

Unfortunately, we can find the sum in finite form only for a very few series. The expression of the sum of a series in terms of a contour integral therefore has much greater importance. One of the methods most frequently employed for this purpose is based on the following theorem.

Theorem 5.2. *Let the function $f(z)$ be regular in the strip $a < \operatorname{Re} z < b$ and let it satisfy there the inequality*

$$|f(x+iy)| \leqslant Me^{\alpha|y|}, \qquad \alpha < 2\pi. \tag{5.1}$$

Then for $k \geqslant a+1$, $n \leqslant b-1$, $n > k$, and for any $0 < \theta < 1$,

$$\sum_{s=k}^{n} f(s) =$$

$$= \int_{k+\theta-1}^{n+\theta} f(x)dx + \frac{1}{2i}\int_{\theta}^{\theta+i\infty} \Big[f(n+z) - f(k-1+z)\Big](\cotan \pi z + i)dz + \tag{5.2}$$

$$+ \frac{1}{2i}\int_{\theta}^{\theta-i\infty} [f(k-1+z) - f(n+z)](\cotan \pi z - i)\, dz.$$

Proof. Let C_h denote the rectangle

$$k-1+\theta < \operatorname{Re} z < n+\theta, \qquad |\operatorname{Im} z| < h,$$

which, in view of the conditions on k and n, is contained in the strip $a < \operatorname{Re} z < b$, and let J be the integral of $f(z) \cotan \pi z$ along C_h. According to the residue theorem, we have

$$J = 2\pi i \sum_{k}^{n} \operatorname*{res}_{z=s} f(z) \cotan \pi z = 2i \sum_{k}^{n} f(s).$$

Next let C_h^+ denote the upper half of C_h, and let C_h^- denote the lower half; here the directions along C_h^+ and C_h^- will be taken to be the direction from the point $k-1+\theta$ to the point $n+\theta$. It is clear that

$$J = \int_{C_h^-} f(z) \cotan \pi z\, dz - \int_{C_h^+} f(z) \cotan \pi z\, dz$$

and

$$J = \int_{C_h^-} f(z)(\cotan \pi z - i)dz + i\int_{C_h^-} f(z)\, dz -$$

$$- \int_{C_h^+} f(z)(\cotan \pi z + i)\, dz + i\int_{C_h^+} f(z)\, dz.$$

However, the integral of $f(z)$ depends only on the endpoints of the contour, so that the integral of $f(z)$ along C_h^+ and C_h^- can be replaced by the integral along the segment $(k-1+\theta,\ n+\theta)$. Thus

$$J = 2i \int_{k-1+\theta}^{n+\theta} f(x)dx + \int_{C_h^-} f(z)(\cotan \pi z - i)dz - \int_{C_h^+} f(z)(\cotan \pi z + i)dz.$$

Moreover,

$$\int_{C_h^+} f(z)(\cotan \pi z + i)dz = \int_{\theta}^{\theta+ih} [f(k-1+z) - f(n+z)](\cotan \pi z + i)dz +$$

$$+ \int_{k-1+\theta+ih}^{n+\theta+ih} f(z)(\cotan \pi z + i)\, dz.$$

Since

$$\left|\int\limits_{k-1+\theta+ih}^{n+\theta+ih} f(z)(\cot \pi z+i)\,dz\right| \leqslant$$

$$\leqslant (n-k+1) \max_{k-1+\theta\leqslant x\leqslant n+\theta} |f(x+ih)|\,|\cot \pi(x+ih)+i|,$$

and since for $h>0$ $\cot \pi(x+ih)+i|<\frac{2}{e^{2\pi h}-1}$, as we showed in Sect. 6, Chap. II, then because of condition (5.1) we have

$$\left|\int\limits_{k-1+\theta+ih}^{n+\theta+ih} f(z)(\cot \pi z+i)\,dz\right| \leqslant (n-k+1)\,Me^{ah}\frac{2}{e^{2\pi h}-1} \to 0$$

$$(h \to +\infty)$$

and

$$\int\limits_{C_h^+} f(z)(\cot \pi z+i)\,dz = \int\limits_{\theta}^{\theta+i\infty} [f(k-1+z)-f(n+z)](\cot \pi z+i)\,dz.$$

The situation is analogous for the integral along C_h^-. Equating the two expressions obtained for J, we arrive at formula (5.2).

Corollary. Let the function $f(z)$ *be regular in the half-plane* $\operatorname{Re} z>0$ *and satisfy the inequality*

$$|f(x+iy)|<\varepsilon(x)\,e^{a|y|},$$

where $\varepsilon(x)\to 0$ *as* $x\to+\infty$*. Then for any* $0<\theta<1$

$$\lim_{n\to\infty}\left\{\sum_{1}^{n} f(s) - \int\limits_{\theta}^{n+\theta} f(x)\,dx\right\} = \frac{1}{2i}\int\limits_{\theta}^{\theta-i\infty} f(z)(\cot \pi z-i)\,dz -$$

$$-\frac{1}{2i}\int\limits_{\theta}^{\theta+i\infty} f(z)(\cot \pi z+i)\,dz.$$

This is sometimes called the *Abel formula.* It is an obvious corollary of formula (5.2), since

$$\left|\int\limits_{\theta}^{\theta\pm i\infty} f(n+z)(\cot \pi z\mp i)\,dz\right| \leqslant$$

$$\leqslant \varepsilon(n+\theta)\int\limits_{0}^{\infty} Me^{-(2\pi-a)y}\,dy \to 0 \qquad (n\to\infty).$$

We next present an example illustrating the use of the Abel formula.

Example 1. We show that the function (see the end of Sect. 1 Chap. IV)

$$F(t)=\sum_{n=1}^{\infty} e^{-\sqrt{n}}\,t^n \qquad (|t|<1)$$

can be continued analytically into the plane with the cross cut $(1, +\infty)$.

We apply the Abel formula by first setting $f(z)=e^{-\sqrt{z}}t^z$. The function t^z is to be understood as $e^{z\ln t}$, where we choose for $\ln t$ the branch satisfying the condition $-\pi+\alpha<\operatorname{Im}\ln t<\pi+\alpha$. This branch is regular in the t-plane with a cross cut along the ray arg $t=\pi+\alpha$. (We may choose α to be any number such that $|\alpha|<\pi$.)

We then have

$$F(t)=\int_{\theta}^{\infty} e^{-\sqrt{x}}\,t^x dx-\frac{1}{2i}\int_{\theta}^{\theta+i\infty}(\operatorname{cotan}\pi z+i)\,e^{-\sqrt{z}}\,t^z\,dz+$$

$$+\frac{1}{2i}\int_{\theta}^{\theta-i\infty}(\operatorname{cotan}\pi z-i)\,e^{-\sqrt{z}}\,t^z dz.$$

The integral

$$\int_{\theta}^{\infty} e^{-\sqrt{x}}\,t^x\,dx$$

converges uniformly in t in the circle $|t|<1$ with a cross cut along the radius $(0,\ e^{i(\pi+\alpha)})$. Rotating the contour of integration, we can continue this integral analytically (on the basis of Theorem 2.1) to the entire t-plane with cross cuts along the rays arg $t=\pi+\alpha$ and $(1, +\infty)$.

The integrals

$$\int_{\theta}^{\theta\pm i\infty}(\operatorname{cotan}\pi z\mp i)\ e^{-\sqrt{z}}\,t^z\,dz$$

converge uniformly in any finite region of the t-plane with a cross cut along the ray arg $t=\pi+\alpha$, since on the line $\operatorname{Re} z=\theta$

$$|e^{-\sqrt{z}}|\leqslant 1, \qquad |t^z|\leqslant|t|^{\theta}\,e^{(\pi+|\alpha|)|\operatorname{Im} z|},$$

and

$$|\operatorname{cotan}\pi z\mp i|\leqslant Me^{-2\pi|\operatorname{Im} z|}.$$

Thus, the function $F(t)$ can be continued analytically to the whole t-plane with cross cuts along the rays arg $t=\pi+\alpha$ and $(1, +\infty)$. However, the number α is subject to only one requirement: $|\alpha|<\pi$. Therefore, if we can show that the function $F(t)$ is unchanged by a circuit around the point 0, we can prove its regularity in the plane with a cross cut $(1, +\infty)$. It is clear from the original formula that $F(t)$ is regular at the point 0. Thus our assertion is proved.

We shall present one more method frequently used for the expression of sums of power series in terms of contour integrals.

Theorem 5.3. *Suppose that the contour L does not pass through the point 0, and that the function $\varphi(t)$ is continuous on L and satisfies*

$$\int_L \frac{|\varphi(t)|}{|t|} |dt| < \infty.$$

If

$$c(x) = \int_L \varphi(t) t^{-x-1} dt \qquad (x \geqslant 0), \tag{5.3}$$

then in any neighborhood of the point 0 we have

$$\sum_0^\infty c(n) z^n = \int_L \frac{\varphi(t)}{t-z} dt.$$

Proof. In (5.3) set $x = n$ $(n = 0, 1, 2, \ldots)$, then multiply by z^n and carry out the summation. If $|z|$ is less than the distance from the point 0 to the contour L, interchange of the order of summation and integration is permissible in view of the uniform convergence of the series and the integral. We then obtain

$$\sum_0^\infty c_n z^n = \int_L \sum_0^\infty \frac{z^n}{t^{n+1}} \varphi(t) dt = \int_L \frac{\varphi(t)}{t-z} dt.$$

This proves the theorem.

Example 2. Let $s > 0$. We show that the function

$$F_s(z) = \sum_1^\infty n^{-s} z^n \qquad (|z| < 1)$$

can be continued analytically to the entire z-plane with cross cut $(1, +\infty)$.

To apply Theorem 5.3 we present the function x^{-s} in the form of the corresponding integral. We now show that

$$x^{-s} = \frac{1}{\Gamma(s)} \int_1^\infty (\ln u)^{s-1} u^{-x-1} du.$$

In fact, substituting $\ln u = \xi / x$, we find

$$\int_1^\infty (\ln u)^{s-1} u^{-x-1} du = \int_0^\infty \left(\frac{\xi}{x}\right)^{s-1} e^{-\xi} \frac{d\xi}{x} =$$

$$= x^{-s} \int_0^\infty \xi^{s-1} e^{-\xi} d\xi = x^{-s} \Gamma(s) .$$

Therefore, Theorem 5.3 gives us

$$F_s(z) = \frac{z}{\Gamma(s)} \int_1^\infty \frac{(\ln u)^{s-1}}{u(u-z)}\, du \qquad (|z| < 1).$$

This last integral is one of the Cauchy type (see Sect. 2), and it represents a function that is regular in a domain not containing points of the contour (i.e., the ray $(1, +\infty)$). This proves our assertion.

If we wish, we can find even more extensive analytic continuations of the function $F_s(z)$ and also investigate its many-valued character in a neighborhood of the point 1.

The basic difficulty of the method described is that we cannot write the result directly in terms of the function $c(x)$, but must first find an integral representation for the function. In many cases this representation can be found by using the inversion formula of the Mellin transform, which will be discussed in Chap. VII. With its aid, the function $\varphi(t)$ can be expressed in terms of the function $c(x)$, although we still use only one contour integral.

6. BASIC FORMULAS RELATING TO EULER'S GAMMA FUNCTION

Very many of the series and integrals that arise in analysis can be expressed in terms of Euler's gamma function. The function $\Gamma(z)$ almost rivals the elementary functions in usefulness in the theory of analytic functions. For this reason we need to supplement somewhat our information about this function.

According to the definition

$$\Gamma(z) = \int_0^\infty x^{z-1} e^{-x}\, dx \qquad (z > 0). \tag{6.1}$$

It was shown in Sect. 5, Chap. II, that this integral converges uniformly in any finite region of the half-plane $\operatorname{Re} z > 0$. We also carried out there an analytic continuation of the function $\Gamma(z)$ to the entire complex plane and showed that $\Gamma(z)$ is regular in the entire plane except at the points $z = 0, -1, -2, \ldots$, at which there are poles of first order.

Integrating (6.1) by parts, we obtain the formula

$$\Gamma(z+1) = z\Gamma(z). \tag{6.2}$$

According to the principle of analytic continuation, this equality is satisfied for all z. It can also be employed for the analytic continuation of $\Gamma(z)$ to the half-plane $\operatorname{Re} z < 0$.

We next demonstrate still another formula suitable for this purpose; namely,

$$\frac{1}{\Gamma(z)} = z e^{-Cz} \prod_{1}^{\infty} \left(1 + \frac{z}{n}\right) e^{-\frac{z}{n}}, \tag{6.3}$$

where C is the so-called Euler's constant

$$C = \lim_{n\to\infty}\left(1 + \frac{1}{2} + \ldots + \frac{1}{n} - \ln n\right).$$

For the proof we note that $\left(1 - \frac{x}{n}\right)^n \to e^{-x}$ as $n \to \infty$ uniformly in x in any finite segment of the positive real axis. Moreover, $0 < \left(1 - \frac{x}{n}\right)^n < e^{-x}$ for $0 < x < n$. Therefore,

$$\lim_{n\to\infty} \int_0^n \left(1 - \frac{x}{n}\right)^n x^{z-1}\, dx = \int_0^\infty x^{z-1} e^{-x}\, dx = \Gamma(z).$$

The integral under the limit sign can easily be evaluated by using integration by parts:

$$\int_0^n \left(1 - \frac{x}{n}\right)^n x^{z-1}\, dx = \frac{n!\, n^z}{z(z+1)\ldots(z+n)}.$$

Thus,

$$\frac{1}{\Gamma(z)} = \lim_{n\to\infty} \frac{z(z+1)\ldots(z+n)}{n!\, n^z} =$$

$$= \lim_{n\to\infty} \left\{ n^{-z} \cdot z\left(1 + \frac{z}{1}\right)\ldots\left(1 + \frac{z}{n}\right)\right\} =$$

$$= \lim_{n\to\infty} \left\{ n^{-z} e^{z\left(1 + \frac{1}{2} + \ldots + \frac{1}{n}\right)}\right\} \lim_{n\to\infty} \left\{ z \prod_{1}^{n} \left(1 + \frac{z}{k}\right) e^{-\frac{z}{k}}\right\}.$$

It is not difficult to show that this infinite product converges uniformly in any finite domain, so that

$$\lim_{n\to\infty} \prod_{1}^{n} \left(1 + \frac{z}{k}\right) e^{-\frac{z}{k}} = \prod_{1}^{\infty} \left(1 + \frac{z}{n}\right) e^{-\frac{z}{n}}.$$

This yields the existence of the limit

$$\lim_{n\to\infty} \left\{ n^{-z} e^{z\left(1 + \frac{1}{2} + \ldots + \frac{1}{n}\right)}\right\} =$$

$$= \exp\left\{ \lim_{n\to\infty} \left[z\left(1 + \frac{1}{2} + \ldots + \frac{1}{n}\right) - z \ln n\right]\right\} = e^{Cz}.$$

We have thus proved formula (6.3) for $z > 0$. By the principle of analytic continuation, the formula is valid for all z.

We now replace z by $-z$ in formula (6.3) and multiply the formula thus obtained by formula (6.3). If we now take into account (5.2), Chap. IV, for the expansion of $\sin z$ in an infinite product, we find

$$\frac{1}{\Gamma(z)\Gamma(-z)} = -\frac{z}{\pi}\sin \pi z.$$

However, according to formula (6.2), $\Gamma(1-z) = -z\Gamma(-z)$, so that we arrive at the formula

$$\Gamma(z)\Gamma(1-z) = \frac{\pi}{\sin \pi z}. \tag{6.4}$$

If in particular we set $z=1/2$, then we obtain $\Gamma(1/2)=\sqrt{\pi}$.

We can easily prove the following integral representation using formula (6.4):

$$\frac{1}{\Gamma(z)} = \frac{1}{2\pi i}\int_L e^{\zeta}\zeta^{-z}\,d\zeta. \tag{6.5}$$

Here L is the boundary of the domain $|\zeta|>\varrho$, $|\arg\zeta|<\pi$, $\zeta^{-z}=e^{-z\ln\zeta}$, and we choose the principal value for $\ln\zeta$.

It is clear that the integral in formula (6.5) converges uniformly in any finite domain, since e^{ζ} approaches zero more rapidly than any power of ζ as $\zeta\to-\infty$. The contour L consists of the circle $|\zeta|=\varrho$ and the ray $(-\infty, 0)$ traversed twice. For $z<1$ the integral along the circle $|\zeta|=\varrho$ approaches zero as $\varrho\to 0$, so that for $z<1$ the contour L can be replaced by the ray $(-\infty, 0)$ traversed twice. We now find the values of the integrand on the upper and lower edges of the cross cut $(-\infty, 0)$. On the upper edge of the cross cut we have $\ln\zeta=\ln|\zeta|+\pi i$ and $\zeta^{-z}=|\zeta|^{-z}e^{-\pi iz}$, and on the lower edge $\ln\zeta=\ln|\zeta|-\pi i$ and $\zeta^{-z}=|\zeta|^{-z}e^{\pi iz}$. Therefore,

$$\frac{1}{2\pi i}\int_L e^{\zeta}\zeta^{-z}\,d\zeta = \frac{e^{\pi iz}}{2\pi i}\int_0^{\infty} x^{-z}e^{-x}dx - \frac{e^{-\pi iz}}{2\pi i}\int_0^{\infty} x^{-z}e^{-x}\,dx =$$
$$= \frac{1}{\pi}\sin\pi z\cdot\Gamma(1-z) = \frac{1}{\Gamma(z)}$$

on the basis of formula (6.4). Formula (6.5) is proved in the same way for $z<1$, but because of the principle of analytic continuation it holds for all z.

Let us now examine the behavior of $\Gamma(z)$ for large z. Stirling's formula, which we derived in Example 2 of Sect. 4, is not fully satisfactory since it is useful only for $\operatorname{Re} z\to+\infty$. Using formula (6.4), we can obtain a formula for $\operatorname{Re} z\to-\infty$. However, this method is not successful if we wish to investigate the behavior of $\Gamma(z)$ near the imaginary axis.

Taking logarithms in formula (6.3), we find

$$\ln\Gamma(z) = Cz + \sum_1^{\infty}\left[\ln\left(1+\frac{z}{n}\right)-\frac{z}{n}\right].$$

From this it readily follows that

$$\frac{d^2}{dz^2}\ln\Gamma(z) = -\sum_0^\infty \frac{1}{(n+z)^2}.$$

Next we note that for $\operatorname{Re} z > 0$

$$-\frac{1}{(n+z)^2} = \int_0^\infty \zeta e^{-\zeta(z+n)}\,d\zeta.$$

Therefore,

$$\frac{d^2}{dz^2}\ln\Gamma(z) = \sum_0^\infty\int_0^\infty \zeta e^{-\zeta(z+n)}\,d\zeta = \int_0^\infty \frac{\zeta e^{-z\zeta}}{1-e^{-\zeta}}\,d\zeta \qquad (\operatorname{Re} z > 0).$$

We can rotate the contour of integration in this formula by the angle $|\arg\zeta| < \frac{\pi}{2} - \delta$, $\delta > 0$, which gives us

$$\frac{d^2}{dz^2}\ln\Gamma(z) = \int_0^{\infty e^{i\theta}} \frac{\zeta e^{-z\zeta}}{1-e^{-\zeta}}\,d\zeta \qquad (\operatorname{Re}(ze^{i\theta}) > 0),\ |\theta| < \frac{\pi}{2}.$$

Using the same reasoning as that at the end of Example 2 of Sect. 4, we can easily arrive at the asymptotic formula

$$\frac{d^2}{dz^2}\ln\Gamma(z) = \frac{c_0}{z} + \frac{c_1\cdot 1!}{z^2} + \ldots + \frac{c_n\cdot n!}{z^{n+1}} + O\left(\frac{1}{z^{n+2}}\right) \tag{6.6}$$

$$(|z| \to \infty,\ |\arg z| \leqslant \pi - \delta),$$

where

$$\sum_0^\infty c_n t^n = \frac{t}{1-e^{-t}}.$$

It is not difficult to obtain $c_0 = 1$, $c_1 = 1.2$.

Integrating formula (6.6), we obtain

$$\frac{\Gamma'(z)}{\Gamma(z)} = \ln z + C' + \frac{1}{2z} + O\left(\frac{1}{z^2}\right) \qquad (z \to \infty,\ |\arg z| \leqslant \pi - \delta),$$

$$\ln\Gamma(z) = z\ln z + (C'-1)z - \frac{1}{2}\ln z + C_1' + O\left(\frac{1}{z}\right)$$

$$(z \to \infty,\ |\arg z| \leqslant \pi - \delta).$$

Equating the last formula with Stirling's formula, we find

$$C' = 0,\quad C_1' = \frac{1}{2}\ln 2\pi.$$

Thus, as $z \to \infty$, $|\arg z| \leqslant \pi - \delta$, we have

$$\frac{\Gamma'(z)}{\Gamma(z)} = \ln z + O\left(\frac{1}{z}\right), \tag{6.7}$$

$$\ln \Gamma(z) = \left(z - \frac{1}{2}\right) \ln z - z + \frac{1}{2} \ln 2\pi + O\left(\frac{1}{z}\right). \tag{6.8}$$

In conclusion we present a few more integrals that can be expressed in terms of $\Gamma(z)$.

Rotating the ray of integration in formula (6.1) until it coincides with the imaginary axis, which is possible on the basis of Jordan's lemma for $0 < z < 1$, we arrive at the formula

$$\int_0^\infty y^{z-1} e^{-iy} dy = e^{-\frac{\pi i z}{2}} \Gamma(z).$$

Splitting this into real and imaginary parts, we obtain

$$\int_0^\infty y^{z-1} \cos y \, dy = \cos \frac{\pi z}{2} \cdot \Gamma(z),$$

$$\int_0^\infty y^{z-1} \sin y \, dy = \sin \frac{\pi z}{2} \cdot \Gamma(z).$$

These formulas are valid for all z for which the integrals concerned converge uniformly, because of the principle of analytic continuation. Thus, the first and second formulas hold for $0 < \operatorname{Re} z < 1$, and the third for $-1 < \operatorname{Re} z < 1$.

Making the substitution $x = u^2$ in formula (6.1), we find

$$\Gamma(z) = 2\int_0^\infty e^{-u^2} u^{2z-1} \, du \qquad (\operatorname{Re} z > 0). \tag{6.9}$$

Multiplying two such integrals together, we find

$$\Gamma(z)\,\Gamma(\zeta) = 4 \int_0^\infty \int_0^\infty e^{-(u^2+v^2)} u^{2z-1} v^{2\zeta-1} \, du \, dv$$

$$(\operatorname{Re} z > 0, \ \operatorname{Re} \zeta > 0).$$

If we transfer to polar coordinates in the double integral, we then find

$$\int_0^\infty \int_0^\infty e^{-(u^2+v^2)} u^{2z-1} v^{2\zeta-1} \, du \, dv =$$

$$= \int_0^\infty \int_0^{\frac{\pi}{2}} e^{-\rho^2} \varrho^{2(z+\zeta)-1} (\cos\theta)^{2z-1} (\sin\theta)^{2\zeta-1} \, d\varrho d\theta =$$

$$= \int_0^\infty e^{-\rho^2} \varrho^{2(z+\zeta)-1} \, d\varrho \int_0^{\frac{\pi}{2}} (\cos\theta)^{2z-1} (\sin\theta)^{2\zeta-1} \, d\theta.$$

According to formula (6.9), this gives us

$$\int_0^{\frac{\pi}{2}} (\cos\theta)^{2z-1} (\sin\theta)^{2\zeta-1}\, d\theta = \frac{1}{2}\,\frac{\Gamma(z)\,\Gamma(\zeta)}{\Gamma(z+\zeta)} \tag{6.10}$$

$$(\operatorname{Re} z > 0,\ \operatorname{Re}\zeta > 0).$$

Substituting $\xi = \cos^2\theta$ in formula (6.10), we obtain

$$\int_0^1 \xi^{z-1} (1-\xi)^{\zeta-1}\, d\xi = \frac{\Gamma(z)\,\Gamma(\zeta)}{\Gamma(z+\zeta)} \qquad (\operatorname{Re} z > 0, \operatorname{Re}\zeta > 0),$$

and substitution of $x = \xi/1-\xi$ gives us still another formula:

$$\int_0^\infty \frac{x^{z-1}}{(x+1)^{z+\zeta}}\, dx = \frac{\Gamma(z)\,\Gamma(\zeta)}{\Gamma(z+\zeta)} \qquad (\operatorname{Re} z > 0, \operatorname{Re}\zeta > 0).$$

The function $\mathrm{B}(z,\ \zeta) = \dfrac{\Gamma(z)\,\Gamma(\zeta)}{\Gamma(z+\zeta)}$ is called Euler's beta function.

CHAPTER VII

The Laplace Transform

The method of integral transforms is one of the most fruitful methods of analysis. The essence of the method is the replacement of the study of a function by the study of its integral transform. As a result, frequently, a complicated equation in $f(x)$ is converted into a simple relation in its integral transform. In general, we shall restrict our attention to the Laplace transform, although in analysis the Fourier and Mellin transforms are employed just as frequently. They differ from the Laplace transform only by an immaterial change of variables.

1. THE INVERSION FORMULA FOR THE LAPLACE TRANSFORM

Suppose that the function $f(x)$ is defined on the whole axis and that the integral

$$F(z)=\int_{-\infty}^{\infty} f(x)\, e^{-xz}\, dx$$

converges, on at least one line $\operatorname{Re} z=c$. The function $F(z)$ is then said to be the *two-sided Laplace transform of the function f(x)* and this relationship is denoted by the formula $f(x) \div F(z)$.

If the function $f(x)$ is defined for $x>0$ and the integral

$$F(z)=\int_{0}^{\infty} f(x) e^{-xz} dx$$

converges in some half-plane $\operatorname{Re} z>c$, then the function $F(z)$ is said to be the *one-sided Laplace transform of the function f(z)* and this relationship is denoted by the formula $f(x) \div F(z)$.

The one-sided Laplace transform has many features in common with power series. We can prove for it a theorem analogous to Abel's first theorem and can introduce the notion of the half-plane of convergence analogous to the notion of circle of convergence for a power series. The two-sided Laplace transform is analogous to the Laurent series. Its domain of convergence is a strip $a < \operatorname{Re} z < b$, which may degenerate into a line for $a = b$. To avoid ambiguity in the case of the two-sided Laplace transform it is necessary to indicate the strip or line of convergence, since the same function $F(z)$ may correspond to different $f(x)$ in different convergence strips. We shall usually assume that the two-sided Laplace transform converges on the imaginary axis, and we shall usually choose as its strip of convergence a strip including the imaginary axis.

It is clear that a formula that permits the recapture of the function $f(x)$ from its Laplace transform has great value. It is analogous to the fomulas for the coefficients of the Laurent series and is called the *inversion formula.*

We prove three theorems about the inversion formula. In the first two theorems, we impose conditions on $F(z)$ sufficient for the validity of the formula, and in the third, on $f(x)$. Note that the inversion formula must have the same form for the two-sided as for the one-sided Laplace transform, since the one-sided transform can be considered as the two-sided transform for a function equal to zero for negative x. (Recall that the formulas for the coefficients also had the same form for both the Taylor and the Laurent series.)

Theorem 1.1. *Let the function $F(z)$ be regular in the strip $a \leqslant \operatorname{Re} z \leqslant b$. If the function F(z) satisfies the condition*

$$F(z) = O(|z|^{-\alpha-1}), \quad 0 < \alpha < 1 \quad (z \to \infty, \ a \leqslant \operatorname{Re} z \leqslant b), \tag{1.1}$$

then the function

$$f(x) = \frac{1}{2\pi i} \int_{c-i\infty}^{c+i\infty} F(z)\, e^{xz}\, dz \qquad (a \leqslant c \leqslant b) \tag{1.2}$$

does not depend on c, and for any $a \leqslant c \leqslant b$ satisfies the inequalities

$$|f(x)\, e^{-cx}| \leqslant M, \quad |f(x)\, e^{-cx} - f(\xi)\, e^{-c\xi}| \leqslant M_1 |x - \xi|^{\alpha}.$$

Moreover, $f(x) \doteqdot F(z)$ $(a < \operatorname{Re} z < b)$ and if $b = +\infty$, then $f(x) = 0$ for $x < 0$ and $f(x) \div F(z)$.

Proof. Since for $z = c + iy$ we have $|e^{xz}| = e^{cx}$, the condition (1.1) ensures absolute and uniform convergence of the integral (1.2) on any finite interval of the x-axis. Moreover,

$$|f(x)| \leqslant \frac{1}{2\pi} \int_{c-i\infty}^{c+i\infty} |F(z)|\, |e^{xz}|\, |dz| = \frac{e^{cx}}{2\pi} \int_{-\infty}^{\infty} |F(c+iy)| dy \leqslant Me^{cx},$$

which gives us the first inequality for the function $f(x)$.

Furthermore,

$$e^{-cx} f(x) - e^{-c\xi} f(\xi) = \frac{1}{2\pi} \int_{-\infty}^{\infty} F(c+iy)(e^{iyx} - e^{iy\xi})\, dy,$$

from which we find

$$|e^{-cx} f(x) - e^{-c\xi} f(\xi)| \leqslant \frac{1}{\pi} \int_{-\infty}^{\infty} |F(c+iy)| \left| \sin \frac{x-\xi}{2} y \right| dy \leqslant$$

$$\leqslant C \int_{0}^{\infty} y^{-\alpha-1} \left| \sin \frac{x-\xi}{2} y \right| dy =$$

$$= C_1 |x-\xi|^{\alpha} \int_{0}^{\infty} \frac{|\sin t|}{t^{\alpha+1}}\, dt = M_1 |x-\xi|^{\alpha},$$

which gives us the second inequality for the function $f(x)$.

Since the integrand $F(z)\, e^{xz}$ approaches zero uniformly as $z \to \infty$ in the strip $a \leqslant \operatorname{Re} z \leqslant b$, an arbitrary deformation can be applied to the contour of integration within this strip. In particular, all countours $\operatorname{Re} z = c$ are equalvalent to one another (see Sect. 1, Chap. VI). This signifies that the function $f(x)$ does not depend on c if $a \leqslant c \leqslant b$.

We now show that $f(x) \risingdotseq F(z)$ $(a < \operatorname{Re} z < b)$. We multiply the function $f(x)$ by $e^{-x\zeta}$ and integrate with respect to x from $-R'$ to R; then we apply formula (1.2) to the function $f(x)$ while choosing $c = a$ for $x > 0$ and $c = b$ for $x < 0$. Since the integral occurring in formula (1.2) converges uniformly, interchange of the order of integration is permissible and we obtain

$$\int_{-R'}^{R} f(x)\, e^{-x\zeta} dx = \frac{1}{2\pi i} \int_{a-i\infty}^{a+i\infty} F(z) \int_{0}^{R} e^{x(z-\zeta)}\, dx\, dz +$$

$$+ \frac{1}{2\pi i} \int_{b-i\infty}^{b+i\infty} F(z) \int_{-R'}^{0} e^{x(z-\zeta)}\, dx\, dz =$$

$$= -\frac{1}{2\pi i} \int_{a-i\infty}^{a+i\infty} \frac{F(z)\, dz}{z-\zeta} + \frac{1}{2\pi i} \int_{b-i\infty}^{b+i\infty} \frac{F(z)\, dz}{z-\zeta} + \varepsilon(a, R, \zeta) - \varepsilon(b, R', \zeta),$$

where

$$\varepsilon(c, r, \zeta) = \frac{1}{2\pi i} \int_{c-i\infty}^{c+i\infty} F(z) \frac{e^{-r(z-\zeta)}}{z-\zeta}\, dz.$$

Setting $a + \delta \leqslant \operatorname{Re} \zeta \leqslant b - \delta$, $\delta > 0$, and putting

$$M' = \frac{1}{2\pi} \max_{a \leqslant c \leqslant b} \int_{c-i\infty}^{c+i\infty} |F(z)|\, |dz|,$$

we find $|\varepsilon(a, R, \zeta)| + |\varepsilon(b, R', \zeta)| \leqslant \frac{M'}{\delta}(e^{-R\delta} + e^{-R'\delta})$; this quantity approaches zero as $R \to +\infty$, $R' \to +\infty$. Thus, taking the limit as R and R' approach $+\infty$, we find that the integral of $f(x)e^{-x\zeta}$ converges uniformly in ζ on the whole real axis for $a+\delta \leqslant \operatorname{Re}\zeta \leqslant b-\delta$, $\delta > 0$ and

$$\int_{-\infty}^{\infty} f(x)e^{-x\zeta}dx = \frac{1}{2\pi i}\int_{b-i\infty}^{b+i\infty} \frac{F(z)\,dz}{z-\zeta} - \frac{1}{2\pi i}\int_{a-i\infty}^{a+i\infty} \frac{F(z)\,dz}{z-\zeta} = \frac{1}{2\pi i}\int_{L} \frac{F(z)dz}{z-\zeta},$$

where L is the boundary of the strip $a < \operatorname{Re} z < b$.

Since the integrand in the last integral approaches zero as $z \to \infty$ in the strip $a \leqslant \operatorname{Re} z \leqslant b$, then, according to Theorem 1.1, Chap. VI, we can apply the residue theorem (or the Cauchy integral formula). The last integral therefore equals $F(\zeta)$ and

$$f(x) \risingdotseq F(z) \qquad (a < \operatorname{Re} z < b).$$

If $b = +\infty$, then the function $F(z)e^{xz}$ is regular in the half-plane $\operatorname{Re} z \geqslant a$ for $x < 0$ and it satisfies there the inequality $F(z) = O\left(\frac{1}{z^{\alpha+1}}\right)$ $(z \to \infty, \operatorname{Re} z \geqslant a)$. Application of Theorem 1.1 of Chap. VI now gives the result that the integral (1.2) equals zero. This proves the theorem.

The conditions used for the proof of Theorem 1.1 are not very convenient for applications. The trouble is that while the function $f(x)$ obtained from the function $F(z)$ is continuous on the whole axis, we more often encounter functions $f(x)$ with discontinuities at $x = 0$. Indeed, when we deal with the one-sided Laplace transform, we then assume that $f(x)$ is equal to zero for $x < 0$ and equal to some other function for $x > 0$.

Therefore we need another theorem imposing different conditions of $F(z)$. We shall have need of the following important lemma for the proof of this theorem as well as for the proof of the third theorem, in which conditions are imposed on $f(x)$.

Lemma 1. *Let the function f(x) be continuous on the entire axis with the possible exception of a countable set of discontinuities having no finite limit points. If*

$$\int_{-\infty}^{\infty} |f(x)|\,dx < \infty,$$

then as $\nu \to \pm\infty$

$$\int_{-\infty}^{\infty} f(x)\,e^{i\nu x}\,dx \to 0.$$

Proof. We first show that the statement of the lemma holds for function $f(x)$ vanishing outside some interval (a, b) and uniformly continuous on this interval. The idea of the proof is based on the rapid oscillation of the function $e^{i\nu x}$ for large ν; in particular, when we change x by π/ν, the function $e^{i\nu x}$ changes sign. Thus we find

$$\int_a^b f(x)\, e^{i\nu x}\, dx = \int_{a-\frac{\pi}{\nu}}^{b-\frac{\pi}{\nu}} f\left(\xi + \frac{\pi}{\nu}\right) e^{i\nu\left(\xi + \frac{\pi}{\nu}\right)}\, d\xi =$$

$$= -\int_{a-\frac{\pi}{\nu}}^{b-\frac{\pi}{\nu}} f\left(\xi + \frac{\pi}{\nu}\right) e^{i\nu\xi}\, d\xi.$$

From this, assuming for the sake of definiteness that $\nu > 0$, we obtain

$$2\int_a^b f(x)\, e^{i\nu x}\, dx = -\int_{a-\frac{\pi}{\nu}}^{a} f\left(x + \frac{\pi}{\nu}\right) e^{i\nu x}\, dx +$$

$$+ \int_{b-\frac{\pi}{\nu}}^{b} f(x)\, e^{i\nu x}\, dx + \int_a^{b-\frac{\pi}{\nu}} \left[f(x) - f\left(x + \frac{\pi}{\nu}\right)\right] e^{i\nu x}\, dx.$$

Each summand on the right side approaches zero: the first two because the length of the interval of integration approaches zero, the third because the integrand approaches zero. This proves our assertion.

To complete the proof of the lemma we need to show that for any $\varepsilon > 0$ we can find an N such that

$$\left| \int_{-\infty}^{\infty} f(x)\, e^{i\nu x}\, dx \right| < \varepsilon \qquad (|\nu| > N).$$

We first choose a number A so large that

$$\int_{|x| > A} |f(x)|\, dx < \frac{\varepsilon}{3}.$$

Note that there are only finitely many discontinuities of the function $f(x)$ on the interval $(-A, A)$. We include these in neighborhoods δ_k sufficiently small so that

$$\sum \int_{\delta_k} |f(x)|\, dx < \frac{\varepsilon}{3}.$$

The choices of A and δ_k are possible because of the absolute integrability of the function $f(x)$ on the entire axis.

After deletion of the δ_k there remain only finitely many intervals, on each of which the function $f(x)$ is continuous. The integral of $f(x)\,e^{i\nu x}$ approaches zero as $\nu \to \pm\infty$ on each of these intervals because of the first result we proved. Therefore, we can choose a number N so large that for $|\nu| > N$ the sum of the integrals of the function $f(x)\,e^{i\nu x}$ on all of the intervals mentioned does not exceed in absolute value the quantity $\frac{\varepsilon}{3}$. Thus, for $|\nu| > N$ we have

$$\left|\int_{-\infty}^{\infty} f(x)\,e^{i\nu x}\,dx\right| \leqslant \int_{|x|>A} |f(x)|\,dx + \\ + \sum \int_{\delta_k} |f(x)|\,dx + \left|\sum \int_{a_n}^{b_n} f(x)\,e^{i\nu x}\,dx\right| < \varepsilon,$$

which completes the proof of the lemma.

Note that the statement of the lemma remains valid also under the sole hypothesis of absolute integrability (we can also apply these remarks to the Lebesgue integral).

Theorem 1.2. *Let $0 < \alpha < 1$ and let the function F(z) be regular in the strip $a \leqslant \operatorname{Re} z \leqslant b$. Furthermore, let F(z) satisfy the conditions*

$$F'(z) = O(z^{-\alpha-1}), \quad F(z) \to 0 \quad (z \to \infty,\ a \leqslant \operatorname{Re} z \leqslant b). \tag{1.3}$$

The inversion formula (1.2) then holds for $x \neq 0$. If we set $g(x) = xf(x)$ (for $x \neq 0$) and set $g(0) = 0$, then the function g(x) satisfies the inequality

$$|e^{-cx}g(x) - e^{-c\xi}g(\xi)| < M|x-\xi|^{\alpha}$$

for any $a \leqslant c \leqslant b$. Moreover, $f(x) \div F(z)$ $(a < \operatorname{Re} z < b)$ and if $b = +\infty$ then $f(x) = 0$ for $x < 0$ and $f(x) \div F(z)$.

Proof. We reduce this theorem to Theorem 1.1. Integrating by parts, we may verify easily that integral (1.2) defining the function $f(x)$ converges for $x \neq 0$. We also obtain the formula

$$g(x) = xf(x) = -\frac{1}{2\pi i}\int_{c-i\infty}^{c+i\infty} F'(z)\,e^{xz}\,dz \qquad (a \leqslant c \leqslant b).$$

It is clear that this last integral also converges for $x = 0$, and that its value is zero when $x = 0$.

In view of (1.3), the function $G(z) = -F'(z)$ satisifes the conditions of Theorem 1.1, so that we obtain the inequality for $g(x)$ and the relation $g(x) \div G(z)$ $(a < \operatorname{Re} z < b)$, i.e.,

$$\int_{-\infty}^{\infty} g(x)\,e^{-xz} = -F'(z) \qquad (a < \operatorname{Re} z < b).$$

We now show that the relation $f(x) \risingdotseq F(z)$ follows from this equality. Setting Re $z=c$ $(a<c<b)$ and integrating the relation obtained for $F'(z)$ with respect to z from ζ to $c+iR$, we find

$$F(\zeta)-F(c+iR)=\int_{-\infty}^{\infty} f(x)\, e^{-x\zeta}\, dx-\int_{-\infty}^{\infty} f(x)\, e^{-cx}\, e^{-iRx}\, dx.$$

It is clear from the inequality for the function $g(x)$ that the function $f(x)\, e^{-cx}$ is absolutely integrable on the entire axis. Thus, as $R\to+\infty$, this last integral approaches zero because of Lemma 1. Since the value of $F(c+iR)$ also approaches zero as $R\to+\infty$ because of condition (1.3), then taking limits as $R\to+\infty$, we arrive at the relation

$$F(\zeta)=\int_{-\infty}^{\infty} f(x)\, e^{-x\zeta}\, dx \qquad (a<\operatorname{Re}\zeta<b).$$

If $b=+\infty$, we apply the same arguments as in Theorem 1.1. This completes the proof.

We shall need one additional notion, which we briefly mentioned before in passing, for the proof of the following theorem.

We shall say that the function $f(x)$ satisfies a Lipschitz condition of order α $(0<\alpha\leqslant 1)$ at the point ξ, if for all x in some neighborhood of the point ξ, we have

$$|f(x)-f(\xi)|<M|x-\xi|^{\alpha}.$$

Theorem 1.3. *Let the function f(x) be continuous on the entire axis with the possible exception of a countable set of points of discontinuity having no finite limit points, and let*

$$\int_{-\infty}^{\infty} |f(x)|\,(e^{-ax}+e^{-bx})\, dx<\infty \tag{1.4}$$

(a and b may coincide). Then the function

$$F(z)=\int_{-\infty}^{\infty} f(x)\, e^{-xz}\, dx \qquad (a\leqslant \operatorname{Re} z\leqslant b) \tag{1.5}$$

is continuous in the strip $a\leqslant \operatorname{Re} z\leqslant b$ *and regular at its interior points (if they exist, i.e., if* $a<b$*). If the function f(x) satisfies a Lipschitz condition of order* $\alpha>0$ *at the point* ξ*, then*

$$\frac{1}{2\pi i}\int_{c-i\infty}^{c+i\infty} F(z)\, e^{\xi z}\, dz=f(\xi) \qquad (a\leqslant c\leqslant b). \tag{1.6}$$

Proof. For $a\leqslant \operatorname{Re} z\leqslant b$ we have $|e^{-xz}|\leqslant e^{-ax}+e^{-bx}$, so that the integrand of formula (1.5) does not exceed the absolutely integrable function $|f(x)|(e^{-ax}+e^{-bx})$ for any value of x. Thus, the integral defining the function $F(z)$ converges uniformly in z in the strip $a \leqslant \operatorname{Re} z \leqslant b$. The properties of the function $F(z)$ follow from this.

To prove formula (1.6) we consider the integral

$$J_{R, R'}(\xi) = \int\limits_{c-iR'}^{c+iR} \left[F(z) - f(\xi)\frac{2ke^{-\xi z}}{z^2-k^2}\right] e^{\xi z}\, dz,$$

where $a \leqslant c \leqslant b$, $k > |c|$.

We have

$$F(z) = \int\limits_{-\infty}^{\infty} f(x)\, e^{-xz}\, dx, \qquad \frac{2ke^{-\xi z}}{z^2-k^2} = \int\limits_{-\infty}^{\infty} e^{-k|x-\xi|-xz}\, dx$$

(we can easily obtain this last relation if we split up the interval of integration into the subintervals $(-\infty, \xi)$ and $(\xi, +\infty)$, and then carry out the integration). Since both integrals converge uniformly on z on the line Re $z=c$ $(a \leqslant c \leqslant b)$, then we can substitute them into the expression $J_{R, R'}(\xi)$ and interchange the order of integration. This yields

$$J_{R, R'}(\xi) = \int\limits_{-\infty}^{\infty} [f(x) - f(\xi)\, e^{-k|x-\xi|}] \int\limits_{c-iR'}^{c+iR} e^{z(\xi-x)}\, dz\, dx.$$

Evaluating the inner integral, we obtain after some simplifications

$$J_{R, R'}(\xi) = \varphi(-R')\, e^{(c-iR')\xi} - \varphi(R)\, e^{(c+iR')\xi},$$

where

$$\varphi(\nu) = \int\limits_{-\infty}^{\infty} g(x)\, e^{i\nu x}\, dx, \quad g(x) = e^{-cx}\frac{f(x) - f(\xi)\, e^{-k|x-\xi|}}{x-\xi}.$$

It is not difficult to verify that if the function $f(x)$ satisfies a Lipschitz condition at the point ξ, then the function $g(x)$ satisfies the conditions of Lemma 1. In fact, it follows from condition (1.4) and the fact that $k > |c|$ that the function $g(x)$ is absolutely integrable on the entire axis with the exception of some neighborhood of the point ξ; furthermore, the Lipschitz condition ensures the absolute integrability of $g(x)$ in a neighborhood of the point ξ. Noting the restrictions placed on the function $f(x)$ in the theorem, we see that the remaining conditions of Lemma 1 are satisfied. Therefore, $\varphi(\nu) \to 0$ as $\nu \to \pm\infty$; consequently, the limit of $J_{R, R'}(\xi)$ as $R \to +\infty$ $R' \to +\infty$, exists and equals zero. This means that

$$\frac{1}{2\pi i}\int\limits_{c-i\infty}^{c+i\infty} F(z)\, e^{\xi z}\, dz = f(\xi)\cdot\frac{1}{2\pi i}\int\limits_{c-i\infty}^{c+i\infty} \frac{2k\, dz}{z^2-k^2} = f(\xi)$$

(the latter integral can easily be evaluated by using the theory of residues: it is equal to one). This proves the theorem.

Remark 1. The inversion formula of the Laplace transform can also be considered as an integral transform. It is easy to check that this inverse integral transform differs only in a few insignificant details from the Laplace transform itself. This means, in particular, that any theorem imposing conditions on $F(z)$ can be turned into a theorem imposing conditions on $f(x)$, and conversely.

Remark 2. The study of the Laplace transform for functions of several variables (on each of the variables) does not lead to any new problems. The inversion formula has the formula

$$f(x_1, \ldots, x_n) = \frac{1}{(2\pi i)^n} \int\limits_{c_1 - i\infty}^{c_1 + i\infty} \cdots \int\limits_{c_n - i\infty}^{c_n + i\infty} F(z_1, \ldots, z_n) e^{x_1 z_1 + \ldots + x_n z_n} dz_1 \ldots dz_n,$$

where

$$F(z_1, \ldots, z_n) = \int\limits_{-\infty}^{\infty} \cdots \int\limits_{-\infty}^{\infty} f(x_1, \ldots, x_n) e^{-(x_1 z_1 + \ldots + x_n z_n)} dx_1 \ldots dx_n.$$

2. THE CONVOLUTION THEOREM AND OTHER FORMULAS

The notion of the convolution of two functions plays an important role in the theory of the Laplace transform.

By the *convolution of the functions f(x) and g(x)* defined on the entire axis, we mean the function

$$(f(x) * g(x)) = \int\limits_{-\infty}^{\infty} f(x - \xi) g(\xi) d\xi = \int\limits_{-\infty}^{\infty} f(\xi) g(x - \xi) d\xi$$

(we shall assume that the integral converges for all x, although this is not always the case).

By the *convolution of the functions f(x) and g(x), defined for* $x > 0$, we mean the function

$$(f(x) * g(x)) = \int\limits_0^x f(x - \xi) g(\xi) d\xi = \int\limits_0^x f(\xi) g(x - \xi) d\xi.$$

If we put $f(x) = 0$ and $g(x) = 0$ for $x < 0$, then we may easily check that this last definition is a special case of the previous one.

There are many diverse theorems on the dependence of the properties of the convolution of two functions on the properties of the functions. (We shall present only one of the simplest*.)

Theorem 2.1. *Let the function* $f(x)e^{a|x|}, a \geqslant 0$, *be uniformly continuous on the whole x-axis, and let the function g(x) have at most a finite number of points of discontinuity on any finite interval. In addition, let*

$$\int_{-\infty}^{\infty} |f(x)|e^{a|x|}dx < \infty, \qquad \int_{-\infty}^{\infty} |g(x)|e^{b|x|}dx < \infty, \quad |b| < a.$$

Then the function $(f(x) * g(x))e^{b|x|}$ *is uniformly continuous on the entire x-axis and*

$$\int_{-\infty}^{\infty} (f(x) * g(x))e^{b|x|}dx < \infty.$$

Proof. We set

$$f_1(x) = f(x)e^{a|x|}, \quad g_1(x) = g(x)e^{b|x|},$$
$$h_1(x) = (f(x) * g(x))e^{b|x|}.$$

Then

$$h_1(x) = \int_{-\infty}^{\infty} f_1(x-\xi)g_1(\xi)\exp(-a|x-\xi| - b|\xi| + b|x|)\,d\xi.$$

We now show that this integral converges uniformly on the entire axis. We first estimate the integrand. In view of the uniform continuity of the function $f_1(x)$ on the entire axis, we have $|f_1(x-\xi)| \leqslant M$. In addition, since $a \geqslant 0$ and $|x-\xi| \geqslant ||x|-|\xi||$, we have

$$-a|x-\xi| - b|\xi| + b|x| \leqslant -a||x|-|\xi|| + |b|\,||x|-|\xi|| =$$
$$= (|b|-a)\,||x|-|\xi|| \leqslant 0.$$

Consequently, the integrand does not exceed $M|g_1(\xi)|$ and in view of the absolute integrability of the function $g_1(x)$ on the entire axis, the integral representing the function $h_1(x)$ converges uniformly on the whole axis.

The uniform continuity of the function $h_1(x)$ follows from the uniform convergence of the integral.

We next prove the absolute integrability of the function $h_1(x)$ on the entire axis. It is evident that

---

*A detailed study of this question can be found in the book: E.C. Titchmarsh, Introduction to the Theory of the Fourier Integrals, Oxford Univ. Press, 1937. Many theorems on convolutions become difficult to formulate without the theory of the Lebesgue integral.

$$\int_{-\infty}^{\infty} |h_1(x)|\, dx \leqslant \int_{-\infty}^{\infty}\int_{-\infty}^{\infty} |f_1(x-\xi)||g_1(\xi)|\, d\xi\, dx.$$

We show now that this double integral converges. It is sufficient for this to show that the integral

$$\iint_{D_r} |f_1(x-\xi)||g_1(\xi)|\, d\xi\, dx \qquad (r \to \infty),$$

has a finite limit. Here D_r is an increasing sequence of domains whose limit as $r \to \infty$ is the whole plane. For the D_r we can take the parallelograms $|\xi| < r$, $|x-\xi| < r$ in the (x, ξ)-plane. We have

$$\iint_{D_r} |f_1(x-\xi)||g_1(\xi)|\, d\xi\, dx = \int_{-r}^{r} |g_1(\xi)| \int_{-r+\xi}^{r+\xi} |f_1(x-\xi)|\, dx\, d\xi =$$

$$= \int_{-r}^{r} |g_1(\xi)|\, d\xi \cdot \int_{-r}^{r} |f_1(\eta)|\, d\eta \leqslant$$

$$\leqslant \int_{-\infty}^{\infty} |g_1(\xi)|\, d\xi \int_{-\infty}^{\infty} |f_1(\eta)|\, d\eta < \infty.$$

Thus, as r increases, the sequence of integrals on the D_r is bounded and monotonically increasing. Thus the integral converges and the theorem is proved.

Remark 1. If we do not assume that the function $f(x)\, e^{a|x|}$ is uniformly convergent on the whole axis, but that it satisfies the condition

$$|f(x)\, e^{ax} - f(\xi)\, e^{a\xi}| < M|x-\xi|^{\alpha} \qquad (0 < \alpha \leqslant 1),$$

then the function $(f(x) * g(x))\, e^{b|x|}$ will also satisfy an analogous condition.

Remark 2. If the functions $f(x)$ and $g(x)$ are zero for $x < 0$, then the values of the convolution on the interval $(0, A)$ depend only on the values of $f(x)$ and $g(x)$ on this interval. There follows easily from Theorem 2.1:

If the function f(x) is continuous for $x \geqslant 0$ and the function g(x) is absolutely integrable on each finite interval, then their convolution

$$(f(x) * g(x)) = \int_0^x f(x-\xi)\, g(\xi)\, dx$$

is continuous for $x \geqslant 0$.

Theorem 2.2. *Let the function f(x) be uniformly continuous on the whole axis, and let the function g(x) have at most a finite number of points of discontinuity on any finite interval; furthermore, let*

$$\int_{-\infty}^{\infty} |f(x)|\, dx < \infty, \qquad \int_{-\infty}^{\infty} |g(x)|\, dx < \infty$$

if $f(x) \doteqdot F(z)$, $g(x) \doteqdot G(z)$, then $(f(x) * g(x)) \doteqdot F(z)\, G(z)$.

Proof. For Re $z=0$ we have

$$(f(x)*g(x)) \div \int_{-\infty}^{\infty} (f(x)*g(x))\, e^{-xz}\, dx =$$

$$= \int_{-\infty}^{\infty} e^{-xz} \int_{-\infty}^{\infty} f(x-\xi)\, g(\xi)\, d\xi\, dx.$$

Just as in the proof of Theorem 2.1, we verify that the double integral

$$\iint_{-\infty}^{\infty} f(x-\xi)\, g(\xi)\, e^{-xz}\, d\xi\, dx \qquad (\mathrm{Re}\, z=0)$$

converges absolutely. Its value can be found by determining the limit of the integral on any increasing sequence of domains D_r. Choosing the domains to be the same parallelograms used in the proof of Theorem 2.1, we obtain the statement of the theorem.

(Note that all our arguments involving the choice of a sequence of domains are used only for the justification of change of the order of integration in the generalized double integral.)

We shall deduce a few interesting corollaries of this theorem.

Theorem 2.2 can be written in the form

$$\int_{-\infty}^{\infty} f(x-\xi)\, g(\xi)\, d\xi = \frac{1}{2\pi i} \int_{-i\infty}^{i\infty} F(z)\, G(z)\, e^{xz}\, dz, \qquad (2.1)$$

where $f(x) \div F(z)$ and $g(x) \div G(z)$.

Next, note that the relation $\overline{f(-x)} \div \overline{F(-\bar{z})}$ follows from the relation $f(x) \div F(z)$. Since on the imaginary axis $-\bar{z}=z$, then, setting $g(\xi)=\overline{f(-\xi)}$, $x=0$, we obtain

$$\int_{-\infty}^{\infty} |f(\xi)|^2\, d\xi = \frac{1}{2\pi} \int_{-\infty}^{\infty} |F(iy)|^2\, dy. \qquad (2.2)$$

This formula is called *Parseval's identity*.

It is frequently possible to solve problems without the use of the inversion formula by means of Theorem 2.2 and other formulas of this type (however, much simpler). Before we give examples of these operations, we introduce a few formulas. They can all be deduced from Theorem 2.2 by means of a suitable generalization, but it is simpler to prove them directly.

We shall have to prove two variants of each of these formulas: for one-sided and two-sided Laplace transforms, since the fomulas for these cases are somewhat different.

1. If $f(x) \div F(z)$, then $xf(x) \div -F'(z)$.

In fact, the integral defining the function $F(z)$ converges in some half-plane Re $z > c$. According to Theorem 4.5, Chapter II, we can differentiate under the integral sign. This gives

$$F'(z) = -\int_0^\infty f(x)\, xe^{-xz}\, dx \qquad (\operatorname{Re} z > c),$$

i.e., $xf(x) \div -F'(z)$.

1. Let*

$$\int_{-\infty}^{\infty} (1 + |x|)\, |f(x)|\, e^{-ax}\, dx < \infty.$$

If $f(x) \div F(z) (\operatorname{Re} z = a)$, then $xf(x) \div -F'(z)$ $(\operatorname{Re} z = a)$.

It is impossible to apply the same argument as that used in the proof of formula 1, for the domain of uniform convergence of the integral has no interior points. However, the condition of absolute integrability of the function $(1 + |x|) f(x)$ ensures the convergence of both the integral defining $F(z)$ and the integral obtained by differentiating under the integral sign. It is therefore legitimate to differentiate under the integral sign, so that we obtain the desired formula.

2. Let

$$\int_0^\infty |f'(x)|\, e^{-ax} < \infty.$$

If $f(x)$ $F(z)$, then $f'(x)$ $zF(z)$ - $f(0)$.

Indeed, for sufficiently large $\operatorname{Re} z$ we have $f(x) e^{-xz} \to 0$ as $x \to +\infty$ and

$$f'(x) \div \int_0^\infty f'(x)\, e^{-xz}\, dx = f(x)\, e^{-xz}\Big|_0^\infty + \\ + z \int_0^\infty f(x)\, e^{-xz}\, dx = -f(0) + F(z).$$

This proves the formula.

2. Let*

$$f(x)\, e^{-ax} \to 0 \qquad (x \to \pm\infty),$$

$$\int_{-\infty}^{\infty} (|f(x)| + |f'(x)|)\, e^{-ax}\, dx < \infty.$$

If $f(x) \div F(z)$ *then* $f'(x) \div zF(z)$ *(Re* $z = a$*).*

This formula is proved in the same way as is the preceding one.

It may appear strange at first glance that formulas 2 and 2* are different, since the one-sided Laplace transform is a special case of the two-sided. The reason for the difference is that the function equal to $f(x)$ for $x \geqslant 0$ and to zero for $x < 0$, is obviously not differentiable if $f(0) \neq 0$. If $f(0) = 0$ (and if $f'(0)$ exists) then formulas 2 and 2* coincide.

We next present an example of the use of the Laplace transform in solving a problem without the use of the inversion formula.

Example 1. We find the solution of the equation

$$y^{(n)}(x) + a_1 y^{(n-1)}(x) + \ldots + a_n y(x) = f(x),$$

under the conditions $y(0) = y'(0) = \ldots = y^{(n-1)}(0) = 0$.

First, we assume that $f(x)$ vanishes for sufficiently large x. Thus, for x sufficiently large, the function $y(x)$ which we seek is the solution of a homogeneous differential equation with constant coefficients, i.e., a linear combination of functions of the form $P_k(x) e^{\lambda_k x}$ ($P_k(x)$ is a polynomial). Thus, the one-sided Laplace transform of the function $y(x)$ exists, as does the Laplace transform of its derivatives.

We put

$$y(x) \div \eta(z), \qquad f(x) \div F(z).$$

Taking account of the condition $y(0) = y'(0) = \ldots = y^{(n-1)}(0) = 0$, we find from formula 2 the relation

$$y'(x) \div z\eta(z), \quad \ldots, \quad y^{(n)}(x) \div z^n \eta(z).$$

Employing the equation for $y(x)$, we find

$$P(z)\eta(z) = F(z) \qquad (P(z) = z^n + a_1 z^{n-1} + \ldots + a_n),$$

or

$$\eta(z) = \frac{F(z)}{P(z)}.$$

The rational function $\frac{1}{P(z)}$ can be expanded as a sum of parital fractions

$$\frac{1}{P(z)} = \sum\sum \frac{A_{m,k}}{(z-\lambda_m)^k}.$$

To find the function $q(x)$ whose one-sided Laplace transform is the function $\frac{1}{P(z)}$, we can solve this problem for each of the partial fractions. Using the evident relation

$$\frac{1}{z-\lambda}=\int_0^\infty e^{\lambda x - xz}\,dx \qquad \left(e^{\lambda x} \div \frac{1}{z-\lambda}\right),$$

we apply formula 1 and get

$$x^k e^{\lambda x} \div \frac{k!\,(-1)^k}{(z-\lambda)^{k+1}}.$$

Thus,

$$q(x)=\sum\sum A_{m,\,k}\,(-1)^k\,(k-1)!\,x^{k-1}e^{\lambda_m x}.$$

Furthermore, from the relation

$$y(x) \div \eta(z), \quad f(x) \div F(z), \quad q(x) \div \frac{1}{P(z)}, \quad \eta(z)=\frac{1}{P(z)}F(z)$$

and using Theorem 2.2, we obtain

$$y(x)=(q(x) * f(x)),$$

i.e.,

$$y(x)=\int_0^x q(x-\xi)\,f(\xi)\,d\xi.$$

Note that the solution depends only on the behavior of the function $f(x)$ on the segment $(0, x)$. Therefore, our assumption that $f(x)=0$ for sufficiently large x did not involve any loss of generality.

There is an extensively developed class of methods of integral transforms: operational calculus, is concerned only with solutions of problems without the use of the inversion formula. A wide variety of formulas is presented in the texts of operational calculus, and frequently they are more convenient than those presented above. All these formulas can be derived from the basic results presented above by one means or another.

We adopt a convenient term from operational calculus:

We call the function $f(x)$ the *original* and its Laplace transform: its *transform*.

3. EXAMPLES OF THE APPLICATION OF THE METHOD

Most of the applications of the method of the Laplace transform lie outside the domain of the theory of analytic functions. Therefore, the examples we study now have little connection with this theory. They are chosen with one purpose in mind: to illustrate the essential points of the method while bringing in as little extraneous material as possible.

Example 1. Let the function $f(x)e^{-b|x|}$, $b<a$, be uniformly continuous on the entire axis. We find a solution of the equation

$$y''(x)-a^2y(x)=f(x) \qquad (a>0)$$

such that the function $y(x)e^{-b|x|}$ is uniformly continuous on the entire axis.

We first assume that the function $f(x)$ equals zero for all values x sufficiently large in absolute value. Then for x sufficiently large $y(x)$ is the solution of the equation $y''=a^2y$, i.e., $y(x)=C_1e^{ax}+C_2e^{-ax}$ (for $x>A$ and $x<-A$ the constants C_1 and C_2 are distinct). The requirement of uniform continuity (and therefore boundedness) for $y(x)e^{-b|x|}$ on the entire axis gives us

$$y(x)=Ce^{-ax} \qquad (x>A), \quad y(x)=C'e^{ax} \qquad (x<-A).$$

It is clear from this that the two-sided Laplace transform exists for the function $y(x)$ and for its derivatives. Setting

$$y(x)\div\eta(z), \qquad f(x)\div F(z),$$

we obtain from the equation

$$(z^2-a^2)\eta(z)=F(z), \qquad \eta(z)=\frac{1}{z^2-a^2}F(z)$$

(by applying formula 2*). However, the function $\frac{1}{z^2-a^2}$ is the transform of the function $\frac{e^{-a|x|}}{2a}$, as may easily be verified by integration. According to Theorem 2.2, the product of the transforms corresponds to the convolution of the originals. Therefore,

$$y(x)=\frac{1}{2a}(e^{-a|x|}*f(x)),$$

or

$$y(x)=\frac{1}{2a}\int_{-\infty}^{\infty}e^{-a|x-\xi|}f(\xi)\,d\xi.$$

Note that the formula obtained is already suitable without any further assumptions. Indeed, it follows from Theorem 2.1 on the properties of the convolution that the function $y(x)e^{-b|x|}$, $b<a$, is uniformly continuous on the entire axis, if the function $f(x)e^{-b|x|}$ has this property.

It is not difficult to show that formula (3.1) gives the unique solution of the problem. In fact, the difference of two solutions is a solution of the equation $y''=ay^2$ and satisfies the condition

$$|y(x)|<Me^{b|x|} \qquad (b<a).$$

It is clear that such a solution of the equation must be identically zero.

Example 2. We find the solution of the integral equation

$$\int_0^x (x-\xi)^{\alpha-1} y(\xi)\, d\xi = f(x) \qquad (0<\alpha<1),$$

where $f(x)$ is any function continuously differentiable for $x \geqslant 0$.

We set

$$y(x) \div \eta(z), \qquad f(x) \div F(z)$$

and note that

$$x^{\nu-1} \div \Gamma(\nu) z^{-\nu} \qquad (\nu>0) \tag{3.2}$$

(we choose the principal value for $z^{-\nu}$), since

$$\int_0^\infty x^{\nu-1} e^{-xz}\, dx = \Gamma(\nu) z^{-\nu} \qquad (\operatorname{Re} z>0,\ \nu>0).$$

Theorem 2.2 on the convolution together with the original formula therefore give us

$$\Gamma(\alpha) z^{-\alpha} \eta(z) = F(z), \qquad \eta(z) = \frac{z^\alpha}{\Gamma(\alpha)} F(z).$$

Let $g(x)$ denote the original of the function $\frac{z^{\alpha-1}}{\Gamma(\alpha)} F(z) = G(z)$. Since according to formula (3.2) with $\nu = 1-\alpha$ we have $x^{-\alpha} \div \Gamma(1-\alpha) z^{\alpha-1}$ and $\Gamma(\alpha)\Gamma(1-\alpha) = \frac{\pi}{\sin \alpha\pi}$ from formula (6.4) of Chap. VI, then we find, using the theorem on convolutions,

$$g(x) = (x^{-\alpha} * f(x)) \frac{\pi}{\sin \alpha\pi} = \frac{\pi}{\sin \alpha\pi} \int_0^x (x-\xi)^{-\alpha} f(\xi)\, d\xi.$$

Since $\eta(z) = zG(z)$, then formula 2 of Sect. 2 yields $y(x) = g'(x) + g(0)$. However, $g(0) = 0$, so that we obtain

$$y(x) = \frac{\pi}{\sin \alpha\pi} \frac{d}{dx} \int_0^x (x-\xi)^{-\alpha} f(\xi)\, d\xi.$$

It may easily be seen by testing that this formula gives us a solution of the integral equation. However, the question of uniqueness requires a supplementary study, which is not so simple.

Example 3. We find the solution of the differential equation

$$\frac{\partial u}{\partial t}=\frac{\partial^2 u}{\partial x^2}, \qquad u(x, 0)=f(x) \qquad (t \geqslant 0, \ -\infty<x<\infty).$$

We set

$$u(x, t) \risingdotseq v(z, t), \qquad f(x) \risingdotseq F(z).$$

Using formula 2* of Sect. 2, we obtain from the equation

$$\frac{\partial v}{\partial t}=z^2 v, \qquad v(z, 0)=F(z).$$

Solving this last equation, we find

$$v(z, t)=e^{z^2 t} F(z).$$

According to the theorem on convolutions, letting $q(x, t)$ denote the original of the function $e^{z^2 t}$, we have

$$u(x, t)=\int_{-\infty}^{\infty} q(x-\xi, t) f(\xi)\, d\xi.$$

We find $q(x, t)$ by applying the inversion formula. Since $e^{z^2 t}$ approaches zero as $\operatorname{Im} z \rightarrow \pm\infty$ for fixed $\operatorname{Re} z$ more rapidly than any power, we can apply Theorm 1.1 and write

$$q(x, t)=\frac{1}{2\pi i} \int_{c-i\infty}^{c+i\infty} e^{z^2 t+xz}\, dz \qquad (-\infty<c<\infty).$$

We choose $c=-\frac{x}{2t}$. Making the substitution $\zeta=z-c$, we easily find

$$q(x, t)=\frac{1}{2\pi i} \int_{c-i\infty}^{c+i\infty} \exp\left[t\left(z+\frac{x}{2t}\right)^2-\frac{x^2}{4t}\right] dz=$$

$$=e^{-\frac{x^2}{4t}} \frac{1}{2\pi i} \int_{-i\infty}^{i\infty} e^{\zeta^2 t}\, d\zeta=\frac{e^{-\frac{x^2}{4t}}}{2\pi} \int_{-\infty}^{\infty} e^{-y^2 t}\, dy=\frac{1}{2} \sqrt{\frac{\pi}{t}}\, e^{-\frac{x^2}{4t}}.$$

The final form of the result is

$$u(x, t)=\frac{1}{2} \sqrt{\frac{\pi}{t}} \int_{-\infty}^{\infty} e^{-\frac{(x-\xi)^2}{4t}} f(\xi)\, d\xi.$$

It is not difficult to verify that this formula gives the desired solution of the equation if $f(x)$ satisfies the condition $|f(x)|<Me^{|x|^{2-\delta}}$.

The question of uniqueness again requires a separate investigattion.

Example 4. We find for the integral equation

$$y(x) = \frac{\lambda}{2}\int_0^\infty e^{-|x-\xi|}y(\xi)\,d\xi \qquad (x > 0),$$

a solution satisfying the condition

$$|y(x)| < Me^{ax} \qquad (a < 1).$$

We set

$$\varphi(x) = \frac{\lambda}{2}\int_0^\infty e^{-|x-\xi|}y(\xi)\,d\xi \qquad (-\infty < x < \infty)$$

and

$$\varphi_+(x) = \begin{cases} \varphi(x), & x \geqslant 0, \\ 0, & x < 0; \end{cases} \qquad \varphi_-(x) = \begin{cases} 0, & x \geqslant 0, \\ \varphi(x), & x < 0. \end{cases}$$

It is clear that, in view of the equation, the function $\varphi_+(x)$ coincides with $y(x)$.

It is easy to obtain the inequality

$$|\varphi(x)| \leqslant Me^{ax-(1-a)|x|} \qquad (-\infty < x < \infty)$$

for the function $\varphi(x)$. The two-sided Laplace transform therefore exists for the function $\varphi(x)$ in the strip $a < \operatorname{Re} z < 1$. We denote it by $\Phi(z)$; we have

$$\Phi_+(z) = \int_0^\infty \varphi(x)e^{-xz}\,dx, \qquad \Phi_-(z) = \int_{-\infty}^0 \varphi(x)e^{-xz}\,dx.$$

The function $\Phi_+(z)$ is regular and bounded in the half-plane $\operatorname{Re} z \geqslant a+\varepsilon$, and $\Phi_-(z)$ has these properties in the half-plane $\operatorname{Re} z < 1-\varepsilon$ (ε is any positive number) and $\Phi(z) = \Phi_+(z) + \Phi_-(z)$ $(a < \operatorname{Re} z < 1)$.

According to Theorem 2.2 on convolutions, we have

$$\Phi(z) = \Phi_-(z) + \Phi_+(z) = \lambda\Phi_+(z)\frac{1}{z^2-1} \qquad (a < \operatorname{Re} z < 1),$$

since the transform of the function $e^{-|x|}$ is the function $\frac{2}{z^2-1}$.

Suppose thet $\lambda < 0$. We then choose a so that $|\operatorname{Re}\sqrt{1+\lambda} < a < 1$. Consider the function

$$\psi(z) = (z-1)\Phi_-(z) = \frac{1+\lambda-z^2}{z+1}\Phi_+(z).$$

On the one hand, the function $\psi(z)$ is regular in the half-plane $\operatorname{Re} z \geqslant a+\varepsilon$ and satisfies the inequality $\psi(z)=O(|z|+1)$ there, since the function $\Phi_+(z)$ is regular and bounded for $\operatorname{Re} z \geqslant a+\varepsilon$. On the other hand, the function $\psi(z)$ is regular and bounded in the half-plane $\operatorname{Re} z \leqslant 1-\varepsilon$ and satisfies the inequality $\psi(z)=O(|z|+1)$ there (we may use the same argument and replace $\Phi_+(z)$ by $\Phi_-(z)$). This means that $\psi(z)$ is regular in the entire plane and $\psi(z)=O(|z|)$ as $z \to \infty$. By Liouville's theorem (see Sect. 2, Chap. IV) we have $\psi(z)=C+C_1 z$. However, as $z \to +\infty$ we have $\psi(z)=o(|z|)$, since $\Phi_+(z) \to 0$ as $z \to +\infty$, as may easily be verified by inspection of its formula. Thus,

$$\psi(z) \equiv C, \qquad \Phi_+(z)=\frac{C(z+1)}{1+\lambda-z^2}.$$

However, $\Phi_+(z)$ is the one-sided transform of the desired solution. Therefore, returning to the original, we find

$$y(x)=(1+\sqrt{1+\lambda})\, e^{x\sqrt{1+\lambda}}-(1-\sqrt{1+\lambda})e^{-x\sqrt{1+\lambda}}.$$

Example 5. We find a fundamental system of solutions for the equation

$$y''(x)+\frac{1}{x}y'(x)+y(x)=0.$$

We seek the solution in the form of a contour integral

$$y(x)=\int_C \varphi(z)\, e^{xz}\, dz,$$

where the contour C is chosen in such a way that the integrand approaches zero sufficiently rapidly as z approaches the endpoints of the contour (or where C is a closed contour). It is clear that we have

$$y'(x)=\int_C z\varphi(z)\, e^{xz} dz, \quad y''(x)=\int_C z^2\varphi(z)\, e^{xz}\, dz$$

and (integrating by parts)

$$x(y''(x)+y(x))=x\int_C (1+z^2)\,\varphi(z)\, e^{xz}\, dz=$$

$$=-\int_C e^{xz}\frac{d}{dz}[(1+z^2)\,\varphi(z)]dz$$

(one term vanishes in view of our assumption about the endpoints of the contour). The equation therefore gives us

$$\int_C \left\{ z\varphi(z) - \frac{d}{dz}[(1+z^2)\varphi(z)] \right\} e^{xz}\,dz = 0.$$

This equation is trivially satisfied if the integrand is zero, i.e., if

$$\frac{d}{dz}[(1+z^2)\varphi(z)] = z\varphi(z).$$

Solving the equation obtained for $\varphi(z)$, we find

$$\varphi(z) = \frac{C}{\sqrt{1+z^2}}.$$

Thus, functions of the form

$$y(x) = \int_C \frac{e^{xz}}{\sqrt{1+z^2}}\,dz$$

are solutions of the original equation if the contour C is chosen in such a way that the integrand approaches zero sufficiently rapidly as z approaches the endpoints of the contour, or if C is a closed contour and $\sqrt{1+z^2}$ is single-valued on C.

We can choose the following contours in order to obtain two linearly independent solutions of the initial equation:

C_1 is the boundary of the domain $|\arg(z-i)| < \pi$, $|z-i| > \varrho$;

C_2 is the boundary of the domain $|\arg(z+i)| < \pi$, $|z+i| > \varrho$.

The integral converges for $\operatorname{Re} x > 0$ since as $z \to \pm i - \infty$, the function e^{xz} approaches zero more rapidly than any power of z.

Setting $\varrho = 0$ and combining the integrals on the two edges of the crosscut into one, we obtain the following formula for the solutions:

$$y_1(x) = e^{ix} \int_0^\infty \frac{e^{-xt}}{\sqrt{t(t+2i)}}\,dt \qquad (\operatorname{Re} x > 0);$$

$$y_2(x) = e^{-ix} \int_0^\infty \frac{e^{-xt}}{\sqrt{t(t-2i)}} \qquad (\operatorname{Re} x > 0).$$

With the help of Theorem 4.1 of Chap. VI we can easily obtain the asymptotic formulas

$$y_1(x) \sim \frac{e^{ix}}{\sqrt{2\pi i x}} \qquad (\operatorname{Re} x \to +\infty),$$

$$y_2(x) \sim \frac{e^{-ix}}{\sqrt{-2\pi i x}} \qquad (\operatorname{Re} x \to +\infty),$$

$y_1(x)$ and $y_2(x)$ are obviously linearly independent.

By rotating the contour (as in Example 2 of Sect. 2, Chap. VI), we can continue the functions $y_1(x)$ and $y_2(x)$ analytically to the whole plane with the exception of the point 0 where these functions have a logarithmic branch point.

We could have chosen the contour C to be the boundary of the domain composed of the plane with a cross cut along the segment $(-i, i)$. This is a closed contour and the function $\sqrt{1+z^2}$ is single-valued on it. The solution of the initial equation corresponding to this contour has the form

$$y(x)=\int_{-1}^{1}\frac{e^{iyx}}{\sqrt{1-y^2}}\,dy.$$

It is clear that the function $y(x)$ is regular on the entire plane.

It is a direct consequence of the general theory that $y(x)$ is a linear combination of the functions $y_1(x)$ and $y_2(x)$.

4. THE GENERALIZED LAPLACE TRANSFORM

Until now we have studied the Laplace transform only for functions satisfying the condition

$$\int_{-\infty}^{\infty}|f(x)|\,e^{-ax}\,dx<\infty$$

for some a. This assumption greatly limits the usefulness of the method in many cases. Thus, for example, in Example 1 of the preceding section, we were able to apply the Laplace transform in obtaining a solution of the problem only after making additional assumptions, which we then hastened to eliminate after obtaining the formulas. In addition to this, we lost the possibility of immediately proving the uniqueness of the solution, and this had to be proved separately. This loss is not significant in the case of rather simple problems; however, the question of the uniqueness of the solution is far from simple in more difficult problems. The proof of this in complicated cases as well as the verification of formulas obtained by operational methods here presents considerable difficulties. In order that he gain an idea of this difficulty, we advise the reader to check the formulas for the solutions which we found in Examples 2 and 3 of the preceding section (we refrain from giving this proof, although we remarked that it is possible).

For these reasons a theory giving a foundation for the introduction of the Laplace transform for functions $f(x)$ not integrable along the entire axis began to be developed a long time ago. However, a theory of the Laplace transform for increasing functions, satisfying those requirements needed for its applications, has been created only recently. With the aid of this theory — it has received the name of the theory of generalized functions — it became possible to solve many problems connected with the existence and uniqueness of solutions of partial differential equations.

Any type of detailed presentation of the theory of generalized functions would lead us too far astray. We limit our discussion to the basic ideas that serve as the foundation for this theory.*

Depending on the requirements arising in the problems to be considered, the Laplace transform may be generalized for various classes of functions. We shall chiefly discuss the Laplace transform of functions that are continuous on some finite interval of the real axis and that are increasing for $x \to \pm\infty$.

As earlier, we shall call the function $f(x)$ the *original* and its Laplace transform—the *transform;* we shall use the same symbolism for this relation: the formula $f(x) \risingdotseq F(z)$, only the meaning of the concept of transform will be somewhat different.

The transform is to be endowed with the following properties:

1. The mappings $F(z)$ and $G(z)$ are assumed to be equal if their originals $f(x)$ and $g(x)$ are identical.

2. The mapping is a linear function of the original, i.e., it follows from the relations $f(x) \risingdotseq F(z)$ and $g(x) \risingdotseq G(z)$ that

$$af(x) + bg(x) \risingdotseq aF(z) + bG(z)$$

for any constants a and b.

3. If the original is continuously differentiable and absolutely integrable on the whole of the real axis, then its transform coincides with the ordinary Laplace transform.

4. We choose some notion of convergence and say that a sequence of transforms is convergent if the sequence of originals converges in the chosen sense.

Having assigned a notion of convergence for the originals, we use this to single out some class of functions (a linear topological space) obtained as limits from continuously differentiable functions that are absolutely integrable on the entire axis. The transform is defined for functions of this class as the formal limit of a sequence of ordinary Laplace transforms. The notion of convergence may turn out to be one for which the limit will exist in some ordinary sense of the term, but it may also turn out that the limit does not exist in any ordinary sense of the term. However, this is not important: we do not require that the transform be a function in the ordinary sense of the word. What is important is that each function of the class constructed correspond to exactly one transform.

We now choose two types of convergence for the originals and examine the classes of functions that arise when these notions of convergence are used.

---

*A detailed presentation of the theory of generalized functions and their applications can be found in the monograph of I.M. Gel'fand and G. E. Shilov, Generalized Functions, 1st and 2nd editions; Generalized Functions. Properties and Operations, Academic Press, N.Y., 1964; Spaces of Ordinary and Generalized Functions, Academic Press, N.Y., 1964.

Example 1. We use the following notion of convergence for the originals: $f_n(x) \longrightarrow 0$ if $f_n(x)$ converges uniformly to zero on each finite interval.

In this case the limit of a sequence of continuously differentiable functions absolutely integrable on the entire axis can be any function continuous at all points of the axis (and only such a function). Indeed, first of all, any continuous function that is absolutely integrable on the entire axis is the uniform limit of continuously differentiable functions that are absolutely integrable in the entire axis. Then it is easy to construct a sequence of continuous functions that are absolutely integrable on the entire axis and that converges uniformly to a given continuous function on any finite interval of the axis. For example, we can take $f_n(x)$ equal to $f(x)$ on the segment $(-n, n)$, zero outside $(-n-1, n+1)$ and linear on the remaining segments.

On the other hand, the limit of a uniformly convergent sequence of continuous functions is again a continuous function.

Example 2. We choose convergence for the originals in the following manner: $f_n(x) \longrightarrow 0$ if for any $\alpha < a$ we have

$$\lim_{n \to \infty} \max_x |f_n(x) e^{-\alpha |x|}| = 0.$$

In this case the limit of a sequence of continuously differentiable functions that are absolutely integrable on the entire axis can be any function $f(x)$ that is continuous on the entire axis and satisfies the inequality

$$|f(x)| < Me^{\alpha |x|}$$

for some $\alpha < a$ (and only such a function). This may easily be proved by using the arguments of Example 1.

We now turn to the question of how to work with this generalized notion of transform and what kind of a role the notion of convergence will play here.

Having assigned the notion of convergence, we obtain a class of originals, each of which may be placed in correspondence with a transform. It would seem that our next step would be to choose a class as broad as possible and then to solve problems. However, the task is not so simple. The choice of the class is determined by the problem to be solved. Roughly speaking, this arises from the fact that the wider the class is, the fewer operations can be done with the transforms.

The fundamental operations that we must be able to carry out with the transforms in order to solve problems are addition of transforms and their multiplication by functions. In the case of generalized transforms, these operations must be understood as follows: each generalized transform is the limit of a sequence of ordinary transforms: operations on these transforms correspond to some kind of operations on their originals; if the sequence of originals on which these operations are carried out converges, then we obtain a convergent sequence of transforms and the corresponding operations are possible on these.

In other words, an operation may be carried out on a transform if the corresponding operation on the convergent sequence of originals preserves the property of convergence. This means that we can carry out operations with the transforms whose corresponding operations on the originals do not lead us out of the class of originals.

It is clear that addition of transforms, which corresponds to addition of originals, does not lead us out of the class of originals.

Multiplication of the transform by the function

$$B(z)=\int_{-\infty}^{\infty}\beta(x)\,e^{-xz}\,dx$$

corresponds to the convolution of the original with the function $\beta(x)$. Thus, one of the fundamental problems in the theory of the Laplace transform is to find classes of functions such that the convolution of two members of the class belongs to the class. This question also plays an important role in the classical theory of the Laplace transform, but its role is even more noteworthy in the theory of generalized Laplace transforms. The answer to this question for the class of originals considered in Example 2 can be immediately obtained from Theorem 2.1 on convolutions:

If the function $\beta(x)$ *satisfies the condition*

$$|\beta(x)|<Me^{-a|x|}\qquad(-\infty<x<\infty),$$

and $f(x)\in S_a$, *then* $(f(x)*\beta(x))\in S_a$.

Here S_a denotes the class of functions described in Example 2.

Let us also consider the problem of multiplying a transform by a power of z.

Multiplication of the transform by z corresponds to the differentiation of the original. Therefore it is not generally admissible to multiply any transform by z. However, if it is known in advance that both the original and its derivative belong to the class of originals, then multiplication by z represents an admissible operation.

We shall not consider any complicated examples of the application of the generalized Laplace transform. We shall consider only one which can be discussed using the study carried out in Example 1 of the preceding section. The arguments that we present in this example are typical of those used in more complicated problems. (We refrain from considering more complicated problems only because we would then have to prove some rather complicated theorems on convolutions, and we shall have no need for these later.)

Example 3. (See Example 1 of Sect. 3.) Let $0\leqslant\alpha<a$ and let $f(x)$ be a function continuous on the entire axis and such that $|f(x)|<Me^{\alpha|x|}$ We show that there exists a unique solution for the equation

$$y''(x)-a^2y(x)=f(x),$$

for which $|y(x)|<M_1e^{a|x|}$, and we find a formula for the solution.
First we set

$$y(x) \doteqdot \eta(z), \quad f(x) \doteqdot F(z)$$

and we then find

$$\eta(z)=\frac{1}{z^2-a^2}F(z).$$

We now determine the class of originals that must be chosen. The function $\frac{1}{z^2-a^2}$ is the transform of the function $\frac{1}{2a}e^{-a|x|}$. Thus we must choose our class of originals so that the convolution of a function $f(x)$ from this class with the function $\frac{1}{2a}e^{-a|x|}$ is also a member of the class. Then $\eta(z)=\frac{F(z)}{z^2-a^2}$ will be the transform of a function from this class of originals and of only one. This means that we can find a unique solution to our problem in any class of originals that is sent into itself under convolution with the function $\frac{1}{2a}e^{-a|x|}$ and that is given by the formula

$$y(x)=\frac{1}{2a}(e^{-a|x|}*f(x))=\frac{1}{2a}\int_{-\infty}^{\infty}e^{-a|x-\xi|}f(\xi)\,d\xi.$$

One such class is known to us. This is the class of functions studied in Example 2. Our conditions correspond exactly to the requirement that the functions $f(x)$ and $y(x)$ belong to this class. It remains only to verify that multiplication of the transform of $y(x)$ by z^2 is admissible. It is clear from the equation that the function $y''(x)$ belongs to the same class as does $y(x)$ and $f(x)$. It is easy to deduce from this that $y'(x)$ (as one of the antiderivatives of $y''(x)$) also belongs to this class. In the same way the equation ensures that $y'(x)$ and $y''(x)$ belong to the same class as do $y(x)$ and $f(x)$, i.e., multiplication of $\eta(z)$ by z and z^2 represent admissible operations.

We have spoken only of the generalization of the Laplace transform to continuous functions that are increasing at infinity. The same idea allows us to generalize also the Laplace transform to functions with weak differentiability properties. It is necessary to choose a notion of convergence consonant with this. Thus, we can construct a theory of the Laplace transform for functions that are square-integrable on the whole real axis, and for even broader classes of functions.

5. THE USE OF ANALYTIC CONTINUATION

It is worth noting that the theory of generalized functions was created for completely determined types of problems and that there is no necessity to apply the theory of generalized functions in any problem in which the Laplace transform of increasing functions is being studied. Moreover, the theory of generalized functions does not even need to be introduced for the purposes of solution in the case of very simple problems of this kind. On the other hand, the classical theory of the Laplace transform deals only with the transforms of increasing functions. One of its methods is closely connected with analytic continuation of integrals.

Let the function $f(x)$ be defined not only for $x>0$, but also in the angle $|\arg x|<\alpha$; suppose further that it satisfies the inequality

$$|f(x)|<Me^{a|x|} \qquad (|x|>1,\ |\arg x|<\alpha)$$

in this angle. Then the function

$$F(z)=\int_0^\infty f(x)\,e^{-xz}\,dx \qquad (\operatorname{Re} z>a)$$

can be continued analytically by rotating the ray of integration as was done in Example 1, Sect. 2, Chap. VI. Here the function $F(z)$ is represented in the half-plane $\operatorname{Re}(ze^{i\theta})>a$, $|\theta|<\alpha$, by the integral

$$F(z)=\int_0^{\infty e^{i\theta}} f(x)\,e^{-xz}\,dx.$$

The function $F(z)$ thus does not depend on the ray chosen for the integration. Therefore, it is natural to call the integral along any ray $\arg x=\theta$ the one-sided Laplace transform of the analytic function, if the function $f(x)$ is regular on this ray. Of course, here we have to be content with the situation in which the same function $f(x)$ may give rise to many different Laplace transforms corresponding to different rays.

It is clear that if we understand the Laplace transform thus, then we can admit an arbitrary rate of growth of the function $f(x)$ on the real axis as long as there is some ray along which $f(x)$ does not grow more rapidly than $e^{a|x|}$. We can even give a meaning to the Laplace transform if we can split $f(x)$ into a sum of a number of functions having rays of exponential growth.

We next prove two theorems concerning this interpretation of the Laplace transform.

Theorem 5.1. *Let the domain D contain some half-plane* $Re(\zeta e^{i\theta})>a$, *let the contour C be the boundary of D and let the function* $\varphi(\zeta)$ *be absolutely integrable on the contour C. If*

$$f(x)=\frac{1}{2\pi i}\int_C \varphi(\zeta)\,e^{x\zeta}\,d\zeta \qquad (\arg x=\theta),$$

then

$$F(z)=\int_0^{\infty e^{i\theta}} f(x)\,e^{-xz}\,dx=\frac{1}{2\pi i}\int_C \frac{\varphi(\zeta)}{\zeta-z}\,d\zeta \qquad (z\in D).$$

If, in addition, the function $\varphi(\zeta)$ *is regular in the domain D, continuous up to its boundary, and* $\varphi(\zeta)\to 0$ $(\zeta\to\infty,\ \zeta\in D)$, *then* $F(z)=-\varphi(z)$.

Proof. Since the domain D contains the half-plane $\mathrm{Re}(\zeta e^{i\theta})>a$, then for $\arg x=\theta$, $\zeta\in C$, we have the inequality $|e^{x\zeta}|\leqslant e^{a|x|}$. Therefore, the integral of the function $f(x)$ converges uniformly in x on any finite part of the ray $\arg x=\theta$, so that the function $f(x)$ is continuous on the ray $\arg x=\theta$. Moreover, it satisfies the inequality

$$|f(x)|\leqslant e^{a|x|}\frac{1}{2\pi}\int_C|\varphi(\zeta)|\,|d\zeta|=Me^{a|x|} \qquad (\arg x=\theta).$$

Consequently, for $\mathrm{Re}(ze^{i\theta})\geqslant a+\delta$ the integral

$$F(z)=\int_0^{\infty e^{i\theta}} f(x)\,e^{-xz}\,dx$$

converges uniformly in z. The usual arguments permit us to show that the order of integration can be inverted. The inner integral is evaluated after this inversion of the order of integration, and we obtain the first formula for $F(z)$. If the function $\varphi(\zeta)$ is regular in the domain D, continuous up to its boundary and if it satisfies the condition $\varphi(\zeta)\to 0$ $(\zeta\to\infty,\ \zeta\in D)$, then we can apply the Cauchy integral formula giving us $F(z)=-\varphi(z)$. This completes the proof.

Theorem 5.2. *Let the domain D contain some half-plane* $\mathrm{Re}(ze^{i\theta})>a$, *let the contour C be the boundary of D. If the function F(z) is regular in the domain D, continuous up to its boundary and if it satisfies the conditions*

$$F(z)\to 0,\quad F'(z)=O(z^{-\gamma-1})\quad (z\to\infty,\ z\in D),\quad 0<\gamma<1,$$

then the function

$$f(x)=-\frac{1}{2\pi i}\int_C F(z)\,e^{xz}\,dz \qquad (\arg x=\theta)$$

is continuous on the ray $\arg x=\theta$, *except for the point 0, and for any* $a'>a$ *it satisfies the inequality*

$$|f(x)|<M|x|^{-\gamma}e^{a'|x|} \qquad (\arg x=\theta).$$

Furthermore,

$$\int_0^{\infty e^{i\theta}} f(x)\, e^{-xz}\, dx = F(z).$$

Proof. We apply Theorem 1.2 to the function $F(ze^{i\theta})$. After some simple manipulations, the inversion formula of the Laplace transform gives us, if we assume that the line $\operatorname{Re}(ze^{i\theta}) = a'$ is the boundary of the half-plane $\operatorname{Re}(ze^{i\theta}) > a'$:

$$f(x) = -\frac{1}{2\pi i} \int_{\operatorname{Re}(ze^{i\theta})=a'} F(z)\, e^{xz}\, dz, \qquad F(z) = \int_0^{\infty e^{i\theta}} f(x) e^{-xz}\, dx.$$

In view of the conditions on $F(z)$, the line of integration $\operatorname{Re}(ze^{i\theta}) = a'$ is equivalent to the contour C. This proves the theorem.

As an application of the theorem proved we shall study an example based on Example 5 of Sect. 3.

Example 1. For the differential equation

$$ny^{(n-1)}(x) + xy(x) = 0 \qquad (n > 2),$$

we find the solution satisfying the initial conditions

$$y(0) = p_0, \quad y'(0) = p_1, \ldots, \; y^{(n-2)}(0) = p_{n-2}.$$

The method of solution that we employ can also be extended to the solution of analogous problems for other differential equations with constant coefficients.

Setting $y(x) \div \eta(z)$ according to formula 2 of Sect. 2, we can write

$$y^{(n-1)}(x) \div z^{n-1}\eta(z) - P(z) \qquad \left(P(z) = \sum_0^{n-2} p_k z^{n-k}\right),$$

$$xy(x) \div -\eta'(z).$$

Therefore, the equation for $y(x)$ gives us the following equation for $\eta(z)$:

$$\eta'(z) - nz^{n-1}\eta(z) = -P(z); \tag{5.1}$$

where $P(z) = p_0 z^{n-2} + \ldots + p_{n-2}$. The solution of equation (5.1) has the form

$$\eta(z) = -e^{z^n} \int_0^z e^{-\zeta^n} P(\zeta)\, d\zeta + Ce^{z^n} \tag{5.2}$$

(C is an arbitrary constant).

It is quite clear that the function $\eta(z)$ is not bounded in any half-plane. We therefore have to split $\eta(z)$ into a sum of functions, each of which is bounded in some half-plane. For this purpose we first study the behavior of the function e^{z^n} in a neighborhood of the point at infinity (e^{z^h} is the solution of the homogeneous equation $\eta'' - nz^{n-1}\eta = 0$). Setting $z = re^{i\varphi}$, we have

$$\ln |e^{z^n}| = \operatorname{Re} z^n = r^n \cos n\varphi.$$

Therefore $e^{z^n} \to 0$ as $z \to \infty$ along the ray $\arg z = \varphi$, if $\cos n\varphi < 0$, and $e^{z^n} \to \infty$ as $z \to \infty$ along $\arg z = \varphi$, if $\cos n\varphi > 0$.

Let D_k be the domain of the z-plane represented by the sector $|z| > R$, $\left(2k - \frac{1}{2}\right)\frac{\pi}{n} - \delta < \arg z < \left(2k + \frac{1}{2}\right)\frac{\pi}{n} + \delta$. (Here $R > 0$ and $0 < \delta < \frac{\pi}{2n}$ is any number.) Let L_k denote the boundary of D_k (Fig. 6). As $z \to \infty$ along the contour L_k the function e^{z^n} approaches zero more rapidly than $e^{-a|z|}$ for any a. Therefore the function

$$\eta_k(z) = \frac{1}{2\pi i}\int_{L_k} e^{\zeta^n}\frac{d\zeta}{\zeta - z} \qquad (\zeta \in D_k),\ k = 0,\ 1, \ldots,\ n-1,$$

is regular in the domain D_k. Moreover, because of the theorem on the analytic continuation of integrals of the Cauchy type (see Sect. 2, Chap. VI), the functions $\eta_k(z)$ can be continued analytically to the entire plane. Just as in Example 1, Sect. 4, Chap. VI, we can obtain the asymptotic formulas

$$\eta_k(z) = \frac{b_k}{z} + O\left(\frac{1}{z^2}\right)$$
$$(z \to \infty,\ z \in D_k),$$
$$\eta_k(z) = \frac{b_k}{z} + e^{z^n} + O\left(\frac{1}{z^2}\right)$$
$$(z \to \infty,\ z \,\overline{\in}\, D_k).$$

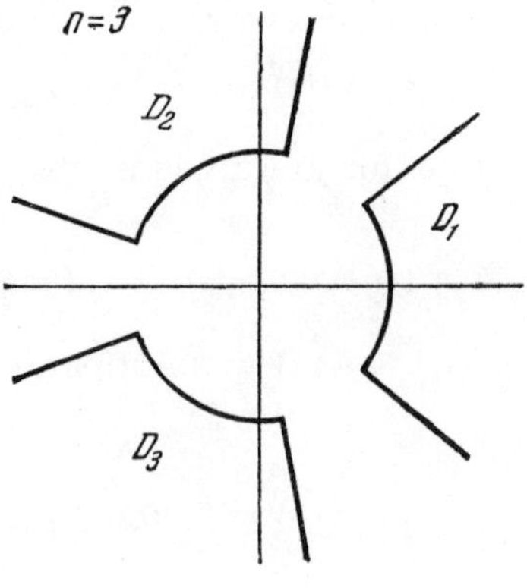

FIG. 6.

According to Theorem 5.1, the functions $\eta_k(z)$ are the Laplace transforms of the functions

$$y_k(x) = \frac{1}{2\pi i} \int_{L_k} e^{\zeta^n + x\zeta} \, d\zeta.$$

We show that the functions $y_k(x)$ are the solutions of the original differential equation. It is sufficient for this to show that each function $\eta_k(z)$ satisfies equation (5.1) for some polynomial of degree $n-2$ on the right side. We have

$$\eta_k'(z) - nz^{n-1}\eta_k(z) = \frac{1}{2\pi i} \int_{L_k} e^{\zeta^n} \frac{d\zeta}{(\zeta - z)^2} - \frac{1}{2\pi i} \int_{L_k} e^{\zeta^n} \frac{nz^{n-1}}{\zeta - z} \, d\zeta,$$

or, carrying out integration by parts in the first integral,

$$\eta_k'(z) - nz^{n-1}\eta_k(z) = \frac{n}{2\pi i} \int_{L_k} e^{\zeta^n} \frac{\zeta^{n-1} - z^{n-1}}{\zeta - z} \, d\zeta =$$

$$= \sum_{s=0}^{n-2} \frac{nz^s}{2\pi i} \int_{L_k} e^{\zeta^n} \zeta^{n-s-2} \, d\zeta,$$

as was required.

Equation (5.1) with some polynomial $P(z)$ of degree $n-2$ on the right side will have exactly n linearly independent solutions, since we have at our disposal $(n-1)$ coefficients for the polynomial $P(z)$ and an arbitrary constant C. The functions $\eta_k(z)$ are n in number and they are linearly independent. It is simpler to verify this with the aid of the asymptotic formulas. It is clear from these that each of the functions $\eta_k(z)$ increase only in its respective angular sector (these angular sectors have no points in common). Therefore, $\eta(z)$, the function of interest to us, can be represented as a linear combination of the functions $\eta_k(z)$. We put

$$\eta(z) = \sum_{k=0}^{n-1} c_k \eta_k(z). \tag{5.3}$$

Then the desired solution $y(x)$ equals

$$y(x) = \sum_{k=0}^{n-1} c_k y_k(x).$$

We still have to find the constant C by using the initial conditions.

We let $z \to \infty$, setting $\arg z = \theta_s = \frac{2\pi s}{n}$. Then, according to the asymptotic formulas for the functions $\eta_k(z)$, we have

$$\eta_s(z) \sim e^{z^n}, \qquad \eta_k(z) = o(1) \qquad (k \neq s).$$

We therefore obtain from formula (5.3):

$$\eta(z) \sim c_s e^{z^n} \qquad \left(z \to \infty,\ \arg z = \theta_s = \frac{2\pi s}{n}\right).$$

On the other hand, from formula (5.2) for $\eta(z)$ we find

$$\eta(z) \sim \left\{ C - \int_0^{\infty e^{i\theta_s}} e^{-\zeta^n} P(\zeta)\, d\zeta \right\} e^{z^n} \qquad (z \to \infty,\ \arg z = \theta_s).$$

Consequently,

$$c_s = C - \int_0^{\infty e^{i\theta_s}} e^{-\zeta^n} P(\zeta)\, d\zeta \qquad \left(\theta_s = \frac{2\pi s}{n}\right).$$

Note that in contrast to the functions $\eta_k(z)$, the functions $y_k(x)$ are linearly dependent. Between them we have the single relation

$$\sum_{k=0}^{n-1} y_k(x) \equiv 0.$$

Therefore, the arbitrary constant C does not appear in the final formula for $y(x)$, which has the form

$$y(x) = \sum_{k=0}^{n-1} \frac{c_k}{2\pi i} \int_{L_k} e^{\zeta^n + x\zeta}\, d\zeta, \qquad c_k = -\int_0^{\infty e^{i\theta_k}} e^{-\zeta^n} P(\zeta)\, d\zeta,$$

where $P(\zeta)$ and L_k have been defined above. It is easy to verify that the integrals converge for all complex values of x.

6. THE MELLIN TRANSFORM

We mentioned at the beginning of the chapter that in analysis along with the Laplace transform several other integral transforms are employed. These differ from the Laplace transform only by minor changes brought about by substitutions. We now wish to say a few words about one of these transforms.

The Fourier transform of the function f(x), absolutely integrable on the entire axis, is the function

$$\varphi(\xi) = \int_{-\infty}^{\infty} f(x)\, e^{ix\xi}\, dx \qquad (-\infty < \xi < \infty).$$

If $F(z)$ is the two-sided Laplace transform of the same function, then we obviously have $\varphi(\xi) = F(-i\xi)$. All properties of the Fourier transform may easily be deduced from this relation by using the properties of the Laplace transform (and conversely). For example, the Fourier transform inversion formula takes the form

$$f(x)=\frac{1}{2\pi}\int_{-\infty}^{\infty}\varphi(\xi)e^{-ix\xi}\,d\xi.$$

The differences in the formulas are so slight that it does not merit discussion.

The difference between the Laplace and Mellin transforms is somewhat greater.

The Mellin transform of the function g(t), defined for positive t and satisfying the condition

$$\int_0^{\infty}|g(t)|\,t^{\varrho-1}\,dt<\infty,$$

is the function

$$G(z)=\int_0^{\infty}g(t)\,t^{z-1}\,dt \qquad (\operatorname{Re} z=\varrho).$$

If we let $F(z)$ denote the two-sided Laplace transform of the function $f(x)=g(e^x)$ then we obtain $F(z)=G(z)$. This relation even permits us to derive all the formulas of the Mellin transform from the formulas of the Laplace transform. The inversion formula for the Mellin transform has the form

$$g(t)=\frac{1}{2\pi i}\int_{\varrho-i\infty}^{\varrho+i\infty}G(z)\,t^{-z}\,dz \qquad (t>0).$$

It is worthwhile to consider the formulas analogous to the formulas of the Laplace transform for the convolution of two functions.

If

$$F(z)=\int_0^{\infty}f(x)\,x^{z-1}\,dx, \qquad G(z)=\int_0^{\infty}g(x)\,x^{z-1}\,dx,$$

and

$$h_1(t)=\int_0^{\infty}f(x)\,g\left(\frac{t}{x}\right)\frac{dx}{x}, \quad h_2(t)=\int_0^{\infty}f(x)\,g(xt)\,dx,$$

then

$$\int_0^{\infty}h_1(t)\,t^{z-1}\,dt=F(z)\,G(z), \quad \int_0^{\infty}h_2(t)\,t^{z-1}\,dt=F(1-z)\,G(z).$$

The proof of these formulas and the derivation of the conditions under which they are valid can easily be carried out by reduction to Theorems 2.1 and 2.2.

In Sect. 5 of Chap. VI we mentioned a method of analytic continuation of a power series based on the use of the Mellin transform. We now are in a position to give a somewhat more detailed discussion of this method.

Theorem 6.1. *Let the function $c(x)$ be regular in the half-plane $\operatorname{Re} x > 0$ and satisfy the conditions*

$$c(x) \longrightarrow 0, \qquad c'(x) = O(x^{-\gamma-1}) \qquad (x \longrightarrow \infty, \ \operatorname{Re} x \geqslant \delta)$$

for any $\delta > 0$ and some $\gamma > 0$. Then the function

$$f(z) = \sum_{n=1}^{\infty} c(n) z^n$$

can be continued analytically to the whole z-plane with a cross cut along the ray $(1, +\infty)$. The analytic continuation is given by the formula

$$f(z) = \frac{z}{2\pi i} \int_1^{\infty} \int_{\delta - i\infty}^{\delta + i\infty} c(x) \frac{t^{-x-1}}{t-z} \, dx \, dt. \tag{6.1}$$

Proof. According to the inversion formula of the Mellin transform (of Theorem 1.2 on the inversion of the Laplace transform), we can write

$$c(-x) = \int_1^{\infty} \varphi(t) t^{x-1} \, dt, \quad \varphi(t) = \frac{1}{2\pi i} \int_{-\delta - i\infty}^{-\delta + i\infty} c(-x) t^{-x} \, dx.$$

In the first formula we put $x = -n$, multiply by z^n and sum on $n \geqslant 1$, which is permissible for $|z| < 1$. After interchange of the order of integration and summation, we obtain

$$\sum_1^{\infty} c(n) z^n = \int_1^{\infty} \sum_1^{\infty} \frac{z^n}{t^{n+1}} \varphi(t) \, dt = z \int_1^{\infty} \frac{\varphi(t)}{t(t-z)} \, dt.$$

The last integral converges uniformly in any closed region of the plane not containing points of the ray $(1, +\infty)$. Thus, we obtain an analytic continuation of the function $f(z)$ to the plane with a cross cut along the ray $(1, +\infty)$. Replacing the function $\varphi(t)$ by its representation in terms of a contour integral, we arrive at formula (6.1). This completes the proof.

The theorem proved shows that the series

$$\sum_1^{\infty} e^{-n^{\alpha}} z^n \ (\alpha < 1), \quad \sum_1^{\infty} n^{-\alpha} (\ln (n+1))^{\beta} z^n \quad (\alpha > 0)$$

can be continued analytically to the entire z-plane with a cross cut along the ray $(1, +\infty)$. If we wish, we can also investigate the behavior of the sum of these series in a neighborhood of the point $z=1$ with the help of formula (6.1).

In conclusion, we present a result (characteristic of the Mellin transform) on the analytic continuation of integrals.

Theorem 6.2. *Let the function $g(t)$ be continuous for $t>0$, let it approach zero more rapidly than any power of t as $t \to +\infty$, and suppose that it can be expanded in a neighborhood of the point $t=0$ in a convergent series*

$$g(t) = \sum_{k=1}^{\infty} c_k t^{\lambda_k} \quad (0<t\leqslant\varepsilon),\ t^{\lambda_k}>0,$$

where $\lambda_1<\lambda_2<\lambda_3<\ldots$ and $\lambda_n \to +\infty$ as $n \to +\infty$. Then the function

$$G(z) = \int_0^\infty g(t)\, t^{z-1}\, dt$$

can be continued analytically to the whole z-plane with the exception of the points $z=-\lambda_n$, at which $G(z)$ has simple poles.

Proof. We set

$$g_n(t) = g(t) - \sum_{k=1}^{n-1} c_k t^{\lambda_k}, \quad H_n(z) = \int_0^1 g_n(t)\, t^{z-1}\, dt.$$

Then in a neighborhood of the point 0 we have

$$|g_n(t)| \leqslant M t^{\lambda_n}.$$

Thus, the integral representing the function $H_n(z)$ converges uniformly in the half-plane $\operatorname{Re} z \geqslant -\lambda_n+\delta$ for any $\delta>0$. Thus, the function $H_n(z)$ is regular in the half-plane $\operatorname{Re} z > -\lambda_n$.

However,

$$G(z) = \int_0^\infty g(t)\, t^{z-1}\, dt =$$

$$= H_n(z) + \int_0^1 \sum_{k=1}^{n-1} c_k t^{\lambda_k+z-1}\, dt + \int_1^\infty g(t)\, t^{z-1}\, dt.$$

The last integral on the right-hand side represents a function regular in the entire z-plane, since, in view of the condition of the theorem, $g(t) \to 0$ as $t \to +\infty$ more rapidly than any power of t. The next to last integral may be evaluated as follows:

$$\int_0^1 \sum_{k=0}^{n-1} c_k t^{\lambda_k+z-1}\,dt = \sum_{k=1}^{n-1} \frac{c_k}{z+\lambda_k} \quad (\mathrm{Re}\, z > 0).$$

Thus, the function $G(z)$ is regular in the half-plane $\mathrm{Re}\, z > -\lambda_n$ with the exception of simple poles at the points $-\lambda_1, \; -\lambda_2, \; \ldots, \; -\lambda_{n-1}$. Since n is arbitrary and $\lambda_n \to +\infty$ as $n \to +\infty$, the theorem is proved.

We point out that we met with a special case of this theorem in the analytic continuation of Euler's gamma function in Chap. II.

CHAPTER VIII

Harmonic and Subharmonic Functions

The theory of harmonic and subharmonic functions plays an essential role in the obtaining of various refined estimates for analytic functions. The basis for obtaining them is the fact that the logarithm of the modulus of a regular function is a subharmonic function, i.e., it does not exceed in value a harmonic function with the same values on the boundary of the domain. Here the so-called Dirichlet problem—the construction of a harmonic function in a domain from the knowledge of its values on the boundary—has great importance. The concept of harmonic measure is employed in obtaining estimates for solutions to the Dirichlet problem.

In the present chapter we study properties of harmonic and subharmonic functions, solve the Dirichlet problem and obtain estimates by using harmonic measure. In concluding the chapter we consider applications to the theory of analytic functions.

1. BASIC PROPERTIES OF HARMONIC FUNCTIONS

We shall discuss only harmonic functions of two variables.

A real-valued function $u(x, y)$ of two real variables x and y is called *harmonic in the domain D,* if it has continuous second partial derivatives in this domain and satisfies *Laplace's equation*

$$\frac{\partial^2 u}{\partial x^2}+\frac{\partial^2 u}{\partial y^2}=0 \qquad ((x, y)\in D). \tag{1.1}$$

For the sake of brevity we shall write $u(z)$ where $z=x+iy$ in place of $u(x, y)$. At times we shall even shift from one notation to the other and retain the same symbol for the function, i.e., we shall assume that $u(x+iy)\equiv u(x, y)$.

We showed in Sect. 1 of Chap. II that the real and imaginary parts of a function $f(z)$ regular in the domain D are harmonic functions in domain D. That the converse of this statement is false for multiply connected domains is shown by the example of the function $\ln|z|$ which is harmonic for $0<|z|<\infty$. We therefore prove a somewhat more complicated statement about the relations between harmonic and analytic functions which is valid also for multiply connected domains.

Theorem 1.1. *For the function $u(z)$ to be harmonic in the domain D it is necessary and sufficient that it be the real part of a function $w(z)$ analytic in the domain D and satisfying the conditions:*

1. the function $w'(z)$ is regular in the domain D;

2. the integral of $w'(z)$ along any closed contour lying in the domain D is equal to a pure imaginary (or zero).

Proof. We begin with the proof of the sufficiency. We must verify that conditions 1 and 2 ensure the single-valuedness of the real part of the function $w(z)$ analytic in the domain D. Since the function $w'(z)$ is regular in the domain, then any element of the analytic function $w(z)$ can be obtained from the initial element by integrating $w'(z)$ along some path lying in domain D. The values of the various elements of $w(z)$ at the same point differ by an integral of $w'(z)$ along some closed path. According to condition 2, this integral is pure imaginary and so its addition does not effect the real part. This proves the sufficiency.

To prove the necessity we have to construct from the given function $u(z)$ a function $w(z)$, analytic in the domain D and having a single-valued real part, and then we have to show that conditions 1 and 2 are fulfilled. To do this we define the function $w'(z)$ by means of the equation

$$w'(x+iy)=u'_x(x, y)-iu'_y(x, y).$$

This function is regular in domain D since it is defined in this domain and its real and imaginary parts satisfy the Cauchy-Riemann equations (here we use Laplace's equation for $u(x, y)$). The antiderivative of a function regular in the domain D is an analytic function in the domain D. We show that the real part of the function $w(z)$ [an antiderivative for $w'(z)$] coincides with $u(z)$ everywhere in D, if it coincides with $u(z)$ at any point $z=\zeta$. We have

$$w(z)=w(\zeta)+\int_{\zeta}^{z} w'(z)\,dz, \quad \operatorname{Re} w(\zeta)=u(\zeta),$$

and, separating out the real part, we find

$$\operatorname{Re} w(z)=u(\zeta)+\int_{\zeta}^{z} u'_x(x, y)\,dx+u'_y(x, y)\,dy.$$

Here we are integrating the total differential $u'_x\,dx+u'_y\,dy=du$, so that the result is independent of the path of integration and equals the difference of the values of the function $u(x, y)$ at the endpoints of the path. Thus,

$$\operatorname{Re} w(z) = u(\zeta) + u(z) - u(\zeta) = u(z).$$

It follows from the single-valuedness of the function $u(z) = \operatorname{Re} w(z)$ that all elements of the function $w(z)$ differ from each other only by pure imaginary numbers at a given point. However, we have already pointed out that these elements differ only by integrals of $w'(z)$ along closed contours. Therefore, the integral of $w'(z)$ along any closed path is a pure imaginary (or zero). This completes the proof.

Remark 1. The essential meaning of Theorem 1.1 is as follows:

to ensure harmonicity for a function u(z) in the domain D it is necessary and sufficient that it be the real part of a function that is analytic in domain D.

Conditions 1 and 2 give necessary and sufficient conditions for the single-valuedness in domain D of the real part of the function $u(z)$ analytic in the domain.

Remark 2. If the domain D is *simply connected*, then a function analytic in the domain is regular in the domain. Therefore, *for harmonicity for a function u(z) in a simply connected domain D it is necessary and sufficient that it be the real part of a function regular in domain D.*

With the help of Theorem 1.1 many questions for harmonic functions can be reduced to the same or other questions for analytic functions. For example, the following result on change of variables has great importance:

Theorem 1.2. *Let the function f(z) be regular in domain D and let its values lie in domain G. If the function U(z) is harmonic in domain G, then the function U(f(z)) = u(z) is harmonic in domain D.*

Proof. If $W(z)$ is an analytic function in domain G for which $U(z) = \operatorname{Re} W(z)$, then the function $w(z) = W(f(z))$ is analytic in the domain D (because, for example, the function $w'(z) = W'(f(z))f'(z)$ is regular in domain D) and we evidently have $u(z) = \operatorname{Re} w(z)$. This proves the theorem.

The following uniqueness theorem also has great importance for the theory of harmonic functions:

Theorem 1.3. *Let u(z) be a harmonic function in domain D. If u(z) = 0 in some neighborhood of the point $\zeta \in D$, then the function u(z) is identically zero.*

Proof. Let $w(z)$ be that analytic function in domain D for which $u(z) = \operatorname{Re} w(z)$. It is easy to verify that

$$w'(z) = u'_x(z) - iu'_y(z).$$

Since $u'_x(z) = u'_y(z) = 0$ in a neighborhood of the point $z = \zeta$, then we also have $w'(z) = 0$ in a neighborhood of the point $z = \zeta$. According to the uniqueness theorem, we have $w'(z) \equiv 0$, i.e., $w(z) \equiv$ const. Consequently, we also have $u(z) \equiv$ const, and since $u(z) = 0$ in a neighborhood of the point $z = \zeta$, then $u(z) \equiv 0$. This completes the proof.

The connection between harmonic and analytic functions plays a very important role in the study of harmonic functions. However, many important properties of harmonic functions can be more simply proved directly. The basis for the majority of direct proofs is a special case of the well-known Green-Ostrogradskiy formula

$$\int_C A(x, y)\,dx + B(x, y)\,dy = \iint_D \left(\frac{\partial B}{\partial x} - \frac{\partial A}{\partial y}\right) dx\,dy \tag{1.2}$$

(D is some domain, C is the boundary of D). The Green-Ostrogradskiy formula is satisfied by any functions $A(x, y)$ and $B(x, y)$ continuously differentiable in D. The special case of this formula of interest to us is called ***Green's formula***. It has the form

$$\int_C \varphi \frac{\partial \psi}{\partial n}\,ds = \iint_D \left(\frac{\partial \varphi}{\partial x}\frac{\partial \psi}{\partial x} + \frac{\partial \varphi}{\partial y}\frac{\partial \psi}{\partial y}\right) dx\,dy + \iint_D \varphi \left(\frac{\partial^2 \psi}{\partial x^2} + \frac{\partial^2 \psi}{\partial y^2}\right) dx\,dy. \tag{1.3}$$

Here $\varphi(x, y)$ and $\psi(x, y)$ have continuous second partial derivatives in D and $\partial\psi/\partial n$ is the derivative of the function $\psi(x, y)$ in the direction of the exterior normal to the curve C, i.e.,

$$\frac{\partial \psi}{\partial n} = \frac{\partial \psi}{\partial x}\cos\theta + \frac{\partial \psi}{\partial y}\sin\theta,$$

where θ is the angle between the exterior normal to the curve C and the x-axis. Since we consider only piecewise smooth curves, the direction of the exterior normal is defined on the entire curve C with the possible exception of a finite number of points.

We can easily obtain formula (1.3) from formula (1.2) if we note that $ds\,(\cos\theta) = dy$, $ds\sin\theta = -dx$ and, consequently,

$$\frac{\partial \psi}{\partial n}\,ds = -\frac{\partial \psi}{\partial y}\,dx + \frac{\partial \psi}{\partial x}\,dy.$$

We now derive a few simple corollaries of Green's formula.

Let the function $\varphi(x, y)$ in formula (1.3) equal unity and let the function $\psi(x, y)$ equal the function $u(x, y)$ harmonic in domain D. Then

$$\int_C \frac{\partial u}{\partial n}\,ds = 0. \tag{1.4}$$

This formula is analogous to Cauchy's theorem for regular functions.

First, put $\varphi(x, y) = u(x, y)$, $\psi(x, y) = v(x, y)$, then put $\varphi(x, y) = v(x, y)$, $\psi(x, y) = u(x, y)$ and subtract the equations obtained using formula (1.3). If $u(x, y)$ and $v(x, y)$ are functions harmonic in domain D, then we find

$$\int_C \left(u \frac{\partial v}{\partial n} - v \frac{\partial v}{\partial n} \right) ds = 0. \tag{1.5}$$

This formula can also be considered as an analog of Cauchy's theorem.

There is also a formula for harmonic functions that is analogous to Cauchy's integral formula for regular functions.

Theorem 1.4. *Let the function $u(z)$ be harmonic in domain D and let it have continuous second partial derivatives in D. If $\zeta \in D$, then*

$$\int_C \left\{ u(z) \frac{\partial}{\partial n} \ln|z-\zeta| - \frac{\partial u}{\partial n} \ln|z-\zeta| \right\} ds = 2\pi u(\zeta) \tag{1.6}$$

(C is the boundary of D). If $\zeta \notin \overline{D}$, then the integral equals zero.

Proof. The function $v(z) = \ln|z-\zeta|$ since it equals the real part of the function $\ln|z-\zeta|$, which is analytic for $0 < |z-\zeta| < \infty$, is harmonic in the entire plane except at the point $z = \zeta$. If $\zeta \notin \overline{D}$, then the function $\ln(z-\zeta)$ is harmonic in the domain D and the integral equals zero by virtue of formula (1.5).

To prove formula (1.6) for $\zeta \in D$, we let D_ϱ denote the domain obtained by removing the circle $|z-\zeta| \leqslant \varrho$ from the domain D (we choose $\varrho > 0$ so small that the circle is contained in domain D). If C_ϱ denotes the boundary of the domain D_ϱ, then in accord with what we said above (since $\zeta \notin \overline{D}_\varrho$)

$$\int_{C_\varrho} \left\{ u \frac{\partial}{\partial n} \ln|z-\zeta| - \frac{\partial u}{\partial n} \ln|z-\zeta| \right\} ds = 0.$$

Since C_ϱ consists of C and the circle $|z-\zeta| = \varrho$, then

$$J = \int_C \left\{ u \frac{\partial}{\partial n} \ln|z-\zeta| - \frac{\partial u}{\partial n} \ln|z-\zeta| \right\} ds =$$

$$= \int_{|z-\zeta|=\varrho} \left\{ u \frac{\partial}{\partial n} \ln|z-\zeta| - \frac{\partial u}{\partial n} \ln|z-\zeta| \right\} ds$$

(the direction in the second integral is chosen to coincide with the direction of a radius from the point $z = \zeta$). It is clear that on the circle $|z-\zeta| = \varrho$ we have $\ln|z-\zeta| = \ln \varrho$ and $\frac{\partial}{\partial n} \ln|z-\zeta| = \frac{\partial}{\partial r} \ln r \Big|_{r=\varrho} = \frac{1}{\varrho}$. Therefore, according to (1.4),

$$J = \frac{1}{\varrho} \int\limits_{|z-\zeta|=\varrho} u(z)\, ds. \qquad (1.7)$$

The left side of the last equality does not depend on ϱ, which means that the right side also does not depend on ϱ. Therefore, it suffices for us to find the limit of the right side as $\varrho \to 0$. This limit equals $2\pi u(\zeta)$, since, according to the mean-value theorem for integrals, the integral equals the value of the function $u(z)$ (at some point of the circle $|z-\zeta|=\varrho$) multiplied by $2\pi\varrho$, and as $\varrho \to 0$ the value of the function $u(z)$ at any point of the circle $|z-\zeta|=\varrho$ approaches $u(\zeta)$. This completes the proof.

Remark 1. We noted that the right side of equality (1.7) does not depend on ϱ and showed that the right side is $2\pi u(\zeta)$. Therefore, in addition to formula (1.6), we also proved the statement bearing the name of the ***theorem of the mean for harmonic functions:***

If the function u(z) is harmonic in the circle $|z-\zeta|<R$, *then*

$$\frac{1}{2\pi\varrho} \int\limits_{|z-\zeta|=\varrho} u(z)\,|dz| = u(\zeta) \qquad (\varrho < R).$$

Remark 2. Formulas (1.5) and (1.6) were proved under the assumption that the functions $u(z)$ and $v(z)$ were harmonic in the domain D and had continuous second partial derivatives in D. This last condition can be considerably weakened if we take into account the fact the integral along the boundary curve of a function continuous up to the boundary of the domain can be approximated with arbitrary accuracy by an integral of this function along a polygonal line contained within the domain (see Sect. 5, Chap. I). In order that the integrand be continuous up to the boundary it is sufficient that the functions $u(z)$ and $v(z)$ be continuously differentiable up to the boundary of the domain D.

This condition can also be weakened somewhat. Namely, formulas (1.5) and (1.6) remain valid if:

the functions u(z) and v(z) are harmonic in the domain D and continuous up to its boundary. The partial derivatives of these functions are continuous up to the boundary of D with the possible exception of a finite number of points $a_1, a_2, \ldots, a_n$, and as $z \to a_k$, $z \to D$,

$$\left|\frac{\partial u}{\partial x}\right| + \left|\frac{\partial u}{\partial y}\right| + \left|\frac{\partial v}{\partial x}\right| + \left|\frac{\partial v}{\partial y}\right| = o(1).$$

The generalized integrals occurring in formulas (1.5) and (1.6) converge.

The validity of these formulas under the above conditions is easily proved by taking the limit as $\varepsilon \to 0$, if we first apply these formulas to the domain D_ε, obtained from D after removal of the parts of the small circles $|z-a_k|<\varepsilon$ contained within it.

It is clear from these considerations that not even continuity of the function $u(z)$ in the closed circle $|z-\zeta| \leqslant \varrho$ is necessary for the validity of the theorem of the mean. We can assume that $u(z)$ has singularities of the same type as were allowed for the partial derivatives of $u(z)$ and $v(z)$ in the previous discussion.

2. SUBHARMONIC FUNCTIONS

Let $u(z)$ be a real-valued function, which may assume the value $-\infty$, and let the function $e^{u(z)}$ be continuous in the domain D. If for any ζ and $\varrho > 0$ for which the circle $|z-\zeta| \leqslant \varrho$ is contained in the domain D, we have

$$u(\zeta) \leqslant \frac{1}{2\pi\varrho} \int\limits_{|z-\zeta|=\varrho} u(z)\,|dz| = \frac{1}{2\pi} \int\limits_{0}^{2\pi} u(\zeta + \varrho e^{i\varphi})\, d\varphi,$$

then the function $u(z)$ is called *subharmonic in the domain D.*

It is evident from the theorem of the mean for harmonic functions (see Remark 1 to Theorem 1.4) that a *function harmonic in domain D is also subharmonic in this domain.*

Let us note a few simple properties of subharmonic functions:

1. *The sum (but not the difference) of two functions subharmonic in the domain D is also a subharmonic function in the domain D. The product of a subharmonic function and a positive constant is a subharmonic function.*

2. *The uniform limit of subharmonic functions in the domain D is a function subharmonic in the domain D.*

3. *If the functions $u_1(z)$ and $u_2(z)$ are functions subharmonic in the domain D, then the function $u(z) = \max\{u_1(z), u_2(z)\}$ is subharmonic in the domain D.*

We shall prove only the third property.

We take any admissible ζ and ϱ. If $u(\zeta) = u_1(\zeta)$, then

$$u(\zeta) = u_1(\zeta) \leqslant \frac{1}{2\pi} \int\limits_{0}^{2\pi} u_1(\zeta + \varrho e^{i\varphi})\, d\varphi \leqslant \frac{1}{2\pi} \int\limits_{0}^{2\pi} u(\zeta + \varrho e^{i\varphi})\, d\varphi,$$

and an analogous statement holds if $u(\zeta) = u_2(\zeta)$.

The following important theorem is called the *maximum principle.*

Theorem 2.1. *Let the function $u(z)$ be subharmonic in the domain D. Let $M = \sup u(z)$. If $u(\zeta) = M$ at the point $\zeta \in D$, then $u(z) \equiv M$.*

In other words:

A nonconstant subharmonic function cannot assume its maximum value inside the domain.

Proof. Let us consider the set E consisting of the points of domain D at which $u(z)=M$. The set E is closed in M since $e^{u(z)}$ is a continuous function and the set of points at which a continuous function assumes a given value is closed. Suppose that there exists a boundary point of the set E contained in the domain D, say, ζ. In view of the closure of the set E, we have $u(\zeta)=M$. Then there exists a ϱ such that the circle $|z-\zeta|<\varrho$ is contained in the domain D and within which are found points not belonging to the set E. The complement of the set E is an open set, so that if $z\notin E$, then there exists some neighborhood of the point z which is not contained in E. Thus, we can choose numbers θ, $\varepsilon>0$ and $\delta>0$, such that

$$u(\zeta+\varrho e^{i\varphi})>M-\varepsilon \qquad (|\varphi-\theta|<\delta).$$

Since for all remaining φ we have $u(\zeta+\varrho e^{i\varphi})\leqslant M$, then

$$\int_0^{2\pi} u(\zeta+\varrho e^{i\varphi})\,d\varphi=\int_{|\varphi-\theta|<\delta} u(\zeta+\varrho e^{i\varphi})\,d\varphi+$$
$$+\int_{\pi>|\varphi-\theta|>\delta} u(\zeta+\varrho e^{i\varphi})\,d\varphi\leqslant 2\delta(M-\varepsilon)+M(2\pi-2\delta)=$$
$$=2\pi M-2\delta\varepsilon<2\pi M.$$

However, according to the definition of subharmonicity, the integral given at the very beginning of the discussion cannot be less than $2\pi u(\zeta)=2\pi M$. This contradiction proves that the set E has no boundary points in the domain D. Thus, the set E is either empty or coincides with D. This proves the theorem.

Remark 1. If $u(z)$ is a harmonic function, then both $u(z)$ and $-u(z)$ are subharmonic functions. Therefore:

A harmonic function different from a constant cannot assume either its maximum or its minimum within the domain of harmonicity.

Remark 2. Let $\varphi(\zeta)=\overline{\lim\limits_{z\to\zeta}}\,u(z)$. If $u(z)$ is continuous at the point ζ, then $\varphi(\zeta)=u(\zeta)$. If C is the boundary of D, then

$$\sup_{z\in D} u(z)=\sup_{\zeta\in C}\varphi(\zeta).$$

Indeed, if $\sup\limits_{z\in D} u(z)=M$, then there exists a sequence of points z_n for which $u(z_n)>M-1/n$, i.e., $u(z_n)\to M$. If ζ_0 is any limit point of the sequence z_n, then we have $u(\zeta_0)=M$. If $\zeta_0\in C$, then $\sup\limits_{\zeta\in C}\varphi(\zeta)\geqslant\varphi(\zeta_0)=M$, and if $\zeta_0\in D$, then, according to Theorem 2.1, $u(z)\equiv M$.

Corollary. Let u(z) be harmonic and let v(z) be subharmonic in domain D. If on the boundary of D we have

$$\overline{\lim_{z\to\zeta}}\,v(z)\leqslant\overline{\lim_{z\to\zeta}}\,u(z) \qquad (\zeta\in C),$$

then also within D we have v(z)⩽u(z).

Indeed, the difference $v(z)-u(z)$ is subharmonic in the domain D (since $-u(z)$ is a subharmonic function in D) and $\overline{\lim\limits_{z\to\zeta}}\,(v(z)-u(z))\leqslant 0$ $(\zeta\in C)$. According to Remark 2, $u(z)\geqslant v(z)$ $(z\in D)$.

It follows from the corollary that the surface $t=v(z)$ lies beneath the surface $t=u(z)$ for all $z\in D$, if this happens for values of z on the boundary of D. In fact, this property of subharmonic functions is the basis for the name.

The following generalized maximum principle has great importance. It shows that the values of the function $\varphi(\zeta)=\overline{\lim\limits_{z\to\zeta}}\,u(z)$ at a countable number of points of the boundary can be disregarded, if we know that our function is bounded in the domain.

Theorem 2.2. *Let the function $u(z)$ be subharmonic and bounded above in a domain D containing at least one interior point. We set*

$$M=\sup_{\zeta\in C,\,\zeta\neq a_n}\ \overline{\lim_{z\to\zeta}}\,u(z),$$

where $a_1, a_2, \ldots,$ is some sequence of points of C (the boundary of D). Then $u(z)<M$ $(z\in D)$ or $u(z)\equiv M$.

Proof. Let b be an interior point of the domain D. For each $\zeta\in C$ we can find a number $A(\zeta)>0$ such that for all z in the domain D we have the inequality

$$A(\zeta)\frac{|z-b|}{|z-\zeta|}<1.$$

Set $A_n=A(a_n)$ and consider the auxiliary function

$$u_\varepsilon(z)=u(z)+\varepsilon\sum_{n=1}^{\infty}\frac{1}{2^n}\ln\left\{A_n\frac{|z-b|}{|z-\zeta|}\right\}.$$

Since the terms following the summation sign are negative, it follows that

$$\overline{\lim_{z\to\zeta}}\,u_\varepsilon(z)\leqslant\overline{\lim_{z\to\zeta}}\,u(z)\leqslant M \qquad (\zeta\neq a_1, a_2, \ldots),$$

and

$$\lim_{z\to a_n}u_\varepsilon(z)=-\infty \qquad (n=1, 2, \ldots),$$

inasmuch as the function $u(z)$ by hypothesis is bounded above and one of the summands approaches $-\infty$ as $z\to a_n$. Therefore, according to Remark 2 to the maximum principle,

$$\sup_{z\in D}u_\varepsilon(z)\leqslant M.$$

Taking the limit as $\varepsilon \to 0$, we find $\sup\limits_{z \in D} u(z) \leqslant M$, which proves the theorem.

The notion of subharmonicity can be considered as a generalization of the notion of (downward) convexity to the case of functions of two variables. Recall that the function $\varphi(x)$ is called *convex (downward) on the segment* (a, b), if $\varphi(x)$ is continuous on this segment and satisfies the inequality

$$\varphi\left(\frac{x_1+x_2}{2}\right) \leqslant \frac{\varphi(x_1)+\varphi(x_2)}{2}.$$

This inequality can be transformed into the inequality

$$\varphi(x) \leqslant \varphi(x_1)\frac{x_2-x}{x_2-x_1} + \varphi(x_2)\frac{x-x_1}{x_2-x_1} \qquad (x_1 \leqslant x \leqslant x_2).$$

For functions with continuous second derivatives a necessary and sufficient condition for (downward) convexity is the condition $\varphi''(x) \geqslant 0$.

If we replace $\leqslant$ by $=$ in either of the inequalities defining downward convexity, then it turns out that such a condition will be satisfied only by a linear function if the function is continuous.

The conditions for subharmonicity are very similar to the conditions for (downward) convexity, except that instead of a segment we have a circle, and instead of linear functions we have harmonic functions. It can be shown without too much difficulty that:

For a function with continuous second partial derivatives to be subharmonic it is necessary and sufficient that it satisfy the condition

$$\frac{\partial^2 u}{\partial x^2} + \frac{\partial^2 u}{\partial y^2} \geqslant 0.$$

This analogy is not the only one connecting the notions of subharmonicity and (downward) convexity.

Theorem 2.3. *If the subharmonic function* $u(x+iy)$ *depends only on* x, *then it is a convex (downward) function of* x.

If the subharmonic function $u(\varrho e^{i\varphi})$ *depends only on* ϱ, *then it is a convex (downward) function of* $\ln \varrho$ *(logarithmically convex function).*

Proof. If the function $u(x+iy)$ depends only on x, then its domain of definition is a strip $a < x < b$. Let $\varphi(x) = u(x+iy)$. The linear function $Ax+B$ is a harmonic function of $x+iy$. Pick x_1 and x_2 such that $a < x_1 < x_2 < b$ and choose constants A and B so that

$$Ax_1 + B = \varphi(x_1), \qquad Ax_2 + B = \varphi(x_2).$$

Then

$$\varphi(x) \leqslant Ax + B \qquad (x_1 \leqslant x \leqslant x_2).$$

In fact, the difference $\varphi(x) - Ax - B$ is a subharmonic function in the strip $x_1 < x < x_2$, is bounded above in this strip and is zero on the boundary of this strip (with the exception of the two points at infinity); thus, Theorem 2.2 is applicable.

Expressing A and B in terms of $\varphi(x_1)$ and $\varphi(x_2)$, we find

$$\varphi(x) \leqslant \varphi(x_1)\frac{x_2 - x}{x_2 - x_1} + \varphi(x_2)\frac{x - x_1}{x_2 - x_1}, \tag{2.1}$$

and this inequality shows that the function $\varphi(x)$ is convex (downward).

We can carry out a similar argument for the case in which the subharmonic function $u(\varrho e^{i\varphi})$ depends only on ϱ. The only difference is that we have to take the function $A \ln \varrho + B$ as the harmonic function depending only on ϱ. The inequality now replacing inequality (2.1) has the form

$$\varphi(\varrho) \leqslant \varphi(r)\frac{\ln \frac{R}{\varrho}}{\ln \frac{R}{r}} + \varphi(R)\frac{\ln \frac{\varrho}{r}}{\ln \frac{R}{r}} \qquad (r \leqslant \varrho \leqslant R). \tag{2.2}$$

This proves the theorem.

We may obtain analogous results by taking other combinations of variables on which the subharmonic function is to depend.

Let us note one more fact, this time without proof, relating subharmonic and convex (downward) functions.

Let the function $u(z)$ be subharmonic in the domain D and let its values be contained in the segment (a, b). If the function $\varphi(x)$ is convex (downward) and does not decrease on the segment (a, b), then the function $\varphi(u(z))$ is subharmonic in domain D.

We are chiefly interested in subharmonic functions because of their connections with analytic functions. The simplest expression of this relationship reads as follows:

The modulus of a function regular in domain D is a function subharmonic in this domain.

For the proof of this statement it is sufficient to note that a regular function $f(z)$ satisfies the theorem of the mean

$$f(z) = \frac{1}{2\pi}\int_0^{2\pi} f(z + \varrho e^{i\varphi})\, d\varphi$$

(for example, because it is satisfied by the real and imaginary parts of $f(z)$, since they are harmonic functions). Taking moduli in the theorem of the mean, we see that the function $|f(z)|$ is subharmonic.

Applying the maximum principle for subharmonic functions to the modulus of a regular function, we find immediately:

Let the function f(z) be regular in domain D with boundary C. We set

$$\varphi(\zeta) = \overline{\lim_{z \to \zeta}} |f(z)| \quad (\zeta \in C), \quad M = \sup_{\zeta \in C} \varphi(\zeta).$$

Then $|f(z)| \leqslant M$ $(z \in D)$, *here the equality sign obtains inside the domain D only if* $f(z) \equiv Me^{i\theta}$ (θ *is a constant).*

Indeed, it follows from the maximum principle for subharmonic functions that $|f(z)| < M$ $(z \in D)$, or $|f(z)| \equiv M$. However, it follows from the identity $\ln|f(z)| \equiv \ln M$ that the conjugate harmonic function $\arg f(z)$ is also a constant. Setting $\arg f(z) = \theta$, we arrive at the statement of our result.

The statement proved is called the *maximum modulus principle for analytic functions.*

The subharmonicity of the modulus of a regular function is usually insufficient for the purpose of obtaining estimates. We shall therefore prove a stronger result.

We first prove the so-called Jensen's formula, of considerable interest in itself.

Lemma. Let the function f(z) be regular in the circle $|z| \leqslant R$ *and let it have zeros there at* $z_1, z_2, \ldots, z_n$ *(each zero is written as many times as its multiplicity). Then*

$$\frac{1}{2\pi}\int_0^{2\pi} \ln|f(Re^{i\varphi})|\, d\varphi = \ln|f(0)| + \sum_1^n \ln\frac{R}{|z_k|}. \tag{2.3}$$

Proof. We consider the auxiliary function

$$f_1(z) = \frac{f(z)}{w_1(z)\ldots w_n(z)},$$

where

$$w_k(z) = \frac{R(z - z_k)}{R^2 - z\bar{z}_k}.$$

We showed in Sect. 2 of Chap. V that the function $w_k(z)$ maps the circle $|z| < R$ conformally onto the circle $|w| < 1$, so that $|w_k(Re^{i\varphi})| = 1$. Thus,

$$|f_1(Re^{i\varphi})| = |f(Re^{i\varphi})|. \tag{2.4}$$

Furthermore, we note that the function $f_1(z)$ is regular in the circle $|z| < R$ and does not vanish there since the product of the functions $w_k(z)$ vanishes at the same points as $f(z)$ (and the zeros all have the same order). According to the theorem of the mean for harmonic functions, we have

$$\frac{1}{2\pi}\int_0^{2\pi} \ln|f_1(Re^{i\varphi})|\,d\varphi = \ln|f_1(0)|.$$

However, in view of Eq. (2.4),

$$\frac{1}{2\pi}\int_0^{2\pi} \ln|f_1(Re^{i\varphi})|\,d\varphi = \frac{1}{2\pi}\int_0^{2\pi} \ln|f(Re^{i\varphi})|\,d\varphi,$$

and

$$\ln|f_1(0)| = \ln|f(0)| - \sum_1^n \ln\frac{R}{|z_k|},$$

and we arrive at the statement of the lemma.

Remark 1. We might just as well have supposed that the function $f(z)$ not only had zeros but also poles $\zeta_1, \zeta_2, \ldots, \zeta_m$ in the circle $|z| < R$. This would have led us to the formula

$$\frac{1}{2\pi}\int_0^{2\pi} \ln|f(Re^{i\varphi})|\,d\varphi = \ln|f(0)| - \sum_1^n \ln\frac{R}{|z_k|} + \sum_1^m \ln\frac{R}{|\zeta_k|}.$$

Remark 2. The presence of zeros or poles on the circle $|z| = R$ does not affect the validity of Jensen's formula. The integral, now a generalized integral, obviously converges and we apply the same reasoning as that given at the end of Sect. 1.

Theorem 2.4. *If the function $f(z)$ is regular in the domain D, then the function $u(z) = \ln|f(z)|$ is subharmonic in the domain D.*

Proof. The function $e^{u(z)} = |f(z)|$ is continuous in the domain D and applying Jensen's formula to the function $f(z+\zeta)$ (with $R = \varrho$), we find the inequality

$$\frac{1}{2\pi}\int_0^{2\pi} u(\zeta + \varrho e^{i\varphi})\,d\varphi \geqslant u(\zeta).$$

Note that Theorem 2.4 actually yields a result stronger than the statement on the subharmonicity of $|f(z)|$. In fact, the function $\varphi(x) = e^{\alpha x}$ is convex (downward) and is increasing for any $\alpha > 0$, so that the subharmonicity of the function $e^{\alpha \ln|f(z)|} = |f(z)|^{\alpha}$ for any $\alpha > 0$ follows from Theorem 2.4 (by use of the result that we introduced just after Theorem 2.3).

We conclude our presentation of the properties of subharmonic functions with the above result; we have refrained from presenting many other properties having no direct connection with the problems of interest to us.*

3. THE DIRICHLET PROBLEM AND POISSON'S INTEGRAL

Dirichlet's problem consists in determining a function harmonic in the domain D and continuous up to its boundary if we are given the values of $f(z)$ on the boundary curve.

We shall attempt to solve an even somewhat more general problem, which we shall also call *Dirichlet's problem.* Namely:

Let D be some domain, bounded by the curve C, and let the function $\varphi(\zeta)$ be continuous everywhere on the curve C with the possible exception of a countable set of points; in addition, let $\varphi(\zeta)$ be bounded on C.

The problem consists in finding a function $u(z)$ harmonic in the domain D and satisfying the conditions:

1. $u(z)$ is bounded in D;
2. $u(z)$ is continuous up to the boundary of D at all points of continuity of the function $\varphi(\zeta)$ and at these points $u(\zeta)=\varphi(\zeta)$.

The function $\varphi(\zeta)$ is called the *boundary function* or the *boundary-value function of the Dirichlet problem.*

Note that it readily follows from Theorem 2.2 (the generalized maximum principle) that *the Dirichlet problem does not have more than one solution.* Indeed, if $u(z)$ and $v(z)$ are two solutions of the Dirichlet problem for the same boundary function $\varphi(\zeta)$, then the function $w(z)=u(z)-v(z)$ is harmonic and bounded in the domain D and

$$\overline{\lim_{z\to\zeta}}\,|w(z)|=0$$

for all $\zeta\in C$ with the possible exception of a countable set of points. Applying Theorem 2.2 to the functions $w(z)$ and $-w(z)$, we find

$$w(z)\leqslant 0, \qquad w(z)\geqslant 0 \qquad (z\in D),$$

i.e., $w(z)\equiv 0$ or $u(z)\equiv v(z)$.

By the *Green's function of the Dirichlet problem for the domain* D we mean the function of two complex variables $G(z,\zeta)$ having the properties:

1. $G(z,\zeta)=\frac{1}{2\pi}\ln|z-\zeta|+g(z,\zeta)$, where the function $g(z,\zeta)$ is a continuous function of two variables for $z\in D$, $\zeta\in D$, bounded in z in D for any $\zeta\in D$ and harmonic in ζ in D for any $z\in D$.

---

*A complete discussion of the properties of subharmonic functions can be found in the monograph of I. I. Privalov, Subharmonic Functions (in Russian), Moscow, ONTI, 1937.

2. The function $g(z, \zeta)$ is continuous in ζ in $\overline{D}$ for any $z \in D$ and $g(z, \zeta') = -\frac{1}{2\pi}\ln|z-\zeta'|$ for any $z \in D$ and ζ' contained in the boundary of D. Thus $G(z, \zeta) = 0$ for any $z \in D$ and ζ contained in the boundary of D.

We can write the solution to the Dirichlet problem with the help of Green's function. We first prove a result having subsidiary value in this direction.

Theorem 3.1. *Let the Green's function of the Dirichlet problem for domain D be continuous up to the boundary of D and let it have first-order partial derivatives in* $\mathrm{Re}\,\zeta = \xi$ *and* $\mathrm{Im}\,\zeta = \eta$ *(except at the point* $\zeta = z$*). Then any function u(z), harmonic in the domain D and continuously differentiable up to its boundary C, can be represented in the domain D in terms of its values on the boundary curve C by means of the formula*

$$u(z) = \frac{1}{2\pi}\int_C u(\zeta)\frac{\partial}{\partial n}G(z, \zeta)\,|d\zeta| \qquad (z \in D). \tag{3.1}$$

Proof. Setting $|z-\zeta| = r$ and taking account of Remark 2 to Theorem 1.4, we obtain from formula (1.6):

$$2\pi u(z) = \int_C \left\{u\frac{\partial \ln r}{\partial n} - \frac{\partial u}{\partial n}\ln r\right\}|d\zeta| \qquad (z \in D),$$

and from formula (1.5)

$$0 = \int_C \left\{u\frac{\partial g}{\partial n} - g\frac{\partial u}{\partial n}\right\}|d\zeta| \qquad (z \in D).$$

Consequently,

$$\int_C \left\{u\frac{\partial G}{\partial n} - G\frac{\partial u}{\partial n}\right\}|d\zeta| = u(z) \qquad \left(G(z, \zeta) = \frac{\ln r}{2\pi} + g(z, \zeta)\right).$$

However, the point ζ is on the boundary of D, so that according to property 2 of Green's function, we have $G(z, \zeta) = 0$. This completes the proof.

In case D is a simply connected domain, the Green's function can easily be expressed in terms of a function which maps the domain D conformally onto the circle $|w| < 1$. Namely:

If $w(z)$ is any function which maps domain D conformally onto the circle $|w| < 1$, then

$$G(z, \zeta) = \frac{1}{2\pi}\ln|w_\zeta(z)|, \qquad w_\zeta(z) = \frac{w(z) - w(\zeta)}{1 - w(z)\overline{w(\zeta)}}. \tag{3.2}$$

Indeed, according to Theorem 2.2 of Chap. V, the function $w_\zeta(z)$ maps the domain D conformally onto the circle $|w| < 1$ and sends the point $z=\zeta$ into the point $w=0$. Therefore, the function $\frac{w_\zeta(z)}{z-\zeta}$ is regular in z in domain D for any $\zeta\in D$ and does not vanish there; moreover, the function $g(z,\ \zeta)=\ln\left|\frac{w_\zeta(z)}{z-\zeta}\right|$ is harmonic in z in domain D for any $\zeta\in D$. That the function $g(z,\ \zeta)$ is a continuous function of two variables can be seen immediately if we express the function $w_\zeta(z)$ in terms of the function $w(z)$.

Since the moduli of complex conjugates are equal,

$$|w_\zeta(z)|=|w_z(\zeta)|,$$

i.e., $G(z,\ \zeta)=G(\zeta,\ z)$, from which it follows that we have harmonicity and continuity in ζ for any $z\in D$. Thus, property 1 of Green's function is satisfied.

Property 2 is also satisfied, for according to the principle of corresponding boundaries, under conformal mapping the function $w_\zeta(z)$ is continuous up to the boundary of D and $|w_\zeta(z)|=1$ if either of the points ζ or z lies on the boundary of D.

Using formula (3.2), we can write a Green's function for simple domains (a circle or a half-plane) in finite form and then carry out a more detailed study of formula (3.1) for the solution of the Dirichlet problem.

If the domain D is the circle $|z|<R$, then, according to Theorem 2.2 of Chap. V, we have

$$w_\zeta(z)=\frac{R(z-\zeta)}{R^2-z\bar{\zeta}},\qquad G(z,\ \zeta)=\frac{1}{2\pi}\ln\frac{R\,|z-\zeta|}{|R^2-z\bar{\zeta}|}.$$

We set $z=re^{i\varphi}$, $\zeta=\varrho e^{i\theta}$. The direction of the exterior normal to the circle $|\zeta|=R$ will be the direction of the radius. Therefore,

$$\frac{\partial}{\partial n}G(re^{i\varphi},\ \varrho e^{i\theta})=\frac{1}{2\pi}\operatorname{Re}\frac{\partial}{\partial\varrho}\ln\frac{R(re^{i\varphi}-\varrho e^{i\theta})}{R^2-\varrho re^{i(\varphi-\theta)}}\bigg|_{\varrho=R}=$$

$$=\operatorname{Re}\left\{\frac{e^{i\theta}}{Re^{i\theta}-re^{i\varphi}}+\frac{re^{i(\theta-\varphi)}}{R^2-Rre^{i(\theta-\varphi)}}\right\}=\frac{R^2-r^2}{R^2+r^2-2Rr\cos(\theta-\varphi)}.$$

Thus, if domain D is the circle $|z|<R$, formula (3.1) takes the form

$$u(re^{i\varphi})=\frac{1}{2\pi}\int_0^{2\pi}\frac{R^2-r^2}{R^2+r^2-2Rr\cos(\theta-\varphi)}u(Re^{i\theta})\,d\theta. \tag{3.3}$$

This formula is called *Poisson's formula* for the circle.

If we take into account that

$$\frac{R^2-r^2}{R^2+r^2-2Rr\cos(\theta-\varphi)}=\operatorname{Re}\frac{Re^{i\theta}+z}{Re^{i\theta}-z}\qquad(z=re^{i\varphi}),$$

then we obtain *Schwarz's formula:*

$$F(z)=\frac{1}{2\pi}\int_0^{2\pi}\frac{Re^{i\vartheta}+z}{Re^{i\vartheta}-z}\operatorname{Re}F(Re^{i\theta})\,d\theta+iC \qquad (|z|<R), \tag{3.4}$$

which allows us to determine the function $F(z)$, regular in the circle $|z|<R$, in terms of the values of its real part on the circle $|z|=R$.

If the domain D is the half-plane $\operatorname{Re} z>0$, then we have

$$w_\zeta(z)=\frac{z-\zeta}{z+\zeta}, \qquad G(z, \zeta)=\frac{1}{2\pi}\ln\left|\frac{z-\zeta}{z+\zeta}\right|$$

and by analogous reasoning we obtain the Poisson formula

$$u(x+iy)=\frac{x}{\pi}\int_{-\infty}^{\infty}\frac{u(i\eta)\,d\eta}{(y-\eta)^2+x^2} \qquad (x>0) \tag{3.5}$$

and the Schwarz formula

$$F(z)=\frac{1}{\pi}\int_{-\infty}^{\infty}\frac{\operatorname{Re}F(i\eta)}{i\eta-z}\,d\eta+iC \qquad (\operatorname{Re} z>0) \tag{3.6}$$

for the half-plane $\operatorname{Re} z>0$.

Until now we have proved all these formulas under the hypothesis that the function $u(z)$ (or $\operatorname{Re}F(z)$) is continuously differentiable in the closed circle or in the closed half-plane (here we include the point at infinity). Now we significantly strengthen this result. We do away with all hypotheses relating to the function $u(z)$ and retain only hypotheses relating to the boundary function.

Theorem 3.2. *Let $f(\theta)$ be a periodic function with period 2π, continuous on the whole axis with the possible exception of a countable closed set of points of discontinuity. The function $u(z)$ given by the formula*

$$u(re^{i\varphi})=\frac{1-r^2}{2\pi}\int_0^{2\pi}\frac{f(\theta)\,d\theta}{1+r^2-2r\cos(\varphi-\theta)} \qquad (r<1),$$

is a harmonic function in the circle $|z|<1$. If the function $f(\theta)$ is continuous at the point $\theta=\theta'$, then $u(z)\to f(\theta')$ as $z\to e^{i\theta'}$. Moreover,

$$m\leqslant u(z)\leqslant M \qquad (|z|<1),$$

where M is the l.u.b. and m is the g.l.b. of the values of the function $f(\theta)$ at the points of discontinuity.

Proof. We begin by proving the inequality for $u(z)$. Under the assumptions made, the integral exists in the ordinary sense (as a limit of Riemann-sums). Therefore, if we split up the interval of integration $(0, 2\pi)$ into the sum of a countable number of nonoverlapping intervals, the integral is equal to the sum of the integrals on these segments. The segment $(0, 2\pi)$ is split up by the points of discontinuity of the function $f(\theta)$ into the sum of a countable number of intervals, on each of which the function $f(\theta)$ is continuous and, thus, satisfies the inequalities $m \leqslant f(\theta) \leqslant M$. The function $1+r^2-2r\cos(\varphi-\theta)$ is positive, so that in obtaining a bound for the integrals on the segments we may replace $f(\theta)$ successively by m and by M. After that, the sum of integrals on the segments may again be replaced by the integral on the segment $(0, 2\pi)$; thus we obtain the inequality

$$m\cdot\frac{1-r^2}{2\pi}\int_0^{2\pi}\frac{d\theta}{1+r^2-2r\cos(\varphi-\theta)} \leqslant u(re^{i\varphi}) \leqslant$$

$$\leqslant M\cdot\frac{1-r^2}{2\pi}\int_0^{2\pi}\frac{d\theta}{1+r^2-2r\cos(\varphi-\theta)}.$$

However,

$$\frac{1-r^2}{2\pi}\int_0^{2\pi}\frac{d\theta}{1+r^2-2r\cos(\varphi-\theta)}=1, \tag{3.7}$$

which is easily verified by substituting $u(z)\equiv 1$ in formula (3.3) (with $R=1$). This also yields the required inequality for our function $u(z)$.

We now prove the harmonicity of the function $u(z)$. Since

$$\frac{1-r^2}{1+r^2-2r\cos(\varphi-\theta)}=\operatorname{Re}\frac{e^{i\theta}+z}{e^{i\theta}-z} \qquad (z=re^{i\varphi}),$$

we have

$$u(z)=\operatorname{Re}F(z), \qquad F(z)=\frac{1}{2\pi}\int_0^{2\pi}\frac{e^{i\theta}+z}{e^{i\theta}-z}f(\theta)\,d\theta.$$

According to Theorem 4.3 of Chap. II, the function $F(z)$ is regular in the circle $|z|<1$, and it follows from this that $u(z)$ is harmonic.

We must show that $u(z)\to f(\theta')$ as $z\to e^{i\theta'}$, on the assumption that the function $f(\theta)$ is continuous at the point $\theta=\theta'$. Employing Eq. (3.7), for this purpose we write

$$u(re^{i\varphi})-f(\varphi)=\frac{1-r^2}{2\pi}\int_0^{2\pi}\frac{f(\theta)-f(\varphi)}{1+r^2-2r\cos(\varphi-\theta)}\,d\theta.$$

The integral of a periodic function over a period does not depend on the point at which the integration is started. Therefore,

$$u(re^{i\varphi})-f(\varphi)=\frac{1-r^2}{2\pi}\int_{-\pi}^{\pi}\frac{f(\varphi+\alpha)-f(\varphi)}{1+r^2-2r\cos\alpha}\,d\alpha.$$

We choose some number $0<\delta<\pi$ and divide up the interval of integration into three parts $(-\pi,\ -\delta)$, $(-\delta,\ \delta)$ and $(\delta,\ \pi)$. We set

$$M'=\sup|f(\theta)|,\qquad \eta(\delta,\ \varphi)=\sup_{|\alpha|<\delta}|f(\varphi+\alpha)-f(\varphi)|.$$

Then,

$$\left|\frac{1-r^2}{2\pi}\int_{-\delta}^{\delta}\frac{f(\varphi+\alpha)-f(\varphi)}{1+r^2-2r\cos\alpha}\,d\alpha\right|\leqslant$$
$$\leqslant\eta(\delta,\ \varphi)\cdot\frac{1-r^2}{2\pi}\int_{-\delta}^{\delta}\frac{d\alpha}{1+r^2-2r\cos\alpha}\leqslant\eta(\delta,\ \varphi),$$

and for the sum of the two remaining integrals we have the inequality

$$\left|\frac{1-r^2}{2\pi}\int_{\delta<|\alpha|<\pi}\frac{f(\varphi+\alpha)-f(\varphi)}{1+r^2-2r\cos\alpha}\,d\alpha\right|\leqslant M'\frac{1-r^2}{1-\cos\delta},$$

since $|f(\varphi+\alpha)-f(\varphi)|<2M'$ and

$$\frac{1-r^2}{2\pi}\int_{\delta<|\alpha|<\pi}\frac{d\alpha}{1+r^2-2r\cos\alpha}<\frac{2(\pi-\delta)}{2\pi}\,\frac{1-r^2}{1+r^2-2r\cos\delta}<$$
$$<\frac{1-r^2}{2-2\cos\delta}=\frac{1}{2}\cdot\frac{1-r^2}{1-\cos\delta}.$$

Thus,

$$|u(re^{i\varphi})-f(\varphi)|\leqslant\eta(\delta,\ \varphi)+M'\frac{1-r^2}{1-\cos\delta},$$

where $0<\delta<\pi$ is some number.

If $z\to e^{i\theta'}$ and the function $f(\theta)$ is continuous at the point $\theta=\theta'$, then $r\to 1$, $\varphi\to\theta'$ and, in addition, $\eta(\delta,\ \theta')\to 0$ as $\delta\to 0$. We have

$$|u(re^{i\varphi})-f(\theta')|\leqslant\eta(\delta,\ \varphi)+M'\frac{1-r^2}{1-\cos\delta}+|f(\theta')-f(\varphi)|.$$

However,

$$\eta(\delta,\ \varphi)\leqslant 2\eta(|\theta'-\varphi|+\delta,\ \theta').$$

Therefore, setting, for example, $\delta=\sqrt[4]{1-r^2}$, we see that $u(z)\to f(\theta')$ as $z\to e^{i\theta'}$. This proves the theorem.

Remark 1. The theorem proved gives the solution of the Dirichlet problem for the circle $|z|<1$ in the precise formulation discussed at the beginning of the section. With the help of conformal mapping, we can reduce the Dirichlet problem for more or less arbitrary simply connected domains to the Dirichlet problem for the circle $|z|<1$. For this we need only employ the theorem of corresponding boundaries under conformal mapping and Theorem 1.2 on the retention of harmonicity under change of variables.

Remark 2. Employing more profound results (to be proved in the next chapter), on corresponding boundaries under conformal mapping, we can show that formula (3.1) also gives a solution to the Dirichlet problem in the form in which it was posed at the beginning of the section. Here we must impose more restrictive conditions on the boundary of the domain D. Namely, we have to assume that the curve C forming the boundary of domain D consists of a finite number of arcs, on each of which the slope of the tangent is subject to a Lipschitz condition.

We return to the question of the solution to the Dirichlet problem for multiply connected domains in the following chapter.

4. HARMONIC MEASURE

Let D be a domain and let E be a set contained in the boundary of this domain. Let $\omega(z, E, D)$ denote the solution of the Dirichlet problem in the domain D with boundary values equal to unity on the set E and zero on the remainder of the boundary of D (if, of course, such a solution exists). We call the function $\omega(z, E, D)$ the *harmonic measure of the set E relative to the domain D at the point z.*

According to Remark 1 to Theorem 3.2, the solution of the Dirichlet problem just posed exists if D is a simply connected domain bounded by a piecewise-smooth curve and E is a finite or even countable set of arcs of this curve.

According to the very definition of the solution of the Dirichlet problem, the function $\omega(z, E, D)$ is a function harmonic in domain D, is bounded in D and is continuous up to the boundary of D at each point of continuity of the boundary function.

It follows from the maximum and minimum principles of harmonic functions that

$$0 \leqslant \omega(z, E, D) \leqslant 1.$$

The equality sign holds for z inside the domain only if either $\omega(z, E, D) \equiv 0$ or $\omega(z, E, D) \equiv 1$.

If the set E is at most countable, then $w(z, E, D) \equiv 0$, and if E differs from the entire boundary of D only by a countable set, then $w(z, E, D) \equiv 1$.

Let us take note of two almost obvious properties of harmonic measure.

If the sets E_1 and E_2 (both situated on the boundary of D) have no common points, then

$$\omega(z,\ E_1+E_2,\ D)=\omega(z,\ E_1,D)+\omega(z,\ E_2,\ D). \tag{4.2}$$

If the function w(z) maps the domain D conformally onto the domain D′ and the set E is sent into the set E′ under this mapping, then

$$\omega(z,\ E,\ D)=\omega(w(z),\ E',\ D'). \tag{4.3}$$

This last property allows us to find easily the harmonic measure in simple cases.

Example 1. Let the domain D_R be the semicircle Re $z>0$, $|z|<R$, and let E_R be a diameter of this circle. We find $\omega(z,\ E_R,\ D_R)$.

Under the mapping $w=\frac{iR-z}{iR+z}$ our semicircle D_R is sent into the quadrant $0<\arg w<\frac{\pi}{2}$, and the diameter of the semicircle into the positive part of the real axis. Denote the quadrant by D' and the positive semiaxis by E', then use formula (4.3). Clearly, this gives us

$$\omega(w,\ E',\ D')=1-\frac{2}{\pi}\arg w=1-\frac{2}{\pi}\operatorname{Im}\ln w.$$

Therefore,

$$\omega(z,\ E_R,\ D_R)=1-\frac{2}{\pi}\operatorname{Im}\ln\frac{iR-z}{iR+z}=1-\frac{2}{\pi}\operatorname{Im}\ln\frac{1+\frac{iz}{R}}{1-\frac{iz}{R}}.$$

For large R and fixed z we can easily obtain the asymptotic formula

$$\omega(z,\ E_R,\ D_R)=1-\frac{1}{R}\cdot\frac{4}{\pi}\operatorname{Re} z+O\left(\frac{1}{R^2}\right).$$

Example 2. Let the domain P_x be the half-strip $|\operatorname{Im} z|<\frac{\pi}{2}$, $\operatorname{Re} z<x$, and let H_x be its right boundary. We find $\omega(z,\ H_x,\ P_x)$.

Under the conformal mapping $w=e^z$ our half-strip is sent into the semicircle Re $w>0$, $|z|<e^x$ and the right boundary goes into the semicircumference. Since the boundary of the semicircle consists of the diameter and the semicircumference, the sum of the harmonic measures of the diameter and the semicircumference relative to the semicircle is equal to one. Therefore, applying the result of Example 1, we find

$$\omega(z,\ H_x,\ P_x)=\frac{2}{\pi}\operatorname{Im}\ln\frac{1+ie^{z-x}}{1-ie^{z-x}}.$$

For large x and fixed z we easily find the asymptotic formula

$$\omega(z,\ H_x,\ P_x)\sim e^{-x}\cdot\frac{4}{\pi}\operatorname{Re} e^z+O(e^{-2x}).$$

The harmonic measure is the solution to the Dirichlet problem only for very special boundary functions; however, with its help it is not difficult to write the solution to the Dirichlet problem for arbitrary boundary functions. Indeed, let D be some simply connected domain, let C be its boundary curve, on which the function $\varphi(\zeta)$ is given (for the sake of simplicity, we assume that it is continuous on C). We choose a sequence of points of C, $\zeta_1, \zeta_2, \ldots, \zeta_n$ ($\zeta_{n+1}=\zeta_1$) in natural order and let C_k denote the part of C contained between points ζ_k and ζ_{k+1}. We consider the sum

$$u_n(z)=\sum_1^n \varphi(\xi_k)\,\omega(z,\ C_k,\ D) \qquad (\xi_k \in C_k).$$

This sum is the solution to the Dirichlet problem in domain D with boundary values equal to $\varphi(\xi_k)$ on C_k, $k=1, 2, \ldots, n$. Let $u(z)$ be the solution to Dirichlet's problem in domain D with boundary values $\varphi(\zeta)$; next we find a bound for $u(z)-u_n(z)$. We have

$$|\varphi(\zeta)-\varphi(\xi_k)|<\eta(C_k), \qquad (\zeta \in C_k),$$

where

$$\eta(C_k)=\sup_{\zeta,\zeta'}|f(\zeta)-f(\zeta')| \qquad (\zeta \in C_k,\ \zeta' \in C_k).$$

According to the maximum and minimum principles for harmonic functions, we find

$$|u(z)-u_n(z)| \leqslant \max_k \eta(C_k).$$

However, $\varphi(\zeta)$ is continuous on C, thus $\max\limits_k \eta(C_k) \to 0$, as the maximum of the length of the C_k approaches zero.

Consequently, the sum of the $u_n(z)$ approaches the function $u(z)$ as a limit as the length of the maximum arc of the C_k approaches zero independently of the method of subdivision and the choice of the points ξ_k on the arcs C_k.

It is natural to denote the limit of the sum of the $u_n(z)$ by the integral*

$$\int_C \varphi(\zeta)\,\omega(z,\ d\zeta,\ D).$$

Thus, the solution to the Dirichlet problem in domain D with boundary function $\varphi(\zeta)$ can be presented in the form

$$u(z)=\int_C \varphi(\zeta)\,\omega(z,\ d\zeta,\ D). \tag{4.4}$$

---

*Integrals of this type are called Stieltjes integrals. A more detailed presentation of the theory of Stieltjes integrals can be found in the book by S. Saks, Theory of the Integral, Dover Publ., N.Y., 1964.

We proved the formula only for continuous functions $\varphi(\zeta)$, but it is clear that the proof can be carried over easily to piecewise continuous, bounded functions.

In particular, setting the function $\varphi(\zeta)$ equal to unity on the set E and to zero on the rest of the boundary of the domain D, we obtain from formula (4.4) the formula

$$\omega(z, E, D) = \int_E \omega(z, d\zeta, D).$$

Comparison of formula (4.4) with formula (3.1) suggests that harmonic measure is closely connected with the Green's function of the Dirichlet problem in domain D. This is actually the case. It is not difficult to express harmonic measure in terms of the harmonic function conjugate to Green's function.

Harmonic measure may be applied in obtaining bounds for analytic functions with the help of the so-called two constants theorem.

Theorem 4.1. *Let the function $f(z)$ be regular in the domain D with boundary C, and let E be some set contained in C. If*

$$\overline{\lim_{z\to\zeta}}\,|f(z)| < m \quad (\zeta \in E), \quad \overline{\lim_{z\to\zeta}}\,|f(z)| < M \quad (\zeta \in C,\ \zeta \overline{\in} E),$$

then

$$\ln|f(z)| < \omega(z, E, D)\ln m + (1 - \omega(z, E, D))\ln M \qquad (z \in D).$$

Proof. The left-hand term of the inequality to be proved is (on the basis of Theorem 2.4) a subharmonic function in domain D and the right-hand term is harmonic. The inequality is satisfied for the limiting values on the boundary, since the function $\omega(z, E, D)$ becomes unity at points of the set E and vanishes at the remaining points of the boundary of D. Applying the maximum principle to the difference of the left- and the right-hand terms of the inequality, we obtain the statement of the theorem.

The exact determination of the harmonic measure occurring in the inequality may turn out to be a very difficult problem. Therefore, estimates for harmonic measure that allow the replacement of complicated quantities by simple ones have great importance in the theory of analytic functions. One of the most important methods of estimating harmonic measure is the so-called *Carleman's principle* or the *principle of extension of domains.*

Theorem 4.2. *Let the domain D' contain the domain D, and let the set E' contained in the boundary of D' contained the set E contain in the boundary of D. Then,*

$$\omega(z, E, D) \leqslant \omega(z, E', D') \qquad (z \in D).$$

Proof. Let us consider both functions on the boundary of D. Both functions are unity at points of the set E. The function

$\omega(z, E, D)$ is zero at the remaining points and the function $\omega(z, E', D')$ is in any case nonnegative (because of (4.1)). Consequently, the inequality to be proved is satisfied on the boundary of D. According to the maximum pinciple, it is therefore satisfied inside the domain.

Note that the principle of extension of domains allows us to find not only upper, but also lower bounds for harmonic measure, for the sum of the harmonic measures of the set E and its conjugate with respect to the entire boundary of domain D is equal to unity. Taking these considerations into account, we can put the principle of extension of domains into the following symmetric form:

The harmonic measure $w(z, E, D)$ increases under extension of the domain D at the expense of part of the boundary not containing points of the set E, while it decreases under extension of the domain at the expense of part of the boundary consisting only of points of the set E.

We prove two theorems due to Lindelöf as an application of the theorem of extension of boundaries. The first reads as follows:

Theorem 4.3. *Let the function $f(z)$ be regular and bounded in the half-plane $\operatorname{Im} z>0$. If there exists a curve L contained in this half-plane such that $f(z) \to a (z\to\infty, z \in L)$, then $f(z)\to a$ uniformly as $z\to\infty$ in any angular sector $\delta \leqslant \arg z \leqslant \pi-\delta$.*

Proof. We choose a point $z_R=2Re^{i\varphi}$, $\delta\leqslant\varphi\leqslant\pi-\delta$, and consider the function $f(z)-a$ in the domain D_R consisting of the connected region of the sector $\operatorname{Im} z>0$, $|z|>R$, intercepted by the curve L and containing the point z_R. Let L_R denote the part of the curve L contained in the boundary of domain D_R, and let $\varepsilon(R)$ and M be the quantities

$$\varepsilon(R)=\sup_{z\in L_R}|f(z)-a|, \qquad M=\sup_{z\in D_R}|f(z)-a|.$$

Applying the two constants theorem to the function $|f(z)-a|$, we find

$$\begin{gathered}\ln|f(z_R)-a|\leqslant\omega(z_R, L_R, D_R)\ln\varepsilon(R)+\\ +(1-\omega(z_R, L_R, D_R))\ln M\leqslant\omega(z_R, L_R, D_R)\ln\varepsilon(R)+\ln^+M,\\ (\ln^+M=\max(\ln M, 0)).\end{gathered}$$

According to the principle of extension of domains, the harmonic measure $\omega(z_R, L_R, D_R)$ does not increase if we replace the domain D_R by the sector $\operatorname{Im} z>0$, $|z|>R$, and the curve L_R by that one of the rays $(R, +\infty)$, $(-\infty, -R)$ which does not form part of the boundary of domain D_R (we denote the sector by D_R' and the curve L_R').

For sufficiently large R we have $\varepsilon(R)<1$ and

$$\ln|f(2Re^{i\varphi})-a|\leqslant\omega(2Re^{i\varphi}, L_R', D_R')\ln\varepsilon(R).$$

The harmonic measure $\omega(2Re^{i\varphi}, L'_R, D'_R)$ can be evaluated, but it is not necessary. It is sufficient to note that it is positive and independent of R for $\delta \leqslant \varphi \leqslant \pi - \delta$. It already follows from this that the theorem holds, since $\varepsilon(R)$ approaches zero as $R \to +\infty$.

We may obtain another theorem of Lindelöf as a corollary of the preceding.

Corollary. Let the function f(z) be regular in the domain D bounded by two curves L_1 and L_2 issuing from the same point and diverging to infinity. If the function is continuous on the curves L_1 and L_2 and

$$f(z) \to a_n \qquad (z \to \infty,\ z \in L_n), \quad n = 1,\ 2,$$

then either the function f(z) is not bounded in the domain D or $a_1 = a_2 = a$ and $f(z) \to a$ as z becomes infinite along any path lying in domain D.

Indeed, let us denote by $z(w)$ the function mapping the half-plane $\operatorname{Im} w > 0$ conformally onto the domain D and sending the point $w = \infty$ into the point $z = \infty$. Consider the function $g(w) = f(z(w))$. If the function $f(z)$ is bounded in the domain D, then the function $g(w)$ is bounded in the half-plane $\operatorname{Im} w > 0$, and it follows from the existence of the limits of $f(z)$ along L_1 and L_2 that the limits of $g(w)$ exist as $w \to \pm\infty$, since the function $z(w)$ maps the real axis into the curve consisting of L_1 and L_2. We now apply Theorem 4.3 to the function $g(w)$, first taking the positive and then the negative half of the real axis as the curve L. This gives us

$$g(w) \to a_1 \qquad (w \to \infty, \qquad 0 \leqslant \arg w \leqslant \pi - \delta)$$

and

$$g(w) \to a_2 \qquad (w \to \infty, \qquad \delta \leqslant \arg w \leqslant \pi).$$

This is possible only in the case that $a_1 = a_2 = a$ and $g(w) \to a$ as w becomes infinite along any path lying in the half-plane $\operatorname{Im} w > 0$. Going over to $f(z)$, we obtain the desired statement.

Using the principle of extension of domains, we can obtain a variety of inequalities satisfied by harmonic measure. We first present a rather deep but intuitive result.

Theorem 4.4. *Let D be a convex domain*), let E be an arc of the boundary curve of this domain. Then*

$$\omega(z,\ E,\ D) \leqslant \frac{1}{\pi}\varphi(z,\ E,\ D),$$

---

*Recall that a domain is called convex, if the segment joining any two points of the domain is contained within the domain.

where $\varphi(z, E, D)$ is the angle intercepted by the arc E at the point z. If D is a half-plane, then the inequality becomes an equality.

Proof. We first prove the last statement of the theorem. It is clear that we can assume without loss of generality that we are dealing with the half-plane $\operatorname{Re} z > 0$ and that the point $z = x$ lies on the real axis. As the arc E we choose the segment (iy_1, iy_2) of the imaginary axis. The harmonic measure can be found with the help of Poisson's integral for the half-plane (see formula (3.5)). This gives us

$$\omega = \frac{x}{\pi}\int_{y_1}^{y_2} \frac{d\eta}{\eta^2 + x^2} = \frac{1}{\pi}\left(\arctan\frac{y_2}{x} - \arctan\frac{y_1}{x}\right).$$

This quantity exactly equals the size of the angle intercepted by the segment (iy_1, iy_2) at the point $z = x$, divided by π. Thus the statement of the theorem is verified for the half-plane.

Note that it is sufficient to prove that the inequality holds for arbitrarily small arc E, since as we add arcs, we also add the harmonic measures and the sizes of the angles intercepted by the arcs. We therefore assume that the arc E is so small that the domain bounded by the arc E and the line segment joining its endpoints does not contain the point z.

Let D_1 denote the line segment joining the endpoints of the arc E, let D_1 be the part of domain D cut off by the segment E_1 and containing the point z, and let G be the half-plane containing the domain E_1 and the line containing the segment E_1 (Fig. 7). According to the principle of extensions of domains, we have

$$\omega(z, E, D) \leqslant \omega(z, E_1, D_1) \leqslant \omega(z, E_1, G),$$

and $\omega(z, E_1, G) = \frac{1}{\pi}\varphi(z, E, D)$, as was proved above. This completes the proof.

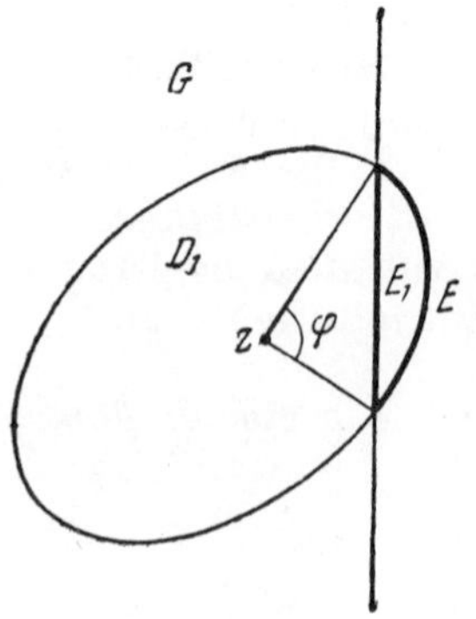

FIG. 7

We can also obtain more refined estimates with the aid of the principle of extension of domains. We show how one of these estimates is obtained while considering the Carleman-Milloux problem.

The following canonical presentation of a problem on obtaining bounds for the harmonic measure is called the *Carleman-Milloux problem.*

Let D be a simply connected domain having a finite, nonempty intersection with any line $\operatorname{Re} z = x$, $a < x < b$. Let D_x denote the connected part of domain D contained in the half-plane $\operatorname{Re} z < x$ and containing a preassigned point ζ $(\operatorname{Re}\zeta < x)$. Let h_x denote the part of the boundary of domain D_x consisting of line segments belonging to the line $\operatorname{Re} z = x$, and let $h(x)$ be the sum of the lengths of these segments.

The problem consists in finding bounds for the value of the harmonic measure $\omega(\zeta, h_x, D_x)$, if the function $h(t)$ is known for $t \leqslant x$.

The following result was obtained by Carleman.

Theorem 4.5. *Let* $\zeta = \xi + i\eta \in D$ *and* $a < \xi < x < b$. *Then*

$$\omega(\xi + i\eta, h_x, D_x) \leqslant \exp\left\{-\frac{4}{\pi}\int_{\xi}^{x}\frac{dt}{h(t)}\right\}.$$

Proof. We take $\xi < \sigma < x$ and consider the two functions $\omega(\zeta, h_x, D_x)$ and $\omega(\zeta, h_\sigma, D_\sigma)$ in the domain D_σ. Both functions are zero on a part of the boundary of domain D_σ which is different from the segment h_σ. Therefore, according to formula (4.4), we can regenerate these functions in terms of the values on the segments h_σ as follows:

$$\omega(\zeta, h_x, D_x) = \int_{h_\sigma}\omega(\sigma + iy, h_x, D_x)\,\omega(\zeta, dy, D_\sigma),$$

$$\omega(\zeta, h_\sigma, D_\sigma) = \int_{h_\sigma}\omega(\zeta, dy, D_\sigma).$$

Subtracting the second equation from the first and dividing by $x - \sigma$, we find

$$\frac{\omega(\zeta, h_x, D_x) - \omega(\zeta, h_\sigma, D_\sigma)}{x - \sigma} = \int_{h_\sigma}\frac{\omega(\sigma + iy, h_x, D_x) - 1}{x - \sigma}\,\omega(\zeta, dy, D_\sigma). \tag{4.6}$$

We can obtain an estimate for the harmonic measure $\omega(\sigma + iy, h_x, D_x)$ occurring in the integral with the aid of the principle of extension of domains. We replace the domain D_x by the half-plane $\operatorname{Re} z < x$, which we denote by G_x. According to the principle of extension of domains, $\omega(\sigma + iy, h_x, D_x) \leqslant \omega(\sigma + iy, h_x, G_x)$. However, according to Theorem 4.4, the harmonic measure $\omega(\sigma + iy, h_x, G_x)$ equals the sum divided by π of the angles intercepted by the segments composing

h_x at the point $\sigma+iy$. For a given sum of the lengths the sum of the sizes of the angles will be greatest when h_x is composed of a single segment symmetric with respect to the line $\operatorname{Im} z=y$. Computing the sizes of the angles in this case, we find

$$\omega(\sigma+iy,\ h_x,\ G_x)\leqslant\frac{2}{\pi}\arctan\frac{h(x)}{2(x-\sigma)}=1-\frac{2}{\pi}\arctan\frac{2(x-\sigma)}{h(x)}.$$

Thus,

$$\omega(\sigma+iy,\ h_x,\ D_x)-1\leqslant-\frac{2}{\pi}\arctan\frac{2(x-\sigma)}{h(x)}.$$

Substituting this inequality into formula (4.6), we find

$$\frac{\omega(\zeta,\ h_x,\ D_x)-\omega(\zeta,\ h_\sigma,\ D_\sigma)}{x-\sigma}\leqslant$$

$$\leqslant-\frac{2}{\pi}\cdot\frac{\arctan\dfrac{2(x-\sigma)}{h(x)}}{x-\sigma}\int_{h_\sigma}\omega(\zeta,\ dy,\ D_\sigma)=$$

$$=-\frac{2}{\pi}\frac{\arctan\dfrac{2(x-\sigma)}{h(x)}}{x-\sigma}\cdot\omega(\zeta,\ h_\sigma,\ D_\sigma).$$

Dividing both sides of the inequality by $\omega(\zeta,\ h_\sigma,\ D_\sigma)$ and taking limits as $x\to\sigma$, we find

$$\frac{d}{d\sigma}\ln\omega(\zeta,\ h_\sigma,\ D_\sigma)\leqslant-\frac{4}{\pi}\cdot\frac{1}{h(\sigma)}.$$

Integrating this inequality with respect to σ from ξ to x and noting that $\omega(\zeta,\ h_\xi,\ D_\xi)=1$, we arrive at the statement of the theorem. (We omit discussion of the question of whether $\omega(\zeta,\ h_\sigma,\ D_\sigma)$ admits a derivative with respect to σ. This problem is easily solved if we make use of the monotonicity of this function; however, it is simpler to prove the last inequality without using the existence of the derivative. We found the inequality with the help of the derivative only for the sake of clarity.)

It is helpful to examine the kind of estimate Theorems 4.4 and 4.5 give for the harmonic measure of the half-strip $\operatorname{Re} z<x$, $|\operatorname{Im} z|<\pi/2$ as $x\to+\infty$.

We obtain from Theorem 4.4

$$\omega(z,\ H_x,\ P_x)\leqslant\frac{2}{\pi}\arctan\frac{\pi}{x-\operatorname{Re} z}\sim\frac{2}{x}\qquad(x\to+\infty).$$

From Theorem 4.5 we obtain

$$\omega(z,\ H_x,\ P_x)\leqslant\exp\left\{-\frac{4}{\pi}\int_{\operatorname{Re} z}^{x}\frac{dt}{\pi}\right\}=e^{-\frac{4}{\pi^2}(x-\operatorname{Re} z)}.$$

The correct estimate (see Example 2) is

$$\omega(z, H_x, P_x) \sim \frac{4}{\pi} e^{-x} \cdot \operatorname{Re} e^z \qquad (x \to +\infty).$$

We show in Sect. 6 how to obtain estimates not differing from the correct ones with the aid of Ahlfor's inequality (see Sect. 6, Chap. V). Using the symmetry principle (see Sect. 2, Chap. X), we can employ Ahlfors' inequality also for the refinement of Carleman's bounds in the Carleman-Milloux problem itself. The refinement, roughly speaking, consists in replacing the multiplier $-4/\pi$ in front of the integral by the multiplier $-\pi$.

5. UNIQUENESS THEOREMS FOR BOUNDED FUNCTIONS

In this and the following sections we shall be concerned with the application of the theory of harmonic and subharmonic functions to various questions of analytic function theory.

We begin by proving several uniqueness theorems for various classes of functions regular in the circle $|z| < R$.

The class of functions regular and bounded in the circle $|z| < R$ is called the *class B*. Here we put

$$B(f) = \sup_{|z| < R} |f(z)|.$$

The class of functions regular in the circle $|z| < R$ and satisfying the condition

$$\sup_{\varrho < R} \int_0^{2\pi} |f(\varrho e^{i\varphi})|^\delta \, d\varphi < \infty,$$

is called the *class* H_δ $(\delta > 0)$. Here we set

$$H_\delta(f, \varrho) = \frac{1}{2\pi} \int_0^{2\pi} |f(\varrho e^{i\varphi})|^\delta \, d\varphi, \qquad H_\delta(f) = \sup_{\varrho < R} H_\delta(f, \varrho).$$

The class of functions regular in the circle $|z| < R$ and satisfying the condition

$$\sup_{\varrho < R} \int_0^{2\pi} \ln^+ |f(\varrho e^{i\varphi})| \, d\varphi < \infty \qquad (\ln^+ x = \max(\ln x, 0)),$$

is called the *class A* or the *class of functions of bounded mode*. Here we set

$$A(f, \varrho) = \frac{1}{2\pi} \int_0^{2\pi} \ln^+ |f(\varrho e^{i\varphi})| \, d\varphi, \qquad A(f) = \sup_{\varrho < R} A(f, \varrho).$$

The presence of the function $f(z)$ in the class B, H_δ or A imposes some type of bound either on the growth of $f(z)$ as z approaches R or on the growth of the coefficients of the Taylor expansion of $f(z)$. However, it is impossible to give necessary and sufficient conditions for the membership of $f(z)$ in these classes in such terms.

It is not difficult to show that class B is the smallest of these classes, that class $H_{\delta'}$ is contained in class H_δ for $\delta' < \delta$ and that class A contains all classes H_δ. (Only the latter assertion is needed in the proof, but it is an immediate corollary of the obvious inequality $\ln^+ x < x^\delta/\delta$.) Since class A is the broadest, most theorems are naturally proved only for it.

The following lemma plays a very important role in all discussions concerning the classes mentioned.

Lemma 1. If the function f(z) is regular for $r_1 < |z| < r_2$, then the functions $H_\delta(f, z)$ and $A(f, z)$, defined above, and also the function

$$L(f, z) = \frac{1}{2\pi}\int_0^{2\pi} \ln|f(ze^{i\varphi})|\, d\varphi$$

are subharmonic functions of z in the annulus $r_1 < |z| < r_2$ and depend only on $|z|$.

Proof. We carry out the proof only for the function $A(f, z)$; the remaining arguments are completely analogous.

Let us note first of all that the function $A(f, re^{i\theta})$ does not depend on θ, since the integral of a periodic function over a complete period is not affected by shift of the initial point of the interval of integration. This also means that the function $A(f, z)$ depends only on $|z|$.

Moreover, the integral of $A(f, z)$ is the limit of Riemann sums

$$S_n(z) = \frac{1}{2\pi}\sum \ln^+ |f(ze^{i\varphi_k})|(\varphi_{k+1} - \varphi_k)$$

(the approach to the limit is uniform in z in any closed annulus contained within the original one). According to property 1 of subharmonic functions (see Sect. 2), a sum of subharmonic functions $S_n(z)$ is a subharmonic function, and according to property 2, the limit of these sums, i.e., the function $A(f, z)$, is also a subharmonic function. This completes the proof.

Corollary. If the function f(z) is regular in the circle $|z| < R$, then the functions $H_\delta(f, \varrho)$, $A(f, \varrho)$ and $L(f, \varrho)$ are nondecreasing functions of ϱ.

This statement follows immediately from the maximum principle for subharmonic functions.

The following theorem shows that the functions of the classes under discussion cannot approach zero very rapidly as z nears the boundary $|z| = R$.

Theorem 5.1. *Let f(z) be a function of bounded mode in the circle* $|z|<R$. *If*

$$\lim_{\varrho\to R}\int_0^{2\pi}\ln|f(\varrho e^{i\varphi})|\,d\varphi=-\infty,$$

then $f(z)\equiv 0$.

Proof. Since $\ln^+ x\geqslant \ln x$ and since $f(z)$ belongs to the class A, it follows that the integral of interest to us is bounded above. Moreover, it follows from the corollary to the lemma that this integral is a nondecreasing function of ϱ. Therefore, the condition of the theorem can be fulfilled only if the integral is $-\infty$ for all ϱ. However, for a function $f(z)$ not identically zero, there exists at least one ϱ for which this integral has a finite value. This means that $f(z)\equiv 0$, as was to be proved.

The theorem proved generalizes a classical uniqueness theorem. Indeed, the classical uniqueness theorem for analytic functions can be formulated as follows:

If the function f(z) is regular at the point $z=a$ *and as* $z\to a$ *f(z) approaches zero more rapidly than any power of* $z-a$, *then* $f(z)\equiv 0$.

It is clear that as z approaches a point of the boundary of the domain of regularity, the function can approach zero more rapidly than any power. Theorem 5.1 places a bound on the rate of approach of $f(z)$ to zero as z approaches a boundary point of the domain, if the function $f(z)$ belongs to one of the classes mentioned. The conditions given in the theorem are not very intuitive, but they have great generality and precision. In the following section, we shall deduce a series of simpler theorems of this type from Theorem 5.1 under the assumption that $f(z)\to 0$ at only one point of the boundary.

The following result is the generalization mentioned of the classical uniqueness theorem.

Theorem 5.2. *Let f(z) be a function of bounded mode in the circle* $|z|<R$, *and let f(z) have zeros at the points* $z_1, z_2, \ldots$ *(each zero is written as many times as its multiplicity). If*

$$\sum_1^\infty (R-|z_n|)=+\infty,$$

then $f(z)\equiv 0$.

Proof. Assume that $f(z)\not\equiv 0$. Then we can assume without loss of generality that

$$f(0)\neq 0. \tag{5.1}$$

Indeed, in place of the function $f(z)$ we can take the function

$g(z)=z^{-m}f(z)$, where m is the multiplicity of the zero of the function at the point $z=0$. It is clear that the function $g(z)$ will also be a function of bounded mode.

We apply Jensen's inequality (see Lemma 1, Sect. 2). It gives us

$$\frac{1}{2\pi}\int_0^{2\pi}\ln|f(\varrho e^{i\varphi})|\,d\varphi=\ln|f(0)|-\sum_{|z_n|<\varrho}\ln\frac{\varrho}{|z_n|}. \tag{5.2}$$

According to the condition of the theorem, if we take limit as $\varrho\to R$, we find

$$\lim_{\varrho\to R}\frac{1}{2\pi}\int_0^{2\pi}\ln|f(\varrho e^{i\varphi})|\,d\varphi=\ln|f(0)|-\sum_1^{\infty}\ln\frac{R}{|z_n|}.$$

But for $0<|z|<R$, we have

$$\ln\frac{R}{|z|}=-\ln\left(1-\frac{R-|z|}{R}\right)=\sum_1^{\infty}\frac{1}{n}\left(\frac{R-|z|}{R}\right)^n>\frac{R-|z|}{R}$$

and, thus,

$$\sum_1^{\infty}\ln\frac{R}{|z_n|}\geqslant\sum_1^{\infty}\frac{R-|z_n|}{R}=+\infty,$$

i.e., $\lim\limits_{\varrho\to R}\int_0^{2\pi}\ln|f(\varrho e^{i\varphi})|\,d\varphi=-\infty$. In view of Theorem 5.1 we have $f(z)\equiv 0$. This completes the proof.

It is possible to show that Theorems 5.1 and 5.2 are exact not only for class A, but for class B as well. This may be done as follows:

If we are given any continuous function $a(\varphi)$ for which

$$\int_0^{2\pi}\ln a(\varphi)\,d\varphi>-\infty,$$

then it is possible to show that the function

$$f(z)=\frac{1}{2\pi}\int_0^{2\pi}\frac{Re^{i\varphi}+z}{Re^{i\varphi}-z}\ln a(\varphi)\,d\varphi \qquad (|z|<R)$$

is regular and bounded in the circle $|z|<R$ and that $|f(z)|\to a(\varphi)$ as $z\to Re^{i\varphi}$.

If we are given any sequence of points z_n satisfying the conditions

$$|z_n|<R, \qquad \sum_1^{\infty}(R-|z_n|)<\infty,$$

then the function

$$f(z)=\prod_{1}^{\infty}\frac{R(z_k-z)}{R^2-z\bar{z}_k}e^{-i\varphi_k} \qquad (\varphi_k=\arg z_k)$$

is regular and does not exceed unity in the circle $|z|<R$; moreover, $f(z_n)=0$.

We leave it to the reader to justify these statements.

There is an interesting result concerning functions of bounded mode that explains why there are no great differences between functions of bounded mode and bounded functions:

*Functions of bounded mode are ratios of bounded functions**.

Classes of functions analogous to the classes B, H_δ and A can be studied not only in the circle $|z|<R$, but also in arbitrary domains. However, taking the result just presented into account, we see that it is possible in the majority of problems to limit the study to functions bounded in some particular domain. If this domain is simply connected, then we can readily obtain results using conformal mapping.

For an example, we present a generalization of Theorem 5.2 to the case of an arbitrary simply connected domain.

Theorem 5.3. *Let D be any simply connected domain, and let w(z) be any function mapping D conformally onto the circle* $|w|<1$. *If the function f(z) is regular and bounded in D and has zeros at the points* $z_1, z_2, \ldots$, *and*

$$\sum_{1}^{\infty}(1-|w(z_n)|)=+\infty,$$

then $f(z)\equiv 0$.

Proof. Consider the function $g(w)=f(z(w))$, where $z(w)$ is the inverse to $w(z)$. The function $g(w)$ is regular and bounded in the circle $|w|<1$ and has zeros at the points $w_k=w(z_k)$, and, moreover, $\sum(1-|w_k|)=\sum(1-|w(z_k)|)=+\infty$. According to Theorem 5.2, $g(w)\equiv 0$. This completes the proof.

The above uniqueness theorem has wide applications in analytic function theory as well as in many other areas of analysis. For an example of these applications we prove a result, well known under the name of *Müntz's theorem* on the completeness of a system of functions $\{x^{\lambda_n}\}$.

Theorem 5.4. If $\lambda_1<\lambda_2<\ldots$ and $\sum\frac{1}{\lambda_n}=+\infty$, then the system of functions $\{x^{\lambda_n}\}$ is complete on the interval $(0, 1)$.

---

*The proof of this and several other interesting results on functions of bounded mode can be found in the book by I. I. Privalov, Boundary Conditions of Analytic Functions (in Russian), Moscow, Gostekhizdat, 1950.

Proof. A system of functions $\{\varphi_n(x)\}$ is called *complete* on the interval (a, b), if there is no function continuous on (a, b) and is orthogonal to all the functions $\varphi_n(x)$.

We assume that $g(x)$ is continuous on the segment $(0,1)$ and is orthogonal to all functions x^{λ_n}, i.e., that

$$\int_0^1 g(x)\, x^{\lambda_n}\, dx = 0 \qquad (n = 1,\ 2,\ \ldots). \tag{5.3}$$

We set

$$G(z) = \int_0^1 g(x)\, x^{z-1} dx.$$

The function $G(z)$ is regular in the half-plane $\operatorname{Re} z > 0$ and bounded, since $|x^z| < 1$ for $0 < x < 1$, $\operatorname{Re} z > 0$. Moreover, it has zeros at the points $z = \lambda_n + 1$ $(n = 1, 2, \ldots)$. We apply Theorem 5.3, and use the function $w = \frac{z-1}{z+1}$ for the function $w(z)$ mapping the half-plane $\operatorname{Re} z > 0$ conformally onto the circle $|w| < 1$. We have

$$\sum (1 - |w(\lambda_n + 1)|) = \sum \left(1 - \frac{\lambda_n}{\lambda_n + 2}\right) = 2 \sum \frac{1}{\lambda_n + 2} = +\infty.$$

Therefore, it follows from Theorem 5.3 that $G(z) \equiv 0$. It is easy to verify that $g(x) \equiv 0$ by using the inversion formula for the Mellin transform (see Sect. 6, Chap. VII). Thus, there does not exist a function continuous on the interval $(0,1)$ and orthogonal to all functions x^{λ_n}, i.e., the system of functions $\{x^{\lambda_n}\}$ is complete on the interval $(0, 1)$. This completes the proof. [The converse of Müntz's theorem is also true, but we omit the proof. Ed.]

We note that one of the problems in the application of Theorem 5.3 is the estimation of the value of $w(z_n)$ as $n \to \infty$. For this purpose we can use the Ahlfors-Warschwskiy inequality (see Sect. 6, Chap. V) for the estimation of conformal mappings near the boundary.

6. THE PHRAGMEN-LINDELÖF THEOREMS

For a second application of the theory of harmonic and subharmonic functions, we prove two rather refined theorems, useful in the most varied circumstances, about the influence of the boundary behavior of functions on the increase and decrease of these functions in infinite domains.

The theorems to be proved do not actually require the regularity of the function, but only the subharmonicity of the function $\ln|f(z)|$, so that if we wish we can easily turn these theorems into statements about subharmonic functions.

Theorem 6.1. *Let G be a simply connected domain having the points $t = \infty$ and $t = 0$ among its boundary points. Let s_ϱ denote the intersection of this domain with the circle $|t| = \varrho$, and let $s(\varrho)$ be* *the length of s_ρ. If the function f(t) is regular in domain G, continuous up to its boundary C (except at the point $t=\infty$) and if f(t) satisfies the conditions*

$$|f(t)| \leqslant 1 \quad (t \in C), \qquad \lim_{\rho \to \infty} \frac{\ln M(\rho)}{\sigma(\rho)} = 0,$$

where

$$M(\rho) = \max_{t \in S_\rho} |f(t)|, \qquad \sigma(\rho) = \exp\left\{\pi \int_1^\rho \frac{du}{s(u)}\right\},$$

then $|f(t)| \leqslant 1$ $(t \in G)$.

Proof. Let $\zeta(t)$ denote a function that maps the domain G conformally onto the half-plane $\operatorname{Re}\zeta > 0$ and that maps the points $t=0$ and $t=\infty$ into the points $\zeta=0$ and $\zeta=\infty$, respectively. Let $t(\zeta)$ denote the inverse of the function $\zeta(t)$. It is clear that these functions are determined to within a constant multiplier.

We choose any point $t_0 \in G$ and a sufficiently large ρ. Let G_ρ be that part of the domain G contained in the circle $|t| < \rho$ and containing the point t_0. For $\rho > |t_0|$ the domain G_ρ is not empty. Let K_ρ denote the image of the domain G_ρ under the mapping $\zeta = \zeta(t)$. The domain K_ρ is bounded by segments of the imaginary axis and some curves L_ρ, the images of the arcs of the circle $|t| = \rho$ contained in s_ρ. Among the curves L_ρ there must be at least one that joins the positive part with the negative part of the imaginary axis. Let L_ρ^* be such a curve; let s_ρ^* be the arc of s_ρ that is the preimage of L_ρ^* and let $s^*(\rho)$ denote the length of s_ρ^*. The domain bounded by the curve L_ρ^* and the line segment joining its endpoints is denoted K_ρ^*, and the preimage of K_ρ^* is denoted by G_ρ^*. (It is worth observing that if the domain G intersects the circle $|t| = \rho$ in precisely one arc, then the starred and unstarred quantities coincide. In the general case $G_\rho^* \supset G_\rho$ and $K_\rho^* \supset K_\rho$, $s_\rho^* \subset s_\rho$ and $s^*(\rho) \leqslant s(\rho)$.)

The domain K_ρ may be imagined as a distorted semicircle. We now determine the radius of the largest semicircle $\operatorname{Im}\zeta > 0$, $|\zeta| < r(\rho)$, contained in domain K_ρ^*, i.e., the quantity

$$r(\rho) = \inf_{t \in s_\rho^*} |\zeta(t)|.$$

We use Ahlfors' inequality for the determination of $r(\rho)$ (see Theorem 6.1, Chap. V). To reduce the problem to the same form as that used in this inequality, we denote by D the image of the domain G under the mapping $z = \ln t$ (the function $\ln t$ is regular in the domain G no matter which branch we choose). Then the function $w(z) = \ln \zeta(e^z)$ maps the domain D conformally onto the strip $|\operatorname{Im} w| < \pi/2$ and the intersections of the domain D with the lines $\operatorname{Re} z = x$ are the images of the domain G with the circles $|t| = e^x$ under the mapping $z = \ln t$. Here the segment θ_x is the image of the arc $s^*_{e^x}$ and

$$\theta(x) = \frac{s^*(e^x)}{e^x}, \qquad \ln r(e^x) = \sup_{z \in \theta_x} \operatorname{Re} w(z).$$

Thus, Ahlfors' inequality gives us

$$r(\varrho) \geqslant \exp\left\{C + \pi \int_0^{\ln \varrho} \frac{dt}{\theta(t)}\right\} = e^C \cdot \exp\left\{\pi \int_1^{\varrho} \frac{du}{s^*(u)}\right\} \geqslant e^C \sigma(\varrho). \tag{6.1}$$

We now turn to the general part of the proof (it is simpler than the auxiliary reasoning that gives the theorem its generality).

Consider the function $F(\zeta) = f(t(\zeta))$ in the domain K^*_ρ. On the imaginary axis we have $|F(\zeta)| \leqslant 1$, since the imaginary axis goes into the boundary of the domain G under the mapping $t = t(\zeta)$, i.e., on C according to the condition of the theorem $|f(t)| \leqslant 1$. On the remaining part of the boundary of the domain K^*_ρ, i.e., on the curve L^*_ρ, the image of the arc s^*_ρ under the mapping $\zeta = \zeta(t)$, we have

$$\sup_{\zeta \in L^*_\rho} |F(\zeta)| = \sup_{t \in s^*_\rho} |f(t)| \leqslant \sup_{t \in s_\rho} |f(t)| = M(\varrho).$$

Applying the two constants theorem (Theorem 4.1) to the function $F(\zeta)$ in domain K^*_ρ with L^*_ρ in place of E, $m = M(\varrho)$ and $M = 1$, we obtain

$$\ln|F(\zeta_0)| \leqslant \omega(\zeta_0, L^*_\rho, K^*_\rho) \ln M(\varrho) \qquad (\zeta_0 = \zeta(t_0)).$$

We showed that the domain K^*_ρ contains the semicircle $\operatorname{Re}\zeta > 0$, $|\zeta| < r(\varrho)$, where $r(\varrho) > C' \sigma(\varrho)$. According to the principle of extension of domains, the harmonic measure $\omega(\zeta_0, L^*_\rho, K^*_\rho)$ does not exceed the harmonic measure of the semicircumference relative to the semicircle $\operatorname{Re}\zeta > 0$, $|\zeta| < r(\varrho)$ (at this point). We calculated the latter in Example 1, Sect. 4, and obtained an asymptotic formula for it (for large radii). This harmonic measure equals

$$\frac{2}{\pi} \operatorname{Im} \ln \frac{r(\varrho) - i\zeta_0}{r(\varrho) + i\zeta_0} \sim \frac{1}{r(\varrho)} \cdot \frac{4}{\pi} \operatorname{Re}\zeta_0 \qquad (r(\varrho) \to \infty).$$

Therefore, in view of inequality (6.1), as $\varrho \to \infty$ for fixed ζ_0 we have

$$\omega(\zeta_0, L^*_\rho, K^*_\rho) \leqslant C_1 \frac{1}{\sigma(\varrho)},$$

and inequality (6.2) gives us

$$\ln|F(\zeta_0)| \leqslant C_1 \frac{\ln M(\varrho)}{\sigma(\varrho)}.$$

According to hypothesis, there exists a sequence $\varrho_n \to \infty$ for which $\frac{\ln M(\varrho_n)}{\sigma(\varrho_n)} \to 0$. Therefore, setting $\varrho = \varrho_n$ in the last inequality and taking limits as $n \to \infty$, we obtain $\ln|F(\zeta_0)| \leqslant 0$. It follows from this that $|f(t_0)| \leqslant 1$ and since t_0 is any point of domain G, we arrive at the statement of the theorem.

Note that if the domain G is of simple form (half-plane, angular sector, strip) or if G is contained in a domain of simple form, the preliminary reasoning with Ahlfors' inequality is unnecessary and the proof becomes completely elementary.

In addition, it is worthwhile to formulate Theorem 6.1 separately for the special case in which G is an angular sector, since this special case arises frequently.

Let the function $f(z)$ be regular in an angular sector of magnitude π/α and let $f(z)$ be continuous up to the sides. If $|f(z)| \leqslant M$ on the sides of the angle, then either $|f(z)| \leqslant M$ inside the angle or

$$\ln \max_{|z|=\varrho} |f(z)| > c^{\alpha} \varrho^{\alpha} (\varrho > \varrho_0)$$

for some $c<0$.

Indeed, for an angle of magnitude π/α we have $s(\varrho) = \pi\varrho/\alpha$ and $\sigma(\varrho) = \varrho^{\alpha}$, so that Theorem 6.1 immediately gives us the desired result. The example of the function $e^{cz^{\alpha}}$ in the angular sector $|\arg z| < \pi/2\alpha$ shows that it is impossible to strengthen the result significantly.

The following theorem relates to the problem of the admissible rate of approach to zero for a function $f(z)$ regular in some domain as the point z approaches a boundary point of this domain. We discussed this problem somewhat in the preceding section in connection with Theorem 5.1. We now give the result proved in that theorem a more intuitive form, although at the cost of some simplifying restrictions; however, in return we are able to extend it to arbitrary domains.

Let us begin with a simplified formulation of Theorem 5.1:

Let the function $f(z)$ be regular in the circle $|z|<1$ and continuous in the circle $|z| \leqslant 1$. If

$$\int_0^{2\pi} \ln |f(e^{i\varphi})| \, d\varphi = -\infty,$$

then $f(z) \equiv 0$.

This statement is actually a simple corollary of Theorem 5.1, since $f(z)$ is bounded (and therefore of bounded mode) in the circle $|z| < 1$, so that it follows obviously from the continuity of $f(z)$ in the circle $|z| \leqslant 1$ that

$$\lim_{\varrho \to 1} \int_0^{2\pi} \ln |f(\varrho e^{i\varphi})| \, d\varphi = \int_0^{2\pi} \ln |f(e^{i\varphi})| \, d\varphi = -\infty.$$

This result can be carried over immediately to other domains with the aid of conformal mapping. We next prove an analogous result for half-planes by first giving the theorem a still simpler and more convenient form.

Theorem 6.2. *Let the function f(z) be regular in the half-plane Re z>0, continuous in the half-plane Re z⩾0 and let f(z) satisfy the condition*

$$\ln|f(z)|<-\nu(|z|) \qquad (\mathrm{Re}\, z\geqslant 0),$$

where $\nu(t)$ is a positive continuous function for $t\geqslant 0$. If

$$\int_1^\infty \frac{\nu(t)}{t^2}\,dt=+\infty,$$

then $f(z)\equiv 0$.

Proof. The function $z=\frac{1+w}{1-w}$ maps the circle $|w|<1$ conformally onto the half-plane $\mathrm{Re}\, z>0$. Therefore, the function $F(w)=f\left(\frac{1+w}{1-w}\right)$ is regular in the circle $|w|<1$ and continuous for $|w|\leqslant 1$. We have

$$\int_0^{2\pi} \ln|F(e^{i\varphi})|\,d\varphi=\int_{-\pi}^{\pi} \ln\left|f\left(\frac{1+e^{i\varphi}}{1-e^{i\varphi}}\right)\right|d\varphi<-2\int_0^{\pi} \nu\left(\cot\frac{\varphi}{2}\right)d\varphi.$$

However,

$$\int_0^{\pi} \nu\left(\cot\frac{\varphi}{2}\right)d\varphi=2\int_0^{\frac{\pi}{2}} \nu(\mathrm{tg}\,\theta)\,d\theta=$$

$$=2\int_0^\infty \frac{\nu(t)\,dt}{1+t^2}\geqslant 2\int_1^\infty \frac{\nu(t)\,dt}{1+t^2}\geqslant 4\int_1^\infty \frac{\nu(t)}{t^2}\,dt=+\infty.$$

According to Theorem 5.1, we have $F(w)\equiv 0$, which means that $f(z)\equiv 0$. This completes the proof.

The following theorem can be proved analogously.

Theorem 6.3. *Let the function f(z) be regular in the strip $|\mathrm{Im}\, z|<\pi/2$, continuous in the strip $|\mathrm{Im}\, z|\leqslant\pi/2$ and let f(z) satisfy the inequality*

$$\ln|f(x+iy)|<-\nu(x) \qquad \left(-\frac{\pi}{2}<y<\frac{\pi}{2}\right),$$

where $\nu(x)$ is a poistive continuous function. If

$$\int_0^\infty \nu(x)\,e^{-x}\,dx=+\infty, \quad mo\ f(z)\equiv 0.$$

Using Warschawskiy's inequality (see Theorem 6.2 of Chap. V), we can obtain a similar result for more or less arbitrary strip regions. In fact:

Let D be the domain defined by the inequalities

$$\varphi(x)-\frac{1}{2}\theta(x)<y<\varphi(x)+\frac{1}{2}\theta(x) \qquad (-\infty<x<\infty),$$

where $\varphi(x)$ and $\theta(x)$ are continuously differentiable functions, for which we assume that

$$|\varphi'(x)|<M, \quad |\theta'(x)|<M, \qquad \int_0^\infty \frac{\theta'^2(x)}{\theta(x)}\,dx<+\infty.$$

Theorem 6.4. *Let the function $f(z)$ be regular in domain D, continuous in $\bar{D}$ and satisfy the inequality*

$$\ln|f(x+iy)|<-\nu(x) \qquad (x+iy\in D),$$

where $\nu(x)$ is a positive continuous function. We set

$$\sigma(x)=\pi\int_0^x \frac{1+\varphi'^2(t)}{\theta(t)}\,dt.$$

If

$$\int_0^\infty \nu(x)\,e^{-\sigma(x)}\frac{dx}{\theta(x)}=+\infty,$$

then $f(z)\equiv 0$.

Proof. Let $w(z)$ denote the function that maps the domain D conformally onto the strip $|\operatorname{Im} w|<\pi/2$ in such a way that $\operatorname{Re} w\to\pm\infty$ as $\operatorname{Re} z\to\pm\infty$. Warschawskiy's inequality (see Theorem 6.2, Chap. V) is satisfied under the hypotheses made concerning $\varphi(x)$ and $\theta(x)$. In our notation this inequality takes the form

$$\operatorname{Re} w(x+iy)-\operatorname{Re} w(a+b)<\sigma(x)-\sigma(a)+C' \qquad (x>a)$$

(the constant C' does not depend on x, y, a, b). Setting $a=0$, $C=C'+\sup_b \operatorname{Re} w(ib)$, we reduce this inequality to the form

$$\operatorname{Re} w(x+iy)<\sigma(x)+C \qquad (x>0). \tag{6.3}$$

Let $z(w)$ denote the inverse to $w(z)$ and set

$$x(u)=\min \operatorname{Re} z(w) \qquad \left(\operatorname{Re} w=u,\ |\operatorname{Im} w|\leq\frac{\pi}{2}\right).$$

Taking for w in inequality (6.3) the value for which $\operatorname{Re} w = u$, $\operatorname{Re} z(w) = x(u)$, we obtain

$$u < \sigma(x(u)) + C. \tag{6.4}$$

We now consider the function $F(w) = f(z(w))$ in the strip $|\operatorname{Im} w| < \pi/2$. It is regular in this strip and continuous in the closed strip. Moreover, it satisfies the inequality

$$\ln|F(u+iv)| = \ln|f(z(u+iv))| < -\nu(x(u)),$$

since $\nu(x)$ is a nondecreasing function. It follows from inequality (6.4) that $x(u) < k(u-c)$, where $k(u)$ is the inverse to $\sigma(x)$ (it is clear that $k(u)$ is a nondecreasing function and that $k(u) \to +\infty$ as $u \to +\infty$). Thus,

$$\ln|F(u+iv)| < -\nu(k(u-c))$$

and

$$e^c \int_c^{\infty} \nu(k(u-c))\, e^{-u}\, du =$$

$$= \int_0^{\infty} \nu(x)\, e^{-\sigma(x)} \sigma'(x)\, dx > \int_0^{\infty} \nu(x)\, e^{-\sigma(x)} \frac{dx}{\theta(x)} = +\infty.$$

According to Theorem 6.3, we have $F(w) \equiv 0$, which means that $f(z) \equiv 0$. This proves the theorem.

We have presented the strongest possible statements of two of the types of theorems, usually called the Phragmen-Lindelöf theorems. These theorems do not exhaust the entire class of Phragmen-Lindelöf theorems used in applications.*

---

*Many theorems of this type are presented in the book by M. A. Evgrafov, Asymptotic Estimates and Entire Functions, Gordon & Breach, N.Y., 1962.

CHAPTER IX

Conformal Mappings of Multiply Connected Domains

Until now we have spoken only of one-to-one conformal mappings, while the theorems on the existence of the mappings and on corresponding boundaries were left without proof. The fact is that the theorems on the existence of mappings turn out to be more complete if we consider mappings of domains by analytic (in general, multiple-valued) functions. Such mappings have a direct connection with many other problems that we solved for simply connected domains with the help of conformal mappings. For example, with their help we can solve the Dirichlet problem for multiply connected domains. Several algebraic problems arise in a natural way in the study of mappings of multiply connected domains by functions analytic in these domains, since a so-called automorphism group is connected with each such mapping. At the end of the chapter we introduce modular functions and briefly discuss the simpler problems of the theory of elliptic and automorphic functions.

1. THE EXISTENCE OF CONFORMAL MAPPINGS

At the end of Sect. 1, Chap. V, we formulated Riemann's theorem on the existence of conformal mappings of simply connected domains into the circle. We left the theorem without proof, since we are now going to prove a more general theorem (due, in a somewhat different formulation, to Poincaré) on the existence of conformal mappings.

We discuss now mappings of a domain D by functions that are not necessarily regular, but are analytic in this domain. In the case in which the domain is simply connected, there is no distinction between such mappings, since according to the monodromy theorem, a function analytic in a simply connected domain is regular in this domain. For multiply connected domains the distinction between these types of mappings is rather great, since functions that are analytic in a multiply connected domain are, in general, multiple-valued there.

We must supplement somewhat our basic information about mappings, as presented in Sect. 1, Chap. V.

Let $f(z)$ be a function analytic in a domain D. By *the image of domain D under the mapping* $w=f(z)$ we mean the totality of values assumed in the domain D by all elements of the function $f(z)$, analytic in the domain D. We denote the image of D by $f(D)$.

Suppose that we are given $w_0 \in f(D)$ and let $f_1(z), \ldots, f_s(z)$ be all those elements of the function $f(z)$ that are analytic in domain D, that are defined in neighborhoods of the points $z_1 \in D, \ldots, z_s \in D$, respectively, and for which $f_k(z_k) = w_0$. (Among the points z_k the same point may appear more than once if the corresponding elements are not identical.) If ν_k is the multiplicity of the root of $f_k(z) - w_0$ at the point z_k and $\nu_1 + \nu_2 + \ldots + \nu_s = m$, then we shall say that *the value* w_0 *is assumed by the function* $f(z)$ *exactly* m *times in domain D.*

If each value $w \in f(D)$ is assumed by the function $f(z)$ analytic in domain D exactly once, then we shall say that the function $f(z)$ is *univalent in domain D.*

We now list the most important properties of mappings by analytic functions and the properties of univalent analytic functions.

Property 1. Let the set G consist of the values w assumed not more than m times by the function f(z) in the domain D. Then G is an open set. In particular, the image of a domain is a domain.

Property 2. Let the function f(z) be analytic and univalent in the domain D, and let the function g(z) be analytic and univalent in the domain f(D). Then the function g(f(z)) is analytic and univalent in domain D.

Property 3. It is necessary and sufficient for the univalency of the function f(z) analytic in the domain D that there exist in the domain f(D) a function $\varphi(w)$ *inverse to f(z), i.e., such that* $\varphi(f(z)) \equiv z$.

All the properties listed are proved in a way completely analogous to that for the corresponding properties of regular functions (see Sect. 1, Chap. V).

Let us say a few words about the covergence of sequences of functions analytic in a domain.

Suppose that we are given a sequence of functions $\{f_n(z)\}$, $n = 1, 2, \ldots$, analytic in a domain D, and suppose that $\varphi_n(z)$ are the initial elements of these functions defined in a neighborhood of the point $z_0 \in D$. Suppose, in addition, that L is any curve issuing from the point z_0 and contained in domain D, and that $\varphi_n(z, L)$ is a regular function on the curve L obtained by analytic continuation of the element $\varphi_n(z)$ along the curve L. We shall say that *the sequence* $f_n(z)$ *converges uniformly within the domain D,* if for some choice of curve L the sequence $\{\varphi_n(z, L)\}$ converges uniformly along this curve.

We next enumerate the properties we need of uniformly convergent sequences of analytic functions.

Property 1. The limit of a sequence of functions analytic in D that converges uniformly in D is a function analytic in D.

Property 2. If $\{f_n(z)\}$ is a sequence of functions analytic in a domain D

$$|f_n(z)| \leqslant M \qquad (z \in D)$$

(the constant M is not to depend on n nor on the choice of the element), then it is possible to choose a uniformly convergent subsequence from the sequence $\{f_n(z)\}$.

Property 3. Let $\{f_n(z)\}$ be a sequence of functions analytic in D and uniformly convergent to the nonconstant function F(z). If each of the functions $f_n(z)$ does not assume any value more than m times, then the function F(z) has the same property.

In particular:

The limit of a sequence of analytic, univalent functions uniformly convergent in D is also an analytic, univalent function or is a constant.

Properties 1 and 2 are proved by following the patterns of the corresponding theorem for regular functions. To illustrate these patterns we prove Property 2.

We pick a point $z_0 \in D$ and a sequence $\{\varphi_n(z)\}$ of initial elements of the functions $f_n(z)$. The functions $\varphi_n(z)$ are bounded in a neighborhood of the point z_0. According to the compactness principle for regular functions (see Theorem 4.6, Chap. II), we can choose from the sequence $\{\varphi_n(z)\}$ a subsequence that converges uniformly in the chosen neighborhood of z_0. Next, we choose some curve L and a point z_1 on it, so close to z_0 that the functions $\varphi_n(z, L)$ are regular in a neighborhood of the point z_1 that has a nontrivial intersection with the neighborhood of z_0. We show that the subsequence $\{\varphi_{n_k}(z, L)\}$ we have chosen also converges uniformly in the neighborhood of the point z_1. According to the compactness principle, we can choose from this subsequence a subsequence that converges uniformly in the given neighborhood of the point z_1. However, the limit of this subsequence must coincide with the limit of the sequence $\{\varphi_{n_k}(z)\}$ in the common part of the neighborhoods of the points z_0 and z_1. This means that the limits of all subsequences of the sequence $\{\varphi_{n_k}(z, L)\}$ must be the same. Hence $\{\varphi_{n_k}(z, L)\}$ converges in a neighborhood of z_1.

After this we choose a point $z_2 \in L$ etc.; proceeding in this way we may verify that the sequence $\{\varphi_{n_k}(z, L)\}$ converges uniformly on the whole curve. Since the choice of the subsequence n_k does not depend on the choice of the curve L, it follows that the subsequence $\{f_{n_k}(z)\}$ converges uniformly in D.

The proof of the last property is even simpler. Let $F_1(z), \ldots, F_s(z)$ be those elements of the limit function of the sequence $\{f_n(z)\}$ for which $F_k(z) - w$ has a zero at the point $z = z_k$. Applying Theorem 6.3, Chap. IV, to each of these elements, we obtain the desired statement.

If the function $f(z)$ is analytic and univalent in a domain D, we say that it effects a *conformal mapping of the domain D onto the domain* $f(D)$.

If the domain D is simply connected, then our new concept of conformal mapping coincides with the old one, since according to the monodromy theorem, the function $f(z)$ is regular in D. However, if the domain D is multiply connected, this concept differs from the old one. When we discuss mappings of multiply connected domains by regular univalent functions, we shall stress this by employing the term: *one-to-one conformal mapping.*

We now present some simple examples of conformal mappings of multiply connected domains.

Example 1. Let us consider the mapping of the annulus $r<|z|<R$ by the function $w=\ln z$, which is analytic in this domain.

Note first of all that the function $\ln z$ is univalent in this domain, since it has an inverse $z=e^w$ which is regular in the entire plane. Thus, the mapping $w=\ln z$ is a conformal mapping and we have only to find the image of the annulus.

We introduce the cross cut $(-R, -r)$ into the annulus. The function $\ln z$ admits a division into regular branches in the annulus with cross cut. Let us study where each of the regular branches of $\ln z$ maps the the annulus with cross cut. Recalling the mappings effected by the elementary functions, we see that the image of the annulus with cross cut is the rectangle

$$\ln r<\operatorname{Re} w<\ln R, \quad -\pi+2\pi k<\operatorname{Im} w<\pi+2\pi k,$$

where the integer k is determined by the choice of the regular branch of $\ln z$. The totality of all these rectangles, supplemented by the images of the cross cut, is the strip $\ln r<\operatorname{Re} w<\ln R$, which is therefore the image of the annulus under the mapping $w=\ln z$.

Note that the image under conformal mapping of a doubly connected domain—the annulus—is a simply connected domain—the strip. That this is possible is due to the fact that the conformal mapping by the analytic function is not one-to-one. Our conformal mapping may be considered as a one-to-one mapping on the strip of the part of the Riemann surface of the logarithm lying above the annulus; this is a simply connected domain.

Example 2. We find a conformal mapping of the circle $|z|<1$, with the point a, $0<|a|<1$, deleted, onto the circle $|w|<1$, whereby the point 0 is sent into the point 0.

First, using a linear fractional transformation, we send the circle $|z|<1$ with deleted point a into the circle $|\zeta|<1$ with deleted center, i.e., into the annulus $0<|\zeta|<1$. This is done with the aid of the function

$$\zeta=\frac{a-z}{1-z\bar{a}}.$$

We next make use of the result of the preceding example, and with the help of the function $t=\ln \zeta$ we map the annulus $0<|\zeta|<1$ conformally onto the strip, which in our case degenerates into the half-plane $\operatorname{Re} t<0$. We now determine into what point of this half-plane the point 0 is sent. Since $t(z)=\ln\frac{a-z}{1-z\bar{a}}$, then $t(0)=\ln a$, where any determination may be taken for $\ln a$.

To obtain the desired mapping we still have to use the linear fractional transformation to map the half-plane Re $t<0$ into the circle $|w|<1$ and to send the point $t=\ln a$ into the point $w=0$. This is done with the help of the function $w=\frac{t-t(0)}{t+t(0)}$. The overall mapping has the form

$$w=w(z)=\frac{\ln\frac{a-z}{1-z\bar{a}}-\ln a}{\ln\frac{a-z}{1-z\bar{a}}+\ln a}.$$

Finally, we find $w'(0)$ for that element of the mapping function $w(z)$ for which $w(0)=0$. We have

$$w'(0)=\frac{1-|a|^2}{a}\cdot\frac{1}{2\ln|a|}.$$

It is easy to check that

$$|w'(0)|>1 \qquad (0<|a|<1).$$

We now turn to the basic aim of the present section—the existence theorem for conformal mappings. We first prove a somewhat weaker form of the theorem.

Theorem 1.1. *Any domain (of the complex plane) having at least one exterior point can be mapped conformally onto the unit circle.*

Proof. We can assume without loss of generality that the point $z=0$ is an interior point and that the point $z=\infty$ is an exterior point of the domain, since we can always achieve this by means of a linear fractional transformation.

We shall construct the function $\varphi(z)$ conformally mapping our domain (we denote it by D) onto the circle $|w|<1$ as the solution of the following extremal problem.

We find among the functions analytic and univalent in domain D and satisfying the conditions

$$f(0)=0, \quad |f(z)|\leqslant 1 \quad (z\in D) \tag{1.1}$$

(the first condition relates to the initial element of the function, the second—to all of them) the one for which the value of $|f'(0)|$ (for the initial element) is the greatest.

For the sake of convenience, we denote by $S(D)$ the set of those functions among which we seek the extremal.

We have to prove two properties:

1) There exists an extremal function in the set $S(D)$.

2) The extremal function effects the desired mappings.

We begin with the proof of statement 1.

Note first of all that the set $S(D)$ is not empty, for D is a bounded domain, so that the function $f(z)=cz$ belongs to $S(D)$ for sufficiently small c. (Recall that $z=\infty$ is an exterior point of D.)

Second, note that the value of $|f'(0)|$ is bounded for the set of functions $S(D)$. Indeed, the domain D contains some circle $|z| \leqslant \varrho$ (the point $z=0$ is an interior point of D). The initial element of any function $f(z) \in S(D)$ is a function regular in this circle. Therefore,

$$f'(0) = \frac{1}{2\pi i} \int_{|z|=\varrho} \frac{f(z)}{z^2}\, dz.$$

Taking moduli and recalling that $|f(z)| \leqslant 1$ for $f(z) \in S(D)$, we obtain $|f'(0)| \leqslant \frac{1}{\varrho}$. We now set

$$\mu = \sup_{f \in S(D)} |f'(0)|.$$

According to the definition of least upper bound, there exists a sequence

$$f_n(z) \in S(D), \quad |f_n'(0)| > \mu - \frac{1}{n} \qquad (n = 1, 2, \ldots).$$

Since $|f_n(z)| \leqslant 1$ $(z \in D)$, according to Property 2 of sequences of analytic functions, we can choose from the sequence $\{f_n(z)\}$ a convergent subsequence. We denote the limit of this subsequence by $\varphi(z)$. According to Property 3, we have $\varphi(z) \in S(D)$, since $|\varphi'(0)| \geqslant \mu$, which means that $\varphi(z)$ is not a constant. Thus,

$$\varphi(z) \in S(D), \quad |\varphi'(0)| = \mu,$$

i.e., the function constructed, $\varphi(z)$, is extremal.

Let us now turn to the proof of statement 2.

Since the extremal function $\varphi(z)$ is univalent and analytic in domain D, it effects a conformal mapping of the domain D onto the domain $\varphi(D)$. In view of the condition $|\varphi(z)| \leqslant 1$ $(z \in D)$, the domain $\varphi(D)$ is contained in the circle $|w| < 1$. We show that it follows from the extremal property of the function $\varphi(z)$ that the domain $\varphi(D)$ coincides with the circle $|w| < 1$.

Indeed, let us assume the opposite. Then the domain $\varphi(D)$ has at least one boundary point a contained in the circle $|w| < 1$.

Consider the function $f(z) = w(\varphi(z))$, where $w(z)$ is the function of Example 2 that maps the circle $|z| < 1$ with deleted point a conformally onto the circle $|w| < 1$ and where $w(0) = 0$. According to Property 2 of univalent functions, $f(z)$ is analytic and univalent in D. Moreover, it satisfies condition (1.1), so that $f(z) \in S(D)$. However,

$$f'(0) = w'(0) \cdot \varphi'(0), \qquad |f'(0)| = |\varphi'(0)| \cdot |w'(0)|,$$

and we have already seen that $|w'(0)| > 1$. This means that $|f'(0)| > |\varphi'(0)|$, which contradicts the result that $\varphi(z)$ is an extremal function. This contradiction proves that $\varphi(D)$ coincides with the circle $|w| < 1$ and completes the proof.

The complete formulation of the existence theorem on conformal mappings reads as follows:

Theorem 1.1*. *Any domain (of the complex plane) having more than two boundary points can be mapped conformally onto the unit circle.*

For the proof of this theorem it is sufficient to construct a function that maps the extended complex plane with three deleted points conformally onto the unit circle. Indeed, once such a function $\zeta(z; a, b, c)$ is constructed (here a, b, c are the deleted points), then we can map any domain D whose boundary contains the points a, b, c into the domain D' contained in the circle $|\zeta| < 1$ by using the function $\zeta = \zeta(z;\ a,\ b,\ c)$. We then map the domain D' onto the circle $|w| < 1$ by using Theorem 1.1, thus obtaining the desired mapping of domain D. The construction of the function $\zeta(z; a, b, c)$ mapping the plane with three deleted points conformally onto the unit circle is a rather complicated problem. We devote Sect. 5 to its construction.

We next note that Theorem 1.1* cannot be strengthened further. Two boundary points is insufficient to ensure the possibility of mapping the domain conformally onto the unit circle (this follows from Theorem 2.4 of Chap. IV). The plane with two points a and b deleted, can be mapped conformally onto the entire finite plane by means of the function $w = \ln \frac{z-a}{z-b}$ (see Example 1).

We still have to resolve the question of uniqueness of the conformal mapping.

Theorem 1.2. *Let* a *be any point of the domain D, and let* θ *be any real number. There exists a unique function* $w(z)$ *that maps the domain* D *conformally onto the circle* $|w| < 1$ *and satisfies the conditions* $w(a) = 0$, *arg* $w'(a) = \theta$ *(for the initial element).*

Proof. Let $w_1(z)$ be a second function satisfying the same conditions. Let $z(w)$ denote the inverse to $w(z)$ and consider the function $g(w) = w_1(z(w))$. The function $g(w)$ is analytic and, according to the monodromy theorem, it is regular in the circle $|w| < 1$ (we choose a branch of the analytic function obtained by analytic continuation of the initial element).

It is clear that the function $g(w)$ satisfies the inequality

$$|g(w)| \leqslant 1 \qquad (|w| < 1).$$

Moreover, $g(0) = 0$ and

$$g'(0) = w_1'(a) \cdot z'(0) = \frac{w_1'(a)}{w'(a)}, \qquad \arg g'(0) = 0.$$

We can assume without loss of generality that $|w'(a)| \leqslant |w_1'(a)|$, since otherwise we could interchange the roles of $w(z)$ and $w_1(z)$. Consequently, the function $g(w)$ is regular in the circle $|w| < 1$ and satisfies the conditions

$$|g(w)| \leqslant 1 \quad (|w| < 1), \qquad g(0) = 0, \qquad |g'(0)| \geqslant 1.$$

Consider the function $\psi(w)=\frac{g(w)}{w}$. It is regular for $|w|<1$, since $g(0)=0$ and $\psi(0)=g'(0)\geqslant 1$. On the other hand, $\overline{\lim\limits_{|w|\to 1}}|\psi(w)|=\overline{\lim\limits_{|w|\to 1}}|g(w)|\leqslant 1$. According to the maximum modulus principle for analytic functions (see Sect. 2, Chap. VIII), this is possible only in the case that $|\psi(w)|\equiv 1$. This in turn is possible only if $\psi(w)\equiv e^{i\alpha}$, and since $\arg\psi(0)=0$, we obtain $\psi(w)\equiv 1$ and $g(w)\equiv w$. Thus, $w_1(z)\equiv w(z)$, which proves the theorem.

Corollary. Let $w_1(z)$ and $w_2(z)$ be initial elements of two functions analytic in a domain D and let them map the domain D conformally onto the circle $|w|<1$ (we assume that these elements are defined in a neighborhood of a given point). Then $w_2(z)=T(w_1(z))$, where $T(w)$ is a linear fractional transformation sending the circle $|w|<1$ into itself.

In fact, the function $w_1(z_2(w))=T(w)$, where $z_2(w)$ is the inverse to $w_2(z)$, effects a conformal mapping of the circle $|w|<1$ onto itself. Since we have already proved Riemann's theorem, we can apply Theorem 2.2, Chap. V, which gives us the desired result.

2. CORRESPONDING BOUNDARIES UNDER CONFORMAL MAPPINGS

Before we can discuss problems related to specific conformal mappings of multiply connected domains by analytic functions, we still have to repay an old debt. Namely, we still have to prove the theorem of corresponding boundaries, which was formulated at the end of Sect. 1, Chap. V.

We first recall the notion of accessible boundary point, which we first introduced in Sect. 1, Chap. IV.

Let D be any bounded domain, and let L be a simple curve contained in D except for its endpoint ζ, which lies on the boundary of D. The pair (ζ, L) determines an *accessible boundary point of domain D*.

Here it is assumed that (ζ, L) and (ζ, L') determine the same accessible boundary point, if the parts of the curves L and L' contained in some neighborhood of the point ζ lie in the same connected component of the intersection of this neighborhood with domain D.

It was already mentioned that for domains bounded by piecewise-smooth curves the notions of accessible boundary point and boundary point coincide, i.e., each point of the boundary of D corresponds to at least one accessible boundary point. In the case of arbitrary points, boundary points that are not accessible boundary points may exist. Let us consider an example.

Let the domain D be the square

$$0<\operatorname{Re} z<2,\ |\operatorname{Im} z|<1,$$

with cross cuts along the vertical segments $\left(\frac{1}{n},\ \frac{1}{n}+i\right)$ $n=1, 2, \ldots.$

Each point of each cross cut (in addition to its free endpoints) corresponds to two accessible boundary points of the domain. Each point of the segment $(0, i)$ corresponds to no accessible boundary point. All remaining boundary points correspond to one accessible boundary point.

We find it more convenient to use a somewhat different definition of accessible boundary point. We define it not in terms of the curves leading up to it, but rather in terms of the connected components of the neighborhoods in which these curves lie. (The difference between these definitions is roughly the same as that between Heine's and Cauchy's definitions of continuity at a point.)

Let ζ be a boundary point of domain D and let $P(\zeta, \varrho), 0<\varrho<\infty$ be a system of domains having the following properties:

1. the domain $P(\zeta, \varrho)$ is a connected subdomain of the intersection of the circle $|z-\zeta|<\varrho$ with the domain D;
2. for any $\varrho>0$ the domain $P(\zeta, \varrho)$ is not empty and has the point ζ as one of its boundary points;
3. for $\varrho'>\varrho$ the domain $P(\zeta, \varrho)$ is contained in the domain $P(\zeta, \varrho')$.

Each system of domains $P(\zeta, \varrho)$ determines a unique accessible boundary point of domain D.

We leave it to the reader to verify the equivalence of these definitions.

It is easy to define the notion of limit of a function at an accessible boundary point with the aid of this new definition.

We shall say that the function $F(z)$, defined in the domain D, *has the limit A as z approaches the accessible boundary point determined by the system* $P(\zeta, \varrho)$, if for any $\varepsilon>0$ we can find a $\delta>0$ such that $|F(z)-A|<\varepsilon$ for $z \in P(\zeta, \delta)$.

The following lemma, similar in content to the uniqueness Theorem 5.1 of Chap. VIII plays a fundamental role in the proof of the corresponding boundaries theorem.

Lemma 1. Let the function $f(z)$ be regular and bounded in the finite simply connected domain D, and let ζ be any boundary point of the domain D. If we have $f(z) \to 0$ as z approaches any boundary point of the domain D contained in the circle $|z-\zeta| \leq r$, then $f(z) \equiv 0$.

Proof. Let D' be any connected component of the intersection of the domain D with the circle $|z-\zeta|<r$, and let Γ be the part of the boundary of D' that is not part of the boundary of D (i.e., that consists of an arc of the circle $|z-\zeta|=r$). It is clear that D' is a simply connected domain having the point ζ as either a boundary or an exterior point (see Fig. 8). The function $f(z)$ is continuous in $\overline{D}'$ if we assume that it is equal to zero on the part of the boundary of D' left after deleting Γ.

Since the domain D' is simply connected and does not contain the point ζ, then the function $w=\sqrt{z-\zeta}$ is regular in D'. Let G denote the image of D' under the mapping $w=\sqrt{z-\zeta}$, and let γ be the image of Γ. The domain G is contained in the circle $|w|<\sqrt{r}$, and γ is part of the circumference $|w|=\sqrt{r}$. Note that at least half of the circumference $|w|=\sqrt{r}$ contains no points of γ, since under the mapping $w=\sqrt{z-\zeta}$ every circumference $|z-\zeta|=r$ goes into a half of the circumference $|w|=\sqrt{r}$.

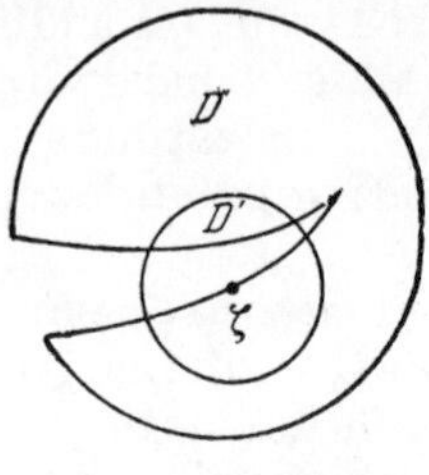

FIG. 8.

Let us consider the function $g(w)=f(\zeta+w^2)$ in domain G. The function $z=\zeta+w^2$, the inverse to $w=\sqrt{z-\zeta}$, maps the domain G conformally onto the domain D'. Thus, the function $g(w)$ is regular in G, continuous in $\overline{G}$ and equal to zero on the part of the boundary of G that is distinct from γ.

According to the maximum principle for subharmonic functions, the function $u(w)=\ln|g(w)|$ does not exceed any given harmonic function in domain G if it does not exceed it on the boundary of G. Moreover, since we have $u(w)=-\infty$ on the part of the boundary of G which is distinct from γ, then this part of the boundary of G does not come into consideration. Thus, the function $u(w)$ does not exceed the function $u_\varepsilon(w)$ harmonic in the circle $|w|<\sqrt{r}$ and defined by means of the following boundary values on the circumference $|w|=\sqrt{r}$.

We set $u_\varepsilon(w)=\ln\varepsilon$, on that half of the circle $|w|=\sqrt{r}$ on which there are no points of γ, on the remaining part we put $u_\varepsilon(w)=\ln M$, where $M=\max_{w\in\gamma}|g(w)|$.

Thus, for any $\varepsilon>0$ we have the inequality $u(w)\leqslant u_\varepsilon(w)(w\in G)$. It is not difficult to give the function $u_\varepsilon(w)$ in closed from, but it is still simpler to note that $u_\varepsilon(w)\to-\infty$ as $\varepsilon\to 0$ for any fixed $w\in G$. Hence, $u(w)\equiv-\infty$, so that $g(w)\equiv 0$ and $f(z)\equiv 0$. This proves the lemma.

Theorem 2.1. *Let D be a finite simply connected domain, let* $\varphi(z)$ *be a function mapping the domain D comformally onto the domain G bounded by the simple closed curve C. As the point z approaches any accessible boundary point of the domain D, the point* $w=\varphi(z)$ *approaches some point of curve C, and, moreover, distinct limits correspond to distinct accessible boundary points.*

Proof. We choose a system $P(\zeta,\varrho)$ determining an accessible boundary point of the domain D and denote by $Q(\zeta,\varrho)$ the image of $P(\zeta,\varrho)$ under the mapping $w=\varphi(z)$. The domain $Q(\zeta,\varrho)$ is contained in the domain G and $Q(\zeta,\varrho)\subset Q(\zeta,\varrho')$ for $\varrho<\varrho'$. Let E denote the intersection of all closed domains $Q(\zeta,\varrho)$, $\varrho>0$. The set E is the union of all limit points of the function $\varphi(z)$ as the point z approaches a given accessible boundary point. Since the mapping $w=\varphi(z)$ is one-to-one, then the set of all limit points of $\varphi(z)$ as z approaches any one of the points of the boundary of D coincides with the curve C. Thus, the set E is part of the curve C. Moreover, all the sets $Q(\zeta,\varrho)$ are connected closed sets, so that their intersections with the set E are also connected closed sets. A connected closed part of the circle C

can be either an arc of this circle or a point. The statement of the theorem says that E is a point of the curve C. To prove this we consider the function $\psi(w)$, inverse to the function $\varphi(z)$, in the domain G. It maps the domain $Q(\zeta, \varrho)$ onto the domain $P(\zeta, \varrho)$, so that for $w \in Q(\zeta, \varrho)$ we have $\psi(w) \in P(\zeta, \varrho)$, i.e., $|\psi(w) - \zeta| < \varrho$. If the set E is an arc of the curve C, then all domains $Q(\zeta, \varrho)$ have this arc in their boundary arc. This means that for any interior point w_0 of arc E we have

$$\psi(w) \longrightarrow \zeta \qquad (w \longrightarrow w_0, \; w \in G).$$

Applying Lemma 1 to the function $\psi(w) - \zeta$, we find $\psi(w) \equiv \zeta$, which is impossible. Thus, the set E is a point $w_0 \in C$ and the limit of the function $\varphi(z)$ as z approaches a given accessible boundary point exists and equals w_0.

We show now that the function $\varphi(z)$ has distinct limits at distinct accessible boundary points. Suppose that we have two distinct accessible boundary points of domain D. We construct a simple curve contained in D and having these points as endpoints. Let L denote this curve, and let Γ be its image under the mapping $w = \varphi(z)$. If the limits of the function $\varphi(z)$ at both accessible boundary points are the same, then Γ is a simple closed curve having only one point in common with the boundary of the domain G. Let G' denote the domain bounded by the curve Γ, and let D' be its preimage under the mapping $w = \varphi(z)$. The boundary of the domain D' consists of the curve L (the preimage of Γ) and of some part of the boundary of D, say, Δ. The set Δ is not empty, for the ends of the curve D determine distinct accessible boundary points of domain L. As z approaches any point of the set Δ, the function $\varphi(z)$ approaches w_0, where w_0 is the unique common point of the curve Γ and the boundary of the domain G. In the set Δ there is a boundary point of D' that, together with one of its neighborhoods, is contained in D'. Applying Lemma 1, we find $\varphi(z) \equiv w_0$, which is impossible. This contradiction proves that the function $\varphi(z)$ must have distinct limits at distinct accessible boundary points. This completes the proof.

Corollary. Let domains D and G be bounded by piecewise-smooth curves, and let $\varphi(z)$ be a function mapping the domain D conformally onto the domain G. Then the function $\varphi(z)$ is continuous up to the boundary of D.

We can assume without loss of generality that the domains D and G are bounded by simple piecewise-smooth curves, for otherwise we can divide D and G into finitely many parts of this type. For domains bounded by simple curves the boundary points are in one-to-one correspondence with the accessible boundary points. According to Theorem 2.1, the function $\varphi(z)$ has a limit at each point of the boundary. This means that the function $\varphi(z)$ is continuous in $\bar{D}$. Our assertion follows from this.

For continuity of the mapping function up to the boundary of the domain we require only that the domain to be mapped be bounded by continuous curves. This result can also be deduced from Theorem 2.1 in approximately the same way; however, for this there are required some rather delicate results from the theory of sets*). We can obtain some information on the smoothness of the mapping function from the smoothness conditions imposed on the boundary curves. We now proceed to prove a theorem of this type. It is based on the following lemma.

Lemma 2. Let the function $w(z)$ map the circle $|z|<1$ conformally onto domain D, which is bounded by the smooth curve C. If $h(\theta)$ is the continuous function equal to the angle between the tangent to the curve C at the point $w(e^{i\theta})$ and the positive x-axis, for each θ, $0\leqslant\theta<2$, then

$$\ln w'(z)=\frac{i}{2\pi}\int_0^{2\pi}\frac{e^{i\theta}+z}{e^{i\theta}-z}\left[h(\theta)-\theta-\frac{\pi}{2}\right]d\theta+C \qquad (2.1)$$

(the choices of the branch of $\ln w'(z)$ and of the function $h(\theta)$ are subject to the same degree of arbitrariness).

Proof. Consider the function

$$g_\varepsilon(z)=\ln\frac{w(ze^{i\varepsilon})-w(z)}{ze^{i\varepsilon}-z}\qquad(\varepsilon>0).$$

This function is regular in the circle $|z|<1$, since in view of the univalence of the function $w(z)$ the numerator and denominator of the fraction always vanish simultaneously. It follows from the corollary to Theorem 2.1 that the function $g_\varepsilon(z)$ is continuous in the circle $|z|\leqslant 1$ for any $\varepsilon>0$. Consequently, it can be generated by the values of its imaginary part on the circumference $|z|=1$. (For this purpose we have to apply Schwarz's formula, Sect. 3 of Chap. VIII, to the function $\frac{1}{i}g_\varepsilon(z)$.)

As $\varepsilon\to 0$, we have

$$g_\varepsilon(z)\to\ln w'(z)\qquad(|z|<1).$$

We next determine what happens to the imaginary part of the function $g_\varepsilon(z)$ as $\varepsilon\to 0$ on the circumference $|z|=1$. We have

$$\operatorname{Im} g_\varepsilon(e^{i\theta})=\arg\{w(e^{i(\theta+\varepsilon)})-w(e^{i\theta})\}-\arg(e^{i(\theta+\varepsilon)}-e^{i\theta}).$$

The first term of the right side is nothing but the angle of inclination of the chord of the curve C joining the points $w(e^{i(\theta+\varepsilon)})$ and $w(e^{i\theta})$. The second term is easy to compute. Its limit as $\varepsilon\to 0$ is $\frac{\pi}{2}+\theta$. The limit of the first term as $\varepsilon\to 0$ is the angle of inclination of the tangent to the curve C at the point $w(e^{i\theta})$, i.e., $h(\theta)$.

---

*) Some results and a detailed bibliography concerning these questions can be found in the book of G.M. Goluzin, Geometric Theory of the Functions of the Complex Variable (in Russian), Moscow, Gostekhizdat, 1952.

Since the passage to the limit is uniform in θ, it can be carried out under the integral sign. This means that the function $\ln w'(z)$ can be found in terms of the function $h(\theta)-\frac{\pi}{2}-\theta$ with the aid of the formula that recaptures a function regular in the circle $|z|<1$ in terms of the values of its imaginary part on the circumference $|z|=1$. This then gives us formula (2.1) and completes the proof.

Theorem 2.2. *Let the function $w(z)$ map the circle $|z|<1$ conformally onto the domain D, bounded by the smooth curve C, and let $z(w)$ be the function inverse to $w(z)$. Then the functions arg $w'(z)$ and arg $z'(w)$ are continuous respectively in the circle $|z|\leqslant 1$ and in the domain D.*

Proof. It follows from lemma that the function $\arg w'(z)$ is a solution to Dirichlet's problem in the circle $|z|<1$ with the boundary function $h(\theta)-\frac{\pi}{2}-\theta$. According to Theorem 3.2 of Chap. VIII, it follows from this that $\arg w'(z)$ is continuous. The continuity of the function $\arg z'(w)$ follows from the formula

$$\arg z'(w)=\arg\frac{1}{w'(z(w))}=-\arg w'(z(w))$$

and from the continuity of the function $z(w)$. This proves the theorem.

It is rather easy with the aid of formula (2.1) to obtain some theorems asserting the continuity of the functions ln $z'(w)$ and ln $w'(z)$ on the basis of some additional conditions on the curve C bounding domain D.

One of the most frequently applied results is the so-called *theorem of Kellog.*

Let the equation of curve C have the form $w=\varphi(s)$ (the parameter s is the arclength of curve C). If (*the function $\varphi(s)$ satisfies the condition*)

$$|\varphi'(s_1)-\varphi'(s_2)|<M|s_1-s_2|^\alpha \qquad (0<\alpha<1),$$

then the functions $w(z)$ and $z(w)$ satisfy the conditions

$$\left|\ln\frac{w'(z_1)}{w'(z_2)}\right|<M_1|z_1-z_2|^\alpha \qquad (|z_1|\leqslant 1,\ |z_2|\leqslant 1),$$

$$|w'(z_1)-w'(z_2)|<M_1|z_1-z_2|^\alpha \qquad (|z_1|\leqslant 1,\ |z_2|\leqslant 1),$$

$$\left|\ln\frac{z'(w_1)}{z'(w_2)}\right|\leqslant M_2|w_1-w_2|^\alpha \qquad (w_1\in\bar{D},\ w_2\in\bar{D}),$$

$$|z'(w_1)-z'(w_2)|\leqslant M_2|w_1-w_2|^\alpha \qquad (w_1\in\bar{D},\ w_2\in\bar{D}).$$

The proof of Kellog's theorem and other theorems of a similar nature can be found in the book already mentioned of G.M. Goluzin, Geometric Theory of Functions of the Complex Variable (in Russian). Moscow, Gostekhizdat, 1952).

---

*) Also see Warschawskiy's article: On differentiability at the boundary in conformal mapping, Proc. Amer. Math, Soc., Vol. 12, No. 4, pp. 614-620, where the most precise results of this type can be found.

We can use the same methods to investigate the behavior of the mapping function on the boundary of the domain when the entire boundary is not smooth, but when the particular arc of interest is smooth.

The behavior of the mapping function at vertices of angular domains, cusps etc., can be studied with the help of the inequalities of Ahlfors and Warschawskiy (see Sect. 6 of Chap. V).

3. THE AUTOMORPHISM GROUP OF A CONFORMAL MAPPING

We now introduce properties of conformal mappings by analytic functions displayed only in mappings of multiply connected domains. These properties are to be formulated with the aid of the notion of group.

A set α is called a *group*, if:

1. there is a multiplication that assigns to any two elements $A \in \alpha$ and $B \in \alpha$ a third element of α, their product AB;

2. the multiplication is associative:

$$(AB)\,C = A\,(BC);$$

3. there exists an identity element in α, i.e., an element I such that for any $A \in \alpha$ we have $AI = IA = A$;

4. for any element A of α there exists an inverse A^{-1}, i.e., an element $AA^{-1} \in \alpha$ such that $AA^{-1} = A^{-1}A = I$.

The set of nonsingular matrices of any given degree is an example of a group.

With a conformal mapping of any domain D onto the circle $|w| < 1$ we can associate a group consisting of the linear fractional transformations mapping the circle $|w| < 1$ into itself. We do this in the following way.

Let $\varphi(z)$ be some function mapping the domain D conformally onto the circle $|w| < 1$, and let $\varphi_0(z)$ be an element of this function defined in some neighborhood of the point $z_0 \in D$. We continue the element $\varphi_0(z)$ along some closed path continued in domain D. We thus obtain some other element $\varphi_1(z)$ of the function $\varphi(z)$. According to the corollary to Theorem 1.2, the initial elements of the two functions mapping the domain D conformally onto the circle $|w| < 1$ are connected by a linear fractional transformation taking the circle $|w| < 1$ into itself. This also holds for the other elements of the given mapping function. Therefore, $\varphi_1(z) = A(\varphi_0(z))$, where $A(w)$ is a linear fraction transformation taking the circle $|w| < 1$ into itself. The totality of all linear fractional transformations corresponding to analytic continuations of the initial element $\varphi_0(z)$ along all possible closed paths contained in D forms a group, if by the product AB we understand the composite transformation: $w \longrightarrow A(B(w))$.

We denote this group by $\gamma(D, \varphi)$ and call it the *automorphism group of the conformal mapping* $w = \varphi(z)$. (The group $\gamma(D, \varphi)$ is independent of the choice of $\varphi_0(z)$.)

The group $\gamma(D, \varphi)$ consists of a countable number of distinct transformations, since the number of distinct elements of an analytic function (at a given point) is countable.

We may also speak of the automorphism group of a conformal mapping of domain D onto any circle (or half-plane).

It is not difficult to observe that the group $\gamma(D, \varphi)$ reduces to the identity element for a simply connected domain D.

For the sake of simplicity, we shall write $\begin{pmatrix} a & b \\ c & d \end{pmatrix} w$ in place of $\frac{aw+b}{cw+d}$. We saw in Sect. 2 that if we connect a matrix A with a linear fractional transformation $A(w)$ in this way, then the matrix AB corresponds to the transformation $A(B(w))$ and the inverse matrix corresponds to the inverse transformation.

If we wish distinct matrices to correspond to distinct transformations, we must normalize them. It is common to study matrices normalized by the conditon

$$ad - bc = 1.$$

It is not difficult to verify that under such a normalization the matrix $\begin{pmatrix} a & b \\ c & d \end{pmatrix}$ corresponding to any linear fractional transformation taking the circle $|w| < 1$ into itself satisfies the conditions:

$$\begin{aligned} a &= \frac{e^{i\theta}}{\sqrt{1-|\alpha|^2}}, & b &= \frac{\alpha e^{i\theta}}{\sqrt{1-|\alpha|^2}}, \\ c &= \frac{\bar{\alpha} e^{-i\theta}}{\sqrt{1-|\alpha|^2}}, & d &= \frac{e^{-i\theta}}{\sqrt{1-|\alpha|^2}}, \end{aligned} \tag{3.1}$$

where θ is some real number and α is some complex number satisfying the condition $|\alpha| < 1$.

We next study several properties of the group $\gamma(D, \varphi)$. We begin with a lemma.

Lemma 1. Let $\varphi(z)$ be some function mapping the domain D conformally onto the circle $|w| < 1$, and let $f(w)$ be the function inverse to $\varphi(z)$. For any transformation $A \in \gamma(D, \varphi)$ we have

$$f(Aw) \equiv f(w) \qquad (|w| < 1).$$

Proof. The function $f(w)$ is regular in the circle $|w| < 1$ and satisfies the condition $f(\varphi(z)) \equiv z$. This means, in particular, that the value of the function $f(\varphi(z))$ does not depend on the particular element chosen for the function $\varphi(z)$. However, Aw and w are none other than the values of two elements of the function $\varphi(z)$ at some point of domain D. Consequently, $f(Aw) = f(w)$, which proves the lemma.

Property 1. Let A be an element of the group $\gamma(D, \varphi)$ distinct from the identity. Then all powers of this element are distinct from one another.

If $A^{n_1} = A^{n_2}$, then, setting $n_2 - n_1 = p$, we have $A^p = I$. Let the element A correspond to the analytic continuation of the function $\varphi(z)$ along the closed path L contained in domain D. It follows from the equality $A^p = I$ that p circuits of the path L in the positive direction lead us back to the initial element of the function $\varphi(z)$. Thus, the image of the curve L traversed p times under the mapping $w=\varphi(z)$ is some closed curve Γ contained in the circle $|w|<1$. In other words, the image of the closed curve Γ under the mapping $z=f(w)$ ($f(w)$ is regular in the circle $|w|<1$ and inverse to $\varphi(z)$) is the curve L traversed p times. Since the curve can be continuously deformed to a point of the circle $|w|<1$, then its image — the curve L traversed p times — can be continuously deformed to a point of domain D, for the image of the circle $|w|<1$ under the mapping $z=f(w)$ is the domain D. However, the curve L traversed p times can be shrunk to a point only if this can be done with the curve L traversed once. The result of analytic continuation is not effected by continuous deformation of the curve. Since the curve can be shrunk to a point in domain D, the continuation along this curve leads us back to the initial element. Thus, the transformation A is the identity transformation. This proves the property.

It follows from Property 1, in particular, that the *group $\gamma(D, \varphi)$ is infinite in the case that D is a multiply connected domain.*

Property 2. Let the group $\gamma(D, \varphi)$ consist of the transformations $A_n (n=0, 1, 2, \ldots)$. The sequence $\{A_n W_0\}$, where $|w_0|<1$, has all its limit points on the circle $|w|=1$.

Indeed, consider the function $f(w)$ inverse to $\varphi(z)$. It is regular in the circle $|w|<1$ and $f(A_n w_0)=f(w_0)$ If the sequence $\{A_n w_0\}$ has a limit point within the circle $|w|<1$, then, according to the uniqueness theorem, $f(w) \equiv f(w_0)$, which is impossible.

With the help of the properties proved we can obtain more detailed information about the matrices of the transformations constituting the automorphism group. Before we prove the result in question, we prove a lemma determining the dependence of the group $\gamma(D, \varphi)$ on the choice of the mapping function $\varphi(z)$.

Lemma 2. Let the group $\gamma(D, \varphi)$ consist of the transformations $A_n (n=0,1, 2, \ldots)$. If $\psi(z)$ is some other function mapping the domain D conformally onto the circle $|w| < 1$, then the group $\gamma(D, \psi)$ consists of the transformations $TA_nT^{-1} (n=0, 1, 2, \ldots)$, where Tw is some linear fractional transformation of the circle $|w| < 1$ into itself.

Proof. According to the corollary to Theorem 1.2, the functions $\varphi_0(z)$ and $\psi_0(z)$, the initial elements of the mapping functions $\varphi(z)$ and $\psi(z)$, are related by the equations

$$\psi_0(z) = T\varphi_0(z), \qquad \varphi_0(z) = T^{-1}\psi_0(z),$$

where Tw is some linear fractional transformation of the circle $|w|<1$ into itself. According to the definition of the automorphism group, any element of the function $\varphi(z)$ can be represented in the form

$$\varphi_n(z) = A_n\varphi_0(z) \qquad (A_n \in \gamma(D, \varphi)).$$

Thus, for any element $\psi_n(z)$ of the function $\psi(z)$ we have

$$\psi_n(z) = TA_n\varphi_0(z) = TA_nT^{-1}\psi_0(z),$$

i.e., $B_n = TA_nT^{-1}$. This completes the proof.

Theorem 3.1. *If $A \in \gamma(D, \varphi)$, then the matrix corresponding to the transformation Aw (and normed by the condition $ad - bc = 1$) must have a repeated eigenvalue equal to either 1 or -1.*

Proof. Let the matrix $A = \begin{pmatrix} a & b \\ c & d \end{pmatrix}$ correspond to the transformation Aw. Since the transformation Aw is a linear fractional transformation of the circle $|w| < 1$ into itself, we can use the relations (3.1) for a, b, c, d. This gives

$$\begin{vmatrix} a - \lambda & b \\ c & d - \lambda \end{vmatrix} = \lambda^2 - 2\lambda\cos\theta + 1.$$

The eigenvalues of the matrix A are the roots of this equation, which are easily found. We can suppose that $\lambda_1 = e^{i\theta}$, $\lambda_2 = e^{-i\theta}$, where $0 \leqslant \theta \leqslant \pi$. If $\theta = 0$ or $\theta = \pi$, we obtain the statement of the theorem. Let us show that no other values of θ are possible.

For $0 < \theta < \pi$ the eigenvalues of the matrix $\lambda_1 = e^{i\theta}$ and $\lambda_2 = e^{-i\theta}$ are distinct. According to a well-known theorem of linear algebra, the matrix can then be put into diagonal form, i.e., presented in the form

$$A = T\begin{pmatrix} e^{i\theta} & 0 \\ 0 & e^{-i\theta} \end{pmatrix} T^{-1},$$

where T is some nonsingular matrix.

There are two possiblilities: whether $\frac{\theta}{\pi}$ is a rational or an irrational number.

If $\frac{\theta}{\pi} = \frac{p}{q}$, where p and q are integers, then

$$A^{2q} = T\begin{pmatrix} e^{2\pi ip} & 0 \\ 0 & e^{-2\pi ip} \end{pmatrix} T^{-1} = I.$$

This is impossible, for according to Property 1 all powers of the matrix A must be distinct.

Let $\frac{\theta}{\pi}$ be an irrational number. The transformation corresponding to the matrix T^{-1} takes the circle $|w| < 1$ into some circle K. We choose a point w_0 that is sent into some nonzero point of circle K and put $w_1 = T^{-1}w_0$. We have

$$A^n w_0 = T\begin{pmatrix} e^{in\theta} & 0 \\ 0 & e^{-in\theta} \end{pmatrix} w_1 = T(e^{2in\theta}w_1).$$

The limit points of the sequence $e^{2in\theta}w_1$ fill the circumference $|w| = |w_1|$, since $\frac{\theta}{\pi}$ is an irrational number. Part of this circumference is contained in the circle K since it passes through the point $w_1 \in K$. Part of the image of the circumference $|w| = |w_1|$ is contained in the circle $|w| < 1$, so that limit points of the sequence $A^n w_0$ are contained in the circle $|w| < 1$. According to Property 2, this is impossible.

Having eliminated the other possibilities, we have thus completed the proof of the theorem.

It is convenient in many problems to employ the notion of fundamental domain of an automorphism group.

Suppose that we are given an m-connected domain D and a function $\varphi(z)$ mapping this domain conformally onto a circle. The boundary of the m-connected domain D consists of m separate pieces $C_0, C_1, \ldots, C_{m-1}$. We assume that C_0 is the exterior boundary of the domain and that $C_1, \ldots, C_{m-1}$ are boundaries of holes. We introduce cuts $L_1, \ldots, L_{m-1}$ into the domain D by connecting the holes with the exterior boundary. We can assume that the cuts do not intersect one another and that their direction is from the hole to the exterior boundary. After introducing the cuts we obtain a simply connected domain D' from the domain D. We select a regular branch of the function $\varphi(z)$ in D', say, $\varphi_0(z)$. Let G_0 denote the image of the domain D' under the mapping $w = \varphi_0(z)$. The domain G_0 is called a *fundamental domain of the automorphism group* $\gamma(D, \varphi)$.

It is clear that there is a large degree of arbitrariness in the definition of fundamental domain.

If the group $\gamma(D, \varphi)$ consists of the transformations A_n, $n = 0, 1, \ldots$ (A_0 is the identity transformation), then the image of the fundamental domain G_0 under the mapping $A_n w$, which takes the circle $|w| < 1$ into itself, is denoted by G_n.

Any one of the domains G_n may be taken for the fundamental domain.

Let us note two important properties of the complete collection of domains G_n.

1. All domains G_n are contained in the circle $|w| < 1$ and any pair has empty intersection.

2. Every point of the circle $|w| < 1$ is either contained in a domain G_n or lies on the boundary of some G_n.

Indeed, in view of the univalence of the conformal mapping, the function $\varphi(z)$ assumes every value in the circle $|w| < 1$ exactly once. The images of the domain D', part of the domain D, under mapping by the various branches of the function $\varphi(z)$ cannot have common points. Statement 1 follows from this.

Each point of the circle $|w| < 1$ is the image of some point of the domain D under the mapping $w = \varphi(z)$. Since each point of domain D is contained in the domain D' or on the boundary of D', we obtain assertion 2.

Applying the same procedure as that used in the construction of the fundamental domain, we can prove an important result on the structure of the automorphism group of a mapping of a finitely connected domain.

Theorem 3.2. *The group $\gamma(D, \varphi)$, where D is an m-connected domain, is generated by the transformations $A_1, A_2, \ldots, A_{m-1}$.*

Proof. Just as in the construction of the fundamental domain, we introduce cuts $L_1, L_2, \ldots, L_{m-1}$ into the domain D by connecting the holes $C_1, C_2, \ldots, C_{m-1}$ with the exterior boundary C_0. The domain thus obtained is denoted D'. The function $\varphi(z)$ mapping the domain D conformally onto one circle $|w|<1$ is split up in the domain D' into a countable number of regular branches, which are obtained from one another by analytic continuation across the cuts L_k. Each cut L_k has two sides: L_k^+ and L_k^-. We select a regular branch of the function $\varphi(z)$ in domain D', say, $\varphi_0(z)$, and denote by $\varphi_k(z)$ the branch of the function $\varphi(z)$ obtained by continuing the branch $\varphi_0(z)$ analytically across the side L_k^+ of cut L_k. We can express the branch $\varphi_k(z)$ in terms of $\varphi_k(z)$ with the help of a linear fractional transformation, which we denote by A_k. The analytic continuation of the function $\varphi_k(z)$ across side L_s^+ of cut L_s can be reduced to analytic continuation of the function $\varphi_0(z)$ across L_s^+; as the result of this we obtain $A_k A_s \varphi_0(z)$. The continuation of the function $\varphi_0(z)$ across side L_k^- of cut L_k can be expressed in terms of the transformation A_k. In fact, as a result of analytic continuation of the function $\varphi_0(z)$ across side L_k^- we obtain the function $A_k^{-1}\varphi_0(z)$, since continuation of the function $\varphi_0(z)$ across L_k^+ and then across L_k^- leads us back to the original function.

Thus, the result of analytic continuation of the function $\varphi_0(z)$ across any sequence of edges L_k^+ or L_k^- can be expressed easily in terms of the transformations corresponding to the analytic continuation of $\varphi_0(z)$ across the various L_k^+. In fact, the matrix of the linear fractional transformation corresponding to the overall continuation is the product of the matrices corresponding to the passage across each cut (the matrices are multiplied in the same order as the order in the sequence of cuts).

Since the analytic continuation of the function $\varphi_0(z)$ along any closed path reduces to a sequence of continuations across cuts, the theorem is proved.

It follows directly from Property 1 that the matrices corresponding to the transformations $A_1, A_2, \ldots, A_{m-1}$, are algebraically independent, i.e., no product of their powers can give the identity matrix (if this product contains some nontrivial power of a matrix A_k).

With the help of the automorphism group we can easily resolve the problem of the possibility of mapping one multiply connected domain conformally on another in a one-to-one fashion.

We shall say that the *groups α and β of linear fractional transformations* (or matrices) *are equivalent*, if there exists a nonsingular matrix T such that the equation

$$B_n = TA_nT^{-1}$$

is satisfied under some ordering of the elements $A_n \in \alpha$ and $B_n \in \beta$.

It follows from Lemma 2 that the groups $\gamma(D, \varphi)$ and $\gamma(D, \psi)$ corresponding to two different mapping functions are equivalent.

Theorem 3.3. *It is necessary and sufficient for the existence of a one-to-one conformal mapping of domain D onto domain D_1 that the groups $\gamma(D, \varphi)$ and $\gamma(D_1, \psi)$ be equivalent.*

This statement is easily proved and we leave this for the reader to carry out himself.

Let us take note of an interesting fact following from this theorem.

The number of distinct types of multiply connected domains capable of being mapped in a conformal and one-to-one fashion onto one another is exactly equal to the number of distinct (nonequivalent) automorphism groups of mappings of these domains onto the circle $|w| < 1$. It follows from Theorem 3.2 that the automorphism group of the mapping of an m-connected domain onto the circle $|w| < 1$ is determined by $3m - 3$ parameters (A_k is the matrix corresponding to a transformation of the circle $|w| < 1$ onto itself). However, two parameters must be subtracted because of equivalence (this is clear from Theorem 3.1). Thus, the number of different types of conformally equivalent domains is determined by not more than $3m-5$ real parameters.

4. THE DIRICHLET PROBLEM AND MAPPING ONTO CANONICAL DOMAINS

Conformal mapping of multiply connected domains by analytic functions can be applied to the solution of the Dirichlet problem for multiply connected domains. We shall discuss only the solution of the Dirichlet problem for multiply connected domains bounded by piecewise-smooth curves $C_0, C_1, \ldots, C_{m-1}$. We shall assume that the curve C_0 is the exterior boundary and that the curves $C_1, C_2, \ldots, C_{m-1}$ are the boundaries of the holes.

The Dirichlet problem can be stated in the same way as for simply connected domains (see Sect. 3, Chap. VIII). Namely:

On the boundary curves of domain D are given m functions $f_0(\zeta), \ldots, f_{m-1}(\zeta)$, continuous on these curves except on a countable closed (and bounded) set of points of discontinuity.

We are required to find a function $u(z)$, bounded and harmonic in the domain D and approaching the function $f_k(\zeta)$ as $z \to \zeta$ $(\zeta \in C_k)$ at any point of continuity of the function $f_k(\zeta)$.

We proved the uniqueness of the solution of the Dirichlet problem for any kind of domain in Sect. 3 of Chap. VIII, but its solvability was established only for simply connected domains.

Assuming that the function $f(\zeta)$ is defined on the set consisting of all the boundary curves, we shall denote the class of functions $f_0(\zeta), \ldots, f_{m-1}(\zeta)$ by the symbol $f(\zeta)$.

We now introduce some additional notations.

Let $w(z)$ be a function mapping the domain D conformally onto the circle $|w|<1$, and let $z(w)$ be the inverse of $w(z)$. Let G_0 denote a fundamental domain of the group $\gamma(D, w)$, and let D' denote the domain D with cross cuts. The domain D' is the image of the domain G_0 under the mapping $z=z(w)$. The group $\gamma(D, w)$ is assumed to consist of the transformation $A_0, A_1, A_2, \ldots$ (where A_0 is the identity transformation), numbered in some order. Let G_ν denote the image of domain G_0 under mapping of the circle $|w|<1$ effected by the linear fractional transformation $w \to A_\nu w$. Let σ_ν denote the collection of arcs of the circle $|w|=1$ contained in the boundary of domain G_ν.

Theorem 4.1. *The function $u(z)$ solving the Dirichlet problem in domain D with boundary function $f(\zeta)$ can be presented in the form $u(z)=v(w(z))$, where*

$$v(\varrho e^{i\varphi}) = \sum_{\nu=0}^{\infty} \frac{1-\varrho^2}{2\pi} \int_{\sigma_\nu} \frac{f(z(e^{i\theta}))\, d\theta}{1+\varrho^2-2\varrho\cos(\varphi-\theta)} \qquad (\varrho<1). \tag{4.1}$$

Proof. First of all let us convince ourselves that the integral occurring in the definition of the function $v(w)$ is well-defined and that the series converges. The function $z(w)$ maps the domain G_0 conformally onto the domain D', and since, according to Lemma 1 of Sect. 3, $z(A_\nu w) \equiv z(w)$, it also maps any domain G_ν conformally onto the domain D'. Moreover, the arcs σ_ν are sent into those parts of the boundary of the domain D' that appear in the boundary of D, i.e., into the boundary curves. According to the corresponding boundaries theorem (see the corollary to Theorem 2.1), the function $z(w)$ is continuous on the arcs σ_ν and the values of $z(e^{i\theta})$ lie on the boundary curves of the domain D. Therefore, the function $f(z(e^{i\theta}))$ is defined and continuous for $e^{i\theta} \in \sigma_\nu$ with the exception of a countable closed set of points of discontinuity. All the remaining integrals may be shown to be well-defined by means of the same arguments.

Since the arcs σ_ν have no points in common (see Property 1, Sect. 3), it is not difficult to show that the series converges uniformly within the circle $|w| \leqslant r < 1$. Each summand is a harmonic function in the circle $|w|<1$. Therefore, the function $v(w)$ is harmonic in the circle $|w|<1$ since it is the sum of a uniformly convergent series of harmonic functions. Moreover, for the function $v(w)$ we have the inequality

$$m \leqslant v(w) \leqslant M \qquad (|w|<1),$$

where

$$m = \inf f(\zeta), \qquad M = \sup f(\zeta).$$

We now prove that the function $u(z)=v(w(z))$ is defined in the domain D. For this purpose we must verify that the value of the function $v(w(z))$ at the point z_0 does not depend on the choice of the element of the function $w(z)$ at this point. Since all elements of the function $w(z)$ are obtained by means of some transformation from the group $\gamma(D, w)$, we have to show that $v(A_n w) \equiv v(w)$ for all $A_n \in \gamma(D, w)$.

To do this we note that the function $v(w)$ is the sum of the series

$$v(w) = \sum_{\nu=0}^{\infty} v_\nu(w),$$

where the function $v_\nu(w)$ is the solution of the Dirichlet in the circle $|w| < 1$ with boundary values $f(z(e^{i\theta}))$ for $e^{i\theta} \in \sigma_\nu$ and zero for all remaining points of the circumference $|w| = 1$. Any transformation $A_n w$ maps the circle $|w| < 1$ into itself, and the sets σ_ν are permuted among themselves. Thus, the function $v(A_n w)$ is the sum of the same series $\sum v_\nu(w)$, but with the terms in a different order. Since the series converges absolutely, the sum is independent of the order of the terms. Consequently, $v(A_n w) \equiv v(w)$, so that the function $u(z) = v(w(z))$ is defined in D.

It is clear that the function $u(z)$ is bounded in domain D. We can easily obtain the harmonicity of function $u(z)$ in domain D from the harmonicity of the function $v(w)$ in the circle $|w| < 1$ with the aid of Theorem 1.1 of Chap. VIII. We still have to show that $u(z) \to f(\zeta)$ as $z \to \zeta$ for any point of continuity of the function $f(\zeta)$. Since $u(z) = v(w(z))$ and the values of $v(w(z))$ do not depend on the choice of the branch of the function $w(z)$, we can take in place of $w(z)$ the branch $w_0(z)$ mapping the domain D' conformally onto the domain G_0. The functions $w_0(z)$ and $z(w)$ are continuous up to the boundaries of the domains D' and G_0, respectively, as a consequence of the theorem of corresponding boundaries. Therefore, as $z \to \zeta'$ (ζ' is a point of one of the boundary curves), we have

$$w_0(z) \to e^{i\theta'}, \qquad z(w) \to \zeta' \qquad (w \to e^{i\theta'}).$$

According to the properties of Poisson's integral (see Theorem 3.2, Chap. VIII), we have

$$v(w) \to f(z(e^{i\theta'})) = f(\zeta')\,(w \to e^{i\theta'})$$

(if θ' is a point of continuity of the function $f(z(e^{i\theta})))$. This proves the theorem.

In the preceding section we found necessary and sufficient conditions under which the domains D and D_1 could be mapped conformally and in a one-to-one manner onto one another. However, we did not solve the problem of which domains of comparatively simple type can be the images of a given m-connected domain. This problem can be solved rather easily by using information about the solution of the Dirichlet problem.

We first consider the case of a doubly connected domain.

Theorem 4.2. *Any doubly connected domain (bounded by piecewise-smooth curves) can be mapped conformally and in a one-to-one manner onto the annulus $r < |w| < 1$. The mapping function is uniquely determined to within a factor of modulus one. (The number r is not preassigned, but is determined by the domain.)*

Proof. We begin with the uniqueness proof. Let the function $w = w(z)$ map domain D, bounded by the piecewise-smooth curves C_0 (the exterior boundary) and C_1 (the boundary of the hole), conformally and in a one-to-one manner onto the annulus $r < |w| < 1$. Here, of course, the curve C_0 goes into the circumference $|w| = 1$ and the curve C_1 into the circumference $|w| = r$.

Since the function $w(z)$ does not vanish in domain D, the function $u(z) = \ln\ |w(z)|$ is harmonic in domain and continuous up to its boundary. Clearly,

$$u(z) = 0 \quad (z \in C_0), \qquad u(z) = \ln r \quad (z \in C_1). \tag{4.2}$$

These conditions completely define the function $u(z)$. The function $\ln w(z)$, analytic in domain D, is determined by the function $u(z)$ to within an arbitrary pure imaginary summand $i\theta$. Thus, the function $w(z)$ is determined by the function $u(z)$ to within a constant mulitplier of modulus one.

We still have to show that the number r is also defined in a unique manner. Let $\zeta(z)$ denote the function analytic in D and having the harmonic measure $\omega(z; C_1, D)$ as its real part, i.e., the solution of the Dirichlet problem in domain D with boundary values equal to zero on C_0 and to unity on C_1. Clearly, we have

$$\ln w(z) = \zeta(z) \ln r, \qquad w(z) = e^{\zeta(z) \ln r}. \tag{4.3}$$

According to Theorem 1.1 of Chap. VIII, the function $\zeta'(z)$ is regular in domain D and the integral of $\zeta'(z)$ along any closed contour contained in D is a pure imaginary number (or zero). Therefore, under analytic continuation of $\zeta(z)$ along a closed path making one circuit of the hole C_1 in the positive direction we add a pure imaginary summand $2\pi i\omega_0$ to the original value of $\zeta(z)$ (the integral of $\zeta'(z)$ along the path mentioned). We see from formula (4.3) that the original value of the function $w(z)$ is multiplied by $e^{2\pi i\omega_0 \ln r}$ under analytic continuation of the function $w(z)$ along any closed path making one circuit of the hole C_1 in the positive direction. Regularity of the function $w(z)$ means that $\omega_0 \ln r = n$. The function $w(z)$ must be not only regular, but also univalent in domain D, i.e., cannot assume the same value twice. It follows from this without great difficulty that the product $\omega_0 \ln r$ must equal ± 1. Since $r < 1$, the sign is also determined and we see that the number r is uniquely determined.

This proves the uniqueness of the mapping. To prove the existence of the mapping we show that the function

$$w_0(z) = e^{\frac{1}{\omega_0}\zeta(z)}$$

effects the desired mapping of the domain D on the annulus

$$r < |w| < 1, \quad \ln r = \frac{1}{\omega_0}.$$

With this goal in mind, we determine what happens to the point $w_0(z)$ as the point z makes a circuit of the curve C_λ on which

$\omega(z, C_1, D)=\lambda$, $0<\lambda<1$. Note that the curve C_λ is a simple curve contained in domain D (the absence of self-intersections follows from the maximum and minimum principles for harmonic functions). As $\lambda \to 0$, this curve approaches C_0, and as $\lambda \to 1$ it approaches C_1. The function $\zeta(z)$ is regular at each point of the curve C_λ, so that the Cauchy-Riemann equations, written in the system of coordinates in which the direction of the x-axis is taken to be the direction of the normal n to the curve C_λ, and the direction of the y-axis is taken to be that of the tangent to C_λ, give

$$\frac{\partial}{\partial s}\operatorname{Im}\zeta(z)=\frac{\partial}{\partial n}\operatorname{Re}\zeta(z) \qquad (\operatorname{Re}\zeta(z)=\omega(z; C_1, D)).$$

If we take for n that direction of the normal that corresponds to increase of λ, then $\frac{\partial}{\partial n}\operatorname{Re}\zeta(z)>0$. Consequently, as we move along the curve C_λ in a direction such that the domain of large values of λ remains on the right, the value of $\operatorname{Im}\zeta(z)$ increases. After a complete circuit, the value of $\operatorname{Im}\zeta(z)$ must increase by $2\pi i\omega_0$. Thus, as the point z carries out a complete circuit of curve C_λ, the point $w_0(z)$ completes one full circuit of the circumference $|w|=e^{\frac{\lambda}{\omega_0}}$. This also means that the function $w_0(z)$ maps domain D, determined by curves C_λ, $0<\lambda<1$, conformally and in a one-to-one manner onto the annulus $e^{\frac{1}{\omega_0}}<|w|<1$, determined by the circumferences $|w|=e^{\frac{\lambda}{\omega_0}}$, $0<\lambda<1$. This completes the proof.

In case $m>2$ there exist no such simple canonical domains as annuli, so that we have to consider canonical domains of many types. We prove a theorem on the mapping of a finitely connected domain onto one of the types of canonical domain—onto a plane with a finite number of vertical cuts. Here we shall not be concerned with refinements connected with insufficient smoothness of the boundary curves.

We begin with some notation.

Let D be an m-connected domain bounded by the curves C_0 (the exterior boundary) and $C_1, C_2, \ldots, C_{m-1}$ (the holes). Let $\zeta_1(z), \zeta_2(z), \ldots, \zeta_{m-1}(z)$ be functions analytic in domain D and having real parts equal to the harmonic measure $\omega(z; C_k, D)$. Let $2\pi i\omega_{ks}$ $(1\leqslant k\leqslant m-1$, $1\leqslant s\leqslant m-1)$ denote the integral of the function $\zeta_k'(z)$ along a simple closed curve making a circuit of the hole bounded by C_s and of no other holes (according to Theorem 1.1, the function $\zeta_k'(z)$ is regular in domain D and its integral along any closed contour is a pure imaginary).

We first prove a fundamental lemma.

Lemma 1. The matrix $\Omega=\|W_{ks}\|$ *is nonsingular.*

Proof. Suppose the contrary. Then it is possible to select a set of real constants $\lambda_1, \lambda_2, \ldots, \lambda_{m-1}$, not all zero, such that the function

$$\zeta(z)=\lambda_1\zeta_1(z)+\ldots+\lambda_{m-1}\zeta_{m-1}(z)$$

is regular in the domain D. Indeed, once the matrix $\|\omega_{ks}\|$ is assumed to be singular, there are constants $\lambda_1\ \lambda_2 \dots \lambda_{m-1}$, not all zero such that $\sum_{s=1}^{m-1} \omega_{ks}\lambda_s = 0$, $(1 \leq k \leq m-1)$, has a nontrival solution. Hence $\int_{C_k} \sum_{s=1}^{m-1} \lambda_s \zeta_s'(z)\,dz = 0$ for each C_k and thus the function $\zeta(z)$ is regular in D.

We now determine which values the function $\zeta(z)$ may assume in the domain D. The values of the function $\zeta(z)$ have zero real part on the curve C_0 and have $\text{Re}\,\zeta(z) = \lambda_s$ on curve C_s. In other words, the image of the boundary of domain D is a set distributed along the lines $\text{Re}\,\zeta = 0$, $\text{Re}\,\zeta = \lambda_s$ $(s = 1, 2, \dots, m-1)$. If the value w does not lie on one of these lines, then according to the argument principle (see Theorem 6.1, Chap. IV) the number of solutions of the equation $\zeta(z) - w$ in the domain D equals the change in $\arg[\zeta(z) - w]$ under a circuit by the point z of the entire boundary of D. However,

$$\underset{C_s}{\text{var}}\{\arg[\zeta(z) - w]\} = 0 \qquad (s = 0, 1, \dots, m-1),$$

since as the point z moves along the curve C_s the point $\zeta(z)$ moves along the line $\text{Re}\,\zeta = \text{const}$ and so cannot pass through the point w. Thus, the change in $\arg[\zeta(z) - w]$ equals zero, i.e., the function $\zeta(z)$ cannot take on the value w in the domain D. Since w is any point not situated on one of the lines $\text{Re}\,\zeta = 0$, $\text{Re}\,\zeta = \lambda_s$ $(s = 1, \dots, m-1)$, this means that the function $\zeta(z)$ can take on only values on these and in the domain D. However, according to Theorem 1.1 of Chap. V, the set of values assumed in a domain by a regular function other than a constant is itself a domain. Consequently, $\zeta(z) \equiv \text{const}$. This is impossible since

$$\text{Re}\,\zeta(z) = 0 \quad (z \in C_0), \qquad \text{Re}\,\zeta(z) = \lambda_s \quad (z \in C_s),$$

if even one of the constants λ_s is distinct from zero. This contradiction proves the lemma.

Theorem 4.3. *Any finitely connected domain D can be mapped conformally and in a one-to-one fashion onto the w-plane with finitely many vertical cross cuts. The mapping function w(z) is uniquely defined if the point* $a \in D$ *that is mapped into* ∞, *a real number A and the number* $c = \lim_{z \to a}\left[w(z) - \frac{A}{z-a}\right]$ *are assigned in advance.*

Proof. Let $u(z)$ denote the solution of the Dirichlet problem in the domain D with boundary values $\text{Re}\,\frac{A}{\zeta - a}$, and let $w_0(z)$ be a function analytic in D and with $u(z)$ as its real part.

We choose real constants $\lambda_1, \lambda_2, \dots, \lambda_{m-1}$ so that the function

$$-w_0(z) + \lambda_1\zeta_1(z) + \dots + \lambda_{m-1}\zeta_{m-1}(z)$$

is regular in domain D. In virtue of Lemma 1, this can be done since the matrix $\Omega = \| \omega_{ks} \|$ is nonsingular.

We show that the function

$$w(z) = \frac{A}{z-a} + c_1 - w_0(z) + \lambda_1 \zeta_1(z) + \ldots + \lambda_{m-1} \zeta_{m-1}(z)$$

(the constant c_1 is chosen so that $w(z) - \frac{A}{z-a} \to 0$ as $z \to a$) effects the desired mapping.

By construction we have

$$\operatorname{Re} w(z) = \mu_s \quad (z \in C_s),$$
$$\mu_0 = \operatorname{Re} c_1, \qquad \mu_s = \operatorname{Re} c_1 + \lambda_s \qquad (s = 1, \ldots, m-1),$$

and, assuming some kind of smoothness for the boundary of D, we can easily show that the imaginary part of $w(z)$ is continuous on the boundary of D. The function $w(z)$ has one simple pole inside D. As in Lemma 1, we verify that the change in arg $[w(z) - w]$ along the entire boundary of D is zero for all values of w not contained in the lines

$$\operatorname{Re} w = \mu_s \qquad (s = 0, 1, \ldots, m-1).$$

This means on the basis of the argument principle that the number of zeros of the function $w(z) - w$ in domain D equals the number of the poles there, i.e., is one. Also, the values of w lying on these lines cannot be assumed more than once by the function $w(z)$ since according to Theorem 1.1 of Chap. V the set of values assumed in a domain by a regular function more than one is an open set. Thus, the function $w(z)$ maps domain D conformally and in a one-to-one fashion onto the entire w-plane from which segments of the indicated vertical lines have been removed.

We must now prove the uniqueness of the mapping function. If $w_1(z)$ and $w_2(z)$ are two mapping functions, then their difference is regular in domain D and is zero for $z = a$. Applying the same arguments to this difference as were applied to the function $\zeta(z)$ in the proof of Lemma 1, we easily obtain $w_1(z) - w_2(z) \equiv 0$.

This completes the proof*.

Simple computations show that it is possible to assign $3m - 5$ real constants in the selection of the type of canonical domain—the same number as was found for an upper bound in Sect. 3.

It is interesting to note that the matrix Ω also is left fixed under one-to-one conformal mappings, but that it contains $(m-1)^2$ real parameters. For $m = 2$ and $m = 3$, the number of parameters in the

---

*We shall not take the time to discuss what kind of smoothness of the boundary is necessary for the validity of the theorem. The theorem is also true even without requirements on the boundary. The proof of this fact and a presentation of many other problems can be found in the book of G. M. Goluzin cited on p. 264.

matrix coincides with $3m-5$; however, it is greater for $m>3$. This means that from >3 there must exist some relations between the elements of matrix Ω.

5. MAPPING OF THE PLANE WITH DELETED POINTS

We devote the present section to the construction of a function that maps the plane with three deleted points conformally onto the circle $|w|<1$. We need this function for the proof of Theorem 1.1*, which was carried out on the assumption of its existence; however, it is of interest in many other connections.

We find it more convenient to construct a function that maps the plane with three deleted points (let us say, the points $z=0$, $z=1$ and $z=\infty$) not onto the circle $|w|<1$, but onto the half-plane $\operatorname{Im}\zeta>0$.

Let G denote the half-plane $|\operatorname{Re}\zeta|<1$, $\operatorname{Im}\zeta>0$ from which have been deleted two semidisks having the segments $(-1, 0)$ and $(0, 1)$ as their diameters.

Let $k(\zeta)$ denote the function mapping the domain G conformally onto the z-plane with a cross cut along the positive part of the real axis so that the points $\zeta=0, 1, \infty$ are sent into the points $z=0, 1, \infty$ on the upper edge of the cross cut. The existence of such a function follows from Theorem 1.1. Moreover, this function can be constructed with the aid of the Schwarz-Christoffel integral (see Sect. 5, Chap. V).

Let $\lambda_0(z)$ denote the function inverse to $k(\zeta)$.

We show that *the analytic function $\lambda(z)$, obtained by analytic continuation of the function $\lambda_0(z)$, is analytic in the z-plane with deleted points $z=0, 1$, and maps it conformally onto the half-plane $\operatorname{Re}\zeta>0$.*

The proof is divided into five steps.

1. We show that *the values of the function $\lambda_0(z)$ in the z-plane with a cross cut along the positive half of the real axis satisfy the relation*

$$\overline{\lambda_0(\bar{z})}=-\lambda_0(z). \tag{5.1}$$

For this purpose we let $\varphi(z)$ denote the function mapping the half-plane $\operatorname{Im} z>0$ conformally onto the half of the domain G, lying to the right of the imaginary axis and sending the points $z=0,\ 1, \infty$ into the points $\zeta=0,\ 1,\ \infty$, respectively. According to Riemann's theorem, such a function exists, and it is not difficult to show with the aid of Theorem 2.1 of Chap. V that it is unique. By virtue of the theorem of corresponding boundaries the function $\varphi(z)$ is continuous in the half-plane $\operatorname{Im} z\geqslant 0$. Under the mapping $\zeta=\varphi(z)$ the negative part of the real axis is sent into the positive part of the imaginary axis. According to the symmetry principle (see Theorem 4.2, Chap. V), the function $\varphi(z)$ can be continued analytically into the half-plane $\operatorname{Im} z<0$ across the negative half of the real axis by setting

$$\varphi(z)=-\overline{\varphi(\bar{z})} \qquad (\operatorname{Im} z<0). \tag{5.1*}$$

The continuation (we retain the notation $\varphi(z)$ for it) is regular in the entire z-plane with a cross cut along the positive half of the real axis and maps this plane with cross cut conformally onto domain G. According to Theorem 2.1, Chap. V, we may uniquely determine the mapping function by assigning three points on the boundary of the domain; thus, $\varphi(z)\equiv\lambda_0(z)$. Hence, Eq. (5.1) follows from Eq. (5.1*).

2. We find the analytic continuation of the function $\lambda_0(z)$ across the segment (0, 1) starting from below (i.e., across the lower edge of the cut).

The mapping $\zeta=\lambda_0(z)$ sends the lower edge of the cross cut (0,1) into the semicircumference $\left|\zeta+\frac{1}{2}\right|=\frac{1}{2}$, $\operatorname{Im}\zeta>0$. Thus, according to the symmetry principle, the analytic continuation of the function $\lambda_0(z)$ across the lower edge of the cross cut (0.1) is possible. As a result of this continuation we obtain another regular branch of the analytic function $\lambda(z)$, which we denote by $\lambda_1(z)$. According to the symmetry principle, the values of $\lambda_0(\bar z)$ and $\lambda_1(z)$ must be symmetric with respect to the circle $\left|\zeta+\frac{1}{2}\right|=\frac{1}{2}$ (since the points $\bar z$ and z are symmetric with respect to the segment (0, 1)). Writing the condition of symmetry with respect to the circle (see Sect. 2, Chap. V), we find

$$\left[\lambda_1(z)+\frac{1}{2}\right]\left[\overline{\lambda_0(\bar z)}+\frac{1}{2}\right]=\left(\frac{1}{2}\right)^2.$$

Employing relation (5.1), we obtain

$$\lambda_1(z)=S\lambda_0(z),\qquad S\zeta=\frac{\zeta}{-2\zeta+1}. \tag{5.2}$$

Let $\lambda_2(z)$ denote the branch of the analytic function $\lambda(z)$ obtained by analytic continuation of the function $\lambda_0(z)$ across the lower edge of the cross cut $(1,+\infty)$; by means of analogous reasoning we find

$$\lambda_2(z)=T\lambda_0(z),\qquad T\zeta=\zeta-2. \tag{5.3}$$

In a completely analogous manner we can obtain the formulas for the analytic continuation of the function $\lambda_0(z)$ across the upper edges of these cross cuts. If we denote by $\lambda_3(z)$ and $\lambda_4(z)$ the branches of the analytic function $\lambda(z)$ obtained by analytic continuation of the function $\lambda_0(z)$ across the upper edges of the cross cuts (0,1) and $(1,+\infty)$, then

$$\lambda_3(z)=S^{-1}\lambda_0(z),\qquad \lambda_4(z)=T^{-1}\lambda_0(z),$$

where S^{-1} and T^{-1} are linear fractional transformations inverse to the transformations S and T, i.e.,

$$S^{-1}\zeta=\frac{\zeta}{2\zeta+1},\qquad T^{-1}\zeta=\zeta+2.$$

3. We show that *the function $\lambda_0(z)$ can be continued analytically along any path not passing through the points $z=0$, 1, ∞, and such that all elements of the analytic function thus obtained have values lying in the half-plane Im $\zeta>0$.*

Let L be any path not passing through the points $z=0$, 1, ∞. When this path crosses the positive part of the real axis for the first time, the function $\lambda_0(z)$ is replaced by one of the following four functions:

$$S\lambda_0(z), \qquad T\lambda_0(z), \qquad S^{-1}\lambda_0(z), \qquad T^{-1}\lambda_0(z).$$

The function in question depends on which edge of which part of the cut we cross. The analytic continuation of each of these four functions can be reduced again to continuation of the function $\lambda_0(z)$ after application of a linear fractional transformation.

It is clear from this that the function $\lambda_0(z)$ can be continued analytically along any path not passing through the points $z=0$, 1, ∞. As a result of continuation we obtain some linear fractional transformation of the function $\lambda_0(z)$. Obviously, this transformation is part of the group generated by the transformations S and T.

Noting that the transformations S and T are mappings of the half-plane Im $\zeta>0$ into itself, we arrive at the desired statement; for the values of the function $\lambda_0(z)$ are contained in the domain G, situated in the half-plane Im $\zeta>0$ and all transformations of the group map this half-plane into itself.

4. We show that *the function $k(\zeta)$, inverse to $\lambda_0(z)$, can be continued analytically into the half-plane Im $\zeta>0$.*

The function $k(\zeta)$ maps the domain G conformally onto the entire z-plane with a cross cut along the positive part of the real axis, so that it assumes real values on the boundary of G. Since the boundary of G consists of lines and circles, this requirement allows us to continue the function $k(\zeta)$ analytically by means of the symmetry principle. Successively continuing the function $k(\zeta)$ analytically across the straight line sides of domain G, we show that the function $k(\zeta)$ is regular in the domain obtained by deletion from the half-plane Im $\zeta>0$ of the semidisks having the segments $(n, n+1)$ as diameters (n is any integer). The function $k(\zeta)$ as before takes on real values on the boundary of this domain. Continuing the function $k(\zeta)$ by means of the symmetry principle across each of the bounding semicircles, we see that the function $k(\zeta)$ is regular in a still larger domain. This domain is also obtained from the half-plane Im $\zeta>0$ by deletion of a countable number of disks having segments of the real axis as diameters. (Under symmetry with respect to a circle with center on the real axis, the real axis is mapped into itself and any circle with center on the real axis is mapped into some other circle with center on the real axis.)

The function $k(\zeta)$ must again assume real values on the boundary of the new domain. Continuing it across all the bounding semicircles, we see that it is regular in a still larger domain of the same form.

Repeating this process an unlimited number of times, we arrive at the conclusion that the function $k(\zeta)$ is regular in the entire half-plane $\operatorname{Im}\zeta > 0$, since at each step of the continuation the radii of the semicircles thrown out is reduced by at least half. (Each new semicircle is the image of one of the old ones under a symmetry transformation with respect to one of the old semicircles; this means that the diameter of any of the new semicircles is contained in the radius of one of the old ones.)

5. *We complete the proof of the statement made at the beginning of the section.*

According to Property 3 of univalent analytic functions (see Sect. 1), the univalence of the function $\lambda(z)$ follows from the regularity of the function $k(\zeta)$, inverse to the function $\lambda(z)$ and analytic in the z-plane with the deleted points $z=0$, 1, ∞. This is true because 3 implies that the image of the z-plane with deleted points $z=0, 1$, ∞ under the mapping $\zeta=\lambda(z)$ is contained in the half-plane $\operatorname{Im}\zeta > 0$.

We must now show that the image of the z-plane with deleted points $z=0$, 1, ∞ under the mapping $\zeta=\lambda(z)$ is the half-plane $\operatorname{Im}\zeta > 0$.

For this we first note that the function $k(\zeta)$ does not assume the values 0, 1, ∞ in the half-plane $\operatorname{Im}\zeta > 0$. Indeed, this is certainly true in the domain G, since it is mapped by $k(\zeta)$ onto the z-plane with a cross cut along the positive half of the real axis. Under continuation of the function $k(\zeta)$ according to the symmetry principle, only the values assumed at the vertices of domain G can be taken on at the vertices of the symmetric domain. Since the vertices of all the symmetric domains are situated on the real axis, we arrive at the desired conclusion.

We next choose any point ζ', $\operatorname{Im}\zeta' > 0$, and find an element of the function $\lambda(z)$ and a point z' such that $\lambda(z')=\zeta'$. To do this we join some point of domain G to the point ζ' by means of a line segment and continue the function $\lambda(z)$ along the path L passing through the point $z=k(\zeta)$, where the point ζ is situated on this line segment. The functions $\lambda_0(z)$ and $k(\zeta)$ are inverse to one another, so that on the whole of path L we have $\lambda(k(\zeta))=\zeta$. Continuation along path L is possible since the function $k(\zeta)$ does not take on the values $0, 1, \infty$. At the end of L we find $\lambda(z')=\zeta'$.

Thus, any value ζ' from the half-plane $\operatorname{Im}\zeta > 0$ is assumed by the function $\lambda(z)$, so that the image of the z-plane with deleted points $z=0$, 1, ∞ under the mapping $\zeta=\lambda(z)$ is the half-plane $\operatorname{Im}\zeta > 0$. We have thus proved that the function $\lambda(z)$ effects the desired mapping.

Construction of the function $\zeta(z; a, b, c)$ used in the proof of Theorem 1.1* does not occasion any difficulty. It is easily generated in terms of the function $\lambda(z)$ with the aid of two linear fractional transformations.

With the aid of the Schwarz-Christoffel formula for the mapping of polygons bounded by arcs of circles, (see the end of Sect. 5, Chap. V), we can show that the function

$$\xi(z)=\frac{1}{\sqrt{\lambda'(z)}}$$

satisfies the differential equation

$$\xi''(z)=\frac{z^2-z+1}{z^2(z-1)^2}\,\xi(z).$$

The function $k(\zeta)$ is related to elliptic functions. This function together with all rational functions of it are called *modular functions.*

Let us note that the domain G with which we began our construction is none other than the fundamental domain of the automorphism group of the mapping $\zeta=\lambda(z)$. We have already constructed the automorphism group—it is generated by the two linear fractional transformations

$$S\zeta=\frac{\zeta}{-2\zeta+1},\qquad T\zeta=\zeta-2.$$

This group can also easily be described by other means. In fact, the matrices of the transformations of this group have the form

$$\begin{pmatrix} a & b \\ c & d\end{pmatrix}\equiv\begin{pmatrix} 1 & 0 \\ 0 & 1\end{pmatrix}\ (\mathrm{mod}\ 2),\qquad ad-bc=1.$$

This group is one of the subgroups of the *modular group,* which consists of all matrices $\begin{pmatrix} a & b \\ c & d\end{pmatrix}$ over the integers satisfying $ad-bc=1$.

The modular functions are special functions possessing a series of properties essentially different from those of the elementary functions. Thus, for example, the function $k(\zeta)$ cannot be continued analytically across the boundaries of the half-plane $\mathrm{Im}\,\zeta>0$—it has for singular points all the points of the real axis.

The profound result, *Picard's theorem,* was first proved with the aid of modular functions.

Theorem 5.1. *A function f(z), meromorphic in the entire finite plane and not assuming three different values is a constant.*

Proof. Suppose that $f(z)\neq a,\ b,\ c$. We consider the function

$$F(z)=\zeta(f(z);\ a,\ b,\ c),$$

where $\zeta(w;a,b,c)$ is a function mapping the w-plane with deleted points $w=a,\ b,\ c$ conformally onto the circle $|\zeta|<1$. Since the function $f(z)$ does not assume the values a, b, c, and the function $\zeta(w;\ a,\ b,\ c)$ has no singular points other than a, b, c, the function $F(z)$ is analytic, and according to the monodromy theorem it must also be regular in the entire finite plane. Moreover, $|F(z)|<1$. According to Liouville's theorem (see Theorem 2.3, Chap. IV), we have $F(z)\equiv$ const, which means that $f(z)\equiv$ const. This completes the proof.

6. AUTOMORPHIC AND ELLIPTIC FUNCTIONS

It is consistent with our discussion of the problems mentioned in Sects. 3 and 5 to present the basic facts from the theory of automorphic functions.

Suppose that we are given a group γ, composed of the linear fractional transformations $A_\nu z$ $(\nu=0, 1, 2, \ldots)$, mapping domain K into itself (the domain may be a circle, a half-plane or the entire finite plane).

If the function $f(z)$, meromorphic in domain K, satisfies the conditions

$$f(A_\nu z) \equiv f(z) \qquad (z \in K, \ A_\nu \in \gamma),$$

then it is called *automorphic with respect to the group.*

Functions automorphic with respect to finite groups (for example, even functions) do not have special properties of great interest.

The simplest class of functions automorphic with respect to an infinite group is the class of periodic functions. These functions are undoubtedly very interesting, but they have been carefully studied and their properties are well known.

When the domain K is the entire finite plane, there exists only one interesting class of automorphic functions—elliptic or doubly periodic functions. Elliptic functions have been studied for a long time in connection with a wide variety of problems of analysis (finding the length of an arc of an ellipse, integrating simple differential equations, etc.). A developed theory of elliptic functions arose before the theory of groups. Elliptic functions were defined at first in terms of elliptic integrals, but it was noted subsequently that it was easier to define them as functions having two periods whose ratio is a complex number.

If the domain K is a circle or a half-plane, we obtain much more interesting classes of automorphic functions since a greater variety of groups is available. The theory of automorphic functions got its start with the study of modular functions, which are closely connected with elliptic functions.

The present development of the theory of automorphic functions came about with the consideration of functions of several complex variables. The basis for this is that while any group of linear fractional transformations is necessarily a subgroup of the group of matrices of second degree, by transferring our consideration to functions of several complex variables we greatly extend the class of possible groups.

We shall not present the theory of automorphic functions in any detail, but shall only prove a few of the simplest theorems related primarialy to elliptic functions.

Just as for automorphism groups, we introduce the concept of fundamental domain for groups γ composed of linear fractional transformations $A_\nu z$ $(\nu=0, 1, 2, \ldots)$ which send the domain K into itself. We say that points z_1 and z_2 of domain K are *congruent,* if there exists a transformation $A_\nu \in \gamma$ such that $z_2 = A_\nu z_1$.

The domain G_0, contained in domain K, is called a fundamental domain of group , if:

1. no two points of domain G_0 are congruent;
2. any point of domain K is congruent either to some point of domain G_0 or to a point on the boundary of G_0.

A great variety of fundamental domains is possible for a given group. We shall assume that a fundamental domain is bounded by a simple piecewise-smooth curve.

Example 1. Let the domain K be the entire finite plane, and let the group consist of linear transformations of the form

$$Az = z + n + im,$$

where G_ν and m are arbitrary integers. Let us find a fundamental domain for this group.

Our group is generated by two transformations, $Sz = z + 1$ and $Tz = z + i$. These transformations are commutative. Therefore, we can construct fundamental domains for the groups γ_1 and γ_2, generated by S and T, respectively, and then take the intersection of the fundamental domains for groups γ_1 and γ_2 as the fundamental domain for our group.

Any curvilinear strip $\varphi(y) < x < \varphi(y) + 1$ is a fundamental domain for group γ_1, and any curvilinear strip $\psi(x) < y < \psi(x) + 1$ is a fundamental domain for the group γ_2. We obtain the simplest fundamental domains if we take $\varphi(y) \equiv 0$ and $\psi(x) \equiv 0$. Their intersection is the square $0 < \operatorname{Re} z < 1$, $0 < \operatorname{Im} z < 1$. This square is also the simplest fundamental domain for our group.

It is possible to show that it is always possible to choose a fundamental domain whose boundary consists of arcs of circles and line segments.

All our theorems will be proved for the case in which the fundamental domain together with its boundary is contained in the domain K. Such fundamental domains are called *compact*. (The theorems can be generalized somewhat, but some restriction of this form is necessary.)

Lemma 1. Suppose that the fundamental domain G_0 of group γ is compact and suppose that there exist nontrivial functions automorphic with respect to this group. Then the boundary of domain G_0 can be broken up into 2m arcs $C_1, \ldots, C_m$, and $C_1', \ldots, C_m'$. For each arc C_s' there exists a transformation $T_s z$, sending arc C_s' into arc C_s with reversal of the direction.

Proof. Let the group γ consist of the transformations $A_\nu z$ $(\nu = 0, 1, 2, \ldots)$ (A_0 is the identity transformation). Let G_ν denote the image of domain G_0 under the mapping $A_\nu z$. According to the definition of fundamental domain, the domains G_ν have no common points and the union of their closures $\overline{G}_\nu$ covers the domain K.

We show that we can find among the G_ν domains having boundary arcs in common with domain G_0.

To prove this we note that the domains G_ν approach the boundary of K as $\nu \to \infty$. Indeed, in the contrary case there would exist a sequence of congruent points $\{z_\nu\}$ having a limit point inside K. This contradicts the existence of nontrivial (i.e., nonconstant) functions $f(z)$ automorphic with respect to group γ; for a nonconstant function $f(z)$ meromophic in domain K cannot assume the same value on a sequence of points having a limit point within K.

Thus, all domains G_ν with sufficiently large index fall within an arbitrarily small neighborhood of the boundary of domain K, and the domain G_0 together with its boundary is contained within K. As a consequence of this, the domain G_0 has common boundaries with only a finite number of domains G_ν.

We choose from among the domains having common boundaries with G_0 those having an arc in common with G_0 (and not just a boundary point). There is an even number of such domains. Indeed, if the transformation $Az \in \gamma$ sends domain G_0 into a domain having a boundary arc in common with G_0, then the transformation $A^{-1}z$ also sends the domain G_0 into a domain having a boundary arc in common with G_0; for the domains G' and G'' obtained from G_0 by transformation with Az and $A^{-1}z$ are distinct.

Let $T_1, \ldots, T_m$ be all those transformations for which the images of domain G_0 under the transformations $T_s z$ and $T_s^{-1}z$ have boundary arcs in common with G_0 and such that there are no repetitions among the transformations $T_1, T_2, \ldots, T_m$ and $T_1^{-1}, T_2^{-1}, \ldots, T_m^{-1}$. Let G_s^* denote the image of domain G_0 under the transformation $T_s z$ and let G_s^{**} denote its image under the transformation $T_s^{-1}z$. Let C_s denote the common part of the boundaries of G_0 and G_0^*, and let C_s' denote the common part of the boundaries of G_0 and G_0^{**}. The direction along C_s and C_s' is taken to coincide with the direction along the boundary of G_0.

It follows from the method of choosing the transformations T_1, T_2, ..., T_m that the union of the arcs C_1, C_2, ..., C_m and C_1', C_2', ..., C_m' is the entire boundary of G_0 and that these arcs have no points in common.

We next determine what happens to arc C_s' under transformation by T_s. Under this transformation the domain G_0 is sent into the domain G_s^* and the domain G_s^{**} (the image of G_0 under the inverse transformation) is sent into the domain G_0. The arc C_s' forming the common boundary of the domains G_0 and G_s^{**} is sent into the common boundary of the domains G_0 and G_s^*. Here the direction of the image of C_s' coincides with the direction along the boundary of G_s^*, i.e., the direction opposite to that of the boundary of G_0. Thus, the transformation T_s sends the arc C_s' into the arc C_s' and reverses the direction. This completes the proof.

Theorem 6.1. *Let the fundamental domain of group* γ *be compact. If the function f(z), automorphic with respect to the group* γ, *has no poles or zeros on the boundary of the fundamental domain* G_0, *then the number of its zeros in* G_0 *equals the number of its poles there.*

Proof. Let C denote the boundary of the fundamental domain G_0. According to Theorem 6.1 of Chap. IV, we have

$$N-P=\frac{1}{2\pi i}\int\limits_C \frac{f'(z)}{f(z)}\,dz,$$

where N is the number of zeros and P is the number of poles of the function $f(z)$ in domain G_0. Let C_s and C_s' denote the arcs of the boundary of G_0 as discussed in Lemma 1. Then

$$\int_{C}\frac{f'(z)}{f(z)}\,dz=\sum_{s=1}^{m}\int_{C_s}\frac{f'(z)}{f(z)}\,dz+\sum_{s=1}^{m}\int_{C'_s}\frac{f'(z)}{f(z)}\,dz. \tag{6.1}$$

We make the substitution $z=T_s(w)$ in the integrals along C'_s, where $T_s(w)$ is the transformation sending arc C'_s into arc C_s with reversal of direction. Then

$$\int_{C'_s}\frac{f'(z)}{f(z)}\,dz=-\int_{C_s}\frac{f'(T_s(w))}{f(T_s(w))}\,T'_s(w)\,dw=-\int_{C_s}\frac{f'(w)}{f(w)}\,dw,$$

since it follows from the fact that $f(z)$ is automorphic that

$$f(T_s(w))\equiv f(w),\quad f'(T_s(w))\,T'_s(w)\equiv f'(w).$$

Consequently, the integrals along C'_s and C_s in formula (6.1) cancel each other out, so that we obtain $N-P=0$. This completes the proof.

Theorem 6.2. *Let the fundamental domain of the group γ be compact. Then any function, automorphic with respect to group γ, and not having any poles either within or on the boundary of the fundamental domain is a constant.*

Proof. Let ζ be any value not assumed by the function $f(z)$ on the boundary of the fundamental domain. Applying Theorem 6.1 to the function $f(z)-\zeta$, we see that the function $f(z)$ also does not assume the value ζ inside the fundamental domain. Thus, the function $f(z)$ can assume only values within G_0 that it assumes on the boundary of G_0. According to Theorem 1.1 of Chap. V, this is impossible unless $f(z)\not\equiv$ const since the image of a domain under mapping by a nonconstant regular function is again a domain. This proves the theorem.

Remark. It is easy to conclude on the basis of the example afforded by Theorem 6.2 that the condition of compactness for the fundamental domain is essential. Indeed, consider the group γ composed of the transformations $A_\nu z=z+2\pi i\nu$ (the domain K is the entire finite plane). A fundamental domain of this group is the strip $0<\operatorname{Im} z<2\pi$, and the functions automorphic with respect to this group are the periodic functions with period $2\pi i$. The fundamental domain is not compact and Theorem 6.2 does not hold, as is shown by the example $f(z)=e^z$.

If there exists a function automorphic with respect to the group γ and having only one pole in the fundamental domain (and not having poles on the boundary of the fundamental domain), then such a function is called *basic*.

Theorem 6.3. *Let the fundamental domain of group γ be compact. If there exists a basic automorphic function $\varphi(z)$, then any other function automorphic with respect to group γ is a rational function of this basic function.*

Proof. Let $f(z)$ be any function automorphic with respect to group γ, and let a and b be two values not assumed by the function $f(z)$ on the boundary of the fundamental domain G_0. Denote the points of the domain at which $f(z)=a$ by $\alpha_1, \alpha_2, \ldots, \alpha_m$, and those at which $f(z)=b$ by $\beta_1, \beta_2, \ldots, \beta_m$ (each point is written a number of times equal to its multiplicity).

Consider the function

$$F(z)=\frac{f(z)-a}{f(z)-b}\cdot\frac{[\varphi(z)-\varphi(\beta_1)]\ldots[\varphi(z)-\varphi(\beta_m)]}{[\varphi(z)-\varphi(\alpha_1)]\ldots[\varphi(z)-\varphi(\alpha_m)]}.$$

This function has no poles either within or on the boundary of G_0, since it can have poles only at points at which either $f(z)=b$ or $\varphi(z)=\varphi(\alpha_s)$, and at these points the zeros of numerator and denominator have the same multiplicity. (According to Theorem 6.1, all zeros of the function $\varphi(z)-\varphi(\alpha)$ are simple, and the number of zeros of the function $f(z)-a$ and $f(z)-b$ is the same.) Thus, according to Theorem 6.2, $F(z)\equiv$const, which proves the theorem.

Thus, if it is possible to construct a basic automorphic function, the structure of the entire class of functions automorphic with respect to a given group becomes clear. Unfortunately, basic automorphic functions are far from readily available, so that it is necessary to have recourse to more complicated constructions for the description of the complete class of automorphic functions.

Let us consider this problem for elliptic functions. By elliptic functions we mean functions automorphic with respect to the group composed of the transformations

$$Az=z+n_1\omega_1+n_2\omega_2,$$

where n_1 and n_2 are arbitrary integers, and ω_1 and ω_2 are given numbers with nonreal ratio. The numbers ω_1 and ω_2 are the periods of the elliptic function.

The fundamental domain for the group is constructed according to the same procedure as in Example 1. The simplest fundamental domain is the parallelogram with vertices $z=0$, $z=\omega_1$, $z=\omega_2$, $z=\omega_1+\omega_2$, which is called the *parallelogram of the periods*. It is clear that this fundamental domain is compact.

There is no basic automorphic function for this class. Indeed, if the function $\varphi(z)$ had one simple pole inside the parallelogram of the periods, then the integral along the boundary of this domain would be equal to the residue at this pole, i.e., would be nonzero. However, the integral along the parallelogram of the periods is zero, since the function $\varphi(z)$ must assume the same values on opposite sides in view of its periodicity, so that the integrals along opposite sides cancel one another.

Thus, the simplest elliptic function can have either one pole of order two or two simple poles within the parallelogram of the periods. Such functions exist.

An elliptic function with one pole of order two at the point $z=0$ is called a Weierstrass $\wp$- function. It is defined by the series

$$\wp(z)=\frac{1}{z^2}+\sum\sum\left\{\frac{1}{(z+n_1\omega_1+n_2\omega_2)^2}-\frac{1}{(n_1\omega_1+n_2\omega_2)^2}\right\}$$

(the summation extends over all nonnegative integers with the exception of the case $n_1=0$ and $n_2=0$). It is not difficult to verify that this series converges uniformly in the entire z-plane with the exception of the points congruent to zero, since the terms commencing with some given one do not exceed in absolute value the terms of the absolutely convergent numerical series

$$\sum\sum\frac{C}{|n_1\omega_1+n_2\omega_2|^3}\qquad\left(\operatorname{Im}\frac{\omega_2}{\omega_1}\neq 0\right).$$

The periodicity of the function $\wp(z)$ with periods ω_1 and ω_2 follows from the fact that the terms of the series are merely regrouped under the replacment of z by $z+\omega_1$ or $z+\omega_2$.

It is clear that $\wp(z)$ is an even function and that $\lim\limits_{z\to 0}\left\{\wp(z)-\frac{1}{z^2}\right\}=0.$

Theorem 6.4. *Any elliptic function with periods w_1 and w_2 can be represented in the form $f(z)=R_1(\wp(z))+\wp'(z)R_2(\wp(z))$, where $R_1(w)$ and $R_2(w)$ are rational functions.*

Proof. Note that the function $\wp(z)$ (or, more precisely, the function $\varphi(z)=\frac{1}{\wp(z)-a}$) is a basic automorphic function for the group composed of the transformations

$$Az=\pm z+n_1\omega_1+n_2\omega_2.$$

Indeed, as a fundamental domain for this group we can take the parallelogram with vertices

$$-\frac{\omega_1}{2},\ \frac{\omega_1}{2},\ \frac{\omega_1+\omega_2}{2},\ \frac{\omega_2-\omega_1}{2}$$

(half of the parallelogram of the periods), in which each value is assumed once in view of the evenness of the function $\wp(z)$.

The functions automorphic with respect to our group are the even elliptic functions with periods ω_1 and ω_2. Thus, according to Theorem 6.3, any even elliptic function is a rational function of $\wp(z)$.

If $f(z)$ is an odd elliptic function, then $\frac{f(z)}{\wp'(z)}$ is an even elliptic function. Therefore, any odd elliptic function can be represented in the form $\wp'(z)R(\wp(z))$. Since any function can be represented as the sum of an even and an odd function, we obtain the statement of our theorem.

We point out that the Weierstrass function is mainly employed in theoretical investigations because of the slow convergence of its series. It is customary in applied problems to use the elliptic functions of Jacobi as well as the so-called theta-functions*).

The relation of elliptic functions to differential equations is of great importance.

Theorem 6.5. *The function $\wp(z)$ satisfies the differential equation*

$$\wp'^2(z) = 4\wp^3(z) - g_2\wp(z) - g_3,$$

where g_2 and g_3 are constants depending on the periods w_1 and w_2.

Proof. The functions $\wp(z)$ and $\wp'(z)$ have no poles other than 0 in the parallelogram of the periods. Therefore, it suffices for the proof of the theorem to verify that the expression

$$\wp'^2(z) - 4\wp^3(z) + g_2\wp(z)$$

has no pole at 0, if we make a suitable choice of the constant g_2. We know that $\wp(z)$ is an even function and that $\wp(z) = \frac{1}{z^2} + o(1)$ $(z \to 0)$. This means that

$$\wp(z) = \frac{1}{z^2} + c_1 z^2 + c_2 z^4 + \dots .$$

From this we find

$$\wp'(z) = -\frac{2}{z^3} + 2c_1 z + \dots,$$

$$\wp'^2(z) = \frac{4}{z^6} - \frac{8c_1}{z^2} + O(1),$$

$$\wp^3(z) = \frac{1}{z^6} + \frac{3c_1}{z^2} + O(1).$$

Setting $g_2 = 20c_1$, we obtain the statement of the theorem.

Note that the square root of Eq. (6.2) can be integrated, and yields the following expression for the function $z(w)$ inverse to the function $\wp(z)$:

$$z(w) = \int_w^\infty \frac{dw}{\sqrt{4w^3 - g_2 w - g_3}}.$$

---

*) The reader may find a presentation of the theory of Jacobi's elliptic functions and the theta-functions in Whittaker and Watson's book "Modern Analysis," 4th edition, Cambridge, England.

CHAPTER X

Extremal Problems and Distribution of Values

In Chap. VIII we discussed methods of obtaining bounds for analytic functions by use of the subharmonicity of the logarithm of the modulus. These methods are far from applicable to all problems; in many cases a much more refined argument is required. In this chapter we present the simplest types of extremal principles employed for obtaining such estimates: the principle of the hyperbolic metric, the symmetrization principle and the principle of the relation between length and area. As applications of these principles we prove a series of distortion theorems for functions univalent in the mean. In the last two sections we prove two fundamental theorems from Nevanlinna's theory of the distribution of values.

1. THE PRINCIPLE OF THE HYPERBOLIC METRIC

To have a conception of the difficulties with which we shall have to deal, let us consider a rather simple problem.

Suppose that we are given a function $f(z)$ that is regular and does not exceed unity in the circle $|z|<1$. How can we strengthen this inequality, if we know also that $|f(a)|\leqslant\alpha<1$ when $|a|\leqslant r<1$?

It is readily observed that the application of the subharmonicity of $\ln f(z)$ in the circle $|z|<1$ gives no new information. Indeed, in the simplest special case where $a=0$ and $\alpha=0$, there exists a subharmonic function $\varepsilon \ln |z|$ equal to $-\infty$ for $z=0$ and as close to zero as we wish (for suitable choice of ε) for all other z in the circle $|z|<1$.

We can obtain a bound for the case $a=0$, $\alpha=0$ by the use of what is called *Schwarz's lemma:*

Lemma 1. If the function f(z) is regular is the circle $|z|<1$ and satisfies the conditions

$$f(0)=0, \qquad |f(z)|<1 \qquad (|z|<1),$$

then

$$|f'(0)| \leqslant 1, \qquad |f(z)| \leqslant |z| \qquad (|z| < 1).$$

We obtain the equality only when the function $f(z) \equiv ze^{i\theta}$.

Proof. Consider the function $\varphi(z)/z = f(z)$. Since $f(0) = 0$, the function $\varphi(z)$ is regular in the circle $|z| < 1$ and $\varphi(0) = f'(0)$ (see, for example, Sect. 2 of Chap. IV). Moreover,

$$\overline{\lim_{|z| \to 1}} |\varphi(z)| = \overline{\lim_{|z| \to 1}} |f(z)|.$$

Applying the maximum principle (see Sect. 2, Chap. VIII), we find: $|\varphi(z)| \leqslant 1$ when $|z| < 1$, and the equality holds only when the function is constant on the entire circle. Going over to $f(z)$, we obtain the statement of the lemma.

Schwarz's lemma is the basis for the principle of the hyperbolic metric, but to go from it to the general formulation of the principle (with the help of which we shall be able to solve the problem in its complete form as well as to treat many more complicated problems) we need some preparation.

Lemma 2. Let w(z) be some function mapping the domain D conformally onto the circle $|w| < 1$. The expression

$$\varrho(z, D) = \frac{|w'(z)|}{1 - |w(z)|^2}$$

is uniquely defined in domain D and does not depend on the choice of the mapping function w(z).

Proof. We must show that the quantity $\varrho(z, D)$ does not change under replacement of the function $w(z)$ by the function

$$w_1(z) = e^{i\theta} \cdot \frac{w(z) - a}{1 - \bar{a}w(z)} \qquad (|a| < 1).$$

(According to the corollary to Theorem 1.2 of Chap. IX, any other function mapping the domain D conformally onto the circle $|w| < 1$ as well as any other branch of this mapping function can be expressed in terms of $w(z)$ with the help of a linear fractional transformation of the circle $|w| < 1$ into itself.)

We have

$$|w_1'(z)| = \frac{1 - |a|^2}{|1 - \bar{a}w(z)|^2} \cdot |w'(z)|$$

and

$$1 - |w_1(z)|^2 = \frac{|1 - \bar{a}w|^2 - |a - w|^2}{|1 - \bar{a}w|^2} =$$

$$= \frac{(1 - \bar{a}w)(1 - a\bar{w}) - (a - w)(\bar{a} - \bar{w})}{|1 - \bar{a}w|^2} = \frac{(1 - |w|^2)(1 - |a|^2)}{|1 - \bar{a}w|^2}.$$

We can easily deduce the statement of the lemma from this.

The quantity $\varrho(z, D)$ is called the *density of the hyperbolic (or invariant) metric in the domain D.*

It is clear that $\varrho(z, D) \to +\infty$ as z approaches the boundary of the domain D. We can show that the function $\varrho(x+iy, D)$ satisfies the differential equation

$$\frac{\partial^2 u}{\partial x^2}+\frac{\partial^2 u}{\partial y^2}=e^{-4u}, \qquad u=\frac{1}{2}\ln \varrho(z, D).$$

The *hyperbolic metric* of the domain D is obtained by defining the *element of hyperbolic length*

$$ds=\varrho(z, D)\,|dz|.$$

After the element of length is given, it becomes possible to speak of the length of a curve or the area of a domain. We can also speak of the distance of two points as being the length of the shortest curve joining them. It is natural to call a curve that realizes this shortest length a line.

Thus, the assignment of a metric to domain D makes this domain a model of some kind of geometric space. It turns out that this space is the Lobachevskian plane. The model becomes especially intuitive if we choose the half-plane $\operatorname{Im} z > 0$ as the domain D. Here the lines are circles with centers on the real axis.

Since the geometry of the Lobachevskian plane is still also called hyperbolic geometry, the metric we have introduced into the domain D is called the hyperbolic metric (another name used is the non-Euclidean metric).

We now present the formulas for the basic quantities in the hyperbolic metric. These formulas follow easily from the definition of the element of length.

The hyperbolic length of the curve L contained in D is equal to

$$\mu(L, D)=\int_L \varrho(z, D)\,|dz|.$$

The hyperbolic area of a domain $S \subset D$ is equal to

$$\Delta(S, D)=\iint_D \varrho^2(z, D)\,dx\,dy.$$

The hyperbolic distance between points $z_1 \in D$ and $z_2 \in D$ is given by

$$r(z_1, z_2; D)=\frac{1}{2}\ln\frac{|1-w(z_1)\overline{w(z_2)}|+|w(z_1)-w(z_2)|}{|1-w(z_1)\overline{w(z_2)}|-|w(z_1)-w(z_2)|},$$

where $w(z)$ is any function mapping D conformally onto the circle $|w|<1$.

One of the fundamental properties of the hyperbolic metric is its invariance under conformal mapping. This property may be stated as follows:

Let the function $\zeta(z)$ map domain D conformally onto domain G. Then

$$\mu(L, D) = \mu(\zeta(L), G),$$
$$\Delta(S, D) = \Delta(\zeta(S), G),$$
$$r(z_1, z_2, D) = r(\zeta(z_1), \zeta(z_2), G).$$

This property follows immediately from the definition. For example, the first of the equations is obtained by a change in the variable of integration, the second by the same method, the third follows from the first.

This property is the basis for calling the hyperbolic metric the invariant metric.

Let us now turn to the formulation of the ***principle of the hyperbolic metric.*** The most frequently used form is stated in the following theorem:

Theorem 1.1. *Let the domains D and G have at least three boundary points. If the function f(z) is regular in the domain D and its values lie in the domain G, then*

$$|f'(z)|\,\varrho(f(z), G) \leqslant \varrho(z, D) \qquad (z \in D).$$

Proof. Let a be any point of domain D and let $b = f(a)$. According to the condition of the theorem, $b \in G$. Let $\zeta(z)$ denote a function that maps the domain D conformally onto the circle $|\zeta| < 1$ and sends the point a into the point 0. Let $z(\zeta)$ denote the inverse to $\zeta(z)$. Analogously, let $t(w)$ denote the function mapping domain G conformally onto the circle $|t| < 1$ and sending the point b into the point 0, and let $w(t)$ be the inverse of this function.

Consider the function

$$g(\zeta) = t(f(z(\zeta))).$$

This function is analytic, and this means that it is also regular in the circle $|\zeta| < 1$. We shall assume that the branch of it that vanishes at the point 0 has been chosen. Evidently, we have

$$g(0) = 0, \qquad |g(\zeta)| \leqslant 1 \qquad (|\zeta| < 1),$$

i.e., the function $g(\zeta)$ satisfies the conditions of Schwarz's lemma. Thus, $|g'(0)| \leqslant 1$ and the equality sign holds only if the function $g(\zeta) \equiv \zeta e^{i\theta}$. However,

$$g'(0) = t'(b) \cdot f'(a) \cdot z'(0),$$

and since $z'(0) = 1/\zeta'(a)$, we obtain

$$|f'(a)| \,.\, |t'(f(a))| \leqslant |\zeta'(a)|.$$

Noting that $t(f(a)) = 0$, $\zeta(a) = 0$, we find

$$|t'(f(a))| = \varrho(f(a), G), \qquad |\zeta'(a)| = \varrho(a, G).$$

The statement of the theorem follows easily from this.

Remark 1. If domain G contains the point at infinity, then the function $f(z)$ is naturally not assumed to be regular but ***meromorphic*** in the domain D.

Remark 2. The statement of Theorem 1.1 remains valid if we assume that the function $f(z)$ is not regular, but ***analytic*** in domain D. This means that the inequality may turn out not to be the best possible for functions regular in the domain D. The easiest way to determine whether this is so is to find an extremal function. If the extremal function is regular in domain D, then it is impossible to strengthen the inequality, but it is possible if it is not regular. Since the extremal function is trivially analytic in domain D, the inequality of Theorem 1.1 is the best possible for a simply connected domain D. Further investigation is required for multiply connected domains.

All the other formulations of the principle of the hyperbolic metric may be deduced easily from Theorem 1.1:

Let the function f(z) be regular in domain D with values in the domain G. Then

$$\mu(L, D) \geqslant \mu(f(L), G),$$
$$\Delta(S, D) \geqslant \Delta(f(S), G),$$
$$r(a, b, D) \geqslant r(f(a), f(b), G).$$

To obtain an idea of the meaning of the inequalities written above, the reader should consider the case in which the domains D and G are the unit circle, $f(z) = z^n$ and L is an arc of the circumference $|z| = r < 1$.

We now study several typical examples of obtaining bounds for analytic functions with the aid of Theorem 1.1. In particular, we shall solve the problem mentioned at the beginning of the section.

Example 1. Let the function $f(z)$ be regular and not exceed unity in the circle $|z| < 1$. We show that

$$|f'(z)| \leqslant \frac{1}{1-|z|^2} \qquad (|z| < 1). \tag{1.1}$$

If the domain B is the unit circle, then

$$\varrho(z, B) = \frac{1}{1-|z|^2},$$

and Theorem 1.1 gives us

$$\frac{|f'(z)|}{1-|f(z)|^2} \leqslant \frac{1}{1-|z|^2} \qquad (|z| < 1), \tag{1.2}$$

from which (1.1) immediately follows. Inequality (1.2) becomes an equality for any function mapping the unit circle conformally onto itself. Since we can find among the functions mapping the unit circle conformally onto itself one that vanishes at any given point of the unit circle, it is impossible to strengthen inequality (1.1) further.

Example 2. Let the function $f(z)$ be regular and not exceed unity in the circle $|z|<1$. We show that if $|f(a)|\leqslant\alpha<1$, where a is some point of the circle $|z|\leqslant r<1$, then

$$|f(z)|\leqslant \qquad (1.3)$$
$$\leqslant\frac{(1+\alpha)(1+r)(1+|z|)-(1-\alpha)(1-r)(1-|z|)}{(1+\alpha)(1+r)(1+|z|)+(1-\alpha)(1-r)(1-|z|)}\quad(|z|<1).$$

We have the equality

$$\frac{1}{2}\ln\frac{1+e^{i\theta}f(z)}{1-e^{i\theta}f(z)}-\frac{1}{2}\ln\frac{1+e^{i\theta}f(a)}{1-e^{i\theta}f(a)}=\int_a^z\frac{e^{i\theta}f'(t)}{1-e^{2i\theta}f^2(t)}\,dt.$$

The path of the integration from a to z is taken to be the line segments $(a,\ 0)$ and $(0,\ z)$. Then

$$\left|\int_a^z\frac{e^{i\theta}f'(t)\,dt}{1-e^{2i\theta}f^2(t)}\right|\leqslant\int_0^a\frac{|f'(t)|}{1-|f(t)|^2}|dt|+\int_0^z\frac{|f'(t)|}{1-|f(t)|^2}|dt|,$$

and applying inequality (1.2), we obtain

$$\frac{1}{2}\left|\ln\frac{1+e^{i\theta}f(z)}{1-e^{i\theta}f(z)}\right|\leqslant\frac{1}{2}\ln\frac{1+|f(a)|}{1-|f(a)|}+\int_0^{|a|}\frac{du}{1-u^2}+\int_0^{|z|}\frac{du}{1-u^2},$$

from which it follows that

$$\left|\ln\frac{1+e^{i\theta}f(z)}{1-e^{i\theta}f(z)}\right|\leqslant\ln\frac{1+\alpha}{1-\alpha}+\ln\frac{1+r}{1-r}+\ln\frac{1+|z|}{1-|z|}.$$

Choosing a number θ such that $e^{i\theta}f(z)=|f(z)|$, we obtain the inequality

$$\ln\frac{1+|f(z)|}{1-|f(z)|}\leqslant\ln\frac{1+\alpha}{1-\alpha}+\ln\frac{1+r}{1-r}+\ln\frac{1-|z|}{1+|z|},$$

from which inequality (1.3) readily follows.

Example 3. Let the function $f(z)$ be regular in the circle $|z|<1$ and not assume negative real values in this circle. We show that

$$\left|\frac{f'(z)}{f(z)}\right|\leqslant\frac{4}{1-|z|^2}\quad(|z|<1)\qquad(1.4)$$

and

$$\left(\frac{1-|z|}{1+|z|}\right)^2\leqslant\left|\frac{f(z)}{f(0)}\right|\leqslant\left(\frac{1+|z|}{1-|z|}\right)^2\quad(|z|<1).\qquad(1.5)$$

Now let the domain D be the circle $|z|<1$ and the domain G be the w-plane with a cross cut along the negative half of the real axis. The function $\zeta=\frac{1-\sqrt{w}}{1+\sqrt{w}}$ maps domain G conformally onto the circle $|\zeta|<1$. Therefore,

$$\frac{|\zeta'(w)|}{1-|\zeta(w)|^2}=\frac{1}{\sqrt{|w|}}\cdot\frac{1}{|1+\sqrt{w}|^2-|1-\sqrt{w}|^2}\geqslant$$

$$\geqslant\frac{1}{\sqrt{|w|}}\frac{1}{(1+\sqrt{|w|})^2-(1-\sqrt{|w|})^2}=\frac{1}{4|w|}$$

and

$$\varrho(w,\ G)\geqslant\frac{1}{4|w|}$$

(this inequality becomes an equality for $w>0$). Since

$$\varrho(z,\ D)=\frac{1}{1-|z|^2},$$

Theorem 1.1 gives us inequality (1.4).

Furthermore,

$$\left|\ln\left|\frac{f(z)}{f(0)}\right|\right|\leqslant\left|\ln\frac{f(z)}{f(0)}\right|=\left|\int_0^z\frac{f'(t)}{f(t)}\,dt\right|\leqslant4\int_0^{|z|}\frac{du}{1-u^2}=2\ln\frac{1+|z|}{1-|z|},$$

from which it follows that

$$-2\ln\frac{1+|z|}{1-|z|}\leqslant\ln\left|\frac{f(z)}{f(0)}\right|\leqslant2\ln\frac{1+|z|}{1-|z|},$$

so that we obtain inequality (1.5).

Let us now return to general questions. In particular, let us note a special case of Theorem 1.1.

Theorem 1.2. *The maximum value for $|f'(a)|$ in the class of functions analytic in the domain D and satisfying the conditions*

$$f(a)=0,\quad |f(z)|\leqslant1\qquad(z\in D),$$

is attained for the function w(z) mapping domain D conformally onto the circle $|w|<1$ and only for this function. This maximum value equals $\varrho(z, D)$.

Proof. It follows from Theorem 1.1 (if the domain G is chosen to be the circle $|w|<1$) that for any function $f(z)$ in the indicated class we have

$$|f'(a)|\leqslant\frac{\varrho(a,\ D)}{\varrho(0,\ G)}=\varrho(a,\ D)$$

(since $\varrho(0,\ |w|<1)=1$). This inequality becomes an equality only for $f(z)=e^{i\theta}w(z)$.

Corollary. If $D \subset D_1$, then $\varrho(z, D) \geqslant \varrho(z, D_1)$ $(z \in D)$, and the equality sign applies only in the case $D \equiv D_1$.

Indeed, the function mapping a larger domain into the circle $|w| < 1$ clearly belongs to the class under discussion for a smaller domain, and the mapping function coincides exactly with the factor $e^{i\theta}$ only when the domains are the same.

It is interesting to observe that the result obtained in Theorem 1.2 is the content of the far from trivial Theorem 1.1 of Chap. IX on the existence of conformal mappings. It turns out that the assumption of the existence of a conformal mapping makes the proof of this result almost trivial.

It is also interesting that the structure of the extremal functions in many extremal problems of the theory of analytic functions can be described with the aid of these or other mapping functions. We shall present two examples of theorems of such a type.

Let D be an m-connected domain. The maximum value of $|f'(a)|$ in the class of functions regular in domain D and satisfying the conditions

$$f(a) = 0, \qquad |f(z)| \leqslant 1 \qquad (z \in D),$$

*is attained for the function w(z) mapping the domain D onto the unit circle with m holes.**

The maximum value of $|f(\zeta)|$ (at a given point of the unit circle) obtained from the class of functions regular in the circle $|z| < 1$ and satisfying the conditions

$$|f(z)| \leqslant 1 \ (|z| < 1), \qquad |f(a_k)| \leqslant \alpha_k < 1 \qquad (k = 1, 2, \ldots, m),$$

*is attained for a function equal to the product of at most m functions mapping the unit circle conformally onto itself.***

The proofs of these results are too complicated to be worth introducing here. The methods employed for their proof are quite close to the classical variational procedures. The presentation of these methods would occupy an entire chapter.

2. THE SYMMETRIZATION PRINCIPLE

In applications of the principle of the hyperbolic metric a problem similar to the following is frequently encountered:

---

*See Goluzin's book, Geometric Theory of the Functions of the Complex Variable (in Russian), Moscow, Gostekhizdat, 1952.

**See the article by S. Ya. Khavinson, Extremal problems for several classes of analytical functions in finite regions, Mat. Sb., Vol. 36 (78), 3, 1955, pp. 445-478.

Let the domain D be the entire plane with a cross cut along some curve beginning at the origin. For what form of the curve is the quantity $\varrho(z, D)$ a minimum?

In the majority of cases it is possible to obtain an answer to such questions with the aid of the following theorem, which is a special case of the so-called symmetrization principle.

Theorem 2.1. *Let domain D be such that on any circle $|z| = \varrho$ for $\varrho \geq r$, there exists at least one point not contained in domain D. Then*

$$\varrho(z, D) \geq \frac{1}{4(|z| + r)}.$$

The equality sign holds only in the case that D is the entire plane with a cross cut along the ray $(-re^{i\varphi}, -\infty e^{i\varphi})$, where $\varphi = \arg z$.

Proof. Let D_r denote the plane with a cross cut along the ray $(-r, -\infty)$. It is clear that it is possible to prove the theorem only in the case that $z = a > 0$. Then the equality $\varrho(a, D) = \frac{1}{4(a+r)}$ is possible only when D coincides with D_r (we may easily deduce that $\varrho(a, D_r) = \frac{1}{4(a+r)}$) by the method of Example 3 of Sect. 1).

Note that in investigating when equality holds we do not need to consider the case in which D is a proper subdomain of D_r. Indeed, in this case we have a stricter inequality (see the corollary to Theorem 1.2).

We show that it is sufficient for the proof of the theorem for any $a > 0$ to construct a function $\varphi(z)$ with the properties:

1. The function $\varphi(z)$ is analytic in domain D.
2. $\varphi(0) = 0$, $|\varphi(z)| \leq 1$ $(z \in D)$.
3. If D is not contained in D_r, we have $|\varphi'(a)| > \frac{1}{4(a+r)}$.

Indeed, according to Theorem 1.1 (cf. Remark 2), for the function $\varphi(z)$ we must have the inequality

$$|\varphi'(a)|\,\varrho(0, G) \leq \varrho(a, D),$$

where G is the domain containing the values of $\varphi(z)$. Because of condition 2, we can take the circle $|w| < 1$ for G, so that

$$\varrho(0, |w| < 1) = 1.$$

Therefore,

$$\varrho(a, D) \geq |\varphi'(a)|,$$

and our statement follows from condition 3, since the problem has already been solved in the case where domain D is contained in D_r. We shall find it somewhat more convenient to construct the function $u(z) = \ln\left|\frac{\varphi(z)}{z-a}\right|$. Note that it is sufficient for us to construct a function $u(z)$ enjoying the following properties:

1*. The function $u(z)$ is harmonic in domain D.

2*. $u(z) \leqslant -\ln|z-a|$ $(z \in D)$.

3*. If D is not contained in D_r, then $u(a) \geqslant \ln \frac{1}{4(a+r)}$.

Indeed, suppose that such a function $u(z)$ has been constructed. Let $w(z)$ denote the function having $u(z)$ as its real part and set

$$\varphi(z) = (z-a)\, e^{w(z)}.$$

This function has the required properties. Condition 1* ensures the fulfillment of condition 1. The fulfillment of condition 2 follows from that of condition 2* (it is evident that $\varphi(a)=0$). Condition 3* implies condition 3 since $|\varphi'(a)| = e^{u(a)}$.

We need the formula

$$\frac{\sqrt{a}}{\pi} \int_0^\infty \frac{\ln|z+x|}{a+x} \frac{dx}{\sqrt{x}} = 2\ln|\sqrt{z}+\sqrt{a}|, \tag{2.1}$$

for the construction of function $u(z)$. This formula holds for any $a>0$ and any z (we take the principal value for $\sqrt{z}$, i.e., $\operatorname{Re}\sqrt{z} \geqslant 0$).

To prove this formula we write

$$\frac{\sqrt{a}}{\pi} \int_0^\infty \frac{\ln|z+x|}{a+x} \frac{dx}{\sqrt{x}} = \frac{\sqrt{a}}{\pi} \int_{-\infty}^\infty \frac{\ln|z+t^2|}{a+t^2}\, dt =$$

$$= \frac{\sqrt{a}}{\pi} \int_{-\infty}^\infty \frac{\ln|t+i\sqrt{z}|+\ln|t-i\sqrt{z}|}{a+t^2}\, dt.$$

Since we can easily obtain

$$\frac{\sqrt{a}}{\pi} \int_{-\infty}^\infty \frac{\ln|t+i\sqrt{z}|}{a+t^2}\, dt = \frac{\sqrt{a}}{\pi} \int_{-\infty}^\infty \frac{\ln|t-i\sqrt{z}|}{a+t^2}\, dt =$$

$$= \ln|\sqrt{z}+\sqrt{a}|,$$

evaluating the integral with the help of residues [see formula (3.7) of Chap. VI], we arrive at the required formula.

We note in particular that for negative z the formula takes on the simpler form:

$$\frac{\sqrt{a}}{\pi} \int_0^\infty \frac{\ln|x-t|}{a+x} \frac{dx}{\sqrt{x}} = \ln(a+t) \qquad (t>0). \tag{2.2}$$

We next consider the construction of the function $u(z)$.

According to the hypothesis of the theorem, on any circle $|z|=\varrho$ with $\varrho \geqslant r$ we can find at least one point z_ϱ not contained in the domain D. We put

$$z_\varrho = -\varrho e^{i\theta(\varrho)}, \qquad -\pi \leqslant \theta(\varrho) \leqslant \pi,$$

and

$$u(z) = -\frac{\sqrt{a+r}}{\pi} \int_0^\infty \frac{\ln|z+(x+r)e^{i\theta(x+r)}|}{a+r+x} \frac{dx}{\sqrt{x}}.$$

We verify that this function satisfies conditions 1*-3*. The integral of the function $u(z)$ converges uniformly in any finite part of the plane, so that $u(z)$ is continuous in the entire plane. The integrand is a harmonic function of z in the entire plane with the exception of the points

$$z = -(x+r)e^{i\theta(x+r)} \qquad (x > 0).$$

Since these points are not in D, the uniform convergence of the integral ensures the harmonicity of function $u(z)$ in D. Condition 1* is fulfilled for the same reasons.

From the obvious inequality

$$\ln|z+(x+r)e^{i\theta(x+r)}| \geqslant \ln|x+r-|z||$$

we find

$$u(z) \leqslant -\frac{\sqrt{a+r}}{\pi} \int_0^\infty \frac{\ln|x+r-|z||}{a+r+x} \frac{dx}{\sqrt{x}}.$$

According to formula (2.2), this gives us $u(z) \leqslant -\ln(a+|z|) \leqslant -\ln|z-a|$, i.e., condition 2* is also satisfied.

For any positive z and ϱ we have the inequality

$$\ln|z+\varrho e^{i\theta}| = \frac{1}{2}\ln\left((z+\varrho)^2 - 4z\varrho\sin^2\frac{\theta}{2}\right) =$$
$$= \ln(z+\varrho) + \frac{1}{2}\ln\left(1 - \frac{4z\varrho}{(z+\varrho)^2}\sin^2\frac{\theta}{2}\right) \leqslant \ln(z+\varrho) -$$
$$- \frac{2z\varrho}{(z+\varrho)^2}\sin^2\frac{\theta}{2}.$$

It follows from this inequality that

$$\ln|a+(x+r)e^{i\theta(x+r)}| \leqslant \ln(a+x+r) - \frac{2a(x+r)}{(a+x+r)^2}\sin^2\frac{\theta(x+r)}{2}.$$

Using this last inequality and formula (2.1), we find

$$u(a) \geqslant -2\ln\left(2\sqrt{a+r}\right) + \frac{2a\sqrt{a}}{\pi}\int_0^\infty \frac{x+r}{(a+x+r)^3}\sin^2\frac{\theta(x+r)}{2}\frac{dx}{\sqrt{x}}.$$

The last integral can vanish only if the function $\theta(x+r)$ is zero almost everywhere. However, in this case no points of D are included in the ray $(-r, -\infty)$, i.e., D is contained in D_r. If D is not contained in D_r, then $u(a) > \ln\frac{1}{4(a+r)}$, i.e., condition 3* already holds. This completes the proof.

In cases where we have to deal with problems similar to the one discussed at the beginning of the section, we can generalize the theorem with the aid of conformal mappings. However, here we have to relinquish the hypothesis that the points not contained in D may not form a connected set.

There exists an even broader generalization of Theorem 2.1, known under the name of the symmetrization principle. We need to introduce a new concept in order to be able to formulate this principle.

We generate a *symmetrized domain D** from a domain D as follows:

If the circle $|z|=\varrho$ intersects the domain D in arcs, the sum of whose lengths is $\theta(\varrho)$, then this circle is to intersect domain D^* in a single arc of length $\theta(\varrho)$ centered at the point $z=-\varrho$ (if the circle $|z|=\varrho$ is entirely contained in D, then the new circle is to be entirely contained in D^*, and conversely).

Thus, we have the inequality*

$$\varrho(z, D) \geqslant \varrho(|z|, D^*) \qquad (z \in D).$$

An analogous inequality may be established for the harmonic measure figuring in the Carlemann-Milloux problem (see Sect. 4, Chap. VIII).

3. BOUNDS FOR FUNCTIONS UNIVALENT IN THE MEAN

As an example of the application of the methods presented we shall study the problem of obtaining exact bounds for functions regular and univalent in the unit circle. Many of these estimates are valid also for a broader class of functions, those univalent in the mean along a circle. Therefore, we first define this class and become acquainted with the simplest properties of the functions in it.

Let $n(w, f)$ denote the number (counting the multiplicity) of zeros of the function $f(z)-w$ in the circle $|z|<1$.

It is necessary and sufficient for $f(z)$ to be univalent in the circle $|z|<1$ that $n(w, f)\leqslant 1$ for any w.

The function $f(z)$ is said to be *univalent in the mean along a circle within the circle* $|z|<1$, if for any $\varrho>0$ we have the inequality**

---

*A proof of the symmetrization principle can be found in the books: W. K. Hayman, "Multivalent Functions," Cambridge Univ. Press, 1958; and G. Polya, "The Isoperimetric Problem in Mathematical Physics," John Wiley, N. Y. 1962.

**It is not difficult to prove that the function $n(w,f)$ is Lebesgue integrable, but we avoid problems dealing with the Lebesgue integral in this book. It is therefore better to understand the integral of the function $n(w,f)$ along the circle $|w|=\rho$ as the limit as $r\to 1$ of the integral of the function $n(r,w,f)$, where $n(r,w,f)$ is the number of zeros of the function $f(z)-w$ in the circle $|z|<r$. The function $n(r,w,f)$ has only a finite number of points of discontinuity for any $r<1$.

$$\int\limits_{|w|=\varrho} n(w, f)\ |dw| \leqslant 2\pi\varrho.$$

It is clear that functions univalent in the circle $|z|<1$ are also univalent in the mean along a circle inside this circle.

Let us take note of two important properties of functions univalent in the mean along a circle.

Property 1. Let the function $z(\zeta)$ map the unit circle conformally onto a domain contained within the unit circle. If the function $f(z)$ is univalent in the mean along a circle within the circle $|z|<1$, then the function $g(\zeta)=f(z(\zeta))$ is also univalent in the mean along a circle within the circle $|z|<1$.

For the proof of the property it is sufficient to note that

$$n(w, f) \geqslant n(w, g),$$

since w' assumed by the function $g(\zeta)$ at the point ζ' is assumed by the function $f(z)$ at the point $z(\zeta')$.

Property 2. Let the function $f(z)$ be regular in the circle $|z|<1$ and univalent in the mean along a circle within this circle. Then there exists a number $d=d(f)$ with the following property:

For any w contained in the circle $|w|<d$ we have $n(w, f)=1$, and on any circle $|w|=\varrho$, $\varrho>d$, we can find a value w_ρ for which $n(w_\rho, f)=0$.

Suppose that there is no point on the circle $|w|=\varrho$ for which $n(w, f)=0$. This is possible only if $n(w, f)=1$ for all w on this circle. However, according to Theorem 1.1, Chap. V, the set of points at which $n(w, f)\geqslant 2$ is an open set. This means that the presence of one point of this set on the circle $|w|=\varrho$ requires the existence of an entire arc of the circle contained in this set, which contradicts the condition

$$\int\limits_{|w|=\varrho} n(w, f)\ |dw| \leqslant 2\pi\varrho,$$

since $n(w, f)\geqslant 1$ for all w on the circle of integration and $n(w, f)\geqslant 2$ on some arc of this circle.

Thus, for any $\varrho>0$ one of the following two possibilities must occur: either $n(w, f)=1$ for all w on the circle $|w|=\varrho$ or there exists a point w_ρ on the circle $|w|=\varrho$ for which we have $n(w_\rho, f)=0$.

We now show that if $n(w, f)=1$ for all w on the circle $|w|=\varrho$, then $n(w, f)=1$ also for all w within the circle $|w|\leqslant\varrho_0$. Indeed, condition $n(w, f)=1$ $(|w|=\varrho_0)$ means that the circle $|w|=\varrho_0$ is the one-to-one image under the mapping $w=f(z)$ of some set L in the circle $|z|<1$. It is clear that the set L can be only a simple closed curve (in view of the continuity of the inverse mapping). Therefore, applying the principle of corresponding boundaries (see Theorem 1.4 of Chap. V), we see that the function $f(z)$ maps the domain bounded by the curve L conformally and in a one-to-one fashion onto the circle $|w|<\varrho_0$.

Next denote the least upper bound of the values of ϱ for which $n(w, f)=1$ for all w such that $|w|<\varrho$ by $d(f)$. It is clear that $d(f)<\infty$, for otherwise the function $f(z)$ maps the circle $|z|<1$ conformally and in a one-to-one manner onto the entire plane, which is impossible. This proves the property.

We cannot find bounds for all functions regular in the circle $|z|<1$ and univalent in the mean along a circle within this circle, but we can find them for some subclasses of this class of functions. One of these subclasses is the set of functions different from zero in the unit circle, another is the set of functions satisfying the conditions $f(0)=0$, $f'(0)=1$.

Theorem 3.1. *If the function f(z) is regular in the unit circle, univalent in the mean along a circle and does not vanish within this circle, then*

$$\left|\frac{f'(z)}{f(z)}\right| \leqslant \frac{4}{1-|z|^2} \tag{3.1}$$

and

$$\left(\frac{1-|z|}{1+|z|}\right)^2 \leqslant \left|\frac{f(z)}{f(0)}\right| \leqslant \left(\frac{1+|z|}{1-|z|}\right)^2. \tag{3.2}$$

The equality sign holds in either of these inequalities only for functions of the form

$$f(z)=A\left(\frac{1+ze^{i\theta}}{1-ze^{i\theta}}\right)^2,$$

where A is any complex and θ is any real number.

Proof. Since the function $f(z)$ does not vanish in the circle $|z|<1$, it follows from property 2 that $d=d(f)=0$. This means that the values of the function $f(z)$ are contained in a domain G having a boundary or an exterior point on every circle $|w|=\varrho$. According to Theorem 1.1, we have

$$|f'(z)|\,\varrho(f(z),\ G) \leqslant \varrho(z,\ |z|<1)=\frac{1}{1-|z|^2},$$

and according to Theorem 2.1, $\varrho(w,\ G) \geqslant 1/4|w|$. The equality sign can hold in the first inequality only when the function $f(z)$ maps the circle $|z|<1$ conformally onto the domain G, and in the second, only when domain G is the plane with a cross cut along the ray $\arg z=\varphi$. Consequently,

$$\frac{|f'(z)|}{4|f(z)|} \leqslant \frac{1}{1-|z|^2},$$

and the equality sign holds only when the function $f(z)$ maps the circle $|z|<1$ conformally onto the w-plane with a cross cut along some ray $\arg z=\varphi$. This gives us inequality (3.1). Inequality (3.2) can be obtained from inequality (3.1) by the method employed in Example 3 of Sect. 1. This completes the proof.

Theorem 3.2. *Let the function $f(z)=z+a_2z^2+\ldots$ be regular and univalent in the mean along a circle within the circle $|z|<1$. Then*

$$\left|z\frac{f'(z)}{f(z)}\right|\leqslant\frac{1+|z|}{1-|z|}. \tag{3.3}$$

The equality sign holds only for functions of the form

$$f(z)=\frac{z}{(1-ze^{i\theta})^2},$$

where θ is any real number.

Proof. It follows from property 2 that the function $f(z)$ cannot vanish more than once if it is to be univalent in the mean in the circle $|z|<1$.

Let $\zeta(z)$ denote a function mapping the circle $|z|<1$ with cross cut along the radius $(0,1)$ conformally onto the circle $|\zeta|<1$, and let $z(\zeta)$ denote its inverse. Consider the function

$$g(\zeta)=f(z(\zeta)).$$

Since the function $f(z)$ vanishes only at 0 and the function $z(\zeta)$ is never zero in the circle $|\zeta|<1$, the function $g(\zeta)$ does not vanish in the circle $|\zeta|<1$. Moreover, the function $g(\zeta)$ is regular and univalent in the mean in the circle $|\zeta|<1$ (according to property 1). Applying Theorem 3.1 to function $g(\zeta)$, we find

$$\left|\frac{g'(\zeta)}{g(\zeta)}\right|\leqslant\frac{4}{1-|\zeta|^2},$$

from which it follows that

$$\left|\frac{f'(z)}{f(z)}\right|\leqslant\frac{4|\zeta'(z)|}{1-|\zeta(z)|^2}=4\varrho(z,\ G_0),$$

where G_0 denotes the unit circle with a cross cut along the radius $(0,\ 1)$. The value of $\varrho(z,\ G_0)$ can be determined directly, but it is simpler to use the equality

$$\varrho(w(z),\ G)\,|w'(z)|=\varrho(z,\ D),$$

where $w(z)$ is a function which maps the domain D conformally onto the domain G and is such that $\varrho(w,\ D_0)=\frac{1}{4w}$ $(w>0)$ (D_0 is the plane with a cross cut along the negative half of the real axis). The function

$w(z)=\frac{1}{2}\left(z+\frac{1}{z}\right)-1$ maps G_0 conformally onto D_0. Therefore,

$$\varrho(z, G_0)=\varrho(w(z), D_0)\,|w'(z)| =$$
$$=\frac{1}{2}\varrho\left(\frac{1}{2}\left(z+\frac{1}{z}\right)-1,\ D_0\right)\left|1-\frac{1}{z^2}\right|$$

and

$$\left|\frac{f'(z)}{f(z)}\right| \leqslant 2\frac{1-|z|^2}{|z|^2}\varrho\left(\frac{1}{2}\left(z+\frac{1}{z}\right)-1,\ D_0\right).$$

Noting that we could have taken in place of $z(\zeta)$ a function differing from it by an arbitrary factor of the form $e^{i\theta}$, we see that we can replace z by $ze^{i\theta}$ in the last inequality and find the minimum value of the right side as θ varies. This gives us

$$\left|\frac{f'(z)}{f(z)}\right| \leqslant 2\frac{1-|z|^2}{|z|^2}\varrho\left(\frac{1}{2}\left(|z|+\frac{1}{|z|}\right)-1,\ D_0\right),$$

i.e., since $\varrho(w, D_0)=\frac{1}{4w}\quad (w>0)$,

$$\left|\frac{f'(z)}{f(z)}\right| \leqslant \frac{1}{|z|}\cdot\frac{1+|z|}{1-|z|}.$$

The possibility of equality can be studied with the help of Theorem 3.1. This completes the proof.

We next present two inequalities which are easy consequences of Theorem 3.2.

Corollary. Let the function $f(z)=z+a_2z^2+\ldots$ *be regular and univalent in the mean along a circle within the circle* $|z|<1$. *Then*

$$|f(z)| \leqslant \frac{|z|}{(1-|z|)^2}, \tag{3.4}$$

$$|f'(z)| \leqslant \frac{1+|z|}{(1-|z|)^3}. \tag{3.5}$$

Indeed, if we write inequality (3.3) in the form

$$\left|\frac{f'(z)}{f(z)}\right| \leqslant \frac{1}{|z|}\cdot\frac{1+|z|}{1-|z|},$$

and choose a number ε sufficiently close to zero and such that arg $\varepsilon=\arg z$, then, after integrating this inequality along the segment of the radius from ε to z, since $f(\varepsilon)\to 0\ (\varepsilon\to 0)$, we find

$$\ln\left|\frac{f(z)}{f(\varepsilon)}\right| \leqslant |\ln f(z)-\ln f(\varepsilon)| \leqslant \ln\frac{|z|}{(1-|z|)^2}-\ln\frac{|\varepsilon|}{(1-|\varepsilon|)^2}.$$

From this we obtain

$$\ln\left|\varepsilon\frac{f(z)}{f(\varepsilon)}\right|\leqslant\ln\frac{|z|}{(1-|z|)^2}-2\ln(1-|\varepsilon|)$$

and, taking limits as $\varepsilon\to 0$, inequality (3.4) follows immediately.

Inequality (3.5) can be obtained by multiplying inequalities (3.3) and (3.4).

As in Theorem 3.2, the case of equality can be studied by referring to Theorem 3.1.

Remark. Letting $z\to 0$ in equality (3.4), we find

$$|f(z)|\leqslant|z|+2|z|^2+O(|z|^3). \tag{3.6}$$

This gives us

$$|a_2|\leqslant 2. \tag{3.7}$$

We can also find a lower bound for $|f(z)|$ and an inequality for the value of $d(f)$.

Theorem 3.3. *Let the function $f(z)=z+a_2z^2+\dots$ be regular and univalent in the mean along a circle inside the circle $|z|<1$. Then*

$$d(f)\geqslant\frac{1}{4} \tag{3.8}$$

and

$$|f(z)|\geqslant\frac{|z|}{(1+|z|)^2}. \tag{3.9}$$

Equality is possible only if $f(z)=\frac{z}{(1-ze^{i\theta})^2}$.

Proof. According to the definition of $d(f)=d$, the domain G containing the values of $f(z)$ has at least one boundary or exterior point on any circle $|w|=\varrho$ for $\varrho\geqslant d(f)$. Applying the same argument as in Theorem 3.1, we obtain the inequality

$$\frac{|f'(z)|}{|f(z)|+d}\leqslant\frac{4}{1-|z|^2}.$$

However, $f(0)=0$, $f'(0)=1$, so that, setting $z=0$, we find $1/d\leqslant 4$. The possibility of equality may be studied by the same method as in Theorem 3.1.

According to the definition of the quantity $d(f)$, the inequality $d(f)\geqslant 1/4$ means that any value of w from the circle $|w|<1/4$ is assumed exactly once by the function $f(z)$ in the circle $|z|<1$.

Inequality (3.9) may be proved by almost the same arguments as those used in Theorem 3.2. Choose some point c in the circle

$|z|<1$ and let $z(\zeta)$ denote a function mapping the circle $|\zeta|<1$ conformally onto the circle $|z|<1$ with a cross cut along the segment of the radius $(c, c/|c|)$ and sending 0 into 0. It is easy to verify that such a function is defined by the equation

$$\frac{ze^{-i\varphi}}{(1-ze^{-i\varphi})^2}=\alpha(c)\frac{\zeta}{(1-\zeta)^2},$$

where

$$\varphi=\arg c, \qquad \alpha(c)=\frac{4|c|}{(1+|c|)^2}.$$

Consider the function $g(\zeta)=\frac{f(z(\zeta))}{z'(0)}$. According to property 1, it is univalent in the mean along a circle inside the circle $|\zeta|<1$, $g(0)=0$, $g'(0)=1$. If $|f(c)|<1/4$, then the function $g(\zeta)$ does not assume the value $\frac{f(c)}{z'(0)}$ in the circle $|\zeta|<1$, since the value $f(c)$ $(f(c)|<1/4)$ is assumed by the function $f(z)$ only at the point c and the function $z(\zeta)$ does not take on the value c in the circle $|\zeta|<1$. However, according to inequality (3.8), we have $d(g)\geqslant 1/4$. This means that either $f(c)|\geqslant 1/4$ or that $|f(c)|\geqslant 1/4|z'(0)|$. Evaluating $z'(0)$, we arrive at inequality (3.9).

The case of equality can be studied in the usual way. This proves the theorem.

If we assume that the function is not merely univalent in the mean, but is actually univalent, then we can also obtain bounds for its derivative in the circle $|z|<1$; in fact, we can obtain both upper and lower bounds. (It is clear that no nontrivial lower bound can be given for the modulus over the entire circle of the derivative of a function univalent in the mean, since the derivative can vanish.)

Theorem 3.4. *If the function* $f(z)=z+a_2z^2+\dots$ *is regular and univalent in the circle* $|z|<1$, *then*

$$\left|z\frac{f'(z)}{f(z)}\right|\geqslant\frac{1-|z|}{1+|z|}, \qquad |f'(z)|\geqslant\frac{1-|z|}{(1+|z|)^3} \tag{3.10}$$

and, furthermore,

$$\left|z\frac{f''(z)}{f'(z)}-\frac{2|z|^2}{1-|z|^2}\right|\leqslant\frac{4|z|}{1-|z|^2}. \tag{3.11}$$

The equality holds only if $f(z)\ \frac{z}{(1-ze^{i\theta})^2}$.

Proof. Consider the function

$$g(\zeta)=f\left(\frac{\zeta+a}{1+\zeta\bar{a}}\right), \quad |a|<1.$$

Since the function $z(\zeta)=\frac{\zeta+a}{1+\zeta\bar{a}}$ maps the circle $|\zeta|<1$ conformally onto itself, the function $g(\zeta)$ is regular and univalent in the circle

$|\zeta|<1$. Applying inequality (3.7) to the function $\frac{g(\zeta)-g(0)}{g'(0)}$ (this function is univalent since $g(\zeta)$ is univalent; univalence in the mean is not preserved under such a mapping), we obtain $|g''(0)|\leqslant 4|g'(0)|$. However,

$$g'(0)=(1-|a|^2)f'(a),$$
$$g''(0)=(1-|a|^2)^2 f''(a)-2\bar{a}(1-|a|^2)f'(a).$$

Thus,

$$|(1-|a|^2)f''(a)-2\bar{a}f'(a)|\leqslant 4|f'(a)|.$$

Multiplying this last inequality by $\frac{1}{|f'(a)|}\cdot\frac{a}{1-|a|^2}$, we obtain inequality (3.11).

Setting $a=\varrho e^{i\varphi}$, we can rewrite (3.11) in the form

$$\left|\operatorname{Re}\left\{e^{i\varphi}\frac{f''(\varrho e^{i\varphi})}{f'(\varrho e^{i\varphi})}\right\}-\frac{2\varrho}{1-\varrho^2}\right|\leqslant\left|e^{i\varphi}\frac{f''(\varrho e^{i\varphi})}{f'(\varrho e^{i\varphi})}-\frac{2\varrho}{1-\varrho^2}\right|\leqslant\frac{4}{1-\varrho^2},$$

from which we find

$$\operatorname{Re}\left\{e^{i\varphi}\frac{f''(\varrho e^{i\varphi})}{f'(\varrho e^{i\varphi})}\right\}\geqslant 2\,\frac{2-\varrho}{1-\varrho^2}.$$

Since

$$\operatorname{Re}\left\{e^{i\varphi}\frac{f''(\varrho e^{i\varphi})}{f'(\varrho e^{i\varphi})}\right\}=\frac{\partial}{\partial\varrho}\operatorname{Re}\{\ln f'(\varrho e^{i\varphi})\}=\frac{\partial}{\partial\varrho}\ln|f'(\varrho e^{i\varphi})|,$$

this inequality means that

$$\frac{\partial}{\partial\varrho}\ln|f'(\varrho e^{i\varphi})|\geqslant 2\,\frac{2-\varrho}{1-\varrho^2}.$$

Integrating this inequality with respect to ϱ from zero to z, we obtain the second part of inequality (3.10), and from it, using inequality (3.4), we readily obtain the remaining inequality.

All the inequalities obtained become equalities only in the case that inequality (3.7) becomes an equality. This can happen only for a function of the type indicated. This completes the proof.

The theory of univalent functions is a highly developed part of the theory of analytic functions. Refined variational methods have been developed in this theory;* one of the simplest of these, permitting us to find some fundamental inequalities, is presented below.

---

*A complete presentation of most of the questions associated with the theory of univalent functions can be found in the books: G. M. Goluzin, Geometric Theory of the Functions of the Complex Variable (in Russian), Moscow, Gostekhizdat, 1952; W. K. Hayman, Multivalent Functions, Cambridge Univ. Press, 1958; this reference Jenkins, Univalent Functions and Conformal Mappings. (Each book presents its side of the question in great detail.)

4. THE PRINCIPLE OF LENGTH AND AREA

We next present yet another method of obtaining bounds for analytic functions. The bounds obtained with its use are somewhat less exact, but in return they are considerably more useful.

We encountered the principle of length and area in Sect. 6 of Chap. V in the derivation of the inequalities of Ahlfors and Warschawskiy. We employed this method in the proof of an estimate, but did not single it out as an independent result. We now give a separate proof of this principle in a more general form.

First of all we must define some new notation.

Suppose that we have a function $f(z)$ regular in the closed domain D, and let D be the image of the domain D under the mapping $w=f(z)$. We shall not assume that the function $f(z)$ is univalent in the domain D, so that the domain G may be covered many times by the values of the function $f(z)$. We shall assume that a one-to-one image of the domain D under the mapping $w=f(z)$ is some Riemann surface S situated above domain G. This Riemann surface is part of the Riemann surface of the function $z(\zeta)$, inverse to the function $f(z)$. Therefore, the function $z(\zeta)$ is univalent on the Riemann surface S and is a one-to-one mapping of S onto G.

If we understand the mapping in this way, then the formulas introduced in Sect. 1, Chap. V, for one-to-one conformal mappings remain valid:

If $D' \subset D$ and S' is a one-to-one image of D' under the mapping $w=f(z)$, then

$$\Delta(S') = \iint_{D'} |f'(z)|^2\,dxdy, \qquad \Delta(D') = \iint_{S'} |z'(w)|^2\,dudv$$

(where $z=x+iy$, $w=u+iv$ and $\Delta(G)$ denotes the area of the domain G).

If C is some curve contained in the domain D and L is its image under the mapping $w=f(z)$, then

$$\mu(L) = \int_C |f'(z)|\,|dz|, \qquad \mu(C) = \int_L |z'(w)|\,|dw|$$

(the length of curve Γ is denoted by $\mu(\Gamma)$).

Theorem 4.1. *Let the function $f(z)$ be regular in the closed domain D. Let λ_ρ denote the set of curves on which $|f(z)|=\varrho$, and let $\lambda(\varrho)$ be the sum of their lengths. We denote by θ_ρ the set of images of the curves λ_ρ under the mapping $w=f(z)$, and by $\theta(\varrho)$ the sum of their lengths. Then*

$$\int_0^\infty \frac{\lambda^2(\varrho)}{\theta(\varrho)}\,d\varrho \leqslant \Delta(D).$$

Proof. According to the formulas presented above, we have

$$\lambda(\varrho) = \int_{\theta_\rho} |z'(w)|\,|dw|.$$

According to the Cauchy-Schwarz inequality,

$$\left[\int FG\,dx\right]^2 \leqslant \int F^2\,dx \int G^2 dx.$$

Setting $F=1,\quad G=|z'(w)|$, we find

$$\lambda^2(\varrho)=\left\{\int_{\theta_\rho}|z'(w)||dw|\right\}^2 \leqslant \theta(\varrho)\int_{\theta_\rho}|z'(w)|^2|dw|$$

or

$$\int_0^\infty \frac{\lambda^2(\varrho)}{\theta(\varrho)}\,d\varrho \leqslant \int_0^\infty \varrho\,d\varrho \int_{\theta_\rho}|z'(\varrho e^{i\varphi})|^2\,d\varphi.$$

However,

$$\int_0^\infty \varrho\,d\varrho \int_{\theta_\rho}|z'(\varrho e^{i\varphi})|^2\,d\varphi = \iint_S |z'(w)|^2\,du\,dv = \Delta(D),$$

which yields the statement of the theorem.

The principle of length and area is employed together with the following inequality, which differs little from the inequality of Ahlfors, for obtaining bounds. It is easier for us to prove this inequality anew, rather than try to relate to the previous notation and hypotheses.

Theorem 4.2. *Let the function $f(z)$ be regular and nonzero in the circle $|z|<1$. We set $f(0)=A$, $|f(a)|=B$. Then*

$$\left|\int_A^B \frac{d\varrho}{\theta(\varrho)}\right| \leqslant \frac{1}{\pi}\left(\ln\frac{1+|a|}{1-|a|}+\pi\right).$$

Proof. We can assume without loss of generality that $0<a<1$ and $A<B$. Consider the function

$$g(\zeta)=f\left(\frac{e^\zeta-1}{e^\zeta+1}\right)$$

in the rectangle D defined by the inequalities

$$-\frac{\pi}{2}<\operatorname{Re}\zeta<b+\frac{\pi}{2},\qquad |\operatorname{Im}\zeta|<\frac{\pi}{2}\qquad \left(b=\ln\frac{1+a}{1-a}\right).$$

It is not difficult to verify that the function $z=\dfrac{e^\zeta-1}{e^\zeta+1}$ maps the strip $|\operatorname{Im}\zeta|<\pi/2$ conformally into the circle $|z|<1$ and that the rectangle D is a part of this circle. Therefore, the functions $\theta(\varrho)$, constructed for rectangle D, and $g(\zeta)$ do not exceed the functions $\theta(\varrho)$, constructed for the circle $|z|<1$, and $f(z)$. Consequently, according to Theorem 4.1, we have

$$\int_A^B \frac{\lambda^2(\varrho)}{\theta(\varrho)}\, d\varrho \leqslant \Delta(D),$$

where the function $\lambda(\varrho)$ is constructed for the rectangle D and the function $g(\zeta)$, and $\theta(\varrho)$ is constructed for the circle $|z|<1$ and the function $f(z)$.

Since the area of the rectangle equals $\pi(b+\pi)$, we obtain the inequality

$$\int_A^B \frac{\lambda^2(\varrho)}{\theta(\varrho)}\, d\varrho \leqslant \pi\left(\ln\frac{1+a}{1-a}+\pi\right). \tag{4.1}$$

Let us estimate the value of $\lambda(\varrho)$. For this purpose we note that the function $|g(\zeta)|$ assumes any value ϱ included between A and B somewhere on the segment $(0, b)$. Let ξ_ρ be that point of the segment $(0, b)$ for which $|g(\xi_\rho)|=\varrho$. One of the curves λ_ρ passes through the point ξ_ρ. It cannot be a closed curve contained in rectangle D. Indeed, the function $g(\zeta)$ does not vanish in this rectangle. Therefore, applying the maximum modulus principle to the functions $g(\zeta)$ and $1/g(\zeta)$ in a domain bounded by some loop of this closed curve, we obtain $|g(\zeta)|\equiv\varrho$, which is impossible. Thus, we may choose a curve from the set λ_ρ and with an endpoint on the rectangle D. However, the distance from any point of the segment $(0, b)$ to the boundary of the rectangle D is not less than $\pi/2$. This means that the length of the curve we have chosen is not less than π, i.e., $\lambda(\varrho)\geqslant\pi$.

Therefore, inequality (4.1) gives us

$$\pi^2\int_A^B \frac{d\varrho}{\theta(\varrho)} \leqslant \pi\left(\ln\frac{1+a}{1-a}+\pi\right).$$

This completes the proof.

It would also be valuable to study somewhat more refined estimates in the case in which the function $f(z)$ vanishes in the circle $|z|<1$, but has at most a finite number of zeros. To obtain an estimate we must determine how to insert into the integral those values of ϱ for which the point ξ_ρ has a distance less than π from a zero of the function $g(\zeta)$.

Let us consider an example that allows us to compare the bounds obtained earlier with those obtained with the help of the principle of length and area.

Example 1. Suppose that the function $f(z)$ is regular and does not vanish in the circle $|z|<1$. We find a bound for $|f(z)|$ under the assumption that $\theta(\varrho)\leqslant 2\pi\varrho$ for all $\varrho>0$.

Theorem 4.2 gives us

$$\left|\int_A^B \frac{d\varrho}{2\pi\varrho}\right| \leqslant \frac{1}{\pi}\left(\ln\frac{1+|z|}{1-|z|}+\pi\right) \qquad (A=|f(0)|,\ B=|f(z)|),$$

or

$$\left|\ln\left|\frac{f(z)}{f(0)}\right|\right| \leqslant 2\left(\ln\frac{1+|z|}{1-|z|}+\pi\right). \tag{4.2}$$

This means that

$$e^{-2\pi}\left(\frac{1-|z|}{1+|z|}\right)^2 \leqslant \left|\frac{f(z)}{f(0)}\right| \leqslant e^{2\pi}\left(\frac{1+|z|}{1-|z|}\right)^2. \tag{4.3}$$

To compare this result with those obtained earlier, we note that the condition $\theta(\varrho) \leqslant 2\pi\varrho$ $(\varrho > 0)$ means that the function $f(z)$ is univalent in the mean along a circle within the circle $|z| < 1$. Indeed, the value of $n(w, f)$ is the number of zeros of the function $f(z) - w$ in the circle $|z| < 1$. This quantity can be considered as the number of sheets of the Riemann surface S above the point w. (The Riemann surface S is the one-to-one image of the circle $|z| < 1$ under the mapping $w = f(z)$.) The curves θ_ρ are none other than the arcs of the circle $|w| = \varrho$ on the Riemann surface S. Each point w of the circle $|w| = \varrho$ occurs in θ_ρ as many times as the number of sheets of the Riemann surface S lying above the point w, i.e., $n(w, f)$ times. Therefore,

$$\theta(\varrho) = \int_{|w|=\rho} n(w, f)\,|dw|$$

and the assumption $\theta(\varrho) \leqslant 2\pi\varrho$ means univalence of the function $f(z)$ in the mean along a circle within the circle $|z| < 1$.

We can compare the result obtained in the example with that of Theorem 3.1, which has the form

$$\left(\frac{1-|z|}{1+|z|}\right)^2 \leqslant \left|\frac{f(z)}{f(0)}\right| \leqslant \left(\frac{1+|z|}{1-|z|}\right)^2.$$

The bounds obtained differ by a factor $e^{2\pi}$. This factor is far from one, but it does not change the order of the growth of the function $|f(z)|$ as $|z| \to 1$. We thus see that Theorem 3.1 is somewhat more exact, but that its proof is considerably more complicated (we also have to take account of the symmetrization principle in its proof).

It is worth pointing out that it is also possible in some cases to obtain exact bounds with the aid of the principle of length and area. Thus, for example, one of the simplest proofs of the inequality $|a_2| \leqslant 2$ for univalent functions is obtained with the aid of the principle of length and area (it is used in the form called the area theorem).

One of the most important features of the principle of length and area is its generality.

We shall present yet another example of the use of the principle of length and area in obtaining a bound for functions p-valent in the mean along a square inside the circle $|z|<1$.

A function $f(z)$ is called p-valent in the mean along a square inside the circle $|z|<1$, if for any $\varrho>0$ we have

$$\iint\limits_{|w|<\varrho} n(w, f)\, du\, dv \leqslant \pi\varrho^2 p.$$

Here as before, $n(w, f)$ is the number of zeros of the function $f(z)-w$ in the circle.

It is easy to verify that a function p-valent in the mean along a circle is also p-valent in the mean along a square, but the converse is false.

Theorem 4.3. *Let the function $f(z)$ be regular, p-valent in the mean along a square and not vanish in the circle $|z|<1$. Then*

$$e^{-2\pi p-\frac{1}{2}}\left(\frac{1-|z|}{1+|z|}\right)^{2p} \leqslant \left|\frac{f(z)}{f(0)}\right| \leqslant e^{2\pi p+\frac{1}{2}}\left(\frac{1+|z|}{1-|z|}\right)^{2p}.$$

Proof. According to Theorem 4.2, we have

$$\left|\int\limits_A^B \frac{d\varrho}{\theta(\varrho)}\right| \leqslant \frac{1}{\pi}\left(\ln\frac{1+|z|}{1-|z|}+\pi\right), \qquad (A=|f(0)|,\ B=|f(z)|).$$

We have to find bounds for the left-hand integral, by using the p-valence of the function $f(z)$ in the mean along a square within the circle $|z|<1$. This condition can be written in the form

$$\int\limits_0^\varrho \theta(t)\, dt \leqslant \pi\varrho^2 p$$

or in the form

$$-\pi\varrho^2 \leqslant \varphi(\varrho) \leqslant 0, \tag{4.4}$$

where

$$\varphi(\varrho) = \int\limits_0^\varrho [\theta(t) - 2\pi t p]\, dt.$$

From the obvious inequality $\frac{x}{a}+\frac{a}{x} \geqslant 2$ we obtain the inequality $\frac{1}{x} \geqslant \frac{1}{a} - \frac{x-a}{a^2}$ and setting $x=\theta(t)$, $a=2\pi t p$, we arrive at the inequality

$$\frac{1}{\theta(t)} \geqslant \frac{1}{2\pi t p} - \frac{\varphi'(t)}{(2\pi t p)^2}.$$

Assuming for the sake of definiteness that $A < B$, we obtain from this inequality

$$\int_A^B \frac{d\varrho}{\theta(\varrho)} \geqslant \frac{1}{2\pi p} \ln \frac{B}{A} - \int_A^B \frac{\varphi'(t)\, dt}{(2\pi t p)^2}.$$

Integrating by parts and employing (4.4), we find

$$\int_A^B \frac{d\varrho}{\theta(\varrho)} \geqslant \frac{1}{2\pi\varrho} \ln \frac{B}{A} + \frac{\varphi(A)}{(2\pi A p)^2} \geqslant \frac{1}{2\pi p} \ln \frac{B}{A} - \frac{1}{4\pi p}.$$

Thus, $\left| \ln \left| \frac{f(z)}{f(0)} \right| \right| \leqslant 2\pi p + \frac{1}{2} + 2p \ln \frac{1+|z|}{1-|z|}$, which proves the theorem.

5. DISTRIBUTION OF VALUES OF ENTIRE AND MEROMORPHIC FUNCTIONS

In the preceding sections we developed methods for obtaining bounds for functions regular in a given domain (usually the unit circle), under one or another hypothesis relating to the distribution of the values assumed by these functions in this domain. We now present some results relating to the distribution of values of functions regular or meromorphic in the entire finite plane (functions regular in the entire finite plane are called entire functions).

We must first introduce some notation for this purpose.

Let the function $F(z)$ be meromorphic in the entire finite plane. Let $n(r, \zeta, F)$ denote the number of zeros of the function $F(z) - \zeta$ in the circle $|z| < r$ (each zero is counted a number of times equal to its multiplicity). Let $n(r, \infty, F)$ denote the number of poles of the function $F(z)$ in the circle $|z| < r$. In addition, let

$$N(r, \zeta, F) = \int_0^r \frac{n(t, \zeta, F) - n(0, \zeta, F)}{t}\, dt + n(0, \zeta, F) \ln r.$$

The function $N(r, \zeta, F)$ is an average measure of the number of times the function $F(z)$ assumes the value ζ in the circle $|z| < r$.

The following function is an average measure of how close the function $F(z)$ is to the value ζ on the circle $|z| = r$:

$$m(r, \zeta, F) = \frac{1}{2\pi r} \int_{|z|=r} \ln^+ \frac{1}{|F(z) - \zeta|} |dz|,$$

$$m(r, \infty, F) = \frac{1}{2\pi r} \int_{|z|=r} \ln^+ |F(z)|\, |dz|.$$

Here $\ln^+ x = \max\{\ln x, 0\}$.

For the sake of brevity in the sequel we shall write $n(r, \zeta, F)$, $N(r, \zeta, F)$ and $m(r, \zeta, F)$ in place of $n(r, \zeta)$, $N(r, \zeta)$ and $m(r, \zeta)$ respectively, if it is clear to which function this notation refers.

It is clear that average characteristics of the type of $N(r, \zeta)$ and $m(r, \zeta)$ can be introduced in many ways. The reason for introducing these particular characteristics is given in the following theorem:

Theorem 5.1. *For any function $F(z)$ meromorphic in the entire finite plane and for any fixed ζ we have the following relation as $r \to \infty$:*

$$m(r, \zeta) + N(r, \zeta) = m(r, \infty) + N(r, \infty) + O(1).$$

Proof. We proved in Sect. 2 of Chap. VIII Jensen's formula

$$\frac{1}{2\pi r} \int\limits_{|z|=r} \ln|f(z)|\,|dz| = \ln|f(0)| + \\ + \sum_{|a_k|<r} \ln\frac{r}{|a_k|} - \sum_{|b_k|<r} \ln\frac{r}{|b_k|},$$

which is valid for any function meromorphic in the circle $|z| \leqslant r$ and not having a zero or a pole at the point 0.

It is easy to express sums in terms of the functions $N(r, 0, f)$ and $N(r, \infty, F)$. In fact,

$$\sum_{|a_k|<r} \ln\frac{r}{|a_k|} = \int\limits_0^r \ln\frac{r}{t}\, dn(t, 0) = \int\limits_0^r \frac{n(t, 0)}{t}\, dt = N(r, 0)$$

(since $n(0, 0) = 0$) and analogously,

$$\sum_{|b_k|<r} \ln\frac{r}{|b_k|} = \int\limits_0^r \frac{n(t, \infty)}{t}\, dt = N(r, \infty) \qquad (n(0, \infty) = 0).$$

Therefore, setting $f(z) = F(z) - \zeta$ and noting that

$$N(r, 0, F-\zeta) = N(r, \zeta, F), \qquad N(r, \infty, F-\zeta) = N(r, \infty, F),$$

we obtain from Jensen's formula

$$\frac{1}{2\pi r} \int\limits_{|z|=r} \ln|F(z)-\zeta|\,|dz| - \ln|F(0)-\zeta| = \\ = N(r, \zeta, F) - N(r, \infty, F). \tag{5.1}$$

This formula also remains valid for $F(0) = \zeta$ or $F(0) = \infty$, only the term $\ln|F(0)-\zeta|$ must be replaced by some other constant, the finding of which we leave to the reader.

Note that

$$\frac{1}{2\pi r}\int_{|z|=r}\ln|F(z)-\zeta||dz| = -\frac{1}{2\pi r}\int_{|z|=r}\ln^{+}\frac{1}{|F(z)-\zeta|}|dz| + \\ +\frac{1}{2\pi r}\int_{|z|=r}\ln^{+}|F(z)-\zeta||dz|.$$

The first term equals $-m(r,\zeta)$ and in view of the evident inequalities

$$\ln^{+}|w|-\ln^{+}|\zeta|-\ln 2\leqslant \ln^{+}|w-\zeta|\leqslant \\ \leqslant \ln^{+}|w|+\ln^{+}|\zeta|+\ln 2$$

for the second term we can write

$$\left|\frac{1}{2\pi r}\int_{|z|=r}\ln^{+}|F(z)-\zeta||dz|-m(r,\infty)\right|\leqslant \ln^{+}|\zeta|+\ln 2.$$

Thus,

$$\frac{1}{2\pi r}\int_{|z|=r}\ln|F(z)-\zeta||dz| = m(r,\infty)-m(r,\zeta)+O(1).$$

Substituting this relation into formula (5.1), we arrive at the statement of the theorem.

The function

$$T(r)=T(r,F)=m(r,\infty)+N(r,\infty)$$

is called the *characteristic function* or the *characteristic meromorphic function* of $F(z)$. The statement of Theorem 5.1 can be formulated as follows:

$$m(r,\zeta)+N(r,\zeta)=T(r)+O(1). \tag{5.2}$$

The theorem proved reveals an interesting symmetry in the distribution of values of a function meromorphic in the entire finite plane:

If some value ζ is assumed by the function $F(z)$ comparatively rarely (i.e., the function $N(r,\zeta)$ is small compared with the function $T(r)$), then the values of the function $F(z)$ must be close to the value ζ.

This uniformity is most simply exhibited in the result that an entire function (i.e., not assuming the value $\zeta=\infty$) approaches infinity along some path leading up to the point at infinity.

This uniformity is easily observed in the behavior of all the elementary functions: for instance, the function e^{z} does not vanish; in return it approaches zero uniformly in the whole half-plane $\operatorname{Re} z<0$.

It is interesting to study the behavior of the functions $m(r, \zeta)$, $N(r, \zeta)$ and $T(r)$ for a rational function $F(z)$.

As $z \to \infty$, a rational function approaches some limit a. If $\zeta \neq a$, then $m(r, \zeta) = O(1)$, and the number of zeros of the function $F(z) - \zeta$ is equal to the degree of the rational function, i.e., to the larger of the degrees of the numerator and denominator (we denote this by k). Thus,

$$T(r) = O(1) + N(r, \zeta) = O(1) + \int_0^r \frac{n(t, \zeta) - n(0, \zeta)}{t} dt + $$
$$+ n(0, \zeta) \ln r = k \ln r + O(1).$$

For $\zeta = a$ the number of zeros of $F(z)$ is less than k and this is compensated by the fact that the function $m(r, \zeta)$ increases as $r \to \infty$.

If $F(z)$ is an entire function, then the growth of the characteristic $T(r)$ is closely connected with the growth of the maximum modulus of $F(z)$ on the circle $|z| = r$, as is shown in the following theorem.

Theorem 5.2. *Let $F(z)$ be an entire function and let $M(r) = \max_{|z|=r} |F(z)|$. Then for any $0 < \theta < 1$ and for sufficiently large r we have*

$$\frac{1-\theta}{1+\theta} \ln M(\theta r) \leqslant T(r) \leqslant \ln M(r).$$

Proof. $N(r, \infty) \equiv 0$ for an entire function, so that

$$T(r) = m(r, \infty) = \frac{1}{2\pi r} \int_{|z|=r} \ln^+ |F(z)| |dz| \leqslant \ln^+ M(r)$$

for sufficiently large r. The right-hand inequality follows from this.

On the other hand, $\ln^+ |F(z)|$ is a subharmonic function in the entire finite plane. This means that in the circle $|z| < r$ it does not exceed the harmonic function constructed in terms of the values of $\ln^+ |F(z)|$ on the boundary of this circle, i.e., on the circumference $|z| = r$. Forming this harmonic function with the aid of Poisson's integral, we find

$$\ln^+ |F(\varrho e^{i\varphi})| \leqslant \frac{r^2 - \varrho^2}{2\pi} \int_0^{2\pi} \frac{\ln^+ |F(re^{i\psi})| \, d\psi}{r^2 + \varrho^2 - 2r\varrho \cos(\psi - \varphi)} \leqslant$$
$$\leqslant \frac{r^2 - \varrho^2}{(r - \varrho)^2} \frac{1}{2\pi} \int_0^{2\pi} \ln^+ |F(re^{i\psi})| \, d\psi.$$

We readily see from this that

$$\frac{r - \varrho}{r + \varrho} \ln M(\varrho) \leqslant \frac{1}{2\pi} \int_0^{2\pi} \ln^+ |F(re^{i\psi})| \, d\psi =$$
$$= \frac{1}{2\pi r} \int_{|z|=r} \ln^+ |F(z)| |dz| = T(r).$$

Setting $\varrho=\theta r$, we obtain the left-hand inequality, which completes the proof.

The rapidity of growth of an entire function seems to be determined by the degree of difficulty of its structure. The characteristic $T(r)$ plays about the same role as in the case of meromorphic functions. The following theorem is analogous to Liouville's theorem (see Sect. 2, Chap. IV).

Theorem 5.3. *If*

$$\varliminf_{r\to\infty} \frac{T(r)}{\ln r}\leqslant m, \tag{5.3}$$

then F(z) is a rational function of degree not greater than m.

Proof. Note that it follows from condition (5.3) that the function $F(z)$ does not have more than m poles. Indeed, otherwise, we have $n(r,\infty)\geqslant\mu>m$ for $r>r_0$ and

$$N(r,\infty)\geqslant\int_{r_0}^{r}\frac{n(t,\infty)-n(0,\infty)}{t}\,dt+n(0,\infty)\ln r\geqslant$$
$$\geqslant\mu\ln r-O(1),$$

from which it follows that $T(r)\geqslant\mu\ln r+O(1)$, contradicting (5.3).

We now construct a proper (the degree of the denominator exceeds that of the numerator) rational function $G(z)$ which has the same poles as $F(z)$ as well as the same principal parts at these poles. Since $G(z)\to 0$ as $z\to\infty$, $m(r,\infty,G)=0$ for sufficiently large r. The function $H(z)=F(z)-G(z)$ has no poles and

$$T(r,H)=m(r,\infty,H)\leqslant m(r,\infty,F)+m(r,\infty,G)+\ln 2\leqslant$$
$$\leqslant T(r,F)+O(1)$$

in view of the obvious inequality

$$\ln^+|a-b|\leqslant\ln^+|a|+\ln^+|b|+\ln 2.$$

According to Theorem 5.2, for the entire function $H(z)$ we have the relation

$$\varliminf_{r\to\infty}\frac{\ln M(r,H)}{\ln r}<\infty,\qquad M(r,H)=\max_{|z|=r}|H(z)|,$$

i.e.,

$$\varliminf_{r\to\infty}\frac{M(r,H)}{r^p}=0$$

for some p. According to Liouville's theorem (see Sect. 2, Chap. IV), the function $H(z)$ is a polynomial. Thus, $F(z)$ is a rational function.

However, we saw that for a rational function of degree k we have the relation $T(r, F) = k \ln r + O(1)$. Consequently, $F(z)$ is a rational function of degree not exceeding m. This completes the proof.

The simplest quantity characterizing the growth of the function $T(r)$ is the number

$$\varrho = \overline{\lim_{r \to \infty}} \frac{\ln T(r)}{\ln r},$$

called the *order of the meromorphic function.*

In view of Theorem 5.2, we can use $\ln M(r)$ in place of the quantity $T(r)$ in determining the order of an entire function.

The functions studied in greatest detail in the theory of entire functions are the functions of finite order, i.e., those for which $0 < \varrho < \infty$.

The theory of entire and meromorphic (especially the theory of entire functions) is one of the most highly developed branches of the theory of analytic functions. However, it is not our aim to discuss even the most basic problems of this theory. This would require at least an entire chapter.*

In this and the following sections we prove two very beautiful results directly related to the theory of distribution of values.

To formulate the first of these results, called the *Denjoy-Carlemann-Ahlfors theorem,* we need the notion of asymptotic value of an entire function:

The number ζ is called an ***asymptotic value of the entire function F(z)***, if there exists a curve L ending at the point at infinity such that $F(z) \to \zeta$ as $z \to \infty$ along curve L.

Theorem 5.4. *The number of distinct (finite) asymptotic values of an entire function of order* ϱ *does not exceed* 2ϱ.

Proof. Let the function $F(z)$ have n distinct finite asymptotic values, and let $L_1, L_2, \ldots, L_n$ be the curves along which the function $F(z)$ approaches the asymptotic values $a_1, a_2, \ldots, a_n$. We can assume without loss of generality that the curves L_k start at the point 0 and have no other point in common. Then the plane is broken up by these curves into n different domains $D_1, D_2, \ldots, D_n$.

According to a theorem of Lindelöf (see the corollary to Theorem 4.3, Chap. VIII), the function $F(z)$ cannot be bounded in any one of the domains D_k, since it has distinct limits as $z \to \infty$ on different sides of the domain D_k.

We can obtain a lower bound for the growth of a function bounded on the boundary of an infinite domain and unbounded within the domain with the aid of the Phragmen-Lindelöf theorem proved in

*Readers wishing to become acquainted with the theory of entire functions can consult the books: A. O. Gel'fand, Calculations of Finite Differences (in Russian), Moscow, Gostekhizdat, 1959; M. A. Evgrafov, Asymptotic Estimates and Entire Functions, Gordon and Breach, N.Y., 1962; B. Ya. Levin, Distribution of the Roots of Entire Functions (in Russian), Moscow, Gostekhizdat, 1956.

Sect. 6 of Chap. VIII (Theorem 6.1). Applying this theorem to the function $F(z)$ in the domains $D_1, D_2, \ldots, D_n$, we obtain

$$\ln \ln M(r) \geqslant \pi \int_1^r \frac{dt}{\theta_k(t)} + C \qquad (k = 1, 2, \ldots, n),$$

where $\theta_k(t)$ is the sum of the lengths of the arcs of the circle $|z| = r$ lying in the domain D_k, and C is a constant independent of r.

Summing these inequalities, we find

$$n \ln \ln M(r) \geqslant \pi \int_1^r \sum_1^n \frac{1}{\theta_k(t)}\, dt + C_1. \tag{5.4}$$

We next find an estimate for the sum occurring in the integrand. According to the Cauchy-Schwarz inequality,

$$\left(\sum a_s b_s\right)^2 \leqslant \sum a_s^2 \cdot \sum b_s^2.$$

If we take into account that

$$\sum_1^n \theta_k(t) = 2\pi t,$$

because the set of the D_k covers the entire plane, we can write

$$2\pi t \sum_1^n \frac{1}{\theta_k(t)} = \sum_1^n \theta_k(t) \sum_1^n \frac{1}{\theta_k(t)} \geqslant \left\{\sum_1^n \sqrt{\theta_k} \cdot \frac{1}{\sqrt{\theta_k}}\right\}^2 = n^2.$$

Thus

$$\sum_1^n \frac{1}{\theta_k(t)} \geqslant \frac{n^2}{2\pi t}.$$

Substituting this estimate into inequality (5.4), we obtain

$$\ln \ln M(r) \geqslant \frac{n}{2} \ln r + C_1,$$

from which it follows from the definition of order that $\varrho \geqslant n/2$. This completes the proof.

That the theorem just proved gives an exact bound is shown by the example

$$F(z) = \int_0^z \frac{\sin t^m}{t^m}\, dt.$$

Indeed, this function has order m, as may readily be seen from the inequality

$$|F(z)| \leqslant |z| e^{|z|^m}.$$

On the other hand, as z approaches infinity along the rays $\arg z = \frac{\pi i s}{m}$ $(s=0, 1, \ldots, 2m-1)$, the function $F(z)$ has the limits

$$\alpha_s = \int_0^{\infty e^{\frac{\pi i s}{m}}} \frac{\sin t^m}{t^m}\, dt = e^{-\frac{m-1}{m}\cdot s\cdot \pi i} \int_0^{\infty} \frac{\sin x^m}{x^m}\, dx =$$

$$= e^{\frac{\pi i s}{m}} \frac{1}{m} \Gamma\left(\frac{1}{m}-1\right) \sin \frac{\pi}{m}.$$

Thus, the function $F(z)$ has $2m$ distinct asymptotic values.

We require one more definition in order to be able to formulate the second result.

By the *defect* of a value ζ we mean the number

$$\delta(\zeta) = \delta(\zeta, F) = 1 - \varlimsup_{r\to\infty} \frac{N(r, \zeta)}{T(r)}.$$

It is clear that we have the inequality $0 \leqslant \delta(\zeta) \leqslant 1$ for all values of ζ, since $0 \leqslant N(r, \zeta) \leqslant T(r) + O(1)$.

The result we shall prove in the following section (the second fundamental theorem of Nevanlinna's theory of distribution of values) states that the sum of the defects of all values of a function meromorphic in the entire finite plane does not exceed two. This result implies in particular the theorem of Picard (see Sect. 5 of Chap. IX) stating that a function meromorphic in the entire finite plane takes on all values, with perhaps one exception, at least twice.

It is instructive to observe that the arguments leading to the validity of this result are simple and striking. We present them here for the case of an entire function $F(z)$ in order to limit discussion to sums of defects with finite value, since for an entire function $\delta(\infty) = 1$.

If $\delta(\zeta) > 0$, this means that

$$\varliminf_{r\to\infty} \frac{m(r, \zeta)}{T(r)} = \delta(\zeta) > 0,$$

i.e., the function $F(z)$ approaches the value ζ quite rapidly as z approaches infinity in some part of the plane. However, if the function itself approaches a constant function in some domain, then its derivative must approach zero in this domain with roughly the same speed. This means that

$$\delta(0, F') \geqslant \sum \delta(\zeta, F), \tag{5.5}$$

where the sum is taken over all defects of finite value. However, according to the definition of defect, we have $\delta(0, F') \leqslant 1$, i.e., the sum of all defects of finite value for the function $F(z)$ does not exceed one, so that the sum of all defects does not exceed two.

Unfortunately, this simple argument turns out to be rather difficult to justify. Even though inequality (5.5) turns out to be correct, its proof requires a great deal of effort. It is easier to prove the theorem without this inequality. Certain interesting regularities have been found in the search for a proof of the second fundamental theorem of Nevanlinna.

6. NEVANLINNA'S THEOREM OF DEFECT

We first consider the geometric meaning of the characteristic $T(r)$ of a meromorphic function.

First of all let us recall some information about the Riemann sphere.

Each point $z = x + iy$ of the complex plane corresponds to the point (ξ, η, ζ) of the sphere $\xi^2 + \eta^2 + \left(\zeta - \frac{1}{2}\right)^2 = \left(\frac{1}{2}\right)^2$. The quantities ξ, η, ζ are related to the coordinates x, y of the plane by the equations

$$\xi = \frac{1}{2}\frac{x|z|}{1+|z|^2}, \quad \eta = \frac{1}{2}\frac{y|z|}{1+|z|^2}, \quad \zeta = \frac{|z|^2}{1+|z|^2}$$

(see Sect. 1, Chap. I). The distance between two points of the Riemann sphere corresponding to the points z and w is equal to

$$k(z, w) = \frac{|w-z|}{\sqrt{1+|z|^2}\sqrt{1+|w|^2}}, \qquad k(z, \infty) = \frac{1}{\sqrt{1+|z|^2}}.$$

Thus, the element of length on the Riemann sphere is equal to

$$ds = \frac{|dz|}{1+|z|^2},$$

and the element of area is equal to

$$d\sigma = \frac{dx\,dy}{(1+|z|^2)^2}.$$

We shall say that the expressions

$$\int_L \frac{|dz|}{1+|z|^2}, \quad \iint_D \frac{dx\,dy}{(1+|z|^2)^2}$$

are the ***spherical length of the curve*** L and the ***spherical area of domain*** D, respectively.

Let us take note of an important and easily verified property of the spherical metric.

The spherical metric is invariant under transformations of the form

$$w = \frac{1 + z\bar{a}}{z - a}.$$

(These transformations correspond to rotations of the Riemann sphere.)

We shall require yet another generalization of Jensen's formula:

Lemma 1. *Let the function* $\varrho(\zeta)$, $\zeta = \xi + i\eta$, *be continuous in the entire plane except at a finite number of points, and let it satisfy the relations*

$$\varrho(\zeta) \geqslant 0, \quad \iint\limits_{-\infty}^{\infty} \varrho(\zeta) \ln^{+} |\zeta| \, d\xi \, d\eta < \infty, \quad \iint\limits_{-\infty}^{\infty} \varrho(\zeta) \, d\xi \, d\eta = 1.$$

We set

$$U(w) = \iint\limits_{-\infty}^{\infty} \varrho(\zeta) \ln |w - \zeta| \, d\xi \, d\eta.$$

$$V(r) = \iint\limits_{-\infty}^{\infty} n(r, \zeta, F) \varrho(\zeta) \, d\xi \, d\eta,$$

where $F(z)$ *is some function meromorphic in the entire finite plane. Then*

$$\frac{1}{2\pi r} \int\limits_{|z|=r} U(F(z)) |dz| =$$

$$= U(F(0)) + \int\limits_{0}^{r} \frac{V(x)}{x} dx - N(r, \infty, F). \tag{6.1}$$

Proof. We employ Jensen's formula in the form in which it was used in the preceding section [see formula (5.1)]

$$\frac{1}{2\pi r} \int\limits_{|z|=r} \ln |F(z) - \zeta| \, |dz| =$$

$$= \ln |F(0) - \zeta| + N(r, \zeta, F) - N(r, \infty, F).$$

We next multiply this formula by $\varrho(\zeta)$ and integrate over the entire plane. In view of the conditions on $\varrho(\zeta)$ all integrals converge uniformly, so that it is permissible to interchange the order of integration. If we recall that for $\zeta \neq F(0)$

$$N(r, \zeta) = \int\limits_{0}^{r} \frac{n(x, \zeta)}{x} dx,$$

then it is easy to obtain the statement of the lemma by integrating over ξ, η.

Remark 1. If $F(0)=\infty$, then $U(F(0))$, as in the ordinary Jensen formula, must be replaced by some other constant.

Remark 2. A rather simple geometric meaning can readily be assigned to the function $V(r)$. To do this we introduce into the complex plane a metric having as its element of length $ds=\sqrt{\varrho(\zeta)}\,|d\zeta|$. Then $\varrho(\zeta)\,d\xi\,d\eta$ is the element of area in this metric. If S_r denotes the Riemann surface that is the one-to-one image of the circle $|z|<r$ under the mapping $w=F(z)$, then $n(r,\zeta)$ is the number of sheets of the Riemann surface S_r situated above the point ζ. Therefore, $V(r)$ is nothing more than the area of the Riemann surface S_r in our metric.

This line of reasoning (see also Sect. 4) permits us to obtain another formula for the function $V(r)$:

$$V(r)=\iint_{|z|<r}\varrho(F(z))\,|F'(z)|^2\,dx\,dy. \tag{6.2}$$

With the help of Lemma 1 it is not difficult now to establish the geometric meaning of the function $T(r,F)$—the characteristic of a function $F(z)$ meromorphic in the entire finite plane.

To do this we set

$$\varrho(\zeta)=\frac{1}{\pi}\cdot\frac{1}{(1+|\zeta|^2)^2}.$$

Then the function $V(r)$ becomes the spherical area of the Riemann surface S_r divided by π. We denote the spherical area of the Riemann surface S_r by $S(r)$. According to Lemma 1, we have

$$\frac{1}{2\pi r}\int_{|z|=r}U(F(z))\,|dz|=U(F(0))+\frac{1}{\pi}\int_0^r\frac{S(x)}{x}\,dx-N(r,\infty).$$

We next find the function $U(w)$. By definition,

$$U(w)=\frac{1}{\pi}\iint_{-\infty}^{\infty}\frac{\ln|w-\zeta|}{(1+|\zeta|^2)^2}\,d\xi\,d\eta=$$

$$=\frac{1}{\pi}\int_0^{\infty}\frac{1}{(1+R^2)^2}\int_{|\zeta|=R}\ln|w-\zeta|\,|d\zeta|\,dR.$$

The inner integral may be evaluated, for instance, by Jensen's formula

$$\frac{1}{2\pi R}\int_{|\zeta|=R}\ln|w-\zeta|\,|d\zeta|=\begin{cases}\ln R & (|w|<R),\\ \ln|w| & (|w|\geqslant R),\end{cases}$$

and after evaluating the integral obtained, we see that $U(w)=\ln\sqrt{1+|w|^2}$.

We thus arrive at the formula

$$\frac{1}{2\pi r}\int\limits_{|z|=r} \ln\sqrt{1+|F(z)|^2}\,|dz| + N(r,\infty) = \frac{1}{\pi}\int\limits_0^r \frac{S(x)}{x}\,dx + \ln\sqrt{1+|F(0)|^2} \tag{6.3}$$

(the formula may be verified in the usual way for $F(0)=\infty$).

It follows from the obvious inequality

$$\ln^+|w| \leqslant \ln\sqrt{1+|w|^2} \leqslant \ln^+|w| + \ln 2$$

that

$$m(r,\infty) \leqslant \frac{1}{2\pi r}\int\limits_{|z|=r} \ln\sqrt{1+|F(z)|^2}\,|dz| \leqslant m(r,\infty) + \ln 2.$$

Therefore,

$$T(r) = m(r,\infty) + N(r,\infty) = \frac{1}{\pi}\int\limits_0^r \frac{S(x)}{x}\,dx + O(1).$$

This formula gives us the geometric meaning we seek for the characteristic of a meromorphic function.

The quantities

$$\mathring{T}(r) = \frac{1}{\pi}\int\limits_0^r \frac{S(x)}{x}\,dx,$$

$$\mathring{m}(r,\zeta) = -\frac{1}{2\pi r}\int\limits_{|z|=r} \ln k(\zeta, F(z))\,|dz|,$$

where

$$k(\zeta, w) = \frac{|\zeta - w|}{\sqrt{1+|\zeta|^2}\sqrt{1+|w|^2}},$$

are called the *spherical form of the characteristic* and the *spherical form of the approximation function*, respectively.

We have a somewhat more exact relation than Theorem 5.1 for the spherical form of the characteristic:

Theorem 6.1. $\mathring{m}(r,\zeta) + N(r,\zeta) = \mathring{T}(r) - \ln k(\zeta, F(0))$.

Proof. For $\zeta=\infty$ the theorem coincides with formula (6.3). To prove the statement for any ζ we consider the function $G(z) = \frac{1+\bar{\zeta}F(z)}{F(z)-\zeta}$ and apply formula (6.3). This gives us

$$\mathring{m}(r,\infty,G) + N(r,\infty,G) = \mathring{T}(r,G) - \ln k(\infty, G(0)).$$

It is clear that $N(r, \infty, G) = N(r, \zeta, F)$, since the poles of the function $G(z)$ are the zeros of the function $F(z) - \zeta$. Furthermore, we have already noted that the transformation $\frac{1+\bar{\zeta}w}{w-\zeta}$ (a rotation of the Riemann sphere) preserves the spherical metric. This means that

$$k(\zeta, F(z)) = k(\infty, G(z))$$

and that $S(x, F) = S(x, G)$ for all x. Therefore,

$$\mathring{m}(r, \infty, G) = \mathring{m}(r, \zeta, F), \quad \mathring{T}(r, G) = \mathring{T}(r, F),$$
$$k(\infty, G(0)) = k(\zeta, F(0)),$$

which completes the proof.

We now turn our attention to the preparation of the proof of Nevanlinna's defect theorem. We first prove a completely elementary lemma.

Lemma 2. *Let $\psi(x)$ be a continuously differentiable, nondecreasing function positive for $x \geqslant a > 0$. For any positive q we have the inequality*

$$\ln \psi'(x) < 2 \ln \psi(x) + q \ln x$$

for all $z \geqslant a$ with the possible exception of a set E for which

$$\int_E x^q \, dx < \infty.$$

Proof. Let E be the set of points on the ray $x \geqslant a > 0$ for which the opposite inequality holds. Then for $x \in E$ we have $\psi'(x) \geqslant x^q \psi^2(x)$ and

$$\int_E x^n \, dx \leqslant \int_E \frac{\psi'(x)}{\psi^2(x)} \, dx \leqslant \int_a^\infty \frac{\psi'(x)}{\psi^2(x)} \, dx \leqslant \frac{1}{\psi(a)} < \infty.$$

This proves the lemma.

We also need the inequality

$$\frac{1}{b-a} \int_a^b \ln \varphi(x) \, dx \leqslant \ln \left\{ \frac{1}{b-a} \int_a^b \varphi(x) \, dx \right\}, \tag{6.4}$$

which is satisfied by any function $\varphi(x)$ that is negative on the segment (a, b). It is the continuous analog of the inequality

$$\sqrt[n]{A_1 \dots A_n} \leqslant \frac{1}{n}(A_1 + \dots + A_n) \tag{6.5}$$

(relating the geometric and the arithmetic means) and is easily obtained from it by a limit process.

The following inequality is fundamental for the proof:

Lemma 3. *Suppose that the conditions of Lemma 1 are satisfied. Then in its notation we have*

$$\frac{1}{2\pi r}\int\limits_{|z|=r} \ln|F'(z)|\,|dz| + \\ + \frac{1}{2\pi r}\int\limits_{|z|=r} \ln\sqrt{\varrho(F(z))}\,|dz| \leqslant \frac{1}{2}\ln\frac{V'(r)}{2\pi r}. \tag{6.6}$$

Proof. We employ formula (6.2) for $V(r)$. We may readily obtain from this that

$$V'(r) = \int\limits_{|z|=r} \varrho(F(z))\,|F'(z)|^2\,|dz|.$$

We next divide both sides of this formula by $2\pi r$ and use inequality (6.4). This gives us the statement of the lemma.

Theorem 6.2. *For any* $\zeta_1, \zeta_2, \ldots, \zeta_n$ *we have the inequality*

$$\sum_1^n \mathring{m}(r, \zeta_k) < 2\mathring{T}(r) + O(\ln \mathring{T}(r) + \ln r)$$

for all r *with the possible exception of a set* E *for which* $\int\limits_E r^q\,dr < \infty$ *for any fixed* $q > 0$.

Proof. The idea of the proof is to choose the function $\varrho(\zeta)$ in the appropriate way and use inequality (6.6).

Note that if the function $\varrho(\zeta)$ is chosen so that the integral representing the function

$$P(w) = \iint\limits_{-\infty}^{\infty} \ln k(w, \zeta)\,\varrho(\zeta)\,d\xi\,d\eta,$$

converges absolutely for all w, then the function $V(r)$ constructed for the chosen function $\varrho(\zeta)$ satisfies the inequality

$$\int\limits_0^r \frac{V(x)}{x}\,dx < \mathring{T}(r) + O(1). \tag{6.7}$$

In fact, let us take the equation proved in Theorem 6.1, multiply it by $\varrho(\zeta)$ and then integrate over the entire plane. Recalling that $\varrho(\zeta) \geqslant 0$, that by definition $\mathring{m}(r, \zeta) \geqslant 0$, that

$$\iint\limits_{-\infty}^{\infty} \varrho(\zeta)\,d\xi\,d\eta = 1$$

and

$$\int_0^r \frac{V(x)}{x}\,dx=\int_0^r\left\{\iint_{-\infty}^{\infty} n(x,\zeta)\,\varrho(\zeta)\,d\xi\,d\eta\right\}\frac{dx}{x}=\iint_{-\infty}^{\infty} N(r,\zeta)\varrho(\zeta)\,d\xi\,d\eta,$$

by definiton of the formula $P(w)$, we can then obtain the inequality

$$\int_0^r \frac{V(x)}{x}\,dx\leqslant \mathring{T}(r)-P(F(0)).$$

Since we require that $|P(w)|<\infty$, inequality (6.7) follows from this inequality.

We now find bounds for the integral

$$J(\varrho, F)=\frac{1}{2\pi r}\int_{|z|=r}\ln\sqrt{\varrho(F(z))}\,|dz|$$

with the help of inequality (6.6). From Lemma 2 we have

$$\ln\frac{V'(r)}{2\pi r}\leqslant 2\ln V(r)+O(\ln r)\qquad (r\,\overline{\in}\,E_1)$$

and

$$\ln V(r)\leqslant 2\ln\int_0^r\frac{V(x)}{x}\,dx+O(\ln r)\qquad (r\,\overline{\in}\,E_2).$$

Consequently, denoting the union of the sets E_1 and E_2 by E, we have

$$\ln\frac{V'(r)}{r}=O(\ln\mathring{T}(r)+\ln r)\qquad (r\,\overline{\in}\,E). \tag{6.8}$$

Furthermore, according to Jensen's formula,

$$\frac{1}{2\pi r}\int_{|z|=r}\ln|F'(z)|\,|dz|=\ln|F'(0)|+N(r,0,F')-N(r,\infty,F')\geqslant$$
$$\geqslant -N(r,\infty,F')+O(1)$$

(since $N(r,0,F')\geqslant 0$). However, $N(r,\infty,F')\leqslant 2N(r,\infty,F)$, since $F'(z)$ has only the poles of $F(z)$ and their multiplicity is not more than doubled. Thus,

$$-\frac{1}{2\pi r}\int_{|z|=r}\ln|F'(z)|\,|dz|\leqslant 2N(r,\infty,F)+O(1). \tag{6.9}$$

Substituting estimates (6.8) and (6.9) into inequality (6.6), we find

$$J(\varrho,F)=\frac{1}{2\pi r}\int_{|z|=r}\ln\sqrt{\varrho(F(z))}\,|dz|<$$
$$<2N(r,\infty)+O(\ln T(r)+\ln r)\qquad (r\,\overline{\in}\,E). \tag{6.10}$$

To complete the proof we have only to make a suitable choice for the function $\varrho(\zeta)$ satisfying the conditions

$$\varrho(\zeta) \geqslant 0, \qquad \iint\limits_{-\infty}^{\infty} \varrho(\zeta)\, d\xi\, d\eta = 1$$

and such that the integral for the function $P(w)$ converges absolutely for all w.

It is not obvious how to choose such a function $\varrho(\zeta)$. For $\varrho(\zeta)$, F. Nevanlinna took the density of the hyperbolic metric for the ζ-plane with deleted points $\zeta_1, \zeta_2, \ldots, \zeta_n$. It was only later that Ahlfors observed that it is possible to take a considerably simpler function for $\varrho(\zeta)$ with the same behavior as $\zeta \to \zeta_s$ and $\zeta \to \infty$. Following Ahlfors, we take the function $\varrho(\zeta)$ to be defined by the equation

$$\ln \sqrt{\varrho(\zeta)} = \ln k(\zeta, \infty) - \sum_{1}^{n-1} \ln k(\zeta, \zeta_s) - 2 \ln \left[-\sum_{1}^{n} \ln k(\zeta, \zeta_s) \right] + C$$

(for convenience in notation we have put $\zeta_n = \infty$, which does not limit the generality in any way). The function $\varrho(\zeta)$ defined by this equation is positive and continuous in the entire plane except at the points ζ_s, in neighborhoods of which we have the asymptotic formulas

$$\varrho(\zeta) \sim \frac{A_s}{|\zeta - \zeta_s|^2 (\ln|\zeta - \zeta_s|)^4} \quad (\zeta \to \zeta_s), \quad s = 1, 2, \ldots, n-1;$$

$$\varrho(\zeta) \sim \frac{A_n}{|\zeta|^2 (\ln|\zeta|)^4} \quad (\zeta \to \infty)$$

(the A_s are some positive constants) for the function $\varrho(\zeta)$.

It is clear from these asymptotic formulas that the integral of $\varrho(\zeta)$ over the entire plane as well as the integral defining the function $P(w)$ converge absolutely. We choose the constant C so that the integral of the function $\varrho(\zeta)$ over the entire plane is unity.

Let us estimate the integral $J(\varrho, F)$ for the function we have chosen. We have $J(\varrho, F) = J_1 - 2J_2 + C$, where

$$J_1 = \frac{1}{2\pi r} \int\limits_{|z|=r} \left[\ln k(F(z), \infty) - \sum_{1}^{n-1} \ln k(F(z), \zeta_s) \right] |dz| = -\mathring{m}(r, \infty) + \sum_{1}^{n-1} \mathring{m}(r, \zeta_s)$$

by definition of $\mathring{m}(r, \zeta)$, and

$$J_2 = \frac{1}{2\pi r} \int\limits_{|z|=r} \ln \left[-\sum_{1}^{n} \ln k(F(z), \zeta_s) \right] |dz| \leqslant$$

$$\leqslant \ln \left\{ -\frac{1}{2\pi r} \int\limits_{|z|=r} \sum_{1}^{n} \ln k(F(z), \zeta_s) \, |dz| \right\} = \ln \sum_{1}^{n} \mathring{m}(r, \zeta_s) = O(\ln \mathring{T}(r))$$

because of inequality (6.4).

Thus, inequality (6.5) gives us

$$\sum_{1}^{n-1} \mathring{m}(r, \zeta_s) - \mathring{m}(r, \infty) < 2N(r, \infty) + O(\ln \mathring{T}(r) + \ln r) \quad (r \overline{\in} E).$$

Adding the quantity $2\mathring{m}(r, \infty)$ to both sides of this equation and recalling that $\mathring{m}(r, \infty) + N(r, \infty) = \mathring{T}(r) + O(1)$ and that $\zeta_n = \infty$, we obtain the statement of the theorem.

We can easily deduce the defect theorem from the theorem just proved.

In fact, we may assume that $F(z)$ is not a rational function, since it is clear for these functions. Therefore, because of Theorem 5.3, we have

$$\ln r = o(\mathring{T}(r)) \qquad (r \longrightarrow \infty).$$

Moreover,

$$\delta(\zeta) = 1 - \overline{\lim_{r \to \infty}} \frac{N(r, \zeta)}{\mathring{T}(r)} = \underline{\lim_{r \to \infty}} \frac{\mathring{m}(r, \zeta)}{\mathring{T}(r, \zeta)}.$$

We next divide both sides of the inequality

$$\sum_{1}^{n} \mathring{m}(r, \zeta_s) < 2\mathring{T}(r) + O(\ln \mathring{T}(r)) \qquad (r \overline{\in} E)$$

by $T(r)$ and take the limit as $r \longrightarrow \infty$ along some sequence of points not contained in the set E. This then gives us

$$\sum_{1}^{n} \delta(\zeta_s) \leqslant 2.$$

A complete presentation of the problems touched upon in the last two sections as well as many other interesting results can be found in the extremely interesting book of R. Nevanlinna, Eindeutige Analytische Funktionen, Springer-Verlag, Berlin, 1957. A survey of the latest results obtained in Nevanlinna's theory of distribution of values is given in the book of H. Wittich, Neuere Untersuchungen über Eindeutige Analytische Funktionen, Springer-Verlag, Berlin, 1955.

Index

Abels's first theorem 12, 178
Abel's formula 168
Absolute integrability, hypothesis of 182
Absolutely convergent series 11
Accessible boundary point 75
Additivity of the integral 20
Ahlfors' inequality 241
Ahlfors' theorem 136
Ahlfors-Warschawski inequality 246
Algebraic singular point 87
Analytic continuation, concept of 42
  principle of 42, 50, 76, 171
  use of 202
Analytic functions 24
  multiple-valued 50
  properties of 24
  theory of 24, 85, 191
Analyticity criteria 38
Antiderivative of an analytic function 37
Archimedean property 2
Area theorem 313
Argument principle 97, 99, 110
Arzelà's theorem 13, 41
Associativity, defined 2
Automorphic functions, theory of 253, 283
Automorphism group 253
  of conformal mapping 266

Basic elementary functions, behavior of 46
Bieberbach, L. 78
Boundary functions, arbitrary 234
Boundary point of set 6
Bounded functions, uniqueness theorems for 241
Bounded mode, class of functions of 241
Branch point 86
  isolated 86
  logarithmic 86
de Bruijn, N. G. 165

Carlemann-Milloux problem 239
Carlemann's bounds 241
Carleman's principle 235
Cartesian coordinates 114
Cauchy-Hadamard formula 12
Cauchy-Riemann equations 25, 112, 214
Cauchy-Schwarz inequality 138, 311
Cauchy-type integrals 153
Cauchy's criterion 10
Cauchy's integral formula 24, 32, 153, 180
  for regular functions 217
Cauchy's theorem 24, 28
  for regular functions 216
Characteristic meromorphic function 317
Chordal distance 5
Circle of convergence 12
Closed domain 6
Closed sets 6
  connected 6
Closure, defined 6
Commutativity, defined 2
Compactness principle for analytic functions 41
Complete analytic function, concept of 50
Complete system of functions 246
Complex numbers 1
  multiplication of 2
  definition of product of 4
Complex plane 2
  extended 4
Complex sphere 4
Concept of limit point 70
Conformal mappings 107
  defined 111
  existence of 253
  near boundary, approximation of 135
  Riemann's theorem on 253
Continuous curve 7
Continuous functions 12
Continuous mappings 107
Contour integrals, analytic continuation of 149
Contour integration 88
Convex function 222
Convolution theorem 185
Corners, defined 8
Corresponding boundaries, principle of 303
Corresponding boundaries, theorem of 112, 232, 273

Darboux sums 22
Defect of a value 322
Definite integrals, evaluation of 154
Denjoy-Carlemann-Ahlfors theorem 320
Derivative of a function 24
Dienes, P. 78
Differentiable functions 24
Dilation coefficient 111
Dirichlet problem 213, 226
  boundary-value function of 226
  for multiply connected domains 253
  Green's function of 226
Distribution of values, theory of 320
Domains, multiply connected 112
  simply connected 112
Downward convexity 222

Element of a function 66
Element of area 111, 112

Element of length 111
Elementary functions, conformal mapping of 118
Elliptic functions, theory of 253, 284
Entire functions, asymptotic value of 320
distribution of values of 315
theory of 85
Equicontinuous sequence of functions 13
Euler's beta function 176
constant 172
formula 3, 44
gamma function 44, 88, 162, 212
Evgrafov, M. A. 165, 252, 320
Existence theorem for conformal mappings 257
Expansion in a Laurent Series 90
Expansion in series 75
Extended complex plane 4
Extension of domains, principle of 235, 236
theorem of 236
Exterior point of set 6

Fabry's theorem 78
Fourier transform 177, 208
Functions univalent in the mean, bounds for 302
Fundamental domains, compact 285
of automorphism group 270

Gel'fand, A. O. 320
Gel'fand, I. M. 199
Generalized functions, theory of 198
Generalized Laplace transforms, theory of 201
application of 201
Goluzin, G. M. 264
Goursat, E. 19
Goursat's theorem 28
Graph of analytic function 70
Green's formula 216
Green-Ostragradski formula 28, 216
Groups, theory of 284

Harmonic functions 27
basic properties of 213
conjugate 27
construction of 213
theory of 213, 215
Harmonic measure 232
concept of 213
Haymon, W. K. 302, 309
Hyperbolic geometry 293
Hyperbolic length, element of 293
Hyperbolic metric, principle of 291
density of 293

Imaginary axis 2
Imaginary number 2
Implicit functions 100
Integral equation, solution of 193
Integral of the function 15
Integral sum 15
Integral transforms, method of 177, 191
Integrals, analytic continuation of 203
asymptotic formulas for 159
Integrals depending on a parameter 20
Interior point of set 5
Invariant metric 294
Inverse functions 100
Inversion formula 178
Isolated branch points 86

Jacobi's elliptic functions 290
Jacobian of a transformation 7
Jensen's formula 224, 225, 316
Jensen's inequality 244
Jordan's lemma 147
theorem 8

Kellog's theorem 265
Khavinson, S. Ya. 298

Laplace's equation 27, 213, 214
Laplace transform 177
application of method of 191
one-sided 177
two-sided 177
Laurent expansions 153
Laurent series 88, 178
coefficients of 178
for a function 91
principal part of 92
regular part of 92
Lebesgue integral 182, 302
Length of curve 9
Levin, B. Ya. 320
Limit of a sequence 9
Limit of poles 85
Limit point of set 5
Limits, finite 9
Lindelöf's theorem 236, 320
Line integrals 15
Linear algebra, theorem of 269
Linear fractional transformations 112, 116
function 111, 112
Liouvilles theorem 82, 132, 196, 283, 319
Lipschitz condition 153, 183, 184, 232
Lobachevskian plane 293
Logarithmic branch point 86

Mappings, basic properties of 107
general information of 107
Jacobian of 112
one-to-one 108
Maximum modulus principle for analytic functions 224
Maximum principle theorem 219
Mean value theorem for integrals 218
Mellin transforms 177, 208, 246
inversion formulas of 171
Meromorphic functions 85, 109
distribution of values of 315
expansion of 93
in series of partial fractions 93
order of 320

Mittag-Leffler function 160
Modular functions 283
Modular group 283
Modulus of a function 223
Modulus of complex number, square of 114
Monodromy theorem 62
Morera's theorem 38, 81
Multiple-valued functions, equality of 60
Multiplicity of a pole 84
Muntz's theorem 245

Neighborhood of a point 5
Nevanlinna, F. 331
Nevanlinna, R. 331
Nevanlinna's theorem of defect 323
  proof of 327
Nevanlinna's theory of distribution values 291
  second fundamental theorem of 322
Newton-Leibniz formula 37
Nondegenerate mapping 6
Non-Euclidean metric 293
Notion of circuit number, definition of 59
Notion of connectedness 70
Notion of nearness 70
Notion of neighborhood 70

One-sheeted points 71
One-to-one transformation 7
Open set 6
  connected 6
Order of a zero, defined 84

Parallelogram of the periods 288
Parametric equation of a curve 7
Parseval's identity 188
Path of integration, length of 95
Periodic function, integral of a 230
Petrovskiy, I. G. 13
Phragmen-Lindelöf theorems 246, 252, 320
Picard's theorem 283, 322
Piecewise smooth curve 8
  with folds 8
Poincaré theorem 253
Poisson's formula 228
Poisson's integral 226, 238, 318
Polya, G. 302
Polya's theorem 78
Power series 12
Principal linear part of transformation 7
Principle of corresponding boundaries 109
Pringsheim's theorem 78
Privalov, I. I. 153, 226, 245

Radius of convergence of series 12
Radius of convergence of Taylor series 78
Real axis 2
Real numbers, concept of 2
Rectifiable curve 9
Regular branch of analytic function 71
Regular functions, concept of 51
  mappings of 108
Relation between length and area, principle of 291, 310
Removal of singularities 80
Residue of a function 88
Residues, defined 88
  theory of 88, 89, 180, 185
Riemann-Schwarz symmetry principle 123
Riemann sphere 4, 107
Riemann sums 242
Riemann surfaces 68
  abstract 69
  construction of 71
  realization of 70
Riemann's theorem 112, 117
Rotation, defined 111
Rouché's theorem 97, 99

Saddle-point method 165
Saks, S. 234
Schwarz-Christoffel integral 128, 279, 282
  transformation 128
Schwarz inequality 3
Schwarz's formula 228, 264
Schwarz's invariant 134
Schwarz's lemma 291
Series, summation of 165
Sets, distance between 5
  intersection of 5
Shilov, G. E. 199
Similarity transformation 111
Simple curves 8
Simple poles 84
Simple zeros 84
Singular points 75
  algebraic 87
  isolated 83
  notations of 75
  of analytic function 70, 76
Sokhotski's theorem 86
Spherical metric 324
Square-integrable functions 202
Stereographic projection 4
Stieltjes integrals 234
  theory of 234
Stirling's formula 164
  derivation of 164
Subharmonic functions 219
  properties of 219
  theory of 213
Sum of the series 11
Symmetric points, examples of 115
Symmetry, concept of 114
Symmetry principle 154
  application of 125

Taylor expansion 242
Taylor series 35, 178
Theorem of the mean for harmonic functions 218, 219
Theory of residues 144
Titchmarsh, E. C. 186
Topological properties 70
Topological surfaces, defined 70
Two-constants theorem 235

Uniform convergence, concept of 10
Uniform convergence of series 23
Uniformly convergent subsequence 13
Uniqueness theorem 41
  application of 42
Univalent functions, theory of 309

Viete's theorem 49

Warschawskiy's inequality 251
Warschawskiy's result 139
Weierstrass' criterion 11
Wittich, H. 331

Zhukovskiy's function 120
  univalence of 121